The Creative Spirit

The Creative Spirit

An Introduction to Theatre

Sixth Edition

Stephanie Arnold

Lewis and Clark College

THE CREATIVE SPIRIT: AN INTRODUCTION TO THEATRE, SIXTH EDITION
Published by McGraw-Hill Education, 2 Penn Plaza, New York, NY 10121. Copyright © 2015
by McGraw-Hill Education. All rights reserved. Printed in the United States of America. 2011,
2008, and 2004. No part of this publication may be reproduced or distributed in any form or by any
means, or stored in a database or retrieval system, without the prior written consent of McGraw-
Hill Education, including, but not limited to, in any network or other electronic storage or trans-
mission, or broadcast for distance learning.

Some ancillaries, including electronic and print components, may not be available to customers outside the
United States.

This book is printed on acid-free paper.

2 3 4 5 6 7 8 9 0 DOC/DOC 1 0 9 8 7 6 5 4

ISBN 978-0-07-351426-0
MHID 0-07-351426-8

Senior Vice President, Products & Markets: *Kurt L. Strand*
Vice President, General Manager, Products & Markets: *Michael Ryan*
Vice President, Content Production & Technology Services: *Kimberly Meriwether David*
Managing Director: *William R. Glass*
Brand Manager: *Sarah Remington*
Marketing Manager: *Kelly Odom*
Editorial Coordinator: *Kanyakrit Vongkiatkajorn*
Director, Content Production: *Terri Schiesl*
Content Project Manager: *Laura L. Bies*
Senior Buyer: *Laura Fuller*
Designer: *Margarite Reynolds*
Cover Images: *From the production of* Eurydice, *South Coast Repertory, 2012*
Content Licensing Specialist: *Brenda Rolwes*
Compositor: *Laserwords Private Limited*
Typeface: *10/12 Janson LT Std*
Printer: *R. R. Donnelley*

All credits appearing on page or at the end of the book are considered to be an extension of the
copyright page.

Library of Congress Cataloging-in-Publication Data

Arnold, Stephanie.
   The creative spirit: an introduction to theatre/Stephanie Arnold, Lewis & Clark College.—Sixth
Edition.
      pages cm
   Includes index.
      ISBN 978–0–07–351426–0—ISBN 0–07–351426–8 (hard copy: acid-free paper) 1. Theater.
2. Drama. I. Title.
      PN1655.A75 2014
      792–dc23

2013036336

The Internet addresses listed in the text were accurate at the time of publication. The inclusion of a
website does not indicate an endorsement by the authors or McGraw-Hill Education, and McGraw-Hill
Education does not guarantee the accuracy of the information presented at these sites.

www.mhhe.com

For Mark and for Daniel

Brief Contents

Contents

PART III

The Nature of Style: Realism and Theatricalism   193

Preface

I wrote *The Creative Spirit* for students like mine, whose interest in live theatre is critical to its future. My goal has been to give students the information they need for an in-depth understanding of the way theatre creates meaning. Rather than using a multitude of examples from plays that students may not have seen, I have chosen to focus on fewer works in greater detail, allowing students to become immersed in the worlds of the plays, the lives of the characters, and the choices involved in bringing these texts to the stage. My teaching has convinced me that students gain the most comprehensive understanding of theatre when plays are presented both in the context of culture and history and in relation to performance.

In order to create this textbook, I turned to my professional colleagues in the theatre and asked for their participation. I selected plays that I thought represented important artistic, philosophical, and social issues and sought out productions of those plays. I sat in on rehearsals and performances. I interviewed playwrights, directors, actors, and designers. I invited theatres to contribute photographs of their productions so that a visual story would accompany a written story. I wove quotes from my interviews through the descriptive material so that the practitioners could be part of a shared dialogue with the students. I tried to create a sense of what it would be like to be in the rehearsal hall and what it would be like to be an audience member at the production. I also considered what kind of historical and social background materials would help students understand the plays that they were reading. Building a substantive cultural context meant considering historical, political, and economic background materials as well as musical and artistic sources. The presentation of

the cultural context could then demonstrate for students the place of the theatre in the development of the community and the way the theatre represents a gathering place of knowledge as well as of individuals.

Four Complete Playscripts

At the core of the text are four complete plays: *Joe Turner's Come and Gone* by August Wilson, *And the Soul Shall Dance* by Wakako Yamauchi, *Angels in America: Millennium Approaches* by Tony Kushner, and *Water by the Spoonful* by Quiara Alegría Hudes. Each play is used to illustrate a chapter theme: in Chapter 3 *Joe Turner's Come and Gone* illustrates the playwright's vision; Chapter 8 includes *And the Soul Shall Dance* as an example of expressing a worldview through realism; in Chapter 10 *Angels in America: Millennium Approaches* is included as an example of expressing a worldview through theatricalism; and in Chapter 13 *Water by the Spoonful* is explored to consider elements of dramatic structure. Together these four works demonstrate the power of contemporary American theatre to address the questions and concerns of our time.

Examples from a Range of Cultures and Periods

In addition to the four complete plays, extended examples from classic and contemporary drama are included throughout. Chapter 1, for example, introduces ritual dramas performed by the Kwakwaka'wakw people of the Pacific Northwest and the Hopi Indians of the Southwestern United States. The chapter also includes an overview of ancient Greek theatre represented through an exploration of Euripides' *Medea*. Medieval mystery cycles, Elizabethan drama, the Beijing Opera of China, European modernism, and American musicals are among the types of drama represented. The primary focus, however, is still the rich diversity of contemporary American theatre. And because the theatre's eloquence depends on visual imagery as well as on language, *The Creative Spirit* is supported by 200 production shots, design sketches, renderings, and drawings that highlight the exciting work of today's theatre artists.

An Integrated Approach: Context and Performance

I have tried to show students how to explore the text of a play as a theatre practitioner might, and how this exploration also enriches their experiences as audience members. Each of the book's four complete playscripts is accompanied by a discussion of the playwright's other works, his or her sources, and the historical and cultural context that informs the play's plot, setting, and characters. "In Context" boxes provide timelines related to the play; for example, a list of key dates in the African American experience offers some background for *Joe Turner's Come and Gone*. Following each playscript is a section on the performance and production of the play at one or more representative American theatres. The theatres range from small, innovative theatres, such as the Eureka Theatre and East West Players, to large regional companies, such as the Oregon Shakespeare Festival, South Coast Repertory, and the Mark Taper Forum, to off Broadway and Broadway playhouses. This integrated approach is most apparent in these "case study" chapters, but I have also discussed cultural context and performance choices in the book's eleven other chapters.

Voices of Theatre Artists

In writing *The Creative Spirit*, I wanted to bring to the forefront the energy, passion, and commitment of artists working in the theatre today.

I wanted students to hear playwrights, actors, designers, and directors explain, in their own words, the choices and methods they use in their work. To obtain this material, I have interviewed more than ninety theatre artists over the course of preparing the six editions of the book. The playwrights Quiara Alegría Hudes, Craig Higginson, and Wakako Yamauchi; directors Marc Masterson, Malcolm Purkey, Oskar Eustis, Davis McCallum, Nancy Keystone, Ping Chong, and Tony Taccone; the actors Zabrina Guevara, Armando Riesco, Liza Colón-Zayas, Sean McNall, and Heather Robison; designers Neil Patel, Gerard Howland, Bruno Louchouarn, Anne Militello, and John Crawford, and choreographer Shen Wei are among the commentators on plays and productions discussed in the text.

Supporting Pedagogical Features

Integrated throughout the book are structured assignments that focus on critical thinking, writing, and creative approaches to advance the students' understanding of theatre and to help students develop essential skills applicable in many areas of their education. All chapters include content-specific exercises for discussion, writing, and creative activity. The project chapter at the end of the book provides students with a guided structure for imagining their own productions and engaging creatively with elements of theatre practice. The project also presents the opportunity for historical research. The appendix of guided writing assignments builds on the approaches of the dramaturg and critic introduced in Chapter 14. Writing assignments include reviewing productions, preparing research materials for display, and conducting interviews. Together the assignments throughout the book provide students with the foundation for appreciating the complexities of theatremaking and for being insightful and sophisticated audience members. With the expanded Web site and revised testing materials, *The Creative Spirit* includes all of the resources for a complete course.

New to the Sixth Edition

- The 2012 Pulitzer Prize winning play, *Water by the Spoonful* by Quiara Alegría Hudes, has been added to Part 4: The Nature of Drama: Structure and Genre. In an entirely new version of Chapter 13, *Water by the Spoonful* introduces students to a young playwright's approach to dramatic structure involving social media as well as thematic concerns related to the struggles of American veterans returning home from the Iraq War. *Water by the Spoonful* is the second play of a trilogy Hudes has written about a young marine, Elliot Ortiz, during and following his tour of combat duty in Iraq. The first play of this trilogy, entitled *Elliot, A Soldier's Fugue* (2007), examines the related experiences of a son, father, and grandfather, during their times of service in three different American wars: Iraq, Vietnam, and Korea. In *Water by the Spoonful* Elliot Ortiz attempts to move beyond the wounds of the Iraq War and the wounds inflicted by his mother's crack addiction. A new way of defining family is achieved by the expanded group of characters in this second play, some of whom are related to each other and some who connect in cyberspace. A scene from *Elliot, A Soldier's Fugue* is included in *The Creative Spirit* as part of the introduction to *Water by the Spoonful*, identifying the themes central to the full trilogy and the way the characters are drawn from Hudes' own family. The introduction to *Water by the Spoonful* also includes a consideration of Hudes' background as a composer who draws on classical and jazz music sources for the innovative structures of her plays. Following the complete text of the play is an analysis of the production of *Water by the Spoonful* at Second Stage in New York City in 2013. The casebook study of the production includes commentary from all of the key artists developed specifically for *The Creative Spirit*. Photographs are included throughout the chapter from *Elliot, A Soldier's Fugue* and *Water by the Spoonful*.

- Chapter 6, The Designers, has been extensively rewritten to focus on the design for a new production of Sarah Ruhl's *Eurydice* produced at South Coast Repertory in Costa Mesa, California under the direction of Marc Masterson in 2012. A group of exceptional designers demonstrate the power of theatrical imagination in interpreting Ruhl's poetic retelling of the story of Orpheus and Eurydice. The design work includes sophisticated sound and video scores showcasing the ability of emerging technologies to support and enhance the work of the actors and the other designers. Fourteen photographs and drawings illustrate the specific contributions of the scenic, costume, lighting, and video designs with commentary from the director and all of the designers to explain the development of the design concept and each of their individual responsibilities. Selections from the sound and music design for the production are presented on *The Creative Spirit's* Web site.

- Although the focus of *The Creative Spirit* continues to be on the American theatre, the international coverage has been expanded to include the contribution of theatre to social change in South Africa. Material on South Africa has been integrated into Chapters 2, 5, 7, and 9. The importance of theatre in resisting apartheid is introduced in the discussion of theatre as a mirror of society in Chapter 2. The work of the great South African playwright and director, Athol Fugard, is presented in Chapter 5 as part of the history of directing. Recent plays that explore the changing identity of South Africa post-apartheid are introduced in Chapter 2 and Chapter 7. And the work of the Handspring Puppet Company from Cape Town, South Africa, has been added to Chapter 9, Understanding Style: Theatricalism. The Handspring Puppet Company became known for its brilliant use of visual art, puppets, and dramatic texts that reflect Brecht, expressionism, and absurdism during the 1980s and 1990s. Most recently

Handspring collaborated on one of the most successful current works of popular theatre, *War Horse*. The importance of theatre festivals in sustaining new artistic movements in South Africa and throughout the world is also addressed. A video about emerging young artists and the Grahamstown National Arts Festival in South Africa made specifically for the sixth edition of *The Creative Spirit* is available on the book's Web site.

- Over fifty new color photographs provide coverage of many exciting new plays and productions of classics including *Elliot, A Soldier's Fugue, Eurydice, The Glass Menagerie, The Island, Master Harold and the Boys, Mies Julie, Once, The Three Sisters, Uncle Vanya, War Horse, Water by the Spoonful,* and *The York Mystery Cycle* (for the London Olympiad in 2012).

- Chapter 15, The Project, has been revised to focus on students' imagining their own production of *Elliot, A Soldier's Fugue* or *Water by the Spoonful*. A new play is no longer included in this chapter.

Supplements

The following supplements are available through a McGraw-Hill sales representative.

- An **Online Learning Center,** located at www.mhhe.com/creativespirit6e, offers interviews with theatre practitioners, a slide show, music, video, chapter quizzes, exercises, and more.

- The **Instructor's Manual and Test Bank** offers a variety of resources for instructors, including assignment ideas; chapter summaries; and multiple-choice, short-answer, and essay questions.

Acknowledgments

As *The Creative Spirit* enters its sixth edition, I am deeply appreciative of the many people who have contributed to its evolution. A large number of theatre artists have given generously of their time in helping to build the case studies of the various productions or in contributing additional interview material. The playwrights, actors, directors, and designers whose insightful commentary is found throughout the text have added immeasurably to the book's specificity and vitality. For the sixth edition it was my pleasure to interview a number of remarkable theatre practitioners. For the production analysis of *Water by the Spoonful,* I had illuminating conversations with playwright Quiara Alegría Hudes, director Davis McCallum, scenic designer Neil Patel, and actors Liza Colón-Zayas, Zabrina Guevara, and Armando Riesco. Many thanks as well to Frances White and the Second Stage staff who helped make arrangements in New York. To develop the design material on *Eurydice* produced by South Coast Repertory in Costa Mesa, California, I spoke with director Marc Masterson and designers John Crawford, Gerard Howland, Bruno Louchouarn, and Anne Militello. Tania Thompson, public relations director at SCR, was an invaluable ally in arranging interviews, background materials, and the beautiful photos to support the discussion of the production. In 2010, I attended the Grahamstown National Arts Festival in South Africa as both a participant and an observer. Gilly Hemphill was wonderful in taking time from her packed schedule to help connect me with a number of prominent South African theatre artists. During the festival I interviewed the artistic director of the Market Theatre, Malcolm Purkey, and the Market's literary manager and dramaturg, Craig Higginson, also a well-known playwright and novelist. I spoke with playwright and director Mandla Mbothwe, playwright and designer Neil Coppen, director Libby Allen, and actors Dorothy Ann Gould and Michael Maxwell. Lynette Marais, who was the executive director of the Grahamstown Festival for many years, was most gracious in providing me with her insights into its history and significance. All of the above practitioners were in the midst of their own demanding productions and yet made time to welcome me into their communities and share their thoughtful and inspired perspectives on the nature of theatrical communication. The opportunity to speak with leading and emerging theatre and art practitioners is one of the great joys of my continued work on

The Creative Spirit. In addition, I particularly want to express appreciation to Kemiyondo Coutinho for our three-year collaboration, which resulted in the production of two new theatre pieces, one of which was presented in Grahamstown. From Kemi, an exceptional actor and playwright, came awareness of life for young people in Africa today. Many theatre companies were most generous in providing new production images for the sixth edition. Thanks to American Repertory Theater, Berkeley Repertory Theatre, the Grotowski Institute, Handspring Puppet Company, the Market Theatre, South Coast Repertory, and York Theatre Royal. And many thanks to Rob Lamb for making the arrangements for the inclusion of the photo of Walpi Village, new to this edition.

A growing number of people have reviewed the manuscript at different stages of the project. A fundamental goal of mine in writing *The Creative Spirit* has been to partner effectively with theatre teachers to provide the most meaningful experience for our students. The review process helps to make that goal possible. I wish to thank the following reviewers for their invaluable comments and suggestions for the sixth edition:

Susan Gilbert
Appalachian State University

Katherine Hammond
Old Dominion University

Keith Hight
College of Southern Maryland

Ray Miller
Appalachian State University

James Murphy
Louisiana State University

Tammy O'Donnell
Prince George's Community College

Russ Schultz
University of Florida

Melissa Ritz
Appalachian State University

Chase Waites
Lone Star College

Anna Ward
Appalachian State University

An additional thanks to Ray Miller at Appalachian State University for taking the time for an extended conversation, which was both enjoyable and helpful.

The editorial staff at McGraw-Hill has continued to provide outstanding support for this book. Instrumental to the sixth edition was the wisdom and dedication of Jessica Holmes, the editorial coordinator. Laura Wilk and Sarah Remington have both served as sponsoring editors and it was my pleasure to work with them. Laura Bies, as production manager, Kathryn DiBernardo as copyeditor, and Jan Fehler as proofreader, have made essential contributions to finalizing the manuscript. The design staff has produced an exceptional finish to the presentation of the material. I am most appreciative of the collaborative relationship with McGraw-Hill and our shared commitment to the sustained development of my book, which continues to grow and change to meet the needs of the field. I also wish to thank two of my students from Lewis & Clark College who worked with me as research assistants, Diana Fox and Marissa Fenley. And thanks to Lewis & Clark College, which has provided grant support for my research assistants over the years and to the Mellon Foundation for supporting my trip to Africa.

Once again, I would like to include a few words about my students. I have been most fortunate in my teaching career to have worked closely with many remarkable students. As I have taught them in acting and dramatic literature classes or directed them in plays, we have had the great joy of making discoveries together, learning from each other, and together reaching an understanding of the value of the theatre in our lives. I salute their talent, their openness, their idealism, and their commitment.

Finally, I acknowledge the support of my family. To my son Daniel Arnold gratitude for our ongoing conversation about the craft of writing. To my husband Mark Prieto my deepest appreciation for his insights into the nature of art over many years and his help in all phases of making this book a reality.

Author's Note

Stephanie Arnold is Professor Emerita of Theatre at Lewis and Clark College where she taught acting, directing, and dramatic literature for twenty-five years. Previously, she taught at the University of California, Riverside and Mills College. At Lewis and Clark College, she also served as Chair of the Theatre Department and Dean of Arts and Humanities. Dr. Arnold's research focuses on the American theatre. Professor Arnold's B.A. is from Stanford University and she holds M.F.A. and Ph.D. degrees in theatre from the University of Wisconsin, Madison. She has directed over forty productions for the theatre, including works by classical and contemporary playwrights, musicals, and opera. Most recently she has directed *Vilna's Got a Golem*, *Jabulile!*, and *Kawuna, You're It*. *Jabulile!* was presented at the 2010 National Arts Festival in Grahamstown, South Africa.

The Nature of Theatre

For thousands of years, in almost all cultures, the theatre has been an essential part of human expression. In his book *The Rainbow of Desire,* the Brazilian theatre director Augusto Boal calls theatre the first human invention because it is through theatre that we step back from ourselves to observe and interpret our own behavior. Through the theatre, we reflect on our experiences and we imagine new possibilities. Making theatre is a way of understanding the world around us and our place in it. We also find this process of projecting ourselves into strange or familiar circumstances immensely entertaining.

In the theatre, the **playwright** and the **actor** together present stories in the form of action. The stage action invites audience members to enter a created, fictional world. The energy of the actors and the energy of the audience fuse to charge the theatre event with an intensity that carries the performance beyond ordinary existence into a magical realm of the human spirit. Into theatre performances we pour our dreams, our myths and stories, our struggles and fears. The conflicts that divide us and the laughter that makes us whole take their place on the stage. We make a journey through space and time that is limited only by our imagination.

Before the electronic age, the theatre provided much or all of a community's dramatic entertainment. Today, drama takes place on small and large screens and over the airwaves as well as in the theatre. But although it has much in common with its electronic relatives, the theatre is distinguished by the very fact that it is a live event dependent on the presence of actor and audience in the same space. The live actor–audience relationship offers countless possibilities for envisioning human experience.

This book presents a study of contemporary American plays and productions as a way of understanding the theatre in our own time. To lay a foundation for this approach, we begin by examining the nature of performance and the way performance responds to deep human needs. We look at the impulse to perform that draws actors onto the stage. We then consider the power of the theatre in society. Just as performance exerts a strong pull on individuals, the theatre generates a forceful presence in the life of a community. By introducing some of the great theatre traditions worldwide, we begin a discussion of the many forms that theatre may take and the complex relationship between theatre and society.

CHAPTER 1

The Impulse to Perform: Origins

As dusk falls, the people gather in the ceremonial house for the Winter Dance. All the members of the community are present, from the oldest to the youngest, as well as honored guests who have arrived by boat to the island village located on a remote waterway. A fire burns in the center of the large dark lodge. Beyond the blazing logs stands a screen painted with images of sea animals, whales and otters and eagles, flickering in the firelight. The screen represents the house of the chief of the undersea kingdom.

A loud, commanding whistle sounds, filling the lodge with its notes and announcing the presence of supernatural forces. A rustling is heard from behind the screen and then a large whale swims into view. Swooping and spouting, the whale glides around the fire, bringing with it the authority of the natural world and an ancient story told many times by the community elders about their ancestor, Born-to-Be-Head-of-the-World. A young man from this village was drawn beneath the sea, where he performed feats of heroism in the undersea kingdom. When he returned, he possessed the knowledge and power of the sea.

A dancer wears the enormous whale mask that recalls one of the forms in which Born-to-Be-Head-of-the-World appeared. The mask is animated by this actor through the movement of his own body and the moving parts of the mask, which the master carver has fashioned for this fantastic creature and which the dancer controls by manipulating strings. The enormous, ferocious mouth drops open and snaps shut. The double tail with flukes, curving forward and back, can be lowered to suggest the motion of a diving whale. An eagle rides on the whale's back and even his wings flap as the whale swims on. Paint and mica make the eyes glow in the firelight and glisten as if they carry drops of water from the sea.

The whale mask shown here was collected by the anthropologist George Hunt in 1901 and would have been used to enact the story of Born-to-Be-Head-of-the-World during the nineteenth century in Hopetown, British Columbia. Made from wood, hide, and rope, this heavy piece, measuring about 7½ feet long and 2½ feet wide, would have required skill and practice to maneuver effectively. This mask is in the collection of the American Museum of Natural History in New York City.

The dancer stops and a further pull of the strings causes the entire face of the whale to give way and open to reveal another presence inside, a large bullhead fish (a sculpin), carved and painted to be both fish and man. This transforming mask and the performance itself are nothing less than a display of the supernatural powers of this community's ancestor, Born-to-Be-Head-of-the-World.[1]

This whale performance is part of the **potlatch** ceremonies of the indigenous peoples of the Pacific Northwest Coast of the United States and the Southwest Coast of Canada, and dates from the nineteenth century and perhaps earlier. It is one example of the many ways storytelling and performance function in almost all human societies. Storytelling is central to the formation of human culture. Myth and metaphor are fundamental, imaginative constructs that we employ to distill human experience. But it is not enough for us to tell our stories through words alone. We are compelled to act them out, to perform our understanding of human behavior and the forces that we believe govern our world. This impulse to perform is an essential part of human nature that appears in our daily interactions as well as in the dramas we put on the stage and on film.

Performance and Human Behavior

If we step back from organized dramas to examine individual behavior, we see that the impulse to perform is part of the way we survive. We adapt to changes in our circumstances by making adjustments in the identity we present to other people. We seek to transform ourselves or to emphasize a compelling characteristic, such as courage or humility, that will carry us safely through danger. The human mind is elastic and imaginative in the construction of identity. Part of growing up depends on observing successful role models and experimenting with identities that make us feel comfortable in the face of changing social pressures or demands. Identity is fluid rather than fixed; we may be one person with our families and quite a different person at work or in public situations. Peer pressure or social conditioning can cause people to adopt various sets of behaviors that make them a recognizable part of a group.

Sometimes we feel that we cannot know certain people until we can break through the masks that they wear to protect themselves or, perhaps, to take us in. Consider on one hand the politician who puts on a different face for every new situation or constituency. We may even doubt that such a person has a core identity at all. On the other hand, we may believe that we cannot really know someone until we

The mask shown in these photographs represents the continuation of the ceremonial traditions of the Kwakwaka'wakw people in the present day. The artist George Hunt Jr. has resumed the carving practices that were almost lost when the cultural practices of Native peoples were suppressed. Today Hunt Jr. makes masks and costumes for the potlatch ritual, which is observed by coastal Native peoples of Southwestern Canada and Northwestern United States. At its height in the nineteenth century, the potlatch ceremony lasted for days. It was a major social occasion involving the immediate community and many invited guests, and was also an essential means of expressing changes in the social order. Rites of passage for the young, marriages, and mourning cycles were all observed through the potlatch. Dramatic performances were a highlight of these gatherings and included elaborately carved masks, spectacular costumes, and astonishing special effects. The transformation mask in these photographs changes from a wolf, in the first image, to a killer whale, in the second, when the performer pulls on strings threaded through both sides of the wolf's long face.

recognize that he or she is made up of different identities. Certainly we understand the great release in letting go of certain "expectations" of behavior and trying out a role that is "nothing like us." In the theatre, actors build on this fundamental human impulse to perform in order to describe and interpret human existence for an audience. As audience members, we take great pleasure in watching the work of actors who have made an art out of an impulse that is part of human nature.

Performance and Role Playing

We begin our study of the theatre by exploring the place of performance in human behavior. What human needs are met through performance? What are the psychological, social, and cultural conditions that motivate performance? Understanding the functions of performance in our lives provides a basis for approaching the professional performance of the actor, whose work is the essence of the theatre.

These children, living in Iraq, use dramatic play to imitate and interpret the violence that governs their lives.

If we observe children at play, we see that many of them pretend to be the adults who are prominent in their lives. Children often start taking roles by "playing house" or "playing school"—pretending to be parents or teachers. Children living in war zones play out the violence that surrounds them at a very early age. Certainly children's imitation of the behavior they observe is a way of learning about or preparing themselves for roles they expect to assume. But there is more to dramatic play than social conditioning.

Imagine a four-year-old boy going out with his mother. Before leaving the house he insists on putting on his cape and strapping on his sword. Whether he sees himself as Superman, Batman, Spiderman, or the latest incarnation of a superhero, his impersonation is a serious business. At four, he is old enough to know that the world can be a threatening place. He is aware that he is physically small and lacks the skills of older children or adults that would give him more control in a dangerous and confusing environment. So he puts on the costume or "signs" of what he recognizes as power. And through wearing the cape and bearing the sword, he takes on a role that enables him to share in the power of his hero.

We recognize in this small boy's actions a pattern of behavior that occurs in a variety of situations and at different ages. Life is difficult and full of obstacles. In certain situations, we enact roles; we make adjustments in the way we present ourselves, particularly in ways that make us feel more powerful. The small child is not concerned about being obvious as he carts around his sword. He wants threatening forces, whether real or imaginary, to be clear about his new identity. As adults we try to be more subtle as we put on the clothes and accessories of power, assume certain postures, and alter our language or vocal intonation. The actor Bill Irwin, whose work is discussed in Chapter 4, says he approaches many of his characterizations by asking himself two questions: (1) "What am I afraid of right now?" (2) "What are all the mechanisms that I'm putting into play to show that I'm not really afraid of that?"[2]

Community Performance

The story of the little boy and his superhero battle gear is one of many examples of individual role playing. But humans also engage in forms of collective dramatic expression that are fundamental to the community. Through **dramatic rituals** we reinforce community values and act out community stories that preserve a way of life. The term *ritual* refers to a ceremonial observation that is repeated in a specified way in order to confer certain benefits on the participants. Rituals are highly symbolic events with densely coded meanings. There are sacred rituals, and there are distinctly secular rituals. Indeed, some of the richest forms of ritual dramatic expression take place as part of religious observances such as the enactment of the birth of Jesus in the Christian community or the observation of the seder meal at Passover in the Jewish community. The Kwakwaka'wakw whale performance at the beginning of the chapter is part of a traditional religious ritual.

La Carpa del Ausente, the 2007 production for Día de los Muertos at the Miracle Theatre in Portland, Oregon, is shown in this photo. Directed by Philip Cuomo, the production combined vaudeville, acrobatics, and political satire enacted by various skeletal characters. The actors are Daniel Moreno, CarlosAlexis Cruz, Matt Haynes, and Jorge Arredondo.

A ritual that is becoming more prevalent in the United States takes place in communities with a Hispanic heritage. *El día de los muertos,* or the Day of the Dead, is observed at the beginning of November as a way of remembering family members who have died and celebrating their lives. The beliefs that underlie the Day of the Dead come first from Aztec worship and embrace a view in which life and death are seen as part of a continuum. Death is accepted rather than abhorred or denied. By tending to family graves and bringing to the cemetery the food and drink enjoyed by those who have died, "the way is prepared for the spirits to return." Far from being a morbid or sad occasion, the day is filled with humor, music, processions, food, and performances. At this time, comic figures of skeletons appear who are engaged in all the activities of life, bright orange marigolds decorate cemeteries, and special breads take over bakeries.

Olga Sanchez is the artistic director of the Miracle Theatre in Portland, Oregon. Each year this theatre celebrates the Day of the Dead with a musical festival or a play that builds on the more personal observations of families. Sanchez sees the Day of the Dead as a "chance to revisit with your ancestors and acknowledge the people who came before us, to hear of their stories, their sacrifices, and their values." The connections to the past help to form more meaningful "personal and community identity."[3]

Weddings and graduations exemplify two types of well-known community rituals. In a traditional wedding, a sacred ritual, the bride, the groom, and the attendants wear elaborate and highly ceremonial clothes, and the couple enact their vows according to the custom of their religious faith. Many believe that such a ceremony strengthens the marriage and subsequently the community, whose members participate as witnesses and join in the celebration; they see the wedding ceremony as essential to the stability of the community. Although rituals tend to change slowly because their form needs to be fixed to be effective, they can also be somewhat flexible. One element of the wedding ritual currently undergoing significant change is giving away the bride. At one time this gesture symbolized shifting authority over a woman from her father to her husband. Today other family members or friends may "give the bride away," or the couple may choose to eliminate this custom altogether.

The secular ritual of the high school graduation is of great significance to towns and cities across the United States. The graduation ceremony is a formal rite of passage for the community's young people, a way for them to be accepted into adulthood. Robes and caps are worn; solemn music is played; the graduates accept their diplomas and congratulations and best wishes for the

In this late nineteenth-century photograph, a kachina ritual observation takes place in the plaza of Walpi Village. Walpi Village, on the First Mesa in Arizona, was settled in the ninth century and is the oldest continuously occupied community in the United States. It is striking to compare the dates relating to the development of medieval European theatre presented later in the chapter with the time frame in which performance rituals were evolving on the North American continent. This photo shows only a modest number of participants; other ceremonies could involve many more community members.

future from their community leaders. Most students play their parts with an unusual amount of dignity. To complement the formality of the actual graduation ceremony, many graduating classes develop their own more ecstatic, freer ritual festivities to mark the significance of this event.

Other secular rituals include sporting events, particularly college and professional football games. Sports fans wear costumes and makeup as part of their identification with the drama enacted on the playing field. Beauty pageants, too, are community rituals, as are parades, such as the gay-pride parades that occur in a number of communities and involve many dramatic elements of costume and impersonation.

Community rituals bind community members together by reinforcing their common history and shared goals. They help shape the yearly calendar and the many rites of passage in the human life cycle. Because the United States is made up of many religious faiths and cultural groups, our national rituals tend to be secular, which may be one reason sports have become so important to us. Nonetheless, some community rituals in the United States are a form of worship that interpret religious history or values and also allow for intense identification with the most sacred beliefs of the community. For some communities, dramatic religious rituals are central to community life and govern a great deal of community activity throughout the year. It is from such entrenched dramatic rituals that many of the major dramatic traditions worldwide have evolved.

We turn to the dramatic rituals of a small Native American community, the Hopi, as a source for our further examination of the impulse to perform. This community has been chosen for two primary reasons: the richness of its ceremonial performances and the fact that its rituals—as well as other Native American ceremonial dramas—represent one of the earliest dramatic forms indigenous to our continent.

Ritual Performance Among the Hopi

In an elaborate sequence of dramatic ceremonies, the Hopi Indians of the southwestern United States represent the *kachinas*, whom they view as their spiritual guardians. According to Dorothy K. Washburn, "Kachinas are the messengers and intermediaries between men and gods."[4] The concept of the kachina is associated with the clouds from which rain falls and with the dead, whom the Hopi believe become part of the clouds and return to earth as rain. The Hopi believe that the intervention of the kachinas will bring rain to the arid landscape of the high desert and ensure the success of their crops.

With their brilliant costumes and **masks** incorporating animal and plant images, the ceremonial dramas make the kachina spirits visible to the Hopi community. Because most elements of the costumes and masks have a symbolic meaning, the Hopi figuratively "wear their world" when they are in their ceremonial dress.[5] For example, different colors represent the different geographic and spiritual directions and the weather and resources represented by those directions. Tortoiseshell rattles refer to the water of the ponds and springs where the tortoises live. Eagle and turkey feathers become the flight of prayers.

Kachina Performances

The kachina ceremonies are central to the Hopi worldview and may have originated as early as

The performance of the kachina cycle binds the Hopi community together through the preservation of a belief system and a way of life. Kachina dolls like the one shown here are carved by Hopi artists as a sacred representation of the kachina ritual. The preferred Hopi word for kachina is *katsina* and, in the plural form, *katsinam*.

the twelfth or thirteenth century. There are more than 300 different kachinas, and kachina rituals are spread over much of the year. From December to July a great epic cycle of kachina performances involves all members of the community in varying responsibilities for the ongoing ritual drama. In fact, the Hopi villages are built around the plazas in which the ceremonial dances take place. The kachina performances are at the center of the community physically as well as spiritually and socially.

Soyal, the first observation of the **kachina cycle,** occurs at the winter solstice, in December, to break the darkness and prepare for the new year. *Niman*, the last ceremony, anticipating a successful harvest, occurs in July. Following this final Home Dance, the kachinas are believed to return to the San Francisco Mountains west of the Hopi villages, where they remain until they rejoin the Hopi at the winter solstice. Between the initiation of the cycle in December and the conclusion in July, the kachinas perform a series of ceremonies in which seeds are planted, children are initiated, community members are taught discipline, and, finally, crops are harvested. Rain, fertility, and maintaining social order are the underlying goals of all kachina activity. The dramatic ritual is a highly complex way of exerting control over the environment—that is, the physical, social, and spiritual world.

The kachina ceremonies are frequently serious and sometimes even frightening. But humor is also an essential part of the ritual; laughter is understood as basic to human survival. Clowns appear among the kachinas, and they offer a critique of negative behavior through **parody** by performing outrageous acts that would be unacceptable outside the ritual observation.

The Hopi Performer

The Hopi man who takes on the persona of a kachina is transformed (women do not participate as performers). He transcends his own being and becomes the kachina spirit that he embodies. He takes on the presence and the power of the kachina and therefore can act for the kachina in the ceremonies. Through the ritual dance, a transaction takes place between the human and the supernatural, a merging of the two levels of existence.

Like personal performance, community performance is very much tied to the quest for power. But in sacred community performance in particular, performers become separated from their status as mere mortal beings. They become elevated. By the nature of their special religious knowledge, their enactment of the ceremony, and their performance skills, they become "magicians" who act on behalf of the other members of the community.

Society and Aesthetic Expression

Throughout the world the impulse to perform, to interpret human existence through the presentation of characters on a stage, has evolved into an astonishing variety of theatre traditions. Just as the human capacity for speech has produced many languages, so the impulse to perform has found expression in many distinct forms. In Indonesia shadow puppets play out complicated stories of kings and battles; in

Traditional theatre throughout the East uses various forms of dance as the foundation for storytelling and dramatic expression. The Odissi style of classical dance from eastern India shown here uses elaborate symbolic costumes as well as makeup and ornaments to complement the skills of the dancer, which take many years of training to master. Isa Prieto is a student working to learn a revived form of this temple dance that has been handed down for as long as 2,000 years.

China animal gods fight with demons as actors in highly stylized makeup and costumes perform a combination of sensational gymnastics and martial arts; in India barefoot women with painted faces, hands, and feet perform eloquent dances made up of densely coded, intricate gestures. Sometimes actors speak; sometimes they dance; sometimes they sing. Actors may wear masks or elaborate symbolic costumes, or they may wear the clothes of everyday life. They may inhabit mythical regions, historical locations, or realistic, contemporary environments. They may use elevated speech and gestures or language and actions that correspond with contemporary behavior.

From culture to culture and continent to continent, the theatre responds to the unique worldviews of differing human communities and develops forms of expression that reflect specific community concerns and community aesthetics. By community concerns, we mean the ideas or subjects of theatre performances. By **community aesthetics,** we mean the actual nature of the elements that construct the performance itself, elements that have precise meaning for a particular community and that contribute to the images with which the community describes itself.

For example, the Hopi kachina performances emphasize the importance of the harvest and the place of the entire agricultural process in maintaining social order. The relationship between agriculture, the natural environment, and the social order of the community is shaped by the proper regard for a spiritual presence. This complex interaction is the subject of the ritual; it is what the dramatic cycle is about. The performances themselves are created through certain sequences of dance steps performed by celebrated characters wearing symbolic costumes and carrying iconographic props, all of which form images that express the Hopi view of the world. These characteristics of performance are part of the aesthetic expression of this particular people. Geography, the physical environment, material culture, family structure, social organization,

history, religion, and philosophy are some of the basic forces that shape artistic expression.

The Collective and Public Nature of Theatre

Sometimes the theatre retells the sacred stories of a community. Sometimes individual playwrights forge the body of work that interprets the life of the social group. Myths, legends, history, contemporary events, and personal experience filtered through the imagination of the playwright may all serve as sources for theatrical expression. Celebrated plays of individual playwrights may come to function as sacred stories, anchoring community values or providing a measure against which new experience can be tested. But whatever balance is struck between sustaining stories and the innovations of individuals, the formation and evolution of the theatre takes place in a public forum in a collective endeavor. A community of artists gathers to present a performance for a community audience.

Theatre as a Social Force

It is particularly the collective and public nature of the theatre that makes it such a potent social force. The theatre is a gathering place for the public presentation of ideas. Because ideas are expressed through characters caught in difficult or dangerous situations, the theatre creates an intensely emotional experience for the audience. And the impact of the work is then magnified by the number of people present. A collective emotional response is a force of enormous energy and can function in different ways. On one hand, theatre can evoke a collective sigh of relief, an emotional release: Sometimes when a group of people have laughed very hard together or cried together, they feel that they can more easily accept the difficulties of their daily lives or the pressures that face the entire community. On the other hand, theatre can generate and focus collective anger or outrage, which can then take form as a revolutionary force.

The relationship between theatre and society is complex because the theatre has so much potential power. Theatre can be a conservative force that contributes to stability and reinforces the status quo, or it can be part of an experimental process through which a society redefines itself. Theatre can release social tensions, or it can lead to social upheaval. Theatre can be part of social debate, part of the free exchange of ideas, or it can be used for the dissemination of propaganda. Because of its unique power as a collective, public form, theatre has always been of great interest to philosophers and governments.

Theatre and Religious Festivals

We now examine the relationship between theatre and society by studying examples of theatres from different nations and different historical periods that have been particularly influential in the development of the modern theatre. We study the subjects and ideas of the particular theatres and the aesthetics of the different styles of performance. As we move from theatre to theatre, we explore some of the issues that have arisen from the volatile relationship between theatre and society: issues of religion and politics, race and gender, social stability and revolution.

Two very different European theatres both developed in conjunction with religious festivals: the Greek theatre of Athens in the fifth century B.C.E. and the medieval mystery cycles, specifically those of England, which reached their high point between 1350 and 1550. Although both of these theatres were associated with community celebrations and ceremonies, the Greek theatre developed into a forum for highly sophisticated philosophical debate about the place of human beings in the universe, whereas the medieval theatre produced a pageant that functioned as a form of devotion, an affirmation of accepted religious beliefs.

The Greek Theatre: Athens, Fifth Century B.C.E.

By the fifth century B.C.E., Athens had become the dominant force in the group of city-states politically, culturally, and geographically linked on the peninsula and islands of Greece. The century produced a dazzling record of the Athenian genius for the arts, for learning, for government, and for the building of an empire. The Athenian theatre and literature of the fifth century B.C.E. has inspired much of the theatre and literature in later eras and throughout the world. The great **tragedies** that came from this period— *Prometheus Bound*, *Oedipus Rex*, *Antigone*, and *Medea*—were intricately bound to the religious as well as the political life of the community.

The Origin of Greek Theatre in the Worship of Dionysus

Early on in the development of theatre in Greece, plays were associated with festivals to honor the god **Dionysus.** There is much debate among theatre historians and anthropologists about whether the plays actually evolved out of ritual worship of Dionysus or whether they grew out of the more secular impulses of individual playwrights. Whatever path the evolution of Greek drama followed, the worship of Dionysus was central to the place of theatre in Greek culture.

Dionysus was the Greek god of the life force; he represented new growth for vegetation, new life for herds and flocks, and fertility for human beings. A god of nature, wine, and fertility, Dionysus was honored in the spring with festivals that celebrated regeneration and renewal. These were ecstatic celebrations in which social inhibitions were supplanted by liberated, intoxicated behavior. The worship of Dionysus supposedly began with his followers' tearing apart his body and eating it in order to absorb his power into themselves. In the spring following the dismemberment of the god, Dionysus was miraculously

Origins of the Theatre in Greece

Date	Event
1300–1200 B.C.E.	Worship of Dionysus introduced to Greece from the Middle East
c. 800 B.C.E.	The *Iliad* and the *Odyssey* composed by Homer
534 B.C.E.	Dramatic competition established at City Dionysia
523–456 B.C.E.	Life of Aeschylus
508 B.C.E.	Athenian democracy established
496–406 B.C.E.	Life of Sophocles
490 B.C.E.	Defeat of the Persians by the Greeks at Marathon
480–406 B.C.E.	Life of Euripides
c. 460–430 B.C.E.	Rule of Pericles
458 B.C.E.	*The Oresteia,* by Aeschylus
441 B.C.E.	*Antigone,* by Sophocles
431 B.C.E.	*Medea,* by Euripides
430 B.C.E.	*Oedipus Rex,* by Sophocles
429–347 B.C.E.	Life of Plato
404 B.C.E.	Athens defeated in Peloponnesian War
384–322 B.C.E.	Life of Aristotle
c. 330 B.C.E.	*The Poetics,* by Aristotle

remarkable similarities are apparent. For both cultures, the drama is central to community observations concerned with renewal and regeneration. The transformation of actors into characters concerned with issues of social and religious order coincides with the transformation of nature to sustain human existence once more. The suffering and rebirth of Dionysus became a model for the theatre, which explores the suffering and triumph of the human community. This transformative function for the drama would recur in the Christian drama of medieval times, when pageants celebrating the Christian history of the world were performed in conjunction with the Corpus Christi festivals held throughout Europe in the late spring to celebrate the sacraments of the church associated with the body of Christ.

Like the Hopi ritual performances, the Greek theatre was part of the soul of the community, essential to the basic fabric of the life of the city-state. Through plays, the Greeks examined the relationships necessary to sustain human existence as they understood it. Family relationships, social organization, the relationships and obligations of individuals to the larger society, and the interplay between human action and the actions of the gods dominated the dramas written by playwrights such as Aeschylus (523–456 B.C.E.), Sophocles (496–406 B.C.E.), and Euripides (480–406 B.C.E.). By raising ethical and political questions, the Greek plays helped shape the emergence of democracy in Athens.

There are, however, significant differences between the kachina cycle and the theatre of Greece. The kachina performances evolved over generations of community participation; no single playwright shaped the ideas and images. By contrast, in the Greek theatre the imagination of the individual playwright was celebrated.

restored to life, resurrected. In its evolution, the worship of Dionysus at first actually involved human sacrifice; later, animals were used for the communion ritual. Stories and songs celebrating the life of Dionysus were added to the ritual observations, which grew into community festivals involving civic and religious activity. Finally, in the sixth century B.C.E., dramas were added to the various activities of the festival of Dionysus, setting the stage for the brilliant Athenian **drama** that would emerge in the fifth century B.C.E.

Although the Greek dramas that came to dominate the festival of Dionysus are profoundly different from the Hopi kachina cycle, certain

The theatre at Epidaurus dates from about 300 B.C.E., which is later than the period we have been studying. However, these well-preserved ruins give a sense of the scale and setting of the theatre of Dionysus in Athens in the fifth century B.C.E. The theatre at Epidaurus seated 14,000 spectators and was known for its excellent acoustics. In spite of the vast size of the theatre, the actors could be heard by everyone present. Our knowledge of Greek theatre practice is based on fragmentary evidence and involves much speculation on the part of theatre historians. We imagine that the actors in the fifth century B.C.E. performed on a circular, unraised playing area, with a wooden building behind, which served as a place to change costumes and masks and from which actors entered and exited the stage. The wooden building might have created the sense of a palace facade. The roof of the scene building also provided a raised level for the appearance of the gods and a crane to facilitate special effects like Medea's final exit in a flying chariot.

The presentation of plays, in fact, took the form of a competition, at the festival known as the **City Dionysia,** and prizes were given each year to the outstanding playwright. Further, the kachina performances reinforce an accepted set of religious beliefs, whereas Greek theatre questioned the nature of fate and the very existence of the gods.

The Greek plays were presented each year over a period of several days. Most traditional work stopped, and 15,000 community members or more would gather on a hill outside the city where a rudimentary theatre had been constructed. From wooden benches built into the hillside, the audience would look down on an open-air playing space. At the back of this circular playing area was a plain stone building that provided for the entrances and exits of the actors and served as a place for costume changes and storage for simple stage machinery. Beyond the theatre lay the sea. The audience and the actors

gathered in the middle of the geographic features that delineated the external boundaries of the Athenian world as they witnessed or acted the plays that probed the internal nature of that world. From early morning to late afternoon, the playwrights staged dramas to entertain, to illuminate, and to reflect on the concerns of the huge audience. We now examine one of the Greek dramas, *Medea*, to explore the merging of ideas and aesthetics in the Greek theatre. Accompanying our discussion of *Medea* are photos from two of the numerous recent productions of this work, which continues to be compelling for modern producers and audiences. Reviews of these productions are included in Chapter 14.

Medea, by Euripides

Medea was written by Euripides in 438 B.C.E. and is one of eighteen of his plays that have survived into our own times. Euripides is known for his concerns with the complexity of human motivation, the difficulty of negotiating love and desire, and the conflicts between men and women. Human behavior out of control is the subject of both *The Bacchae* and *Hippolytus*. Euripides has also written eloquently about the destructive nature of war in the often-produced *Trojan Women*.

With characters drawn from well-known Greek mythology, *Medea* focuses on the obsessive passion of the title character, Medea, for her husband, Jason. The play is both the intimate and the public telling of the breakdown of a marriage. As a domestic story, the plot is familiar. A married man leaves his wife, the mother of his children, for a younger woman. Euripides' rendering of this material not only portrays the shifting terms of a relationship but also presents a struggle for power and self-preservation. The younger woman Jason hopes to marry, Glauce, is the daughter of the king of Corinth. By marrying her, Jason stands to inherit a throne. Medea faces losing her husband, and as the play begins, she is threatened with banishment. Furthermore, she bears the weight of a complicated history. Early in their relationship, so devoted was Medea to Jason that she committed murder and alienated her own family in order to help him obtain and then escape with the legendary Golden Fleece. Now, she is regarded as an outsider, a barbarian, among the majority population, the Greeks. For Jason, his alliance with Medea is no longer useful. He sees her as a dangerous and disruptive force. Medea sees the man for whom she sacrificed home and family abandoning her to a life in which she will be alone with neither a country nor friends to support her. The explosive conflict between husband and wife results in the deaths of their children, an outcome that has both personal and symbolic significance. Euripides' *Medea* tells a bloody story of revenge and murder as disturbing as some of today's films. Violence in the drama and in the conduct of human affairs is not a uniquely contemporary phenomenon.

Staging Conventions

Every theatre has its own conventions, which are understood and accepted by performers and audience members alike. **Theatrical conventions** are the unique devices of dramatic construction and performance that facilitate the presentation of stories on the stage. One convention in Greek theatre was that no more than three actors appeared on the stage at any one time; another was that the actors always wore masks. Although we know some of the major conventions followed in Greek performance, many others are unrecorded or are the subject of continuing intense debate. However, using evidence from the plays themselves as well as from other writings, artwork, and archaeological investigation, we can imagine some aspects of a performance.

Male Actors   We know that women did not participate in the Greek theatre in any way. All the roles, male and female, were played by men. Therefore, the central role of Medea would have been played by a man, as would the Nurse and the chorus of Corinthian women. We also know that the Greeks used a small number of actors, two or three, to perform all the individual speaking parts in any particular play; so actors usually played more than one role. In imagining a performance of *Medea* in its own time, we must shift our contemporary perspective to envision two or three men onstage at a time, wearing masks and costumes to indicate the roles they are assuming. One of the actors would probably have played only Medea because this character is onstage throughout most of the play. All the other roles—Nurse, Tutor, Creon, Jason, and Aegeus—would have been divided between two additional actors. After an actor finished one scene or section of the play, he would exit to change his costume and mask so that he could appear as another character. *Medea* is clearly structured with two-person scenes in order to allow the third actor to exit and prepare to reenter in another role.

IN CONTEXT

Mythological Background

Jason sails on the ship *Argo* to find the Golden Fleece, which is in the possession of King Aeetes of Colchis. Medea is the daughter of Aeetes and the granddaughter of the Sun. With her mixed ancestry, human and divine, she has the powers of a sorcerer. She falls deeply in love with Jason and resolves to become his partner in his quest for the Golden Fleece. To help Jason escape from her father's pursuit, she kills her brother Apsyrtus and cuts his body into pieces, forcing her father to stop to gather the scattered remains of his dead son. Medea then tricks the daughters of Pelias, king of Iolkos, into killing their father, who had promised to restore Jason's inheritance in exchange for the fleece. Medea and Jason must flee once again and travel to Corinth, where Euripides' play takes place.

Character Relationships in the Play

Creon   (king of Corinth, killed by Medea)

Glauce   (Jason's new bride, killed by Medea; does not actually appear onstage)

Medea   Jason

2 sons

(killed by Medea)

Aegeus (king of Athens; tricked by Medea into giving her refuge following her crimes in Corinth)

Members of Medea's household

Nurse

Tutor

In general, the same actor could play a man, a woman, and a god all within a few scenes. This particular staging convention reveals a great deal about Greek society. In a story about marriage and betrayal, jealousy and infanticide, the central character, who is held up as a psychological study of a woman in extreme circumstances, was written by a man to be played by a man. Furthermore, the audience would have been composed largely or completely of men.

Offstage Violence   The murders in *Medea* bring us to a particularly noteworthy convention of Greek theatre. All the violence was performed offstage. Frequently, dead bodies were wheeled onstage on a special wagon called the **ekkyklema.** The audience heard in gory detail from messengers about the violent encounters

that resulted in the loss of life, and they saw the reactions of the other characters. But the Greek audience did not witness the fight scenes, the murders, and the dismemberments that played a prominent part in their dramas and that have essentially taken center stage in contemporary plays and films.

During the course of this play, Medea commits two atrocious crimes. First she sends a gift to Jason's new wife, Glauce: a beautiful dress and crown infused with poisonous chemicals that bring the girl to a fiery death when she puts them on. The poison also envelops Glauce's father, Creon, when he tries to rescue her. Following the murders of Glauce and Creon, Medea kills her own sons by Jason. In the play, as it is written by Euripides, none of this violence takes place onstage. The episode of the poisonous dress is described in graphic detail by the Messenger in a speech of over two pages which he delivers to Medea:

> Blood mingled with fire dripped from the top of her head, her flesh melted from her bones like teardrops of resin as your poisons gnawed invisibly.[6]

The cries for help of Medea's children are heard from offstage, and then their dead bodies are revealed in the chariot in which Medea makes her exit at the end of the play, pulled through the sky by dragons.

The Mask   Another convention of the Greek theatre that sharply contrasts with contemporary theatre practice is the use of the mask. The mask has been a vital element of theatrical expression in a variety of cultures and had a number of significant functions in the Greek theatre. For the Greeks the mask had practical implications as well as aesthetic ones. As our discussion of *Medea* demonstrates, masks allowed one actor to play a number of roles. The same actor may have played Creon and Jason or the Nurse and Aegeus. Masks also enabled male actors to play female roles. And masks allowed mortals to play the roles of the gods, projecting the power and authority of Olympian deities. Because the Greek plays took place in huge outdoor theatres, the mask also increased the visibility of the actor, who would have been at a considerable distance from many of those in the audience. And in the case of the Greeks, the mask put yet more emphasis on the importance of the voice in conveying the meaning of the text and holding the audience's attention.

The mask also significantly affected the nature of acting. Whereas contemporary performance is frequently dominated by the personality and appearance of the actor, the use of masks in the Greek theatre put the emphasis in performance on the character rather than on the actor. The mask allowed the character to emerge as an entity separate from the actor who wore it.

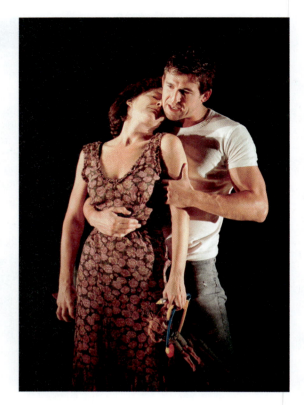

Fiona Shaw plays Medea and Jonathan Cake plays Jason in a production of *Medea* directed by Deborah Warner for the Abbey Theatre of Ireland in 2002. This production emphasizes Medea's obsession with her husband and the intensity of their sexual relationship. The play is placed in a contemporary setting and the chorus speeches are divided between individuals rather than spoken in unison. The realism of the domestic conflict takes precedence over the mythical dimensions of the story. Note the children's toys in Medea's left hand.

The mask shifted the actor's focus to his voice and gestures, although the positioning of the head would have been eloquent in the absence of changing facial expression. In the Greek theatre, the gestures and body positions would have had to be large and striking to communicate across the vast space of the amphitheatre. The most sharply drawn contrast with performance today would be to the close-up of the actor in a film

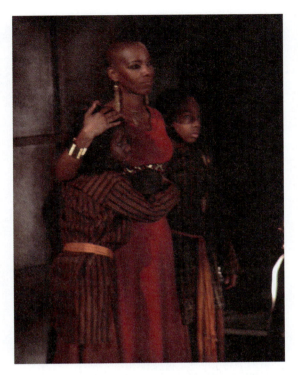

Medea, played here by April Yvette Thompson, clings to her children, played by Brian Gilbert and Laron Griffin, in the production of *Medea* staged by the Classical Theatre of Harlem in 2005. The director Alfred Preisser incorporated dance and music throughout the performance, using the movement and chanting of the chorus to provide a rhythmic underscoring and strong visual images to accompany the actions of the main characters, reinforcing the mythological background.

where the most subtle and natural expressions of the face suggest great depth of feeling. The eyes that turn inward, the mouth that trembles slightly—these can convey significant meaning. The Greek actor had to work with an entirely different apparatus and on a much larger scale to make his meaning clear.

Any actor who wears a mask experiences some degree of transcendence as he or she identifies with the spirit of the mask. For actors such as the Hopi or the Kwakwaka'wakw engaged in a religious ceremony, the mask is an essential intermediary that transports the actor into the spirit world. In more secular performances, masks can still have the effect of lifting the actors out of themselves to identify with the essence of what the masks represent. Finally, for the audience, masks transform the stage or playing space into a magical world inhabited by larger-than-life characters who prompt a shift in the audience's consciousness. The audience members feel that they are in the presence of powerful, archetypal figures who bring a cosmic drama onto the stage.

The Chorus   The **chorus,** like the mask, was another convention of the Greek theatre. Although audiences today are familiar with singing choruses of all kinds, they might find a speaking or chanting chorus on the contemporary stage somewhat strange. A group of twelve to fifteen characters dressed alike and speaking in unison would not seem to represent the world as we see it. But for the Greek audience, the chorus was an expected part of the theatre experience. The chorus first appeared in early religious festivals, when groups of fifty would sing choral hymns in honor of Dionysus. Some theatre historians believe tragedy had its beginning when one of the chorus members initiated a dialogue between himself—as a single speaker or character—and the rest of the chorus. This legendary first speaker, Thespis, is the source of the word **thespian,** meaning actor.

Sometimes the Greek chorus spoke in **dialogue** and sometimes in longer poetic passages. In the sections of dialogue, the chorus played opposite major characters, asking questions and then listening, serving as a confidant who allowed the central characters to explain themselves. The chorus in *Medea* is made up of Corinthian women who remain sympathetic to Medea throughout the play, relating the painful history of Medea and Jason's relationship and then, as the action progresses, pleading with Medea not to kill her children.

Choral passages also contained many references to other mythological situations, and these allowed the playwright to expand on the significance of the immediate dramatic conflict. He built a complex background through the choral commentary.

In addition to functioning as both a character and a storyteller, the chorus had rhythmic and visual functions. The choral sections were accompanied by music and had their own meter, which contrasted with the dialogue episodes and heightened the growing tensions. The staging of the choruses involved intricate choreography and were an important part of the visual spectacle.

In *Medea*, a tormented woman kills her enemies and kills her own children. But performed in its own time, the horror of the play was contained by the formal nature of the presentation. The masked male actor portraying Medea was surrounded by the masked members of the chorus who chanted their responses, while the violent actions took place offstage.

The Greek theatre of Athens in the fifth century B.C.E. reinforced the existing social structure and celebrated Athenian democracy. But it was also a theatre of questions. The playwrights recognized that life is full of contradictions and that the future can be neither predicted nor controlled. The dramas that have come down to us call the community to account for its actions and charge individuals with responsibility for their choices. Characters struggle toward self-knowledge, but their view is frequently distorted by arrogance and passion. Wisdom follows only from catastrophic suffering.

The Medieval Mystery Cycle

Medieval society was organized largely around the Catholic Church, and it was as part of religious observation that the theatre developed in medieval Europe. The great medieval **mystery cycles** that were staged across western Europe from the thirteenth century to the sixteenth are a fascinating example of a religious theatre tradition that depended on the same kind of broad community participation found in the Hopi kachina cycle.

Initiated by the Catholic Church in the tenth century to make Christian teachings more accessible to a largely illiterate population, the mystery cycles dramatizing the Christian history of the world grew into elaborate pageants associated with the late spring festivals of Corpus Christi. Towns in England, France, Germany, Italy, and Spain all staged similar variations of these performances, which focused on biblical events from the creation of the world to the birth and crucifixion of Jesus to the last judgment. The number of episodes presented ranged from forty to as many as one hundred. Not only did the normal work of the communities cease during the time the plays were performed—as it did during the City Dionysia in Athens and as it continues to do during the kachina cycle in Hopi communities—the entire town was responsible for the presentation of the elaborate sequence of plays.

Staging and Production: A Community Endeavor

In England, production of the plays was organized through the business community and specifically through workers' unions known as guilds. Different guilds were responsible for the production of the different plays. In fact, the work of a particular guild would sometimes relate to the subject of its assigned play: The boatwrights produced *Noah's Ark*, and the bakers were responsible for *The Last Supper*.

The individual playlets of the English cycles were staged on **pageant wagons,** or carts that were drawn through the town by horses, each wagon essentially a miniature traveling stage. In the town of York, for example, forty plays were presented beginning at the earliest morning light and continuing far into the night. Each play was performed at twelve different sites throughout

During the 2012 Cultural Olympiad presented concurrently with the London Olympic Games, the people of York, one of the most celebrated sites of the early medieval mystery cycles, staged a major revival of their city's mystery plays. The plays were originally staged in York from the 1300s to 1569 when they were suppressed during the Reformation. About 1,500 community members worked to create the production shown in this photo. Two casts of 250 actors each performed, almost 200 musicians accompanied the performance, and hundreds of local residents sewed costumes and built scenery, just as the community would have gathered to produce the plays in medieval times. The episode shown in the photo is the story of the Flood, with the wooden structure in the center representing the Ark, while the figures with umbrellas create the rolling motion of the sea. The play was staged in the ruins of St. Mary's Abbey, a monastery that was closed at the same time the mystery plays were suppressed and gradually crumbled, leaving only some of the arched stone walls. Seats for 1,400 spectators were set up around the grounds of the Abbey for the performance, which lasted three hours. The adaptation of the text was written by Mike Kenny, Ferdinand Kingsley played God and Jesus, Graeme Hawley played Satan, and the co-directors were Damian Cruden and Paul Burbridge.

the town. People would gather at the designated locations along the "parade" route, and the plays would come to them. Food and music added to the air of great festivity and celebration.

The involvement of the guilds in the production of the plays is not unlike the corporate sponsorship of contemporary entertainments, including parades. The huge nationally televised

The Los Angeles Theatre Center has created a contemporary performance honoring the Virgin of Guadalupe, entitled *La Virgen de Guadalupe: Dios Inantzin,* that draws on traditions tied to the Catholic mystery or miracle plays in combination with Aztec performance traditions that pre-date the arrival of Europeans in the Americas. Presented annually in the Cathedral of Our Lady of the Angels, a church seating 3,000 people, the play is performed in both Spanish and Nahuatl, the Aztec language, and is a Christmas celebration for Los Angeles area residents of Hispanic heritage. The Director Jose Luis Valenzuela says, "the intent of this piece has been that every year we can come together and have a performance of a play that is ours and is built by us together as a community."[7] The goal of the performance is to empower the community in addition to reinforcing culture and faith.

parades, such as the Tournament of Roses parade on New Year's Day in Pasadena, California, with its flower-covered floats, and the Macy's Thanksgiving Day parade in New York, with its gigantic balloon characters, are supported by both commercial enterprises and city and state governments.

However, perhaps closer in spirit to the community involvement in the medieval mystery cycles is the small-town parade on the Fourth of July or another day dear to the heart of a local community. The high school bands, groups of riders on horseback, veterans, civic dignitaries, Shriners, and floats sponsored by local businesses—all represent community institutions and community values. The people who line the parade route recognize their friends and neighbors in the parade, and they clearly understand the significance of the celebration.

The kind of community effort that was required to produce the medieval mystery cycles is hard for us to imagine, because most of our elaborate entertainments are put on by professionals and involve a variety of commercial considerations. Over a hundred male actors, and sometimes several hundred, were involved in the mystery plays, as were dozens of men to build scenery and arrange the stage or pageant wagons. Numerous musicians played during or between episodes. And a director and technicians in charge of special effects coordinated the many participants. The undertaking was so complex and demanding of community resources that productions took place only every few years rather than annually.

Aesthetic Expression: A Shared, Sacred Language

We have seen that the Greek theatre of the fifth century B.C.E. developed a distinct life of its own in part because of the brilliant playwrights who shaped the ideas in the plays and the conventions of performance. In fact, the Greek playwrights directed their own plays, thereby exercising virtually complete control over the material. The medieval theatre, in contrast, was guided by no such original thinking. Rather, it can be seen as one element in an overall pattern of aesthetic expression influenced by the Catholic Church. Because artwork was done for the glory of God, the artists, including visual artists, were all anonymous. We know neither the names of the playwrights nor the identity of the artisans who made the glorious stained glass windows of the great medieval cathedrals. Art was seen as a collective effort of devotion rather than as something done for personal aggrandizement. Instead of focusing on individual innovation or style, artists used the same system of signs and symbols that had evolved within the church and that functioned as a kind of sacred language or writing understood by the entire community. The theatre and the various forms of visual art all used the same subjects, the same ideas of organization, the same details of character, and the same symbols of religious significance.

Story and Symmetry We have already observed that the mystery cycles were organized in an **episodic,** or processional, manner, constituting a number of separate incidents all related to one epic story. The visual art forms of the time, such as stained glass windows and paintings, were also structured as a group of individual panels with episodes or story incidents all related to one larger theme. Within each panel the figures were organized in a symmetrical and hierarchical manner. For example, three angels at the top of a panel might be balanced by three devils at the bottom, or a certain number of virtuous characters might be depicted to the right of Jesus, with a comparable number of sinners to the left. Functioning as a background in many of these visual images was often a small building or emblematic structure that indicated the location of the scene. The same small buildings became the scenic units placed on the pageant wagons. The arrangement and spacing of the characters probably drew on the same principles of symmetry and hierarchy.

Performance and Special Effects The simplicity and order of the staging, however, did not restrict the exuberance of the performances, which were far from stiff religious exercises. The point of the performances was to give the audience a chance to identify with Christ's suffering, to feel the power of the miracles and the degradation of the devils and those who had sinned. The central subject of the entire pageant was salvation itself. To have a powerful and useful effect on the audience, the staging had to be clever, magical, lively, and humorous.

Much effort went into the staging of special effects, such as fire, flying angels, ascensions, flowing water, and the bouncing head of St. John the Baptist. One of the most popular parts of the spectacle was the hell mouth, a gaping, monstrous structure emitting smoke and fire and discharging devils in fantastic costumes out into the audience. And the small plays themselves all had compelling details of human interest that connected the situations of the characters to the immediate hardships and joys experienced by those in the audience.

The Role of the Mystery Cycles in Medieval Society

There are several ways to view the relationship of the Christian mystery cycles to society. On one level they must be seen as a celebration that gave people a break from their routine tasks and a chance to work together to re-create primary community stories. Participants had the double satisfaction of contributing their own skills to the performances and enjoying the results of their neighbors' contributions. Although the mystery plays quickly grew beyond the walls of the church buildings themselves, they served to tie the church and community together. The plays reinforced people's faith by allowing community members to identify with Christ's suffering and triumph and to act on their devotion through the production of the plays.

At the same time, the plays served the interests of the ruling classes and the Catholic Church. They reinforced the social organization of the time, which held people in rigidly structured hierarchical positions with almost no possibility of upward mobility. The plays were full of lessons based on accepting one's position in society no matter what the degree of poverty or deprivation;

The mystery cycles were performed in a holiday atmosphere. Music, food, large crowds, and the interruption of work contributed to the audience's anticipation of the performance. Fire, smoke, and the appearance of devils who interacted with the audience all made for very lively entertainment.

the true rewards of human existence, the plays taught, were to be received in the hereafter.

The relationship of the mystery cycles to society can be seen clearly in the changes that occurred in England in the sixteenth century. In medieval times the mystery cycles benefited both church and state, but after the Protestant Reformation (beginning in 1511), the religious theatre became embroiled in the political upheavals of the day. In England, Henry VIII broke with the pope in 1534 over issues of autonomy in general and divorce in particular. His daughter, Elizabeth I, governed a nation with an expanding sense of national identity and power and a newly established Church of England, which allowed Christian worship without papal interference. Up to this time, the performance of the mystery cycles had reinforced a strong Catholic presence in England. Worried that continued performances would provide a rallying ground for supporters of the pope and Catholicism, the English government set about eliminating the mystery cycles. Manuscripts recording the plays were destroyed, regulations against religious performances onstage were enforced, and plays expressing Catholic views were not licensed. The mystery cycles, long considered a fundamental part of English society, were suppressed when they no longer served the interests of the state.

 # Summary

Performance is a vital part of human expression that may involve playing roles in daily life, participating in community rituals, or working as a professional actor. Performance is an essential human activity that relates to successful personal adaptation. Children use performance to test new roles; adults use performance to adjust to changes in their circumstances. Much of the shifting of roles in daily life relates to our attempts to become more powerful.

Through dramatic rituals, communities reach out to supernatural forces to secure control over their environment. Ceremonial performances, such as the kachina cycle of the Hopi, are central to the social and religious organization of the community. The individual who takes on a ceremonial role goes through a process of transformation.

The power of the theatre derives from its collective public nature, from the combined energies of the community of artists and the community audience. Theatre addresses issues of religion and politics, gender and race, social stability and revolution. It functions as a mirror to society, reflecting the themes and subjects that concern the people and the forms of aesthetic expression deemed appropriate and acceptable in that community.

Some theatre traditions developed in association with religious festivals. The theatre of Athens in the fifth century B.C.E. arose from festivals celebrating the transformative powers of Dionysus, god of the life force. Performed outdoors in natural amphitheatres overlooking the sea, the Greek dramas provided the occasion for thousands of Athenians to gather for a few days every year to experience community myths and legends in the form of drama. Greek theatre employed certain well-understood conventions of performance, including the mask and the chorus. Through drama, the Greeks explored difficult questions about human existence. *Medea*, by Euripides, explores troubled relationships between individuals and the chaos generated by unchecked passion and relentless ambition.

Like Greek theatre, the medieval mystery cycles were religious in origin and purpose. Every few years, community members, working through their guilds, re-created the story of Christianity in a series of playlets presented during the late spring festival of Corpus Christi. Plays were staged on pageant wagons that moved from place to place in the town. The conventions of the medieval theatre were derived from the shared, sacred language of signs and symbols used to evoke and represent Christianity. Stories were simple and told in episodic fashion, both in the plays and in medieval visual art forms such as stained glass windows; the works of playwrights and artists were anonymous and emphasized order and symmetry. In the medieval cycles, religious meaning merged with the humorous and exuberant performances to create an event that was highly entertaining as well as deeply moving. The plays reinforced the hierarchical structure of medieval society with stories that encouraged obedience and humility.

Topics for Discussion and Writing

1. The purpose of this exercise is to examine the way "personal performance" is used in everyday life. Choose "nonactors" for your observations. Where do you see people performing in daily life? That is, under what circumstances do people make some kind of switch in how they present themselves, taking on a different role, putting on a mask, or dramatically aggrandizing their behavior? What is the purpose of the "performance"? Observe people in five different situations. Write approximately one-half page for each observation.

2. Discuss the ways in which the Hopi kachina cycle benefits the Hopi community. Do you know of any dramatic ceremonial performances that are part of your community?

3. Greek tragedies involved a great deal of violence. However, all the violent incidents took place offstage and were then described in detail to the audience by messengers who had witnessed the violence. The dead bodies were also frequently brought onstage as a display of what had happened. What reasons might the Greeks have had to place the violence offstage? What do you think the effect would have been on the audience? What would happen to contemporary drama and films if the violence occurred offstage? What is the effect of onstage and onscreen violence on audiences today?

CHAPTER 2

Theatre as a Mirror of Society

The Professional Theatre

The Greek theatre of the fifth century B.C.E. and the medieval mystery cycles were both associated with religious festivals and appeared only seasonally. The plays in both cases were community endeavors involving large numbers of community members and resources. The production of plays was considered a civic and religious responsibility and brought together religious leaders, civic leaders, business interests, and community members. The participants in the performances themselves consisted of a few semiprofessional theatre practitioners, but the majority were nonprofessionals.

We turn now to two professional theatres with different aesthetics and different conditions of performance: the theatre of Shakespeare and the **Beijing Opera** (also called the Chinese opera). Unlike the Greek and medieval theatres, both of these theatres involved professional practitioners engaged full-time in the production of plays. Commercial considerations were vital to the financial well-being of each theatre. Attracting a regular and substantial paying audience and securing the patronage of the aristocracy were equally important. Although the theatres of Shakespeare and the Beijing Opera represent extremely different cultural traditions, they share staging conventions that focus on the abilities of actors working on a bare stage to engage the imagination of the audience.

The Elizabethan Theatre

Elizabeth I, the daughter of Henry VIII by Ann Boleyn, came to the English throne in 1558. She inherited the English crown when England was entering an era of adventure and expansion, when the spirit of the Renaissance was firing the English imagination. But her reign began in the shadow of English civil wars, the Wars of the Roses, that had bled the nation during the preceding century. And Elizabeth faced an ongoing religious struggle between Protestants and Catholics, initiated when her father, Henry VIII, broke with the pope in 1534 and established himself as head of the Church of England. Elizabeth reigned for almost fifty years, until 1603, and she did much to stabilize the nation, creating an atmosphere conducive to spectacular achievements in science, exploration, and the arts. But she held together a contentious society that would return to civil war some years following her death, and there was a price to be paid for the peace that she maintained.

The Theatre in Society

The Elizabethan theatre inherited much both from the Greek theatre and from the medieval theatre that immediately preceded it, but its place in the English society of the late sixteenth century and early seventeenth century was quite different from the place of those theatres in their societies. The production of Greek and medieval plays merged religious observation with performances that entertained as they reinforced community values. Regular citizens were involved at every level of the productions, so productions were community-based and amateur in nature. In both Greece and medieval Europe, theatre festivals were held at special times of the year when the normal life of the community stopped to allow the presentation of plays.

In contrast, Elizabethan theatre was a secular theatre operated by professional actors and playwrights who supported themselves with their theatre activities year-round. This secular theatre interpreted the ambitions and the tremendous changes in worldview of the age. Elizabethan theatre was fascinated by the power struggles of kings and the inner turmoil provoked by such struggles. But in spite of seizing on the political maneuverings of the human community as one of its principal subjects, the theatre was cautious in keeping its distance from the political debates that swirled around the throne of Elizabeth I.

IN CONTEXT

Tudor and Jacobean England

Date	Event
1455–1485	Wars of the Roses
1485	Battle of Bosworth in which Richard III is defeated by the first Tudor king, Henry VII
1509–1547	Reign of Henry VIII (father of Elizabeth I)
1534	Henry VIII breaks with the pope and founds the Church of England
1547–1553	Reign of Edward VI
1553–1558	Reign of Mary I
1558–1603	Reign of Elizabeth I
1588	Defeat of the Spanish Armada by the English navy
1564–1623	Life of Shakespeare
c. 1590–1610	Shakespeare's theatre career in London
1603–1625	Reign of James I (referred to as the Jacobean period)

The film *Elizabeth* (1999), with Cate Blanchett in the title role, chronicled the evolution of Elizabeth I into a monarch with an iron will, strong enough to withstand the threats to her throne and the power struggles surrounding her. In a remarkable performance, Blanchett begins as a lively and emotional girl and gradually builds up her defenses until she withdraws behind the mask of the invulnerable queen. Elizabeth I brought considerable stability to England, allowing the theatre, including the work of William Shakespeare, to flourish.

The unique circumstances of the late sixteenth century in England afforded the opportunity for a national theatre. The intellectual and artistic curiosity of the Renaissance prepared the way for sophisticated plays such as those of Shakespeare. The stability of the long reign of Elizabeth I allowed the economy to prosper, and with it the theatre. The patronage of the nobility protected playwrights and actors and allowed them to continue to work, even when some religious and civic leaders saw the theatre as either a moral danger or an actual physical danger through the spread of the plague. The growth of London—with a population of 200,000, the largest city in Europe—provided a lively audience eager for frequent theatre performances. And the English language, already rich in expressive words and rhythmic possibilities, was open to the playwright's inventive vocabulary and phrasing, unfettered by rigid rules or academic restrictions.

The Nature of Elizabethan Drama

Elizabethan drama focused on the complexity of human motivation. The human mind and human action were placed center stage. Human action was played out against a background of religious and political concerns, but it was the internal struggles of the characters that became the major subject of the drama. The most compelling characters from Elizabethan drama were those whose vision for themselves outreached their abilities to live the lives they imagined. It was the drama of an age of human possibility, full of startling opportunities for the expansion of human understanding, underscored by the expansion of the European nations on the high seas and on vast, distant continents. The unknowns were enormous, but the possibilities were exhilarating. A new view of human existence was emerging from Renaissance philosophy and science; at the same time, however, medieval thinking still persisted.

A play that offered an illuminating prologue for the Elizabethan dramas to follow, particularly the plays of William Shakespeare, was *Doctor Faustus*, by Christopher Marlowe. *Doctor Faustus* explores the mind of a man with a consuming ambition to understand the nature of the world and the universe. But his science proves to be no more than a magician's tricks. Faustus's hope for the mind of man shatters his faith in God. He dies in despair, unable to achieve the heights of human understanding that he envisions but also unable to repent for his desire to know. In his quest for knowledge, he is damned by his own conscience as well as the prevailing morality of his society. Faustus has lost the comfort of the medieval worldview, a view that he has yet to escape.

Doubts and questions also torment Shakespearean characters whose burning ambitions lead them to ill-conceived courses of action. Macbeth pursues a course of murder to gain the crown but cannot silence his conscience. King Lear divides up his kingdom in order to receive the adulation of his daughters and is driven mad by the consequences of his actions. In his greatest play, Shakespeare creates a character, Hamlet, who is forced to deal with the murderous ambition of his uncle Claudius. The play explores the questioning mind of a character who cannot make sense of the political and philosophical issues confronting him.

William Shakespeare

As we examine Elizabethan theatre, we focus on William Shakespeare, the playwright whose soaring achievements became synonymous with the age. A number of other playwrights, such as Christopher Marlowe and Ben Jonson, contributed to the vitality and brilliance of this remarkable period of theatre, but as the theatre became central to Elizabethan and Jacobean England, so Shakespeare became central to the theatre.

Although images of Shakespeare exist, he continues to be an elusive historical figure, known through the eloquence of his plays but not through substantial biographical materials. We can only imagine the life he led in London as a member of the Lord Chamberlain's Men who sometimes wrote as many as three plays a year to keep up with the demands of his company and his audience.

Shakespeare's Career   Shakespeare's career in the theatre illuminates the characteristics of the professional London stage of the late sixteenth century and the early seventeenth. Between approximately 1590 and 1610 Shakespeare wrote thirty-seven plays that together are considered the greatest achievement of any playwright in the history of world theatre.

Shakespeare emerged from an obscure background in Stratford to become one of the important members of the Lord Chamberlain's Men, a small but prominent professional theatre company in London. As part of this company, Shakespeare was an actor, a shareholder, a part owner of the Globe Theatre, and, most significantly, a playwright. Shakespeare's membership and participation in the Lord Chamberlain's Men greatly facilitated his career as a playwright. He worked with a company that had a continuing need for new material, and he knew the strengths and weaknesses of the company, the specialized skills of individual members, and the range of the different actors. In fact, he knew who would play the roles as he wrote them—which actor excelled at comedy, which actor had a good singing voice, which boy actor was available to play a woman's role, and how many lines he could be expected to handle. There was a continuous interplay

Michael Cumpsty plays Richard III in this 2007 production at the Classic Stage Company, directed jointly by Cumpsty and Brian Kulick. Cumpsty plays Richard as a seductive villain who successfully overcomes his opposition with charm before he turns to murder. The play was performed on an open stage with the only scenic element large crystal chandeliers that were raised or lowered by the actors to create a throne room, a forest, or even an undersea environment. The use of the chandeliers was a modern variation of the flexible staging employed in Shakespeare's time.

between the playwright and the company as he crafted his work to take advantage of the gifts of his fellow company members.

The Sources of Shakespeare's Plays

Shakespeare was not an original story maker. Rather, he was a genius at taking materials from other sources—historical chronicles, romances, and even other plays—and dramatizing them for his company, his theatre, and his lively audience, which consisted of royalty, aristocrats, merchants, and laborers. Written histories of the dynastic struggles that led to the triumph of the House of Tudor provided the material for his

chronicling of the English kings. His comedies were modeled on the Latin comedies of Plautus and on Italian romances; his tragedies were derived from violent stories and plays of revenge. But no matter how indebted he may have been to his sources, Shakespeare's particular genius—his brilliant language, his facility with plot and action, and his deep understanding of human nature expressed through his unparalleled array of characters—allowed him to bring a series of dramas to the stage that made his company the most successful in London.

Although the struggle for political power was a prominent subject of his plays, Shakespeare generally managed to focus on character rather than on political analysis, which might have been seen as commentary on the national debate over succession. One of the most striking of his history plays, *The Tragedy of Richard III*, however, reveals the manipulation of history in the drama. Drawing on the distortions in Thomas More's biography of Richard III, also repeated in the Holinshed *Chronicles* (histories of England, Scotland, and Ireland), Shakespeare created a portrait of a monstrous, misshapen villain who murders the two boys who are the true heirs to the throne and slashes his way across England to revenge himself for his bitter life. As a study of evil, *Richard III* conveniently justifies the killing of Richard by Henry VII and Henry's subsequent usurpation of the throne. Henry VII was the grandfather of Shakespeare's sovereign, Elizabeth I. The portrait of Richard III immortalized by Shakespeare obviously justifies the presence of Elizabeth on the throne. That Richard was actually far different from Shakespeare's character has generally been lost to history, so vivid was Shakespeare's rendering of his villain.

Elizabethan Staging

The Globe and Other Theatres

A cluster of professional theatres was built across the River Thames from the city of London, just beyond the jurisdictional reach of a city government that was dubious about the wisdom of a growing theatrical presence. But theatre owners saw profit to be made from theatrical entertainments that drew 3,000 spectators at a time to their large, round, wooden theatres. The most famous of these public commercial theatres, the Globe, was the home of Shakespeare's company, the Lord Chamberlain's Men, from 1599 to 1609. The name of the Globe not only reflected the circular shape of the theatre but also described the way the physical structure of the theatre contained the universe as the Elizabethans saw it. And this point of view, encompassed by the theatre building, echoed the same combination of medieval and Renaissance thinking as did the structure of the plays.

Because the theatre was partly open to the sky, the stage was protected by a canopy that might have had stars painted on it to represent the heavens. The stage platform itself was the world, the level of human endeavor; and the area below the stage, accessible through trapdoors, suggested hell, with its ghosts and spirits. This hierarchical representation was similar to the understanding of the universe expressed by the medieval stage. The difference was the expansion of the human arena, where most of the action took place.

Of the three theatres discussed so far, the medieval theatre had the most elaborate scenic effects. The Elizabethan stage—like the stage of the Beijing Opera discussed later in this chapter—was an empty space with minimal stage properties: a table, a chair, banners. It was through the playwright's eloquent language that the Elizabethan actor defined the space.

Language as an Element of Staging

Like the Greek theatre, the Elizabethan stage relied on vivid, energetic, and evocative **language** to fill the stage space and shape the **action.** In scene after scene, the playwright framed the action with only a few poetic words to create setting or time of day. In *Hamlet*, the sunrise is created with the following memorable lines:

But, look, the morn, in russet mantle clad,
Walks o'er the dew of yon high eastern hill.[1]

In *King Lear*, a storm is created when Lear pours out a description of the weather that also describes the breaking of his heart:

LEAR: Blow, winds, and crack your cheeks! Rage!
　Blow!
You cataracts and hurricanoes, spout
Till you have drench'd our steeples, drown'd
　the cocks!
You sulph'rous and thought-executing fires,
Vaunt-couriers of oak-cleaving thunderbolts,

The Globe Theatre was built for the Lord Chamberlain's Men and was the site of the premiere performances of some of Shakespeare's most famous plays. This photo shows a reconstruction of the Globe, built on the south bank of the Thames River, that is now used for theatre performances in London. In Elizabethan times the Thames served as a boundary between the city of London and the theatres that by law were kept outside the city limits. This photo shows a production of *Coriolanus* with Jonathan Cake in the title role under the direction of Dominic Dromgoole, performed at the Globe Theatre in 2006.

Singe my white head! And thou, all-shaking thunder,
Strike flat the thick rotundity o' th' world!
Crack nature's moulds, all germens spill at once
That makes ingrateful man![2]

The entering or exiting of characters indicated a change of scene, and frequently characters referred to their next destination as they went. All the information needed by the audience to follow the action was contained in the language. The importance of the language points to an audience prepared to listen closely to the words and rapidly process verbal cues, although there were certainly visual cues as well.

The performance of Shakespeare depended on the imagination of the audience. *Henry V* opens with a prologue in which a character called Chorus asks the audience to fill in the images suggested by the actors so that the stage might become a battlefield where a few actors become armies led by kings:

Piece out our imperfections with your thoughts;
Into a thousand parts divide one man,
And make imaginary puissance;

Think, when we talk of horses, that you see them
Printing their proud hoofs i' th' receiving earth.
For 'tis your thoughts that now must deck our
    kings,
Carry them here and there, jumping o'er times,
Turning the accomplishment of many years
Into an hour-glass.[3]

As suggested in these lines, Elizabethan plays involved numerous characters acting out complicated events in rapidly shifting locations over extended periods of time. This expansiveness of space and time was a direct inheritance from the medieval stage, which told the entire history of the Christian world in a single production. The Greek drama, in contrast, generally offered a concentrated representation of human experience, portrayed by only a few characters in one location in a very compressed passage of time: human action reduced to its essence. Shakespeare and his contemporaries looked to show the variations of human action by writing complex plays with multiple plots or subplots. To accomplish this sweeping presentation of action, the Elizabethan stage depended on the alertness of its audience and the language of the playwright.

Acting in Elizabethan Dramas

The professional English actor was a master of speech. In discussions of Elizabethan acting, the most famous acting teacher was Shakespeare himself, who through the character of Hamlet instructs a group of traveling actors on their craft:

Speak the speech, I pray you, as I pronounced it
to you, trippingly on the tongue; but if you
mouth it, as many of your players do, I had
as lief the town-crier had spoke my lines.[4]

Hamlet goes on to emphasize a natural acting style, performed with moderation rather than exaggeration.

Nor do not saw the air too much with your hand,
thus, but use all gently; for the very torrent,
tempest, and, as I may say, the whirlwind

of passion, you must acquire and beget a
temperance that may give it smoothness. . . .
Suit the action to the word, the word to the
action; with this special observance, that
you o'erstep not the modesty of nature. For
anything so overdone is from the purpose of
playing, whose end, both at the first and now,
was and is, to hold, as 'twere, the mirror up to
nature; to show virtue her own feature, scorn
her own image, and the very age and body of
the time his form and pressure.[5]

In fact, the actor would frequently perform very close to the audience, again more like the medieval theatre than the Greek. The platform stage extended into the audience space, and audience members would have stood on three sides of the stage pressing close against it. The actor playing at the edge of the stage would have been able to address the audience easily and intimately in his soliloquies and asides. Even the audience seated in boxes placed around the walls of the audience space would have been close enough to the stage to observe the details of character action. The proximity of the audience to the actors suggests that broad gestures and exaggerated speech were unnecessary. Furthermore, the indication is that the speech was delivered with considerably more speed than it would be today, making a broad style of delivery impossible to maintain.

The Beijing Opera of China

China is a nation with ancient origins that date back to around 4000 B.C.E. The theatre has played a significant part in the rich Chinese cultural heritage for more than 3,000 years and has taken many forms over that remarkable span of time. The relatively recent form that we examine here, the Beijing Opera, draws on many earlier theatre movements or styles but is usually recognized as being established in 1790. It was at the eightieth birthday party of the reigning emperor in that year that new forms of performance were introduced to Beijing, the capital of China.

A Formal Society

The teachings of Confucius, who lived in the fifth century B.C.E., at the same time as the major Greek playwrights, provided the foundation for the organization of Chinese society. Confucian ideas of family, respect for and deference to elders, acceptance of one's place in the hierarchy, and the importance of formal codes of conduct evolved over a period of centuries into a society governed officially by a vast bureaucracy and internally by a complex and pervasive network of rules and obligations. Although Confucius adhered to ideals that included democracy, what resulted from the modifications of his principles led to a society committed to conformity as a way of maintaining social stability.

At the center of Chinese society was the extended family. The effective functioning of the family as the basic social and political unit depended on the observation of intricate rules that governed relationships and the demonstration of appropriate regard for the elders who headed the family and the ancestors who had preceded them. The dramas of the Beijing Opera took this organization of the family as one of its major subjects. The theatre developed its own precise rules of style and detailed codes for the presentation of character types in response to the formal organization of Chinese society.

Playwrights and Plays

Like the Greek dramatists and Shakespeare, the playwrights for the Beijing Opera drew on earlier sources, such as historical novels, myths, and legends. But the goal of the Chinese dramatist was not to create a work that would stand on its own philosophical or poetic merit but to provide a vehicle for the actor. The Chinese playwright was an anonymous arranger of a text, bringing together functional passages that would support the actor's creation. And the audience members who gathered in large restaurant-like theatres, drinking tea and eating during the performances,

did not hang on every word but paused in their noisy activity to pay close attention only to the most exciting or clever parts.

The plays were loosely divided into two areas of focus: civil plays that dealt with domestic and social situations and military plays that maximized the opportunity for the action of warriors, outlaws, and demons. Plays were constructed around a set of instantly recognizable stock characters: four categories—male, female, painted-face, and comic—were divided into representative types whose characteristics were predetermined through generations of performances. A male character could be the hero, the official, the warrior, or the patriarch. A female character could be the virtuous and demure woman, the lively but untrustworthy woman, the warrior woman, or the matriarch. As in the Greek, medieval, and Elizabethan theatres, men played the women's roles, and because these were professional actors, female impersonation became a highly refined art. The gender issues related to female impersonation were complicated further by the social and sexual position of the male actors who undertook these roles in Chinese society. We return to the issue of female impersonation later in the chapter.

The painted-face characters brought the fantastic, the grotesque, and the supernatural into the world constructed by the Chinese theatre. Animal gods, outlaws, and warriors were given a larger-than-life appearance with bold and colorful makeup applied in such strong patterns that it functioned much like a mask. Finally, the comic roles included characters who contradicted expectations: the elderly soldier who was foolish rather than wise, the peasant who was cunning rather than simple.

A Language of Gesture

Although the form of the Beijing Opera is absolutely distinct from the other major forms of theatre in Asia, such as the **kabuki** theatre of Japan,

The Beijing Opera and Chinese History

Date	Event
1644	Manchus conquer China. China is ruled by Manchu dynasties until 1911.
1790	Beijing Opera introduced at the eightieth birthday celebration of Emperor Ch'ien Lung.
1911	Revolution breaks out against dynastic rule. After 1911, women slowly begin to appear on the stage in traditional plays as well as more Westernized drama.
1912	China becomes a republic. A period of great instability begins, involving continuous military and political struggles over the next thirty-seven years, including feuding warlords, Japanese invasion, and civil war between Chiang Kai-shek and the communists.
1921	Creation of the Communist Party.
1930/1935	The actor Mei Lan-Fang tours Japan, the United States, and Russia, where he is seen by Bertolt Brecht.
1937	War with Japan.
1942	Talks at Yan'an Forum on Art and Literature, during which Mao Zedong presents his theories of art and theatre serving the political cause.
1949	Communist takeover of China.
1966	Cultural Revolution. Harshest period of censorship of the arts under supervision of Mao's wife, Jiang Qing. Substitution of model plays for traditional Chinese theatre.
1976	Death of Mao. Overthrow of the "gang of four." Revival of traditional theatre forms.
1978	New openness.
1989	Massacre at Tiananmen Square. Crackdown against democracy movement.
1990s	Acceleration of social change.
2008	Summer Olympics in Beijing.

the **kathakali** theatre of India, and the dance drama of Bali, certain basic principles guide all the traditional theatres of Asia. Just as text is the dominating force in the Western theatre, so gesture is the language of the actor in the Eastern theatre. In the West, the scripts of famous playwrights have been handed down through the centuries, and theatre is largely a verbal, language-based art. In Asian theatre, the gestures, stylized and intricate, convey codes of meaning that can be "read" by an audience just as plainly as we in the West can interpret the actor's speech.

The text of the Beijing Opera may lack the power of the finest writing for the Western stage; similarly, the use of character types may have precluded the development of highly individualized, psychologically developed characters such as Oedipus and Hamlet, whose struggles have made them central to Western culture. But the Beijing Opera developed a poetry of theatrical

The heroine prepares for battle in this scene from *The Peony Pavilion,* which demonstrates the way the intensity of the gestural acting style combined with brilliant costumes and elaborate makeup provides the visual expression of Chinese opera without the use of any scenic background. Women now perform in traditional Chinese theatre with the same impressive skills as men.

expression that we cannot yet approximate. And the speech of Asian theatre, which is totally unlike Western conversational stage speech, is as stylized and removed from the everyday world as the actor's movement patterns.

Acting and Staging

The movement and the speech or singing of the Asian theatre demand a technical proficiency achievable only after years of the most disciplined training, which begins when the actors are children. It is through such rigorous training that the physical interpretation of a role can be passed from generation to generation, even over centuries.

With the conventions of the Chinese theatre in mind, we can imagine a performance of the Beijing Opera in the mid-nineteenth century. The actor stood alone on a bare platform stage. Although elaborate scenery was in use throughout European and American theatres at this time, in the Beijing Opera there were no clever scenic elements to capture the audience's imagination, no special lighting effects to focus their attention. The actor had to use his own resources to create everything that the audience would see. And for this, the actor was singularly well prepared. With a few steps he crossed an invisible threshold and entered a new room or building. With a flick of his whip he rode a nonexistent horse; with a swaying motion he was carried down the river in an imaginary boat. Dressed in sumptuously embroidered robes and wearing an elaborate wig and headdress, the Chinese actor created a compelling presence.

Later in the performance the subtle pantomime that created both environment and action gave way to more spectacular choreography. A battle scene took place, and the combatants seemed to come flying across the stage. With enormous swords in hand, the actors performed acrobatic feats that had the audience shouting approval. Bodies hurtled about the stage at unbelievable speeds, performing multiple flips and somersaults in the air, akin to the flights of Olympic gymnasts. All the action, the entrances and exits, the pantomimed sequences, and the acrobatic choreography were accompanied by musicians seated in view of the audience playing drums, gongs, cymbals, flutes, and traditional Chinese string instruments. The actors' lines, which had their own stylistic patterns, were sung and chanted rather than spoken.

A few basic pieces of furniture were all that helped designate location. A table and two chairs in different configurations changed the scene from a palace to a law court to a bedroom or indicated a wall, a bridge, or a mountain. A stagehand whose invisibility was an accepted convention of the Chinese theatre appeared as needed to reposition the furniture or to add or remove the few additional props that gave further definition to the changing space. The flexible approach to staging meant that performances could easily accommodate multiple locations and shifting conditions, such as time of day and weather. This style of performance emphasized the bond between the actor's skill and the audience's imagination. It also depended heavily, as so many performance traditions do, on a body of theatrical conventions accepted and understood by all participants in the dramatic event.

The Beijing Opera and the Communist Revolution

The history of the Beijing Opera in the twentieth century was closely intertwined with the rise of the Communist Party to power and its subsequent cultural policies. In the first part of the twentieth century approximately 3,000 opera companies performed the traditional repertoire throughout China. A typical company was a private commercial endeavor organized around one or more star performers that played regular engagements in a theatre and also was hired to perform for various festivals, both public and private.

The most famous company was headed by the actor Mei Lan-Fang, who was revered throughout China for his brilliant performances and for the innovations he brought to the traditional theatre form. Mei Lan-Fang also achieved an international reputation by undertaking a series of tours with his company in the 1920s and the 1930s to Japan, the United States, and Russia. He made an enormous impression on Western theatre practitioners, particularly the German director and playwright Bertolt Brecht, who would become one of the defining forces in twentieth-century theatre.

The Chinese communists saw the arts as essential to their goals for transforming Chinese society. From the early days of communist activity in China, Mao Zedong and his followers encouraged the development of a political theatre that would serve the revolutionary cause. In 1942, seven years before the communists came to power in China, Mao officially articulated his theories about the relationship between politics and art and literature at the Yan'an Forum on Art and Literature. According to his view, the only acceptable function for art was to celebrate and serve the proletariat:

> If everyone agrees on the fundamental policy of art serving the workers, peasants, and soldiers and on how to serve them, such should be adhered to by all our workers, our schools,

publications, and organizations in the field of literature and art and in all our literary and artistic activities. It is wrong to depart from this policy. Anything at variance with it must be duly corrected.

The implications of this policy would be as wrenching for the Beijing Opera as the upheaval and strife generated by Mao and his wife, Jiang Qing, would be for the Chinese nation as they reformed what they perceived to be the corruptions of the past. Jiang Qing, who had been an actor before she became a communist leader, brought both personal and ideological concerns into her drive to dominate the arts in China. Because of its enormous popularity, the Beijing Opera was targeted as a major vehicle for communist propaganda. During the **Cultural Revolution** (1966 to 1976), the traditional Beijing Opera was almost completely suppressed and replaced with eight model plays that dealt with contemporary themes and emphasized heroic, sacrificial actions on behalf of the revolution and the workers. Enormous sums of money and human resources were lavished on the development of the model productions. Productions such as *The Red Lantern* and *The White-Haired Girl* demonstrated the class struggle at the heart of the Chinese revolution and clearly identified the corrupt, capitalist enemies of the people.

Although these plays are not without strong characters and rising tension, they are extremely didactic. And although the model productions held the attention of audiences during this intense period of upheaval in China, they undermined the ability of the opera form to sustain itself when the political winds changed. The old actors and stories were gone. Audiences became wary of overtly political theatre. The model productions had laid no groundwork for the development of new material, and the companies had no other plays available with which to attract audiences.

The manipulation of the Beijing Opera to present communist propaganda had the long-term effect of practically destroying the theatre form itself; this development was not unlike the elimination of the mystery cycles in Elizabethan England as part of the government's policy to create a nation removed from the pope's influence. In China, the Beijing Opera was appropriated to promote the social change envisioned by Mao Zedong and his wife, Jiang Qing.

These examples are far from unique. Many societies, past and present, have sought to manipulate the theatre for political ends. Some societies have persecuted and even murdered actors and playwrights, and some cultures have worshiped them, sometimes simultaneously. Actors and playwrights have been slaves and they have been military leaders and heads of state. They have been social outcasts and the confidantes of kings.

For example, in the United States in the mid-twentieth century, fear of communism prompted the United States Congress to call playwrights and screenwriters, actors and directors before the House Committee on Un-American Activities (HUAC) to answer questions about their political affiliations. Without due process or proof of laws being broken, theatre and film practitioners were sent to jail or were blacklisted. They were blocked from further participation in film or play making until this committee was discredited for its attempts to control the free expression of ideas, an overt contradiction of one of our nation's founding principles.

The Theatrical Mirror

The Chinese opera, like the Elizabethan theatre, the Greek theatre, and the medieval theatre, was at the center of its society. All four of these theatres functioned as the mirror that, in Hamlet's words, revealed the "form and pressure" of "the very age and body of the time." The performance traditions and the subjects of the plays reflected the concerns of the community and the way the community understood and expressed itself.

Thus far we have observed the way the theatre has reflected religious beliefs, political organization, and social relationships. As we try to understand what the theatre has to tell us about the past, we are struck particularly by one theatrical convention shared by all of these theatres from vastly different periods and with extremely different political and religious points of view: Although women characters appeared on the stage, all the female roles were written and played by men.

In the theatres that we have studied in the first two chapters, women did not participate in any way except as audience members. The exclusion of women from participation in the theatre reflected a significant aspect of a social organization that excluded women from the public discourse. Just as women did not vote, hold office, or participate in the educational system or the government—with the exception of Elizabeth I—so they were not allowed to be part of the theatre as playwrights or actors. Women characters were presented, but women did not represent themselves through writing or acting. The female behavior constructed onstage was considered appropriate or even ideal. But men created all the images that represented women, both physically and psychologically.

Today, some theatre historians and social critics see this representation of women by men as an absence. That is, any actual sense of women was completely missing. The female characters were part of a man's world but not part of a woman's world. The female characters may have become erotic objects for the male characters or they may have reflected male attitudes toward women, but they did not genuinely represent the actual nature and concerns of women themselves.

In the Greek theatre, masks and costumes designated the gender of the characters, and because three actors played all the individual roles, actors moved back and forth between male and female characters. In the unmasked Elizabethan theatre, boys or young men played the female roles. In the Beijing Opera, elaborate makeup, costuming, and wigs were used to complete the illusion. In the Asian theatre, Chinese or Japanese actors were designated at an early age to take female roles, and their whole training focused on techniques of impersonation. These actors, called *dan* in the Beijing Opera, then played female roles throughout their careers.

By being excluded from the early forms of theatre, women lost a valuable opportunity to participate in the life of the community. Their voices were not heard, and so there was a serious distortion of what both women and men in a given society saw as "believable" female behavior. Because the theatre functions as a major source of culturally accepted gender identity, ideas or models of behavior were generated that defined women's roles and women's nature, even though women had no part in their creation. Demeaning stereotypes are often substituted for truthful representation when people are not able to speak for themselves. Conversely, inclusion in the theatre, in the making of a community's stories, is one of the most powerful ways to change a society from within.

Theatre and Social Change

South Africa

We turn to another part of the world, South Africa, to examine a further dimension of the relationship between theatre and social change. Through much of the twentieth century, South Africa pursued some of the most repressive government policies in modern history. Blatant segregation based on race was used to divide black and white citizens, to determine where people could live and with whom they could associate. Employment conditions and labor options open to people of color were dictated by the white minority government to the black majority of South Africans. Extreme poverty, lack of

Timeline of South African History and Apartheid

Date	Event
Origins:	Research identifies South Africa as one of the earliest areas, possibly the earliest area, inhabited by human ancestors, millions of years ago. Modern humans have lived in South Africa for as long as one hundred thousand years or more.
1652	First European settlement.
1800	Acceleration of colonization by British and Dutch people resulting in land dispossession for African people.
1948	Apartheid institutionalized as the governing apparatus of South Africa by the Boer leadership, which legalized the systematic segregation of races that had been developing since 1910 when the Union of South Africa was established. Black citizens forced to live in townships and home-lands facing censorship and brutal repression involving imprisonment and murder.
1950s	Athol Fugard (born 1932) begins his work as a playwright and a director.
1960	Sharpville Massacre: killing of unarmed black Africans (69 killed, 180 injured) who protested against the pass laws which restricted where black Africans could live and what employment was open to them.
	International movement of sanctions against South Africa expands following Sharpville Massacre.
1961	Fugard's first major play, *The Blood Knot*.
1962	Nelson Mandela (born 1918), leader of the African National Congress, arrested and eventually sentenced to life in prison. Mandela served much of his twenty-seven years of imprisonment on Robben Island.
1963–64	Rivonia Trial in which 10 leaders (black and white) of the African National Congress were tried for acts of sabotage against the state for trying to overthrow apartheid.
1973	First performance of *The Island*.
1976	Soweto Uprising: massive student protests at being forced to use the Afrikaan language (Dutch derived) instead of native African languages. Of the eleven languages currently recognized as official South African languages today, Afrikaan is spoken as a mother tongue by 13.3% of the population; English is spoken as a mother tongue by 8.2% of the population. Most of the remaining people speak an African language as their first language.
1977	Law student and black power leader Steven Biko dies in police custody. Following the death of Steven Biko most nations embrace sanctions against South Africa with the exception of the governments of the United States and Great Britain, although many citizens of both nations joined in various forms of boycotts.
1986	The United States Congress votes in favor of sanctions against South Africa over the veto of President Ronald Reagan.
1990	Nelson Mandela released from prison.
1991	Nelson Mandela elected president of the African National Congress and apartheid begins to be dismantled.

Date	Event
1994	Nelson Mandela elected president of South Africa in the first democratic elections with black citizens granted voting rights.
1996	Truth and Reconciliation Commission hearings.
1998	*Ubu and the Truth Commission.*
2010	*The Girl in the Yellow Dress.*
2012	*Mies Julie.*

education and opportunity, separation of families, as well as brutal work and living conditions were the result of *apartheid*, a network of laws established to privilege and enrich residents of European descent through the exploited labor and enforced servitude of black citizens. Resistance to apartheid resulted in persecution, arrest, imprisonment, and sometimes death. The system of apartheid was so brutal that until 1990 South Africa was considered an outcast from the international community of nations. It is only in the last twenty-five years that South Africa has attempted to govern itself democratically and transform the living conditions of its people. We are witnessing a process of change that is ongoing; many of the traumatic consequences of South Africa's turbulent history still need to be overcome. But instead of erupting into civil war, South Africa has found the beginning of a path toward a peacefully constituted multicultural society with a redistribution of power and privilege. This is a story of social change for our own time in which we can see the power

of the theatre's contribution to the re-making of a nation: first through resistance and protest and then through the forging of a new identity.

The Island was first produced at a tiny, radical theatre called The Space in Cape Town in 1973. This photo shows a recent revival of the play in 2013 at The Market Theatre in Johannesburg, which is one of the leading theatres in South Africa. The original actors were John Kani and Winston Ntshona, who collaborated with the director Athol Fugard in writing the play. The current revival is being directed by John Kani, with his son, Atandwa Kani, now acting the role of John originated by his father. The other actor is Nat Ramabulana. Although much of the play presents the hostile world governed by irrational conditions at the Robben Island prison, this scene shows the intense comradery between the two characters. They have just finished an exhausting day of digging and transporting sand, "grotesquely futile labor." They have been humiliated and beaten by the guard they call Hodoshe, green carrion fly. "I was sentenced to Life brother, not bloody Death!" Now they attempt to revive their spirits by enacting an imaginary phone call to old friends in a bar they frequented in happier times. With resilient good humor, they joke with their imaginary friends, and then more poignantly, ask to be remembered to their wives and children.

In the 2013 revival of *The Island* at the Market Theatre, the two prisoners stage a scene from *Antigone* as an entertainment for the other prisoners. Winston, played by Nat Ramabulana, takes on the character of Antigone, which at first he refuses to do. "I didn't walk with those men and burn my bloody passbook in front of that police station, and have a magistrate send me here for life so that he can dress me up like a woman and make a bloody fool of me." But Winston comes to recognize that his act of resistance, burning his passbook, is like Antigone's act of resistance, burying the body of her dead brother, against the decree of her uncle, the king. The two actors express the ideas that Sophocles wrote two thousand five hundred years ago as a warning against tyranny in Greece. The words of Sophocles take on a haunted meaning when they are adjusted to the justice system that sentences men to life on Robben Island. The actor, Atwanda Kani, who plays John, also plays the role of Creon.

Theatre and Resistance to Apartheid

In 1970 a white playwright who was also a theatre director began to work with two black actors on a play about justice and the prison system in South Africa. The very nature of their collaboration, blacks and whites working together, was prohibited. The subject of their play was a dangerous one: the human rights violations and the brutality with which political prisoners were treated on Robben Island. Robben Island was an infamous and remote island prison, seven miles out to sea from Cape Town, where incarceration was used to suppress dissent. At the time that the play was presented, Nelson Mandela, the leader of the opposition to apartheid, had already been imprisoned on Robben Island for a number of years. The audiences for this play also gathered in contradiction to the laws of South Africa, which prohibited the mixing of the races in public assembly. The production of *The Island* was one of the boldest examples of theatre performances, occurring in a number of cities at this time, aimed at breaking down barriers between the people who participated and encouraging black and white resistance to the increasingly repressive measures of the South African government. The presentation of these plays was an act of courage and a form of empowerment.

The development of *The Island* was innovative for other reasons. It was not the work of a single playwright but was devised by the three participants through improvisation and then arranged as a written text. The participants were the playwright, Athol Fugard, and the actors, John Kani and Winston Ntshona. All three knew a number of people who were or had been imprisoned on Robben Island, so the details of the play were drawn from actual experience. And the three collaborators also drew on another source for their story about the resistance to tyranny, the play *Antigone* by the Greek playwright Sophocles. A member of their theatre company, the Serpent Players, had been arrested and sent to Robben Island while they were rehearsing *Antigone* some years earlier. He had performed speeches for the other prisoners from Sophocles' play, and this episode also became part of *The Island*. In *The Island* the two characters determine to put on a scene from *Antigone* as part of one night's prison

The Handspring Puppet Company of Cape Town produced *Ubu and the Truth Commission* in response to the actual hearings conducted by Bishop Tutu on the crimes committed during apartheid. The piece combined puppetry, performance by live actors, music, animation, and documentary footage. Puppets, such as the one in the photo, represented the witnesses who testified at the hearings. Live actors spoke verbatim testimony while the puppets performed restrained actions such as the stirring of soup. The puppets enlarged the presence of the witnesses to a metaphoric and universal stature. The simple demeanor of the witness puppets with their excruciating stories was juxtaposed with another performance dynamic. Two live actors played characters taken from an absurdist play by Alfred Jarry entitled *Ubu Roi,* first produced one hundred years before the South African adaptation. Pa and Ma Ubu are vulgar, obscene, loud, and greedy, a representation of corrupt leaders desperate to save themselves now that their power has been stripped away. Pa and Ma Ubu are grotesque and wildly funny, adding a surprising element of humor to a deeply painful subject. Jane Taylor wrote the text for the play.

entertainment. They stage the scene where the king, Creon, sentences his niece to death for defying his orders not to give her brother, who has been killed, an honorable burial. The play sets two different battles between the rights of the individual and the abuse of the power of the state against each other. In the foreground is the daily struggle of two humble prisoners not to be crushed by a prison system that would take away their identities as individual human beings of worth. Their struggle is amplified by

the commitment of a young woman to love and honor her dead brother according to religious law even though the king believes her brother is a traitor to the state. And behind both stories, all audience members would have recognized the fight of Nelson Mandela, imprisoned on Robben Island, to bring about a new day in South Africa.

The Island inspired other politically engaged theatre pieces and theatre practices in South Africa and contributed to the growing resistance in South Africa to apartheid. And because it was

The Girl in the Yellow Dress is set in Paris where a French-Congolese student, Pierre, played by Nat Ramabulana, is studying English with a British teacher, Celia, played by Marianne Oldham. Inspired by Ovid's myth of Echo and Narcissus, the play is foremost about "a young man trying to survive a troubled relationship." The romantic struggle of the couple shifts between witty exchanges and damaging accusations and revelations. The male/female conflict can be seen in terms of a power struggle connected to gender, to politics, to class, and to race. Written by Craig Higginson and directed by Malcolm Purkey for the Market Theatre, the play premiered in 2010 at the Grahamstown International Arts Festival in South Africa before touring to Scotland and Sweden. Since then new productions have been staged in New York and Chicago.

Not only did new, inclusive democratic policies need to be implemented, but the terrible damage done by apartheid had to be recognized and redressed.

In 1994 Nelson Mandela was elected president of South Africa. Two years later in 1996, under the leadership of Bishop Desmond Tutu, the Truth and Reconciliation Commission (TRC) was established to hold hearings across the country where witnesses were at last given the opportunity to testify about the atrocities they had experienced and government officials, prison guards, police, and soldiers were offered amnesty in exchange for detailing and acknowledging their crimes. The Truth and Reconciliation Commission hearings were the beginning of a healing process that is still in its early stages. As

also performed widely outside of South Africa, it helped further galvanize international public opinion that helped bring economic and cultural sanctions against the South African government.

Truth and Reconciliation

In 1989 the new leader of South Africa's government, William de Klerk, realized that the situation in South Africa was unsustainable with the disenfranchisement of so many of its citizens and world opinion unanimously opposed to its policies. In a stunning reversal, Nelson Mandela, whom many people feared would die in prison, was released. His political party, the African National Congress, which had been banned, was legitimized. Groups that had been violently opposed began to seek ways to work together.

the theatre was essential to the resistance during apartheid, now it has another role to play as South Africans reexamine their bitter history and work to establish new relationships between the racial, ethnic, and language groups that make up this richly multicultural nation. Jane Taylor, who wrote the text for the play *Ubu and the Truth Commission*, shown on previous page, says, "that through the arts some of the difficult and potentially volatile questions, such as why we betray or abuse each other, could be addressed without destabilizing the fragile legal and political process of the TRC itself."[6]

Mandla Mbothwe is a director working with the Magnet Theatre in Cape Town. In 2010, more than a decade after *Ubu and the Truth Commission* was first presented, he produced a play in collaboration with his actors entitled *The Wound* of a Healer (*Inxeba Iomphilisi*). Mbothwe emphasizes the significance of individuals telling their personal stories, an experience initiated by the Truth and Reconciliation Commission.

> All of us South Africans were given bandages to bandage our wounds. But our wounds were never healed; our wounds were never really attended to. At this point in South Africa, the bandage is leaking. The production rips off the bandage and deals with the wound, cleans it. It's going to be painful, but you can't pass that stage. You cannot put the stories in archives. It's very early. One can't do it alone. We need an audience to watch when we rip off the bandage.

South African plays have also begun to embrace other themes, moving beyond the focus on the terrors of apartheid and the catastrophes left in its wake. South Africa, often referred to as the rainbow nation, is a country that formally recognizes eleven different languages. Ethnic groups with substantial histories in South Africa include indigenous African peoples as well as descendants of English, Dutch, Lithuanian, Indian, and other immigrant groups. Plays have begun to explore the many identities and histories represented within the South African population, as well as the new perspectives on social relationships within this rapidly transforming nation and between South Africa and other parts of the world.

Malcolm Purkey has been the director of the Market Theatre in Johannesburg for the last nine years, which produced the revival of *The Island* shown in photographs in this chapter. The Market Theatre was a major artistic force in the opposition to apartheid and remains one of the leading theatres in South Africa today. Purkey emphasizes the seismic shift in the landscape of South African thought.

> We live in a society that's in a new kind of a crisis. Democracy has thrown up new ways of seeing the world, and our theatre must engage with those. People have a great hunger to see reflections of themselves, to have light thrown on where we are in the world, how we are making progress.

Craig Higginson, a playwright and dramaturg at the Market Theatre, explains that no one play can represent the experience of the nation.

> We sometimes say that it's not in any one play that you will see a picture of South Africa, but in the dialogue between the different plays.[7]

Because of the unique contribution that theatre in South Africa makes to its own country and the world theatre, we will return to other plays from South Africa in later chapters in the book.

Conclusion

When we look at nations like China and South Africa, we can see in contemporary situations ways that theatre is used for government propaganda or to bring about revolutionary social change. In the United States theatre has often been part of the debate about social issues. At the time of the American Civil War, dramatic versions of Harriet Beecher Stowe's novel *Uncle Tom's Cabin* were performed all over the country and had a significant impact on the struggle to abolish slavery. During the Vietnam War in the 1960s and early 1970s, theatre was an important part of the national dialogue about the legitimacy of that conflict and was a vital part of the efforts that brought that war to an end. Today as a nation we are involved in debates about subjects like immigration, gender identity, equal opportunity, substance abuse, and the environment, as well as issues of war and peace.

Many theatre practitioners believe that the stories we tell in the theatre should be part of our national discussion. The plays included in this book, *Joe Turner's Come and Gone*, *And the Soul Shall Dance*, *Angels in America*, and *Water by the Spoonful*, are first and foremost examples of strong theatrical storytelling concerned with the human condition. But each, in its own way, also focuses on different areas of the American experience and the challenges we face early in the twenty-first century.

Summary

Unlike the Greek and medieval theatres, which were basically religious and depended on community participation, Elizabethan theatre and the Beijing Opera were secular and professional. Elizabethan drama focused primarily on human motivation and the internal struggles of psychologically complex characters. Reflecting the curiosity and expansiveness of the Renaissance, Elizabethan drama took on the whole realm of human endeavor. The vitality of Elizabethan drama came from vivid and poetic language, most highly regarded in the works of William Shakespeare. Performing on a bare platform stage during Shakespeare's time, the actors were able to create a continually changing panorama of events and locations through the playwright's expressive words.

Before the Cultural Revolution (from 1966 to 1976), Chinese plays focused on domestic, social, and military situations, supporting the existing values of society. The Chinese playwright's goal, however, was not to create an immortal work but to provide a vehicle for the highly trained Chinese actor. The Beijing Opera was a theatre of stylized gesture and choreographed, acrobatic movement. The conventions of this theatre included a refined movement vocabulary that conveyed meaning just as spoken scripts do in Western theatre.

Theatre has always reflected religious belief, social organization, and issues of concern to the community. In the twentieth century, the theatre began to question the construction of identity in relation to race and gender. In South Africa the theatre played a vital role in exposing the catastrophic inequities of racial politics and has begun to explore the emerging identities of people whose position in society has been drastically altered. No matter what its specific concerns, however, theatre is a community endeavor with the power to reinforce, to celebrate, to challenge, and to sustain.

Topics for Discussion and Writing

1. On the basis of the examples discussed in the chapter, what differences do you find between religious and secular theatre?

2. What makes theatre a useful tool for propaganda?

3. The chapter discusses the exclusion of actual women from the theatres of the past. How were women represented on the stage? What conventions were used to create female characters? Are there any such conventions used today for the representation of women or men in the theatre, in film, or on television?

● For suggested readings and other resources related to this chapter, please visit **www.mhhe.com/creativespirit6e**

The Nature of Performance
The Theatre Practitioners

In Chapters 1 and 2 we considered the centrality of theatre for societies earlier than our own, societies in which dramas could only be presented live, not through the film media prevalent today. We now shift our attention to the significance of the theatre in modern society, particularly the American theatre, and the work that must be done to realize theatre productions on the contemporary stage. As we expand our references to American playwrights and productions, we quickly see that no one playwright speaks for the nation as Shakespeare did in Elizabethan England; nor do we have a national theatre like the Greek and medieval theatres, with a set of myths and signs recognized by everyone. Furthermore, the American theatre is not dominated by a particular place or group of producers. For many decades the center of the American theatre was considered to be New York City. The acceptance of any new play depended on a production in one of the prestigious theatres clustered on and around **Broadway.** Other parts of the nation would see what Broadway had sanctioned through touring productions or the gradual passage of successful plays to smaller theatres around the country. But the energy of the American theatre is no longer focused in one geographic area. Although New York is certainly still a leader in the development of plays and performance styles, large and small theatres play a vital part in communities throughout the country and collectively help to form an evolving idea of the American theatre.

Producing theatre depends on a collaborative process, usually begun by a playwright who is joined by actors, a director, and designers. In this section of the book, we turn our attention to the work of these theatre practitioners. First we examine the way the contributions of the different participants come together to develop ideas, images, dramatic action, and characters. Through a study of the play *Joe Turner's Come and Gone* by August Wilson in a production at the Oregon Shakespeare Festival, we explore the playwright's creation and then the collective effort of producing the play for an audience. We see the play as a work of art and an exploration of historical and social issues.

Following the discussion of the play in production, we take a closer look at the unique arts of the actor, the director, and the designers. We separate and examine the special abilities and skills required of each theatre artist and the kinds of training necessary to prepare for the intense demands of theatre work. Whether a playwright, a performer, a director, or a visual artist, every theatre practitioner shares the need to merge creativity and discipline, intuition and analysis, imagination and technique. Only through years of training does the skilled artist emerge.

CHAPTER 3

The Playwright's Vision

Looking at *Joe Turner's Come and Gone*

by August Wilson

When August Wilson was a fifteen-year-old high school student living in Pittsburgh with his mother, he wrote a paper on Napoleon for his history class. The quality of the paper was so high that the teacher had two responses: He gave the paper an A+, and he told the young African American student that he would have to prove that the work in the paper was really his. Wilson pointed to the bibliography and footnotes but otherwise refused to plead his case. The teacher then changed the grade to an F. On that day, August Wilson quit school and never went back.

He turned instead to the public library and began to educate himself through the books he found there. And at age twenty he began his writing career, first as a poet and then as a writer of short stories. As a young man who had been rejected by the institutions of white culture, he began "remaking the world in his own image through the act of writing."[1] But while he responded to his own experiences, he also started listening to the stories and experiences of the people he met on the street, people such as the elderly black men who hung around the cigar store, "swapping tales, discussing the day's headlines, arguing and needling."[2] Their lives and memories were long, going back to the postslavery days in the South and the great migration to the North.

Eventually Wilson would prove that he had a rich and unique way of presenting history: the history of African Americans, too frequently left out of American history books. Wilson ultimately turned to playwriting in order to present this history on the stage, where his characters could come to life and share their revelations with audiences across the country.

In the early 1980s Wilson began writing a cycle of plays chronicling African American life in the United States. These plays interpret periods of history through the stories of ordinary people rather than the powerful or famous individuals who are usually considered historical figures. For each decade of the twentieth century, Wilson focused on a representative group of characters whose struggles and dreams reflect the events and attitudes of the larger society. Just before his death in 2005, Wilson completed the tenth and final play of this ambitious cycle. In his first play, *Ma Rainey's Black Bottom*, originally produced in 1984 and set in the 1920s, Wilson explores the world of black jazz musicians who seek recognition for themselves and ownership of the music that they are making. *Ma Rainey's Black Bottom* takes place in Chicago; it is the only one of the ten plays not set in Pittsburgh's Hill District, where Wilson grew up. *Fences* looks at life in the America of the 1950s. A former baseball player, forced by racial circumstances to become a garbage hauler, battles with his son to justify his own life.

In *The Piano Lesson*, representing the 1930s, a brother and sister fight over the fate of the old family piano. Carved on the piano are the faces of relatives who were slaves. By selling the piano, the brother hopes to make enough money to buy land and secure a place for himself in America. For the sister, the piano symbolizes the presence of their ancestors, a presence that she cannot part with.

In *Two Trains Running*, the characters gather in Memphis Lee's diner, where they find the determination in each other's company to take their places with dignity in the hostile urban environment of Pittsburgh in 1969. *Seven Guitars*, set in 1940s Pittsburgh, returns to the struggles of a musician, this time the singer and guitar player Floyd Barton, and the events that led up to his death.

King Hedley II looks at the struggles of an ex-convict trying to make a life for himself in the 1980s. *Jitney*, written in 1979, was recently revised and given a new series of productions beginning in 1996. Set in the 1970s, *Jitney* reflects the tensions of inner-city life through the world of unlicensed cab drivers who drive their "jitneys" through the decaying streets of Pittsburgh, beyond the boundaries of the legal taxi trade. The last two plays written by Wilson, *Gem of the Ocean* and *Radio Golf*, provide the beginning and the ending for the ten-play, 100-year cycle. *Gem of the Ocean*, placed at the

THE AUTHOR SPEAKS

August Wilson

To write is to fix language, to get it down and fix it to a spot and have it have meaning and be fat with substance. It is in many ways a remaking of the self in which all of the parts have been realigned, redistributed, and reassembled into a new being of sense and harmony. You have wrought something into being, and what you have wrought is what you have learned about life, and what you have learned is always pointed toward moving the harborless parts of your being closer to home. To write is to forever circle the maps, marking it all down, the latitude and longitude of each specific bearing, giving new meaning to something very old and very sacred—life itself.[3]

Wining Boy plays the family piano while Boy Willie, seated center, and his sister, Berniece, fume at each other about the piano's future. Boy Willie has already tied a rope around the piano in preparation to move it to be sold. Berniece refuses to allow the piano to be taken from the house. The family members torn from each other during slavery are carved on the front and sides of the piano. All of the characters are burdened in different ways by this history. The actors are Chuck Cooper, Jason Dirden, Brandon J. Dirden, Roslyn Ruff, and Eric Lenox Abrams in the 2012 production of *The Piano Lesson* directed by Ruben Santiago-Hudson for the Signature Theatre in New York. Productions of August Wilson plays are staged frequently all over the United States.

opening of the twentieth century in 1904, features a mystical 300-year-old character, Aunt Ester, who lives at 1839 Wylie Avenue and has the power to cleanse people's souls. *Radio Golf,* placed at the end of Wilson's century in 1997, returns to the house on Wylie Avenue, now an impediment to high-rise development. *Joe Turner's Come and Gone,* set in 1911, follows *Gem of the Ocean* chronologically, and like that play brings us characters who are close to the experience of slavery.

The focus of this chapter is the artistic vision of the playwright, a vision that emerges from the playwright's imagination and is shaped by the playwright's personal history and responses to cultural influences. By studying the text of *Joe Turner's Come and Gone* and a production of the play at the Oregon Shakespeare Festival, we explore the foundation of August Wilson's work and the way his vision is realized in performance. The entire text of the play is included in the chapter.

Exploring the Text of *Joe Turner's Come and Gone*

Joe Turner's Come and Gone is about the aftermath of slavery, about the damage done to the spirit, which must be healed before people can take their rightful place in the world. Following the end of slavery, white plantation owners resorted to new forms of forced labor. The worst of these continuing injustices was the chain gang. The play's central character, Herald Loomis, has just served seven years on Joe Turner's chain gang in Tennessee. Now he has come North to search for his wife, from whom he was separated when he was kidnapped and imprisoned by Joe Turner. He joins a group of characters he meets at a boardinghouse in Pittsburgh, most of whom are part of the migration of African Americans leaving the South in search of a better life.

Plot and Characters: A Meeting of Two Worlds

The play begins in Seth and Bertha Holly's boardinghouse, where two dollars a week pays for a room, two meals a day, and a fried chicken dinner on Sunday. The boardinghouse is a haven for struggling young black men and women, charged with energy and full of longing, trying to make a start in a northern city. Bertha provides the roomers with biscuits and sensible counsel. Bynum, a "rootworker," offers his own special wisdom accompanied by herbs and powders. The transient characters look to Seth and Bertha for the practical necessities of life. Bynum offers them a mystical vision to help them find themselves. Everyone at the boardinghouse has a story to tell, and the characters share their tales around the big dining table.

IN CONTEXT

August Wilson's Dramatic Cycle

Play (first production date)	Decade Represented
Gem of the Ocean (2003)	1900s
Joe Turner's Come and Gone (1986)	1910s
Ma Rainey's Black Bottom (1984)	1920s
The Piano Lesson (1987)	1930s
Seven Guitars (1995)	1940s
Fences (1985)	1950s
Two Trains Running (1990)	1960s
Jitney (1982)	1970s
King Hedley II (2001)	1980s
Radio Golf (2005)	1990s

The contentious but cheerful atmosphere of the boardinghouse is interrupted by the arrival of a threatening stranger. He is as withdrawn and abrupt as the other characters are open and at ease. In his long dark coat and hat, the stranger, Herald Loomis, keeps himself hidden. For Herald Loomis the chain gang has been an extension of slavery, and he hides the torment and shame of that legacy. Joe Turner and the chain gang represent all 300 years of slavery, with its endless sorrow and dislocation. The ghost of Joe Turner haunts Herald Loomis. The play's title says that Joe Turner has "come and gone." But for Herald Loomis, Joe Turner is not yet gone. Loomis must rid himself of the ghost of Joe Turner before he can find himself and begin life as a free man.

Historical and Cultural Contexts of the Play

In creating this remarkable play, which is both a social document and the dramatization of a heroic struggle, August Wilson is responding to

Joe Turner's Come and Gone continues to be given distinguished productions across the country. This photo is from the 2008 production at the Berkeley Repertory Theatre, directed by Delroy Lindo, who played Herald Loomis in the first Broadway production. The scene shows the characters dancing the Juba, which takes place at the end of Act 1. The actors are Barry Shebaka Henley, Kim Staunton, Don Guillory, and Brent Jennings. In 2009 the play was given a celebrated production at Lincoln Center in New York City attended by Barack and Michelle Obama, the President and First Lady of the United States.

a unique cultural context—that is, the personal, historical, social, and artistic forces that combine to create his particular perspective. That perspective is shaped by the experiences of being a black American as well as through the inspiration of other artists. For example, Wilson came of age in the explosive 1960s, when black cultural awareness led to a major reassessment of American history and the relationship of black Americans to the society in which they lived. For Wilson, ideas

of "self-determination, self-respect, and self-defense" became crucial to his outlook.[4]

During this time he also discovered the **blues,** which provided an oral and a musical rendering of the history and texture of black American life. As we will discuss shortly, Wilson's fascination with great blues artists such as Bessie Smith led him to the work of another artist, this time a painter, Romare Bearden. Bearden had found a way to create visual narratives out of

IN CONTEXT

The African American Experience

Date	Event
1518	African people first brought to New World as slaves by Spaniards.
1619	First African slaves in North America arrive in Virginia on a Dutch ship.
1860	Slaves number 3.5 million in the United States, about one-third the total population of slaveholding states.
1860–1865	Civil War.
1863	Lincoln's Emancipation Proclamation, freeing slaves in Confederate states.
1865	Thirteenth Amendment to the Constitution, prohibiting slavery in the United States.
1865–1877	Reconstruction: Federal government is involved in governing former Confederate states.
1880	Beginning of Jim Crow legislation in the South, legalizing segregation and discrimination, including the loss of voting rights for black American citizens. The Jim Crow laws were part of the institutionalized oppression that shut off economic opportunity for southern African Americans.
1890–1930	Migration of African Americans from rural South to urban North.

the life sung about in the blues. Wilson wanted to put the life of the blues into a dramatic verbal form just as Bearden had created visual stories through paint and collage.

We begin our study of *Joe Turner's Come and Gone* by examining in this section the historical and cultural contexts of the play; in the following section we look at some of August Wilson's sources. The historical and cultural contexts and Wilson's personal sources will help us to understand the world of this particular play and at the same time provide insight into the creative process of the playwright in making theatre.

Theatre as History

The theatre has always been a major repository of history. Some plays, such as Shakespeare's histories, interpret the lives and actions of actual historical figures—in Shakespeare's case, the kings who preceded Elizabeth I. Some plays feature legendary characters who symbolize the conflicts and concerns of their own times. Greek tragedies are full of larger-than-life characters such as the mythological heroes who fought the Trojan War.

By using a historical frame, August Wilson gives us something of the past and something of the present. In the case of *Joe Turner's Come and Gone*, he gives us certain information about life for African Americans at the turn of the century: the harshness of labor conditions in the South, from sharecropping to the chain gang; a sense of life on the road for a migrating people searching for a more fulfilling life; and the difficulties of remaking life yet once again, this time in northern cities eager for African American labor but resistant to sharing wealth and accepting cultural difference. Wilson also shows us individuals engaged in a struggle to gain control of their own lives and to make connections with others that will sustain them. That struggle, of course, continues today and includes all of us.

The Aftermath of Slavery: Peonage and Sharecropping

Following the Civil War, African Americans experienced a period of promise. But the promise of freedom quickly turned to the reality of reenslavement. Across the South, horrifying new forced-labor practices emerged to compensate for the loss of slave labor. Particularly in the production of cotton, turpentine, and tobacco, black Americans were forced to work as part of prison gangs or under circumstances known as peonage. White employers would claim that black workers owed them money for rent or wages that had been advanced and would then insist that the workers remain in their employment until the debt was discharged. Obligations were frequently manipulated so that the worker could never be free of debt. The peonage system was dominated by violence. A worker who tried to escape would be hunted and beaten or shot. Any form of resistance could result in imprisonment or lynching.

In Wilson's play, Herald Loomis's wife tries to keep up their sharecropper's plot when he is sentenced to the chain gang. Sharecroppers farmed on land owned by someone else and paid their rent with part of their crop. Sharecropping was part of the vicious cycle that kept black Americans in debt and unable to achieve any economic security or independence. In the play, Martha finds she cannot meet the sharecropper's obligation alone and goes to live with her mother. But "trouble" follows her, and the growing violence motivates her to take to the road. The migrating characters who gather at the Pittsburgh boardinghouse contrast sharply with Herald Loomis, a man bound by both physical and spiritual chains.

Migration to the North

Several of the plays in this book deal with the consequences of migration. Although each play examines the realities of migration for specific communities, migration is in fact one of the essential experiences that have shaped U.S. history and culture. We all share in the process and

In 1940 the artist Jacob Lawrence created a remarkable series of sixty paintings that he called "The Migration Series," chronicling the massive movement of African Americans from the South to the North. Lawrence saw the paintings as a "portrait" of himself and his family. Reproduced here is the panel numbered "18" and entitled "The migration gained in momentum."

consequences of migration, from the migration from South to North represented in *Joe Turner's Come and Gone* to the migration that has brought groups of immigrants to the United States from all over the world and has set off large movements across the continent from east to west.

The year 1911, the time period of *Joe Turner's Come and Gone*, represents the early stages of African American migration to the North. Beginning in 1890 hundreds of thousands of black Americans moved from the farms and plantations of the South to the cities of the North, a process accelerated by factory employment needs during World War I. By 1930, the African American populations of New York, Chicago, Detroit, and Pittsburgh had doubled and then tripled, as southern blacks fled from the poverty and violence that followed the period of Reconstruction after the end of the Civil War.

They brought the energy and strength that had made southern agriculture flourish in the eighteenth and nineteenth centuries to the growing industrial base that would shape American life in the twentieth century. Although the journey was one of hope and optimism, it was begun in fear and deprivation and was characterized by the confusion of a people uprooted first from their ancestral home, Africa, and then driven out of their second home by massive economic and social discrimination and repression.

The Metaphor of the Road

Herald Loomis has suffered more than any of the other characters in August Wilson's play. But all the characters share in this history of violence and intimidation. That is why the metaphor of the road becomes so important to the play. Freedom of movement, the chance to move on in search of opportunity, the chance to settle your own land and determine your own future—these ideas have always been synonymous with America.

The road is one of the dominant images of August Wilson's play as the characters set out on journeys of discovery. The road, of course, suggests the passage from the South to the North. And although the road connects people to new opportunities and new ways of seeing the world, for Wilson's characters the journey also serves as a process of searching to find oneself. For black Americans leaving the South, the road had another significant meaning as well. It represented a freedom of movement that had been denied them in slavery and then by the forced labor symbolized in the Joe Turner chain gang. The road, then, symbolizes a celebration of life and possibility.

The Oral Tradition

Beginning in the southern plantation fields, enslaved Africans—who were cut off from almost all cultural expression—adapted African work songs to their brutal new environment. Forbidden the use of their eloquent drums, the displaced Africans poured all their heartache into song. These slave songs were a collective expression of oppression and sorrow. After the Civil War, as black Americans farmed alone or took to the road in search of work, the collective songs of the fields were elaborated and reinterpreted by the individual: "Each man had his own voice, and his own way of shouting—his own life to sing about."[5]

But poverty, lack of opportunity, and violence still characterized life for black Americans. By 1890 these songs of overcoming hardship, of lost love, of loneliness, of determination not to be defeated had become the blues. Throughout the South, on the docks, on the rivers, on the railroads, on the farms, and in the woods, the blues became a crucial form of communication, a way of rebuilding a collective sense of the black American experience. The blues were concerned with social issues and personal problems; they offered a social critique and a form of rebellion or resistance. They were also the basis for social gatherings that brought the community together to dance and sing and shout. These social gatherings were an opportunity for communal emotional expression, for letting go of feelings, just as the lyrics of the blues provided a communal text, an oral, rather than a written, history that described the lives of people who had the doors of literacy closed in their faces.

In his book *Looking Up at Down*, William Barlow explains the importance of the oral tradition to the development of culture:

> The legions of folk musicians and songsters who created and sustained the blues in their infancy were African American variations on the famous West African "griot" tradition. The griots were talented musicians and folklorists designated to be the oral carriers of their people's culture. . . . The griots

functioned as "the libraries" of West African tribal societies "by supporting among themselves generations of living books." A well-known West African proverb states: "When an old man dies, a library burns to the ground."

The African American songsters who synthesized the blues from earlier genres of black folk music were descendents of the griots, carrying forward the historical and cultural legacy of their people even while they were setting a new agenda for social discourse and action.[6]

In his own way, as a theatre artist, August Wilson continues the griot tradition. He has become a storyteller of the African American experience. He tells his stories through dramas rather than songs, although musical rhythms and structures run through his plays. And his characters are storytellers, using myths and personal stories like jazz improvisations to underscore the meanings of the plays. He reaches back to African sources for his mythology and metaphors, and those African traditions and rituals still shine through the evolving African American identity.

The Playwright's Sources

Bessie Smith and Romare Bearden

In creating his theatrical interpretation of the black experience in America, Wilson has placed himself in a broad tradition of African American culture that includes the blues and visual art. Wilson explains that the songs of Bessie Smith and the paintings and collages of Romare Bearden are of primary importance to him because it was in the work of these two artists that he found himself. In the following excerpt from his foreword to a book about the work of Romare Bearden, Wilson discusses the impact of Smith and Bearden on his own life and art:

> In 1965, as a twenty-year-old poet living in a rooming house in Pittsburgh, I discovered Bessie Smith and the blues. It was a watershed event in my life. It gave me a history. It provided me with a cultural response to the world

Bessie Smith, known as the queen of the blues, toured widely and made numerous recordings, becoming one of the most popular singers of the early twentieth century.

> as well as the knowledge that the text and content of my life were worthy of the highest celebration and occasion of art . . . . The blues gave me a firm and secure ground. It became, and remains, the wellspring of my art.[7]

In 1977, twelve years after he became a student of Bessie Smith and the blues, Wilson was introduced to the art of Romare Bearden. He describes his response to viewing a collection of Bearden's work called *The Prevalence of Ritual:*

> What for me had been so difficult, Bearden made seem so simple, so easy. What I saw was black life presented on its own terms, on a grand and epic scale, with all its richness

and fullness, in a language that was vibrant and which, made attendant to everyday life, ennobled it, affirmed its value, and exalted its presence. It was the art of a large and generous spirit that defined not only the character of black American life, but also its conscience.

I called to my courage and entered the world of Romare Bearden and found a world made in my image. A world of flesh and muscle and blood and bone and fire. A world made of scraps of paper, of line and mass and form and shape and color, and all the melding of grace and birds and trains and guitars and women bathing and men with huge hands and hearts, pressing on life until it gave back something in kinship. Until it gave back in fragments, in gesture and speech, the colossal remnants of a spirit tested through time and the storm and the lash. A spirit conjured into being, unbroken, unbowed, and past any reason for song—singing an aria of faultless beauty and unbridled hope.[8]

A work of Romare Bearden's appears in this book; the blues, however, must be heard. The text of one of Bessie Smith's most famous recordings, "Nobody Knows You When You're Down and Out," demonstrates the simple eloquence of the blues form. The words printed here are the lyrics written by the composer Jimmy Cox. If you listen to the Bessie Smith recording, you will hear her personalized version of the lyrics.

> I once lived the life of a millionaire,
> Spending my money, I didn't care,
> Always taking my friends out for a good time,
> Buying champagne, gin and wine.
> But just as soon as my dough got low,
> I couldn't find a friend, no place I'd go,
> If I ever get my hands on a dollar again,
> I'm gonna squeeze it and squeeze it—till the eagle grins.
> NOBODY KNOWS YOU WHEN YOU'RE DOWN AND OUT,
> In your pocket, not one penny
> And your friends you haven't any.
> And soon as you get on your feet again,

> Ev'rybody is your long lost friend.
> It's mighty strange, without a doubt,
> BUT NOBODY WANTS YOU—WHEN YOU'RE DOWN AND OUT—
> NOBODY WANTS YOU—WHEN YOU'RE DOWN AND OUT.[9]

Smith sang with all the collective anguish of a people who had survived one of the most wrenching dislocations in human history. The song that first captured Wilson's heart, "Nobody in Town Can Bake a Sweet Jellyroll Like Mine," shows the exuberance and humor of the blues. These songs capture both the history and the consciousness of a people. Bearden added a visual component to that history. Smith and Bearden and Wilson are all connected to what is called the black oral tradition. This black oral tradition is descended from an African culture in which drumming and storytelling were primary means of communicating.

Mill Hand's Lunch Bucket

August Wilson found the central character of *Joe Turner's Come and Gone* in Romare Bearden's *Mill Hand's Lunch Bucket* (1978), one of a series of artworks that Bearden called *Pittsburgh Memories*. Bearden and Wilson share a common geographic history as well as certain artistic concerns. Through collage and painting, Bearden expressed his own interpretation of the historical period that Wilson wanted to write about. Bearden explored images of the life led by black Americans going to work in the steel mills of Pittsburgh, where he himself had grown up.

Mill Hand's Lunch Bucket shows a house that becomes the boardinghouse in *Joe Turner's Come and Gone*. Coming down the stairs in the painting is a young man full of energy, his large hand reaching for the lunch bucket on a small table at the foot of the stairs. He may very well be the model for Jeremy, who works building roads in Wilson's play. Seated at the dining table at the center of the scene is another man, hunched over

Mill Hand's Lunch Bucket by Romare Bearden (1911–1988) provided the inspiration for many of the characters in *Joe Turner's Come and Gone*. This artwork exemplifies Bearden's technique of layering images through collage and painting to give extraordinary life and feeling to the figures he created. Bearden's paintings and collages represent the African American experience in both a tropical southern landscape and the industrial cities of the North. He had a particular interest in jazz, which he expressed through numerous studies of musicians. The vibrant color of Bearden's work and his eloquent combination of materials are responsible for his growing reputation as one of the great American artists of the twentieth century.

and weary. Both men wear the asbestos coats and hats necessary to protect against the heat of the furnaces at the steel mills. The original caption of the collage, "The mills went 24 hours a day with three 8-hour shifts," suggests that what we see in the contrasting figures is one man who is just leaving for his shift and another who has just returned, too exhausted even to remove his heavy asbestos coat. However, August Wilson saw far more than a story of grinding labor in the steel mills. Although the painting takes its title from the strong, extended hand reaching for the lunch bucket, it was the seated man who captured Wilson's attention:

> I began to wonder, who was this figure of the abject man sitting in a posture of defeat. It occurred to me that all the people in the painting were going out, and they were going to leave this man alone just when what he needed most was human contact.[10]

Folk Sources and W. C. Handy

Wilson created a background for the figure who moved him so deeply in the Bearden collage from a folk blues song called "Joe Turner's Come and Gone," which, of course, inspired the play's title:

They tell me Joe Turner's come and gone
Ohhh Lordy
They tell me Joe Turner's come and gone
Ohhh Lordy
Got my man and gone
Come with forty links of chain
Ohhh Lordy
Come with forty links of chain
Ohhh Lordy
Got my man and gone[11]

W. C. Handy toured the country as a musician and bandleader before becoming a composer, producer, and music historian.

The musician W. C. Handy collected such folk songs and used them as the basis for his own compositions. In 1916 he wrote his own version of the "Joe Turner Blues," which was suggested by several earlier versions of songs about Joe Turner, Joe Turney, or Joe Tunney, as this historical figure was variously called. Joe Turner was notorious for kidnapping black men for work on chain gangs. In his autobiography, *The Father of the Blues*, W. C. Handy tells the story of Joe Turner, who was, in fact, the brother of a governor of Tennessee:

> Joe had the responsibility of taking Negro prisoners to the penitentiary at Nashville. Sometimes he took them to the "farms" along the Mississippi. Their crimes, when indeed there were any crimes, were usually very minor, the object of the arrests being to provide needed labor for spots along the river. As usual, the method was to set a stool-pigeon where he could start a game of craps. The bones would roll blissfully til the required number of laborers had been drawn into the circle. At that point the law would fall upon the poor devils, arrest as many as were needed for work, try them for gambling in a kangaroo court and then turn the culprits over to Joe Turner. That night there would be weeping and wailing among the dusky belles. If one of them chanced to ask a neighbor what had become of the sweet good man, she was likely to receive the pat reply, "They tell me Joe Turner's come and gone."[12]

The story that W. C. Handy relates could be the story of Herald Loomis. Drawing inspiration from the songs of Bessie Smith, the collage paintings of Romare Bearden, and stories such as W. C. Handy's, August Wilson has created his own vision of the migration of African American people from the South to the North through the journey of Herald Loomis and his fellow travelers, who arrive at a boardinghouse in Pittsburgh in the early twentieth century.

Joe Turner's Come and Gone

AUGUST WILSON

CHARACTERS

Seth Holly, owner of the boardinghouse
Bertha Holly, his wife
Bynum Walker, a rootworker
Rutherford Selig, a peddler
Jeremy Furlow, a resident
Herald Loomis, a resident
Zonia Loomis, his daughter
Mattie Campbell, a resident
Reuben Scott, a boy who lives next door
Molly Cunningham, a resident
Martha Loomis, Herald Loomis's wife

SETTING

August, 1911. A boardinghouse in Pittsburgh. At right is a kitchen. Two doors open off the kitchen. One leads to the outhouse and SETH's workshop. The other to SETH's and BERTHA's bedroom. At left is a parlor. The front door opens into the parlor, which gives access to the stairs leading to the upstairs rooms.

There is a small outside playing area.

THE PLAY

It is August in Pittsburgh, 1911. The sun falls out of heaven like a stone. The fires of the steel mill rage with a combined sense of industry and progress. Barges loaded with coal and iron ore trudge up the river to the mill towns that dot the Monongahela and return with fresh, hard, gleaming steel. The city flexes its muscles. Men throw countless bridges across the rivers, lay roads and carve tunnels through the hills sprouting with houses.

From the deep and the near South the sons and daughters of newly freed African slaves wander into the city. Isolated, cut off from memory, having forgotten the names of the gods and only guessing at their faces, they arrive dazed and stunned, their heart kicking in their chest with a song worth singing. They arrive carrying Bibles and guitars, their pockets lined with dust and fresh hope, marked men and women seeking to scrape from the narrow, crooked cobbles and the fiery blasts of the coke furnace a way of bludgeoning and shaping the malleable parts of themselves into a new identity as free men of definite and sincere worth.

Foreigners in a strange land, they carry as part and parcel of their baggage a long line of separation and dispersement which informs their sensibilities and marks their conduct as they search for ways to reconnect, to reassemble, to give clear and luminous meaning to the song which is both a wail and a whelp of joy.

ACT ONE

Scene One

The lights come up on the kitchen. BERTHA busies herself with breakfast preparations. SETH stands looking out the window at BYNUM in the yard. SETH is in his early fifties. Born of Northern free parents, a skilled craftsman, and owner of the boardinghouse, he has a stability that none of the other characters have. BERTHA is five years his junior. Married for over twenty-five years, she has learned how to negotiate around SETH's apparent orneriness.

SETH: (at the window, laughing.) If that ain't the damndest thing I seen. Look here, Bertha.

BERTHA: I done seen Bynum out there with them pigeons before.

SETH: Naw . . . naw . . . look at this. That pigeon flopped out of Bynum's hand and he about to have a fit.

(BERTHA crosses over to the window.)

He down there on his hands and knees behind that bush looking all over for that pigeon and it on the other side of the yard. See it over there?

BERTHA: Come on and get your breakfast and leave that man alone.

SETH: Look at him . . . he still looking. He ain't seen it yet. All that old mumbo jumbo nonsense. I don't know why I put up with it.

BERTHA: You don't say nothing when he bless the house.

SETH: I just go along with that 'cause of you. You around here sprinkling salt all over the place . . . got pennies lined up across the threshold . . . all that heebie-jeebie stuff. I just put up with that 'cause of you. I don't pay that kind of stuff no mind. And you going down there to the church and wanna come home and sprinkle salt all over the place.

BERTHA: It don't hurt none. I can't say if it help . . . but it don't hurt none.

SETH: Look at him. He done found that pigeon and now he's talking to it.

BERTHA: These biscuits be ready in a minute.

SETH: He done drew a big circle with that stick and now he's dancing around. I know he'd better not . . .

(SETH bolts from the window and rushes to the back door.)

Hey, Bynum! Don't be hopping around stepping in my vegetables.

Hey, Bynum . . . Watch where you stepping!

BERTHA: Seth, leave that man alone.

SETH: (coming back into the house.) I don't care how much he be dancing around . . . just don't be stepping in my vegetables. Man got my garden all messed up now . . . planting them weeds out there . . . burying them pigeons and whatnot.

BERTHA: Bynum don't bother nobody. He ain't even thinking about your vegetables.

SETH: I know he ain't! That's why he out there stepping on them.

BERTHA: What Mr. Johnson say down there?

SETH: I told him if I had the tools I could go out here and find me four or five fellows and open up my own shop instead of working for Mr. Olowski. Get me four or five fellows and teach them how to make pots and pans. One man making ten pots is five men making fifty. He told me he'd think about it.

BERTHA: Well, maybe he'll come to see it your way.

SETH: He wanted me to sign over the house to him. You know what I thought of that idea.

BERTHA: He'll come to see you're right.

SETH: I'm going up and talk to Sam Green. There's more than one way to skin a cat. I'm going up and talk to him. See if he got more sense than Mr. Johnson. I can't get nowhere working for Mr. Olowski and selling Selig five or six pots on the side. I'm going up and see Sam Green. See if he loan me the money.

(SETH crosses back to the window.)

Now he got that cup. He done killed that pigeon and now he's putting its blood in that little cup. I believe he drink that blood.

BERTHA: Seth Holly, what is wrong with you this morning? Come on and get your breakfast so you can go to bed. You know Bynum don't be drinking no pigeon blood.

SETH: I don't know what he do.

BERTHA: Well, watch him, then. He's gonna dig a little hole and bury that pigeon. Then he's gonna pray over that blood . . . pour it on top . . . mark out his circle and come on into the house.

SETH: That's what he doing . . . he pouring that blood on top.

BERTHA: When they gonna put you back working daytime? Told me two months ago he was gonna put you back working daytime.

SETH: That's what Mr. Olowski told me. I got to wait till he say when. He tell me what to do. I don't tell him. Drive me crazy to speculate on the man's wishes when he don't know what he want to do himself.

BERTHA: Well, I wish he go ahead and put you back working daytime. This working all hours of the night don't make no sense.

SETH: It don't make no sense for that boy to run out of here and get drunk so they lock him up either.

BERTHA: Who? Who they got locked up for being drunk?

SETH: That boy that's staying upstairs . . . Jeremy. I stopped down there on Logan Street on my way home from work and one of the fellows told me about it. Say he seen it when they arrested him.

BERTHA: I was wondering why I ain't seen him this morning.

SETH: You know I don't put up with that. I told him when he came . . .

(BYNUM enters from the yard carrying some plants. He is a short, round man in his early sixties. A conjure man, or rootworker, he gives the impression of always being in control of everything. Nothing ever bothers him. He seems to be lost in a world of his own making and to swallow any adversity or interference with his grand design.)

What you doing bringing them weeds in my house? Out there stepping on my vegetables and now wanna carry them weeds in my house.

BYNUM: Morning, Seth. Morning, Sister Bertha.

SETH: Messing up my garden growing them things out there. I ought to go out there and pull up all them weeds.

BERTHA: Some gal was by here to see you this morning, Bynum. You was out there in the yard . . . I told her to come back later.

BYNUM: (To SETH.) You look sick. What's the matter, you ain't eating right?

SETH: What if I was sick? You ain't getting near me with none of that stuff.

(BERTHA sets a plate of biscuits on the table.)

BYNUM: My . . . my . . . Bertha, your biscuits getting fatter and fatter.

(BYNUM takes a biscuit and begins to eat.)

Where Jeremy? I don't see him around this morning. He usually be around riffing and raffing on Saturday morning.

SETH: I know where he at. I know just where he at. They got him down there in the jail. Getting drunk and acting a fool. He down there where he belong with all that foolishness.

BYNUM: Mr. Piney's boys got him, huh? They ain't gonna do nothing but hold on to him for a little while. He's gonna be back here hungrier than a mule directly.

SETH: I don't go for all that carrying on and such. This is a respectable house. I don't have no drunkards or fools around here.

BYNUM: That boy got a lot of country in him. He ain't been up here but two weeks. It's gonna take a while before he can work that country out of him.

SETH: These niggers coming up here with that old backward country style of living. It's hard enough now without all that ignorant kind of acting. Ever since slavery got over with there ain't been nothing but foolish-acting niggers. Word get out they need men to work in the mill and put in these roads . . . and niggers drop everything and head North looking for freedom. They don't know the white fellows looking too. White fellows coming from all over the world. White fellow come over and in six months got more than what I got. But these niggers keep on coming. Walking . . . riding . . . carrying their Bibles. That boy done carried a guitar all the way from North Carolina. What he gonna find out? What he gonna do with that guitar? This the city.

(There is a knock on the door.)

Niggers coming up here from the backwoods . . . coming up here from the country carrying Bibles and guitars looking for freedom. They got a rude awakening.

(SETH goes to answer the door. RUTHERFORD SELIG enters. About SETH's age, he is a thin white man with greasy hair. A peddler, he supplies SETH with the raw materials to make pots and pans which he then peddles door to door in the mill towns along the river. He keeps a list of his customers as they move about and is known in the various communities as the People finder. He carries squares of sheet metal under his arm.)

Ho! Forgot you was coming today. Come on in.

BYNUM: If it ain't Rutherford Selig . . . the People finder himself.

SELIG: What say there, Bynum?

BYNUM: I say about my shiny man. You got to tell me something. I done give you my dollar . . . I'm looking to get a report.

SELIG: I got eight here, Seth.

SETH: (Taking the sheet metal.) What is this? What you giving me here? What I'm gonna do with this?

SELIG: I need some dustpans. Everybody asking me about dustpans.

SETH: Gonna cost you fifteen cents apiece. And ten cents to put a handle on them.

SELIG: I'll give you twenty cents apiece with the handles.

SETH: All right. But I ain't gonna give you but fifteen cents for the sheet metal.

SELIG: It's twenty-five cents apiece for the metal. That's what we agreed on.

SETH: This low-grade sheet metal. They ain't worth but a dime. I'm doing you a favor giving you fifteen cents. You know this metal ain't worth no twenty-five cents. Don't come talking that twenty-five cent stuff to me over no low-grade sheet metal.

SELIG: All right, fifteen cents apiece. Just make me some dustpans out of them.

(SETH exits with the sheet metal out the back door.)

BERTHA: Sit on down there, Selig. Get you a cup of coffee and a biscuit.

BYNUM: Where you coming from this time?

SELIG: I been upriver. All along the Monongahela. Past Rankin and all up around Little Washington.

BYNUM: Did you find anybody?

SELIG: I found Sadie Jackson up in Braddock. Her mother's staying down there in Scotch-bottom say she hadn't heard from her and she didn't know where she was at. I found her up in Braddock on Enoch Street. She bought a frying pan from me.

BYNUM: You around here finding everybody how come you ain't found my shiny man?

SELIG: The only shiny man I saw was the Nigras working on the road gang with the sweat glistening on them.

BYNUM: Naw, you'd be able to tell this fellow. He shine like new money.

SELIG: Well, I done told you I can't find nobody without a name.

BERTHA: Here go one of these hot biscuits, Selig.

BYNUM: This fellow don't have no name. I call him John 'cause it was up around Johnstown where I seen him. I ain't even so sure he's one special fellow. That shine could pass on to anybody. He could be anybody shining.

SELIG: Well, what's he look like besides being shiny? There's lots of shiny Nigras.

BYNUM: He's just a man I seen out on the road. He ain't had no special look. Just a man walking toward me on the road. He come up and asked me which way the road went. I told him everything I knew about the road, where it went and all, and he asked me did I have anything to eat 'cause he was hungry. Say he ain't had nothing to eat in three days. Well, I never be out there on the road without a piece of dried meat. Or an orange or an apple. So I give this fellow an orange. He take and eat that orange and told me to come and go along the road a little ways with him, that he had something he wanted to show me. He had a look about him made me wanna go with him, see what he gonna show me.

We walked on a bit and it's getting kind of far from where I met him when it come up on me all of a sudden, we wasn't going the way he had come from, we was going back my way. Since he said he ain't knew nothing about the road, I asked him about this. He say he had a voice inside him telling him which way to go and if I come and go along with him he was gonna show me the Secret of Life. Quite naturally I followed him. A fellow that's gonna show you the Secret of Life ain't to be taken lightly. We get near this bend in the road . . .

(SETH enters with an assortment of pots.)

SETH: I got six here, Selig.

SELIG: Wait a minute, Seth. Bynum's telling me about the secret of life. Go ahead, Bynum. I wanna hear this.

(SETH sets the pots down and exits out the back.)

BYNUM: We get near this bend in the road and he told me to hold out my hands. Then he rubbed them together with his and I looked down and see they got blood on them. Told me to take and rub it all over me . . . say that was a way of cleaning myself. Then we went around the bend in that road. Got around that bend and it seem like all of a sudden we ain't in the same place. Turn around that bend and everything look like it was twice as big as it was. The trees and everything bigger than life! Sparrows big as eagles! I turned

around to look at this fellow and he had this light coming out of him. I had to cover up my eyes to keep from being blinded. He shining like new money with that light. He shined until all the light seemed like it seeped out of him and then he was gone and I was by myself in this strange place where everything was bigger than life.

I wandered around there looking for that road, trying to find my way back from this big place . . . and I looked over and seen my daddy standing there. He was the same size he always was, except for his hands and his mouth. He had a great big old mouth that look like it took up his whole face and his hands were as big as hams. Look like they was too big to carry around. My daddy called me to him. Said he had been thinking about me and it grieved him to see me in the world carrying other people's songs and not having one of my own. Told me he was gonna show me how to find my song. Then he carried me further into this big place until we come to this ocean. Then he showed me something I ain't got words to tell you. But if you stand to witness it, you done seen something there. I stayed in that place awhile and my daddy taught me the meaning of this thing that I had seen and showed me how to find my song. I asked him about the shiny man and he told me he was the One Who Goes Before and Shows the Way. Said there was lots of shiny men and if I ever saw one again before I died then I would know that my song had been accepted and worked its full power in the world and I could lay down and die a happy man. A man who done left his mark on life. On the way people cling to each other out of the truth they find in themselves. Then he showed me how to get back to the road. I came out to where everything was its own size and I had my song. I had the Binding Song. I choose that song because that's what I seen most when I was traveling . . . people walking away and leaving one another. So I takes the power of my song and binds them together.

(SETH enters from the yard carrying cabbages and tomatoes.)

Been binding people ever since. That's why they call me Bynum. Just like glue I sticks people together.

SETH: Maybe they ain't supposed to be stuck sometimes. You ever think of that?

BYNUM: Oh, I don't do it lightly. It cost me a piece of myself every time I do. I'm a Binder of What Clings. You got to find out if they cling first. You can't bind what don't cling.

SELIG: Well, how is that the Secret of Life? I thought you said he was gonna show you the secret of life. That's what I'm waiting to find out.

BYNUM: Oh, he showed me alright. But you still got to figure it out. Can't nobody figure it out for you. You got to come to it on your own. That's why I'm looking for the shiny man.

SELIG: Well, I'll keep my eye out for him. What you got there, Seth?

SETH: Here go some cabbage and tomatoes. I got some green beans coming in real nice. I'm gonna take and start me a grapevine out there next year. Butera says he gonna give me a piece of his vine and I'm gonna start that out there.

SELIG: How many of them pots you got?

SETH: I got six. That's six dollars minus eight on top of fifteen for the sheet metal come to a dollar twenty out the six dollars leave me four dollars and eighty cents.

SELIG: (Counting out the money.) There's four dollars . . . and . . . eighty cents.

SETH: How many of them dustpans you want?

SELIG: As many as you can make out them sheets.

SETH: You can use that many? I get to cutting on them sheets figuring how to make them dustpans . . . ain't no telling how many I'm liable to come up with.

SELIG: I can use them and you can make me some more next time.

SETH: Alright, I'm gonna hold you to that, now.

SELIG: Thanks for the biscuit, Bertha.

BERTHA: You know you welcome anytime, Selig.

SETH: Which way you heading?

SELIG: Going down to Wheeling. All through West Virginia there. I'll be back Saturday. They putting in new roads down that way. Makes traveling easier.

SETH: That's what I hear. All up around here too. Got a fellow staying here working on that road by the Brady Street Bridge.

SELIG: Yeah, it's gonna make traveling real nice. Thanks for the cabbage, Seth. I'll see you on Saturday.

(SELIG exits.)

SETH: (To BYNUM.) Why you wanna start all that nonsense talk with that man? All that shiny man nonsense.

BYNUM: You known it ain't no nonsense. Bertha know it ain't no nonsense. I don't know if Selig know or not.

BERTHA: Seth, when you get to making them dustpans make me a coffeepot.

SETH: What's the matter with your coffee? Ain't nothing wrong with your coffee. Don't she make some good coffee, Bynum?

BYNUM: I ain't worried about the coffee. I know she makes some good biscuits.

SETH: I ain't studying no coffeepot, woman. You heard me tell the man I was gonna cut as many dustpans as them sheets will make . . . and all of a sudden you want a coffeepot.

BERTHA: Man, hush up and go on and make me that coffeepot.

(JEREMY enters the front door. About twenty-five, he gives the impression that he has the world in his hand, that he can meet life's challenges head on. He smiles a lot. He is a proficient guitar player, though his spirit has yet to be molded into song.)

BYNUM: I hear Mr. Piney's boys had you.

JEREMY: Fined me two dollars for nothing! Ain't done nothing.

SETH: I told you when you come on here everybody know my house. Know these is respectable quarters. I don't put up with no foolishness. Everybody know Seth Holly keep a good house. Was my daddy's house. This house been a decent house for a long time.

JEREMY: I ain't done nothing, Mr. Seth. I stopped by the Workmen's Club and got me a bottle. Me and Roper Lee from Alabama. Had us a half pint. We was fixing to cut that half in two when they came up on us. Asked us if we was working. We told them we was putting in the road over yonder and that it was our payday. They snatched hold of us to get that two dollars. Me and Roper Lee ain't even had a chance to take a drink when they grabbed us.

SETH: I don't go for all that kind of carrying on.

BERTHA: Leave the boy alone, Seth. You know the police do that. Figure there's too many people out on the street they take some of them off. You know that.

SETH: I ain't gonna have folks talking.

BERTHA: Ain't nobody talking nothing. That's all in your head. You want some grits and biscuits, Jeremy?

JEREMY: Thank you, Miss Bertha. They didn't give us a thing to eat last night. I'll take one of them big bowls if you don't mind.

(There is a knock at the door. SETH goes to answer it. Enter HERALD LOOMIS and his eleven-year-old daughter, ZONIA. HERALD LOOMIS is thirty-two years old. He is at times possessed. A man driven not by the hellhounds that seemingly bay at his heels, but by his search for a world that speaks to something about himself. He is unable to harmonize the forces that swirl around him, and seeks to recreate the world into one that contains his image. He wears a hat and a long wool coat.)

LOOMIS: Me and my daughter looking for a place to stay, mister. You got a sign say you got rooms.

(SETH stares at LOOMIS, sizing him up.)

Mister, if you ain't got no rooms we can go somewhere else.

SETH: How long you plan on staying?

LOOMIS: Don't know. Two weeks or more maybe.

SETH: It's two dollars a week for the room. We serve meals twice a day. It's two dollars for room and board. Pay up in advance.

(LOOMIS reaches into his pocket.)

It's a dollar extra for the girl.

LOOMIS: The girl sleep in the same room.

SETH: Well, do she eat off the same plate? We serve meals twice a day. That's a dollar extra for food.

LOOMIS: Ain't got no extra dollar. I was planning on asking your missus if she could help out with the cooking and cleaning and whatnot.

SETH: Her helping out don't put no food on the table. I need that dollar to buy some food.

LOOMIS: I'll give you fifty cents extra. She don't eat much.

SETH: Okay . . . but fifty cents don't buy but half a portion.

BERTHA: Seth, she can help me out. Let her help me out. I can use some help.

SETH: Well, that's two dollars for the week. Pay up in advance. Saturday to Saturday. You wanna stay on then it's two more come Saturday.

(LOOMIS pays SETH the money.)

BERTHA: My name's Bertha. This my husband, Seth. You got Bynum and Jeremy over there.

LOOMIS: Ain't nobody else live here?

BERTHA: They the only ones live here now. People come and go. They the only ones here now. You want a cup of coffee and a biscuit?

LOOMIS: We done ate this morning.

BYNUM: Where you coming from, Mister . . . I didn't get your name.

LOOMIS: Name's Herald Loomis. This my daughter, Zonia.

BYNUM: Where you coming from?

LOOMIS: Come from all over. Whicheverway the road take us that's the way we go.

JEREMY: If you looking for a job, I'm working putting in that road down there by the bridge. They can't get enough mens. Always looking to take somebody on.

LOOMIS: I'm looking for a woman named Martha Loomis. That's my wife. Got married legal with the papers and all.

SETH: I don't know nobody named Loomis. I know some Marthas but I don't know no Loomis.

BYNUM: You got to see Rutherford Selig if you wanna find somebody. Selig's the People finder. Rutherford Selig's a first-class People finder.

JEREMY: What she look like? Maybe I seen her.

LOOMIS: She a brownskin woman. Got long pretty hair. About five feet from the ground.

JEREMY: I don't know. I might have seen her.

BYNUM: You got to see Rutherford Selig. You give him one dollar to get her name on his list . . . and after she get her name on his list Rutherford Selig will go right on out there and find her. I got him looking for somebody for me.

LOOMIS: You say he find people. How you find him?

BYNUM: You just missed him. He's gone downriver now. You got to wait till Saturday. He's gone downriver with his pots and pans. He come to see Seth on Saturdays. You got to wait till then.

SETH: Come on, I'll show you to your room.

(SETH, LOOMIS, and ZONIA exit up the stairs.)

JEREMY: Miss Bertha, I'll take that biscuit you was gonna give that fellow, if you don't mind. Say, Mr. Bynum, they got somebody like that around here sure enough? Somebody that find people?

BYNUM: Rutherford Selig. He go around selling pots and pans and every house he come to he write down the name and address of whoever lives there. So if you looking for somebody, quite naturally you go and see

him . . . 'cause he's the only one who know where everybody live at.

JEREMY: I ought to have him look for this old gal I used to know. It be nice to see her again.

BERTHA: (Giving JEREMY a biscuit.) Jeremy, today's the day for you to pull them sheets off the bed and set them outside your door. I'll set you out some clean ones.

BYNUM: Mr. Piney's boys done ruined your good time last night, Jeremy . . . what you planning for tonight?

JEREMY: They got me scared to go out, Mr. Bynum. They might grab me again.

BYNUM: You ought to take your guitar and go down to Seefus. Seefus got a gambling place down there on Wylie Avenue. You ought to take your guitar and go down there. They got a guitar contest down there.

JEREMY: I don't play no contest, Mr. Bynum. Had one of them white fellows cure me of that. I ain't been nowhere near a contest since.

BYNUM: White fellow beat you playing guitar?

JEREMY: Naw, he ain't beat me. I was sitting at home just fixing to sit down and eat when somebody come up to my house and got me. Told me there's a white fellow say he was gonna give a prize to the best guitar player he could find. I take up my guitar and go down there and somebody had gone up and got Bobo Smith and brought him down there. Him and another fellow called Hooter. Old Hooter couldn't play no guitar, he do more hollering than playing, but Bobo could go at it awhile.

This fellow standing there say he the one that was gonna give the prize and me and Bobo started playing for him. Bobo play something and then I'd try to play something better than what he played. Old Hooter, he just holler and bang at the guitar. Man was the worst guitar player I ever seen. So me and Bobo played and after a while I seen where he was getting the attention of this white fellow. He'd play something and while he was playing it he be slapping on the side of the guitar, and that made it sound like he was playing more than he was. So I started doing it too. White fellow ain't knew no difference. He ain't knew as much about guitar playing as Hooter did. After we play awhile, the white fellow called us to him and said he couldn't make up his mind, say all three of us was the best guitar player and we'd have to split the prize between us. Then he give us twenty-five cents. That's eight cents apiece and a penny on the side. That cured me of playing contest to this day.

BYNUM: Seefus ain't like that. Seefus give a whole dollar and a drink of whiskey.

JEREMY: What night they be down there?

BYNUM: Be down there every night. Music don't know no certain night.

BERTHA: You go down to Seefus with them people and you liable to end up in a raid and go to jail sure enough. I don't know why Bynum tell you that.

BYNUM: That's where the music at. That's where the people at. The people down there making music and enjoying themselves. Some things is worth taking the chance going to jail about.

BERTHA: Jeremy ain't got no business going down there.

JEREMY: They got some women down there, Mr. Bynum?

BYNUM: Oh, they got women down there, sure. They got women everywhere. Women be where the men is so they can find each other.

JEREMY: Some of them old gals come out there where we be putting in that road. Hanging around there trying to snatch somebody.

BYNUM: How come some of them ain't snatched hold of you?

JEREMY: I don't want them kind. Them desperate kind. Ain't nothing worse than a desperate woman. Tell them you gonna leave them and they get to crying and carrying on. That just make you want to get away quicker. They get

to cutting up your clothes and things trying to keep you staying. Desperate women ain't nothing but trouble for a man.

(SETH enters from the stairs.)

SETH: Something ain't setting right with that fellow.

BERTHA: What's wrong with him? What he say?

SETH: I take him up there and try to talk to him and he ain't for no talking. Say he been traveling . . . coming over from Ohio. Say he a deacon in the church. Say he looking for Martha Pentecost. Talking about that's his wife.

BERTHA: How you know it's the same Martha? Could be talking about anybody. Lots of people named Martha.

SETH: You see that little girl? I didn't hook it up till he said it, but that little girl look just like her. Ask Bynum.

(To BYNUM.) Bynum. Don't that little girl look just like Martha Pentecost?

BERTHA: I still say he could be talking about anybody.

SETH: The way he described her wasn't no doubt about who he was talking about. Described her right down to her toes.

BERTHA: What did you tell him?

SETH: I ain't told him nothing. The way that fellow look I wasn't gonna tell him nothing. I don't know what he looking for her for.

BERTHA: What else he have to say?

SETH: I told you he wasn't for no talking. I told him where the outhouse was and to keep that gal off the front porch and out of my garden. He asked if you'd mind setting a hot tub for the gal and that was about the gist of it.

BERTHA: Well, I wouldn't let it worry me if I was you. Come on get your sleep.

BYNUM: He says he looking for Martha and he a deacon in the church.

SETH: That's what he say. Do he look like a deacon to you?

BERTHA: He might be, you don't know. Bynum ain't got no special say on whether he a deacon or not.

SETH: Well, if he the deacon I'd sure like to see the preacher.

BERTHA: Come on get your sleep. Jeremy, don't forget to set them sheets outside the door like I told you.

(BERTHA exits into the bedroom.)

SETH: Something ain't setting right with that fellow, Bynum. He's one of them mean-looking niggers look like he done killed somebody gambling over a quarter.

BYNUM: He ain't no gambler. Gamblers wear nice shoes. This fellow got on clodhoppers. He been out there walking up and down them roads.

(ZONIA enters from the stairs and looks around.)

BYNUM: You looking for the back door, sugar? There it is. You can go out there and play. It's alright.

SETH: (Showing her the door.) You can go out there and play. Just don't get in my garden. And don't go messing around in my workshed.

(SETH exits into the bedroom. There is a knock on the door.)

JEREMY: Somebody at the door.

(JEREMY goes to answer the door. Enter MATTIE CAMPBELL. She is a young woman of twenty-six whose attractiveness is hidden under the weight and concerns of a dissatisfied life. She is a woman in an honest search for love and companionship. She has suffered many defeats in her search, and though not always uncompromising, still believes in the possibility of love.)

MATTIE: I'm looking for a man named Bynum. Lady told me to come back later.

JEREMY: Sure, he here. Mr. Bynum, somebody here to see you.

BYNUM: Come to see me, huh?

MATTIE: Are you the man they call Bynum? The man folks say can fix things?

BYNUM: Depend on what need fixing. I can't make no promises. But I got a powerful song in some matters.

MATTIE: Can you fix it so my man come back to me?

BYNUM: Come on in . . . have a sit down.

MATTIE: You got to help me. I don't know what else to do.

BYNUM: Depend on how all the circumstances of the thing come together. How all the pieces fit.

MATTIE: I done everything I knowed how to do. You got to make him come back to me.

BYNUM: It ain't nothing to make somebody come back. I can fix it so he can't stand to be away from you. I got my roots and powders, I can fix it so wherever he's at this thing will come up on him and he won't be able to sleep for seeing your face. Won't be able to eat for thinking of you.

MATTIE: That's what I want. Make him come back.

BYNUM: The roots is a powerful thing. I can fix it so one day he'll walk out his front door . . . won't be thinking of nothing. He won't know what it is. All he knows is that a powerful dissatisfaction done set in his bones and can't nothing he do make him feel satisfied. He'll set his foot down on the road and the wind in the trees be talking to him and everywhere he step on the road, that road'll give back your name and something will pull him right up to your doorstep. Now, I can do that. I can take my roots and fix that easy. But maybe he ain't supposed to come back. And if he ain't supposed to come back . . . then he'll be in your bed one morning and it'll come up on him that he's in the wrong place. That he's lost outside of time from his place that he's supposed to be in. Then both of you be lost and trapped outside of life and ain't no way for you to get back into it. 'Cause you lost from yourselves and where the places come together, where you're supposed to be alive, your heart kicking in your chest with a song worth singing.

MATTIE: Make him come back to me. Make his feet say my name on the road. I don't care what happens. Make him come back.

BYNUM: What's your man's name?

MATTIE: He go by Jack Carper. He was born in Alabama then he come to West Texas and find me and we come here. Been here three years before he left. Say I had a curse prayer on me and he started walking down the road and ain't never come back. Somebody told me, say you can fix things like that.

BYNUM: He just got up one day, set his feet on the road, and walked away?

MATTIE: You got to make him come back, mister.

BYNUM: Did he say goodbye?

MATTIE: Ain't said nothing. Just started walking. I could see where he disappeared. Didn't look back. Just keep walking. Can't you fix it so he come back? I ain't got no curse prayer on me. I know I ain't.

BYNUM: What made him say you had a curse prayer on you?

MATTIE: 'Cause the babies died. Me and Jack had two babies. Two little babies that ain't lived two months before they died. He say it's because somebody cursed me not to have babies.

BYNUM: He ain't bound to you if the babies died. Look like somebody trying to keep you from being bound up and he's gone on back to whoever it is 'cause he's already bound up to her. Ain't nothing to be done. Somebody else done got a powerful hand in it and ain't nothing to be done to break it. You got to let him go find where he's supposed to be in the world.

MATTIE: Jack done gone off and you telling me to forget about him. All my life I been looking for somebody to stop and stay with me. I done already got too many things to forget about. I take Jack Carper's hand and it feel so rough and strong. Seem like he's the strongest man in the world the way he hold me. Like he's bigger than the whole world and can't nothing bad get to me. Even when he act mean sometimes he still make everything seem okay with the world. Like there's part of it that belongs just to you. Now you telling me to forget about him?

BYNUM: Jack Carper gone off to where he belong. There's somebody searching for your doorstep right now. Ain't no need you fretting over Jack Carper. Right now he's a strong thought in your mind. But every time you catch yourself fretting over Jack Carper you push that thought away. You push it out your mind and that thought will get weaker and weaker till you wake up one morning and you won't even be able to call him up on your mind.

(BYNUM gives her a small cloth packet.)

Take this and sleep with it under your pillow and it'll bring good luck to you. Draw it to you like a magnet. It won't be long before you forget all about Jack Carper.

MATTIE: How much . . . do I owe you?

BYNUM: Whatever you got there . . . that'll be alright.

(MATTIE hands BYNUM two quarters. She crosses to the door.)

You sleep with that under your pillow and you'll be alright.

(MATTIE opens the door to exit and JEREMY crosses over to her. BYNUM overhears the first part of their conversation, then exits out the back.)

JEREMY: I overheard what you told Mr. Bynum. Had me an old gal did that to me. Woke up one morning and she was gone. Just took off to parts unknown. I woke up that morning and the only thing I could do was look around for my shoes. I woke up and got out of there. Found my shoes and took off. That's the only thing I could think of to do.

MATTIE: She ain't said nothing?

JEREMY: I just looked around for my shoes and got out of there.

MATTIE: Jack ain't said nothing either. He just walked off.

JEREMY: Some mens do that. Womens too. I ain't gone off looking for her. I just let her go. Figure she had a time to come to herself. Wasn't no use of me standing in the way. Where you from?

MATTIE: Texas. I was born in Georgia but I went to Texas with my mama. She dead now. Was picking peaches and fell dead away. I come up here with Jack Carper.

JEREMY: I'm from North Carolina. Down around Raleigh where they got all that tobacco. Been up here about two weeks. I likes it fine except I still got to find me a woman. You got a nice look to you. Look like you have mens standing in your door. Is you got mens standing in your door to get a look at you?

MATTIE: I ain't got nobody since Jack left.

JEREMY: A woman like you need a man. Maybe you let me be your man. I got a nice way with the women. That's what they tell me.

MATTIE: I don't know. Maybe Jack's coming back.

JEREMY: I'll be your man till he come. A woman can't be by her lonesome. Let me be your man till he come.

MATTIE: I just can't go through life piecing myself out to different mens. I need a man who wants to stay with me.

JEREMY: I can't say what's gonna happen. Maybe I'll be the man. I don't know. You wanna go along the road a little ways with me?

MATTIE: I don't know. Seem like life say it's gonna be one thing and end up being another. I'm tired of going from man to man.

JEREMY: Life is like you got to take a chance. Everybody got to take a chance. Can't nobody say what's gonna be. Come on . . . take a chance with me and see what the year bring. Maybe you let me come and see you. Where you staying?

MATTIE: I got me a room up on Bedford. Me and Jack had a room together.

JEREMY: What's the address? I'll come by and get you tonight and we can go down to Seefus. I'm going down there and play my guitar.

MATTIE: You play guitar?

JEREMY: I play guitar like I'm born to it.

MATTIE: I live at 1727 Bedford Avenue. I'm gonna find out if you can play guitar like you say.

JEREMY: I plays it sugar, and that ain't all I do. I got a ten-pound hammer and I knows how to drive it down. Good god . . . you ought to hear my hammer ring!

MATTIE: Go on with that kind of talk, now. If you gonna come by and get me I got to get home and straighten up for you.

JEREMY: I'll be by at eight o'clock. How's eight o'clock? I'm gonna make you forget all about Jack Carper.

MATTIE: Go on, now. I got to get home and fix up for you.

JEREMY: Eight o'clock, sugar.

(The lights go down in the parlor and come up on the yard outside. ZONIA is singing and playing a game.)

ZONIA:

*I went downtown
To get my grip
I came back home
Just a pullin' the skiff*

*I went upstairs
To make my bed
I made a mistake
And I bumped my head
Just a pullin' the skiff*

*I went downstairs
To milk the cow
I made a mistake
And I milked the sow
Just a pullin' the skiff*

*Tomorrow, tomorrow
Tomorrow never comes
The marrow the marrow
The marrow in the bone.*

(REUBEN enters.)

REUBEN: Hi.

ZONIA: Hi.

REUBEN: What's your name?

ZONIA: Zonia.

REUBEN: What kind of name is that?

ZONIA: It's what my daddy named me.

REUBEN: My name's Reuben. You staying in Mr. Seth's house?

ZONIA: Yeah.

REUBEN: That your daddy I seen you with this morning?

ZONIA: I don't know. Who you see me with?

REUBEN: I saw you with some man had on a great big old coat. And you was walking up to Mr. Seth's house. Had on a hat too.

ZONIA: Yeah, that's my daddy.

REUBEN: You like Mr. Seth?

ZONIA: I ain't see him much.

REUBEN: My grandpap say he a great big old windbag. How come you living in Mr. Seth's house? Don't you have no house?

ZONIA: We going to find my mother.

REUBEN: Where she at?

ZONIA: I don't know. We got to find her. We just go all over.

REUBEN: Why you got to find her? What happened to her?

ZONIA: She ran away.

REUBEN: Why she run away?

ZONIA: I don't know. My daddy say some man named Joe Turner did something bad to him once and that made her run away.

REUBEN: Maybe she coming back and you don't have to go looking for her.

ZONIA: We ain't there no more.

REUBEN: She could have come back when you wasn't there.

ZONIA: My daddy said she ran off and left us so we going looking for her.

REUBEN: What he gonna do when he find her?

ZONIA: He didn't say. He just say he got to find her.

REUBEN: Your daddy say how long you staying in Mr. Seth's house?

ZONIA: He don't say much. But we never stay too long nowhere. He say we got to keep moving till we find her.

REUBEN: Ain't no kids hardly live around here. I had me a friend but he died. He was the best friend I ever had. Me and Eugene used to keep secrets. I still got his pigeons. He told me to let them go when he died. He say, "Reuben, promise me when I die you'll let my pigeons go." But I keep them to remember him by. I ain't never gonna let them go. Even when I get to be grown up. I'm just always gonna have Eugene's pigeons.

(Pause.)

Mr. Bynum a conjure man. My grandpap scared of him. He don't like me to come over here too much. I'm scared of him too. My grandpap told me not to let him get close enough to where he can reach out his hand and touch me.

ZONIA: He don't seem scary to me.

REUBEN: He buys pigeons from me . . . and if you get up early in the morning you can see him out in the yard doing something with them pigeons. My grandpap say he kill them. I sold him one yesterday. I don't know what he do with it. I just hope he don't spook me up.

ZONIA: Why you sell him pigeons if he's gonna spook you up?

REUBEN: I just do like Eugene do. He used to sell Mr. Bynum pigeons. That's how he got to collecting them to sell to Mr. Bynum. Sometime he give me a nickel and sometime he give me a whole dime.

(LOOMIS enters from the house.)

LOOMIS: Zonia!

ZONIA: Sir?

LOOMIS: What you doing?

ZONIA: Nothing.

LOOMIS: You stay around this house, you hear? I don't want you wandering off nowhere.

ZONIA: I ain't wandering off nowhere.

LOOMIS: Miss Bertha set that hot tub and you getting a good scrubbing. Get scrubbed up good. You ain't been scrubbing.

ZONIA: I been scrubbing.

LOOMIS: Look at you. You growing too fast. Your bones getting bigger everyday. I don't want you getting grown on me. Don't you get grown on me too soon. We gonna find your mamma. She around here somewhere. I can smell her. You stay on around this house now. Don't you go nowhere.

ZONIA: Yes, sir.

(LOOMIS exits into the house.)

REUBEN: Wow, your daddy's scary!

ZONIA: He is not! I don't know what you talking about.

REUBEN: He got them mean-looking eyes!

ZONIA: My daddy ain't got no mean-looking eyes!

REUBEN: Aw, girl, I was just messing with you. You wanna go see Eugene's pigeons? Got a great big coop out the back of my house. Come on, I'll show you.

(REUBEN and ZONIA exit as the lights go down.)

Scene Two

It is Saturday morning, one week later. The lights come up on the kitchen. BERTHA is at the stove preparing breakfast while SETH sits at the table.

SETH: Something ain't right about that fellow. I been watching him all week. Something ain't right, I'm telling you.

BERTHA: Seth Holly, why don't you hush up about that man this morning?

SETH: I don't like the way he stare at everybody. Don't look at you natural like. He just be staring at you. Like he trying to figure out something about you. Did you see him when he come back in here?

BERTHA: That man ain't thinking about you.

SETH: He don't work nowhere. Just go out and come back. Go out and come back.

BERTHA: As long as you get your boarding money it ain't your cause about what he do. He don't bother nobody.

SETH: Just go out and come back. Going around asking everybody about Martha. Like Henry Allen seen him down at the church last night.

BERTHA: The man's allowed to go to church if he want. He say he a deacon. Ain't nothing wrong about him going to church.

SETH: I ain't talking about him going to church. I'm talking about him hanging around outside the church.

BERTHA: Henry Allen say that?

SETH: Say he be standing around outside the church. Like he be watching it.

BERTHA: What on earth he wanna be watching the church for, I wonder?

SETH: That's what I'm trying to figure out. Looks like he fixing to rob it.

BERTHA: Seth, now do he look like the kind that would rob the church?

SETH: I ain't saying that. I ain't saying how he look. It's how he do. Anybody liable to do anything as far as I'm concerned. I ain't never thought about how no church robbers look . . . but now that you mention it, I don't see where they look no different than how he look.

BERTHA: Herald Loomis ain't the kind of man who would rob no church.

SETH: I ain't even so sure that's his name.

BERTHA: Why the man got to lie about his name?

SETH: Anybody can tell anybody anything about what their name is. That's what you call him . . . Herald Loomis. His name is liable to be anything.

BERTHA: Well, until he tell me different that's what I'm gonna call him. You just getting yourself all worked up about the man for nothing.

SETH: Talking about Loomis: Martha's name wasn't no Loomis nothing. Martha's name is Pentecost.

BERTHA: How you so sure that's her right name? Maybe she changed it.

SETH: Martha's a good Christian woman. This fellow here look like he owe the devil a day's work and he's trying to figure out how he gonna pay him. Martha ain't had a speck of distrust about her the whole time she was living here. They moved the church out there to Rankin and I was sorry to see her go.

BERTHA: That's why he be hanging around the church. He looking for her.

SETH: If he looking for her, why don't he go inside and ask? What he doing hanging around outside the church acting sneaky like?

(BYNUM enters from the yard.)

BYNUM: Morning, Seth. Morning, Sister Bertha.

(BYNUM continues through the kitchen and exits up the stairs.)

BERTHA: That's who you should be asking the questions. He been out there in that yard all morning. He was out there before the sun come up. He didn't even come in for breakfast. I don't know what he's doing. He had three of them pigeons line up out there. He dance around till he get tired. He sit down awhile then get up and dance some more. He come through here a little while ago looking like he was mad at the world.

SETH: I don't pay Bynum no mind. He don't spook me up with all that stuff.

BERTHA: That's how Martha come to be living here. She come to see Bynum. She come to see him when she first left from down South.

SETH: Martha was living here before Bynum. She ain't come on here when she first left from down there. She come on here after she went back to get her little girl. That's when she come on here.

BERTHA: Well, where was Bynum? He was here when she came.

SETH: Bynum ain't come till after her. That boy Hiram was staying up there in Bynum's room.

BERTHA: Well, how long Bynum been here?

SETH: Bynum ain't been here no longer than three years. That's what I'm trying to tell you. Martha was staying up there and sewing and cleaning for Doc Goldblum when Bynum came. This the longest he ever been in one place.

BERTHA: How you know how long the man been in one place?

SETH: I know Bynum. Bynum ain't no mystery to me. I done seen a hundred niggers like him. He's one of them fellows never could stay in one place. He was wandering all around the country till he got old and settled here. The only thing different about Bynum is he bring all this heebie-jeebie stuff with him.

BERTHA: I still say he was staying here when she came. That's why she came . . . to see him.

SETH: You can say what you want. I know the fact of it. She come on here four years ago all heartbroken 'cause she couldn't find her little girl. And Bynum wasn't nowhere around. She got mixed up in that old heebie-jeebie nonsense with him after he came.

BERTHA: Well, if she came on before Bynum I don't know where she stayed. 'Cause she stayed up there in Hiram's room. Hiram couldn't get along with Bynum and left out of here owing you two dollars. Now, I know you ain't forgot about that!

SETH: Sure did! You know Hiram ain't paid me that two dollars yet. So that's why he be ducking and hiding when he see me down on Logan Street. You right. Martha did come on after Bynum. I forgot that's why Hiram left.

BERTHA: Him and Bynum never could see eye to eye. They always rubbed each other the wrong way. Hiram got to thinking that Bynum was trying to put a fix on him and he moved out. Martha came to see Bynum and ended up taking Hiram's room. Now, I know what I'm talking about. She stayed on here three years till they moved the church.

SETH: She out there in Rankin now. I know where she at. I know where they moved the church to. She right out there in Rankin in that place used to be a shoe store. Used to be Wolf's shoe store. They moved to a bigger place and they put that church in there. I know where she at. I know just where she at.

BERTHA: Why don't you tell the man? You see he looking for her.

SETH: I ain't gonna tell that man where that woman is! What I wanna do that for? I don't know nothing about that man. I don't know why he looking for her. He might wanna do her a harm. I ain't gonna carry that on my hands. He looking for her, he gonna have to find her for himself. I ain't gonna help him. Now, if he had come and presented himself as a gentleman—the way Martha Pentecost's husband would have done—then I would have told him. But I ain't gonna tell this old wild-eyed mean-looking nigger nothing!

BERTHA: Well, why don't you get a ride with Selig and go up there and tell her where he is? See if she wanna see him. If that's her little girl . . . you say Martha was looking for her.

SETH: You know me, Bertha. I don't get mixed up in nobody's business.

(BYNUM enters from the stairs.)

BYNUM: Morning, Seth. Morning, Bertha. Can I still get some breakfast? Mr. Loomis been down here this morning?

SETH: He done gone out and come back. He up there now. Left out of here early this morning wearing that coat. Hot as it is, the man wanna walk around wearing a big old heavy coat. He come back in here paid me for another week, sat down there waiting on Selig. Got tired of waiting and went on back upstairs.

BYNUM: Where's the little girl?

SETH: She out there in the front. Had to chase her and that Reuben off the front porch. She out there somewhere.

BYNUM: Look like if Martha was around here he would have found her by now. My guess is she ain't in the city.

SETH: She ain't! I know where she at. I know just where she at. But I ain't gonna tell him. Not the way he look.

BERTHA: Here go your coffee, Bynum.

BYNUM: He says he gonna get Selig to find her for him.

SETH: Selig can't find her. He talk all that . . . but unless he get lucky and knock on her door he can't find her. That's the only way he find anybody. He got to get lucky. But I know just where she at.

BERTHA: Here go some biscuits, Bynum.

BYNUM: What else you got over there, Sister Bertha? You got some grits and gravy over there? I could go for some of that this morning.

BERTHA: (Sets a bowl on the table.) Seth, come on and help me turn this mattress over. Come on.

SETH: Something ain't right with that fellow, Bynum. I don't like the way he stare at everybody.

BYNUM: Mr. Loomis alright, Seth. He just a man got something on his mind. He just got a straightforward mind, that's all.

SETH: What's that fellow that they had around here? Moses, that's Moses Houser. Man went crazy and jumped off the Brady Street Bridge. I told you when I seen him something wasn't right about him. And I'm telling you about this fellow now.

(There is a knock on the door. SETH goes to answer it. Enter RUTHERFORD SELIG.)

Ho! Come on in, Selig.

BYNUM: If it ain't the People finder himself.

SELIG: Bynum, before you start . . . I ain't seen no shiny man now.

BYNUM: Who said anything about that? I ain't said nothing about that. I just called you a first-class People finder.

SELIG: How many dustpans you get out of that sheet metal, Seth?

SETH: You walked by them on your way in. They sitting out there on the porch. Got twenty-eight. Got four out of each sheet and made Bertha a coffeepot out the other one. They a little small but they got nice handles.

SELIG: That was twenty cents apiece, right? That's what we agreed on.

SETH: That's five dollars and sixty cents. Twenty on top of twenty-eight. How many sheets you bring me?

SELIG: I got eight out there. That's a dollar twenty makes me owe you . . .

SETH: Four dollars and forty cents.

SELIG: (Paying him.) Go on and make me some dustpans. I can use all you can make.

(LOOMIS enters from the stairs.)

LOOMIS: I been watching for you. He say you find people.

BYNUM: Mr. Loomis here wants you to find his wife.

LOOMIS: He say you find people. Find her for me.

SELIG: Well, let see here . . . find somebody, is it?

(SELIG rummages through his pockets. He has several notebooks and he is searching for the right one.)

Alright now . . . what's the name?

LOOMIS: Martha Loomis. She my wife. Got married legal with the paper and all.

SELIG: (Writing.) Martha . . . Loomis. How tall is she?

LOOMIS: She five feet from the ground.

SELIG: Five feet . . . tall. Young or old?

LOOMIS: She a young woman. Got long pretty hair.

SELIG: Young . . . long . . . pretty . . . hair. Where did you last see her?

LOOMIS: Tennessee. Nearby Memphis.

SELIG: When was that?

LOOMIS: Nineteen hundred and one.

SELIG: Nineteen . . . hundred and one. I'll tell you, mister . . . you better off without them. Now you take me . . . old Rutherford Selig could tell you a thing or two about these women. I ain't met one yet I could understand. Now, you take Sally out there. That's all a man needs is a good horse. I say giddup and she go. Say whoa and she stop. I feed her some oats and she carry me wherever I want to go. Ain't a speck of trouble out of her since I had her. Now, I been married. A long time ago down in Kentucky. I got up one morning and I saw this look on my wife's face. Like way down deep inside her she was wishing I was dead. I walked around that morning and every time I looked at her she had that look on her face. It seem like she knew I could see it on her. Every time I looked at her I got smaller and smaller. Well, I wasn't gonna stay around there and just shrink away. I walked out on the porch and closed the door behind me. When I closed the door she locked it. I went out and bought me a horse. And I ain't been without one since! Martha Loomis, huh? Well, now I'll do the best I can do. That's one dollar.

LOOMIS: (Holding out dollar suspiciously.) How you find her?

SELIG: Well now, it ain't no easy job like you think. You can't just go out there and find them like that. There's a lot of little tricks to it. It's not an easy job keeping up with you Nigras the way you move about so. Now you take this woman you looking for . . . this Martha Loomis. She could be anywhere. Time I find her, if you don't keep your eye on her, she'll be gone off someplace else. You'll be thinking she over here and she'll be over there. But like I say there's a lot of little tricks to it.

LOOMIS: You say you find her.

SELIG: I can't promise anything but we been finders in my family for a long time. Bringers and finders. My great-granddaddy used to bring Nigras across the ocean on ships. That's wasn't no easy job either. Sometimes the winds would blow so hard you'd think the hand of God was set against the sails. But it set him well in pay and he settled in this new land and found him a wife of good Christian charity with a mind for kids and the like and well . . . here I am, Rutherford Selig. You're in good hands, mister. Me and my daddy have found plenty Nigras. My daddy, rest his soul, used to find runaway slaves for the plantation bosses. He was the best there was at it. Jonas B. Selig. Had him a reputation stretched clean across the country. After Abraham Lincoln give you all Nigras your freedom papers and with you all looking all over for each other . . . we started finding Nigras for Nigras. Of course, it don't pay as much. But the People finding business ain't so bad.

LOOMIS: (Hands him the dollar.) Find her. Martha Loomis. Find her for me.

SELIG: Like I say, I can't promise you anything. I'm going back upriver, and if she's around in them parts I'll find her for you. But I can't promise you anything.

LOOMIS: When you coming back?

SELIG: I'll be back on Saturday. I come and see Seth to pick up my order on Saturday.

BYNUM: You going upriver, huh? You going up around my way. I used to go all up through there. Blawknox . . . Clairton. Used to go up to Rankin and take that first righthand road. I wore many a pair of shoes out walking around that way. You'd have thought I was a missionary spreading the gospel the way I wandered all around them parts.

SELIG: Okay, Bynum. See you on Saturday.

SETH: Here, let me walk out with you. Help you with them dustpans.

(SETH and SELIG exit out the back. BERTHA enters from the stairs carrying a bundle of sheets.)

BYNUM: Herald Loomis got the People finder looking for Martha.

BERTHA: You can call him a People finder if you want to. I know Rutherford Selig carries people away too. He done carried a whole bunch of them away from here. Folks plan on leaving plan by Selig's timing. They wait till he get ready to go, then they hitch a ride on his wagon. Then he charge folks a dollar to tell them where he took them. Now, that's the truth of Rutherford Selig. This old People finding business is for the birds. He ain't never found nobody he ain't took away. Herald Loomis, you just wasted your dollar.

(BERTHA exits into the bedroom.)

LOOMIS: He say he find her. He say he find her by Saturday. I'm gonna wait till Saturday.

(The lights fade to black.)

Scene Three

It is Sunday morning, the next day. The lights come up on the kitchen. SETH sits talking to BYNUM. The breakfast dishes have been cleared away.

SETH: They can't see that. Neither one of them can see that. Now, how much sense it take to see that? All you got to do is be able to count. One man making ten pots is five men making fifty pots. But they can't see that. Asked where I'm gonna get my five men. Hell, I can teach anybody how to make a pot. I can teach you. I can take you out there and get you started right now. Inside of two weeks you'd know how to make a pot. All you got to do is want to do it. I can get five men. I ain't worried about getting no five men.

BERTHA: (Calls from the bedroom.) Seth. Come on and get ready now. Reverend Gates ain't gonna be holding up his sermon 'cause you sitting out there talking.

SETH: Now, you take the boy, Jeremy. What he gonna do after he put in that road? He can't do nothing but go put in another one somewhere. Now, if he let me show him how to make some pots and pans . . . then he'd have something can't nobody take away from him. After a while he could get his own tools and go off somewhere and make his own pots and pans. Find him somebody to sell them to.

Now, Selig can't make no pots and pans. He can sell them but he can't make them. I get me five men with some tools and we'd make him so many pots and pans he'd have to open up a store somewhere. But they can't see that. Neither Mr. Cohen nor Sam Green.

BERTHA: (Calls from the bedroom.) Seth . . . time be wasting. Best be getting on.

SETH: I'm coming, woman! (To BYNUM.) Want me to sign over the house to borrow five hundred dollars. I ain't that big a fool. That's all I got. Sign it over to them and then I won't have nothing.

(JEREMY enters waving a dollar and carrying his guitar.)

JEREMY: Look here, Mr. Bynum . . . won me another dollar last night down at Seefus! Me and that Mattie Campbell went down there again and I played contest. Ain't no guitar players down there. Wasn't even no contest. Say, Mr. Seth, I asked Mattie Campbell if she wanna come by and have Sunday dinner with us. Get some fried chicken.

SETH: It's gonna cost you twenty-five cents.

JEREMY: That's alright. I got a whole dollar here. Say Mr. Seth . . . me and Mattie Campbell talked it over last night and she gonna move in with me. If that's alright with you.

SETH: Your business is your business . . . but it's gonna cost her a dollar a week for her board. I can't be feeding nobody for free.

JEREMY: Oh, she know that, Mr. Seth. That's what I told her, say she'd have to pay for her meals.

SETH: You say you got a whole dollar there . . . turn loose that twenty-five cents.

JEREMY: Suppose she move in today, then that make seventy-five cents more, so I'll give you the whole dollar for her now till she gets here.

(SETH pockets the money and exits into the bedroom.)

BYNUM: So you and that Mattie Campbell gonna take up together?

JEREMY: I told her she don't need to be by her lonesome, Mr. Bynum. Don't make no sense for both of us to be by our lonesome. So she gonna move in with me.

BYNUM: Sometimes you got to be where you supposed to be. Sometimes you can get all mixed up in life and come to the wrong place.

JEREMY: That's just what I told her, Mr. Bynum. It don't make no sense for her to be all mixed up and lonesome. May as well come here and be with me. She a fine woman too. Got them long legs. Knows how to treat a fellow too. Treat you like you wanna be treated.

BYNUM: You just can't look at it like that. You got to look at the whole thing. Now, you take a fellow go out there, grab hold to a woman and think he got something 'cause she sweet and soft to the touch. Alright. Touching's part of life. It's in the world like everything else. Touching's nice. It feels good. But you can lay your hand upside a horse or a cat, and that feels good too. What's the difference? When you grab hold to a woman, you got something there. You got a whole world there. You got a way of life kicking up under your hand. That woman can take and make you feel like something. I ain't just talking about in the way of jumping off into bed together and rolling around with each other. Anybody can do that. When you grab hold to that woman and look at the whole thing and see what you got . . . why, she can take and make something out of you. Your mother was a woman. That's enough right there to show you what a woman is. Enough to show you what she can do. She made something out of you. Taught you converse, and all about how to take care of yourself, how to see where you at and where you going tomorrow, how to look out to see what's coming in the way of eating, and what to do with yourself when you get lonesome. That's a mighty thing she did. But you just can't look at a woman to jump off into bed with her. That's a foolish thing to ignore a woman like that.

JEREMY: Oh, I ain't ignoring her, Mr. Bynum. It's hard to ignore a woman got legs like she got.

BYNUM: Alright. Let's try it this way. Now, you take a ship. Be out there on the water traveling about. You out there on that ship sailing to and from. And then you see some land. Just like you see a woman walking down the street. You see that land and it don't look like nothing but a line out there on the horizon. That's all it is when you first see it. A line that cross your path out there on the horizon. Now, a smart man know when he see that land, it ain't just a line setting out there. He know that if you get off the water to go take a good look . . . why, there's a whole world right there. A whole world with everything imaginable under the sun. Anything you can think of you can find on that land. Same with a woman. A woman is everything a man need. To a smart man she water and berries. And that's all a man need. That's all he need to live on. You give me some water and berries and if there ain't nothing else I can live a hundred years. See, you just like a man looking at the horizon from a ship. You just seeing a part of it. But it's a blessing when you learn to look at a woman and see in maybe just a few strands of her hair, the way her cheek curves . . . to see in that everything there is out of life to be gotten. It's a blessing to see that. You know you done right and proud by your mother to see that. But you got to learn it. My telling you ain't gonna mean nothing. You got to learn how to come to your own time and place with a woman.

JEREMY: What about your woman, Mr. Bynum? I know you done had some woman.

BYNUM: Oh, I got them in memory time. That lasts longer than any of them ever stayed with me.

JEREMY: I had me an old gal one time . . .

(There is a knock on the door. JEREMY goes to answer it. Enter MOLLY CUNNINGHAM. She is about twenty-six, the kind of woman that "could break in on a dollar anywhere she goes." She carries a small cardboard suitcase, and wears a colorful dress of the fashion of the day. JEREMY's heart jumps out of his chest when he sees her.)

MOLLY: You got any rooms here? I'm looking for a room.

JEREMY: Yeah . . . Mr. Seth got rooms. Sure . . . wait till I get Mr. Seth.

(Calls.) Mr. Seth! Somebody here to see you!

(To MOLLY.) Yeah, Mr. Seth got some rooms. Got one right next to me. This a nice place to stay, too. My name's Jeremy. What's yours?

(SETH enters dressed in his Sunday clothes.)

SETH: Ho!

JEREMY: This here woman looking for a place to stay. She say you got any rooms.

MOLLY: Mister, you got any rooms? I seen your sign say you got rooms.

SETH: How long you plan to staying?

MOLLY: I ain't gonna be here long. I ain't looking for no home or nothing. I'd be in Cincinnati if I hadn't missed my train.

SETH: Rooms cost two dollars a week.

MOLLY: Two dollars!

SETH: That includes meals. We serve two meals a day. That's breakfast and dinner.

MOLLY: I hope it ain't on the third floor.

SETH: That's the only one I got. Third floor to the left. That's pay up in advance week to week.

MOLLY: (Going into her bosom.) I'm gonna pay you for one week. My name's Molly. Molly Cunningham.

SETH: I'm Seth Holly. My wife's name is Bertha. She do the cooking and taking care of around here. She got sheets on the bed. Towels twenty-five cents a week extra if you ain't got none. You get breakfast and dinner. We got fried chicken on Sundays.

MOLLY: That sounds good. Here's two dollars and twenty-five cents. Look here, Mister . . .?

SETH: Holly. Seth Holly.

MOLLY: Look here, Mr. Holly. I forgot to tell you. I likes me some company from time to time. I don't like being by myself.

SETH: Your business is your business. I don't meddle in nobody's business. But this is a respectable house. I don't have no riffraff around here. And I don't have no women hauling no men up to their rooms to be making their living. As long as we understand each other then we'll be alright with each other.

MOLLY: Where's the outhouse?

SETH: Straight through the door over yonder.

MOLLY: I get my own key to the front door?

SETH: Everybody get their own key. If you come in late just don't be making no whole lot of noise and carrying on. Don't allow no fussing and fighting around here.

MOLLY: You ain't got to worry about that, mister. Which way you say that outhouse was again?

SETH: Straight through that door over yonder.

(MOLLY exits out the back door. JEREMY crosses to watch her.)

JEREMY: Mr. Bynum, you know what? I think I know what you was talking about now.

(The lights go down on the scene.)

Scene Four

The lights come up on the kitchen. It is later the same evening. MATTIE and all the residents of the house, except LOOMIS, sit around the table. They have finished eating and most of the dishes have been cleared.

MOLLY: That sure was some good chicken.

JEREMY: That's what I'm talking about. Miss Bertha, you sure can fry some chicken. I thought my mama could fry some chicken. But she can't do half as good as you.

SETH: I know it. That's why I married her. She don't know that, though. She think I married her for something else.

BERTHA: I ain't studying you, Seth. Did you get your things moved in alright, Mattie?

MATTIE: I ain't had that much. Jeremy helped me with what I did have.

BERTHA: You'll get to know your way around here. If you have any questions about anything just ask me. You and Molly both. I get along with everybody. You'll find I ain't no trouble to get along with.

MATTIE: You need some help with the dishes?

BERTHA: I got me a helper. Ain't I, Zonia? Got me a good helper.

ZONIA: Yes, ma'am.

SETH: Look at Bynum sitting over there with his belly all poked out. Ain't saying nothing. Sitting over there half asleep. Ho, Bynum!

BERTHA: If Bynum ain't saying nothing what you wanna start him up for?

SETH: Ho, Bynum!

BYNUM: What you hollering at me for? I ain't doing nothing.

SETH: Come on, we gonna Juba.

BYNUM: You know me, I'm always ready to Juba.

SETH: Well, come on, then.

(SETH pulls out a harmonica and blows a few notes.)

Come on there, Jeremy. Where's your guitar? Go get your guitar. Bynum say he's ready to Juba.

JEREMY: Don't need no guitar to Juba. Ain't you never Juba without a guitar?

(JEREMY begins to drum on the table.)

SETH: It ain't that. I ain't never Juba with one! Figured to try it and see how it worked.

BYNUM: (Drumming on the table.) You don't need no guitar. Look at Molly sitting over there. She don't know we Juba on Sunday. We gonna show you something tonight. You and Mattie Campbell both. Ain't that right, Seth?

SETH: You said it! Come on, Bertha, leave them dishes be for a while. We gonna Juba.

BYNUM: Alright. Let's Juba down!

(The Juba is reminiscent of the Ring Shouts of the African slaves. It is a call and response dance. BYNUM sits at the table and drums.

He calls the dance as others clap hands, shuffle and stomp around the table. It should be as African as possible, with the performers working themselves up into a near frenzy. The words can be improvised, but should include some mention of the Holy Ghost. In the middle of the dance HERALD LOOMIS enters.)

LOOMIS: (In a rage.) Stop it! Stop!

(They stop and turn to look at him.)

You all sitting up here singing about the Holy Ghost. What's so holy about the Holy Ghost? You singing and singing. You think the Holy Ghost coming? You singing for the Holy Ghost to come? What he gonna do, huh? He gonna come with tongues of fire to burn up your woolly heads? You gonna tie onto the Holy Ghost and get burned up? What you got then? Why God got to be so big? Why he got to be bigger than me? How much big is there? How much big do you want?

(LOOMIS starts to unzip his pants.)

SETH: Nigger, you crazy!

LOOMIS: How much big you want?

SETH: You done plumb lost your mind!

(LOOMIS begins to speak in tongues and dance around the kitchen. SETH starts after him.)

BERTHA: Leave him alone, Seth. He ain't in his right mind.

LOOMIS: (Stops suddenly.) You all don't know nothing about me. You don't know what I done seen. Herald Loomis done seen some things he ain't got words to tell you.

(LOOMIS starts to walk out the front door and is thrown back and collapses, terror-stricken by his vision. BYNUM crawls to him.)

BYNUM: What you done seen, Herald Loomis?

LOOMIS: I done seen bones rise up out the water. Rise up and walk across the water. Bones walking on top of the water.

BYNUM: Tell me about them bones, Herald Loomis. Tell me what you seen.

LOOMIS: I come to this place . . . to this water that was bigger than the whole world. And

I looked out . . . and I seen these bones rise up out the water. Rise up and begin to walk on top of it.

BYNUM: Wasn't nothing but bones and they walking on top of the water.

LOOMIS: Walking without sinking down. Walking on top of the water.

BYNUM: Just marching in a line.

LOOMIS: A whole heap of them. They come up out the water and started marching.

BYNUM: Wasn't nothing but bones and they walking on top of the water.

LOOMIS: One after the other. They just come up out the water and start to walking.

BYNUM: They walking on the water without sinking down. They just walking and walking. And then . . . what happened, Herald Loomis?

LOOMIS: They just walking across the water.

BYNUM: What happened, Herald Loomis? What happened to the bones?

LOOMIS: They just walking across the water . . . and then . . . they sunk down.

BYNUM: The bones sunk into the water. They all sunk down.

LOOMIS: All at one time! They just all fell in the water at one time.

BYNUM: Sunk down like anybody else.

LOOMIS: When they sink down they made a big splash and this here wave come up . . .

BYNUM: A big wave, Herald Loomis. A big wave washed over the land.

LOOMIS: It washed them out of the water and up on the land. Only . . . only . . .

BYNUM: Only they ain't bones no more.

LOOMIS: They got flesh on them! Just like you and me!

BYNUM: Everywhere you look the waves is washing them up on the land right on top of one another.

LOOMIS: They black. Just like you and me. Ain't no difference.

BYNUM: Then what happened, Herald Loomis?

LOOMIS: They ain't moved or nothing. They just laying there.

BYNUM: You just laying there. What you waiting on, Herald Loomis?

LOOMIS: I'm laying there . . . waiting.

BYNUM: What you waiting on, Herald Loomis?

LOOMIS: I'm waiting on the breath to get into my body.

BYNUM: The breath coming into you, Herald Loomis. What you gonna do now?

LOOMIS: The wind's blowing the breath into my body. I can feel it. I'm starting to breathe again.

BYNUM: What you gonna do, Herald Loomis?

LOOMIS: I'm gonna stand up. I got to stand up. I can't lay here no more. All the breath coming into my body and I got to stand up.

BYNUM: Everybody's standing up at the same time.

LOOMIS: The ground's starting to shake. There's a great shaking. The world's busting half in two. The sky's splitting open. I got to stand up.

(LOOMIS attempts to stand up.)

My legs . . . my legs won't stand up!

BYNUM: Everybody's standing and walking toward the road. What you gonna do, Herald Loomis?

LOOMIS: My legs won't stand up.

BYNUM: They shaking hands and saying goodbye to each other and walking every which-away down the road.

LOOMIS: I got to stand up!

BYNUM: They walking around here now. Mens. Just like you and me. Come right up out the water.

LOOMIS: Got to stand up.

BYNUM: They walking, Herald Loomis. They walking around here now.

LOOMIS: I got to stand up. Get up on the road.

BYNUM: Come on, Herald Loomis.

(LOOMIS tries to stand up.)

LOOMIS: My legs won't stand up! My legs won't stand up!

(LOOMIS collapses on the floor as the lights go down to black.)

ACT TWO

Scene One

The lights come up on the kitchen. BERTHA busies herself with breakfast preparations. SETH sits at the table.

SETH: I don't care what his problem is! He's leaving here!

BERTHA: You can't put the man out and he got that little girl. Where they gonna go then?

SETH: I don't care where he go. Let him go back where he was before he come here. I ain't asked him to come here. I knew when I first looked at him something wasn't right with him. Dragging that little girl around with him. Looking like he be sleeping in the woods somewhere. I knew all along he wasn't right.

BERTHA: A fellow get a little drunk he's liable to say or do anything. He ain't done no big harm.

SETH: I just don't have all that carrying on in my house. When he come down here I'm gonna tell him. He got to leave here. My daddy wouldn't stand for it and I ain't gonna stand for it either.

BERTHA: Well, if you put him out you have to put Bynum out too. Bynum right there with him.

SETH: If it wasn't for Bynum ain't no telling what would have happened. Bynum talked to that fellow just as nice and calmed him down. If he wasn't here ain't no telling what would have happened. Bynum ain't done nothing but talk to him and kept him calm. Man acting all crazy with that foolishness. Naw, he's leaving here.

BERTHA: What you gonna tell him? How you gonna tell him to leave?

SETH: I'm gonna tell him straight out. Keep it nice and simple. Mister, you got to leave here!

(MOLLY enters from the stairs.)

MOLLY: Morning.

BERTHA: Did you sleep alright in that bed?

MOLLY: Tired as I was I could have slept anywhere. It's a real nice room, though. This is a nice place.

SETH: I'm sorry you had to put up with all that carrying on last night.

MOLLY: It don't bother me none. I done seen that kind of stuff before.

SETH: You won't have to see it around here no more.

(BYNUM is heard singing offstage.)

I don't put up with all that stuff. When that fellow come down here I'm gonna tell him.

BYNUM: (singing)

Soon my work will all be done
Soon my work will all be done
Soon my work will all be done
I'm going to see the king.

BYNUM: (Enters.) Morning, Seth. Morning, Sister Bertha. I see we got Molly Cunningham down here at breakfast.

SETH: Bynum, I wanna thank you for talking to that fellow last night and calming him down. If you hadn't been here ain't no telling what might have happened.

BYNUM: Mr. Loomis alright, Seth. He just got a little excited.

SETH: Well, he can get excited somewhere else 'cause he leaving here.

(MATTIE enters from the stairs.)

BYNUM: Well, there's Mattie Campbell.

MATTIE: Good morning.

BERTHA: Sit on down there, Mattie. I got some biscuits be ready in a minute. The coffee's hot.

MATTIE: Jeremy gone already?

BYNUM: Yeah, he leave out of here early. He got to be there when the sun come up. Most working men got to be there when the sun come up. Everybody but Seth. Seth work at

night. Mr. Olowski so busy in his shop he got fellows working at night.

(LOOMIS enters from the stairs.)

SETH: Mr. Loomis, now . . . I don't want no trouble. I keeps me a respectable house here. I don't have no carrying on like what went on last night. This has been a respectable house for a long time. I'm gonna have to ask you to leave.

LOOMIS: You got my two dollars. That two dollars say we stay till Saturday.

(LOOMIS and SETH glare at each other.)

SETH: Alright. Fair enough. You stay till Saturday. But come Saturday you got to leave here.

LOOMIS: (Continues to glare at SETH. He goes to the door and calls.) Zonia. You stay around this house, you hear? Don't you go anywhere.

(LOOMIS exits out the front door.)

SETH: I knew it when I first seen him. I knew something wasn't right with him.

BERTHA: Seth, leave the people alone to eat their breakfast. They don't want to hear that. Go on out there and make some pots and pans. That's the only time you satisfied is when you out there. Go on out there and make some pots and pans and leave them people alone.

SETH: I ain't bothering anybody. I'm just stating the facts. I told you, Bynum.

(BERTHA shoos SETH out the back door and exits into the bedroom.)

MOLLY: (To BYNUM.) You one of them voodoo people?

BYNUM: I got a power to bind folks if that what you talking about.

MOLLY: I thought so. The way you talked to that man when he started all that spooky stuff. What you say you had the power to do to people? You ain't the cause of him acting like that, is you?

BYNUM: I binds them together. Sometimes I help them find each other.

MOLLY: How do you do that?

BYNUM: With a song. My daddy taught me how to do it.

MOLLY: That's what they say. Most folks be what they daddy is. I wouldn't want to be like my daddy. Nothing ever set right with him. He tried to make the world over. Carry it around with him everywhere he go. I don't want to be like that. I just take life as it come. I don't be trying to make it over.

(Pause.)

Your daddy used to do that too, huh? Make people stay together?

BYNUM: My daddy used to heal people. He had the Healing Song. I got the Binding Song.

MOLLY: My mama used to believe in all that stuff. If she got sick she would have gone and saw your daddy. As long as he didn't make her drink nothing. She wouldn't drink nothing nobody give her. She was always afraid somebody was gonna poison her. How your daddy heal people?

BYNUM: With a song. He healed people by singing over them. I seen him do it. He sung over this little white girl when she was sick. They made a big to-do about it. They carried the girl's bed out in the yard and had all her kinfolk standing around. The little girl laying up there in the bed. Doctors standing around can't do nothing to help her. And they had my daddy come up and sing his song. It didn't sound no different than any other song. It was just somebody singing. But the song was its own thing and it come out and took upon this little girl with its power and it healed her.

MOLLY: That's sure something else. I don't understand that kind of thing. I guess if the doctor couldn't make me well I'd try it. But otherwise I don't wanna be bothered with that kind of thing. It's too spooky.

BYNUM: Well, let me get on out here and get to work.

(BYNUM gets up and heads out the back door.)

MOLLY: I ain't meant to offend you or nothing. What's your name . . . Bynum? I ain't meant to say nothing to make you feel bad now.

(BYNUM exits out the back door.)

(To MATTIE.) I hope he don't feel bad. He's a nice man. I don't wanna hurt nobody's feelings or nothing.

MATTIE: I got to go on up to Doc Goldblum's and finish his ironing.

MOLLY: Now, that's something I don't ever wanna do. Iron no clothes. Especially somebody else's. That's what I believe killed my mama. Always ironing and working, doing somebody's else's work. Not Molly Cunningham.

MATTIE: It's the only job I got. I got to make it someway to fend for myself.

MOLLY: I thought Jeremy was your man. Ain't he working?

MATTIE: We just be keeping company till maybe Jack come back.

MOLLY: I don't trust none of these men. Jack or nobody else. These men liable to do anything. They wait just until they get one woman tied and locked up with them . . . then they look around to see if they can get another one. Molly don't pay them no mind. One's just as good as the other if you ask me. I ain't never met one that meant nobody no good. You got any babies?

MATTIE: I had two for my man, Jack Carper. But they both died.

MOLLY: That be the best. These men make all these babies, then run off and leave you to take care of them. Talking about they wanna see what's on the other side of the hill. I make sure I don't get no babies. My mama taught me how to do that.

MATTIE: Don't make me no mind. That be nice to be a mother.

MOLLY: Yeah? Well, you go on, then. Molly Cunningham ain't gonna be tied down with no babies. Had me a man one time who I thought had some love in him. Come home one day and he was packing his trunk. Told me the time come when even the best of friends must part. Say he was gonna send me a Special Delivery some old day. I watched him out the window when he carried that trunk out and down to the train station. Said if he was gonna send me a Special Delivery I wasn't gonna be there to get it. I done found out the harder you try to hold onto them, the easier it is for some gal to pull them away. Molly done learned that. That's why I don't trust nobody but the good Lord above, and I don't love nobody but my mama.

MATTIE: I got to get on. Doc Goldblum gonna be waiting.

(MATTIE exits out the front door. SETH enters from his workshop with his apron, gloves, goggles, etc. He carries a bucket and crosses to the sink for water.)

SETH: Everybody gone but you, huh?

MOLLY: That little shack out there by the outhouse . . . that's where you make them pots and pans and stuff?

SETH: Yeah, that's my workshed. I go out there . . . take these hands and make something out of nothing. Take that metal and bend and twist it whatever way I want. My daddy taught me that. He used to make pots and pans. That's how I learned it.

MOLLY: I never knew nobody made no pots and pans. My uncle used to shoe horses.

(JEREMY enters at the front door.)

SETH: I thought you was working? Ain't you working today?

JEREMY: Naw, they fired me. White fellow come by told me to give him fifty cents if I wanted to keep working. Going around to all the colored making them give him fifty cents to keep hold to their jobs. Them other fellows, they was giving it to him. I kept hold to mine and they fired me.

SETH: Boy, what kind of sense that make? What kind of sense it make to get fired from a job where you making eight dollars a week and all it cost you is fifty cents. That's seven dollars and fifty cents profit! This way you ain't got nothing.

JEREMY: It didn't make no sense to me. I don't make but eight dollars. Why I got to give him fifty cents of it? He go around to all the colored and he got ten dollars extra. That's more than I make for a whole week.

SETH: I see you gonna learn the hard way. You just looking at the facts of it. See, right now, without the job, you ain't got nothing. What you gonna do when you can't keep a roof over your head? Right now, come Saturday, unless you come up with another two dollars, you gonna be out there in the streets. Down up under one of them bridges trying to put some food in your belly and wishing you had given that fellow that fifty cents.

JEREMY: Don't make me no difference. There's a big road out there. I can get my guitar and always find me another place to stay. I ain't planning on staying in one place for too long noway.

SETH: We gonna see if you feel like that come Saturday!

(SETH exits out the back. JEREMY sees MOLLY.)

JEREMY: Molly Cunningham. How you doing today, sugar?

MOLLY: You can go on back down there tomorrow and go back to work if you want. They won't even know who you is. Won't even know it's you. I had me a fellow did that one time. They just went ahead and signed him up like they never seen him before.

JEREMY: I'm tired of working anyway. I'm glad they fired me. You sure look pretty today.

MOLLY: Don't come telling me all that pretty stuff. Beauty wanna come in and sit down at your table asking to be fed. I ain't hardly got enough for me.

JEREMY: You know you pretty. Ain't no sense in you saying nothing about that. Why don't you come on and go away with me?

MOLLY: You tied up with that Mattie Campbell. Now you talking about running away with me.

JEREMY: I was just keeping her company 'cause she lonely. You ain't the lonely kind. You the kind that know what she want and how to get it. I need a woman like you to travel around with. Don't you wanna travel around and look at some places with Jeremy? With a woman like you beside him, a man can make it nice in the world.

MOLLY: Molly can make it nice by herself too. Molly don't need nobody leave her cold in hand. The world rough enough as it is.

JEREMY: We can make it better together. I got my guitar and I can play. Won me another dollar last night playing guitar. We can go around and I can play at the dances and we can just enjoy life. You can make it by yourself alright, I agrees with that. A woman like you can make it anywhere she go. But you can make it better if you got a man to protect you.

MOLLY: What places you wanna go around and look at?

JEREMY: All of them! I don't want to miss nothing. I wanna go everywhere and do everything there is to be got out of life. With a woman like you it's like having water and berries. A man got everything he need.

MOLLY: You got to be doing more than playing that guitar. A dollar a day ain't hardly what Molly got in mind.

JEREMY: I gambles real good. I got a hand for it.

MOLLY: Molly don't work. And Molly ain't up for sale.

JEREMY: Sure, baby. You ain't got to work with Jeremy.

MOLLY: There's one more thing.

JEREMY: What's that, sugar?

MOLLY: Molly ain't going South.

(The lights go down on the scene.)

Scene Two

The lights come up on the parlor. SETH and BYNUM sit playing a game of dominoes. BYNUM sings to himself.

BYNUM: (Singing.)

They tell me Joe Turner's come and gone
Ohhh Lordy
They tell me Joe Turner's come and gone
Ohhh Lordy
Got my man and gone

Come with forty links of chain
Ohhh Lordy
Come with forty links of chain
Ohhh Lordy
Got my man and gone

SETH: Come on and play if you gonna play.

BYNUM: I'm gonna play. Soon as I figure out what to do.

SETH: You can't figure out if you wanna play or you wanna sing.

BYNUM: Well sir, I'm gonna do a little bit of both.

(Playing.)

There. What you gonna do now?

(Singing.)

They tell me Joe Turner's come and gone
Ohhh Lordy
They tell me Joe Turner's come and gone
Ohhh Lordy

SETH: Why don't you hush up that noise.

BYNUM: That's a song the women sing down around Memphis. The women down there made up that song. I picked it up down there about fifteen years ago.

(LOOMIS enters from the front door.)

BYNUM: Evening, Mr. Loomis.

SETH: Today's Monday, Mr. Loomis. Come Saturday your time is up. We done ate already. My wife roasted up some yams. She got your plate sitting in there on the table.

(To BYNUM.) Whose play is it?

BYNUM: Ain't you keeping up with the game? I thought you was a domino player. I just played so it got to be your turn.

(LOOMIS goes into the kitchen, where a plate of yams is covered and set on the table. He sits down and begins to eat with his hands.)

SETH: (Plays.) Twenty! Give me twenty! You didn't know I had that ace five. You was trying to play around that. You didn't know I had that lying there for you.

BYNUM: You ain't done nothing. I let you have that to get mine.

SETH: Come on and play. You ain't doing nothing but talking. I got a hundred and forty points to your eighty. You ain't doing nothing but talking. Come on and play.

BYNUM: (Singing.)

They tell me Joe Turner's come and gone
Ohhh Lordy
They tell me Joe Turner's come and gone
Ohhh Lordy
Got my man and gone
He come with forty links of chain
Ohhh Lordy

LOOMIS: Why you singing that song? Why you singing about Joe Turner?

BYNUM: I'm just singing to entertain myself.

SETH: You trying to distract me. That's what you trying to do.

BYNUM: (Singing.)

Come with forty links of chain
Ohhh Lordy
Come with forty links of chain
Ohhh Lordy

LOOMIS: I don't like you singing that song, mister!

SETH: Now, I ain't gonna have no more disturbance around here, Herald Loomis. You start any more disturbance and you leavin' here, Saturday or no Saturday.

BYNUM: The man ain't causing no disturbance, Seth. He just say he don't like the song.

SETH: Well, we all friendly folk. All neighborly like. Don't have no squabbling around here. Don't have no disturbance. You gonna have to take that someplace else.

BYNUM: He just say he don't like the song. I done sung a whole lot of songs people don't like. I respect everybody. He here in the house too. If he don't like the song, I'll sing something else. I know lots of songs. You got "I Belong to the Band," "Don't You Leave Me Here." You got "Praying on the Old Campground," "Keep your Lamp Trimmed and Burning" . . . I know lots of songs.

(Sings.)

Boys, I'll be so glad when payday come
Captain, Captain, when payday comes
Gonna catch that Illinois Central
Going to Kankakee

SETH: Why don't you hush up that hollering and come on and play dominoes.

BYNUM: You ever been to Johnstown, Herald Loomis? You look like a fellow I seen around there.

LOOMIS: I don't know no place with that name.

BYNUM: That's around where I seen my shiny man. See, you looking for this woman. I'm looking for a shiny man. Seem like everybody looking for something.

SETH: I'm looking for you to come and play these dominoes. That's what I'm looking for.

BYNUM: You a farming man, Herald Loomis? You look like you done some farming.

LOOMIS: Same as everybody. I done farmed some, yeah.

BYNUM: I used to work at farming . . . picking cotton. I reckon everybody done picked some cotton.

SETH: I ain't! I ain't never picked no cotton. I was born up here in the North. My daddy was a freedman. I ain't never even seen no cotton!

BYNUM: Mr. Loomis done picked some cotton. Ain't you, Herald Loomis? You done picked a bunch of cotton.

LOOMIS: How you know so much about me? How you know what I done? How much cotton I picked?

BYNUM: I can tell from looking at you. My daddy taught me how to do that. Say when you look at a fellow, if you taught yourself to look for it, you can see his song written on him. Tell you what kind of man he is in the world. Now, I can look at you,

Mr. Loomis, and see you a man who done forgot his song. Forgot how to sing it. A fellow forget that and he forget who he is. Forget how he's supposed to mark down life. Now, I used to travel all up and down this road and that . . . looking here and there. Searching. Just like you, Mr. Loomis. I didn't know what I was searching for. The only thing I knew was something was keeping me dissatisfied. Something wasn't making my heart smooth and easy. Then one day my daddy gave me a song. That song had a weight to it that was hard to handle. That song was hard to carry. I fought against it. Didn't want to accept that song. I tried to find my daddy to give him back the song. But I found out it wasn't his song. It was my song. It had come from way deep inside me. I looked long back in memory and gathered up pieces and snatches of things to make that song. I was making it up out of myself. And that song helped me on the road. Made it smooth to where my footsteps didn't bite back at me. All the time that song getting bigger and bigger. That song growing with each step of the road. It got so I used all of myself up in the making of that song. Then I was the song in search of itself. That song rattling in my throat and I'm looking for it. See, Mr. Loomis, when a man forgets his song he goes off in search of it . . . till he find out he's got it with him all the time. That's why I can tell you one of Joe Turner's niggers. 'Cause you forgot how to sing your song.

Loomis: You lie! How you see that? I got a mark on me? Joe Turner done marked me to where you can see it? You telling me I'm a marked man. What kind of mark you got on you?

(BYNUM begins singing.)

Bynum:

They tell me Joe Turner's come and gone
Ohhh Lordy
They tell me Joe Turner's come and gone
Ohhh Lordy
Got my man and gone

Loomis: Had a whole mess of men he catched. Just go out hunting regular like you go out hunting possum. He catch you and go home to his wife and family. Ain't thought about you going home to yours. Joe Turner catched me when my little girl was just born. Wasn't nothing but a little baby sucking on her mama's titty when he catched me. Joe Turner catched me in nineteen hundred and one. Kept me seven years until nineteen hundred and eight. Kept everybody seven years. He'd go out hunting and bring back forty men at a time. And keep them seven years.

I was walking down this road in this little town outside of Memphis. Come up on these fellows gambling. I was a deacon in the Abundant Life Church. I stopped to preach to these fellows to see if maybe I could turn some of them from their sinning when Joe Turner, brother of the Governor of the great sovereign state of Tennessee, swooped down on us and grabbed everybody there. Kept us all seven years.

My wife Martha gone from me after Joe Turner catched me. Got out from under Joe Turner on his birthday. Me and forty other men put in our seven years and he let us go on his birthday. I made it back to Henry Thompson's place where me and Martha was sharecropping and Martha's gone. She taken my little girl and left her with her mama and took off North. We been looking for her ever since. That's been going on four years now we been looking. That's the only thing I know to do. I just wanna see her face so I can get me a starting place in the world. The world got to start somewhere. That's what I been looking for. I been wandering a long time in somebody else's world. When I find my wife that be the making of my own.

Bynum: Joe Turner tell why he caught you? You ever asked him that?

Loomis: I ain't never seen Joe Turner. Seen him to where I could touch him. I asked one of

them fellows one time why he catch niggers. Asked him what I got he want? Why
don't he keep on to himself? Why he got
to catch me going down the road by my
lonesome? He told me I was worthless.
Worthless is something you throw away.
Something you don't bother with. I ain't
seen him throw me away. Wouldn't even let
me stay away when I was by my lonesome.
I ain't tried to catch him when he going
down the road. So I must got something he
want. What I got?

SETH: He just want you to do his work for him.
That's all.

LOOMIS: I can look at him and see where he big
and strong enough to do his own work. So
it can't be that. He must want something he
ain't got.

BYNUM: That ain't hard to figure out. What he
wanted was your song. He wanted to have
that song to be his. He thought by catching
you he could learn that song. Every nigger he
catch he's looking for the one he can learn
that song from. Now he's got you bound
up to where you can't sing your own song.
Couldn't sing it them seven years 'cause you
was afraid he would snatch it from under
you. But you still got it. You just forgot how
to sing it.

LOOMIS: (To BYNUM.) I know who you are. You
one of them bones people.

(The lights go down to black.)

Scene Three

The lights come up on the kitchen. It is the following morning. MATTIE and BYNUM sit at the
table. BERTHA busies herself at the stove.

BYNUM: Good luck don't know no special time
to come. You sleep with that up under your
pillow and good luck can't help but come
to you. Sometimes it come and go and you
don't even know it's been there.

BERTHA: Bynum, why don't you leave that gal
alone? She don't wanna be hearing all that.
Why don't you go on and get out the way
and leave her alone?

BYNUM: (Getting up.) Alright, alright. But you
mark what I'm saying. It'll draw it to you just
like a magnet.

(BYNUM exits up the stairs as LOOMIS enters.)

BERTHA: I got some grits here, Mr. Loomis.

(BERTHA sets a bowl on the table.)

If I was you, Mattie, I wouldn't go getting all
tied up with Bynum in that stuff. That kind of
stuff, even if it do work for a while, it don't
last. That just get people more mixed up than
they is already. And I wouldn't waste my time
fretting over Jeremy either. I seen it coming.
I seen it when she first come here. She that
kind of woman run off with the first man got
a dollar to spend on her. Jeremy just young.
He don't know what he getting into. That
gal don't mean him no good. She's just using
him to keep from being by herself. That's the
worst use of a man you can have. You ought
to be glad to wash him out of your hair. I
done seen all kind of men. I done seen them
come and go through here. Jeremy ain't
had enough to him for you. You need a man
who's got some understanding and who willing to work with that understanding to come
to the best he can. You got your time coming. You just tries too hard and can't understand why it don't work for you. Trying to
figure it out don't do nothing but give you a
troubled mind. Don't no man want a woman
with a troubled mind.

You get all that trouble off your mind and
just when it look like you ain't never gonna
find what you want . . . you look up and it's
standing right there. That's how I met my
Seth. You gonna look up one day and find
everything you want standing right in front
of you. Been twenty-seven years now since
that happened to me. But life ain't no happy-
go-lucky time where everything be just like
you want it. You got your time coming. You
watch what Bertha's saying.

(SETH enters.)

SETH: Ho!

BERTHA: What you doing come in here so late?

SETH: I was standing down there on Logan Street talking with the fellows. Henry Allen tried to sell me that old piece of horse he got.

(He sees LOOMIS.)

Today's Tuesday, Mr. Loomis.

BERTHA: (Pulling him toward the bedroom.) Come on in here and leave that man alone to eat his breakfast.

SETH: I ain't bothering nobody. I'm just reminding him what day it is.

(SETH and BERTHA exit into the bedroom.)

LOOMIS: That dress got a color to it.

MATTIE: Did you really see them things like you said? Them people come up out the ocean?

LOOMIS: It happened just like that, yeah.

MATTIE: I hope you find your wife. It be good for your little girl for you to find her.

LOOMIS: Got to find her for myself. Find my starting place in the world. Find me a world I can fit in.

MATTIE: I ain't never found no place for me to fit. Seem like all I do is start over. It ain't nothing to find no starting place in the world. You just start from where you find yourself.

LOOMIS: Got to find my wife. That be my starting place.

MATTIE: What if you don't find her? What you gonna do then if you don't find her?

LOOMIS: She out there somewhere. Ain't no such thing as not finding her.

MATTIE: How she got lost from you? Jack just walked away from me.

LOOMIS: Joe Turner split us up. Joe Turner turned the world upside-down. He bound me on to him for seven years.

MATTIE: I hope you find her. It be good for you to find her.

LOOMIS: I been watching you. I been watching you watch me.

MATTIE: I was just trying to figure out if you seen things like you said.

LOOMIS: (Getting up.) Come here and let me touch you. I been watching you. You a full woman. A man needs a full woman. Come on and be with me.

MATTIE: I ain't got enough for you. You'd use me up too fast.

LOOMIS: Herald Loomis got a mind seem like you a part of it since I first seen you. It's been a long time since I seen a full woman. I can smell you from here. I know you got Herald Loomis on your mind, can't keep him apart from it. Come on and be with Herald Loomis.

(LOOMIS has crossed to MATTIE. He touches her awkwardly, gently, tenderly. Inside he howls like a lost wolf pup whose hunger is deep. He goes to touch her but finds he cannot.)

I done forgot how to touch.

(The lights fade to black.)

Scene Four

It is early the next morning. The lights come up on ZONIA and REUBEN in the yard.

REUBEN: Something spookly going on around here. Last night Mr. Bynum was out in the yard singing and talking to the wind . . . and the wind it just be talking back to him. Did you hear it?

ZONIA: I heard it. I was scared to get up and look. I thought it was a storm.

REUBEN: That wasn't no storm. That was Mr. Bynum. First he say something . . . and the wind it say back to him.

ZONIA: I heard it. Was you scared? I was scared.

REUBEN: And then this morning . . . I seen Miss Mabel!

ZONIA: Who Miss Mabel?

REUBEN: Mr. Seth's mother. He got her picture hanging up in the house. She been dead.

ZONIA: How you seen her if she been dead?

REUBEN: Zonia . . . if I tell you something you promise you won't tell anybody?

ZONIA: I promise.

REUBEN: It was early this morning . . . I went out to the coop to feed the pigeons. I was down on the ground like this to open up the door to the coop . . . when all of a sudden I seen some feets in front of me. I look up . . . and there was Miss Mabel standing there.

ZONIA: Reuben, you better stop telling that! You ain't seen nobody!

REUBEN: Naw, it's the truth. I swear! I seen her just like I see you. Look . . . you can see where she hit me with her cane.

ZONIA: Hit you? What she hit you for?

REUBEN: She says, "Didn't you promise Eugene something?" Then she hit me with her cane. She say, "Let them pigeons go." Then she hit me again. That's what made them marks.

ZONIA: Jeez man . . . get away from me. You done see a haunt!

REUBEN: Shhhh. You promised, Zonia!

ZONIA: You sure it wasn't Miss Bertha come over there and hit you with her hoe?

REUBEN: It wasn't no Miss Bertha. I told you it was Miss Mabel. She was standing right there by the coop. She had this light coming out of her and then she just melted away.

ZONIA: What she had on?

REUBEN: A white dress. Ain't even had no shoes or nothing. Just had on that white dress and them big hands . . . and that cane she hit me with.

ZONIA: How you reckon she knew about the pigeons? You reckon Eugene told her?

REUBEN: I don't know. I sure ain't asked her none. She say Eugene was waiting on them pigeons. Say he couldn't go back home till I let them go. I couldn't get the door to the coop open fast enough.

ZONIA: Maybe she an angel? From the way you say she look with that white dress. Maybe she an angel.

REUBEN: Mean as she was . . . how she gonna be an angel? She used to chase us out her yard and frown up and look evil all the time.

ZONIA: That don't mean she can't be no angel 'cause of how she looked and 'cause she wouldn't let no kids play in her yard. It go by if you got any spots on your heart and if you pray and go to church.

REUBEN: What about she hit me with her cane? An angel wouldn't hit me with her cane.

ZONIA: I don't know. She might. I still say she was an angel.

REUBEN: You reckon Eugene the one who sent old Miss Mabel?

ZONIA: Why he send her? Why he don't come himself?

REUBEN: Figured if he send her maybe that'll make me listen. 'Cause she old.

ZONIA: What you think it feel like?

REUBEN: What?

ZONIA: Being dead.

REUBEN: Like being sleep only you don't know nothing and can't move no more.

ZONIA: If Miss Mabel can come back . . . then maybe Eugene can come back too.

REUBEN: We can go down to the hideout like we used to! He could come back everyday! It be just like he ain't dead.

ZONIA: Maybe that ain't right for him to come back. Feel kinda funny to be playing games with a haunt.

REUBEN: Yeah . . . what if everybody came back? What if Miss Mabel came back just like she ain't dead? Where you and your daddy gonna sleep then?

ZONIA: Maybe they go back at night and don't need no place to sleep.

REUBEN: It still don't seem right. I'm sure gonna miss Eugene. He's the bestest friend anybody ever had.

ZONIA: My daddy say if you miss somebody too much it can kill you. Say he missed me till it liked to killed him.

REUBEN: What if your mama's already dead and all the time you looking for her?

ZONIA: Naw, she ain't dead. My daddy say he can smell her.

REUBEN: You can't smell nobody that ain't here. Maybe he smelling old Miss Bertha. Maybe Miss Bertha your mama?

ZONIA: Naw, she ain't. My mamma got long pretty hair and she five feet from the ground!

REUBEN: Your daddy say when you leaving?

(ZONIA doesn't respond.)

Maybe you gonna stay in Mr. Seth's house and don't go looking for your mama no more.

ZONIA: He say we got to leave on Saturday.

REUBEN: Dag! You just only been here for a little while. Don't seem like nothing ever stay the same.

ZONIA: He say he got to find her. Find him a place in the world.

REUBEN: He could find him a place in Mr. Seth's house.

ZONIA: It don't look like we never gonna find her.

REUBEN: Maybe he find her by Saturday then you don't have to go.

ZONIA: I don't know.

REUBEN: You look like a spider!

ZONIA: I ain't no spider!

REUBEN: Got them long skinny arms and legs. You look like one of them Black Widows.

ZONIA: I ain't no Black Widow nothing! My name is Zonia!

REUBEN: That's what I'm gonna call you . . . Spider.

ZONIA: You can call me that, but I don't have to answer.

REUBEN: You know what? I think maybe I be your husband when I grow up.

ZONIA: How you know?

REUBEN: I ask my grandpap how you know and he say when the moon falls into a girl's eyes that how you know.

ZONIA: Did it fall into my eyes?

REUBEN: Not that I can tell. Maybe I ain't old enough. Maybe you ain't old enough.

ZONIA: So there! I don't know why you telling me that lie!

REUBEN: That don't mean nothing 'cause I can't see it. I know it's there. Just the way you look at me sometimes look like the moon might have been in your eyes.

ZONIA: That don't mean nothing if you can't see it. You supposed to see it.

REUBEN: Shucks, I see it good enough for me. You ever let anybody kiss you?

ZONIA: Just my daddy. He kiss me on the cheek.

REUBEN: It's better on the lips. Can I kiss you on the lips?

ZONIA: I don't know. You ever kiss anybody before?

REUBEN: I had a cousin let me kiss her on the lips one time. Can I kiss you?

ZONIA: Okay.

(REUBEN kisses her and lays his head against her chest.)

What you doing?

REUBEN: Listening. Your heart singing!

ZONIA: It is not.

REUBEN: Just beating like a drum. Let's kiss again.

(They kiss again.)

Now you mine, Spider. You my girl, okay?

ZONIA: Okay.

REUBEN: When I get grown, I come looking for you.

ZONIA: Okay.

(The lights fade to black.)

Scene Five

The lights come up on the kitchen. It is Saturday. BYNUM, LOOMIS, and ZONIA sit at the table. BERTHA prepares breakfast. ZONIA has on a white dress.

BYNUM: With all this rain we been having he might have ran into some washed-out roads. If that wagon got stuck in the mud he's liable to be still upriver somewhere. If he's upriver then he ain't coming until tomorrow.

LOOMIS: Today's Saturday. He say he be here on Saturday.

BERTHA: Zonia, you gonna eat your breakfast this morning.

ZONIA: Yes, ma'am.

BERTHA: I don't know how you expect to get any bigger if you don't eat. I ain't never seen a child that didn't eat. You about as skinny as a bean pole.

(Pause.)

Mr. Loomis, there's a place down on Wylie. Zeke Mayweather got a house down there. You ought to see if he got any rooms.

(LOOMIS doesn't respond.)

Well, you're welcome to some breakfast before you move on.

(MATTIE enters from the stairs.)

MATTIE: Good morning.

BERTHA: Morning, Mattie. Sit on down there and get you some breakfast.

BYNUM: Well, Mattie Campbell, you been sleeping with that up under your pillow like I told you?

BERTHA: Bynum, I done told you to leave that gal alone with all that stuff. You around here meddling in other people's lives. She don't want to hear all that. You ain't doing nothing but confusing her with that stuff.

MATTIE: (To LOOMIS.) You all fixing to move on?

LOOMIS: Today's Saturday. I'm paid up till Saturday.

MATTIE: Where you going to?

LOOMIS: Gonna find my wife.

MATTIE: You going off to another city?

LOOMIS: We gonna see where the road take us. Ain't no telling where we wind up.

MATTIE: Eleven years is a long time. Your wife . . . she might have taken up with someone else. People do that when they get lost from each other.

LOOMIS: Zonia. Come on, we gonna find your mama.

(LOOMIS and ZONIA cross to the door.)

MATTIE: (To ZONIA.) Zonia, Mattie got a ribbon here match your dress. Want Mattie to fix your hair with her ribbon?

(ZONIA nods. MATTIE ties the ribbon in her hair.)

There . . . it got a color just like your dress.

(To LOOMIS.) I hope you find her. I hope you be happy.

LOOMIS: A man looking for a woman be lucky to find you. You a good woman, Mattie. Keep a good heart.

(LOOMIS and ZONIA exit.)

BERTHA: I been watching that man for two weeks . . . and that's the closest I come to seeing him act civilized. I don't know what's between you all, Mattie . . . but the only thing that man needs is somebody to make him laugh. That's all you need in the world is love and laughter. That's all anybody needs. To have love in one hand and laughter in the other.

(BERTHA moves about the kitchen as though blessing it and chasing away the huge sadness that seems to envelop it. It is a dance and demonstration of her own magic, her own remedy that is centuries old and to which she is connected by the muscles of her heart and the blood's memory.)

You hear me, Mattie? I'm talking about laughing. The kind of laugh that comes from way deep inside. To just stand and laugh and let life flow right through you. Just laugh to let yourself know you're alive.

(She begins to laugh. It is a near-hysterical laughter that is a celebration of life, both its pain and its blessing. MATTIE and BYNUM join in the laughter. SETH enters from the front door.)

SETH: Well, I see you all having fun.

(SETH begins to laugh with them.)

That Loomis fellow standing up there on the corner watching the house. He standing right up there on Manila Street.

BERTHA: Don't you get started on him. The man done left out of here and that's the last I wanna hear of it. You about to drive me crazy with that man.

SETH: I just say he standing up there on the corner. Acting sneaky like he always do. He can stand up there all he want. As long as he don't come back in here.

(There is a knock on the door. SETH goes to answer it. Enter MARTHA LOOMIS [PENTECOST]. She is a young woman about twenty-eight. She is dressed as befitting a member of an Evangelist church. RUTHERFORD SELIG follows.)

SETH: Look here, Bertha. It's Martha Pentecost. Come on in, Martha. Who that with you? Oh . . . that's Selig. Come on in, Selig.

BERTHA: Come on in, Martha. It's sure good to see you.

BYNUM: Rutherford Selig, you a sure enough first-class People finder!

SELIG: She was right out there in Rankin. You take that first righthand road . . . right there at that church on Wooster Street. I started to go right past and something told me to stop at the church and see if they needed any dustpans.

SETH: Don't she look good, Bertha.

BERTHA: Look all nice and healthy.

MARTHA: Mr. Bynum . . . Selig told me my little girl was here.

SETH: There's some fellow around here say he your husband. Say his name is Loomis. Say you his wife.

MARTHA: Is my little girl with him?

SETH: Yeah, he got a little girl with him. I wasn't gonna tell him where you was. Not the way this fellow look. So he got Selig to find you.

MARTHA: Where they at? They upstairs?

SETH: He was standing right up there on Manila Street. I had to ask him to leave 'cause of how he was carrying on. He come in here one night—

(The door opens and LOOMIS and ZONIA enter. MARTHA and LOOMIS stare at each other.)

LOOMIS: Hello, Martha.

MARTHA: Herald . . . Zonia?

LOOMIS: You ain't waited for me, Martha. I got out the place looking to see your face. Seven years I waited to see your face.

MARTHA: Herald, I been looking for you. I wasn't but two months behind you when you went to my mama's and got Zonia. I been looking for you ever since.

LOOMIS: Joe Turner let me loose and I felt all turned around inside. I just wanted to see your face to know that the world was still there. Make sure everything still in its place so I could reconnect myself together. I got there and you was gone, Martha.

MARTHA: Herald . . .

LOOMIS: Left my little girl motherless in the world.

MARTHA: I didn't leave her motherless, Herald. Reverend Tolliver wanted to move the church up North 'cause of all the trouble the colored folks was having down there. Nobody knew what was gonna happen traveling them roads. We didn't even know if we was gonna make it up here or not. I left her with my mama so she be safe. That was better than dragging her out on the road having to duck and hide from people. Wasn't no telling what was gonna happen to us. I didn't leave her motherless in the world. I been looking for you.

LOOMIS: I come up on Henry Thompson's place after seven years of living in hell, and all I'm looking to do is see your face.

MARTHA: Herald, I didn't know if you was ever coming back. They told me Joe Turner had you and my whole world split half in two. My whole life shattered. It was like

I had poured it in a cracked jar and it all leaked out the bottom. When it go like that there ain't nothing you can do put it back together. You talking about Henry Thompson's place like I'm still gonna be working the land by myself. How I'm gonna do that? You wasn't gone but two months and Henry Thompson kicked me off his land and I ain't had no place to go but to my mama's. I stayed and waited there for five years before I woke up one morning and decided that you was dead. Even if you weren't, you was dead to me. I wasn't gonna carry you with me no more. So I killed you in my heart. I buried you. I mourned you. And then I picked up what was left and went on to make life without you. I was a young woman with life at my beckon. I couldn't drag you behind me like a sack of cotton.

LOOMIS: I just been waiting to look on your face to say my goodbye. That goodbye got so big at times, seem like it was gonna swallow me up. Like Jonah in the whale's belly I sat up in that goodbye for three years. That goodbye kept me out on the road searching. Not looking on women in their houses. It kept me bound up to the road. All the time that goodbye swelling up in my chest till I'm about to bust. Now that I see your face I can say my goodbye and make my own world.

(LOOMIS takes ZONIA's hand and presents her to MARTHA.)

Martha . . . here go your daughter. I tried to take care of her. See that she had something to eat. See that she was out of the elements. Whatever I know I tried to teach her. Now she need to learn from her mother whatever you got to teach her. That way she won't be no one-sided person.

(LOOMIS stoops to ZONIA.)

Zonia, you go live with your mama. She a good woman. You go on with her and listen to her good. You my daughter and I love you like a daughter. I hope to see you again in the world somewhere. I'll never forget you.

ZONIA: (Throws her arms around LOOMIS in a panic.) I won't get no bigger! My bones won't get no bigger! They won't! I promise! Take me with you till we keep searching and never finding. I won't get no bigger! I promise!

LOOMIS: Go on and do what I told you now.

MARTHA: (Goes to ZONIA and comforts her.) It's alright, baby. Mama's here. Mama's here. Don't worry. Don't cry.

(MARTHA turns to BYNUM.)

Mr. Bynum, I don't know how to thank you. God bless you.

LOOMIS: It was you! All the time it was you that bind me up! You bound me to the road!

BYNUM: I ain't bind you, Herald Loomis. You can't bind what don't cling.

LOOMIS: Everywhere I go people wanna bind me up. Joe Turner wanna bind me up! Reverend Tolliver wanna bind me up. You wanna bind me up. Everybody wanna bind me up. Well, Joe Turner's come and gone and Herald Loomis ain't for no binding. I ain't gonna let nobody bind me up!

(LOOMIS pulls out a knife.)

BYNUM: It wasn't you, Herald Loomis. I ain't bound you. I bound the little girl to her mother. That's who I bound. You binding yourself. You bound onto your song. All you got to do is stand up and sing it, Herald Loomis. It's right there kicking at your throat. All you got to do is sing it. Then you be free.

MARTHA: Herald . . . look at yourself! Standing there with a knife in your hand. You done gone over to the devil. Come on . . . put down the knife. You got to look to Jesus. Even if you done fell away from the church you can be saved again. The Bible say, "The Lord is my shepherd I shall not want. He maketh me to lie down in green pastures. He leads me beside the still water. He restoreth my soul. He leads me in the path of righteousness for His name's sake. Even though I walk through the shadow of death—"

LOOMIS: That's just where I be walking!

MARTHA: "I shall fear no evil. For Thou art with me. Thy rod and thy staff, they comfort me."

LOOMIS: You can't tell me nothing about no valleys. I done been all across the valleys and the hills and the mountains and the oceans.

MARTHA: "Thou preparest a table for me in the presence of my enemies."

LOOMIS: And all I seen was a bunch of niggers dazed out of their woolly heads. And Mr. Jesus Christ standing there in the middle of them, grinning.

MARTHA: "Thou annointest my head with oil, my cup runneth over."

LOOMIS: He grin that big old grin . . . and niggers wallowing at his feet.

MARTHA: "Surely goodness and mercy shall follow me all the days of my life, and I shall dwell in the house of the Lord forever."

LOOMIS: Great big old white man . . . your Mr. Jesus Christ. Standing there with a whip in one hand and tote board in another, and them niggers swimming in a sea of cotton. And he counting. He tallying up the cotton. "Well, Jeremiah . . . what's the matter, you ain't picked but two hundred pounds of cotton today? Got to put you on half rations." And Jeremiah go back and lay up there on his half rations and talk about what a nice man Mr. Jesus Christ is 'cause he give him salvation after he die. Something wrong here. Something don't fit right!

MARTHA: You got to open up your heart and have faith, Herald. This world is just a trial for the next. Jesus offers you salvation.

LOOMIS: I been wading in the water. I been walking all over the River Jordan. But what it get me, huh? I done been baptized with blood of the lamb and the fire of the Holy Ghost. But what I got, huh? I got salvation? My enemies all around me picking the flesh from my bones. I'm choking on my own blood and all you got to give me is salvation?

MARTHA: You got to be clean, Herald. You got to be washed with the blood of the lamb.

LOOMIS: Blood make you clean? You clean with blood?

MARTHA: Jesus bled for you. He's the Lamb of God who takest away the sins of the world.

LOOMIS: I don't need nobody to bleed for me! I can bleed for myself.

MARTHA: You got to be something, Herald. You just can't be alive. Life don't mean nothing unless it got a meaning.

LOOMIS: What kind of meaning you got? What kind of clean you got, woman? You want blood? Blood make you clean? You clean with blood?

(LOOMIS slashes himself across the chest. He rubs the blood over his face and comes to a realization.)

I'm standing! I'm standing. My legs stood up! I'm standing now!

(Having found his song, the song of self-sufficiency, fully resurrected, cleansed and given breath, free from any encumbrance other than the workings of his own heart and the bonds of the flesh, having accepted the responsibility for his own presence in the world, he is free to soar above the environs that weighed and pushed his spirit into terrifying contractions.)

Goodbye, Martha.

(LOOMIS turns and exits, the knife still in his hands. MATTIE looks about the room and rushes out after him.)

BYNUM: Herald Loomis, you shining! You shining like new money!

The lights go down to BLACK.

Producing *Joe Turner's Come and Gone*

The Construction of Meaning through Collaboration

Theatre production is a unique process that is unlike the creation of visual art, music, or literature. The creation of a stage production is an **interpretive art** and a **collaborative art.** The beginning point is the playwright's **script.** But a script is not a blueprint with all the details precisely recorded. The playscript essentially expresses a drama through dialogue.

In the case of *Joe Turner's Come and Gone*, in addition to the dialogue, Wilson's script outlines basic stage directions, the characters' entrances and exits and other important movements, and the nature of the physical space. It also provides hints of character description. For example, Wilson tells us that Seth is in his early fifties, a skilled craftsman, and that he has a certain "stability." We also learn from the script that Bertha is slightly younger than Seth and that "she has learned to negotiate around Seth's apparent orneriness." Wilson gives us no details of their appearance or their dress.

The script identifies a boardinghouse as the setting and details the layout of the downstairs rooms and the placement of the doors. Most of the play takes place in the kitchen and the parlor, with two short scenes for the children in the garden. There is no specific description of the architectural style of the house, no indication of painting or wall decor, no discussion of the style or the quantity of furniture, and, perhaps most important, no description of the atmosphere created by the combination of the physical details of place.

The playwright begins a process that must be joined by a director, actors, and designers. Together they will interpret the playwright's work by filling in details of character, action, scenery, costumes, lighting, and sound. All are creative artists in their own right. But in the theatre, no one person's work stands alone. Only when the play is fully realized on the stage with an audience present does theatre actually exist.

Working closely with the **director,** who guides the process, the designers and actors give physical shape, a concrete reality, to the playwright's vision. They study the text closely to grasp the playwright's intentions. And then they use their particular talents as a group to create a theatrical event that expresses their understanding of the truth in the playwright's text. This is an enormously complex task, with many people responsible for different parts of the production, all working under the strictest of deadlines. The curtain must go up on the scheduled day, at the scheduled hour.

In the following pages we explore the process of staging *Joe Turner's Come and Gone* at the Oregon Shakespeare Festival in Ashland, Oregon. We begin to analyze the nature of the work done by the director, the actors, and the designers. We look at the collaborative process, the ways in which people work together; and also at the process of interpretation, how expressive choices are made. An examination of the production process will also give us further insights into the meaning of *Joe Turner's Come and Gone*.

The Oregon Shakespeare Festival

Ashland, Oregon, is a small, picturesque town of 30,000 people located in the mountains of southern Oregon. Much of the life of the community revolves around the Oregon Shakespeare Festival, located in the center of the town. The Shakespeare Festival is the largest not-for-profit theatre of its kind in the United States. Other theatres that we examine in this book are in the heart of large cities such as New York, Los Angeles, or Seattle. Attending the theatre in Ashland, however, is a quieter, more reflective experience than going to the theatre in a fast-paced city at the end of a workday or as part of one's daily activities. The actors who perform *Joe Turner's Come and Gone* will have the full attention of their audience as they give life to the world that August Wilson has created.

Although the festival, which began in 1935, was originally dedicated to the plays of Shakespeare, it now presents the works of many other playwrights as well. Recent seasons have offered a total of eleven plays, with about one-third by Shakespeare. For eight months of the year, from late February to October, plays are performed on the festival's three stages.

Many of the audience members at the festival are residents of Ashland or Oregonians from Portland (about four hours away) and closer, smaller communities. But the entire population of Oregon, 3.9 million, would fit into New York City or Los Angeles many times over. It is the out-of-state and even international visitors who enable this large, complex organization to maintain its many enterprises. People come to Ashland from all over the world specifically to go to the theatre. Most people will spend several days and see more than one play. This is why the festival produces plays in **repertory**—that is, a number of plays are produced at once and then performed in rotation. During the same week, theatre-goers might be able to attend performances of *Joe Turner's Come and Gone*, a Shakespearian tragedy, a nineteenth-century French farce, and another new American play. In 1993 the festival's 600-seat Angus Bowmer Theatre opened the season with *Joe Turner's Come and Gone*.

The Actors at Work

Understanding the Play

The actors sit around a large table quietly reading the play to one another. Some of them know each other well. They have worked together for years in this small Oregon town. A few of

---

THEATRE TALENTS AND SKILLS

Starting Points in the Rehearsal Process

1. Careful reading of the play and research into the historical time period
2. Joint reading of the play and discussion of the characters' history and motivation
3. Repetition of and response to the language
4. Physicalization
5. Music

---

the actors are new. They have come to Ashland for the first time as part of the *Joe Turner* cast, although they will stay in Ashland to take part in other plays. The director, Clinton Turner Davis, who leads the discussion, has come from New York just to direct this play. Most of the actors are working with Davis for the first time.

During this first phase of the **rehearsal** process, called **table work,** the actors do not get up and start to move around the stage until the director, Davis, feels that they have asked enough questions and explored enough possible answers about the history and motivation of each character. Why does each character make certain choices? What is behind the words the characters speak? The answers may change a number of times, and more questions will certainly arise. But each actor must have a starting point for the thread that leads him or her from moment to moment during the course of the play.

The discussion shifts to the character of Herald Loomis, and Davis leans toward Derrick Lee Weedon, the actor who is playing Loomis.

CLINTON TURNER DAVIS: What did you feel, what was going through your mind when you went back, when you were released from the chain gang and you went back home and Martha wasn't there? All right now, think of that moment, and nonverbally say the first thing that comes into your mind, nonverbally.[13]

J. P. Phillips portrays Seth, "just a regular American guy trying to be decent."

Weedon pauses and then an anguished, choking sound comes from his throat. Davis says softly, "Remember that sound. We'll use that later." What begins as a sound, an inarticulate expression of loss and rage, becomes a point of departure for the passion that drives Herald Loomis through the course of the play.

J. P. Phillips, playing Seth, is intrigued by the connection of Seth to Booker T. Washington, an African American educator who during the 1910s advocated separating the races and focusing on vocational education for African Americans. Phillips strongly believes that Seth is simply a man "searching for the American dream and trying to prove his decency. He's just a regular American guy trying to be decent."

Davis is eager for the actors to begin the process of building the inner life of their characters as he poses a variety of questions to open up the discussion. But he also welcomes the answer "I don't know."

> **CLINTON TURNER DAVIS:** "I don't know" is sometimes the most empowering answer because it frees the air. And likewise if the actors ask me a question and I don't have an answer, I'll tell them, "I don't know." We have to reveal ourselves to each other and build trust in that revelation.

As they approach Wilson's characters and the world of the play, Davis and the cast also discuss significant events of the times and background source materials. Sitting around that large table, in the quiet, empty rehearsal hall, the actors spread out pictures of Pittsburgh from the early 1900s. They look at photographs of houses, the clothing of the period, and people at work. They share readings from W. E. B. Dubois's essential work *The Souls of Black Folk*, which explores the political and economic structures of the time and their consequences for black Americans. They read from the work of Zora Neale Hurston to expand their awareness of the language spoken by Wilson's characters and for information on traditional religious practice. Davis shares his studies of the Yoruban culture of western Nigeria, which he feels is the appropriate source for the Juba and for Bynum's incantations. After three days of questions and discussion and reading and rereading the play, the actors know enough about the inside of their characters to get the play "up on its legs." They also know most of their lines.

The Rehearsal Process

The next week and a half is spent working on the **blocking**—that is, all of the actors' movements around the stage that make up the physical action of the performance. Not all directors have lengthy discussions with the actors before they start the blocking rehearsals; some have individual discussions with actors, and some have no discussions at all. But for Davis, it is crucial that the actors arrive at an understanding of the play together and that their understanding be informed by the history and the texture of the times as well as their own emotional and intellectual responses to their characters.

The continuing discussion about the play is one of the ways that the director and the actors collaborate to create meaning. The discussion is also a way of building trust between the members of the company. This way of working depends on shared responsibility rather than on competition or a hierarchical structure. Ultimately, the director must make certain decisions and keep examining the performance to ensure that the playwright's ideas are being communicated. But Davis encourages the actors to take risks, to try out new ideas, to contribute their own thoughts.

> **CLINTON TURNER DAVIS:** When you work with an ensemble, it is essential to have a high degree of trust, and the earlier you can create that, the stronger the working environment will be. I try not to impose my views too early on because I think too often the actors feel that they are just the instrument of the director. An autocratic director will tell the actor what to do, when to do it, where, why, and how. And so the actors spend more time trying to contort and mold themselves into his concept of the characters without totally understanding why. It can be frightening.

An atmosphere of trust and receptivity gives the actors a freedom that many believe allows them to do their best work.

> **LEWAN ALEXANDER (BYNUM):** The collaborative way that he worked—he encouraged, really demanded, input, not only in what we were doing with our own characters but the shape of the play, how we saw certain scenes develop. It was really a collaborative effort, and that's very rare.

> **TAMU GRAY (BERTHA):** I was given an opportunity to really concentrate on the craft, to concentrate on the art, to be empowered as an actor in the rehearsal hall. We worked in a respectful and truly collective and community-based way. We walked into the rehearsal hall with a sense of play and a desire to play and a willingness to play that I've not seen anywhere else.

Sometimes when the actors enter the rehearsal room, Davis has music playing.

> **CLINTON TURNER DAVIS:** We listened to gospel tapes, down-home revival, really backwoods revivals where you just had a cappella singing started by the traditional starter of the church. They would wail into it and ultimately discover the communal harmony. And since we had started rehearsal right after Christmas, we had Quincy Jones's interpretation of Handel's Messiah—A Soulful Celebration. Through that recording Quincy has given a complete history of African American music. Other times we listened to jazz or blues. Sometimes we'd have the music playing to set the mood when the actors would come in in the morning or when we would take a break. This would keep us in a specific context.

Davis sees music as part of the texture of the play, the connection to the oral tradition discussed in the first part of this chapter. But he also recognizes a musical structure in the language itself, a poetry in the rhythm of the speeches and the telling of the stories. For J. P. Phillips, who plays Seth, the music has to start with the language:

> **J. P. PHILLIPS:** I'm looking for words and minding the language. You take the playwright's words and you add breath and bring the words to life and reveal what the playwright is trying to say.

BW Gonzalez, who portrays Mattie, also sees the language as the starting point for building character:

> **BW GONZALEZ:** What I feel I do as an actor is like painting. I paint the portrait through the words. The words create the images that I need to paint the portrait of the character.

Bynum (LeWan Alexander) tells Mattie Campbell (BW Gonzalez) to push thoughts of Jack Carper out of her mind.

Physical Characterization

The actors also work to create a specific physical presence for their characters. Although there are many different approaches to the physicalization of a character, we look at the problems faced by the young actor LeWan Alexander in approaching the much older character of Bynum. In 1993 Alexander was in his early thirties. The script gives Bynum's age as early sixties. That presents the actor not only with a large span of years to bridge physically, but also with a significant gap in experience to bridge emotionally.

LEWAN ALEXANDER (BYNUM): Everyone in the play was already cast before Christmas of last year, and they were to start rehearsals at the beginning of January, except for me. I knew

I wasn't in the play. I wasn't cast. They were still looking for Bynum, and I got a call about a week before Christmas to see if I wanted to play Bynum. And I said to Henry Woronicz, the artistic director of the Festival, "Oh, thanks, Hank, but I can't do that role. That's just way out of my range." He said, "Well, it's either you or someone that we're going to find, so why don't you give yourself a couple of days to think about it?" Well, I didn't sleep that night, and I called him ten hours later and said, "Yeah, I'd like to do it." The main reason that I balked, which is also the reason that I decided to accept, was the fact that not only is he thirty years my senior, but the nature of the man and what he's connected to was very far from my own personal experience. Just the thought of a conjure man, a rootworker, is very foreign to me. It was quite a challenge. I started in the rehearsal process with three things, three physical things. My grandfather died when I was very young, but I remember how he used to sit in a chair. I remember that and the way he used to slump and the way he used to eat, particularly bread. I picked those things up from him. There was a homeless man in Milwaukee that I used to observe a lot. He would never pick up his feet when he walked, and he always walked with his head very low, shoulders slumped. And he had a beard that was very gray, and it was kind of curly around him. The script says that Bynum is very connected to the earth, and I wanted his center of gravity to be very low so that it's easy for him to get down to the ground if he needs to.[14]

The director and the actors work together to create an atmosphere that makes the world of the play gradually come alive for them. They study the play and its times. They explore the specific nature of each character, and his or her personal history, objectives, or goals. They begin with individual moments in the stage life of each character and work to build a coherent whole that makes sense of everything the characters say and do. For example, the actor playing Loomis may start with what he has lost and the search for his wife, but ultimately it is himself that he seeks. They focus on the language and the way the rhythms of speech shape character. They listen to music that feeds the work on rhythm and creates a certain atmosphere. They create a physical presence. All of the director's and the actors' preparations are aimed at refining their understanding of the playwright's text and making imaginative choices that will make this understanding clear to an audience.

Staging the Juba

Our summary of the rehearsal process for *Joe Turner's Come and Gone* is far from a complete description of the actors' work. In later chapters we expand our discussion of the nature of acting as we examine other productions and study other actors' work. At this point we pursue the way the director and actors work together to interpret the playwright's text for the audience through staging. We examine the director's blocking of a crucial section of the play to see how the action combines with speech to create meaningful images. For Davis, the Juba is at the center of the play and leads directly to Herald Loomis's first major revelation: his vision of bones rising up out of the water at the end of act 1. The interruption of the Juba by Loomis's entrance sharply escalates the conflict between the characters and exposes the depth of Loomis's despair. We see in physical terms the crippling of his soul by slavery.

The Juba begins after Sunday dinner with all the boardinghouse characters present except Loomis. Together Seth and Bynum organize the other characters.

SETH: . . . Come on, Bertha, leave them dishes be for a while. We gonna Juba.

BYNUM: Alright. Let's Juba down! (act 1, scene 4)

The stage directions describe the Juba as

reminiscent of the Ring Shouts of the African slaves. It is a call and response dance. BYNUM sits at the table and drums. He calls the dance as others clap hands, shuffle and stomp around

the table. It should be as African as possible, with the performers working themselves up into a near frenzy. The words can be improvised, but should include some mention of the Holy Ghost. (act 1, scene 4)

Drumming and Dancing

In staging the Juba, Davis begins with the drum. He explains that drumming is at the heart of African communication and language. According to Davis, one of the greatest deprivations in slavery was the loss of the drum. Drumming was forbidden by slaveowners, who couldn't understand but sensed the power of the drum to speak across the distances and carry the voices, the language, of the African captives from plantation to plantation. For Davis, then, the drumming in the Juba is part of reestablishing communication after the end of slavery, a way of developing community.

The stage directions suggest that Bynum use the dining table as his "drum." After discussing with the cast various possibilities for household items that could be used as drums, Davis settles on the table as the "gbedu," a big, deep-timbred royal drum. The table is the hearth, the center of nurturing and community, and is therefore appropiate to serve as the instrument of communication. Davis establishes that Bynum will sit at the table and drum on the tabletop while the others dance in a processional circle around him. The circle is suggested by the descriptions of Bynum's ceremonies at the beginning of the play:

SETH: He done drew a big circle with that stick and now he's dancing around. (act 1, scene 1)

Davis sees power and completeness in the many symbolic associations of the circle that spatially and visually contribute to the harmony he is trying to develop rhythmically.

Once the basic image is established for the cast, Davis works with the actors on African rhythms to be clapped and dance steps that they may use, some of which have African origins and some of which are associated with religious observation in

Loomis (Derrick Lee Weedon) destroys the Juba celebration with his vision of the "bones people," which is a symbolic telling of both his personal history and the larger history of a people brought across the sea into slavery.

the United States, such as Pentecostal worship. The ceremony represents a merging of African and Christian worship. After Bynum begins his drumming, Davis asks each actor to enter the Juba in order of the age and importance of his or her character to the household. Seth is first as the owner of the house, and Zonia is last as a visiting child. The actors are free to improvise off the basic rhythm and off the basic dance steps to increase the density of sound and movement.

Text and Verbal Improvisation

In addition to the drumming and dancing of the Juba, there is also a whole verbal score to be improvised. Davis asks the cast to approach their words for the Juba section as a kind of personal prayer, a statement of their needs at that particular point in the play. Through a combination of improvised speech, chanting, and song, they call upon the "Spirit" to provide guidance in their lives. Once the actors have begun to develop this verbal text or score for the Juba, Davis adds one more element: He translates some of the actors' improvised words into Dutch, French, Spanish, German, and Portuguese, all languages of the slave traders who carried African people on their ships. The words come out as a kind of genetic memory of the experience of slavery.

Herald Loomis (Derrick Lee Weedon) describes his paralyzing vision of bones rising from the water to Bynum (LeWan Alexander) in the Oregon Shakespeare Festival production of *Joe Turner's Come and Gone.*

launches Herald Loomis into his soul-searing vision. Loomis, who has collapsed to the floor, sees a vision of bones that sink into the ocean and then are washed ashore as black people. Bynum, trying to get Loomis to his feet, tells him that the "bones people" have risen and taken to the road. But Loomis is crushed by the vision and cannot rise. Loomis is reexperiencing the Middle Passage, the holocaustic journey of Africans crossing the ocean to become slaves. The Juba establishes a memory of the passage into slavery that sets the context for Loomis's breakdown.

The many levels of meaning that emerge from a piece of staging that lasts only a few minutes demonstrate one of the fundamental aspects of theatrical communication: stage images are constantly built with many layers of expression, some visual, some verbal, some rhythmic, some psychological or emotional. The audience receives complex information from these images that are so much more than a mere sequence in the storytelling process.

The Meaning of the Juba

In this particular production, then, the Juba has a number of structural and thematic functions. In terms of the **plot,** it is an activity that brings the characters together following their Sunday dinner. Even though they come from widely different backgrounds and have very different goals for themselves, they all know the Juba. It is an informal household religious observation, a ceremony that celebrates an African heritage fused with Christianity and allows for an emotional release following the daily struggle for survival. For the characters it is also a way of focusing their particular search during the course of the play. In addition, the Juba is a symbolic representation of the obstacles the characters have overcome to arrive at this point in their journeys. The languages of the slave traders and the recovery of the drum introduce references to slavery that will become explosive after Herald Loomis's entrance.

The Juba builds a sense of community and harmony that will be broken by Herald Loomis. It also builds all the tensions of act 1 to a high level of intensity, a "frenzy" that essentially

Expanding the Stage Image: The Work of the Designers

The intensity of the actors' movement and language should be riveting for the audience in the sequence at the end of act 1 that we have been discussing. All of the actors' skills are engaged at a high level to create a spellbinding moment of revelation. In the Juba the actors create a sense of community, using the whole stage. Then the

The rendering of the scene design by Mike Fish for *Joe Turner's Come and Gone* communicates the feeling and atmosphere of the set as well as the definition of the space, the placement of the furniture, and the details of place. After the designer creates the scenic images, the scene shop constructs the actual set from technical drawings.

The scene design is transformed into the actual setting for *Joe Turner's Come and Gone.* The warmth of the kitchen is placed against the smokestacks of industrial Pittsburgh. The table offers a gathering place for the characters and becomes the center of the play's action.

The Set Design

In the **rendering** of the set designed by Mike Fish, we can see the placement of the table center stage and get some idea of its relative size. In developing a **ground plan** for the set (the placement of the furniture, doors, and walls), Fish as **scene designer** and Davis as director need to create a space that (1) allows the characters a sense of intimacy produced by being in the warmth of Bertha's kitchen and (2) provides a space that is big enough and spacious enough for the characters to eat together at the dining table and then to be able to dance around it in the Juba sequence. The placement of the table center stage makes it the primary visual focus and also allows for the action described in the previous section. The set design must first support the characters' actions

harmony of the stage picture is destroyed by Herald Loomis's entrance, and the focus narrows until we see only Bynum and Loomis and finally only Loomis. The consequences of slavery come crashing down on us as we see the torment for Herald Loomis when he says, "I got to stand up" and then, "My legs won't stand up! My legs won't stand up!" The primary focus is on the actors, but the work of the designers is essential in supporting and completing the images the actors create.

and movements required by the play. It must provide spaces that allow the appropriate physical relationships between characters.

As the characters eat their Sunday dinner and then begin the Juba, we in the audience sense the comfort provided by the boardinghouse kitchen. The set helps create an atmosphere that is warm and inviting. There is a large fireplace; there is also a stove. The colors are reds and browns and antique rose. And precise attention is paid to detail.

> **MIKE FISH:** It was a very large house but at the same time it had to be very, very intimate because this is Bertha's house and it had all her little knick-knacks. When I furnished the house I was very careful to put details: the Civil War, little precious mementos, little porcelain figures, a sign above the mantel, "God Bless This Home."

The set design also reveals the time and place. Fish shapes the space with nineteenth-century architectural details and furnishes it with period antiques that are purchased or are reproduced in the scene shop. The time and place are also strongly reinforced by the use of a painted backdrop that rises above the three-dimensional structure of the house. Behind the house we see the smokestacks of the Pittsburgh steel mills. The backdrop places us in an industrial setting and reminds us that the boardinghouse must protect its occupants against the urban factory world. Even as we see the family gathering and ritual observation, with its African origins, held in the safety of the kitchen, the reality of Pittsburgh in 1911 looms behind. We see that the characters face an enormous task of integrating experiences and realities.

THEATRE TALENTS AND SKILLS

Summary of Basic Design Functions

A. Set
   1. Reflects time period
   2. Gives sense of place
   3. Creates appropriate atmosphere
   4. Creates space that provides for necessary character action and movement
   5. Creates space that allows the appropriate physical relationships between characters
B. Costuming
   1. Reflects time period
   2. Reveals class and background of characters
   3. Demonstrates individuality of characters
   4. Highlights contrasts between characters
C. Lighting
   1. Creates visibility
   2. Creates atmosphere
   3. Works with pacing and rhythms of actors to establish overall rhythm of the play

All build visual metaphors.

The Costume Design

The costumes play a very important part in creating a sense of the time period and in defining the class and individuality of the characters. As the characters gather for their Sunday dinner and then the Juba, we see them in their "good" clothes, which are nicer but well-worn versions of their work clothes. These are proud people who have to work extremely hard for everything they have. The goal of the **costume designer**, Candice Cain, is to create the effect of real clothing.

> **CANDICE CAIN:** I didn't want them to be "costumes." I called them clothes the whole

The costume design for Mattie Campbell by Candice Cain shows the contrast with Herald Loomis.

unbalanced the household since his first appearance. The character is in a fury, and his visual presence is a critical part of his disruptive force.

> **CANDICE CAIN:** When Loomis walked into that room, I wanted him to suck up everybody's energy, every bit of energy that was in there. The playwright says he comes in a black coat, but you have to find out why that is. All those layers that he wears. There's almost an ecclesiastical feel, and his coat is so solid and so dark and so mysterious. And then that hat with the five-inch brim.

Loomis is the only character in black; the other characters wear a variety of lighter and brighter colors—blues, greens, and browns. Loomis is wearing large, heavy pieces of clothing that hide the outline of his body. His shape is that of the huge coat and the broad hat. The clothing of the other characters is much more formfitting, suggesting that these are ordinary human beings. They also have much more visible details on their clothes—ruffles, buttons, suspenders—giving them a smaller-scale presence. Nothing breaks the line of Loomis's silhouette. Visually, when Loomis is not onstage, all the other characters emerge as individuals. When Loomis enters, the other characters become a group.

The Lighting Design

The **lighting designer,** Jim Sale, had much to do with creating the atmosphere for the Juba sequence. Slowly, as the characters start to dance and shout, the lights change from the warm, realistic light of the kitchen to a strange, moody light, casting strong shadows. The lights for the Juba build gradually so that the audience becomes aware of the shifting mood but not the mechanics. But then, on Loomis's entrance, the lights shift instantly to the bright, realistic light.

> **JIM SALE:** It's almost like he came in and flipped on a light switch, his energy came in so strong.

time. There was a lot of work to do after the clothing was built and fit. We even ill-fitted some of the clothing, so it didn't look perfect. We worked with sandpaper, we worked with paint, we worked with washing and dyeing. You know when they washed their clothes, they used washboards. A lot of the petticoats were actually real petticoats from the period. And I chose some style lines earlier than when the play is set because these people had these clothes for a long period of time.

One of the major design issues for the costume designer in *Joe Turner's Come and Gone* is establishing a strong contrast between Herald Loomis and all the other characters. He destroys the harmony of the Juba with his entrance, just as he has

JOE TURNER'S COME AND GONE

JOE TURNER'S COME AND GONE

The costume designer Candice Cain begins her work by sketching ideas for the costumes of the characters. The silhouette of each character emerges from the sketches. The costume sketches are for Jeremy Furlow *(left)* and Herald Loomis *(right)*. Following discussions with the director and the other designers, sketches are developed into detailed color renderings, accompanied by fabric swatches that indicate the texture and pattern of the different fabrics that will make up each costume.

The designers work continuously with the director and the actors to create a coherent interpretation of the playwright's work. They create images in space, using materials that add layers of meaning to the images created by the actors. Their work goes far beyond illustrating time and place. All the design areas contribute to visual metaphors that define the world of the play. The warmth of Bertha's kitchen juxtaposed with the imposing Pittsburgh skyline of factory smokestacks sets the stage for the struggles of the characters to find a place for themselves. Shadows contrast with the light as Herald Loomis emerges from the dark clothes—in which he hides himself and which weigh him down—to embrace a reborn, expansive sense of himself.

Conclusion: History and Meaning in *Joe Turner's Come and Gone*

At the beginning of the chapter we introduced August Wilson as a dramatic historian. In examining Wilson's sources, we outlined the history of African Americans that forms the background for the play, a history that includes forced labor and migration. Within the play itself, however, Wilson presents an understanding of history that goes beyond the facts of the chain gang and the movement of African Americans to the urban areas of the North. That history is built from the actions of all the characters, as each searches for

This photograph of the first entrance of Herald Loomis demonstrates the way the heavy, severe costume contributes to the power of the character's appearance.

Loomis becomes what his name suggests. He becomes the "luminous," shiny man of Bynum's vision from act 1. Together, the quests of Loomis and Bynum can be seen to represent a large movement from slavery to freedom that suggests both the hundreds of years of American slavery and the internal journey of the individual. Herald Loomis cannot begin his life until he finds a way to cut the ties that bind him, to cleanse himself of the pollution of slavery. This he does symbolically by cutting himself with a knife at the end of the play and bleeding for himself. He has regained the song of himself, a "song of self-sufficiency."

Bynum cannot die "a happy man, a man who done left his mark on life" until he helps bring about the liberation of Herald Loomis that transforms him into the shiny man. A celebration of freedom echoes in the final line of the play, which is spoken by Bynum: "Herald Loomis, you shining! You shining like new money!"

Family and Inheritance: The Way from the Past to the Future

This movement toward freedom and affirmation is the overarching history that the play expresses. But this history of the journey out of slavery is framed by the views of Seth, the northern African American born in freedom; and of the People Finder, Rutherford Selig, who is the descendant of slave traders. The house where the play takes place belongs to Seth, a man born free, unburdened by the baggage of slavery. His history is tied to a father who could leave him the inheritance of a house and a strong sense of himself, in spite of the fact that he is still unable to start his own business.

Seth fears the decency of his house, his history, will be compromised by the turmoil that Loomis brings with him. He rejects Loomis even though he and Bertha have committed their dwelling as a home for people who have nowhere else to go. Because Seth and Bertha have no children of their own, in a symbolic way,

what is most precious in life and what has been lost. Multiple stories are told, and so what we might call a multidimensional view of history emerges from the play. This multidimensional vision of history begun in the text by Wilson is given physical shape in production by the imaginative work of the actors, director, and designers.

The Quest for Self

The central action of the play is Herald Loomis's search for himself, which is connected to Bynum's search for the "shiny man." In fact, what they seek is the same. By the end of the play, they become the parents of the children of slavery, creating a family out of the separated individuals who come to stay at the boardinghouse. In the making of this hybrid family, two different histories of life in America confront each other, and the conflict is strongest in the struggle between Seth and Loomis.

Seth and Bertha represent the only coherent sense of family in the play. One of Wilson's major concerns in *Joe Turner's Come and Gone* is the breakdown of the family under slavery and under the various forms of oppression that followed slavery. The destruction of the Loomis family is central to the events of the play, but most of the other characters are also alone and seeking some form of family. Mattie Campbell is particularly poignant in her search for Jack Carper, the father of her two babies who died as infants. The characters are cut off from the future until they can resolve issues of family, particularly in terms of building relationships that will sustain children.

Under these circumstances, the inheritance from parents takes on tremendous importance. Seth's inheritance of a house from his father has literally given him a place in the world. Bynum has inherited wisdom from his father, even though it comes to him in a vision. And Mattie Campbell, for all her loneliness, is sustained by the memory of her mother. The question of family and inheritance finally focuses on Zonia. Herald Loomis has been desperate to find his wife so that he can regain his bearings. But he cannot begin anew for himself until he secures Zonia's proper inheritance, which is to know both of her parents.

The nature of inheritance for the African American characters contrasts uneasily with the inheritance of the Selig family. They too are searchers, but the search has been connected to the enslavement of Africans. The legacy of searching passed from father to son in this family began with the transportation of slaves, progressed to the hunting of runaway slaves, and ends with Rutherford Selig, who charges for reuniting the very people his family has worked for generations to tear apart. However, in the end, even Rutherford Selig becomes part of the circumstances that finally allow the play's title to be true for Herald Loomis. Joe Turner indeed has come, and at last he is gone.

Summary

The American playwright August Wilson chronicled African American history by writing a play for each decade of the twentieth century. Inspired by the blues songs of Bessie Smith and the paintings and collages of Romare Bearden, Wilson saw his plays as part of an oral tradition. In the production of Wilson's play *Joe Turner's Come and Gone* by the Oregon Shakespeare Festival, the vision of the playwright was expressed by the interpretive work of other theatre artists.

Joe Turner's Come and Gone focuses on the migration of African Americans to the North shortly after the turn of the century. The journey of migration is both an actual and a metaphoric search for a better way of life following emancipation. Part of that search involves the process of separation and re-creation of families that touches all of the characters' lives. For Herald Loomis, the journey of migration becomes a way of reclaiming himself after having been enslaved physically and spiritually on the chain gang.

Theatre production is a collaborative process in which theatre practitioners work closely together to interpret the playwright's script. Director, actors, and designers study the play and its context and then make imaginative contributions to shaping the production onstage. The production of the play at the Oregon

Shakespeare Festival demonstrated the way meaning is constructed through theatrical communication. The scene designer created an environment that would support the action of the play and locate the characters first in the comfortable atmosphere of the boardinghouse and second against the much harsher background of industrial Pittsburgh. The costume designer gave the characters a sense of time, social class, and individuality through the garments she designed; she also used color and silhouette to separate Herald Loomis from the other characters. The lighting designer shifted the mood onstage through color and shadow to reinforce the qualities expressed by the characters. The director and the actors worked together to shape characters and interactions that would give life to the stories Wilson weaves together, ultimately focusing on the stories of Loomis and Bynum as they merge into one "song" of freedom.

 # Topics for Discussion and Writing

1. What is meant by the oral tradition? Can music, painting, and drama all be part of an oral tradition? Is it a contradiction to consider a play with a written text to be part of an oral tradition? What aspects of *Joe Turner's Come and Gone* support its placement in an oral tradition?

2. What is the effect of including the long stories in the text of *Joe Turner's Come and Gone*? How do the stories affect the rhythm of the play and the audience's or reader's response? Choose one of the stories, and write a short essay that includes your responses to the following questions: (a) What do we come to learn about the character from the story? (b) What images in the story make the strongest impression on you? (c) How does the story relate to the events of the play and the play's meaning?

3. What is the relationship of the play to Christianity? Many of the characters are Christian. Herald Loomis is a deacon of the church, and yet he makes a very strong statement about slave labor, associating the gang boss with Jesus Christ. How are we to understand his outburst? Is the attack on religion or hypocrisy?

● For suggested readings and other resources related to this chapter, please visit **www.mhhe.com/creativespirit6e**

CHAPTER 4

The Art of the Actor

In Chapter 3 we studied the collaboration among playwright, director, actors, and designers in producing *Joe Turner's Come and Gone.* We began with the work of the playwright, August Wilson, but, in fact, at the center of the theatre is the work of the actor. If everything that was not absolutely necessary to the theatre were stripped away, we would be left with the actor, a simple playing space, and the audience. The impulse to perform, discussed at the beginning of this book, is the essential force of the theatre. The work of all of the other theatre practitioners builds on the impulse to perform: the creation of stories for the actor to play; costumes to enhance or define the actor's body; scenery and light to provide an environment for the action; music and sound to build atmosphere, mood, and energy.

In the 2005 Broadway production of Martin McDonagh's play *The Pillowman,* Billy Crudup plays Katurian, a character devoted to the gruesome fairy tales he invents. Here he attacks his disabled brother, Michal, played by Michael Stuhlbarg. Of his character Crudup says, "I've never played someone who was as grotesquely distorted by his own history."[1] Crudup's character, part enthusiastic storyteller and part monster, draws the audience through the twists and turns of the play with black humor that shocks in its savage details. Crudup must invest this character with the passion and intensity to account for Katurian's startling actions.

The Presence of the Actor

In Chapter 1 we examined the transformation of the Hopi when they are inhabited by the kachina spirits, and we considered the transformation of the Greek actor through the mask. Whether or not an idea of the supernatural or a mask is part of the process, the actor always undergoes a transformation when appearing onstage in front of an audience. The actor becomes more than an ordinary person going about daily life. The actor in performance becomes a presence charged with energy and vitality who transmits a heightened sense of life to the audience. As the actor opens up to greater emotional and sensory awareness, the audience members also experience heightened awareness. The actor is able to project a sense of character life across the stage space and the auditorium space to reach the audience. The actor invents a world onstage that audience members may also inhabit through their imaginations.

David Warrilow, an actor known for his adventurous work in the plays of Samuel Beckett and in exploratory theatre forms, sees the actor-audience relationship as a matter of trust:

> If I as an actor invest myself to the best of my ability in the work I have chosen to present—if I give it my best energy—then there's a chance that the audience can trust what is going on on stage. If I hold back, if I sit in judgment on myself or the material or the audience, then there is less chance that the audience is going to be justified in trusting and therefore joining the experience. If the actor is willing to go through some kind of transmutation, then the audience can, too.[2]

Frequently the actor's presence is described as a kind of double or triple existence. On the stage the actor is always present in his or her own person. In addition to this elemental self, the actor creates a character who has his or her own boundaries separate from those of the actor's own person. The performer projects a double representation of self and character. A third layer of the actor's presence might be considered a critical facility that the actor uses to step back from the performance and view it from the audience's perspective, making adjustments and modifications as necessary. BW Gonzalez, who played Mattie Campbell in *Joe Turner's Come and Gone*, describes the actor's state of mind as one of "hyperawareness."[3] Stephen Spinella, who played Prior in *Angels in America* at the Eureka Theatre, at the Mark Taper Forum, and on Broadway, discussed in Chapter 10, says that he is always aware of his own presence on the stage and the presence of the audience:

> I am absolutely, completely conscious of the audience. I feel what they are doing. I'm completely conscious of what's going on in my body. It's the height of reality. I actually feel as though I'm suspended above myself or in back of myself and my body. Everything is moving and doing exactly what it should be doing. And I'm saying to myself, "Now do this," making little tiny artistic choices.[4]

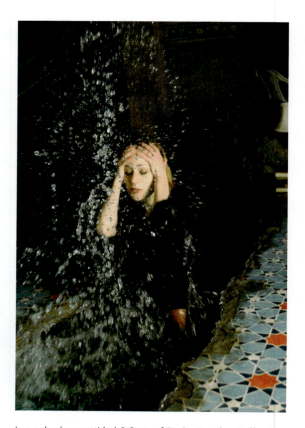

In a solo show entitled *9 Parts of Desire,* Heather Raffo plays nine different Iraqi women characters. She must shift between ages and character circumstances, between speech patterns and physicality. Each character is so vivid that they all seem to be present onstage by the end of the performance, listening to the stories of the other characters. Raffo developed the text for the play by drawing on her interviews with ordinary Iraqi citizens over a period of ten years. The play creates a social document about life in Iraq before and after the American military intervention through the characters' different perspectives on the upheavals that define their lives. The play, which has toured widely, was first performed at the Manhattan Ensemble Theater in 2004 under the direction of Joanna Settle.

The actor commands the attention of the audience by bringing concentrated and explosive energy onto the stage. The actor brings the stage space to life and sweeps the audience up in the

WORKING IN THE THEATRE

Summary of the Actor's Responsibilities

- To study the text
- To memorize lines and blocking quickly
- To bring new ideas to the rehearsal process on a daily basis
- To work openly with the director and other actors
- To be creative in rehearsal
- To constantly refine and adjust character development
- To work with consistent high energy
- To maintain health and flexibility of voice and body
- To sustain freshness in performance and execute repeated performances at a consistent level of quality

vitality of the performance. This energy is part of the actor's charisma. In this respect, the actor is like an athlete or a rock star. For the actor, the energy may be less overtly displayed than for a football receiver leaping to make a catch or a popular singer dancing in front of the microphone. But high-voltage energy is present nonetheless, and the audience senses the electricity generated by the actor's presence.

Because of the unique nature of live performance—with the very real connection between performer and audience—the actor receives energy from the audience just as the audience is energized by the actor's presence. For BW Gonzalez, the energy generated by the audience contributes directly to her readiness to begin the play.

> Before I say my first line, once I feel the energy of the audience, I feel perfectly at home on the stage.[5]

Sean McNall, who recently played Hamlet, believes Shakespeare intended a personal relationship between Hamlet and the audience to be an essential part of the play, particularly in the soliloquies such as the one presented in the photograph on page 116:

> In *Hamlet* you reach out to the audience and you cast the audience in a certain way so you know to whom you are speaking and the reason why you need to address them at this moment. With this particular part, the audience became a kind of conscience, a touchstone. Having the audience on my side was of great importance. But I had to assume that they weren't simply on my side. So when I had the opportunity to reach out to them, I was always making a case. Suddenly, I had all this different energy coming at me.[6]

Stephen Spinella sees the audience energy as a major catalyst for his performance:

> The theatrical event requires the overwhelming focus of the audience. The actors, who have acquired that attention through control of the space and the moment, have power, and if the muse is with them, that power makes them soar.[7]

The actor Heather Robison, whose photograph appears on page 123, sees the audience as the final defining factor in the theatre event:

> The play doesn't work without the audience. That's when the play first lives. The audience is the last character of the play and you live and breathe with them.[8]

James Earl Jones also uses the analogy of flight to describe the propulsion that the audience brings to the performance:

> All acting, at its best, is about entering the stage and, spiritually, going to the edge of that cliff that is the proscenium, acknowledging there is an energy there, and like a sky-diver, pushing yourself off. You trust the thermal waves of energy that the audience is and you soar.[9]

The Actor's Craft

The vitality and talent of the actor are contained and shaped through the development of technique. We expect musicians to study and practice for many years to perfect skills on the piano, the cello, or the saxophone and to acquire subtleties of musicianship. Dancers, too, commit themselves to a training schedule of many hours a day to develop their physical abilities and artistry. In the same way, technique is essential to the actor working on the stage.

We can easily summarize the skills that most actors work to achieve and maintain. The vocal technique of the actor involves the ability to control and project the voice, to speak with richness of tone and nuance of expression, to enunciate with clarity at all times, to use dialects and accents with authenticity, to maintain a healthy voice that doesn't succumb to overuse, to give the language of Shakespeare or August Wilson its own style and rhythm, to speak for the characters and the playwright with authority and imagination. Physical technique allows the actor to move with grace; to command the stage space; to change posture, gestures, and body rhythms to create a range of characters; to present a sense of period style; to perform at a high level of intensity every day; to achieve the appropriate degree of relaxation and freedom from tension; to dance or juggle or walk on stilts.

However, performance skills alone do not make an actor. The words *alchemy* and *magic* are frequently used to describe the way the actor animates the skills of performance and gives life to a dramatic text or situation. Analogy is often used to describe acting because it is difficult to define the actor's process with precision. First, many forces intervene: the text, the director, the other actors, the rehearsal structure and duration, the playing space. Second, acting is such a personal and individual endeavor that it can be impossible to identify with certainty what has taken place internally to produce the result that the audience sees. Some choices are conscious; some are the result of intuitive responses to the text or the rehearsal situation. To investigate the components of the actor's work, we begin with the phases the actor goes through before arriving at a performance in front of an audience: the audition, individual preparation for the role, and the rehearsal.

The Work of the Actor

Competing for Roles: The Audition

One of the harshest and must grueling aspects of the actor's profession is the **audition.** Acting is a highly competitive business. There are many more actors and aspiring actors than there are acting opportunities at every level of theatre

The actors warm up in rehearsal for a production of *Apollo* directed by Nancy Keystone at Portland Center Stage in 2009. The actors perform a complex sequence of exercises that build stamina and flexibility and also provide a way for them to connect to the images in the play and physically and emotionally to one another. One of the cast members, Richard Gallegos, explains: "The warm-up brings us into the rehearsal room, into a collective energy, and it establishes a common vocabulary. It encompasses the body, the breath, and the psyche. It completely makes us a unit."[10]

The professional actor is a kind of magician who can do what we, the audience, cannot. Bill Irwin has an extensive background in mime and dance that also includes studying at the Clown College of Ringling Brothers Barnum and Bailey Circus. In fact, he began his acting career as a clown with the Pickle Family Circus. He then began to develop his own magical "new vaudeville" pieces, such as *Largely New York* (1989) shown here, that have no spoken text and depend on the broad, comic physicality of the actor to communicate.

and film production, in part because of the passion that actors feel about their work and in part because of the large rewards for the few "stars." To enter the competition for roles or places in training programs, actors must participate in auditions.

The audition allows directors and casting directors to see how different actors may fill a certain role or to see which actors complement each other as a group to make an **ensemble.** Because auditions are usually set up to screen a large number of people, the actors are allotted very little time to convince those making the casting decisions of their "rightness" for the part and the depth of their talent. For example,

the Yale School of Drama auditions 900 aspiring actors for its graduate training program. Of those 900, only 16 students are offered places. Likewise, hundreds of dancers and singers may audition for the roles in the chorus of a Broadway musical, and smaller theatres attract scores of actors to their auditions.

Furthermore, auditions may call for unique combinations of talents. Susan Stroman auditioned actors for both the recent revival of *Oklahoma!* (1999) and the new production of *The Producers* (2001). For *Oklahoma!* the actors had to sing and dance and then do a monologue. For *The Producers* they also had to be able to tell jokes. Richard Gallegos, who appears as the Ghost of

Sean McNall is a young actor who won an Obie (Off Broadway) award in 2008 for sustained excellence in performance. He is shown here playing Hamlet in the Pearl Theatre's 2007 production directed by Shep Sobel. McNall has been a member of the Pearl Theatre's resident acting company since 2003, which reflects his goal of being an actor in an ongoing repertory company rather than participating in a continuous sequence of auditions. "What I don't like about the way the business of theatre works is that every production and every performance, particularly in New York, is an audition for the next performance. Some people are able to be creative with the thrill of that. But I think that is a detriment to the creative spirit because that's where people find out what they're good at and then they craft and hone exactly what they're good at, in much the same way that we try to make the best "product." We turn ourselves into a product and we sell that product. This is the model that many of us work with and I'm just not attracted to that. So being in a company gives me this opportunity to be bad, to fail, to do something radically different for a change. Time and time again, that is rewarding."[11]

the Prisoner of Camp Dora in the photograph of *Apollo* on page 130, recalls a memorable audition experience:

> For six years I did the *Wild Wild Wild West Stunt Show* at Universal Studios. When I auditioned, I didn't know what I was getting myself into. I thought they wanted me to tumble and do a couple of cartwheels. They took us into this big warehouse at Universal Studios. There were about 300 of us. They unveiled this huge platform that was about twenty feet high and there was a big fall pad. They wanted us to climb up there and do a forward fall. I was scared out of my mind. The majority of them were actual stunt men. Somehow I weaseled myself into this audition and made the cut. I was there and I just had to breathe in. I remember climbing the ladder and saying to myself, "waiting tables, stunt show, waiting tables . . ." and the next thing I knew, my body was in the air and I did it and I got the job. It was crazy.[12]

Directors pride themselves on being able to recognize almost instantly the qualities that they seek for a certain role. Gordon Davidson, former artistic director of the Mark Taper Forum, says, "I have a feeling within a minute of the audition that you know whether you're in the presence of talent or not."[13] The composer and lyricist Stephen Sondheim can judge singing ability in sixteen measures, or even in eight or four bars of a song.[14] This tendency toward immediate judgment puts enormous pressure on the actor in the audition to deliver a knockout performance. Actors, in fact, study auditioning techniques as part of their career preparation and constantly work to hone their auditioning skills.

Some auditions may involve the presentation of set pieces that the actors have had a chance to study and prepare in detail in advance of the audition. Actors perform monologues or songs of their own choosing for graduate training programs, repertory theatre, or summer stock opportunities—all situations that require actors to take multiple roles. Actors try to choose

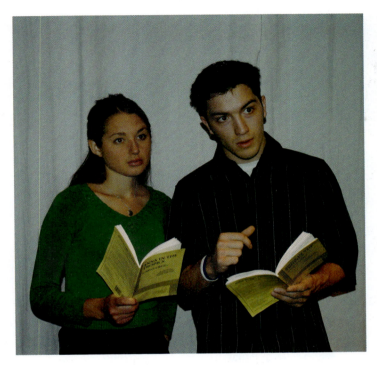

Sage Howard and Brandon Zerr-Smith audition for a production of *Anna in the Tropics* at Lewis and Clark College with scripts in hand. They receive feedback from the director before reading the scene again. Actors are strongly encouraged to study the full text before auditioning for a play.

one of the most important factors that directors try to ascertain in the audition:

> Directors want to come away from an audition knowing that they're going to be able to work with the actor, and that the actor is imaginative enough and well-trained enough to handle different directions. They also need to get a feel for what the actor will be like to work with for an extended period of time.[15]

material from well-respected plays and musicals, but also material that directors may not have already seen hundreds of times. The pieces also need to be well suited to the actor and show the range of the actor's abilities.

A dramatic audition consisting of two contrasting monologues is frequently limited to four minutes. A singing audition may be limited to thirty-two measures of music. In that scant time, actors must show their understanding of the text, their speech or singing skills, their energy, and their ability to reach an audience. The actor must jump into the heart of the character and the play and deliver the lines or the song with all the passion and intensity of a performance, usually without the help of a supporting cast, set, or costumes. The audition also reveals how much training the actors have, their stage presence, and their openness. Jack Bowdan, who casts for Broadway and television, emphasizes that the ability to take direction is

Some auditions focus on cold readings of scenes from the play that is going into production. In this situation, with minimal preparation, actors must read from the script, often with a stage manager or some other member of the production staff who is not an actor as their scene partner. The producer Stuart Ostrow believes that although the cold reading is "the best of a worst lot," its benefits outweigh the drawbacks:

> What it does first and foremost is tell you about the intelligence quotient of the actor. And I would always opt for an intelligent actor, even though he may be wrong for the part. In the creation of a play, that cold reading leads to an understanding about the actor's capacity for imagination and creativity.[16]

If the actor gets through the initial phase of the audition and is called back for further readings, then the process opens up in interesting

James Earl Jones transformed his physical appearance to play the boxer Jack Jefferson in *The Great White Hope* (1967) at the Arena Stage in Washington, D.C. The physical training involved in preparing for the role of a boxer also provided psychological insight into the character. James Earl Jones and Jane Alexander, shown here, also re-created their stage roles for the film version of Howard Sackler's play.

ways, depending on the type of production and the producing company. Interviews, group improvisations, and extended readings with other potential cast members may all be part of the "callback." But first, actors must show that they have enough talent, skill, flexibility, and commitment to stand out from the crowd. No matter how stressful or disappointing the audition process may be, all actors must struggle through the ordeal of auditioning if they are to work. Tamu Gray, who played Bertha in *Joe Turner's Come and Gone*, summarizes the feelings of many actors when she says, "You must raise an amazing amount of courage to go out and audition, but that makes you even stronger because you do it."[17]

Preparing for the Role

When a part has been secured, actors may go to extraordinary lengths to prepare for their roles. They might read histories and biographies or study real-life situations, or they might immerse themselves in the actual circumstances of characters' lives before they try to re-create or interpret those circumstances on the stage or in front of the camera. Sometimes actors transform themselves physically, losing or gaining weight or participating in intense physical training to reshape their bodies or learn difficult physical skills.

James Earl Jones is an actor known for his distinguished performances in the plays of Shakespeare, the South African Athol Fugard,

The Necessary Skills and Talents of the Actor

- Interest in human nature
- Keen observation
- A good memory
- Concentration
- Imagination
- The drive to appear on the stage in front of an audience
- The ability to create characters and interpret dramatic situations
- A strong, expressive voice
- An expressive face and body
- High energy and physical stamina
- The ability to work openly as part of a group process
- Discipline

and August Wilson, as well as for his film work, including the famous voice of Darth Vader in *Star Wars*. To play the role of Jack Jefferson, a boxer, in *The Great White Hope*, by Howard Sackler, Jones undertook the training of a fighter:

> I didn't have the bulk of a fighter but I had the sineviness, the flexibility. In Washington D.C., when we were at the Arena Stage, I had a trainer named Bill Terry who was a former fighter. He took me through the life of a boxer-in-training. Every morning you get up, you run a certain number of miles, you go to the gymnasium, you consume certain kinds of liquids and foods that are good for strength and endurance.

Jones then shaved his beard and his head as part of his mental and physical preparation:

> At this point the physical training I had been doing came into focus and I was a different person. By then I had learned, with the director Ed Sherin's encouragement, to walk and behave physically, unconsciously like an athlete, which I'm not. By the time I finished the run of the play and the film, I hated the training. I was not good at diets and I wanted to be free to eat what I thought my body was crying out for in terms of sustenance.[18]

The Rehearsal Process

In Chapter 3, we reviewed the work of the actors as they rehearsed *Joe Turner's Come and Gone*. We saw them studying the text, memorizing lines, seeking the characters' motivation, developing the characters' relationships, rehearsing blocking patterns, and finding the speech rhythms that would give authenticity to their characters and bring passion and eloquence to the playwright's words.

What happens in rehearsal is a very intricate process of give-and-take between the actors and the director. For a production to have vitality and originality, the rehearsal must be a time of exploration. Discoveries must be made about the characters and their relationships. Staging ideas are tested and discarded. Rhythms and pacing are built and adjusted.

The Actor's Commitment   Acting is extraordinarily hard work. It is a physical and mental process that requires great physical stamina and high energy. Actors must be able to remember their lines, work creatively, and be open and receptive to one another and the director. They must come to rehearsal well rested and fully alert, able to concentrate intensely on the work at hand, whether it is repeating a sword fight many times or discovering the intimate rhythms of a love scene. At each rehearsal, actors must be prepared to try out new approaches to line readings and blocking or to refine choices that have already been made. Rehearsals demand at least as much from the actors as performances; and, for some, rehearsals are the most satisfying part of the production process.

In *Hamlet*, the actor playing Ophelia must find a way to express the character's desperation resulting from the death of her father and her rejection by Hamlet. But the reactions of the other characters are essential to building the belief that she is, as Claudius says, "divided from herself," and in her brother Laertes's words, "a document in madness." In this photo, Laertes reacts with dismay as he tries to comprehend his sister Ophelia's incoherent speeches. Laertes is played by David L. Townsend and Ophelia by Jolly Abraham in the 2007 Pearl Theatre production of *Hamlet* directed by Shep Sobel.

Kathleen Chalfant, who played multiple roles in *Angels in America*, including the part of Ethel Rosenberg, describes rehearsals as a way of pulling a role or a text apart in order to put it back together again:

> In order to learn to act you must take apart something that happens faster than thought, break it into its component parts, and then put it back together. That's also what rehearsal is, breaking down a speech or a reaction, and then getting it close to the speed at which a human being actually does it. Quite often, plays are just a little slower than life because you've added a step, the breaking down. The trick is to act as quickly as you think, which is not necessarily a function of speed. When you're doing it properly, it often feels as though you have all the time in the world. Then you can allow yourself to be entirely taken, with no conscious control. That's what being in the moment means. In order to be prepared to give yourself over to the moment, you have to have done all the work beforehand: knowing the words backwards and forwards, knowing where you're supposed to stand, and more importantly, knowing what the character is doing at every turn and why she does it.[19]

Action and Reaction   In rehearsal, actors discover their actions and their reactions. Much of their work depends on playing actions that communicate a passionate expression of life's defining moments. The action may be contained in a speech such as Hamlet's "To be, or not to be, that is the question," or Bynum's story of the "shiny man." The action may be physicalized through gesture—for example, when the actor playing Herald Loomis cuts himself with the knife or when the actor playing Juliet drinks the sleeping potion.

But as important as the actors' actions are the actors' reactions. Much of what actors create comes through reaction, through response, through seeing and believing. Actors bring a sense of the environment onto the stage; they feel the weather—the cold wind blowing through the cracks of a dilapidated house or the stifling heat of an urban summer. They experience the weariness of the passing of time, see the opulence of a ballroom or the emptiness of a Beckett landscape. Most of all, through reaction, actors give reality to the characters of the other actors onstage. They make these characters believable for the audience by the way that they watch and register the truth of what they have seen. They recognize loss, and they recognize triumph. They feel a threat and respond to an invitation. The art of acting has to do with creative expression and with the construction of belief.

Improvisation **Improvisation** is a useful rehearsal method for enhancing belief and creating imaginative actions. It is used with increasing frequency in many different kinds of production situations. Improvisation can be defined as spontaneous invention that goes beyond the scripted material to explore aspects of character or situation. Actors may do group improvisations at the beginning of rehearsals as a warm-up. They may also use improvisation to solve acting problems or to generate staging ideas. Improvisation is also an important method for establishing creative rapport between actors. Most acting students now have considerable exposure to improvisation as a fundamental part of their training.

One of the most common improvisations involves playing a scene in the actors' own words instead of the playwright's scripted words. This technique allows actors to work through scene content and to explore areas of the characters' relationships. For example, there may be an argument between two characters that lasts two minutes or less in the actual play. The two actors involved might then improvise a much longer argument to explore the sources of the tension between their characters. Their improvisation might even involve extreme physical interactions to help shape the verbal exchange. The scripted

In this photo from *The Piano Lesson,* Boy Willie has persuaded his friend Lymon to help him move the piano so that it can be sold. However, the characters find that they are unable to budge the piano from its spot. The two actors must be convincing in their efforts to push or lift the piano and they must react to one another's attempts as if they are using all of their strength and still failing to move the piano at all. Jason Dirden, to the left of the piano, plays Lymon, and Brandon J. Dirden plays Boy Willie in the 2012 production directed by Ruben Santiago-Hudson for the Signature Theatre.

argument might be set at a dining room table or in a court of law, where restrained behavior is expected, but to get to the strong feelings underlying the situation, the two actors might improvise some physical interaction while saying their lines. They might begin a tug-of-war or shoving match to heighten their responses to each other. The actors then use the intensity generated by the physicalization of the conflict in their verbal exchanges when they play the argument as scripted in the more confined situation.

Improvisation can also take the form of a game. Actors often invent situations in which, for example, the weather, the age of the characters, or the nature of the relationships keeps changing. Actors also improvise stories in which one person begins with a single word or a sentence and then the other actors add pieces to the developing narration. Improvisation can also involve invented languages in which the actors communicate for long periods of time through made-up words. Susan Stroman, whose work as a director and choreographer is discussed in Chapter 11, on musical theatre, has dancers who have no lines to speak create "back stories" to give each of them more character detail and a sense of individual development when they dance their roles.

Improvisation is also used with increasing frequency today to create the actual play text or dramatic structure. Instead of a playwright who provides a complete script before the rehearsal process has begun, the actors, in collaboration with the director, invent both the plot elements and the text together. *The Island*, discussed in Chapter 2 was developed through improvisation as were many parts of *Apollo*, a large-scale performance piece considered in this chapter.

Improvisation is a liberating technique for actors that encourages spontaneity and quickness and can deepen relationships with the other actors in a production. Most of all, by immersing themselves completely in the given circumstances, actors use improvisation to increase their commitment to the truth of the situation.

The Rehearsal Schedule   In **equity theatres** (theatres with more than 100 seats in which all actors are paid according to a union contract), rehearsals last eight hours a day. At the Oregon Shakespeare Festival, which must rehearse several plays at once because actors perform in repertory, rehearsals are held in four-hour units. Actors may rehearse two different plays in one day or rehearse for one play during the day and perform a different play during the evening. In **equity waiver theatres** (theatres with fewer than 100 seats that are not governed by union regulations), rehearsals may last several hours each evening after actors finish their other jobs.

The standard rehearsal process for a play begins with the reading aloud of the script by the company. Sometimes the actors read their parts; sometimes the director reads to the actors. The objective of the reading is for all the actors to hear the words as a starting point for their work. The actors are neither expected nor encouraged to have defined their characters at the first reading. Decisions made too early in the process may impede the work to be done. First readings are not meant to be performances and can sometimes seem very flat.

The work done after the first reading is usually referred to as "table work." It involves the kind of discussion, questioning, and rereading of the play that we observed in the early rehearsals of *Joe Turner's Come and Gone*. During the table work, the director might present the actors with background materials as well as establish the directorial concept or interpretation of the play that will be pursued.

Collaboration with the Designers   Sometimes the designers participate during this phase by showing the actors a model of the set and costume sketches, or "renderings." The participation of the designers helps the actors to imagine the world of the play being constructed and contributes to their own work on their characters. The costume designer's interpretation of a character in terms of silhouette,

For *The Belle's Strategem* produced in 2005 at the Oregon Shakespeare Festival under the direction of Davis McCallum, Heather Robison played a character that she says "asked her to be three different people." The play originally written by Hannah Cowley in 1780 is about views of love and marriage and involves the central character disguising herself to test the heart of the man she hopes to marry. Robison says the role "pulled on every bit of training I've ever had, from movement and speech and text analysis to dance and all of my circus training." Robison collaborated closely with the costume designer Deborah Dryden and found the costume designs were essential to the shift in her character from a proper member of society to a "gauche, country bumpkin," appearing in a petticoat, "with all of her formality and the preconceived ideas of what a lady should be in that time period stripped away. I found it very freeing to wear something so risqué and dangerous. Then she has permission to do anything."[20]

color, weight and texture of fabric, and accessories has enormous implications for the actors' own work in defining character. The presentation of the designers' work gives the actors a sense of the visual style of the production and makes clear the physical realities and practical requirements of the set and costumes: how many steps they will have to navigate, how long a skirt will be, what colors their character will wear. Joe Mantello, who played the role

of Louis in *Angels in America*, found costume choices to be an important part of the foundation for his character work:

> Louis is always looking to be judged. Tony Kushner, the playwright, and I always saw Louis wearing oversized boy clothes that he could disappear into when things got hard, when he was being judged. . . . Louis is swimming in his clothes. They make him look like he just wouldn't grow up. . . . In rehearsal

I always wore an overcoat or a scarf that I made sure was too big for me.[21]

Early on in the rehearsal process, the actors will start wearing **rehearsal costumes.** Doing so allows them to practice with the limitations created by their particular costume pieces and also to experience the feelings generated by wearing particular items of clothing and undergarments. The difference between wearing a baseball cap and wearing a bowler hat or between a cotton bandana and a velvet hat with feathers is enormous. Likewise, a change in shoes from cowboy boots to wing tips or from tennis shoes to high heels makes a huge difference not only to posture and style of walking but most significantly to how the actor feels. The designers' input feeds the actors' creative process. BW Gonzalez recently played Lady Macbeth in *Macbeth*, written by William Shakespeare. She began the rehearsal process wearing boots but found that the boots made her "too masculine." They "stopped her energy and blocked the sensuality" she and the director had determined were central to the character. Ultimately she wore sandals for most of the play and was barefoot in the famous sleepwalking scene.[22]

Approaches to Acting

Actors take many different approaches to their work on a role. Frequently, for the same production, actors work in different ways and use a combination of techniques they find useful. Ultimately, the style of acting throughout the production must be consistent. That is, the audience must perceive that all the actors are in the same play.

The Internal Approach

In a simplified overview of approaches to acting, we can distinguish between a psychological, internal approach and a technical, external approach. The **internal acting approach** involves identifying as closely as possible with the character

The actors in *Dying City* must deal with a very complicated subtext. Kelly is the young widow of a soldier killed in Iraq. Peter, the twin brother of Kelly's husband, has arrived unannounced at her apartment. The play unravels a secret past as it explores the sexual relationships of the characters. Diane Davis, seated, plays Kelly and Ryan King, standing, plays Peter, in *Dying City* by Christopher Shinn at Hartford Stage under the direction of Maxwell Williams in 2008. Ryan King also plays Peter's twin brother Craig in flashbacks to the past.

to be played. This internal approach is associated with the acting innovations developed by Konstantin Stanislavsky (see Chapter 7). Actors using a psychological method look for areas of the character's life that somehow correspond to their own experiences. They draw on their own personal histories and reactions to contribute to the life they create for the character. Actors working internally view the character as having a life beyond what is contained in the play text; they may develop an autobiography that provides them with a sense of the character's past. They investigate motivation in great depth to discover what the character wants from the other characters at any given moment in the play. They fill in the "subtext"—that is, what thoughts occur behind or between the character's lines but go unspoken. The subtext is translated into a stream of consciousness called the "inner monologue" that becomes the actor's silent text. The subtext is not expressed verbally but is communicated through vocal tone, gesture, or facial expression. The actors work to feel the emotions of the character's situation as if they were in the character's place. They are constantly asking why, constantly seeking the source or cause of behavior. Physical choices follow from psychological exploration, and it is this physicalization that reflects the character's state of mind.

The External Approach

In contrast to the internal approach, some actors work technically to give characterization a clear, external shape. Much of our discussion of acting thus far has centered on the actor's identification with the character. When actors seek ways of linking their inner lives with the inner life of the character, they are in the realm of psychological acting. Because so much of American theatre and American actor training depends on an internal, psychological approach, it is harder for us to understand the nature and validity of external, technical approaches to acting.

The **external acting approach** has more to do with conscious choices about how language is to be spoken, which physical details to emphasize, and how emotional content is to be expressed. The actor creates a structure for character through imagination and analysis but not through psychological identification. Under such circumstances, a character's emotion may be created through the manipulation of the actor's expressive abilities rather than through

the actor's actual emotional response. For actors who begin with an external approach, the speaking of the text is frequently the foundation for their work. Character emerges from the investigation of the language, the content and sounds of the words, the rhythm and phrasing. Brandon Dirden, seen in the photo of the two actors moving the piano on page 121, says that actors must follow the rhythm that August Wilson writes into his language. "I think Wilsonian actors can embrace all of the beauty of the language and know it's in the language and not outside . . . This is not me doing something to the language, this is the language doing something to me."[23] Bill Irwin begins by creating an oversize physical reality for the character. But actors who work externally can also be conscious of the needs and goals of their character, what we have called objectives or motivation; although Irwin takes a physical approach to characterization, he acknowledges that he is always aware of what his character wants. An external choice often unlocks a strong emotional response.

Acting Cordelia in *King Lear*

To further explore the concepts of internal and external acting approaches we consider here possible approaches to the role of Cordelia in Shakespeare's *King Lear*. In the opening scene of the play, Lear's youngest daughter, Cordelia, faces the most difficult decision of her life. Her father, King Lear, has decided to give up his throne and divide his kingdom among his three daughters. He has assembled his daughters and the entire court to make a public ceremony out of his abdication of the throne. But he is looking for a show of adulation from his children in exchange for his apparent generosity in giving them a share of the lands and property. The king insists that his three daughters respond to his demand, "Which of you shall we say doth love us most." In responding to this manipulative ploy, Cordelia must either compromise her own beliefs to satisfy her father's vanity, or she must

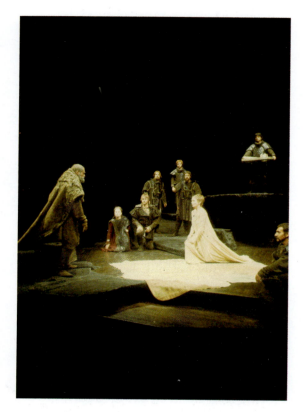

This photo shows the moment early in Act 1 of Shakespeare's *King Lear* when King Lear asks his daughter Cordelia to declare how much she loves him. King Lear is played by Len Cariou and Cordelia is played by Blair Brown in the 1974 production directed by Michael Langham at the Guthrie Theater in Minneapolis. The stage picture makes clear who holds the power in this scene and underscores the vulnerability of Cordelia's position as she tries to find a truthful answer to her father's perplexing question.

a devoted and faithful daughter, but she knows that human beings have multiple loyalties and multiple claims on their affections. Because she is about to be married herself, she is acutely aware that her love must be divided.

CORDELIA: Unhappy that I am, I cannot heave
My heart into my mouth. I love your Majesty
According to my bond, no more nor less.
. . . .
                              Good my lord,
You have begot me, bred me, loved me. I
Return those duties back as are right fit,
Obey you, love you, and most honor you.
Why have my sisters husbands if they say
They love you all? Haply when I shall wed,
That lord whose hand must take my plight
      shall carry
Half my love with him, half my care and
      duty.
Sure I shall never marry like my sisters,
To love my father all.[24]

An actor playing Cordelia who works internally might carefully consider and construct a family history, particularly focusing on Cordelia's relationship with her father. She might invent situations in which Cordelia has acquiesced to her father in the past, encouraging him in his belief that she will follow his desires in this scene. The actor might even imagine situations in which Lear and Cordelia have clashed before in order to explore the dynamics of the power struggle between them. The nature of the relationship might be worked out together by the actors playing Lear and Cordelia. Then when Cordelia speaks to Lear, the actor can use this history as a reference point; she can work to project a sense of what has already passed between them.

As part of an internal process, the actor might also look for her own emotional connections to the situation in two different ways. She might imagine what it would be like to be faced with such a dilemma. By making the pressures of Lear's demands seem real, feelings of her own might surface. The actor might also go back

disappoint him publicly to maintain her own integrity. Her two sisters, Goneril and Regan, make elaborate declarations of love, and Lear rewards them each with a third of his kingdom. But although Cordelia loves her father far more than do her sisters, she cannot offer the kind of false praise he seeks.

In the following two speeches, Cordelia tries to explain her position. She loves her father as through her own personal history to a time when she faced a difficult choice or defied an authority figure with whom she had a close relationship, such as her own father or mother. This process is called "substitution"—the actor uses feelings she recalls from her own experiences as the foundation for the character's responses in the play.

The actor might also work on the character's thought process to create a flow of ideas and responses that we have identified as the inner monologue. She might create a stream-of-consciousness dialogue with herself and the other characters. An example of a brief inner monologue might come before the line "Unhappy that I am." The actor might think but not speak, "His moment of glory . . . that look on his face . . . he will never forgive me for this." She might even improvise parts of the inner monologue aloud during some rehearsals.

The actor who approaches the role of Cordelia externally might begin with the language, the rhythm and sounds of the words. For example, the line "I cannot heave my heart into my mouth" expresses the essence of Cordelia's anguished situation. The words *heave, heart,* and *mouth* have long vowel sounds and soft consonants, giving the words weight and emotional depth as the starting point for the presentation of the character. The phrasing of the line "you have begot me, bred me, loved me" is answered by the rhythm in "I . . . obey you, love you and most honor you." The repeated "me" of the first line is linked to the repeated "you" of the second line, tying Cordelia's life to her father's. The insertion of "and most" before the third verb in the sequence adds emphasis to Cordelia's expression of respect for her father. Cordelia's straightforward declaration of her position in short, patterned syllables is followed by a question, "Why have my sisters husbands . . . ?" which offers a distinct contrast to the tone of the preceding three lines, challenging her sisters' sincerity. Careful analysis of the linguistic structure and the meaning of the words—as well as intuitive responses to the sounds and patterning of the words—yields a character foundation that emerges from Shakespeare's language rather than from an analysis of situation and character psychology.

In either case, before an actor can play Cordelia, there are many questions to be answered. How much control is the character consciously exerting over her own emotions? Are the two speeches played directly to Lear, or is part of the longer speech played to the two sisters? Is Cordelia challenging her father's authority, or is she warning her father of the consequences of taking her sisters' speeches for the truth? Is Cordelia trying to plead her case or prove her point? Is the longer speech a passionate accusation directed at the hypocrisy of Regan and Goneril or a restrained defense of principle? Does she want to expose her sisters as liars or force Lear to see his own vanity? In order to play these few short lines, the actor has many choices to make, whether she uses internal or external techniques for creating character.

Gestural Acting

Today is an explosive time for the actor. Method acting, associated with Stanislavsky and American realism, is being reconsidered from many sides. Experimental theatre companies, performers, and directors are exploring intriguing alternatives to or variations on traditional internal approaches to acting. Acting programs now offer remarkably eclectic courses of study that include dance, Asian theatre, improvisation, games, circus techniques, singing, and speech as well as character analysis and development. The actor has various sources to draw on, some of which strongly reject psychological motivation as part of character development.

In the production of *And the Soul Shall Dance* at East West Players, discussed in Chapter 8, hooded figures dressed in black who are identified by the Japanese term **kuroko** act in a style that does not have a psychological base. Although a primary function of the kurokos is to change the scenery, these actors are far more than stagehands. Their performance is choreographed; their expressive language is based on movement, not words. They embody forces such as the wind rather than detailed human characters. The technique they use in production is based on dance training and the disciplines of Asian theatre.

Asian theatre forms and acting techniques have had a growing influence on many Western theatres and theatre artists, not just on theatres with an Asian cultural base such as East West Players. Some actor training programs teach forms of Asian martial arts in combination with a movement vocabulary influenced by the kabuki or nō theatres of Japan, the Beijing Opera, or Indian kathakali. Eastern approaches to performance may be combined with Western dramatic literature—for example, in kabuki productions of Shakespeare.

Acting in *Apollo*

Drawing on new directions in actor training and theatre production, the director Nancy Keystone and a group of actors have formed a theatre company, Critical Mass, to develop theatre pieces in which movement is as important to the performance as the text. Nancy Keystone explains her goals for the staging of *Apollo*, their most recent production:

> Theatre is a very physical medium. But most of the time what we see is people acting from the neck up. The body is forgotten. Actors as living beings in front of a living audience have great potential for physical expression. One of the goals of *Apollo* was to create a piece in which movement told as much of the story as anything else, to present information—narrative, aesthetic, thematic information—nonverbally. A life lived onstage is a full and extreme life. An actor will do extraordinary things as a character living the events of the play. When we are creating and developing the piece, what I do to prepare, since there is no script, is to write a foundation for the play through exercises. The exercises explore physical states and psychic states which we believe are at the core of the story we're trying to tell.[25]

For this 2009 production, the actors used their bodies to convey actions such as astronauts floating weightless in space, living characters haunted by the dead, or confrontations over civil rights.

Gestures combined with simple props constructed themes through their repetition from character to character, such as the use of handkerchiefs to wipe hands and consciences clean or the wrapping and unwrapping of bundles of ashes

Space flight is celebrated in Part 1 of *Apollo* as the characters imagine a rocket trip to the moon. The weightlessness of the astronauts is created only through the actors balancing upside down on plain metal chairs with their floating arms and legs magnified by the light in this 2009 production at Portland Center Stage, directed by Nancy Keystone. The actors are Richard Gallegos, Andy Hirsch, Jeffrey Johnson, Nick Santoro, and Christopher Shaw.

IN CONTEXT

Apollo: Thematic Development

Apollo, an epic theatre piece composed in three parts, develops themes rather than building a tightly knit plot. The themes are connected to key aspirations in American history: the desire to conquer space and the struggle for civil rights. Geographically, the production moves between Germany in the 1930s and 1940s and the United States in the 1950s and 1960s. But ultimately the focus is on Huntsville, Alabama, where German scientists and engineers were brought following World War II to help develop the American space program and where African Americans were engaged in attempts to integrate public institutions and secure voting rights. The desire to glorify human ingenuity through sending rockets to the moon is seen against the desire to honor human dignity through fighting for equal rights. A consuming quest for power is seen against a consuming quest for freedom. The text for *Apollo* is drawn from historical documents, as well as the improvisation of the actors and the scripting of the director. The production depends on elaborate uses of sound and music, projected slides and film, and choreographed stage movement, in addition to spoken text and character action.

Part 1: *Lebensraum*

Part 1 celebrates a fantasy view of rocket history with glimpses of the development of German technology before and during World War II and America's love affair with space flight. Werner von Braun, a key character, appears with both Hitler and Walt Disney as he sells first Germany and then the United States on his vision to reach the moon.

Part 2: *Gravity*

The mood of the play shifts, as Part 2 uncovers the history of the slave labor used by the Germans to build their V-2 rockets and the war crimes of Germans brought to the United States to satisfy America's desire to win the space race and put a man on the moon. U.S. prosecutor Eli Rosenbaum confronts German engineer Arthur Rudolph about his past, as they examine the contents of some of the 3,000 file boxes that form the set for Part 2 of the play. The revelations bring to light the way the U.S. government put its determination to succeed in space ahead of the nation's laws.

Part 3: *Liberation*

The Nazi "rocketeers" begin their work in Huntsville, Alabama, at the same time that the momentum of the civil rights struggle is increasing, with attempts to integrate lunch counters and then the University of Alabama. Although many historical figures appear in the play, such as Werner Von Braun, Governor George Wallace, Robert Kennedy, and the Reverend Ralph Abernathy, the play focuses, in the end, on a fictional character, David McCadden. He becomes one of the first black students to integrate the University of Alabama and eventually joins NASA to work on the Apollo space program.

to recall lives lost to violence. Sometimes the actors played characters exchanging dialogue; sometimes they were part of an abstracted choreographic sequence. Some scenes were emotionally charged; some were parody. Each of the twelve actors played multiple roles and they needed to shift instantly between characters and between different uses of their acting skills. In order to develop their approach for *Apollo*, Keystone and the actors spent eight years studying research materials and exploring ideas through exercises and improvisations that were distilled and refined to become the scenes of the play.

One of the characters played by Richard Gallegos in *Apollo*, the Ghost of the Prisoner from Camp Dora, is seen kneeling on the table

An American prosecutor, Eli Rosenbaum, one of the characters played by Andy Hirsch, interrogates Arthur Rudolph, one of the characters played by Christopher Shaw, about his past as director of an underground factory in Germany which built V-2 rockets in *Apollo* (2009). The Ghost of the Prisoner of Camp Dora, Richard Gallegos, represents the atrocities of the past, which have been evaded while Rudolph was a leader in the American space program.

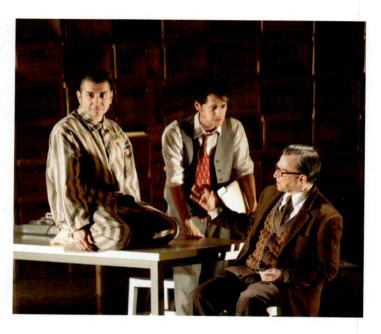

in the photograph on this page. This character represents the many people who worked at forced labor building rockets for the Nazis during World War II. In *Apollo* the "Prisoner" has returned from the dead to personify the past of a German rocket scientist, Arthur Rudolph, who faces deportation from the United States for war crimes. Richard Gallegos describes the external process involved in developing the presentation of his character:

> In the beginning Nancy Keystone told me, "you're not reliving these moments; you are now of the other world. You are drifting by. You are here for a purpose and then you leave. You are simply telling, so you can't have too much emotional connection."
>
> I found the physicality of the character first, the master gesture, the voice. The center of him is the core of my body, just above the pelvis. I wanted to find a gliding quality for him physically. So when he's walking, it's almost like he's moving through space without even touching the ground. He's just an energy that is hovering and not really quite in time movement-wise with everybody else.[26]

A synopsis of *Apollo* is included in this chapter for reference, since we discuss this production here and in Chapter 5.

Whatever the style of the play, the actor's process is both highly individual and subject to fluctuation. Actors usually combine various techniques in their work, and there may be many subtle shifts in the degree of actual emotional engagement in the role at various stages of the rehearsal and performance process. Actors constantly integrate various sources of information and inspiration into their creation of a role. All the work focuses on the creation of stage life that is original and truthful and that the actor can play with maximum conviction. No matter what the approach, good actors achieve complete concentration on the moment being played. As Valerie Spencer, a member of the *Apollo* cast, says:

> For me, I have to be completely in the now. Completely in the present, just in my body, on the stage, or backstage doing what I'm doing. I can't start thinking, "what if, what if, what if," or it will be a train wreck. If I'm changing my clothes, I'm listening to what's going on onstage. I can't be thinking ahead or daydreaming. I can't let my mind wander. I have to be completely focused on the task. It requires absolute concentration and focus and determination. A complete giving myself over to the ride.[27]

Mary-Louise Parker, seen here in *Dead Man's Cell Phone* by Sarah Ruhl (2007). Parker emphasizes that process is the way actors sustain the freshness of their work when doing a long run. "The idea that I've got a role completely doesn't fit in with my philosophy. It's never something to be fully arrived at. It's just something to experience, to keep flexing and testing and to grow with, rather than to fully find."[28]

The Performance

The purpose of all the actor's training and all the work in rehearsal is to provide the foundation for performance. A well-rehearsed play provides the actor with the control and confidence to give a fully energized and completely detailed performance, to be open to audience responses and to make adjustments for the unexpected that always occurs with live performance. Sometimes the run of a play lasts a few weeks or a few months. Sometimes an actor may appear in the same play for years. The final, crucial element of the actor's work is finding ways to sustain the performance over the entire run no matter how long that may be.

Theatre and Film

Far more than other theatre practitioners, actors working in the United States today frequently alternate between the theatre and film work. Most actors appreciate the depth and variety of the characters written for the stage and the way acting in the theatre stretches their skills. Prominent actors who appear in both theatre and film include Cate Blanchett, Billy Crudup, Clare Danes, Charles Dutton, Bill Irwin, Laura Linney, Liam Neeson, Mary-Louise Parker, Kevin Spacey, and Meryl Streep.

The difference between acting in the theatre and acting on film is usually described in terms of scale. In film acting, the camera comes to the actor. Actors then work to open their responses but not to enlarge them. In the theatre, the actor crosses a distance to reach the audience. The size of the performance must respond to the size of the stage and the auditorium. Stage actors need to contain their instincts to be expansive when they are working on a film, and film actors must increase their energy and the breadth of their response when they appear on the stage. Ray Ford, who appeared in *Apollo*, trained as a stage actor and then found he needed to acquire new techniques to act in film and television:

> For the theatre, my intensity needs to land at the back of the house. In a TV show, my intensity just needs to make it a few inches away from my face. So it's the same work, the same preparation, but the delivery is different. It took me two years in L.A. to learn how to do that.[29]

The film actor is aware at all times of the camera lens, both the width of the shot and the focus. Acting must be concentrated in the body parts seen by the camera—the face or a hand, for example, in a close-up. Film actors compose their actions and reactions in synchronization with the size and movement of the lens. Like so many other aspects of the actor's craft, working with the camera is a technical skill to be learned and practiced.

VALERIE SPENCER: In film you're playing to a lens and are always conscious of being watched and photographed; of how your image is being picked up; how you look and the angle of your head. You have to be considerate of that stuff because it's splayed on a huge wall.[30]

Some actors find the financial rewards and the exposure of film acting to be more attractive than the work itself. For actors, film work usually involves more waiting than acting. Setups for stunts or special effects require an extraordinary amount of preparation. Sometimes the waiting depends on the weather or the light. Sometimes huge numbers of extras must be organized. Although the work of the actor is usually the most visible expression of the medium, the actor's work is scheduled around the needs of an elaborate technical process.

Films are frequently shot out of sequence. Actors may have to play a climactic moment at the end of the story before they have filmed the incidents that lead up to that point. The film actor learns only the lines that are necessary to the scene currently being filmed. There is no need to learn all the lines at once or to retain lines from scenes that have been completed. The film editor is responsible for organizing and making sense of the pieces of film that have been shot. The editor constructs what the viewer sees of the plot and the actor's progression. Of this fragmented way of working, Cate Blanchett says, "The challenge is to be able to shape a performance when the process is so piecemeal."[31] Sometimes actors who appear in the same movie never meet during the filming process.

Although the amount of rehearsal time for films varies widely, there is never as much rehearsal time as there is for most plays, and sometimes there is no rehearsal time at all. Sarah Jessica Parker says, "In the theatre, everything you do is about acting. In the movies, it's about a fifth, or an eighth."[32] Valerie Spencer brings us full circle to the connection with the audience in explaining what the film experience lacks for the actor:

First and foremost it's the connection to the audience. You are telling a story and communicating essential truths about the human condition. If you are brave enough and have the opportunity, you can look out and see the faces of the people, read their reactions, and feel the pulse of their energy coming back to you. Perhaps theatre is the most human art form because it communicates from person to person in the same room.[33]

Summary

The art of the actor is the primary force of the theatre. For theatre to exist, in its essential form, only an actor, a playing space, and an audience are required. When actors appear on the stage, they undergo a transformation. Because actors convey concentrated energy and heightened awareness, they seem larger than life. Through their charismatic presence, they inspire the audience's belief in the stage action.

Years of demanding training in voice, movement, textual analysis, character development, and improvisation lay the foundation for performance in front of an audience. Beyond the challenges of actor training, the opportunity to work in the theatre depends on successfully competing for roles in the audition process. Once an actor has been cast, prerehearsal preparation may involve physical training or body reshaping in addition to research and study of the text. Actors immerse themselves in their roles during the rehearsal period.

The rehearsal is a collaborative process of discovery guided by the director. Approaches to character development during rehearsals may include improvisation as well as psychological acting techniques and external acting techniques. Improvisation involves the spontaneous creation of character, action, and dialogue. Improvisation may be used as a way to explore the playwright's text, to develop rapport between actors, or to generate staging ideas. The goal of internal acting is identification with the character that grows out of the actor's own personal experience as well as the actor's imaginative placement of himself or herself in the character's situation. External technique refers to the shaping of character through the manipulation of language and the construction of physical details of posture, movement, and appearance. Gestural acting, a more stylized form of acting that uses abstracted movements to capture the essence of character,

reflects the growing influence of Asian performance styles on American theatre.

Many actors today work in both theatre and film. Acting in the theatre demands a more expansive presentation that is scaled to the size of the theatre. In contrast, acting on film emphasizes subtleties and nuances, which the camera can capture close up. Acting in the theatre involves an integrated, sequential process of rehearsal and performance. Film acting, on the other hand, is a more fragmented process in which action is often shot out of sequence. Actors working on the same film may never meet. On the stage, the actor organizes the details of the performance; in film, the editor has considerable control over how the actor's performance will ultimately be seen.

Topics for Discussion and Writing

1. What is meant by the actor's presence? How would you describe your own response to performances you have witnessed that you would call charismatic?

2. Attend a theatre performance at your university or college. Where do you notice the actors' success in creating belief through their reactions? What do they help you to see or be aware of? Look for reactions to physical circumstances and to the actions of the other characters.

3. Choose one of these short scenes from *Joe Turner's Come and Gone:* Seth and Bertha (page 60) or Molly and Jeremy (page 84). Explore the subtext in the scene you have chosen. What thoughts may be behind the lines that the characters do not verbalize? Choose a section of lines and write an inner monologue that an actor might think as he or she plays the lines. How might the inner monologue affect the way the lines themselves are spoken?

● For interviews with some of the actors in this chapter and *"Apollo* in Performance," as well as suggested readings and other resources, please visit **www.mhhe.com/creativespirit6e**

CHAPTER 5

The Director

The actor brings the playwright's characters to life and secures the vital connection to the audience. The designers create an environment for the actor's presence. Uniting all the elements of the performance—script, acting, set, costumes, lights, music, and sound—into a meaningful whole is the business and the art of the director. The director Libby Appel says, "It is the director's job to illuminate the play for the audience."[1] The director creates a theatrical language, a language of space and movement and sound that coherently communicates the ideas of the production to the audience. The director and critic Harold Clurman, one of the founders of the Group Theatre (the American theatre of the 1930s dedicated to new realistic plays) and a major force in the American theatre for fifty years, calls the director the "author" of the stage action:

> That action speaks louder than words is the first principle of the stage; the director, I repeat, is the "author" of the stage action. Gestures and movements, which are the visible manifestations of action, have a different specific gravity from the writer's disembodied ideas. Theatrical action is virtually a new medium, a different language from that which the playwright uses, although the playwright hopes that his words will suggest the kind of action that ought to be employed. The director must be a master of theatrical action, as the dramatist is the master of the written concept of his play.[2]

The History of the Director

The actor and the playwright are as old as the theatre itself. The designer, in the form of a stage machinist, mask maker, or costumer, is also connected to ancient traditions in the theatre. But the position of the director is a relatively recent addition to the process of theatre production. In earlier times the playwright or a leading actor was responsible for coordinating the production and placing the actors on the stage. In the Greek, medieval, Elizabethan, and Chinese theatres, traditions and conventions were firmly established, and therefore questions of stylistic interpretation were not an issue. Productions did not strive for historical authenticity in representing earlier periods; nor was there an array of acting approaches to choose from.

The Director and the Development of Realism

The position of the director came into being in the Western theatre during the nineteenth century in response to certain shifts in the nature of the theatre. The director filled needs created by (1) an interest in a more detailed representation of place and character history—the movement called realism, which attempted to put a sense of daily life on the stage—and (2) the profusion of theatre styles that arose in response to realism.

As playwrights such as Ibsen and Chekhov began to write realistic plays in which environment deeply affected character feeling and action, the authenticity of the environment became very important. Exact details of costume were also necessary to place the characters accurately in their situations. Actors couldn't simply go to their own wardrobes and choose costumes they thought would be suitable or glamorous. And the psychological motivation and subtext implied by the plays needed careful development by an ensemble of actors, not a presentation by individuals all eager to draw attention to their own particular expertise. Someone was needed to coordinate the production elements of the realistic stage, and this is where the director first appeared.

The Duke of Saxe-Meiningen
George II, duke of Saxe-Meiningen (1826–1914), the leader of a small duchy in what would become Germany, contributed considerable resources and energy to

Stanislavsky's production of *The Seagull* for the Moscow Art Theatre demonstrates the profusion of details in early realism. Rooms were fully structured with walls, doors, and windows. Furnishings and accessories defined character background and also provided many opportunities for naturalistic character action. Stanislavsky maintained that the settings were as important for the actors as for the audience in providing a sense of the environment.

Anton Chekhov (center) reads *The Seagull* to the actors of the Moscow Art Theatre. The director Konstantin Stanislavsky sits immediately to Chekhov's right. Poor health curtailed Chekhov's participation in the development of these famous first productions of his plays. Much of his interaction with the company was reduced to correspondence.

the development of the Meiningen court theatre. Taking on the role of director himself, he was determined to reclaim the theatre from haphazard production practices and the excesses of popular leading actors indulged by a star system in which all elements of a production were dedicated to showing off their talents. In collaboration with his third wife, Ellen Franz, an actor, and with Ludwig Chronegk, who functioned as codirector, the duke built his company on principles that became influential throughout Europe. The actors were hired to be part of an ensemble; an actor who played a leading role in one production might be part of the crowd in the next. Costumes and settings were carefully researched and constructed with great attention to period detail. All the elements of the production were coordinated in a unified presentation. Between 1874 and 1890, the company toured from England to Russia, eventually presenting forty-one plays. European theatre practitioners who subsequently pursued the nuances and subtleties of realism in acting and staging had the integrated productions of the Meininger Players as a foundation for their efforts.

Konstantin Stanislavsky   The most famous and influential director of this early realistic period was Konstantin Stanislavsky. As we observed in our discussion of the internal approach to acting in Chapter 4, Stanislavsky's psychological approach to character development asked actors to behave onstage as if they were living the circumstances of the characters' lives. Stanislavsky defined himself as a director in 1898, when he and his partner Vladimir Nemirovich-Danchenko undertook the direction of Anton Chekhov's first major play, *The Seagull*, at their theatre, the Moscow Art Theatre.

The Seagull had failed in its first production at another theatre because no one had recognized that changes in production methods were necessary to make a success of Chekhov's play. In its initial production, Chekhov's delicate play, which involves the struggles of a small group of characters to be recognized as artists while they also seek to resolve failed love relationships, was performed at the footlights with speeches played melodramatically out to the audience. Stanislavsky recognized the need to turn the characters toward each other. Stanislavsky saw that building an ensemble of the actors would help to create the links between the characters' lives so crucial to Chekhov's dramatic intent. An ensemble could create the essential rhythms of action and speech that together would build a rhythmic structure for the play and draw the audience into its rising and falling breath. Stanislavsky believed that ensemble acting would give the lives of all the characters equal weight and interest rather than having the dramatic material be dominated by the performance of a star.

Stanislavsky also worked to physicalize in small, realistic details the inner, spiritual lives of the characters and to create an atmosphere of setting and sounds that would give the appearance of reality and provide a believable environment for the action. Here he was very concerned about the objects handled by the actors, such as cigarettes and walking sticks, as well as with sound effects such as birdcalls and cricket chirps.

Stanislavsky built a recognizable world for the play through a profusion of details taken from daily life. But to make sense of the physical details and the characters' realistic actions, Stanislavsky recognized the need to discover or identify what he called the **spine** of the play—that is, the central action or central idea that draws together all the smaller plot incidents and all the separate character actions.

As a young director, Stanislavsky followed a method of preparation that some directors still use. He made copious notes of actions and business, diagrams of the actors' placement onstage, sketches of settings, and lists of sound effects and properties. He determined the details and the shape of the production in advance of the rehearsal period with the idea that the actors would be told or taught what to do. The process of discovery was his alone. Later in his directing career, however, Stanislavsky came to see the need for the actors to assume more responsibility for the creative work of building characters. Stanislavsky's revised view of the discovery process is one that many directors adhere to today. Although most contemporary directors immerse themselves in a process of preparation for months or even years before they begin rehearsals, they view the rehearsal process as a journey of discovery that is embarked upon in a spirit of partnership between the actors and the director. The British director Peter Brook, known for his bold interpretation of classical works and highly original new pieces, stresses the importance of spontaneity in the rehearsal process:

> I make hundreds of sketches of the scenery and the movements. But I do this merely as an exercise, knowing that none of it is to be taken seriously the next day. . . . If I were to ask actors to apply the sketches that I did three days or three months earlier, I would kill everything that can come to life at the moment in rehearsal.[3]

The Director and the Determination of Style

Although the position of director emerged in response to developments of realism, the role of the director as a theatre artist who gives a production a clear stylistic point of view that integrates all the elements of the performance became fundamental to the multiplicity of styles that

For this production of Chekhov's play, *Uncle Vanya,* the designer David Borovsky dispensed with the walls and the interior details of realism that we see in the photograph of Stanislavsky's production of *The Seagull* shown on page 136. The house in which the characters live is suggested by a few pieces of furniture. The rural atmosphere of the play is indicated by the haystacks that hover around the characters. The production, directed by Lev Dodin for the Maly Drama Theatre of St. Petersburg, was first produced in 2003 and is shown here in a photograph from a performance at the Brooklyn Academy of Music in 2010. The actors include Sergey Kuryshev and Elena Kalinina. Dodin says of the spatial arrangement in an interview in *The Village Voice,* "We both wanted the space to breathe, to convey the ringing purity of the change of seasons." There is a sense that the characters are suspended in the environment, rather than confined by it.

followed realism. It is the director who decides how a play is to be interpreted, whether it is a classic play from an earlier era or a new play. For example, a director can choose to set *Hamlet* in twelfth-century Denmark, in seventeenth-century England, in a contemporary time frame, or in the future. A production can follow Elizabethan staging practice that frankly acknowledges the presence of the audience, or it can use the convention of the "fourth wall" (an imaginary barrier between the actors and the audience across the front of the stage) to seal the characters in their own world. A director can choose to emphasize the central character's philosophical questioning or the struggles of power politics. In the words of Brook:

> Many years ago it used to be claimed that one must "perform the play as Shakespeare wrote it." Today the absurdity of this is more or less recognized: nobody knows what scenic form he had in mind. All that one knows is that he wrote a chain of words that have in them the

Peter Brook has done his own adaptation of *Hamlet,* in collaboration with Marie-Helene Estienne, in which he cut and rearranged the text. The entire play was performed by only eight actors, without intermission. In the Brook production, the play became even more tightly focused on Hamlet himself, played by Adrian Lester. The stage was defined only by an orange carpet with a few large stools and cushions moved around by the actors to provide a sense of the change of scenes.

possibility of giving birth to forms that are constantly renewed. There is no limit to the virtual forms that are present in a great text.[4]

And the plays of Anton Chekhov, for whom Stanislavsky created intricately realistic productions full of detailed properties and sound effects, could be interpreted with abstract settings that emphasize the symbolic content of the plays. Although some, including the playwright himself, have disagreed with Stanislavsky's interpretations of Chekhov's plays, Stanislavsky defined the position of the director as one who interprets the playwright's creation. Other directors have moved beyond the idea of collaboration with a playwright to view themselves as the primary creators of the theatrical event.

The Visionary Director: Jerzy Grotowski and the Poor Theatre

In 1959, sixty years after Stanislavsky began his work on *The Seagull,* Jerzy Grotowski, a Polish director, began an experimental theatre in Opole, Poland. Six years later, in 1965, Grotowski's Laboratory Theatre moved to the larger city of Wroclaw, Poland. Throughout its existence, the experimental Laboratory Theatre would be subsidized through state and city resources. Although the subsidy was hardly lavish, it did provide a level of basic support that such an experimental company could not expect

in the United States. The following discussion of Grotowski's theatre practice is based on his career in Poland, before he shifted the site of his work to the United States and then to Italy.

Like Stanislavsky, Grotowski was devoted to reforming actor training. But instead of employing Stanislavsky's internal acting system, aimed at producing the most naturalistic performance, Grotowski sought an approach to acting that would maximize the expressive power of the actor's total instrument. Grotowski wanted to train actors to use their voices and bodies in astonishing ways to communicate a heightened expression of human experience:

> At a moment of psychic shock, a moment of terror, of mortal danger or tremendous joy, a man does not behave "naturally." A man in an elevated spiritual state uses rhythmically articulated signs, begins to dance, to sing.[5]

Grotowski's rigorous and athletic program of actor training was based on his own studies of Western acting styles and methods, including Stanislavsky's; and Eastern theatres, including the Chinese opera, the Indian kathakali, and the Japanese nō theatre. Although the training depended on stretching vocal and physical capacity to extraordinary limits, the goal was not simply technical brilliance. Grotowski

In this photo from the 1964 Grotowski production of *Akropolis* (version III, Opole), we see the stripped down nature of the "poor theatre." The actors wear costumes made from burlap bags with holes torn in them and lined to suggest the naked bodies of the actors underneath. They are all dressed identically in heavy work boots and cloth hats to indicate the uniform of the concentration camp where all individuality has been lost. The stage is merely wooden boards, the set made of old wires and pipes. The acting style relies on extreme gestures and grimace-like facial expressions, abstracted expressions of grief and suffering. The characters are going though the motions of living. The violin, the one actual musical instrument in the play, is used as counterpoint to scenes of brutality, a hint of a former civilization. The actors are Zygmunt Molik and Rena Mirecka.

In his 1904 play, *Akropolis,* Stanislaw Wyspianski examined the relationship of Poland to the forces of Western culture. In the play statues representing religious, literary, and historical icons come to life, culminating in the resurrection of Christ. Grotowski placed scenes from Wyspianski's play in a Nazi concentration camp, to show the collapse of human civilization rather than its resurrection. In this photo, a grotesque wedding procession takes place, with the pipe carried by the actor in front used to represent the bride. During the course of the play, the actors use pipes like the one they are carrying to build a crematorium, which they climb into at the end of the play. Grotowski demanded a total commitment from the participants to his methods of actor training and this production was rehearsed for two years before being given public presentations. The actors are Zygmunt Molik, Ryszard Cieslak, Mieczyslaw Janowski, Andrzej Bielski, Gaston Kulig, and Rena Mirecka in *Akropolis* version III at Opole in 1964.

encouraged a process that would allow actors to reveal themselves, to strip away the "life-masks" that they use to protect themselves, so that the spectators would be encouraged to look deeply into themselves as well.

The actor training was essential to Grotowski's own work as a director, which involved staging plays with an entirely different emphasis from that used in the realistic theatre. Grotowski was interested in creating theatre performances that explored myths and archetypal characters as they confronted or illuminated the experiences of the members of his theatre company and the experiences of his audiences, the people of Poland:

> I am very fond of texts which belong to a great tradition. For me, these are like the voices of my ancestors and those voices which come to us from the sources of our European culture.[6]

He was particularly concerned, for example, about the legacy of World War II for Poland and about the presence of Nazi concentration camps such as Auschwitz on Polish land and their effect on the collective Polish psyche. For one of his plays, *Akropolis*, Grotowski arranged a text—based on the play by Stanislaw Wyspianski—that brought together mythical figures from throughout Western history who, in the production, became inmates in a concentration camp. During the course of the production, the characters constructed a crematorium that they all entered at the end of the performance. Ludwik Flaszen, who was the literary adviser of the Laboratory Theatre, writes that the production of *Akropolis* asked the question, "What happens to human nature when it faces total violence?"[7]

As a director, Grotowski believed that the text should be part of the production but not necessarily the dominating force. He maintained that a director should be able to reshape a text or bring several texts together and create a collage of pieces of plays. With this approach, the director goes beyond being the partner of the playwright in developing the production of a play. The director essentially becomes the author. It is the director's imagination that creates the foundation for what happens on the stage.

Grotowski believed that the director should also shape the stage space, the actor–audience relationship, as he or she shapes the text and the actors' work. In his own attempt to bring the actors and audience as close together as possible, Grotowski created a new spatial arrangement for each of the productions of the Polish Laboratory Theatre. For a production of *Doctor Faustus*, the audience sat at long tables while the actors moved around the tables and even performed on top of them. The tables were to suggest the Last Supper. For *The Constant Prince*, the audience members looked down from their seats, raised slightly behind a fence, as if they were at a bullfight or in a surgical operating theatre. The fence was used to suggest that the audience was looking at something "forbidden."[8]

Through the Laboratory Theatre, Grotowski was able to control all the elements of the performance to realize his vision of the theatre. Like the spatial arrangement of the actor-audience placement that we have just discussed, all the physical elements of set, costumes, and properties had an abstract and symbolic quality. Grotowski was adamant that the theatre should leave lavish and high-tech production values to the film industry and focus instead on the most stripped-down, basic materials that could support the actors' work. Found objects, reworked fabrics or clothes, and bare lights served as the design elements of his **poor theatre.** Only those objects or costume pieces that served the actor were incorporated. Nothing was used merely for the purposes of decoration, mood, or background.

The Playwright as Director: Athol Fugard

Stanislavsky's approach to directing was based on finding a truthful way to present the work of the playwright. Grotowski saw the writing of the playwright as material to be manipulated to suit the vision of the director. Another major figure of twentieth and twenty-first century theatre brings the work of the playwright and the director together in a third way. Athol Fugard, introduced in Chapter 2, was initially an actor and then a director before he became one of the leading playwrights of the modern era. When he began to write plays, he also continued his career as a director, directing most of the premieres of his own plays and a number of their subsequent productions. Between 1956 and 2010, Fugard wrote thirty-three plays and directed numerous productions of them. He continues as an active playwright and director today. Adapted to his own purposes, Fugard followed some of the realistic foundations of Stanislavsky and at the same time he was inspired, like Grotowski, to reduce the elements of theatre production to their simplest forms.

The early plays of Athol Fugard were produced under very difficult circumstances. There was no money to purchase materials, hire designers, or pay for theatre space. Sometimes the actors' names were announced from the stage because there was no money for programs. The actors were often under police scrutiny and some of their participation resulted in arrest and imprisonment. Keeping the sets and costumes to a bare minimum

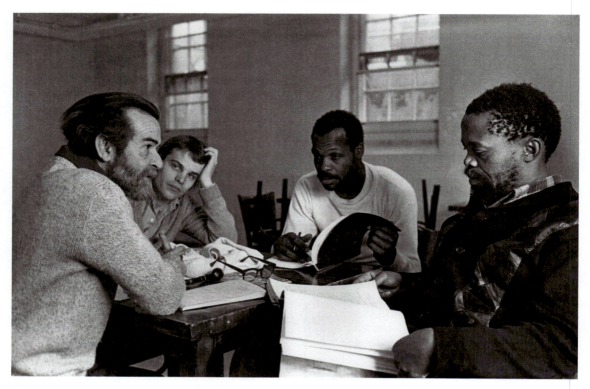

Athol Fugard is shown here with the actors Zeljko Ivanek (Harold), Danny Glover (Willie), and Zakes Mokae (Sam) at the first rehearsal for the world premiere production of *Master Harold and the Boys* at Yale University in 1982. This was the first of the plays written and directed by Fugard that had its premiere production outside of South Africa. The character Harold is based on Fugard's memories of himself as a young man, a character who is caught between two visions of the world. In one vision, he reciprocates the kindness and familiarity shown to him by Willie and, most of all by Sam, who has become his surrogate father. In the other, he embraces a racist perspective, lashing out at these two generous characters and humiliating them to try to offset his own emptiness. The play is set simply in the tea room owned by Hally's parents where Sam and Willie are waiters, arranging the furniture and dishes for the next day's customers, and Harold is doing his homework. Central to the physical action of the play, the two older men practice dance steps for a ballroom competition they plan to enter. In his review of the production in the *New York Times,* Frank Rich writes, "Mr. Fugard's point is simple enough: Before we can practice compassion—before we can, as Sam says, 'dance life like champions'—we must learn to respect ourselves."

was a necessity. What was important was the presentation of stories that revealed the struggles of characters trying to survive in a world rapidly losing its humanity. Fugard was concerned with the brutality of life in apartheid South Africa, but his focus was not specifically on a social critique so much as on the nature of human connections and ultimately human isolation. He wanted to make a place for actors to create and for audiences to see

stories that touched their own lives. "My aesthetic probably comes out of having a theatre in South Africa with nothing, but even if I had resources, my inclination may not be to use them."

Stanislavsky was interested in the details of everyday human behavior and he used a profusion of reference points in elaborate sets, costumes, and properties that gave the appearance of actual places. Fugard selected a few basic objects, the most utilitarian furnishings for set, and basic clothing pieces for costumes. Grotowski was interested in rough found materials to create his environments and properties, and in contrast to Stanislavsky's realistic presentation of human behavior, Grotowski used theatricalized metaphors. Old pipes and pieces of metal became a crematorium. Fugard also used a rough aesthetic, but the few pieces he chose had a much closer correspondence to actual life. The idea for a play or an acting exercise might come from an object like a coat, taken off at the last moment by a man about to be sent to prison, to be left for his family, or a camera used to preserve the identities of common people, or a passbook that must be carried at all times with official stamps in it declaring where a person might live or work. The rehearsal work for *The Island* represented by production photos in Chapter 2 began with Fugard repeatedly folding a blanket in half for the two actors to stand on until there was barely room for both of them to fit on it. The small square of fabric became the space of the play, a prison cell that was both physical and mental.

Fugard explains through his notebooks and in interviews that he has written plays in order to work with actors and, furthermore, that the gestural possibilities of the actor are as important in expressing the ideas of his plays as the words. Essential to composing his plays are the theatre space itself and the silence that surrounds the words. "I would take away the words from him if a simple gesture,

Angels of Swedenborg, originally produced by Ping Chong in 1985 and again in 2011, is a mixed media theatre piece focusing on the conflict between the search for spiritual enlightenment and the temptations of the material world.

a simple pause—the way he put on a sock, the way he took off his scarf and rolled it and put it into his raincoat pocket—said it all."[9] "I have always regarded the completed text as being only a half-way stage to my ultimate objective—the living performance and its particular definition of space and silence."[10]

Directing the Theatre of Mixed Media: Ping Chong

Thus far we have identified three models of approaches to directing: the director who is committed to a partnership with the playwright (Stanislavsky), the director who draws on a variety of sources but is the primary creator of the theatrical event (Grotowski), and the director who is also the playwright (Fugard). Ping Chong is a director who has yet another approach to the creation of work for the stage. He believes in guiding a collective of artists to devise the performance and being free to draw on all the resources of the theatre to lift the audience into an otherworldly view of human existence when appropriate. Ping Chong (1946–) is an American theatre director with an international perspective and an extensive

Undesirable Elements is a series of works produced by Ping Chong since 1992. It is an example of the docudrama form, which uses the testimony of actual people. Each new installment represents a form of collective storytelling by a group of individuals in a different city—in the United States or elsewhere—drawn together by Ping Chong to explore their concerns with identity and isolation. The staging is the essence of simplicity: the actors seated in a semicircle of chairs, in order to put full emphasis on the stories they tell of their own lives. In *Cry for Peace: Voices from the Congo,* Congolese refugees offer first-person testimony about their own experiences of "brutality, loss, and regeneration" in Congo to promote "healing, reconciliation, and justice," in material arranged by Ping Chong and Kyle Buss in 2010. The performers are Cyprien Mihigo, Emmanuel Ndeze, Beatrice Neema, Kambale Syaghuswa, Mona de Vestel, and Dina Ndeze Mahirwe.

background in dance, film, and the visual arts. In fact, he identifies himself "as an artist *in* the theatre, not a theatre artist."[11] Chong was born in Canada and raised in New York City's Chinatown. He studied filmmaking and graphic design before joining Meredith Monk to collaborate with her on experimental dance theatre pieces. In 1975, he founded Ping Chong and Company, dedicated to creating theatre works that address cross-cultural issues and explore new means of theatrical communication. He rejects what he sees as an outdated reliance on realism in the American theatre.

A lot of what goes on in the theatre isn't theatre, in my opinion. It doesn't transform the stage. It doesn't turn it into magic or poetry. The American theatre is largely nineteenth-century naturalism and that's antiquated. We live in a cyber world, a fragmentary world, a world of electronic sound.

Chong and his collaborators—writers, actors, designers, dancers, puppeteers, animators, and video artists—set out to address contemporary issues with contemporary forms, unafraid to integrate ancient storytelling devices with the most recent technology or to combine adventurous uses of the three-dimensional stage space with imaginative projected imagery from video or animation.

As a director, Ping Chong is interested in changing the terms of theatrical communication. He therefore willingly seeks out new collaborative partners and stages performances in new locations. Thematically Chong has been concerned with exploring what it means to be an outsider, how we are affected by perceptions of difference, and what the consequences of those perceptions may be for individuals and communities. He has moved from reflecting on the condition of being apart in his early pieces to work that articulates the need for connection. Recently, Chong's work has embraced two different kinds of storytelling: one that offers a highly theatrical and symbolic form of the presentation through puppets, intricate scenic arrangements, and projected animation; and one rooted in the actual words of people who appear onstage to speak of their own personal experiences.

Elizabeth LeCompte

The director Elizabeth LeCompte leads a collective process with the Wooster Group, an experimental theatre company that also devises

The Wooster *Hamlet* is a recent production directed by Elizabeth LeCompte. The actors perform the play of *Hamlet* in front of a famous, earlier filmed version of this play starring Richard Burton. The Wooster actors mimic the staging and gestures of the film, creating a dialogue between the live action and the film. LeCompte and the Wooster Group work with complex technology that is a major factor in the company's aesthetic. Scott Shepherd plays Hamlet, with Richard Burton seen behind him on the screen.

new theatre works. The performances of the Wooster Group interweave materials from many sources, including play texts, autobiographies, poetry, letters, personal biographical contributions from the actors, and group improvisation. All of the members of the group help generate material for their pieces, but LeCompte makes the final decisions about what will be included.

> I like to run a tight ship. I like to have the final say, not so much because I want the power of it, but because otherwise I lose my way. These workers bring this material to me, and I sift and siphon through it. It isn't that some material is better than other material. I use it when it links up to something very particular with me, when it extends my vision.[12]

A collaborative approach to devising material has become increasingly prominent in the development of new work for the theatre, and directors engaged with this process have a variety of ways of providing leadership.

The Director at Work

We will now continue to explore the work of the director identified in the first model, in which the director is committed to truthfully interpreting the work of the playwright. However even the role of this director is still in flux, and there is much disagreement about how much a director should impose on a production and how much should emerge from collaboration. Declan Donnellan directed the London production of *Angels in America: Millennium Approaches* by Tony Kushner, which preceded the play's Los Angeles and New York productions. (*Angels in America* is presented in Chapter 10.) The playwright, Tony Kushner, participated in the rehearsal process in London, and his presence led to considerable tension between Kushner and the director. Donnellan reports that he and Kushner "almost killed each other," in part over a disagreement about the role of the director:

I was much freer with the actors than Tony expected. There was one great row when Tony asked why a certain actor was standing to say a line when it was very clear from the written line that she should be sitting down. I said that I hadn't even noticed that she was standing up because the scene varied from day to day, and Tony couldn't believe that I wouldn't control whether an actor should stand or sit. He thought this showed a terrible lack of respect for detail. But I told him that on the whole it was for the actor to make the detail, it's up to me to make sure that the actors know what they are doing, which is very different from telling them to stand or sit.[13]

The director Bertolt Brecht was outspoken about his theories of epic theatre as they applied to acting methods and scenic presentation. But in rehearsal he was famous for sitting quietly while the actors worked and making only brief suggestions when they had finished.

Describing the process the director uses is even more difficult than pinning down the process and methods that actors use to create roles and give performances. Directing is studied and discussed less than acting is. Far fewer people are involved as directors than as actors, and the path of the director is a highly individual one. We can identify only the kinds of tasks that a director must accomplish, and we can form an overview of the directing process by describing the approaches used by some prominent directors. Frequently, the views and the methods used by one director contradict those of another director.

Choosing the Play

Directors usually have some choice about what they are going to direct, and they tend to choose plays they care deeply about. They choose plays that connect to their understanding of the world, plays that make sense to them. A play that is a good choice for one director may not work for another. A director may admire and enjoy a particular play and yet lack an inner understanding of the work that would lead to a successful

WORKING IN THE THEATRE

Summary of the Director's Responsibilities

- To choose the play
- To study the play and the historical context, possibly in collaboration with a dramaturg
- To develop a "concept" for the production in collaboration with the designers
- To audition and cast the actors
- To guide the work of the actors:

  To establish an acting style

  To block the play

  To clarify character development and the characters' relationships

  To build the play's rhythm in order to maximize audience involvement

- To maintain an atmosphere that is conducive to the creative work of all involved
- To guide the work of all participants to a timely and coherent readiness for performance

production. Although some directors are hired for a theatre season for which the plays have already been selected, most theatre practitioners and producers recognize the importance of the connection between the director and the script. If the director is to interpret the world of the play for an audience, then the playwright's vision must appeal to the director's imagination and understanding of human nature.

Davis McCallum, who directed *Water by the Spoonful*, the play that is the focus of Chapter 13, explains why he was drawn to an earlier work of the playwright, Quiara Alegría Hudes.

I remember reading the play on the subway and getting just ten pages into it, the very first scene, which involves three different time periods and these three different men

remembering their war experiences and I thought this is a playwright who is musical and poetic and yet you believe the characters are real and you could walk up on stage and introduce yourself to them. I would be thrilled to work on this play.

Marc Masterson, the artistic director of South Coast Repertory Theatre, chose to direct *Eurydice* by Sarah Ruhl, a production to be explored through its design in the next chapter because of the challenges presented by its lyrical construction and the open-ended nature of the decisions to be made. The play offered a process of discovery.

I love the material with its many challenges. The play kept opening up where the possibilities of how to do the story kept us all engaged through a four-week rehearsal period, which is a great sign of an interesting and worthy play.

Lloyd Richards, who directed the original productions of many of August Wilson's plays, found that the beliefs articulated by Wilson's characters coincided with his own understanding of human nature. Richards says of reading the plays for the first time:

There were characters in the play that were well delineated. And the things that they were talking about, I believed. So the playwright, in a sense, was speaking for me as well as to me.[14]

Richards was drawn to Wilson's artistry in expressing a moral position: "He has a very deep sense of social responsibility. He is a repository of unlimited stories which reveal human experience."[15] And the rhythmic structure of the plays inspired Richards's directorial approach: "August Wilson is music. I directed all of his pieces as if they were music."[16]

When directors have a feel for certain material, they sometimes direct a play more than once. Libby Appel, who first directed *Macbeth* in 1987, felt compelled to return to it at the Oregon Shakespeare Festival in 2002 because she had come to a new understanding of this work.

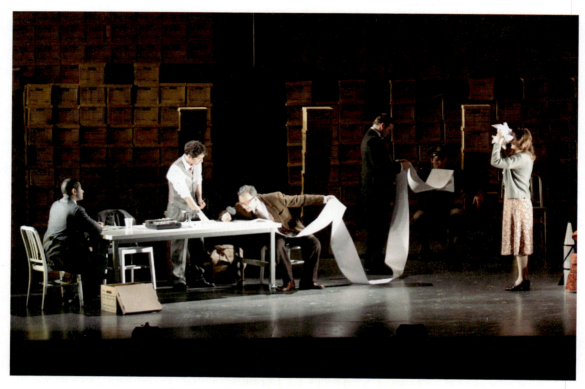

In Part 2 of *Apollo* at Portland Center Stage in 2009, the actors search in the file boxes for evidence about the past of Arthur Rudolph. Three thousand boxes filled the stage and were moved by the actors to create the stage environment. All of the props used by the actors were discovered in the boxes. Andy Hirsch, standing center, plays the prosecutor, Eli Rosenbaum. Chris Shaw, seated with the magnifying glass, plays Arthur Rudolph. Valerie Spencer, holding the bundle of handkerchiefs, plays the daughter of Arthur Rudolph, and Jeffrey Johnson, standing with his back to the audience, plays the ghost of Werner von Braun. The director Nancy Keystone was also the scene designer for *Apollo;* the metaphoric use of the boxes informed both her work with the actors and her shaping of the space.

I've always wanted to do it differently, in a way that would focus on the psychology of the event. I wanted to take it out of the spectacular epic and put it in a smaller space to concentrate on the thought processes of the characters.[17]

Since directing *Joe Turner's Come and Gone* at the Oregon Shakespeare Festival, Clinton Turner Davis has directed Wilson's play for the Milwaukee Repertory Theatre and the New Federal Theatre in New York City. Tisa Chang, the artistic director of the Pan Asian Repertory Theatre in New York, directed *And the Soul Shall Dance*, discussed in Chapter 8, twice and produced a third production over a period of fifteen years. She says that she is drawn to Yamauchi's work because of the truth she recognizes in the characters:

And the Soul Shall Dance is so special because it has very strong women's roles. Emiko is a woman who is utterly unfulfilled, unsatisfied, but has great yearnings, intellectual yearnings, artistic yearnings, and very deep feelings, emotional and sensual. There's nothing false, the sexuality, the brutality. Yamauchi really is the central figure and she was writing about issues that were very daring. *And the Soul Shall Dance* is also remarkable because it seems to speak to so many different people at once. We've had audiences, Italian, Jewish, all say, "This is my story."

The play is an actor's paradise. These roles are so meaty. And until then most of the roles for Asian actors on the American stage were abysmally stereotypical images.[18]

The Director's Initial Response to the Play

Just as actors go through a process of discovering the essence or inner life of the characters they will play, so directors go through their own process of discovering the essence or inner life of the play. They build their own understanding of the world of the play before they attempt to communicate their responses to other members of the production team. Directors use many approaches for exploring a play's images, textures, rhythms, characters, and possible meanings. Directors analyze characters' motivation, but they also listen to music and look at paintings. They study thematic developments, and they also read history. They travel to cities and even foreign countries in search of landscapes or ways of life or performance traditions that may serve the needs of the production. The directorial process is analytical, but it is also intuitive and imaginative.

Creating Metaphors

As a director approaches a play, he or she begins a process of discovering a metaphor, or image, that will translate the ideas of the play into a stage language. The metaphor is a way of expressing the most compelling ideas of the play in a concentrated form that will become a guide for the work of all the theatre artists involved in the production. A metaphor is an analogy, or comparison, a symbolic way of expressing the action of the play. The founding director of the American Conservatory Theatre in San Francisco, William

Ball, emphasizes the need for a single, strong metaphor to guide the work on the production:

> I have learned from my own experiences and from my observations of the work of other directors that the more clear and striking the metaphor, the more unified and powerful the production.[19]

Building metaphors was central to the director Nancy Keystone's work on the production of *Apollo* that was introduced in Chapter 4. One of the subjects of this play was the history of the German scientists who were brought to the United States to work on the American space program after World War II.

> When I'm thinking about a play, metaphor is one of the key ways of developing the work. An example would be Part 2 of *Apollo*. When we first developed Part 2, we were dealing a lot with history, with the Holocaust, and with concentration camp victims, and crimes of the Third Reich. Approximately 20,000 people died in the V-2 rocket factory where some of the German engineers worked. This was the key ethical issue of the story. My first thought was could we have 20,000 of something onstage? What would that be? And then, also, what's the main action of this piece? The main action is the search for the truth. When we started, there were two characters who were researchers, who were searchers. It felt to me like they were digging through archives, digging through the past. So I thought, what if we have a bunch of file boxes onstage, and the file boxes create the environment and everything comes out of the file boxes. That thought is what led to this design. The first time that we performed this part of the play was a workshop in a very small theatre. We had 200 file boxes, and they really filled up the space. Justin Townsend, who is the lighting designer, is also a very close collaborator. He had the idea of creating a wall with these boxes at the front of the stage. The piece would start with this wall and the actors would then remove the boxes. We found that just thrilling to contemplate.

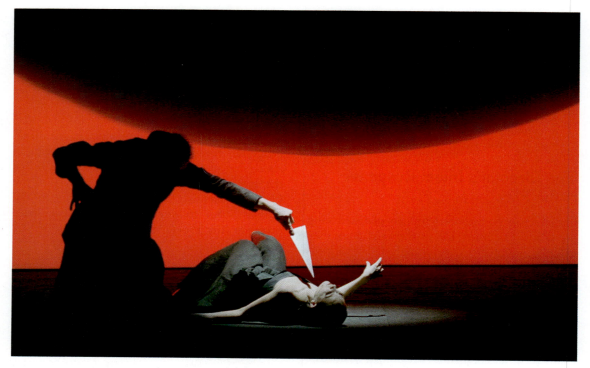

Robert Wilson creates a vivid and horrifying image of violence using the actor's body position and the light to convey the intensity of the moment in his 2002 production of *Wozyeck,* produced in collaboration with the Betty Nansen Teatret of Denmark, with music by Kathleen Brennan and Tom Waits. Wilson is known for his use of visual metaphor as a central expressive device in his productions.

The actors then become manipulators of the environment. That's how it started. I think now we have almost 3,000 file boxes. That's an example of how the conception of the set and the ideas of the piece intersect.[20]

The formulation of a metaphor is a process initiated by the director but very much dependent on the collaboration between the director and the designers. Exactly who will define the nature of the stage imagery, and at what point in the process a central metaphor can be determined, varies from production to production and depends on the working dynamics of the production team.

For a new production, the process of formulating a metaphor, involving the director and the designers, is usually begun well in advance of the work involving the actors. However, in certain situations when the production process takes months or even years, the designers may work in rehearsal with the actors and make design decisions and changes as the production evolves. Theatrical metaphors must be strong enough to provide a physical shape to a production and open-ended enough that they will engage the imaginations of the theatre artists and the audience members.

Directorial images have a visual component that is crucial to the designers, and the images usually include a sense of the stage action as well that will guide the director in the blocking of the actors. At the Oregon Shakespeare Festival in 2002, the director and designers for the production of *Macbeth* looked for a simple, concentrated image around which to build their work. Shakespeare's *Macbeth* is about the ambition of the title character to become king and then to keep the crown at any cost. This ambition transforms Macbeth from a heroic soldier into a bloody murderer who strikes king and servant, friend and foe, woman and child in a desperate course of spiraling violence. The first key decision made by the director, Libby Appel, was to do the play in the round with the audience surrounding the stage (see page 167).

> I knew that I wanted an empty space and that it was just about the actors telling the story. I wanted the audience to be as "cabined, cribbed, confined" as Macbeth is—so that they would feel the claustrophobia of the small space with Macbeth. There's no escape.

Aware that only minimal visual effects would be possible, the director and the designers turned to the language of the play, the many references to blood, summed up in the following lines spoken by Macbeth, as the source for the production's guiding metaphor:

Will all great Neptune's ocean wash this blood
Clean from my hand? No. This my hand
    will rather
The multitudinous seas incarnadine,
Making the green one red.[21]

First they decided that a bucket or pool of blood would be placed center stage, and all the action would revolve around it.

> It grew into this pool of blood that became the cauldron, "fire burn and cauldron bubble." And the whole of the round, the theatre, is the cauldron. And we're all in this cauldron together.

Once the idea of placing a pool of blood onstage was established, the costume designer, Deborah Dryden, concluded that the costumes should be white in order to show the blood. This decision then evolved into the idea that the "blood should be accumulated all the way through the play with every bloody deed multiplied." The costumes became a canvas that would be painted with the murderous actions of the characters. Finally, the movement director, John Sipes, responsible for staging the fight sequences, saw that the pool

of blood onstage should govern the fight choreography. Rather than using swords, the fighting was stylized, with the characters dipping into the pool and marking each other with blood where a blow would have opened a wound.

Working with the Actors

Casting

The first crucial contact the director has with the actors comes during the auditions. Choosing actors wisely is essential to the success of the entire enterprise. Sometimes actors will be chosen at the kind of open auditions discussed in Chapter 4. Sometimes actors are invited to read for a play, and

BW Gonzalez is seen here as Lady Macbeth in the sleepwalking scene wearing the white costume designed by Deborah Dryden to show the bloody misdeeds committed by the Macbeths during the course of the play. The production was directed by Libby Appel at the Oregon Shakespeare Festival in 2002.

sometimes actors whom the director has worked with before are simply asked to take a part. Actors in a repertory situation such as the Oregon Shakespeare Festival are cast in several parts for different plays, all at the beginning of the season.

The director must choose actors who are suited to the roles in the play, who have good work habits, and who will work well in the particular configuration of the cast. The right balance and chemistry among the cast members are as important as the talents of individual actors. **Typecasting,** the selection of certain actors because they have a certain physical appearance and personality, is still entrenched in some areas of the American theatre, particularly in musicals and summer stock. Although a presence that makes the character believable is essential, more and more directors seek actors who will bring insight and creativity to a role rather than a preconceived physical appearance.

Nontraditional Casting

A recent development in the American theatre involves a rethinking of approaches to casting in terms of race. This shift has resulted in part from the increased participation in the theatre of actors and directors from diverse ethnic groups as well as increased social awareness on the part of theatre producers and directors.

Contemporary productions frequently combine actors from different racial backgrounds—even when they are playing members of the same family. Such casting is currently referred to as "nontraditional" or "color-blind casting." The director assumes in this kind of casting that the best actor should be cast for the role and that the audience will respond to the group of characters, not to the racial difference of the actors. In some productions, characters are cast specifically with race in mind to bring out certain ideas in the text. As we reevaluate where we are as a nation in terms of race, casting in the theatre will serve as a way of expressing and addressing the diversity of the U.S. population.

The Work Environment

At the heart of the director's responsibilities in the production of a play is his or her work with the actors. This process begins with the audition and continues through the rehearsal period and the first performances. From the beginning of the auditions, the director is responsible for creating an atmosphere that is conducive to the creative work of all involved, that ensures respectful consideration of the actors' efforts, and that recognizes the vulnerability inherent in the acting process. Because the actors' progress during the rehearsal period depends on their making open and honest responses, the director must be protective of the working environment. Rehearsals are usually closed to outside observers, who might make inappropriate commentary or inhibit the actors' work by making them feel that they are "performing" before they have completed their foundation work. The actors must trust the director; otherwise the process is imperiled. The director who shouts or humiliates an actor immediately shuts down the lines of communication.

The rehearsal should be a time when risks are taken and discoveries are made about the characters' deepest feelings and most compelling motivations. Hidden desires, buried secrets, burdens of the past, and ambitions for the future must be teased out during the rehearsal process. The actors must be open not only to the director and themselves but also, perhaps most of all, to each other. The connections between the actors drive a play forward and create a sense of an imagined world come to life. And it is the responsibility of the director to encourage the bonding of the actors and to guide them in making sense of the characters' relationships.

We have already looked at a number of directorial approaches in our discussion of the production process at different theatres and in the chapter on acting. Although the director usually has a planned structure for the rehearsal process, involving table work, blocking, and character development, the creativity and spontaneity

The lunch counter scene in *Apollo* directed by Nancy Keystone was developed through improvisation. In this violent encounter, played out in slow motion, the man standing repeatedly mimes hitting the seated characters, who, each time they are hit, fall forward. The stage picture makes clear the relationship between the characters and the shift in who is occupying the space and the price to be paid to take a seat at the table. The actors include Ray Ford, J. Karen Thomas, Richard Gallegos, Nick Santoro, Angie Browne, Valerie Spencer, Lorne Green, Brandon Ford Green, and Russell Edge.

of the director in rehearsals are as important as the creativity of the actors. The director must respond in the moment to the contributions and questions of the actors and the progress of the work. The director may stop a scene that is problematic to set up an improvisation in an attempt to get at deeper, more committed responses from the actors. Or the director may make suggestions for stage business that will physicalize a character's motivation.

The director always functions as the actor's audience to confirm what is being clearly communicated and to help clarify moments when the actor's intention is unclear. The director must maintain the company's focus and do whatever is necessary to inspire a continuous high level of energy and creativity. Although the director may be watching the action quietly, in fact she or he must match and encompass the energy of everyone on the stage.

Improvisation

Nancy Keystone, the director of *Apollo*, used improvisation to generate both the text and staging for many of the scenes in this production. The photograph on this page shows a moment from a scene in Part 3 of *Apollo*, representing the attempt to integrate lunch counters in Alabama during the civil rights movement. The finished scene was performed with no words and structured through the precise repetition of the gestures of a group of archetypal white characters used to eating in a segregated restaurant. The characters repeat the motions of entering the diner, eating, and exiting, all in speeded up time, until the rhythm and pace of their movements is broken by the entrance of an African American character. The pace then shifts to extreme slow motion as more African American characters take seats at the lunch counter in spite of the hostile responses with which they are met. The actor Ray Ford, who appears seated at the table on the left in the front, describes the development of the scene:

> The lunch counter sequence was born as an improv. Nancy came in and said, "Ok, here's two tables, it's a lunch counter. You be the chef, you be the cook, you be the waitress, and everyone else be the customers." So we did that improv for a couple of hours. It starts off just as an acting exercise, but there comes a moment where your reality sort of

drops away and you're really there. When you're doing an improv for two hours, your defenses are down, and it completely shifts the energy, not just in the actor, but in the entire room. I remember leaving that night and we were all just completely wiped out and exhausted. But you just go there. You completely go there. It's just about that action of walking into this diner where you're not welcome, and what that feels like on both sides. That was all we had to work with for a long time. There still are no words in that scene, you know, it wasn't like we were playing it out. And we would flip roles, blacks played whites, whites played blacks, to see what that felt like. It's all about the feeling underneath all of that.[22]

Staging the Play

The director's own particular eloquence is expressed through the staging of the play. The director must arrange the actors in the theatrical space and develop sequences of actions that account for the necessary actions required by the script. But this staging of action through spatial relationships goes far beyond serving the practical needs of the script. Like designers, directors should be spatial artists. They compose in space and time with the actors and the scenic elements to interpret the ideas of the play.

The director arranges what is called the **stage picture,** the arrangements of actors onstage to communicate character relationships. But unlike a photograph, the stage picture cannot remain static and still hold the audience's attention. Characters cannot appear like posed statues. The stage picture must be dynamic, ever-changing. And the composition of the stage picture must direct the audience's attention to the important character or characters while also making clear the relationships among the group of characters. Blocking a play is far more complicated and subtle than merely getting the actors on and off the stage and getting them to do interesting things.

Focus

One of the most important components of directorial composition is focus. By the arrangement of the actors' bodies in the theatrical space the director must guide the audience's attention to a specific actor or to the point on the stage where key actions, reactions, or line deliveries will take place. A film director uses the camera to focus the spectator's attention. With a close-up shot, the camera singles out the significant actor and makes sure that the slightest response is registered clearly for the audience's appreciation. A long shot is used to give a view of the whole scene and then, through editing, the film cuts from actor to actor as the director wishes the spectator's attention to shift from character to character.

Stage directors, however, cannot employ such editing techniques. The audience views the

In this photograph, one character reads to a group of workers, sitting at imaginary tables cutting tobacco and rolling cigars, to help them pass their work day. Focus is directed to the character of the reader because he is standing while the other characters are seated and he is also elevated above them. The reader is dressed more formally than the workers and he is placed center and looks directly out while the chairs of the workers are angled in different directions. By placing the reader behind the other characters, the audience can also see their responses as they listen to the story. By raising or lowering lights on individual characters, including the reader, focus can be heightened or shifted. The reader Juan Julian is played by Francisco Gattorno. The other actors are Denise Quiñones, Tatiana Vecino, Grettel Trujillo, Raúl Durán, and Gil Ron. The production is the Spanish language translation of *Anna in the Tropics* by Nilo Cruz, *Ana en el Tropico,* produced in 2004 at Repertorio Español under the direction of René Buch.

full stage space continuously and remains at a constant distance from the stage. The director achieves focus through the placement of characters in relation to one another on the stage. Contrast in the visual presentation of the characters is one of the director's most important compositional tools. A character dressed differently from all the other characters and placed prominently attracts focus. A character separated from a group of characters becomes the focal point. Contrast can also be achieved by elevating or lowering the position of the actors onstage. A character who stands while everyone else sits receives focus; and as long as the character is plainly visible, a character who sits or even falls to the floor while everyone else stands receives the focus. A character raised up higher yet on stairs or an elevated platform will receive the focus if the other characters onstage are on a lower level. The focus of the actors will also direct the focus of the audience. If all the actors are looking at one character, the audience's attention will follow. Actors may also lean their bodies toward a particular character, or they may hold objects that direct the audience to look in a particular direction. The photograph of Herald Loomis on the floor at the end of act 1 of *Joe Turner's Come and Gone* demonstrates several of the principles of stage focus (see page 101).

Spatial Composition and Character Development

In addition to focus, another major function of directorial composition is the communication of character relationships and character development. William Ball compares his spatial work with actors to choreography:

> Picturization is similar to choreography in that the body positions reveal the relationships, independent of the words. My productions usually bear a slight resemblance to ballets, because I tend to picturize as intensely as possible. For example in my production, when the script calls for two people

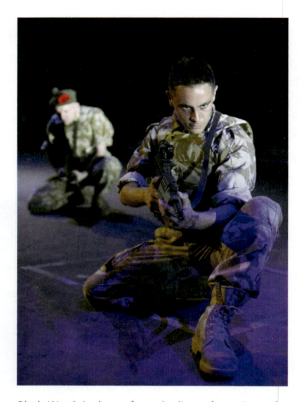

Black Watch is drawn from the lives of members of a 300-year-old Scottish Army regiment that saw repeated duty in the Iraq War as allies of the United States. The play begins in a pub setting where the characters have gathered on their return home. The audience is shocked when suddenly a hand punches through the top of the pub's pool table and men in combat uniforms begin climbing up out of the table. This is almost like a reverse image of the figures at the end of *Akropolis* climbing down into the crematorium. Drawing on both military formation marches and fight sequences, the co-directors Steven Hoggett and John Tiffany place the characters in individual and collective battles with enemies that continue long after the troops are back on Scottish soil. Originally a production of the National Theater of Scotland in 2007, *Black Watch* has toured widely in the United States.

seated on opposite sides of a table, the one who is winning is usually climbing over the table, and the one who is losing is sliding under the other side.[23]

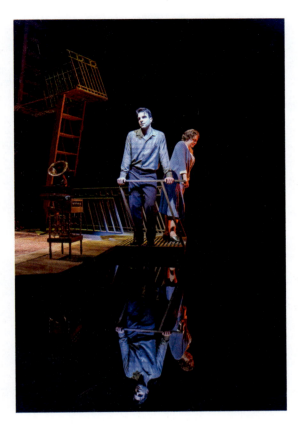

For the 2013 production of *The Glass Menagerie* at the American Repertory Theatre in Cambridge, Massachusetts, John Tiffany and Steven Hoggett used the images of glass and reflection to build a fragile world of memory. Far from the explosive movement used in *Black Watch*, they focused instead on the repetitions of small actions that play continuously in the memory of the narrator, Tom, who abandoned his mother and sister years ago. A moat surrounds part of the stage, separating the characters from both the larger world and the present, and the moat allows the characters to be reflected like glass figurines set on a mirrored surface. Zachary Quinto plays Tom; Cherry Jones plays Amanda Wingfield. The set and costumes are by Bob Crowley; the lighting designer is Natasha Katz.

By expressing the essence of character relationships and individual character development spatially, the director provides a visual telling of a play's story or a visual score just as the playwright's script provides a verbal score. The audience reads the nature of relationships or changes in relationships by the placement of the characters in space and their physical interactions. How close together or far apart are the characters? Do they face each other, or do they face away? Do they touch each other or avoid physical contact? Do the play's events bring the characters together, or do they push the characters apart? Does one character dominate the space while the other shrinks into a less important or a restricted part of the space? Does one character move freely through the space while the other is hesitant? Does one character lead while the other follows? *The progression*, the evolution of the spatial placements, is crucial in defining the progression of the character relationships or character development. Does an independent character who has kept herself apart come to depend on the character she has avoided? Does a character who has moved aggressively through the whole stage space come to occupy a smaller and smaller part of the stage as his power is stripped away?

Plays frequently have strong spatial implications built into their structure that give directors the starting point for their work. A battle for the stage space occurs in a number of plays. The confrontation between the Angel and Prior in act 2, scene 2 of *Perestroika* is a fight for Prior's soul that is realized in physical terms. In *Joe Turner's Come and Gone*, Seth wants to force Loomis out of his house while Loomis is determined to keep his place. In contrast, the sharing of the stage space is central to the supportive character relationships of a play such as *And the Soul Shall Dance*.

Recently a British choreographer and director, Steven Hoggett, has become known for taking a new approach to spatial composition and character development through a movement vocabulary that pushes recognizable physical interactions to extreme or even dangerous dimensions. Starting with the emotional crises of the characters or the difficult predicaments in which they find themselves, he works with the actors to generate gestures or movement sequences that approach the psychological and physical edge. Hoggett uses neither a traditional dance style nor a fixed idea of actor training. Rather he seeks to find the deepest and most truthful physical response to the characters' circumstances. Steven Hoggett is the co-director with Scott Graham of a British company called Frantic Assembly. His work has also been widely seen in the United States. He has served as the choreographer in collaboration with director John Tiffany of a group of diverse theatre pieces that have each broken new ground in the expressive use of movement and spatial composition in theatrical storytelling. These pieces include *Black Watch* in which explosive combat encounters give reality to the lives of Scottish soldiers in Iraq; *Peter and the Starcatcher*, a super-charged comedy where the actors change size, change gender, change from humans to animals, from children to pirates, by only transforming their physicality to account for their new characters; *Once*, the 2011 Broadway musical in which all of the actors are also musicians and all of the movement must be done with musical instruments in hand; and most recently, a 2013 production of Tennessee Williams's *The Glass Menagerie*, that finds original rhythms and gestures to open up the fragility of each character and to locate the play as an inescapable and haunting memory.

Rhythm and Pacing

A play progresses through character development and conflict, through visual imagery, and through rhythm. The rhythmic development and pacing of a play are also the director's responsibilities. A play has a number of rhythmic components. Each actor's speeches have a certain rhythm, as do each actor's movements. Rhythm is in fact an important part of character development. Character rhythms feed into the overall rhythm and pace of the play. Pace is simply the speed at which the production moves. The pace of the play must be slow enough for the audience members to comprehend the information they are receiving but fast enough to maintain a sense of forward drive and excitement. Plays frequently accelerate in pace to build the intensity of conflict or certain moments of revelation. Or the pace may be slowed considerably to allow the characters and the audience to reflect on some catastrophic event. Pacing that is relentlessly fast is exhausting for an audience, just as pacing that is too slow drains away the audience's energy. The pacing of a play is a crucial way of drawing the audience into the drama unfolding before it.

Preparing the Play for Performance

The goal of all the work on a production is always performance. The rehearsal process has its own accelerated pacing as the production moves toward opening night. According to schedule, rehearsals shift from exploration to a tentative shape, from changing and adding details to a completed form. "Run-throughs" of acts and then the whole play take the place of minute work on character and scenes. Rehearsals during which the actors may call for their lines are replaced by rehearsals without interruptions or lapses of concentration. The director brings the play to a point where the actors have confident control of their material and pacing just in advance of the "technical rehearsals."

During the **technical rehearsals** the actors' work receives less focus as the director's attention shifts to the lighting **cues,** the final appearance of the costumes, and the look and movement of the set. It is during the technical rehearsals that all the details of the production, so long in the planning and development phases, are brought together to create the effect that the director has envisioned. Lighting cues may need to be adjusted and set changes rehearsed until they take an acceptably brief amount of time. The director's capacity to attend to myriad details while moving toward performance is most severely tested at this stage of the process.

After the technical rehearsals and dress rehearsals, **preview** performances are given to allow the actors to finish their work on the play in the presence of an audience. (The preview audience consists of people who have been invited or those who have bought tickets at reduced prices.) The director continues to work closely with the actors during the preview performances to refine pacing and timing and to make sure that clarity has been achieved. This is the final stage of the director's involvement. When the play officially opens—the moment that all the director's energies have been focused on—the production belongs to the actors, who will continue to draw on the foundation built during the rehearsal process. The director's work is finished.

The Director's Training

Becoming a director is not unlike training to become an orchestra conductor. Conductors usually study several musical instruments for years before they take on the responsibility for a whole group of musicians. Similarly, directors must have expertise in several areas of theatre before they assume responsibility for coordinating an entire production. Sometimes directors begin their work in the theatre as actors, and their preparation then includes their own work in performance as well as their observation of the methods of the different directors they have worked with. Sometimes directors

begin as stage managers, obtaining a foundation in the organization of production details as well as production oversight. Some directors start as scene designers, gaining experience that gives them a strong visual sense. And there are also examples of successful directors who begin as dancers and choreographers. Choreographic skills are extremely important in the placement of actors on the stage and in the development of spatial relationships. Many directors also have a strong musical background, either as practicing musicians or as scholars of periods and styles of music. Whatever the director's starting point, the successful director must develop skills in all the areas mentioned.

In addition to those directors who work their way up through theatre companies, there are directors who receive their training from undergraduate and graduate theatre programs. Graduate study in directing usually focuses on the M.F.A. degree, although there are Ph.D. programs that also have a directing component. Frequently, graduate schools expect students to have worked in the theatre as directors before entering their programs. In graduate school, directing students study the analysis of plays and directing methods and often scene design, costume design, and lighting design. Studying the design areas not only builds visual skills but also provides a vocabulary and a point of view that facilitate the crucial dialogue between directors and designers. Graduate programs in directing usually involve a minimum of three years of study.

Summary

The director is the "author" of the stage action, the theatre practitioner who unifies all the elements of performance. Sometimes the director functions as the primary interpreter of the playwright's work, and sometimes the director

composes both the drama and the theatrical presentation of the drama.

The modern history of the director began in the late nineteenth century with George II, duke of Saxe-Meiningen. Directing numerous productions that were influential throughout Europe, the duke emphasized the integration of the elements of spectacle and the authenticity of period costumes and settings. At the turn of the century, Konstantin Stanislavsky developed his directorial approach in his work with the plays of Anton Chekhov, which Stanislavsky believed required an ensemble of actors and a more "natural" acting style than had been used previously. Stanislavsky began as a dictatorial director but gradually involved the actors in a more creative partnership.

During the 1960s, Jerzy Grotowski developed the Laboratory Theatre in Wroclaw, Poland. Grotowski had as much influence on the theatre of the latter part of the twentieth century as Stanislavsky had on theatre earlier in the century. Grotowski used the texts of playwrights as a springboard for his own ideas and frequently combined more than one source. He was committed to what he called the "poor theatre," using only the simplest, roughest materials for sets and costumes. The actors trained by Grotowski practiced a physical form of acting heavily influenced by Asian performance techniques. Athol Fugard exemplifies the playwright who directs his own plays. Ping Chong draws together live actors, puppets, and various forms of electronic media to create multidisciplinary works tied to the experiences of different communities who participate in the performances.

Today, directors take widely differing approaches to staging plays and working with actors. Directors such as Clinton Turner Davis work to interpret the playwright's text. Robert Wilson structures a visual presentation of an idea to which he adds text. Elizabeth LeCompte directs the productions of the Wooster Group in which all participants contribute to the shape of the text and the interpretation of that text. Many directors rely on the creative contributions of the actors, although some expect the actors to follow the director's expressive choices.

Directors prefer to have the freedom to choose plays that they find inspiring. Through a collaborative process, the director and the designers evolve a metaphor, or image, that guides the work on the production. The director selects actors who are suited to the roles of the play and the style of the production. The director is responsible for creating a rehearsal atmosphere that encourages the actors to be open with one another and to take creative risks.

In rehearsal, the director faces two major tasks: to guide the interpretive work of the actors and to stage the play's action. Through the arrangement of the actors on the stage, the director clarifies the character relationships and the plot elements. The director pays close attention to the expression of the play's rhythms through the actors' speeches, movements, entrances and exits, and the pacing of their interactions. During the technical rehearsals and preview performances, the director works with the designers, the technical staff, and the crews to finalize all details of the production.

Topics for Discussion and Writing

1. Review the principles of directorial composition related to focus. Find photographs and paintings of groups of people in which the composition is arranged to focus on one or only a few people. Use magazines, newspapers, collections of photographs, or books on painters, but do not use photographs of theatre productions. Bring five pictures to class that clearly establish focus, each through a different element of composition and contrast. Examine the pictures together to see the range of possibilities for spatial composition assembled by the class. What kinds of statements about relationships do the photographs convey? If space and time permit, select some of the most striking compositions and re-create the relationships between the people in the photographs using members of the class.

2. Observe people in different situations and environments to see how they respond to each other in terms of space. Choose one situation that involves a significant negotiation over space, and write a short paper in which you describe the nature of the interaction. For example, you might observe someone trying to maneuver someone else to get the largest share of the space or the most comfortable chair. Someone conducting a job interview might dominate the space while the interviewee takes up as little space as possible. People involved in an argument might try to assert themselves by expanding their physical position. Find a spatial interaction that you think communicates strong motivations, and write a detailed description of approximately one page.

● For interviews with some of the directors in this chapter and "*Apollo* in Performance," as well as suggested readings and other resources, please visit **www.mhhe.com/creativespirit6e**

CHAPTER 6

The Designers

Stage Design—the work of the scene designer, the costume designer, the lighting designer, the sound designer, and the video or projection designer—is an essential part of what makes the audience experience in the theatre a magical one. Stage design, together with the presence of the actor, creates a world apart from the day-to-day existence outside the theatre's boundaries. The designers create a poetry of space, visual and aural, that brings the stage to life with startling images and creates an eloquent foundation for the actor's work.

The stage speaks with color and shape, with light and shadow, with music and sound. The flight of an angel, a boardinghouse seen against a city skyline, a rolling piece of tumbleweed, the haunting sound of a Japanese *shakuhachi* flute, the lyrics of a blues song—these images from productions discussed in this book appeal to the senses. The designers engage the audience with sensory information to locate the actor physically and psychologically and to support the ideas of the text.

The photo on this page represents a central image in the play *Eurydice* by Sarah Ruhl. On the day of her wedding to Orpheus, Eurydice falls from the upper story of a highrise apartment building. The stage directions indicate that Eurydice is transported to the underworld in an elevator and inside the elevator it is raining. In collaboration with the director, the designers must imagine what this moment of transition from the world above to the world below looks like and sounds like. Is there an actual elevator? How strange or terrifying is this journey for the character who is a very young woman? How does the style of the elevator fit in with the rest of the design elements for the play? Where is design necessary for the most vivid telling of this story, where would it get in the actors' way? In 2012, Marc Masterson, the artistic director of South Coast Repertory, and a group of designers set out to solve the special challenges of Sarah Ruhl's play in a process we will highlight as we analyze the art and craft of design for the stage.

In the photo on the opposite page, Eurydice's arrival in the underworld is meant to surprise the audience. Only moments before, she was seen on a bare stage in her wedding dress. All of a sudden, the light turns to deep shades of purple and green and a whirring sound is heard from high above. The elevator, which has been invisible to this point, appears and begins to descend from 45 feet above the stage floor. The door opens and Eurydice re-enters, now dressed for a journey, her umbrella open, the rain falling down. Eurydice is played by Carmela Corbett. The scenic design is by Gerard Howland; the costume design is by Soojin Lee; Anne Militello is the lighting designer. The sound design is by Bruno Louchouarn.

Stagecraft and the Theatre

The actor and the director are artists who are made for the theatre. Their skills and talents are wholly claimed by the theatre itself. Designers, on the other hand, have skills and talents that they share with other visual artists, sound artists, and craftspeople. Scene designers have drafting and construction skills. Costume designers work with fabrics and have cutting, sewing, and dyeing skills. Many scene and costume designers also have extensive training in drawing, painting, sculpture, or architecture. Lighting designers create with a broad range of electrical instruments and control systems. Sound designers work with music, sound effects, recording equipment, and amplifiers. Video and projection designers have expertise with cameras, digital editing, and image manipulation. If designers do not sew or do carpentry or work with electricity themselves, they must clearly understand the

The characters in this photograph are called the Stones. In Sarah Ruhl's play *Eurydice,* they inhabit the underworld. According to the director Marc Masterson, they are "the embodiment of the dead, complacent, and craving quiet. Over time, they have become part of the rock the earth is set on."[1] The designers were faced with the challenge of creating an environment for characters who are fixed in place, have a limited ability to move, and need to seem as they have been in this place for a very long time. The actors are Michael Manuel, Bahni Turpin, and Patrick Kerr.

properties of the materials they incorporate in their designs. But no matter how many overlapping abilities designers share with visual artists, musicians, digital technology experts, or craftspeople, like actors and directors they are interpretive artists whose creativity must be used to shape the world of the play or the theatre piece. A designer's work of art does not stand alone onstage as an individual creation but interprets the ideas of the play with materials just as the actors shape ideas with their voices and bodies.

Much of our discussion of the theatre has to do with the serious interpretation of serious subjects. But whether the subject is comedy or tragedy, spontaneity and playfulness are crucial to theatre work and part of the theatre's great appeal to its participants. The possibility for creative problem solving, for tackling curious challenges that most people never have the opportunity to take on, is part of the basic work of the stage designers and technicians. The following examples demonstrate some of the intriguing problems designers and technicians are called on to address.

- For *Eurydice* one of the design problems was to provide a visual interpretation of characters who are meant to represent stones.

- For the New York production of *Angels in America*, discussed in Chapter 10, the staff faced the problem of flying the angel in such a way that she could perform her aerial gymnastics without catching her wires in her very elaborate costume.

- For *Apollo* (Chapters 4 and 5), for each performance the crew needed to stack 3,000 boxes across the stage, many of which would then be moved by the actors. The boxes needed to be arranged in a precise order because some contained props that had to be accessed by the actors.

- For the Wooster *Hamlet* (Chapter 5), the technical director Boskurt Karusu had to dress in a costume at each performance in case he needed to go onstage and fix malfunctioning media equipment.

- For the production of *Macbeth* discussed in Chapter 5, the costume designer Deborah Dryden needed to find white fabric for the costumes that could be stained with "blood" at each performance and then washed and dried for the next performance, sometimes on the same day when there was a matinee as well as an evening show.

- For *Water by the Spoonful* (Chapter 13), the scene, lighting, and projection design needed to guide the audience in tracking scenes that alternated between actual time and space, where the characters faced each other, and virtual space, where the characters were communicating online.

Bodies need to disappear and ghosts walk the earth; costumes and sets must be changed in a matter of seconds; ships must sail across the sea; or a mountain must give the appearance of snow and ice. Theatrical design requires continuous imaginative thinking, first to visualize the image in response to the needs of the play and then to come up with the technological solution that will make it possible.

The Theatrical Space

The first condition that governs the work of all the designers is the nature of the theatrical space, the relationship between the audience and the stage. The size and atmosphere of theatres in the United States vary widely, from the traditional elegance of Broadway to the modern comfort of large regional theatres such as the Oregon Shakespeare Festival and the Mark Taper Forum to the small and sometimes cramped spaces of equity waiver theatres such as East West Players (Chapter 8) and the Eureka Theatre (Chapter 10).

The common denominator for all theatre spaces is their three-dimensionality. In contrast, movie audiences sit in front of a large flat screen on which filmed images give the impression of dimensional space, but that sense of depth is in fact an illusion created by the camera. In the theatre, the dimensionality of the stage space is actual. For this reason, the audience space and the stage space can be arranged in different configurations. The audience relationship to the screen at the movies, however, always remains the same.

The Proscenium Theatre or End Stage

In many large theatres, such as the Oregon Shakespeare Festival's Bowmer Theatre and Broadway theatres, the audience sits opposite the stage, facing what is called the **proscenium** or **end stage.** A proscenium theatre is a theatre constructed in a rectangular form with the stage at one end of the rectangle. The stage opening follows the rectangular form of the space as if the audience were looking through one end of a box. The audience's view is shaped by a framing device that defines the rectangular opening called the **proscenium arch.** The proscenium arch is like a picture frame. The stage frame of the proscenium masks the mechanics of the backstage operations and creates a clearly defined theatrical space that is particularly suited to realism. The opening of the proscenium arch can be covered by a curtain,

The Argyros Stage is a contemporary version of a proscenium theatre that is part of the group of theatre spaces that make up South Coast Repertory in Costa Mesa, California. This is the theatre in which the production of *Eurydice* we are studying was staged. Because it holds only 336 seats, the Argyros is ideally suited for intimate theatre productions. The proscenium stage began its evolution in the Italian court theatre of the sixteenth century at a time when painted scenery and lavish special effects became an increasingly important part of stage spectacle. The audience members in a proscenium theatre all share the same view of the performance.

The theatre shown in this photograph is part of the Hartford Stage Company in Hartford, Connecticut. This theatre can be transformed into either a thrust configuration or a proscenium configuration. The play being performed in the thrust configuration is *Water by the Spoonful,* which we will study in Chapter 13. Notice the depth of the stage platform, where characters can be seen one behind the other at some distance, and the minimal use of scenic elements except in the upstage area. The thrust stage is historically connected to the Greek and Shakespearean theatres, where the audience was placed around three sides of the stage. A thrust stage allows for a close relationship between actors and audience members.

which also functions as a masking device to allow scene changes out of the view of the audience. Today, however, many styles of theatre other than realism are presented on proscenium stages, such as the surreal and lyrically written play *Eurydice.* Rectangular stages that lack a curtain or even a defined frame are referred to as end stages.

Thrust, Arena, and Black Box Stages

In contrast to the seating arrangement in a proscenium theatre, some theatres are designed to allow the audience to sit on three sides of the stage, which may be rectangular or rounded in its shape. The three-sided arrangement is called a **thrust stage.** The thrust stage extends into the audience, and different sections of seating look across to other seating areas. The audience members in a thrust situation are much more aware of the presence of other audience members than they would be in an end stage arrangement and are therefore more likely to be conscious of their own presence in a theatre watching a play. When the audience sits surrounding the entire stage space, the configuration is referred to as **arena staging** or **theatre in the round,** whether the

The Oregon Shakespeare Festival has three different stage spaces including a flexible space shown here in an arena configuration for the production of *Macbeth* in 2002. The pool of blood in the center was the only constant scenic element in this production except for the structure of the stage itself. Two chairs were brought on for the banquet scene to suggest the thrones of the Macbeths. Arena stages are surrounded on all sides by audience seating. The arena stage emerged from performance traditions in which ceremonial plays were performed in community plazas. The morality plays of medieval times, at which audience members sat on the hillsides of a natural amphitheatre, are one of the best-known historical uses of arena staging. Today the arena stage provides an intimate relationship between actors and audience members. Scenic elements must be carefully scaled and arranged to protect the audience's view.

stage space is an actual circle or a square with the audience on four distinct sides.

Theatre architecture is frequently permanent; that is, a theatre building is constructed so that the actor–audience relationship always remains the same. Sometimes a theatre plant will have more than one stage as South Coast Repertory and the Oregon Shakespeare Festival do; this arrangement allows the staging of plays in different kinds of spaces. Sometimes a theatre space will be constructed specifically so that the stage space

itself can be flexible. Small theatres and colleges frequently have what are called **black box** spaces that can be arranged differently depending on the needs of the specific production.

An exciting opportunity for theatre practitioners occurs with the use of **found spaces** as performance venues. Rather than fitting the production into a traditional configuration of stage and audience, found spaces inspire creative approaches to the actor–audience relationship and unique design possibilities. Found spaces may be inside or outside, public or private. Churches, department stores, factories, garages, train stations, packing plants, and armories have all been turned into theatres. Sometimes the space not only provides architectural opportunities but also carries with it historical and sociological significance that relates to the themes of the play.

The Implications of Theatre Architecture for Designers

Thrust and arena stages have neither the masking of the proscenium arch nor curtains that can block the stage from the audience's view. Therefore, all set changes must be done in view of the audience. In the production of *And the Soul Shall Dance* at East West Players (Chapter 8), the set changes were performed by costumed actors, kurokos, whose choreographed movements were an integral part of the play and were important for the audience to see. In *Angels in America* (Chapter 10), the actors themselves changed the set, but during scene changes they projected a neutral persona rather than portraying one of their characters from the play. In other productions, the lights are dimmed for the set changes,

This production of *Waiting for Godot* was staged in a ruined house in the Gentilly neighborhood of New Orleans shortly after Hurricane Katrina. The actors used both the house and the street to perform Samuel Beckett's play about characters waiting for a figure of salvation, who never comes. Setting the play in an abandoned house and the street is an example of using a found space to produce theatre. The producers wanted to call attention to the sense of abandonment felt by many who remained in New Orleans after the hurricane and provide a way for residents to gather together to support each other. Wendell Pierce plays Vladimir and J. Kyle Manzay plays Estragon in the production directed by Christopher McElroen in 2007.

which are performed by stagehands in dark clothes who move quickly and quietly across the stage space, changing or rearranging the set as efficiently as possible. In theatres with sophisticated physical plants and large budgets, scenic units may be moved mechanically across the stage or on a revolving platform, or they may be flown in from above. The movement of scenery in musicals is frequently choreographed to the music and becomes part of the visual spectacle.

Each spatial configuration makes different kinds of demands on the designers. In an end stage arrangement, the audience cannot see the back of set pieces, which therefore do not have to be finished; in theatre in the round, however, every object on the stage has to be completely finished because it can be seen from all angles. Towering set pieces or backgrounds can be used on proscenium stages or at the back of a thrust stage, whereas set pieces on an arena stage must be designed not to block the view of anyone in the audience. All kinds of ingenious solutions have been developed for arena stages to allow the audience to look over or through stage objects. Costumes and properties become the design focus in arena or thrust staging. The size of the stage and the size of the audience area are also important factors in determining the scale of the scenery and the detail of the sets and costumes.

Three-Dimensional Space

Although the shape of each stage configuration presents unique problems and opportunities, the basic notion of three-dimensional space remains the same. The director and the designers are composing in space. The costume designer and the lighting designer are particularly concerned with shaping the body of the actor. The costume designer creates a silhouette; the lighting designer molds that silhouette. The scene designer creates the physical environment that contains and defines the figures shaped by the costume designer and the lighting designer. The director creates meaningful relationships between the figures of the actors within the space defined by the set designer. Ultimately, the lighting designer unifies all the stage elements, including the figure of the actor.

The History of Scene Design

The history of scene design moves back and forth between periods featuring open theatre spaces with little scenic definition and periods when the scenic environment was of utmost importance to the presentation of the drama. The Greek theatre in the fifth century B.C.E., the Elizabethan theatre, and the Chinese theatre are all examples of theatres that used neutral playing spaces defined through character action, language, or minimal use of properties. The Roman and the medieval theatres began to show considerable interest in scenic effect. But it was in the court theatres of the Renaissance and Baroque periods throughout Europe that stage design generated great enthusiasm and remarkable ingenuity. Some of the leading inventors and artists of the time—including Leonardo da Vinci—contributed their skills to the theatre.

To imagine the energy and resources that went into the effects of the Renaissance theatre, the contemporary film industry provides a useful comparison. Film studios spend tens of millions of dollars on intergalactic special effects, stunts, models of cities or spaceships, hundreds or thousands of elaborate costumes, and the most advanced technology in cameras and sound. This was the kind of fascination that swept the court theatres and later the public theatres. During the Renaissance not only was perspective scenery painted lavishly with palatial interiors or mythical lands, but stunning special effects were also executed, with dazzling results. Fifty angels at a time could rise to the heavens on cloud units called **glories.** The stage floor could be made to resemble the ocean, with dolphins and whales diving through the waves. Mythical figures flew across the stage on the backs of animals or birds.

Buildings collapsed, and actors appeared in the midst of flames. Stupendous costumes matched the scenic invention.

In the nineteenth century, the introduction of scenic realism was a continuation of the Renaissance ideal of an integrated scenic background or environment for the drama. But the realistic stage focused on the limitations of human existence rather than on the fantasies dramatized in earlier centuries. And in the hands of American directors and designers of the late nineteenth century and the early twentieth century, such as Steele MacKaye and David Belasco, realism turned into a spectacle of its own, with rivers running across the stage and fifteen-minute sunsets.

Design for the contemporary theatre includes the aesthetics of both the open, neutral playing space and some form of elaborate scenic background. Broadway musicals usually use very elaborate scenic effects, as do the productions of Robert Wilson, although with different goals and a different impact on the audience. Contemporary productions of Shakespeare are frequently, although not exclusively, produced on some kind of open stage, relying on the talents of the actors and the language they speak to express the essence of the world of the play. And elements of the two approaches can be combined in different ways. In both types of staging, the work of the costume and lighting designers has a great deal to do with completing the visual statement of the production. On an open stage, however, the costumes and lights take on particular expressive significance.

At the beginning of the twentieth century, when a fusion of realism and spectacular effects dominated the European and American theatres, a quiet Swiss scene designer, Adolphe Appia (1862–1928), proposed a radical change in scene design. Appia was an idealist searching for a way to merge music, acting, scenery, and light into an integrated expression of the drama. Appia's research in the theatre was aimed at finding the most eloquent way to stage the operas of Richard Wagner. His conclusions about the possibilities of the stage space in combination with new uses of lighting had a lasting effect on the development of scenic and lighting practices throughout the twentieth century.

Appia advocated a return to the idea of the open playing space and the elimination of painted scenery and all realistic objects. However, rather than the flat platform of the Elizabethan or Chinese stages, Appia thought that the stage floor should be broken up into various levels that would help shape the movement of the actor. Through a combination of ramps, steps, and playing areas of different heights, Appia designed a **terrain** for the action of the drama that would have rhythmic as well as visual implications.

A multilevel stage provides many expressive possibilities for arranging groups of actors. The stage picture formulated by the director is greatly facilitated when the possible positions for the actors are increased vertically as well as horizontally. Steps and ramps also provide for movement patterns and in fact dictate a rhythm of movement through the number of steps and the distances that may be measured in the actors' movements. Appia was interested in supporting the moving figure of the actor as the focus of the performance. He believed in stripping away unnecessary details of spectacle because they detracted from a focus on the actor.

He encouraged the use of light instead to bring color to the stage and create mood and atmosphere through the creative use of shadows. Foremost in his writings on the theatre were his observations on the way that light can define and reveal the moving figure of the actor. Experimentation with the expressive possibilities of light was in its infancy. Appia understood the potential of light as a transformative element in theatre design that would take on a new partnership with both the drama and the actor. The photo of *The Glass Menagerie* at the end of Chapter 5 reflects the influence of Appia on modern stage design.

Scene Design Today

Eurydice at South Coast Repertory

Scene design today may emphasize an elaborate scenic background or an architectural shaping of space. The scenic elements may be realistic or abstract; they may be constructed of simple or highly finished materials. The design may acknowledge the architectural definitions of the theatre or attempt to disguise or transfigure the space. The design may incorporate digitally produced, projected images or use only dimensional, tactile materials. To explore some of the concepts of theatre architecture and scene design that have been introduced thus far, we return to the scene design for *Eurydice* at South Coast Repertory.

First we must begin with the script that is the foundation for the production. To craft her play *Eurydice*, the playwright, Sarah Ruhl, turned to the myth of Orpheus and Eurydice. The story has been told in many versions since its origin in ancient Greece and later in the re-telling by the Roman poet, Ovid, in his collection *Metamorphoses*. In the traditional story, Orpheus, who is known as the world's greatest musician, falls deeply in love with Eurydice. On their wedding day, a catastrophe occurs. Eurydice is bitten by a snake and she dies. Determined to bring Eurydice back to life, Orpheus travels to the underworld to find her, where he plays such beautiful music that Hades, lord of the underworld, relents. Eurydice may leave the underworld as long as she follows behind Orpheus during their return journey to the world of the living, and he does not look back at her. But Orpheus is unable to keep from looking at Eurydice, and when he does, Eurydice dies a second death and is lost to Orpheus forever.

The director, Marc Masterson, points out that Sarah Ruhl's version of *Eurydice* "is a traditional story unconventionally told." Ruhl changes the plot in two major ways. Historically, the story is told from Orpheus's point of view. But as the title of the play tells us, this is Eurydice's story. And Ruhl introduces a new character into the mix, Eurydice's father, who is waiting for her when she arrives in the underworld. In fact, as the playwright acknowledges, she wrote this play in part to work through her grief at the loss of her own beloved father who died when she was twenty. Ruhl explains, "I wanted to write something where I would be allowed to have a few more conversations with him." For the director, "that is where the heart of the story lies. When Eurydice reaches the underworld and is able to reconnect with her father and her memory and her childhood, she has the connection with her father that she never really had in life. Orpheus is more or less a supporting character." Ultimately, this is a story of a daughter's love for her father, which she must address before she can move on in other ways. When Eurydice comes to know her father better during their shared time in the underworld, she also comes to know herself.

As important as the plot is to the work the director and designers will do on this play, the tone and style of the playwright will guide them in the choices they make. The playwright approaches with a light touch a sequence of events that could be relentlessly disturbing for the audience. The characters are odd and quirky, comic moments occur frequently in the dialogue and the action, and the language is lyrical, full of poetic images.

MARC MASTERSON: The poetry is not just linguistic. She does some wonderful things to ignite your visual imagination. When Orpheus reaches the gates of hell, she has a stage direction that says, "raspberries, peaches, and plums drop from the ceiling." And another stage direction says, when Orpheus turns around and looks at Eurydice on his way back up, "the world falls away." These kind of stage directions lead you toward a kind of visual poetry. We ended up not having any raspberries, peaches, and plums. But the writer is creating surreal images that gave us permission to render the world in a particular way.

Summary of the Designers' Responsibilities

- *Costume and scene designers*—prepare sketches and then color renderings of sets and costumes to provide visual definition of designs; develop complete designs that meet the needs of the production, the theatre, and the budget
- *Lighting designer*—prepare a light plot that indicates the position and angle of all lighting instruments; arrange for any additional instruments or materials for special effects
- *Sound designer*—identify cues and collect or compose sounds or musical pieces

All designers:

- Read the play carefully and research possible sources
- Collaborate with the director and the other designers to arrive at a production concept
- Prepare appropriate breakdown of design elements (blueprints, elevations, hookups) to allow support technicians to construct sets and costumes and to hang lights and prepare cues
- Attend rehearsals to monitor necessary changes in designs
- Maintain a dialogue with other designers and the director
- Supervise the construction of sets and costumes, and where appropriate, execute the most difficult processes such as painting and dyeing
- Work through the period of technical and dress rehearsals to make all necessary adjustments

Masterson began his work with the designers four or five months before *Eurydice* was to open at South Coast Repertory in September of 2012. Previous to his joining SCR, Masterson was the artistic director for eleven years of the renowned Actors Theater of Louisville. Since he had moved recently to a new part of the country, he was eager to collaborate with west coast theatre practitioners, and so the designers he invited to work on *Eurydice* were all new to him and new to each other, although some had worked previously at SCR. They didn't yet have a shorthand for communicating with each other that some creative teams develop when they have spent years working together. But what was most important to Masterson was finding "people who were eager to think outside the box, who could do a complex collaboration involving different mediums." In the early developmental process, the designers met individually with Masterson, who communicated the evolving design ideas to the rest of the group. The work with the scenic designer, Gerard Howland, came first.

Design that Supports the Action of the Play

The first task of the scene designer is to support the action of the play. A playing space must be shaped that will provide for the specific actions called for in the play. Do the actors need to run in and out of many doors? Is there a mountain that must be climbed? In the case of *Eurydice*, two underlying actions must be accounted for: in some way the characters must be able to move from up to down, and there must be a way to express simultaneous action in the upper and the lower worlds. A third crucial need has to do with water. In mythology and in Sarah Ruhl's play, there is a River of Forgetfulness. Characters must dip themselves in the river to wash away their memories of the world above and take their leave of life.

For the 2012 production *Eurydice*, Gerard Howland, the scene designer, needed to create a terrain that would allow the director to stage all of the essential moments of this play. The creation of this terrain was both conceptual and practical. After a number of meetings, Howland and Masterson spent one afternoon walking around the stage together, discussing ways that the actors could travel between two worlds that would represent states of mind as much as they represented physical places. From this session, the basic design ideas emerged that are represented in the **ground plan** shown above.

The floor of the stage itself was built to account for the shift in locations. Note the blue line that curves across the stage from **stage right** to **stage left.** This line represents the River of Forgetfulness and divides the stage into two sections, one of which is elevated 6 inches above the other. There are now two major playing areas of different heights, which could be used to indicate different locations. And when the contoured edge of the upper platform was lit, the river appeared. To the downstage right of the curving line is a rectangular platform outlined in red. When Orpheus lay down on this platform, it tipped up on a steep angle and he slid beneath

the stage floor as if he was shooting down into Hades, where he could search for Eurydice. The three boxes outlined in green represent openings cut into the floor through which the Stones emerged in their mirrored boxes. All of these logistical arrangements could be achieved because there is considerable depth underneath the playing level of the stage and the scene shop had the resources to build a complete stage floor just for this production with its special traps and moving pieces. In the upstage center area of the ground plan is a larger square outlined in purple. This represents the elevator shaft that extended up 45 feet to provide for Eurydice's dramatic descent into the underworld. Together these elements provided the director with the fundamental stage positions to tell the story of the play, with both eloquence and with the simplicity that he thought was in keeping with the evocative nature of the script.

As the design process moved forward, Marc Masterson made the decision to include video as part of the language of the production. From the beginning he knew that sound and music would be needed to create an "aural landscape" for the story. When he determined that video would also be used "in the form of underscoring" like the music, another challenge was created for the scene designer, to build screens into the stage space that could be seen by all audience members and complement the positioning of the actors. Two screens were installed, one on either side of the elevator shaft. The use of video created its own set of logistical complications as well as interesting opportunities for expressive images, to be discussed later in the chapter. One of the challenges for the scene designer occurred in creating an effect of falling rain. Water images are an essential part of the texture of this play, sounds of dripping water, a faucet from which Eurydice drinks, the river in the underworld, and many instances of rain, not just in the elevator. To provide rain as a backdrop to significant parts of the action, Howland designed a water wall constructed of lines of monofilament along which water would run to create a sense of rain. The water wall needed to be positioned so the video projects could be seen clearly enough through these lines. And sometimes a rain effect was projected onto the video screen at the same time that actual water flowed down the water wall, heightening the effect. Look at the close-up photo of the Stones on page 163 to see the water lines behind them.

Sometimes the scene designer provides a great deal of imagery that will define the world of the play. In the case of *Eurydice* much of the imagery was to be filled in by the other designers. What Howland did focus on in the scene design was the imagery of water. In addition to the water wall, he designed a framing device for the stage that responded to an idea for the set stated simply in the script as "some rusty exposed pipes." Howland created a sculptural effect of drainpipes that surrounded the entire stage space. These pipes suggested the continuous presence of water, but not water that is a renewal of life, water that wears away at life. The rain pipes conjured water that seeps into the ground and travels to underground places, such as the River of Forgetfulness. The endless drip of loneliness or longing, the falling of water that obscures the view and dampens the spirits.

Costume Design

The costume designer creates through fabric, color, and texture. The materials used range from sumptuous brocades and hand-painted fabrics to clothing found in thrift shops, from delicate laces to metal. Hats, wigs, feathers, and jewelry are just some of the many accessories that add detail and style to a character's presentation. Distortion of the actor's body may be achieved through padded costume pieces, masks, or makeup. Costumes may present a dazzling vision of a fairy-tale world or show poverty and deprivation. The costumes may place the characters in terms of time, place, and social status, or the costumes may be symbolic rather than realistic.

The costume designer Angela Wendt begins her work by asking herself questions:

> Who are these people and what do the clothes mean to them? How do they decide to put on a particular piece of clothing? What does it say about their attitude toward other people and the world? Even though I do research beforehand, I always leave myself the freedom to wait until I've seen the actors themselves, gotten to know them a little bit, so I can pick costumes that support their artistic choices.[2]

Stylistic Unity

Whatever period and style are established for the costumes in a play, the costume designer must approach the characters as a group. Costumes usually have a coherent sense of style as a unit and clearly express visual relationships between the characters in terms of color, line, shape, and texture. Within the group, individual identities are established through contrast and variations in the silhouettes, colors, and materials. Together a group of costumes can be "read" to reveal hierarchical relationships based on wealth or power, differences in age and background, and relationships between smaller units of characters, such as families.

The Psychology of Character

The costume designer has a most interesting responsibility in helping the actor to define what could be called the psychology of character. The clothes we wear have a great deal to say about how we see ourselves and about how we wish to be seen or perceived by others. Joe Mantello, who

played Louis in *Angels in America*, imagined his character choosing clothes that were too big for him, clothes that the character "could disappear into when things got bad." On the other hand, Molly Cunningham in *Joe Turner's Come and Gone* is a character who wants to be noticed. The other characters comment on the appeal of her appearance, but she is also careful not to go too far with the impression that it creates. She says of herself, "Molly don't work. And Molly ain't up for sale." The image she presents of herself through the choices the costume designer makes is quite different from the costume image for Mattie Campbell, who is filled with self-doubt, even though the two characters are both young women and come from very similar socioeconomic backgrounds.

There are people who gain security by carefully following social conventions. Dressing "correctly" in the most acceptable manner, therefore, could be an important character statement. For a rebellious character, choosing the way the character breaks the rules in terms of clothing becomes an interesting challenge for the costume designer. For example, Hamlet continues to wear mourning attire out of respect for his father after the rest of the court, particularly his mother and his uncle-stepfather, have returned to their everyday clothes. His solemn clothes become a point of contention between him and his uncle, Claudius; and their disagreement is a very important issue for the costume designer. In consultation with the director, the costume designer must connect the individuation of the characters to internal as well as external considerations.

The Costume Designer and the Actor

The character definition expressed through costume must support rather than impede the actor's work. A character grows and changes during the course of a play. The audience should be surprised by revelations as the play progresses. The costume designer must allow room for character development rather than make such an obvious statement that the actor's choices are limited or entirely predictable. The definition of character becomes a collaboration between the designer and the actor, with the designer's work enhancing and focusing the creativity of the actor. In the musical *Contact*, the lead dancer wears a yellow dress that was redesigned and constructed nine times during the last two weeks of rehearsal to make sure the fabric and the cut of the dress would accommodate the actor's movement, shown on page 368.

This photo shows the first meeting of the Nasty Interesting Man and Eurydice on her wedding day. His appearance strongly suggests that she should beware. But Eurydice is drawn away from her relationship with Orpheus by the pull of a message from her father. The Nasty Interesting Man is played by Tim Cummings; Eurydice is played by Carmela Corbett. Soojin Lee is the costume designer.

Costume Design for *Eurydice*

For *Eurydice*, the costume designer Soojin Lee was faced with a set of challenges that would have a major influence on both the work of the actors and the choices to be made by the other designers. Some of the characters in the play come from what we would consider the real world and some come from a netherworld that is in large part defined by the characters who reside there: the Stones and the Lord of the Underworld. The playwright, Sarah Ruhl, offers the director and the designers a significant and tantalizing clue to her view of the underworld. In the stage directions she writes, "The underworld should resemble the world of Alice in Wonderland more than it resembles Hades." In fact, in this production the costume designer's responsibility for determining the nature of the underworld was increased because the set design was more

After Eurydice arrives in the underworld and is reunited with her father, she receives a visit from the Lord of the Underworld who comes to visit her riding a red tricycle and dressed as an overgrown child. He both threatens her and tries to seduce her and finally forces her to whisper in his ear, all the creepier for his bizarre appearance. At this point, we see a hint of the playwright's reference to Alice in Wonderland in Eurydice's suit, which could be seen as an adult version of what Alice might have worn when she went down the rabbit hole in Lewis Carroll's story, and the child's costume which could suggest Tweedledum and Tweedledee.

This photo shows the full power of the Lord of the Underworld when he has attained overwhelming size and authority. He dwarfs the stage and all of the other characters. Eurydice's father has washed away his memories and lies dead in the River of Forgetfulness in the contoured part of the stage. Eurydice appears extremely vulnerable with her jacket removed and her arms bare, as the Lord of the Underworld insists that he has grown into a man and that she will become his bride. Ultimately, this is a choice that Eurydice rejects. When the Lord of the Underworld exits to prepare for this bitter wedding, Eurydice makes her final farewell to Orpheus and joins her father in the river. In addition to the other actors already named, Eurydice's father is played by Timothy Landfield.

structural than imagistic. Together, the director and the costume designer had to imagine a visual expression for the Stones that would weigh down the mortal characters who encountered them, and a set of incarnations for the Lord of the Underworld that was genuinely threatening.

Furthermore, in designing the characters from the underworld, Lee was faced with additional problems. In this production the director determined that the Stones would be fixed in place. Therefore all the information that could be communicated about them visually needed to be built into their first entrance. And because the

actors' movement would be limited and they are only seen from the waist up, she needed to give their costumes a great deal of detail to help the actors sustain their performances. In developing her design ideas for the Stones, Lee began by researching images of "stones and rocks that appeared to have human qualities such as rock formations in Arizona and coastal rocks shaped by wind and surf." She then integrated ideas about rocks with a mixture of costume elements from different time periods to create a sense of characters who have lived through hundreds of years of history and like stones have

In sequence, the moment in this photo comes before the previous scene with the enormous figure of the Lord of the Underworld. Eurydice is following Orpheus out of hell when she turns to him and calls his name, which causes him to turn and look at her. Here we see the impact of the simple approach to the costumes for Eurydice and Orpheus, particularly in comparison to the previous scene. The characters are young and very human, both grappling with what it means to be in love and to commit yourself to a lifetime with another person. In this moment, Eurydice fully realizes that this is not a decision she is ready to make. She cannot yet take leave of her father. The costumes sequenced here demonstrate the way the surreal and symbolic telling of Sarah Ruhl's story fits with the human struggles of the central characters. Orpheus is played by Alex Knox.

accumulated various bits and pieces from the forces they have encountered. This presentation of an archaeological layering extended to the wigs and makeup of the Stones as well, with all of the pieces stiffened to complete the rock-like state of the characters' existence. The costumes were also actually constructed in gray and brown earth tones related to rocks in nature. Their green appearance in the photos and throughout the play was the result of a lighting design choice to use saturated green as one of the fundamental colors of the underworld.

The most disturbing character in the play, the Nasty Interesting Man who is also the Lord of the Underworld, goes through an extensive metamorphosis during the course of the play, in distinct contrast to the unchanging appearance of the Stones. He wears four different costumes that represent different stages of Eurydice's interactions with him. She first encounters him in the real world on her wedding day when he persuades her to leave her wedding for a party at his high-rise apartment by promising to give her a letter sent by her father. It is during this episode that Eurydice takes her fateful fall into the underworld. He then appears to her as a petulant and manipulative child riding a tricycle. From the child, he grows into a rock and roll guitarist, ready to challenge Orpheus in the realm of music making. This third version of the character was an addition of this production that is not described in the script. And finally he expands into a towering figure of the devil himself.

Soojin Lee interpreted the characters of Eurydice, Eurydice's father, and Orpheus as everyday mortals and used the hints of the time period that Ruhl provides in the script from the 1930s to 1950s as the guideline for the style of their clothes. By keeping these costumes quite simple, she provided starting points for character development, but gave the actors a great deal of room to build their roles through their acting choices in order to draw the audience members into a deepening awareness of what is at stake for them. Orpheus and Eurydice's father change very little in terms of their appearance. Eurydice's costume goes through subtle but important changes that support but don't define the growth of the character, leaving the actor in control of her psychological journey.

Lighting Design

Light is one of the most powerful influences on human existence. The rhythm of our lives is guided by the cycles of day and night and the lengthening and shortening of days as the seasons change. Summer light is different in intensity from winter light. Light that is filtered by trees and leaves is different from uninterrupted light that glares off water or sand or snow. The light of dawn is often seen as a promise, a beginning; the light of dusk may be seen as a closing or a fading. The beauty of sunrise and sunset offers unending variation and inspiration. Moonlight suggests romance, but a shadow across the moon may seem ominous. We gather around candles and fires because they break the darkness. Light is one of the most expressive tools available to the theatre, and audience members carry with them thousands of impressions and associations with light.

Light has always been a central metaphor in the drama because the effects of light are deeply embedded in the human psyche. Blanche DuBois in Tennessee Williams's *A Streetcar Named Desire* is frightened by the light. She needs to cover the lightbulb to soften the marks of age on her face but also to hide the signs of fear. Ibsen's characters are strongly affected by the Norwegian light; the short winter days of a northern country made gloomier yet by constant rain coming off the fjords play a significant part in the characters' outlook and the mood of the plays. *The Oresteia*, by Aeschylus, begins with the flare of a beacon that signals the end of the Trojan War. The metaphor that guides the entire trilogy is that of light coming out of the darkness. Romeo is drawn to the light in Juliet's window. For him, she becomes the sun and the "envious moon" grows "pale with grief."

The History of Light in the Theatre

It is easy to divide the history of light in the theatre into three periods. Early theatres were located outdoors and relied on natural light. Beginning in the Renaissance there were indoor theatres, which were lit by candles and eventually by gaslight. The modern era of theatre can be dated from the introduction of electric lighting on the stage. With the auditorium darkened and intense light focused on the stage, the realm of the audience became separated from the realm of the actors. And the nature of theatre spectacle was completely transformed by the ability of light to isolate, to create contrasts of light and shadow, to mold the body of the actor, to project a dimensional sense of color rather than the flat color of painted scenery.

However, expressive uses of light surely predated the modern theatre. There is some speculation that in ancient Greece *The Oresteia*

The Necessary Skills and Talents of Designers

- Interest in a collaborative process
- Fascination with dramatic literature and the work of actors
- Strong imagination
- Curiosity
- Flexibility
- Stamina and discipline
- Openness to varied materials and approaches
- Advanced artistic abilities
- Advanced technical abilities

would have been staged early in the morning to allow the natural dawn to express the daybreak that begins the play. The earliest versions of the Christian mystery plays were sung as part of church services and therefore would have been dimly lit by candles and the filtered light coming through windows, thus creating a mood of mystery and reverence far different from the mood set by the late spring light that would have shone brightly on the more exuberant outdoor productions. Lanterns and torches have been used throughout the history of the theatre. But the lighting technology that began in the nineteenth century and has advanced exponentially since then has given light in the theatre an entirely new expressive capacity.

The Lighting Designer's Materials

The lighting designer works with electrical instruments of different shapes and sizes that are placed at various angles to create a design through light. Side light shapes the actors' bodies. Front light illuminates their faces. Follow-spots

are used, particularly in musicals, to highlight and isolate an individual character.

Colored gels are placed across the lighting instruments to change the mood of the light and to interact appropriately with the color choices of the scene designer and the costume designer. Blue is usually considered a cool color, and yellow and straw are warmer, more cheerful colors. A choice from hundreds of gel colors allows the lighting designer to achieve very subtle gradations of color effect. Patterned stencils, or gobos, can also be placed inside lighting instruments to fragment the light and create special effects on the floor or other flat surfaces. Backlighting of actors behind scrims can create a dance of shadows. And projections can be used on various surfaces to provide moving imagery.

The Light Plot and Light Cues

The lighting designer is responsible for creating a light plot, which charts the placement of lighting instruments to meet the needs of the production. Following the completion of the light plot, the lighting designer works closely with the director in developing a sequence of light cues for the production. Each change in light during the course of a production is recorded as a separate cue. In a realistic production, lights may change to indicate changes in the time of day or the weather or to reflect changes in onstage light sources such as candles or chandeliers. Lights also change to reflect mood, to shift focus to different parts of the stage, to emphasize an important entrance, or to create a special effect.

Visibility

Although the lighting design is the last piece of the production puzzle to be fitted into place, it is by no means less important than the work of the scene and costume designers. The light unifies the stage space and the figures of the actors. The visibility of the actors, particularly their faces, depends on the proper use of light. Sometimes lighting designers and directors are drawn to moody, dimly lit effects. But audiences cannot appreciate what they cannot see, and eyestrain rapidly increases general fatigue, making otherwise attentive and involved audience members restless.

Focus

The lighting designer and the director work closely together to guide the audience members' focus. The lighting designer reinforces the director's arrangement of the actors to highlight crucial characters or stage locations. A musical comedy star about to start her song is lit by a spotlight. A doorway receives a special light in anticipation of an important character's entrance. The central figure in a group is picked out with light. As important as the presence of light in establishing focus is the absence of light. Lowering lights on one area of the stage and bringing them up on a new area will redirect the audience's focus.

The Rhythm of Light

The lighting designer Joan Arhelger says that the lighting designer makes a large contribution to building the rhythm of a play, musical, or opera.

> The light breathes. Without movement of the light, the stage and the piece, itself, become static. Our eyes expect change. Every piece has a rhythm to it like music. Is it a love song? Do things flow like a gentle rain or like lightning or thunder? Where are the stepping-stones in the telling of the story? Which ones need a memorable visual moment? The lighting designer must be concerned with how fast things change, the length of the builds, and the timing of the climactic moments.[3]

The lighting for *A Chorus Line* was shaped in response to the dancing and the music. All of the 128 cues were called (initiated) by the stage manager in time to the music. Rather than following a verbal script or cueing the lights off lines spoken by the actors, the stage manager followed the music score and called the cues so that the change in lights would coincide with changes in the music or moments in the dance. The timing of the light cues is a critical aspect of performance and is as carefully set and rehearsed as anything that happens on the stage.

Light usually has a rhythmic function in the theatre even for plays that are not musicals. The rhythm of the lights is created not only through the timing of the changes in the lights but also through the length of time taken for each cue. Light cues are done on timed counts, and the pace of the counting must respond to the pacing of the

In this close-up photo of Eurydice's arrival in the underworld, the angle of the light turns the actor's face into a mask. Notice also the way the light hits the rain falling in the elevator, which together with the face lighting makes the figure appear ghostly.

performance. Sometimes a light cue will be executed rapidly to give visual punch to the moment being played. In contrast, fading up the light on a ten count or longer gives an entirely different effect. Robert Wilson is known for the very slow, meditative movement in his productions. Extremely long, meticulously counted light cues are an enormously important part of his aesthetic.

Here we see the Lord of the Underworld in the third stage of his character progression when he has become a heavy metal guitarist. He is lit as a garish Las Vegas-style entertainer. The sound designer Bruno Louchouarn used rock and roll themes throughout the play in association with this character. At this moment in the play, Orpheus has arrived at the gates of hell and the Lord of the Underworld tries to overwhelm him with the pulse of his musical attack. Note also the hand extensions with elongated fingers that have been added to the costume, further distorting the character.

Although we can summarize the equipment used in theatrical lighting and the basic functions of light in the theatre, Anne Militello, the lighting designer for *Eurydice*, explains that working with light is neither predictable nor easy. The light is alive in ways that scenic and costume materials are not and consequently it brings an extremely important dynamic to the stage.

> When you're a lighting designer, you've got nuts and bolts to deal with, you've got electricity, you've got loads of equipment, you've got budget. And when you put it together, sometimes you've got unknowns. A light doesn't always behave like you think it's going to. You have to be able to roll with it and shape it and mold it and conform it to what you want to do. You've got to fight with the beast and tame it. It's wild! It's an electromagnetic form of energy. It's not a hard piece of scenery, or a piece of fabric, that you know what it's going to do. So there's a magic that goes on when you are making a lighting design.

Conceptualizing with Light

The light in *Eurydice* was essential to establishing the kind of world in which the play takes place. The movement of the actors through the space, down the elevator or through the floor, told us this is a surprising place where the usual rules of human existence do not apply. Space is fluid and can change instantly from the world above to the world below. The costumes of the Stones and the Lord of the Underworld also contributed to the strangeness of Eurydice's journey, funny at times, but also grotesque. Through color changes, variations in degree of saturation, shadows, shifting the angles of the instruments, changes in the rhythm of the light cues, and special effects, the light had a major function in establishing how much separation there was between the world above and the world below, how threatening the forces were that beset Eurydice, and when she had control over her own circumstances.

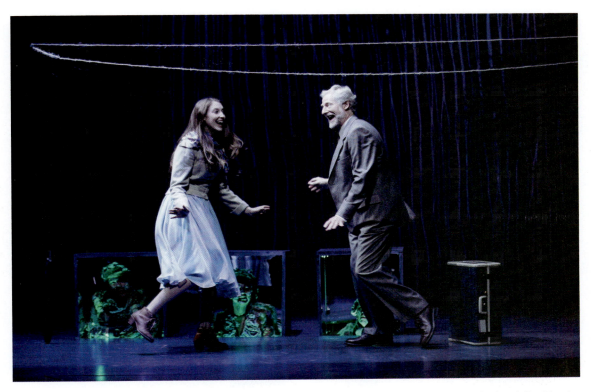

Here Eurydice and her father dance together in the string house that he has made for her. The space is further defined by the bright rectangle of light on the floor. Their faces glow and the Stones fade somewhat into the background.

Mood, Atmosphere, and Psychology of Character

For a play like *Eurydice* with rapidly changing moods as well as locations, the light became a principal part of the storytelling, guiding us through the journey of the characters, placing them both geographically and emotionally. Strongly contrasting colors were used in association with different characters and different kinds of situations. Militello describes her work on this play as a way of painting with light. For example, Militello says she saw the underworld as a "lonely place, where time is forgotten." With the lights she wanted to "capture some kind of isolation, a feeling of being trapped." When Eurydice enters the underworld

she was lost, foreign. I lit her face from below with soft light, making her look not like herself. I wanted her eyes to be dark; the world that she was coming into was empty. So I hollowed out her eyes. I took away her sparkle and gave her a very cold light; it was raining and dank. But at the same time, around the elevator shaft was a kind of magic, green crystal color. As if she had brought in the light with her. I wanted it to look like a surreal painting.

In consultation with the director, Militello decided to use a deeply saturated green for the Stones.

Because they're stones, they are stuck, they're confined, they can't move very well. So they are only in one atmosphere, which we decided should be a kind of sickly green.

They are gathering moss, they are not being wiped, and they are in the ground, like mold growing. I wanted to light them from below so the light source they had was buried with them in the ground.

Militello added a deep red to the lighting palette with the entrances of the Lord of the Underworld.

When the Lord of the Underworld comes in and is offering all these wonderful vices, I just made it as garishly colorful as possible. Almost like Las Vegas, it is sin city and garish and horrible. But it's in the guise of being this sparkly, colorful, enticing atmosphere. In the upper world, he's camouflaged himself. But we don't want to give it away until we see where he lives.

In contrast to the saturated light of many of the moments in the underworld, Militello interpreted the scenes of Eurydice and her father with a brighter, cleaner light. Although their time together also takes place in the underworld, these characters find a way to create a protected space for themselves. Eurydice's father makes a small house for her from string to shelter her from the turmoil outside. Obviously the string is a fragile form of protection.

I felt that there was a sweetness to the confinement. They are in a house where they are happy together. But they're sheltered and they're separated. So I shuttered the light in and I actually made a hard rectangle on the floor, so it was bright white within the space, with blue around them that didn't seep into their little string room. They were illuminated by their own excitement with each other. But for me it wasn't a warm happiness. It was weird, distorted. There was something foreboding about it. Confinement and coldness.

Finally, Militello created a lighting approach for Orpheus that set him off from the other characters, as if he is ultimately separated from the drama of Eurydice and her father.

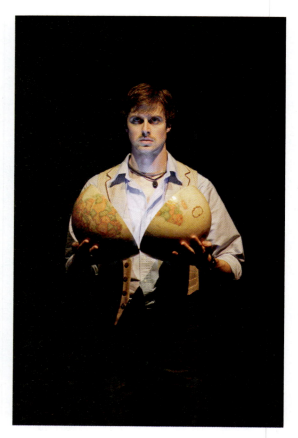

In this photo Orpheus studies the globe looking for Eurydice. His face is lit by the light source in the globe as well as the front light described by lighting designer Anne Militello. These lighting effects combine to create the sensation that Orpheus is suspended in space.

With Orpheus, I was trying to keep him separated and keep him romantic. And as a lighting designer, you also take your cue from the facial structure of an actor. He has a beautiful face, with deep-set eyes. I really wanted to see his eyes so I had to lower the angle of the light a little. His eyes were difficult to work with because I had such high angles with the front light, which I was trying to keep off the projection screen. So I had to be strategic about how I lit him, because I wanted him to appear as the angelic hope of the whole thing.

In addition to her conversations with the director about his vision of the play, Militello was strongly influenced in her design choices and the rhythm of her cueing by the sound design of Bruno Louchouarn. During the late rehearsal process, she made a number of adjustments to the lights in order to interpret what she was hearing musically. In part because she also designs rock and roll tours, she says, "I'm used to hearing music and reacting instantly. Sometimes instinct and impulse is what fuels some of the most effective work. So as I heard it, I lit it. In rehearsals."

Video Design

Exploring the Character's Unconscious

Before the lights dim on the audience for the opening of the play, a pair of narrow eyes with a yellow tinge, haunting and mysterious, appear on the stage right projection screen. They hint of a cat's eyes or perhaps a snake or possibly the devil. A much larger eye appears on the other projection screen. It is a woman's eye filling half of the screen. The face that holds the eye is blended into abstraction, only the eye is clearly from a human face. At first the image seems to be still, but then extremely slowly

the eye blinks. The eyes dissolve into clouds, then waves. Bird-calls blend with sounds of the ocean. We are at the beach. The actors playing Orpheus and Eurydice enter and the play begins with Orpheus proposing to Eurydice by tying a string around her finger. In the next scene, Eurydice's father enters imagining that he is in attendance at Eurydice's wedding. Behind him on the projection screen, Eurydice's face appears as if it is suspended in a drop of water. Eurydice's face returns to the projection screen in different versions throughout the play haunting both Orpheus and her father.

Video, exemplified by the images described above, was the fourth crucial design component in building the visual environment for Sarah Ruhl's play. The director chose to incorporate video into this production because of the way it could be used to explore the unconscious of the characters, their memories, and fragments of thought too elusive to be represented by words. The video designer, John Crawford, was concerned about the "non-narrative elements" of the play that created a "multi-layered exploration of relationships between human beings that went well beyond the story of Orpheus and

This photo represents the way the play and the production bring together the living and the dead, and actuality and memory. Orpheus and Eurydice dance at their wedding. Eurydice's father who is dead dances upstage of her, suggesting that she may be missing his presence at her wedding and remembering him. He, too, has his own longing for her, as she appears behind him on the video screen in a diffused film version of the dance being done in real time on the stage.

Eurydice or Eurydice and her father." Projected images of interior moments could "provide a livening of the set and the lighting in a way that only video could do." John Crawford spent ten years as a theatre director and then ten years studying computer science before embarking on a career that brought both fields together in the area of intermedia design for the arts.

The photo on page 185 shows a video image of Eurydice dancing at her wedding that relates to her father's attempts to reconnect with her across the vast chasm created by his death. He is imagining what her wedding would be like at the same time that the wedding is actually taking place. Father and daughter continue to seek each other in spite of the apparent finality of his death. Crawford used video to add visual detail to the characters' perceptions of each other and themselves in the father–daughter relationship and in the relationship between Orpheus and Eurydice. He wanted to explore what he saw as both physical and emotional distance. He says of Eurydice and Orpheus, "Maybe they didn't know each other that well and the play might have some connection to Orpheus's projections of who he thinks Eurydice is and Eurydice's projections of who she thinks Orpheus is."

When Eurydice dies and is transported to the underworld, Orpheus writes her a sequence of letters which he reads aloud. As their separation continues, he begins to question his certainty about everything. Orpheus says, "I thought: Eurydice is dead. Then I thought—who is Eurydice? . . . and I thought: who am I?" John Crawford explains, "I felt it was important to show how Eurydice was inhabiting, not so much his memory, but his vision of her, who she might be."

To amplify the sense of Orpheus's struggle to keep hold of some part of Eurydice following her death, Crawford created a different view of Eurydice's face to be projected during each one of the letters Orpheus reads. The faces become the woman Orpheus is trying to envision and whom he continues to lose as the play progresses.

In composing these strange faces, Crawford drew on the imagery of string used in the construction of the string house, which provides a temporary dwelling for Eurydice in the underworld (see page 183) and in the stringed instruments that Orpheus plays—string that is fragile, string that can break or unravel. Crawford discusses the process through which he created Orpheus's visions of Eurydice's face, just one of the sets of imagery he created for the production.

I began by shooting some close-up video of Eurydice's face. She is looking *for* Orpheus or imagining that she is looking *at* Orpheus. And then I chose several sections that I was particularly interested in. We only shot two or three minutes of video and I used the computer technology to create super slow motion, where instead of having a two second chunk of video, we would have a 30 second chunk of video. So the first step was creating the super slow motion. And then I used the technology called the particle system to create these strings, which I composited with the face in such a way that it started to look like the face was made of string. Or maybe, more accurately, I think it looked like the face was sketched on a string background. I wanted to come up with the feeling of something hand drawn, something not representational, but a little bit sketchy, the way our memory can sometimes be, where parts of it come in and out of our consciousness. I also had this idea of sand-memory, the way sand can kick up and obscure things. I created what I am calling the sand of memory by compositing dots with the string face in a way that gave you the feeling that the face was disintegrating. And these rendered faces were alive because they were not just a static frame, they were this super slow motion. We would get to see something like very slow blinking that put us into a different time world. I think sometimes that's when video can be most effective; when it's not competing with the real world and trying to show us real time and real space, but where it gives us the ability to perceive time slowing down or time speeding up.

The Integration of Video into the Production Process

The use of filmed imagery, including live figures in action, still images, and animation, is seen in a range of theatre productions today. From Broadway musicals to experimental site-specific pieces to a theatre work such as *War Horse*, discussed in Chapter 9, that combines large puppets with actors to an intimate play such as *Eurydice*, theatre practitioners are exploring the opportunities that filmed imagery offers to heighten theatrical expression. The use of video introduces another complex element with its own special properties that must be brought into balance with the rest of the production.

JOHN CRAWFORD: It's very important to find ways that the video supports the vision of the production rather than competes with it. And in this we really have to use two languages: the language of film and the language of the theatre. It's hard to create video that doesn't steal attention away from the production. You have to think of the time scale; you have to think of the size of the video, the fact that a video screen is almost always bigger than the actors. For example, if you put someone's face on a video screen, the nose of that face on the video screen might be as big as the whole actor is in real space. If all we're doing is watching a film, the scale is not a problem because we get used to the fact that a face can be large on the screen in the cinema or on the screen of our TV at home. But when you're trying to combine real three-dimensional people with these two-dimensional synthesized images, it becomes necessary to pay close attention to scale and to time. If you have video that is in the same tempo as the stage time, there can be a feeling of competition. Sometimes video can be most effective when it goes into a different time, when it stretches or compresses time.

Like the choices of the lighting designer, the video designer will see how the video pieces work with the production for the first time during technical rehearsals. Therefore a great deal of fast paced, creative video composition needs to be done shortly before the production opens.

JOHN CRAWFORD: I was making a lot of adjustments all the way through the tech process. Because almost all of the images are synthesized to one degree or another, they are rendered on the computer, sometimes laboriously one frame at a time. I was rendering through the entire tech process. We would finish tech at ten or eleven each night. Then I would go back to my studio and work on editing the video elements for a couple of hours and then I would set them up to render on the computer overnight. I would bring the new versions into rehearsal, see how things were working, and then after the rehearsal go back and do some more rendering. I also had multiple computers in the theatre, so I was able to do some changes to the video design as the rehearsal progressed. It was a race against time to get—not so much the big strokes—but the subtleties that are crucial to making the piece work.

Unifying the Production Through Sound

Music and sound effects have always been fundamental to theatre performance. Musical accompaniment or onstage orchestras are associated with almost all theatre traditions. Simple but ingenious solutions to sound effects can be traced to the earliest performances. A storm effect was created by snapping or shaking a metal thunder sheet; rolling wooden balls simulated the hooves of approaching horses; a slapstick accompanied the mock violence of comedy. These are all faithful elements of backstage equipment from centuries past. However, the technological advances in electronic recording equipment—first records and tape recorders and then compact discs and computerized sound applications—have completely revolutionized the way sound is produced and used in the theatre.

The sound designer now creates a sound score for a performance just as a lighting designer creates a light plot and a sequence of lighting cues. In fact, sound design shares many key functions with lighting design in the shaping of a production: deepening the mood of a scene, building the rhythm of the action, guiding transitions, providing special effects to define or punctuate important moments. For the production of *Eurydice*, the sound was as important as the light in drawing all of the elements of the production together.

The Materials of Sound Design

Sound design encompasses all of the **aural** components of a theatre production not created by the speaking voices of the actors. The sound designer may compose music for traditional instruments or on an electronic keyboard or synthesizer. The sound designer may record actual sounds such as a car door slamming or a dog barking or produce sounds through the creative manipulation of sound-producing objects. To create the score for *Eurydice*, the sound designer Bruno Louchouarn did all of these things.

Bruno Louchouarn is an accomplished musician with a broad interest in musical styles from many different cultures and from classical music to rock and roll. He plays a variety of instruments: guitar, viola, clarinet, saxophone, flute, and numerous percussion instruments. There is even a bagpipe in his studio. He is also a composer and a computer scientist and he delights in experimenting with either ordinary or unusual items that have the capacity to make interesting and convincing sounds.

In addition to the composition of music and sound, the sound designer is responsible for the amplification of sound through microphones and speakers. For some theatre productions, such as musicals, all of the actors are miked throughout the performance and wear visible microphones as part of the production aesthetic. For *Eurydice*, the actors wore hidden microphones that were used in only a few moments to create special effects such as vocal reverberation. But the placement of speakers was very important to the *Eurydice* sound design even though the play was performed in a relatively small theatre. Just as the actors entered from different places and the light shifted from area to area and came from different angles, to achieve the effect of sound that was integrated into the movement of the storytelling, the sound needed to originate in different parts of the stage space. Therefore a number of speakers were located strategically around the space. A speaker was placed at the top of the 45-foot-high elevator shaft that was used to play the first cue in the sequence of cues accompanying the descent of the raining elevator. Other speakers were placed at different heights, on the sides of the stage and at the back, as well as on the floor.

> **BRUNO LOUCHOUARN:** All the stream sound comes from speakers that are placed at ground level, so the sound basically is slithering, is hugging the ground. And reinforced by the visual, your mind hooks on it and you really feel they are in the water.

Composing and Producing the Score

For a production like *Eurydice*, Bruno Louchouarn saw himself as a storyteller who was developing musical themes to support the character arcs and action of the play.

> **BRUNO LOUCHOUARN:** There are a few big themes that are in the sound. They are traceable and they will help people relate. I think very structurally. I do sound design as part of the whole thing. But you can't have more than a few themes or people get very confused.

Louchouarn developed four major themes or motifs for the *Eurydice* score. The first theme was generated by the idea that Orpheus is a musician who is composing a gift of music for Eurydice. This theme began with gentle harp music and built into a construction of twelve melodies. The instrumentation used had a "floating" quality "because the whole world where they are is so ethereal and immaterial." The brash and vulgar Lord of the Underworld had a theme that contrasted sharply with the ethereal music associated with Orpheus. Louchouarn composed a progression of rock and roll to parallel the development of the character from a grotesque child to the immensely threatening figure at the end of the play. For the Stones, he used percussion instruments and the sounds of stones rather than a more traditional composition to create a sound that was "dry and different and rustling." And finally Louchouarn was particularly struck by the action of the play with the downward movement of all of the characters from the world above to the world below. "So there was this idea of coming down forever and ever and that being eerie and unsettling. So I worked out the descent musically." For all of the themes the music was produced through a blend of real instruments, most of which Louchouarn played himself, and instrumental music that was re-synthesized.

In addition to the four major themes related to the characters, one of the other major contributions of the sound score was to help establish the water imagery that is foundational to the play. Louchouarn had a number of strategies for creating sonic impressions of water. He recorded live sounds of rain falling, of water running through downspouts, even of water in his bathtub. He says water is "gentle and terrifying." He created cascades of water and drops of water. He used pebbles to "*imitate* drops of water because they have a very definite sound that is more energetic than (actual) drops of water." He used bells, and the harp, and glasses to make pinging sounds of water that are different than the "spooky sound of dripping reverberating in a cave." He also explains how important it was to shape the sound of water with interruptions.

> Water sounds are noise. So it can be a disaster. It can cover the voice of the actors. It can really fatigue the listener. So you want to have details that come in and out. So it has spaces: you read it and then it disappears.

Integration of the Sound Design into the Production

The musical score for *Eurydice* was so important to the production that it was introduced into the rehearsal process in advance of the technical rehearsals so that the actors would be familiar with the timing of the cues and also be able to use the sound to help build their performances.

> **BRUNO LOUCHOUARN:** You really want the actors to like the sound and the music so they will play with it and lean on it. They're going to spend a while with it and they can actually modulate their performances, which is hard.

For the composer, being present during rehearsals provided the opportunity to hear the music in conjunction with the actors' voices and experience the rhythms of the spoken language and the tempos of the actors' movements. Louchouarn attended rehearsals weekly from the beginning and then brought the score into the final week of rehearsals before tech.

> **BRUNO LOUCHOUARN:** I will have my ear buds and I will play music in my ear buds with their voices, because the voices of the actors will decide everything, the quality, the energy, where they are in the scene. The music is modulated by what the actors are saying. And sometimes I think, this is going to work, and it doesn't work and sometimes I think this is going to be great and it works. You don't want to cover the actors.

The early introduction of the music provided a testing process that supported the ongoing discussion between the director and the composer about the development of the score. And working with such a complex sound score during rehearsals allowed the stage manager to become familiar with this set of cues before also having to work with both the light cues and the video cues. Once the technical rehearsals began, Louchouarn still had many adjustments to make.

BRUNO LOUCHOUARN: This is sort of my specialty, these really complicated shows with a lot of music. Right from the get go, I write many variations of what I'm going to have in various tempos, all on separate tracks. In rehearsal, I am able very quickly to take away some instruments, move things, move entry points. It's very flexible. So I'm able to change things very quickly.

The work that Bruno Louchouarn does with musical instruments, synthesizers, computers, and sound amplification equipment is highly technical and relies on years of training and

experience. But he speaks for all of the designers whose work is discussed in this chapter when he emphasizes that the starting point for their creative efforts in working in the theatre begins with the ideas in the play.

> Technique is always important in music, in sound, in everything. But technique will always follow the concept and the imagination. It starts with ideas. What you're going to do on every project is you're going to learn. Listen to your collaborators. Collaboration is the hardest thing and the most wonderful thing.

 # Summary

Stage designers communicate the essence of a play through visual and aural forms. Although designers share skills with visual artists, craftspeople, and musicians, the goal of the stage designer is to provide a foundation for the actor, not to create art that exists for its own sake. Designers are highly imaginative in their selection of materials and their uses of technology. They may use advanced electronic and computer technologies and sophisticated methods for forming plastic or metal. They may engage in time-consuming sequences of painting, dyeing, distressing, or otherwise transforming fabric or wood. They may scavenge old material or objects from secondhand sources. Designers must combine a capacity for creating eloquent images with a capacity for practical, technological applications. They are inventors as well as artists.

The designer's work is heavily influenced by the nature of the theatrical space. The proscenium theatre is constructed in a rectangular form with the stage at one end of the rectangle. The proscenium arrangement provides the greatest degree of separation between audience and actor. In a thrust theatre the audience sits

on three sides of the stage, and an arena stage has audience members on four sides of a square or completely surrounding a circular stage space. A black box theatre is a flexible space that can be arranged in any of the preceding configurations. Large pieces of scenery and complicated scenic effects are appropriate on a proscenium stage. For thrust and arena stages, scenery must be designed so that it will not block the view of audience members. The back of scenery for a proscenium stage need not be finished. In contrast, a scenic piece on an arena stage must be finished because it will be seen from all angles.

The costume designer is concerned with establishing the period and background of the characters through silhouette and the textures of the fabrics. The costume designer establishes the individuality of characters as well as the relationships between groups of characters. He or she enhances the actor's presence without restricting the possibilities for character development.

The lighting designer unifies all the visual elements of the performance, bringing together the costumed figure of the actor and the scenic environment. The lighting designer is concerned with visibility, atmosphere, focus, and rhythm. Lighting contributes to the movement of the performance in time and also shapes stage space.

The video designer adds to the visual communication developed by the scene, costume, and lighting designers through the projection of images that can include film of live action, still photographs, or animation. Video can be projected onto screens integrated into the set design or on other surfaces including elements of either the set or the costumes. Video can provide specific information about location or historical context, but it can also add a special dimension to theatre production through the exploration of psychology or the unconscious of the characters through the inventive manipulation of imagery.

Because of rapidly advancing technology, sound design is becoming an increasingly important part of theatre production. Sound design includes the expressive area of environmental sound, such as music and sound effects; and the area of reinforcement, which involves the amplification of the actors' voices. Sound design parallels lighting design in unifying the expressive elements of the production.

Stage designers work closely together to develop a coherent production in which the design elements complement each other in terms of style, color, scale, degree of detail, and mood. The designers interpret the world of the play through visual and aural images that communicate to the audience members' senses and intellects. The stage design may be dazzling and opulent or simple and suggestive. Theatre production depends on the imagination of the designers to transform the stage space into a magical world that reveals the play in physical terms and that enhances the actors' potential.

 # Topics for Discussion and Writing

1. *Costume:* The following writing assignment explores the concept of the psychology of character used by costume designers. Begin by observing the clothing choices made by people in different locations and situations. Consider the impressions created by the clothing choices that you observe, and consider what you perceive to be the intended impressions. For example, one person may choose clothes to create an impression of power but instead project a sense of uncertainty; yet another person may be very effective in creating an aura of power. Select three people who have made distinct clothing and style choices that project a strong sense of character. Describe the choices in detail. Include your own interpretation of what is communicated to you about each person by the construction of his or her appearance. Write a one-half-to-one-page description of each observation.

2. *Light:* Bring notes to class for discussion on the following: (a) Choose an interesting outdoor location. Observe the light at three different times during the day and, if possible, under different weather conditions. (b) Choose three interior locations—such as a store, restaurant, or house—with distinctly different lighting. What kind of lighting is used in each location? Are the light sources natural or artificial? How bright is the light? Is the light soft or harsh? How does the lighting affect the appearance and mood of each space?

3. *Sound:* (a) Over the course of several days, keep a log of sounds that you hear. How many sounds did you hear that you are not normally aware of? How did the various

sounds affect your mood? What kinds of qualities do you associate with the different sounds? What sounds are soothing? What sounds are irritating? What emotional characteristics does a specific sound convey? For example, what emotion does a loud automobile horn in a traffic jam convey? Make a list of sounds that seem to have an emotional component. Include some that involve the human voice and some that do not. (b) Creating a soundscape: Work in groups of four or five. Bring interesting soundmakers to class. Using the soundmakers, as well as vocal sounds and hand sounds, compose a "soundscape" that suggests a specific location, such as a harbor, an amusement park, or a bar. Your soundscape may have individual words in it but no descriptive phrases. Think of your composition as a collage in which sounds will be layered. Some will repeat; some will fade in and out. Each soundscape should last thirty seconds. While performing the soundscapes for class members, have them close their eyes.

(c) Creating a sound story: After warming up with the soundscape, create a short dramatic story with a beginning, middle, and end, using only sound. The sound stories can be performed live or taped. Use dialogue sparingly or not at all. For example, the subject of a sound story could be a burglary that begins with the sound of cautious footsteps, followed by the rattling of a doorknob, the prying of a lock, and the breaking of glass. Other sounds might include drawers being opened and closed, papers being shuffled, and coins clinking. Breathing and muttered voices might also be used. The story could conclude with a police siren, running footsteps, and shouting. Experiment with different soundmakers to create the most interesting and vivid sounds, keeping in mind that the actual object being represented may not make the most convincing sound effect. The sound story should last from thirty to ninety seconds. Length, however, is not as important as creating an intriguing sequence of sounds.

● For interviews with some of the designers in this chapter and music segments from *Eurydice*, as well as suggested readings and other resources, please visit **www.mhhe.com/creativespirit6e**

The Nature of Style
Realism and Theatricalism

T he play is central to the expression of ideas in the theatre. Through stylistic choices playwrights give shape to their particular understanding of the human condition. The play's vocabulary, the arrangement of the words, the rhythm of the speeches, the details of the characters' lives and actions— all contribute to the way a story is told, or what we call the style of the play. In creating their dramas, playwrights draw on their own life experiences as well as traditions from both the American drama and the dramas of other nations. In Part Three we approach the examination of style by

studying the history of two major dramatic traditions: realism and theatricalism. Then we consider the works of two additional playwrights: Wakako Yamauchi and Tony Kushner. We focus on the style of the expressive elements in their plays and the way those elements are arranged to create meaning, expanding the discussion of American playwriting begun with the study of *Joe Turner's Come and Gone.*

After examining the work of the playwright, we study the way the play's meaning is further defined throughout the production process. We see that the choices of directors, actors, and designers also have stylistic significance and shape the ideas communicated to the audience. We look at Wakako Yamauchi's play *And the Soul Shall Dance,* in production at East West Players and Northwest Asian American Theatre; and Tony Kushner's play *Angels in America,* in production at the Eureka Theatre. Through the text and performance of these plays, we examine issues of self-determination and self-knowledge, family, social equality, American politics and history, race, and gender. We see the assumptions that are challenged through the plays and the contributions the plays make to social change.

Following our discussion of *Angels in America,* we expand our study of theatricalism through an exploration of the American musical theatre. We consider some of the ways music and dance are used to heighten theatrical expression and the evolution of the musical form to encompass increasingly adventurous content. Analyzing the creation of musical theatre also allows us to add the work of the composer, the lyricist, and the choreographer to our assessment of the work of theatre practitioners.

CHAPTER 7

Understanding Style: Realism

In theatrical communication, the distinctive manner in which a playwright chooses to describe, express, interpret, or present her or his worldview is referred to as **style.** A playwright makes stylistic choices, as do the theatre practitioners who mount productions. Many plays are written in one style; others, however, are written in mixed styles. Furthermore, although the goal in much theatre production is to stage a play according to the style indicated by the script, some productions seek to interpret or reinterpret material by staging a play in a different style.

Since the early twentieth century, American theatre has been dominated by the style known as **realism.** Realistic plays explore social and economic problems, psychological issues, and the personal struggles of ordinary people. Realistic productions attempt to give the audience members a sense that they are watching real life rather than a theatrical event. It is as if a "fourth wall" has been removed and the audience members are looking in at actual events. Realism is a style we frequently see on television and in movies. It is, however, only one of numerous styles seen in the American theatre.

This chapter focuses on the characteristics of realism and the realistic theatre. We begin by identifying realistic elements in *Joe Turner's Come and Gone* and considering the use of realism in film. We then examine the historical context for the development of realism and some of the most important European and American playwrights and theatre practitioners of the realistic school.

Introduction to Realism

Most forms of theatre are an exploration of some truth about human existence. Realism seeks to construct truth through an accumulation of surface detail. Realists are guided by the supposition that if we understand enough of the "facts," if we see enough of the details, we will be able to make sense of the situation. And if we see the details of the environment in which characters live or the psychological forces that affect them, we will understand why they behave as they do.

In realistic plays, audience members forget that they are in a darkened auditorium and feel transported to the locale of the play: a restaurant, a home, or a business. Functional furniture, sinks with running water, stoves that cook real food, and working radios and televisions all help to create the "illusion" that the audience sees and hears occurrences of daily life.

This illusion is heightened by the fact that the actors perform their actions, play their parts, as if the audience were not present. They do not look directly at audience members or speak to them. They address each other as if no one else were present to overhear them. If the actors do look out to where the audience is seated, they may create the impression that they are looking out a window into a garden or onto railroad tracks or into another part of the defined space. In strict realism, the actors do not acknowledge the audience's presence.

The language in realistic plays echoes the language of daily life. Characters use language that seems to come from the streets, the corner bar, or the workplace—what we can call the vernacular. Realistic plays are also frequently concerned with the way the past shapes the present. For some playwrights, heredity is an important element in the characters' identity; often, past secrets are of primary significance in understanding the characters' present. For other playwrights, environment is the crucial factor.

Realistic Elements in *Joe Turner's Come and Gone*

For August Wilson's *Joe Turner's Come and Gone*, realism is clearly a useful means of expression. The past is a crucial factor in this play, particularly the past of slavery and the chain gang. Herald Loomis's past is buried in his flesh and bones; it is a bitter secret that must be revealed before he can move into the present and then the future as a free man.

Heredity is also important. Seth inherited property and values from his father, an inheritance that puts him in a unique position. Bynum has a different kind of inheritance from his father. He has inherited a song, a way of being in the world, a vision of life's possibility. Seth contrasts sharply with most of the other characters, who have been disinherited by slavery and the political upheavals in the American South. They are cut off from the past as they try to find the basics of making a living and some sense of family or companionship.

The world that *Joe Turner's Come and Gone* presents is a daily struggle for survival. The play's environment is life as it is lived day to day in the boardinghouse. Food is prepared and eaten. Bertha's biscuits and coffee keep everyone going. Seth makes dustpans for Selig and works in his own garden. Money and sheets of metal change hands. Seth's conversations with his tenants also focus on money and the rules of the house. The basics of living arrangements and work arrangements give the play its underlying rhythm. The clatter of life—cooking, tools against metal, dishes on the table—blends with the earthy language of the characters, as Wilson employs the speech patterns and expressions of characters from a particular time and place.

A tone of sensuality also contributes to the vital atmosphere of the boardinghouse in all of the male–female relationships, most noticeably in the interactions between Jeremy and Mollie, who exude sexual energy. August Wilson constructs his play with an earthy realism to give us a richly detailed view of African American life at a turning point in American history. Although our focus at this point is on realism, we must not fail to recognize other stylistic elements in *Joe Turner's Come and Gone*, such as the mythic background that Bynum establishes with his story of the shiny man, and the larger-than-life symbolic struggle that Herald Loomis goes through to gain control of his own destiny.

Realism in Film

Realism has found its most receptive medium in film. A brief discussion of realism and film will help to further define the nature of realism. Film can create the appearance of reality far more completely than most theatre productions can. The camera, in fact, is frequently positioned at what would be the fourth wall. It becomes the silent witness that carries the audience into the most private or intimate of circumstances.

Because a film audience cannot interrupt film actors, cannot alter what is fixed on the screen, the illusion is never broken. During the course of a film, actors cannot forget their lines, because scenes are reshot to achieve a perfection that is neither possible nor even desirable in the theatre. Enormous amounts of money and energy go into building elaborate sets full of intricate, concrete details that simulate "real" spaces, whether they are homes or western towns or space stations. Alternatively, the actors and film crew often go on location and use actual places; they take over houses, public buildings, and city streets to create a realistic effect. A whole city may form the set for a car chase. Real vehicles are blown up to create the effect of car crashes. Mangled bodies and disturbing amounts of stage blood are carefully arranged to create the illusion of death and destruction. Of course, we are also aware that films can overload the senses with such an excess of spectacular realism that they lose any feeling of actuality.

The perfectability of realism in film is one of the reasons theatre practitioners do not try to create completely realistic productions. In the early part of the century, when film was in its infancy, entire restaurants or rivers with flowing water were created onstage, but rarely do we see this kind of elaborate attempt at realism in today's theatre.

By presenting an accumulation of externally observed details of human action and environment, realism gives us one view of human existence. Other styles of theatrical communication (such as expressionism; see Chapter 9) might move inside the characters' psyches and present a world shaped by distortion and exaggeration, or they might focus on large symbolic actions rather than minute details, or they might emphasize the political context of human action rather than an in-depth exploration of individual characters' lives. Today, theatrical performances are unlikely to follow only one style or another; styles tend to be mixed, reflecting the sense that we experience the world around us in different ways at the same time.

Origins of Realism

During the nineteenth century the theatre underwent profound changes, in both the subjects that playwrights chose for their plays and the style in which plays were written and performed. Before that time, as we discussed earlier in the book, serious dramas were written about royal or noble families or about religious figures. The histories or conflicts involving kings and gods were considered representative of the concerns of the entire society. Only **comedies** focused on the lives of average citizens or those who were disenfranchised, and then the focus was on human weakness.

In the nineteenth century, however, a movement began that was aimed at making the lives of middle-class and poor characters the focus of serious drama. The world inhabited by these characters was made more tangible by the use of language that seemed to come from overheard daily conversations.

In earlier styles, environment was indicated by suggestion or theatrical conventions, or backgrounds were created for the actors' presentations by a kind of generalized decoration. In the Greek theatre, for example, the scene building suggested the palace of whatever royal family was the subject of the play, and new characters were indicated by changes in masks. In the Elizabethan theatre, the throne room of the king was indicated by bringing on a chair, or a battlefield was created by the entrance of soldiers carrying banners. The audience's imagination was crucial to completing the stage image.

Decorative backgrounds became popular after the introduction of **perspective** painting by the Italians in the early seventeenth century. They were used in opera, court masques, or pageants, and then in the romantic drama of the eighteenth and early nineteenth centuries. Images of gardens or palaces were painted on flat scenic pieces that were arranged **upstage**

(the area of the stage farthest away from the audience) to create a pictorial background for the actors.

But as the drama began to consider the struggles of working people, the theatre shifted in its style of presentation in order to place those struggles in actual three-dimensional environments rather than on bare stages or in front of painted backgrounds. The material environment became a crucial factor in character development. The lives of characters living in harsh circumstances, speaking the informal language of the workplace and the home, presented in seemingly real environments, also generated the development of a new acting style. Actors and directors sought a more natural style of acting that would make

Hedda Gabler by Henrik Ibsen offers a psychological study of a nineteenth-century woman who struggles with the restrictions of middle-class society. Played here by Cate Blanchett in a production by the Sydney Theatre Company (2006), Hedda seeks power through manipulating those around her because she is too frightened of scandal to lead an independent life.

sense of the changes playwrights were bringing to the drama. No longer could actors be expected to stand at the front edge of the stage and declaim their lines with grand gestures directly to the audience. Actors had to move upstage to give the appearance that they lived in the onstage furnishings and speak to each other conversationally as if the audience were not there. This new fusion of subject matter and performance became the basis for the realistic style of theatre. A working definition of *realism* might be theatre that seeks to give the appearance of everyday life.

The Social Background of Realism

Realism occurred at a particular point in human history and served as an artistic crossroads, as a representation of the intersection of various developments in philosophical, social, and scientific thought. It is no coincidence that dramas began to portray the "common" man or woman at the same time democratic governments began to replace kings ruling by "divine right." Nor is it surprising that as advances in science and technology fueled the industrial revolution, the theatre would include more evidence of the material world. The study of human psychology also had its counterpart in the theatre, as playwrights, directors, and actors probed the sources of human behavior and looked to heredity and environment to explain why human beings act as they do. And as social reformers began to consider the inequitable distribution of wealth and the consequences of poverty, the impact of social circumstances on the development of character became an important consideration in the theatre as well.

Realism became a dominant force in the theatre as society became interested in questions of how individuals are defined by or overcome the limitations placed on them by the circumstances of their history, their environment, their social positions, and their relationships. In examining realism, however, it is always crucial to remember that although realistic plays are constructed to give the appearance of reality, realism is a theatrical style involving artistic choices; it is not life itself.

European Realism

Henrik Ibsen

The Norwegian playwright Henrik Ibsen (1828–1906) profoundly changed the nature of the European theatre when he wrote a group

Before being recognized as one of the leading playwrights of the late nineteenth century, Henrik Ibsen worked in almost every capacity in the theatre, directing plays, building scenery, and selling tickets. In addition to writing twelve plays that provided the foundation for realism in the theatre, Ibsen wrote verse plays such as *Peer Gynt* and symbolic plays such as *The Wild Duck*.

One of the early realistic plays was *An Enemy of the People* by the Norwegian playwright Henrik Ibsen. Shown here in a production directed by Trevor Nunn in 1998, Ian McKellan portrays Dr. Stockmann, a character trying to persuade his fellow citizens that the mineral baths on which the town depends for revenue must be shut down because the water is polluted.

metaphors for the characters' lives: warm but stifling rooms filled with wood stoves, rocking chairs, and needlework; or colder spaces furnished with thick, heavy couches and draperies, the windows looking out on endless rain or withered leaves.

of plays during the latter part of the nineteenth century that focused on social problems and the struggle of individuals to resist the social, religious, and familial restrictions of a tightly structured, hierarchical society. Writing about surprisingly contemporary subjects such as pollution, venereal disease, and women's rights, Ibsen brought onto the stage problems and concerns that shifted the emphasis of theatrical content. In *An Enemy of the People* (1882), for example, a town furiously turns on the doctor who exposes the pollution in the community water system because the citizens fear that their lucrative spa business will be ruined. In *A Doll's House* (1879), a woman chooses to leave her husband and children rather than go on living the charade of a doll wife in a doll's house.

Ibsen looked at the daily lives of middle-class characters as they dealt with the need to earn a living, to provide properly for their children, to find meaningful work, to establish satisfying relationships. And he placed his characters in the environment of the middle class, replacing flat, painted scenery with the detailed furnishings of three-dimensional houses. The settings became

August Strindberg

Whereas Ibsen focused on the struggle between individual self-determination and social restrictions, his fellow Scandinavian August Strindberg (1849–1912), from Sweden, laid bare the highly charged emotions of couples caught in love–hate relationships. Strindberg's characters tear at each other using words as weapons to wound or destroy each other in what frequently becomes a fight to the death. The American critic Ruby Cohn has called these verbal battles "dialogues of cruelty."[1]

In Strindberg's play *The Father* (1887), the Captain is tormented by his own unfounded doubts about his daughter's paternity. A power struggle with his wife, Laura, over the direction of their daughter's education and upbringing turns into a nightmarish conflict of manipulation and attack. Laura's cleverness in outmaneuvering her husband sends him into a violent rage that becomes her proof that he is unfit to remain in the household.

Strindberg's play *Miss Julie* (1888) adds class conflict to sexual conflict. The aristocratic mistress of a wealthy house, Miss Julie, is seduced

August Strindberg's early plays are known for their combination of detailed naturalism and emotional explosiveness. This photo of a new adaptation of *Miss Julie* (*Mies Julie*) by the playwright Yael Farber demonstrates the intensity of a conflicted sexual relationship. Farber sets the play in post-apartheid South Africa to explore the fierce struggles with identity experienced by black and white characters and the difficulties in finding balance in the newly reconstituted nation. The production was originally staged by the Baxter Theatre Centre of Capetown and premiered at the Grahamstown National Arts Festival, both in South Africa, before traveling to St. Ann's Warehouse in New York where this photo was taken in 2012. Mies Julie is played by Hilda Cronje, John is played by Bongile Mantsai, and his mother (in this adaptation) Christin is played by Thoko Ntshinga. Yael Farber is also the director. Many critics feel that this new adaptation provides Strindberg's play with its most compelling presentation for a contemporary audience.

by the valet, Jean. Their struggle for domination in the relationship results in her suicide. This brief and intense relationship unleashes bitter, insulting denunciations from both characters that alternate with painful admissions of dependency. Strindberg's pessimistic examination of male–female relationships was in part meant to answer Ibsen's apparent championship of women's rights.

Anton Chekhov

The third major playwright in the development of European realism was the Russian Anton Chekhov (1860–1904). Chekhov finished his medical degree and supported himself and his family as a writer during his student days, before he turned to writing as his primary occupation. He wrote numerous short stories and sketches,

Anton Chekhov's medical training and his own problems with tuberculosis seemed to make him an especially acute observer of human interactions. He approached his characters with an objectivity that revealed human weakness in all of them. He was sympathetic to his characters yet gently exposed their hypocrisy and vanity.

and at the end of his career and his short life he wrote the four plays that established his unique place in the theatre.

Chekhov's plays have neither the complicated plots of Ibsen nor the emotional fireworks of Strindberg. In fact, very little seems to happen in Chekhov's plays. The characters barely hear each other, so absorbed are they by their own concerns. In *The Cherry Orchard* (1904), for example, a group of characters gather at the family estate supposedly to prevent the sale of their beloved cherry trees. But while they gossip and give sad little parties and fret endlessly over their own failures, the cherry orchard slips away, sold to a developer who will cut down the trees for summer cottages. The developer was once a peasant on the very land that he has purchased. As a friend of the family members, he has tried to advise them on ways to save the cherry orchard, but they are incapable of hearing him. Chekhov's characters speak passionately about love, but lasting relationships prove to be as elusive for them as the ability to save the cherry orchard.

Although much in Chekhov's plays is very painful, the plays are actually full of humor. By juxtaposing incongruous incidents and exposing the foolishness of characters who take themselves too seriously, the Chekhovian world shifts constantly between evoking sympathy and evoking laughter. Chekhov concentrated on the small details of his characters' lives and wrote dialogue that frequently goes unanswered because the characters are more interested in what they have to say than in listening to each other. Although Chekhov chose each detail carefully, his plays lack the obvious buildup of increasing tension and the exciting plot development that shape the dramas of Ibsen and Strindberg. But because of the seeming randomness of the actions and dialogue, Chekhov's plays may be the most realistic, the most like life. And yet the construction of the worldview through carefully selected objects and actions gives a heightened sense of life that takes on a poetic quality.

American Realism

Realism was the dominant style of American theatre in the first half of the twentieth century. Lillian Hellman (1905–1984), Arthur Miller (1915–2005), and Tennessee Williams (1911–1983) consolidated and shaped the foundation of American realism during the 1930s and 1940s. Hellman and Miller were particularly concerned with the moral positions of their characters, whereas Williams wrote about

The Three Sisters by Anton Chekhov is shown in a 2013 production directed by Les Waters at Berkeley Rep. Note the realistic detail of the interior and the characters engaged in a variety of different pursuits: dancing, drinking, playing cards. The characters' hopes for a lively evening are soon to be disappointed when Natasha enters to insist their revelry will wake her sleeping children. The actors include Alex Moggridge and Heather Wood. The set design is by Annie Smart; costume design by Ilona Somogyi.

highly sensitive characters struggling to reconcile personal longing with the harsh and judgmental society surrounding them. Hellman and Williams also brought issues of gay and lesbian sexuality onto the stage, startling their audiences, given the taboos concerning such subjects at the time.

Lillian Hellman

Lillian Hellman's first major play, *The Children's Hour*, was produced in New York in 1934. The play is the story of two young women teachers whose lives are ruined by a lie told by a restless student looking for attention. In both *The Children's Hour* and *The Little Foxes* (1939), which looks at the greed and exploitation inherent in American capitalism, Hellman was concerned with characters who are aware of a wrong being perpetrated but who do not step forward, thereby leaving a void that is quickly filled by slander and manipulation. The kind of realism used by Hellman in her plays is reminiscent of Ibsen, with an emphasis on the concrete details of the characters' lives and a plot in which one incident causes the next.

Clifford Odets (1906–1963) was a founding member of the Group Theatre, a company instrumental in the development of realism in playwriting and acting in the United States. Among the plays he wrote for the Group Theatre was *Golden Boy*, about a young man torn between a career as a violinist and the seductive world of boxing with its opportunities for adulation and immediate wealth. The play was revived on Broadway in 2012 in a production that was noted for the realism of the boxing sequences as well as the contrast between the world of gamblers and fight managers and the struggling family of Joe Bonaparte. In this photo, Joe, Seth Numrich, has begun to achieve the success he craves including the affection of Lorna Moon, played by Yvonne Strahovski. The production was directed by Bartlett Sher for Lincoln Center Theater.

Arthur Miller continued to be a force in American theatre and film until shortly before his death in 2005. A highly regarded revival of *Death of a Salesman,* with Brian Dennehy playing Willy Loman, was produced on Broadway in 1999. It was followed by a new production of *The Crucible,* about the Salem witch trials, in 2002 with Liam Neeson and Laura Linney. Miller also participated in the adaptation of his play *A View from the Bridge* into an opera, which premiered in 1999 and continues to be produced at opera houses around the country. And more recently he wrote a new play, *Resurrection Blues,* produced in 2002 at the Guthrie Theater in Minneapolis, which in Miller's words is about "the commercialization of everything."

Poetic Realism: Arthur Miller and Tennessee Williams

Arthur Miller and Tennessee Williams transformed the realism of Hellman's work by focusing on a psychological exploration that places the characters' memories and fantasies onstage.

Williams's *A Streetcar Named Desire* (1947) and Miller's *Death of a Salesman* (1949) begin in what seem to be realistic family situations but then change the point of view by moving inside the minds of characters who are beginning to slip away from reality. The plays shift back and forth between the present and the past, and it becomes impossible to know if what the characters remember is truth or illusion.

In *Death of a Salesman* the walls actually dissolve, allowing the space to become as flexible as

Biff (John Malkovich) tries to convince his father Willy (Dustin Hoffman) that neither of them was meant to be a leader of men, in Arthur Miller's most famous play, *Death of a Salesman,* produced here in 1984.

the title character's mind. In *A Streetcar Named Desire* symbolic characters enter the seemingly realistic stage space. The imagery and structure of Miller's and Williams's plays inspired memorable productions directed by Elia Kazan and designed by Jo Mielziner in a style that came to be known as **poetic realism.** For decades, this style was considered the most eloquent representation of American drama.

Arthur Miller's first play, *All My Sons* (1947), is a traditional, realistic family drama that concerns the corrosive effect of greed on the human spirit and the need for individuals to take responsibility, both for the larger society and for their families. In this play, the father, Joe Keller,

has sold flawed aircraft parts to the government during World War II. His partner, a less forceful man, goes to prison when this fraud is exposed. Although Keller continues to proclaim his innocence, his own son, a pilot in the war, disappears in combat, unable to live with the knowledge of his father's crime against all the young pilots destined to fly unsafe equipment.

Miller took the essence of the family drama from *All My Sons*, the conflict between fathers and sons, and expanded its dimensions in his play *Death of a Salesman*. In this play, the father, Willy Loman, is driven to suicide by the fear that he has failed his son, Biff. Biff, who was full of promise until his senior year in high school, has spent his adult life drifting from job to job, and even serving a stint in prison for stealing. Through flashbacks we see Willy's obsession with Biff's youth and Willy's attempt to defend the lesson that he repeatedly taught him: to create an image for yourself in a world in which everything is for sale rather than build a base of accomplishment.

Although the play critiques the notion of success in the United States as measured by dollar signs, it also looks again to the theme of responsibility for one's children and the children of the nation. Here Miller presents a character cut off from his roots, cut off from his heritage, who consequently does not know what to teach his own children.

Tennessee Williams came to prominence as a playwright with his play *The Glass Menagerie* (1944). The central character, Tom, ultimately abandons his domineering mother and fragile sister in order to make a life for himself. The mother, Amanda, lives through exaggerated memories of her own youth as a much sought-after southern belle, while the sister, Laura, lives in an imaginary world she shares with her glass figurines. Laura is too mentally unstable to cope

with life beyond the shabby family apartment; she is a complete contradiction of her mother's fantasy that a gentleman caller will appear to marry her and transform all their lives.

In *A Streetcar Named Desire*, Williams explores the disintegration of a young woman, Blanche Dubois, who retreats further and further into a world of illusions to block out her own failures and the failures of those around her to live up to a code of gentility from a bygone era. When her reduced circumstances force her to move in with her sister, Stella, and brother-in-law, Stanley, the tensions between the characters explode in Stanley's sexual assault on Blanche and her final collapse.

Konstantin Stanislavsky and Realistic Acting

The new realistic dramas of the nineteenth century prompted actors to rethink the nature of their craft. The most influential figure in the development of a new approach to acting was Konstantin Stanislavsky (1863–1938), an actor who became a prominent stage director and teacher as cofounder and artistic director of the Moscow Art Theatre. Stanislavsky directed the initial productions of all of Chekhov's plays. It was in part from his work with Chekhov that Stanislavsky evolved his approach to acting—one appropriate to the subtlety

In the 2013 production of *The Glass Menagerie* at American Repertory Theatre in Cambridge, Laura loses herself in the beauty of her glass unicorn, which allows her to retreat from the demands of living in the real world. Laura is played by Celia Keenan-Bolger.

Tracy Letts' play *August: Osage County* explores the tensions and secrets of a large family that gathers in their mother's home when her husband mysteriously disappears. With the bitterness of the mother, Violet Weston, at the heart of the family's dysfunction, revelations of alcoholism, drug addiction, and sexual misconduct run through the characters' attacks on each other. Letts writes with biting humor as well as verbal savagery, building on the family dramas that have been at the center of American realism. The production shown in this photo was first staged at Steppenwolf Theater in Chicago and then on Broadway under the direction of Anna Shapiro in 2007.

character would emerge in his or her place. He proposed an internal rather than an external approach to character development.

From Stanislavsky's work has come the idea that one of the major sources for character development should be the life of the actor. That is, the actor should draw on personal experiences and relationships to provide the foundation for the character's inner life. The actor should also study the role closely to discover a network of objectives—motivations that can then carry the actor from moment to moment. At all times the actor must know what the character's intention is. The actor may then invent strategies or tactics to achieve the objective. Each objective, together with the actions and words involved in playing that objective, is considered a **beat.** A role is composed of a sequence of beats that together form a coherent **through line** for the character. The character's dominant motive, or the **superobjective,** will make sense of all the smaller objectives that feed into the particular focus of the character.

In developing this internal acting approach, Stanislavsky was particularly concerned with keeping actors in an alert and creative frame of mind to offset the numbness that he believed resulted from the endless repetitions of the same lines and actions in rehearsals and performances. Stanislavsky also looked to maximize actors' concentration so they could focus on their creative work rather than on the distractions of playing in front of an audience.

In the United States in the 1930s, theatre practitioners associated with the Group Theatre (a company dedicated to the production of works

and introspection of Chekhov's characters. This approach has become a mainstay of realistic theatre and film.

The ideas suggested by Stanislavsky have come to be organized into something of a system that is frequently referred to as **method acting.** In his own time, however, Stanislavsky was continuously reviewing and adjusting his approach. Stanislavsky believed that the actor should look for ways to identify as closely as possible with his or her character, to undergo a transformation in which the actor would disappear and the by new playwrights and to the development of a new acting style) became interested in Stanislavsky's work, which they adapted for the American theatre. Lee Strasberg, Stella Adler, and Morris Carnovsky contributed their interpretations of an internal approach to acting, and their modifications of Stanislavsky's work became the basis for much American acting both on the stage and in film. Many contemporary American productions continue to reflect this influence, such as the productions of *The Piano Lesson* and *Dying City* shown on pages 48 and 124, in addition to the acting preparation that we have discussed for *Joe Turner's Come and Gone* and for *And the Soul Shall Dance.*

Furthermore, the effect of Stanislavsky's work is felt worldwide. Shortly after American actors went to Russia to meet with Stanislavsky, a Chinese director, Jiao Juyin, studied Stanislavsky's writings and began to translate realistic Russian plays into Chinese. In 1952, Jiao became a founding member of the Beijing People's Art Theatre (BPAT), which was modeled on Stanislavsky's Moscow Art Theatre. At the BPAT, Jiao introduced his understanding of Stanislavsky's method as the foundation for performing in the spoken-language drama of China. According to this leading figure in Chinese directing, acting, and playwriting, "Distinguished characterization comes out of profound inner experiences."[2] However, in order to create a distinctly Chinese presentation for realistic drama, Jiao also promoted integrating some performance traditions from Chinese folk art, including *xiqu*, the Chinese opera. In addition to interest in Chekhov, the Chinese have found the plays of Henrik Ibsen to offer insight into the social struggles of their country and have produced his plays, particularly *A Doll's House*, since early in the twentieth century. In 1983, Arthur Miller was invited to come to the BPAT to direct *Death of a Salesman* and so contributed an Americanized idea of realistic acting to the evolving spoken-language theatre in China. Today, Lin Zhaohua, the current director of the BPAT, affirms that Stanislavsky is still the guiding force behind the acting approach of his company, both for the growing number of plays written by Chinese playwrights and the international repertoire.[3]

Summary

The theatrical style called realism includes elements of both playwriting and production. Realistic plays are concerned with social problems and the struggles that characters undergo to overcome difficulties of circumstance. The relationship of the present to the past is important, as is the connection between cause and effect. Realistic plays present incidents, characters, and language that appear to come from daily life. The truth of a situation is expressed through observable, external details of character and situation.

Among the European playwrights whose work formed the foundation of the realistic style are Henrik Ibsen, August Strindberg, and Anton Chekhov; American playwrights who developed a realistic theatre in this country include Lillian Hellman, Arthur Miller, Clifford Odets, and Tennessee Williams. In the work of Miller and Williams we see an evolution of a style based on realism that becomes more poetic in its expression. Konstantin Stanislavsky's work on an internal approach to acting, which emphasized the actor's identification with the character's psychological motivation, provided the basis for much American acting on the stage and in films today.

Topics for Discussion and Writing

1. What is meant by the term *realism?* What are examples of realistic elements in *Joe Turner's Come and Gone?* What is the most realistic play or film that you have seen recently?

2. Anton Chekhov writes dialogue in which the characters do not listen to each other, and frequently one character responds by saying things unrelated to the subject of another character. Listen to several different groups of people talking together under different circumstances. Where do you see examples of Chekhov's observation that people are so absorbed by their own problems and concerns that they fail to hear the concerns of others?

3. If Ibsen were to write social problem plays today, what kinds of social problems might he address?

● For suggested readings and other resources related to this chapter, please visit **www.mhhe.com/creativespirit6e**

CHAPTER 8

Expressing a Worldview through Realism

Looking at *And the Soul Shall Dance*

by Wakako Yamauchi

Wakako Yamauchi is another contemporary American playwright working in the realistic style. Yamauchi's plays have been compared to those of Anton Chekhov because of the small but precisely chosen details with which she renders her characters' lives and the quiet anguish that the

characters express. Her plays also focus on a group of characters rather than on a central individual. And like Tennessee Williams, whom she acknowledges as a major influence, Yamauchi creates plays with a heightened, lyrical quality.

We turn now to an exploration of the play *And the Soul Shall Dance,* by Wakako Yamauchi, with a focus on its realistic elements. Following the text of the play we analyze two different productions: one at East West Players in Los Angeles and the other at Northwest Asian American Theatre in Seattle. In our analysis of these productions, we take a close look at the development of performance techniques used in realistic staging.

The Muratas (Sharon Omi and Nelson Mashita) face the hardships of immigrant life by relying on each other's strength and will to endure, in the production staged by East West Players, directed by Jim Ishida.

Exploring the Text of *And the Soul Shall Dance*

Like August Wilson's *Joe Turner's Come and Gone*, Wakako Yamauchi's *And the Soul Shall Dance* gives us a detailed view of a particular time and place in the United States. The play examines a brief passage of time in the life of an eleven-year-old girl, Masako, through what seems to be a memory of childhood. As Masako returns to this critical moment in her formative years, we experience with her the life of Japanese immigrants to the United States in the 1930s.

On the surface the play presents the harsh realities of immigrant life, of lives circumscribed by U.S. laws that preclude citizenship and land ownership, of a people who have left their homeland and find themselves out of place in their new circumstances. Underneath the story of survival is another story of longing for a life that is more than mere drudgery. For the adult characters, the longing is to return to Japan. For the child, Masako, the longing concerns a desire to create her own identity, to find her own place in the culture that is so alien to her parents.

And the Soul Shall Dance juxtaposes the contrasting experiences of two Japanese immigrant families farming the Imperial Valley in California during the 1930s. Each family suffers hardships. One carries on with grace and humor because the family relationships are intact; the warm regard of the parents for each other and their daughter creates a refuge from the economic struggle and the cultural isolation. The other family builds a closed world of alcoholism and abuse that deepens their dislocation.

Plot and Characters

And the Soul Shall Dance has a simple plot that follows the encounters of the two families over a period of about one year. The Muratas and the Okas are brought together when the Murata bathhouse burns down because of Masako's carelessness. When the Muratas are invited to use the Okas' bathhouse, the bitter secrets of the Oka family begin to emerge.

Mr. Oka has a daughter, Kiyoko, in Japan whom he has not seen for years. Kiyoko feels abandoned by Oka, and he is desperate for money to bring her to the United States. Kiyoko is the daughter of a previous, happier marriage. As a young man, Oka was married to his current wife's sister, who died after her husband had emigrated to the United States in search of a better life for his small family. The dead woman's sister, Emiko, left Japan under mysterious circumstances. She was married to Oka by proxy after her sister's death and sent to the United States by her parents. The second Oka marriage has degenerated into hostility and recrimination.

Emiko Oka emerges as a most surprising character. She is an alcoholic who drinks and smokes openly. She flouts all traditional standards of Japanese decorum. At the same time, she is devoted to the traditional Japanese arts of dance and music. The arranged marriage is a disaster for both husband and wife. Emiko is already on the edge of madness at the beginning of the play. The arrival of the daughter, Kiyoko, leads directly to catastrophe for her stepmother-aunt, Emiko.

Personal, Cultural, and Historical Contexts of the Play

The Play as Memory

Although the play is obviously about the contrasting lives of the two families, the point of view is that of Masako, the Muratas' daughter. The play consists of events that would have made a significant impression on an adolescent girl and that still seem worth telling by the adult that Masako has become. At the end of the play, Masako's mother, Hana, points to this memory when she says,

> Maybe someday when you're grown up, gone away, you'll . . . remember yourself as this little girl . . . remember this old house, the ranch, and . . . your old mama. . . . (act 2, scene 5)

And the Soul Shall Dance takes the playwright back to her earliest memories of her own family history, to a time when her sense of herself as an artist began to unfold. As an artist, Yamauchi aspired to transcend the limitations of the first-generation Japanese immigrants in America, known as *Issei*. Yamauchi originally wrote *And the Soul Shall Dance* as a short story but later adapted it as a drama. The original short story makes the point of view of memory very clear in its opening words:

> It's all right to talk about it now. Most of the principals are dead, except, of course, me and my younger brother, and possibly Kiyoko Oka, who might be near forty-five now because, yes, I'm sure of it, she was fourteen then. I was nine, and my brother about four,

Distraught, Emiko (Dawn A. Saito) holds an empty can that no longer contains her savings. The money that she hoped would take her back to Japan has been spent by her husband, Oka, to "Americanize" his daughter. This production is by the Pan Asian Repertory Theatre.

so he hardly counts. Kiyoko's mother is dead, my father is dead, my mother is dead, and her father could not have lasted all these years with his tremendous appetite for alcohol and pickled chiles—those little yellow ones, so hot they could make your mouth hurt—he'd eat them like peanuts and tears would surge from his bulging thyroid eyes in great waves and stream down the coarse terrain of his face.[1]

The play approaches the issue of memory through Masako's position in the structure of the scenes. She is the only character who appears in almost every scene, and frequently we see her as she is watching the other characters. The play, then, is about the startling entrance of the Oka family into Masako's consciousness and her assessment of their strangeness in relation to the accepted "normalcy" of her own family. Masako, who seeks a wider view of life than can be imagined or accommodated in the safety of her own home, finds tantalizing possibilities in the aberrant behavior of the elusive neighbor, Emiko. The importance of the memory lies in the way Emiko's rebellion and her life as an artist, as eccentric as both may be, serve to open up possibilities for Masako. The memory is the beginning of Masako's consciousness of herself as an artist.

The play builds layers of feeling as Masako's memory intersects with the memories of Emiko and Masako's mother, Hana. The empathetic child is able to enter these other memories and consider what they may mean for her future. Emiko's memory is of beauty and grace. She lives in her memory of herself dancing and singing, studying the arts of Japanese high culture. And, most significantly, this memory of classical training allows her to sustain a memory of love and desire. She lives for the man she would have chosen for herself if her family had not intervened because he was unacceptable to them.

Hana is also sustained by her memories. She too longs to return to Japan. But instead of indulging in the past, she suppresses her memories in order to function in the present. She consciously chooses practical solutions, even though we see that under other circumstances she would have cultivated her imagination for more than survival.

Personal History

Both the short stories and the plays of Wakako Yamauchi are largely autobiographical. Yamauchi

---

IN CONTEXT

Legislation Restricting Asian Immigration

Date	Act
1790	Naturalization Law: declared only whites eligible to become naturalized citizens of the United States.
1882	Chinese Exclusion Act: barred immigration of Chinese nationals.
1913	First Alien Land Law (California): declared Japanese immigrants could lease land for a period of no more than three years; barred purchase of land by Japanese immigrants.
1920	Second Alien Land Law (California): barred lease or purchase of land by individual Japanese nationals or corporations.
1922	U.S. Supreme Court decision in the *Ozawa* case: decided that a Japanese national whom the Court deemed qualified in every other way for citizenship could be denied citizenship because he was not white.
1924	National Origins Act (Immigration Act of 1924): barred immigration of aliens ineligible for citizenship—that is, barred nonwhites; aimed particularly at Japanese, who were consequently barred from immigration to the United States for the next twenty-eight years, until 1952; excluded all Asian immigrants except Filipinos.
1934	Tydings-McDuffie Act: limited Filipino immigration to the United States to fifty people per year.
1942	Executive Order 9066, President Franklin D. Roosevelt: ordered incarceration of all West Coast people of Japanese heritage; of the 120,000, two-thirds were American citizens by birth.[2] Both Wakako Yamauchi and Chiura Obata were interned.

The history of Japanese Americans in the United States is particularly marked by their internment during World War II. The artist Chiura Obata interpreted that experience in drawings and paintings. This painting, created in 1943, is entitled *Topaz War Relocation Center by Moonlight* and shows the darkening sky over the remote settlement of barracks. In 1965 Obata wrote the following of the internment ordeal. "The biggest difficulty was not being able to work fully toward our hopes and expectations. Other than that, anything physical or the desert storms, those things were secondary. The biggest hardship was when we wanted to do something, we couldn't let our ability grow, and we couldn't contribute to society."[3]

was born in 1924 in Westmoreland, California. Both of her parents were *Issei*. The playwright is, in fact, Masako, the child whose memory forms the basis for the play. Yamauchi's childhood was spent moving from one shabby rented farm to another as her parents struggled with the precariousness of being part of an unwelcome immigrant community.

Yamauchi's mother was eighteen or nineteen in 1920, when she came to the United States. Her father, thirteen years older than her mother, was thirty-two. Theirs was an arranged marriage that resulted from financial developments. Yamauchi's mother came from the merchant class, as did her father. Her maternal grandfather was a tea packer. Her paternal grandfather made fish cakes. Yamauchi's maternal grandfather had many daughters but no son to inherit the family business and carry forth the family name. Therefore, the grandfather "adopted" a son-in-law and gave him his name (much like the character Oka in *And the Soul Shall Dance* who tells the story of giving up his own name for that of his father-in-law).

But then a son was born to Yamauchi's grandfather and his second wife. For the son-in-law, seeing his inheritance slip away to the new baby was too much to bear, and he embezzled the family money, leaving the business bankrupt. So Yamauchi's mother had no financial prospects to offer potential suitors, and the grandfather accepted the one proposal that she received from a young man who had returned to Japan to marry and then take his new wife to California.

The young couple had neither the skills nor the background that would prepare them for the life they would face in California. Nor did they have relatives to turn to. Everything would depend on their own ingenuity and hard work. Their lives were governed by laws such as the California Alien Land Law, which barred Japanese immigrants from buying property, and the naturalization statutes and Supreme Court decisions that specifically excluded Asian immigrants from becoming American citizens. Because they could not own land and were forced to move every two or three years, many of the Japanese immigrant farmers had to grow annual crops such as carrots, which were particularly vulnerable to drought and rain, rather than planting more stable nursery stock such as fruit trees.

Prejudice, Discrimination, and Internment

Prejudice against Asians in the United States was encouraged by a combination of business and union interests, the political maneuvering of state and national legislators, and powerful media interests such as the Hearst newspapers. The precarious position of Asian immigrants was forged by contradictions in the workings of the nation. The country was eager for Asian labor to build the railroads and to work in the canneries and the fields. Although the nation would prosper from the backbreaking labor of Asian nationals and the farming techniques they introduced to irrigate the dry valleys of California, it was unwilling to treat Asian workers equally under the laws or to provide them the opportunities enjoyed by "white" residents. Comparisons to current debates about immigration, particularly with respect to Latin American immigrants, are unavoidable.

An extremely prejudicial attitude toward Japanese and Chinese people was well established on the West Coast long before the Japanese bombed Pearl Harbor in 1941 and the U.S. government incarcerated all West Coast Japanese nationals and Japanese Americans in detention camps. The internment of the "Japanese," fully

---

THE AUTHOR SPEAKS

Wakako Yamauchi

Why does anyone write? To record a time, maybe; to get things right.[4]

. . .

My mother died and I felt I had to put something down for my daughter to remember me because mothers don't tell their kids everything; but at least if she read my stories, my plays, she'd know what kind of person I am . . . or was.[5]

Wakako Yamauchi wrote about the incarceration of Japanese Americans during World War II in her play *12-1-A*. The title refers to the barracks in which the central characters live at the camp in Poston, Arizona. Here, the characters arrive at the camp with the one suitcase each they are allowed to bring and the identification tags they are required to wear. Becky Roscher, May Cha, Brian Kameoka, Chisao Hata, Phil Duong, S. H. Kim, and Tsune Tateoka play the characters who must learn to survive a new form of dislocation, in a production directed by Stephanie Arnold in 1999. The set design is by Mark Prieto.

two-thirds of whom were American citizens by birth, remains one of the travesties of American democracy. Among the many disturbing aspects of this infamous episode in American race relations are two that reveal the prevailing American attitude toward Asian immigrants at this time. One is that many West Coast Americans profited from the acquisition of possessions of Japanese Americans who were incarcerated. The other is that Americans of German (European) descent were not treated as enemies of the nation.

The Play as Social Document

Like the writing of August Wilson, the plays and short stories of Wakako Yamauchi have great value as social documents as well as works of art. They record the experiences and events that shaped the lives of a group of people whose history has gone largely unrecorded. Whereas some historians write about the events they experience firsthand in journals or diaries, Yamauchi has recorded her history in short stories, plays, and, more recently, memoirs.

Yamauchi's work as a writer is both historical and personal. She explores her own evolving consciousness as an artist and as a woman at the same time that she explores the family and community life for Japanese immigrants and Japanese Americans at different stages of their American history. Yamauchi is particularly concerned with gender issues, as the men and women in her stories and plays make awkward and frequently unsuccessful attempts to adapt

The artist Chiura Obata documented the internment experience of Japanese Americans in drawings and paintings, as Wakako Yamauchi recorded the experience in plays. Obata was interned at Topaz, Utah; Yamauchi at Poston, Arizona. In this drawing, Obata shows the wind blowing a kind of smoky dust into the barracks room occupied by his family. The scene is reminiscent of the character action in *12-1-A* or in *And the Soul Shall Dance.* The characters do everything in their power to maintain a sense of normalcy and dignity while facing an overwhelming struggle with the environment. *Dust Storm in the Barracks* was a drawing made in 1942.

nature. For the women characters this stifling of ambitions is part of a pattern in which they are forced to assume the responsibility for their families' survival while the men abandon the struggle.

Evoking a World Through Detail

And the Soul Shall Dance presents characters caught between cultures whose memories of the past constantly seep into the present. Yamauchi has chosen the small moments of her characters' lives as the most revealing reflections of the deep disturbance caused by this cultural collision. Through a realistic approach to the material world, the playwright gives us concrete details that bring to life the two cultures that exert such strong pulls on the characters.

The plot of *And the Soul Shall Dance* revolves around key objects. The bathhouse burns to the ground. Oka must sell his horse to raise money for Kiyoko's passage by ship from Japan. The families listen to memory-laden records on the Victrola. Oka takes the money that Emiko has been saving to return to Japan and spends it on Americanizing and pampering his daughter with clothes, trips to the hairdresser, and movies. The realistic plotting of the play concludes with Emiko's painful attempts to sell her kimonos to Hana and Masako.

The focus on these objects defines the world of the play very carefully. The period, the culture of the characters, and their economic circumstances are quickly established. Motives and values are also defined in relation to this presentation of the material world. Oka, desperate for affection, does for his daughter what he cannot do for his wife. He surrounds her with American "luxuries"; he tries to overcome his cultural isolation by creating the appearance that he and Kiyoko are part of America, that they fit in. Emiko will sell her most treasured possessions, her kimonos, before she will give up her dream

their relationships from Japanese expectations to the demands and shifting cultural perspectives of their new circumstances. The plays and stories are full of misunderstood and unfulfilled sexual longing. Male and female characters frequently fail to understand each other's aspirations; and they stifle rather than nurture individual development, particularly of an artistic or intellectual of recovering the sense of herself that she projects onto Japan.

Another characteristic of realism is that the objects used in the play and the material concerns, such as crop failure and financial worries, not only ground the lives of the characters in a particular time and place and form an integral part of the plot structure but also have symbolic significance. *And the Soul Shall Dance* is dense with objects that communicate layers of meaning. For example, the food and drink—the sake, chiles and tea—that Hana puts on the table are signs of a functioning home, of warmth and nourishment. In contrast, Emiko refuses to make tea. The absence of food at the Okas' house symbolizes the emptiness of the dwelling; the family members fail to nurture each other. The illegal liquor they brew and the cigarettes Emiko smokes are poisonous substitutes for the missing food. The parents' addictions are part of the profound dysfunction of the family. At the same time that the cigarettes indicate a self-destructive attitude, they are also an important symbol of Emiko's rebellion against her husband and the accepted Japanese social structure.

Even the hairstyles of the two daughters have extremely important symbolic value. Kiyoko is transformed by a permanent wave in act 2 of the play. The processed curly hair says a great deal about the father–daughter relationship and the movement of Oka and Kiyoko toward an image of assimilation. The permanent wave suggests the fabrication of a value system to cover the confusion brought on by their dislocation. The permanent wave is also a weapon in the war between husband and wife. Oka revenges himself on Emiko by spending on Kiyoko the money that Emiko has hoarded to return to Japan. Additionally, the permanent wave provides a way of acknowledging the firm foundation of the Murata family. Hana shows her love and regard for her daughter and also her own strength and stability when she says simply to Masako at the end of the play, "Your hair is so black and straight . . . nice."

The use of objects to develop the symbolic meaning of the play leads to one final conclusion about realism. The careful selection of lifelike details highlights the characters' experiences. Realism, in fact, has its own poetic quality. A movement of the spirit is expressed in the precisely chosen actions and objects that contain the essence of the characters' lives. The appearance of reality becomes a concentrated view of a particular way of life. In *And the Soul Shall Dance*, the simplicity of the play's structure, delicately rendered like Japanese brush painting, presents an almost lyrical impression of memory and longing.

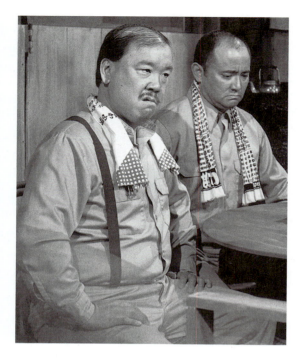

And the Soul Shall Dance

WAKAKO YAMAUCHI

CHARACTERS

MURATA, 40, *Issei* farmer
HANA, 35, *Issei* wife of Murata
MASAKO, 11, *Nisei* daughter of the Muratas
OKA, 45, *Issei* farmer
EMIKO, 30, wife of Oka
KIYOKO, 14, Oka's daughter

Kokoro Ga Odoru	**And the Soul Shall Dance**
Akai kuchibiru	Red lips
Kappu ni yosete	Press against a glass
Aoi sake nomya	Drink the green wine
Kokoro ga odoru	And the dreams will dance
Kurai yoru no yume	In the dark night
Setsu nasa yo	Dreams are unbearable
Aoi sake nomya	Drink the green wine
Yume ga odoru	And the soul shall dance
Asa no munashisa	The morning's truth

Yume wo chirasu	Scatter the dreams
Sora to kokoro wa	Sky and soul
Sake shidai	Are suspended by wine
Futari wakare no	In the separation
Samishisa yo	The desolation
Hitori sake nomya	Drink the wine
Kokoro ga odoru	And the soul shall dance

ACT ONE

Scene 1

Summer afternoon, 1935. Interior of the Murata house. The set is spare. There are a kitchen table, four chairs, a bed, and on the wall, a calendar indicating the year and month: June 1935. A doorway leads to the other room. Props are: a bottle of sake, two cups, a dish of chiles, a phonograph, and two towels hanging on pegs on the wall. A wide wooden bench is outside.

The bathhouse has just burned to the ground due to MASAKO's carelessness. Offstage there are sounds of MURATA putting out the fire. Inside, HANA MURATA, in a drab house-dress, confronts MASAKO (in summer dress). MASAKO is sullen and defiant.

HANA: How could you be so careless, Masako? You know you should be extra careful with fire. How often have I told you? Now the whole bathhouse is gone. I told you time and again—when you stoke a fire, you must see that everything is swept into the fireplace.

(MURATA enters. He is in old work clothes. He suffers from heat and exhaustion.)

MURATA: (coughing) Shack went up like a match-box. This kind of weather dries everything . . . just takes a spark to make a bonfire out of that dry timber.

HANA: Did you save any of it?

MURATA: No. Couldn't.

HANA: (to MASAKO) How many times have I told you . . .

(MASAKO moves nervously.)

MURATA: No use crying about it now. *Shikata ga nai.* It's gone now. No more bathhouse. That's all.

HANA: But you've got to tell her. Otherwise she'll make the same mistake. You'll be building a bathhouse every year.

(MURATA removes his shirt and wipes off his face. He throws his shirt on a chair and sits at the table.)

MURATA: *Baka!* Ridiculous!

MASAKO: I didn't do it on purpose.

(MASAKO goes to the bed. She opens a book. HANA follows her.)

HANA: I know that, but you know what this means? It means we bathe in a bucket . . . inside the house. Carry water in from the pond, heat it on the stove . . . we'll use more kerosene.

MURATA: Tub's still there. And the fireplace. We can still build a fire under the tub.

HANA: (shocked) But no walls! Everyone in the country can see us!

MURATA: Wait till dark then. Wait till dark.

HANA: We'll be using a lantern. They'll still see us.

MURATA: Angh! Who? Who'll see us? You think everyone in the country waits to watch us take a bath? Hunh! You know how stupid you sound? Who cares about a couple of farmers taking a bath at night?

HANA: (defensively) It'll be inconvenient.

(HANA is saved by a rap on the door. OKA enters. He is short and stout. He wears faded work clothes.)

OKA: Hello! Hello! *Oi!* What's going on here? Hey! Was there some kind of fire?

(HANA rushes to the door to let OKA in. He stamps the dust from his shoes and enters.)

HANA: Oka-san! You just wouldn't believe . . . We had a terrible thing happen.

OKA: Yeah. Saw the smoke from down the road. Thought it was your house. Came rushing over. Is the fire out?

(MURATA half rises and sits back again. He's exhausted.)

MURATA: (gesturing) *Oi, oi.* Come in. Sit down. No big problem. It was just our bathhouse.

OKA: Just the *furoba,* eh?

MURATA: Just the bath.

HANA: Our Masako was careless, and the *furoba* caught fire. There's nothing left but the tub.

(MASAKO looks up from her book, pained. She makes a small sound.)

OKA: Long as the tub's there, no problem. I'll help you with it.

(He starts to roll up his sleeves.)

MURATA: What . . . now? Now?

OKA: (heh-heh) Long as I'm here.

HANA: Oh, Papa. Aren't we lucky to have such friends?

MURATA: (to HANA) We can't work on it now. The ashes are still hot. I just now put the damned fire out. Let me rest a while. (to OKA) *Oi,* how about a little sake? (gesturing to HANA) Make sake for Oka-san.

(OKA sits at the table. HANA goes to prepare the sake. She heats it, gets out the cups, and pours it for the men.)

MURATA: (continuing) I'm tired . . . I am tired.

HANA: Oka-san has so generously offered his help . . .

(OKA is uncomfortable. He looks around and sees MASAKO sitting on the bed.)

OKA: Hello, there, Masako-chan. You studying?

MASAKO: No, it's summer vacation.

MURATA: (sucking in his breath) Kids nowadays . . . no manners.

HANA: She's sulking because I had to scold her.

(MASAKO makes a small moan.)

MURATA: Drink, Oka-san.

OKA: (sipping) Ahhhh . . . That's good.

MURATA: Eh, you not working today?

OKA: No-no. I took the afternoon off today. I was driving over to Nagata-san's when I saw this big black cloud of smoke coming from your yard.

HANA: It went up so fast.

MURATA: What's up at Nagata-kun's? (to HANA) Get out the chiles. Oka-san loves chiles.

(HANA opens a jar of chiles and puts them on a plate. She serves them and gets out her mending basket and walks to MASAKO. MASAKO makes room for her.)

OKA: (helping himself) Ah, chiles.

(MURATA waits for an answer.)

OKA: (continuing) Well, I want to see him about my horse. I'm thinking of selling my horse.

MURATA: Sell your horse?

OKA: (scratching his head) The fact is, I need some money. Nagata-san's the only one around made money this year, and I'm thinking he might want another horse.

MURATA: Yeah, he made a little this year. And he's talking big . . . big! Says he's leasing twenty more acres this fall.

OKA: Twenty acres?

MURATA: Yeah. He might want another horse.

OKA: Twenty acres, eh?

MURATA: That's what he says. But you know his old woman makes all the decisions at that house.

(OKA scratches his head.)

HANA: They're doing all right.

MURATA: Heh. Nagata-kun's so henpecked, it's pathetic. Peko-peko. (He makes henpecking motions.)

OKA: (feeling the strain) I better get over there.

MURATA: Why the hell you selling your horse?

OKA: Well . . . a . . . I need cash.

MURATA: Oh yeah. I could use some too. Seems like everyone's getting out of the depression but the poor farmers. Nothing changes for us. We go on and on planting our tomatoes and summer squash and eating them. Well, at least it's healthy.

HANA: Papa, do you have lumber?

MURATA: Lumber? For what?

HANA: The bath . . .

MURATA: (impatiently) Don't worry about that. We need more sake now.

(HANA rises wearily.)

OKA: You sure Nagata-kun's working twenty more?

MURATA: Last I heard. What the hell, if you need a few bucks, I can loan (you) . . .

OKA: A few hundred. I need a few hundred dollars.

MURATA: Oh, a few hundred. But what the hell you going to do without a horse? Out here a man's horse is as important as his wife.

OKA: (seriously) I don't think Nagata will buy my wife.

(The men laugh, but HANA doesn't find it so funny. MURATA glances at her. She fills the cups again. OKA makes a half-hearted gesture to stop her. MASAKO watches the pantomime carefully. OKA finishes his drink.)

OKA: (continuing) I better get moving.

MURATA: What's the big hurry?

OKA: Like to get the horse business done.

MURATA: Eh . . . relax. Do it tomorrow. He's not going to die, is he?

OKA: (laughing) Hey, he's a good horse. I want to get it settled today. If Nagata-kun won't buy, I got to find someone else.

OKA: (continuing) You think maybe Kawaguchi-kun . . .?

MURATA: No-no. Not Kawaguchi. Maybe Yamamoto.

HANA: What is all the money for, Oka-san? Does Emiko-san need an operation?

OKA: No-no. Nothing like that.

HANA: Sounds very mysterious.

OKA: No mystery, Missus. No mystery. No sale, no money, no story.

MURATA: (laughing) That's a good one. "No sale, no money, no . . ." Eh, Mama . . . (He points to the empty cups.)

HANA: (filling the cups, muttering) I see we won't be getting any work done today. (to MASAKO) Are you reading again? Maybe we'd still have a bath if you . . .

MASAKO: I didn't do it on purpose.

MURATA: (loudly) I sure hope you know what you're doing, Oka-kun. What'd you do without a horse?

OKA: I was hoping you'd lend me yours now and then. (He looks at HANA.) I'll pay for some of the feed.

MURATA: Sure! Sure!

OKA: The fact is, I need that money. I got a daughter in Japan, and I just got to send for her this year.

(HANA leaves her mending and sits at the table.)

HANA: A daughter? You have a daughter in Japan? Why, I didn't know you had children. Emiko-san and you . . . I thought you were childless.

OKA: (scratching his head) We are. I was married before.

MURATA: You son-of-a-gun!

HANA: (overlapping) Is that so? How old is your daughter?

OKA: Kiyoko must be . . . fifteen now. Yeah, fifteen.

HANA: Fifteen! Oh, that *would* be too old for Emiko-san's child. Is Kiyoko's-san living with relatives in Japan?

OKA: (reluctantly) With grandparents. Shizue's parents. (pause) Well, the fact is, Shizue—that's my first wife—Shizue and Emiko were sisters. They come from a family with no sons. I was a boy when I went to work for them . . . as an apprentice. They're blacksmiths. Later I married Shizue and took on the family name—you know, *yoshi*—because they had no sons. My real name is Sakakihara.

MURATA: Sakakihara! That's a great name!

HANA: A magnificent name!

OKA: No one knows me by that here.

MURATA: Should have kept that—Sakakihara.

OKA: (muttering) I don't even know myself by that name.

HANA: And Shizue-san passed away and you married Emiko-san?

OKA: Oh. Well, Shizue and I lived with the family for a while, and we had the baby—you know, Kiyoko. (He gets looser with the liquor.) Well, while I was serving apprentice with the family, they always looked down their noses at me. After I married, it got worse.

HANA: (distressed) Worse!

OKA: That old man . . . (unnnnh!) Always pushing me around, making me look bad in front of my wife and kid. That old man was the meanest . . . ugliest . . .

MURATA: Yeah, I heard about that apprentice work—*detchi-boko*. Heard it was damned humiliating.

OKA: That's the God's truth!

MURATA: Never had to do it myself. I came to America instead. They say *detchi-boko* is blood work.

OKA: The work's all right. I'm not afraid of work. It's the humiliation! I hated them! Pushing me around like I was still a boy. Me, a grown man! And married to their daughter!

(MURATA and HANA groan in sympathy.)

OKA: (continuing) Well, Shizue and I talked it over, and we decided the best thing was to get away. We thought if I came to America and made some money . . . you know, send her money until we had enough, and I'd go back and we'd leave the family . . . you know, move to another province . . . start a small business, maybe in the city . . . a noodle shop or something.

MURATA: That's everyone's dream. Make money, go home, and live like a king.

OKA: I worked like a dog. Sent every penny to Shizue. And then she dies. She died on me!

(HANA and MURATA observe a moment of silence in respect for OKA's anguish.)

HANA: And you married Emiko-san.

OKA: I didn't marry her. They married her to me! Right after Shizue died.

HANA: But Oka-san, you were lu(cky) . . .

OKA: Before the body was cold! No respect. By proxy. The old man wrote me that they were arranging a marriage by proxy for me and Emiko. They said she'd grown to be a beautiful woman and would serve me well.

HANA: Emiko-san *is* a beautiful woman.

OKA: And they sent her to me. Took care of everything! Immigration, fare, everything.

HANA: But she's your sister-in-law. Kiyoko's aunt. It's good to keep the family together.

OKA: That's what I thought. But hear this: Emiko was the favored one. Shizue was not so pretty, not so smart. They were grooming Emiko for a rich man—his name was Yamato—lived in a grand house in the village. They sent her to schools; you know, the culture thing: the dance, tea ceremony, you know, all that. They didn't even like me, and suddenly they married her to me.

MURATA: Yeah. You don't need all that formal training to make it over here. Just a strong back.

HANA: And a strong will.

OKA: It was all arranged. I couldn't do anything about it.

HANA: It'll be all right. With Kiyoko-san coming . . .

OKA: (dubiously) I hope so. (pause) I never knew human beings could be so cruel. You know how they mistreated my daughter? After Emiko came here, things got from bad to worse, and I never had enough money to send to Kiyoko and . . .

MURATA: They don't know what it's like here. They think money's picked off the ground here.

OKA: And they treated Kiyoko so bad. They told her I forgot about her. They told her I didn't care . . . said I abandoned her. Well, she knew better. She wrote to me all the time, and I always told her I'd send for her . . . as soon as I got the money. (He shakes his head.) I just got to do something this year.

HANA: She'll be happier here. She'll know her father cares.

OKA: Kids tormented her for being an orphan.

MURATA: Kids are cruel.

HANA: Masako will help her. She'll help her get started at school. She'll make friends. She'll be all right.

OKA: I hope so. She'll need friends. (He tries to convince himself he's making the right decision.) What could I say to her? Stay there? It's not what you think over here? I can't help her? I just have to do this thing. I just have to do this one thing for her.

MURATA: Sure.

HANA: Don't worry. It'll work out fine.

(MURATA gestures to HANA. She gets the sake.)

MURATA: You talk about selling your horse, I thought you were pulling out.

OKA: I wish I could. But there's nothing else I can do.

MURATA: Without money, yeah.

OKA: You can go into some kind of business with money, but a man like me . . . no education . . . there's no kind of job I can do. I'd starve in the city.

MURATA: Dishwashing, maybe. Janitor.

OKA: At least here we can eat. Carrots, maybe, but we can eat.

(They laugh. HANA starts to pour more wine.)

OKA: I better not drink anymore. Got to drive to Nagata-san's yet. (He walks over to MASAKO.) You study hard, don't you? You'll teach Kiyoko English, eh? When she gets here . . .?

HANA: Oh, yes, she will.

MURATA: Kiyoko-san could probably teach her a thing or two.

OKA: She won't know about American ways.

MASAKO: I'll help her.

HANA: Don't worry, Oka-san. She'll have a good friend in our Masako.

(They move to the door.)

OKA: Well, thanks for the sake. I guess I talk too much when I drink. (He scratches his head and laughs.) Oh. I'm sorry about the fire. By the way, come to my house for your bath . . . until you build yours again.

HANA: Oh, a . . . thank you. I don't know if . . .

MURATA: Good, good! I need a good hot bath tonight.

OKA: Tonight, then.

MURATA: We'll be there.

HANA: (bowing) Thank you very much. *Sayonara.*

OKA: (nodding) See you tonight.

(OKA leaves. HANA faces MURATA as soon as the door closes.)

HANA: Papa, I don't know about going over there.

MURATA: (surprised) Why?

HANA: Well, Emiko-san . . .

MURATA: (irritated) What's the matter with you? We need a bath and Oka's invited us over.

HANA: (to MASAKO) Help me clear the table.

(MASAKO reluctantly leaves her book.)

HANA: (continuing) Papa, you know we've been neighbors already three, four years, and Emiko-san's never been very hospitable.

MURATA: She's shy, that's all.

HANA: Not just shy. She's strange. I feel like she's pushing me off. She makes me feel like—I don't know—like I'm prying or something.

MURATA: Maybe you are.

HANA: And never puts out a cup of tea . . . If she had all that training in the graces . . . why, a cup of tea . . .

MURATA: So if you want tea, ask for it.

HANA: I can't do that, Papa. (pause) She's strange. . . . I don't know . . . (to MASAKO) When we go there, be very careful not to say anything wrong.

MASAKO: I never say anything anyway.

HANA: (thoughtfully) Would you believe the story Oka-san just told? Why, I never knew . . .

MURATA: There're lots of things you don't know. Just because a man don't . . . don't talk about

them, don't mean he don't feel . . . don't think about . . .

HANA: (looking around) We'll have to take something. There's nothing to take. Papa, maybe you can dig up some carrots.

MURATA: God, Mama, be sensible. They got carrots. Everybody's got carrots.

HANA: Something . . . Maybe I should make something.

MURATA: Hell, they're not expecting anything.

HANA: It's not good manners to go empty-handed.

MURATA: We'll take the sake.

(HANA grimaces. MASAKO sees the phonograph.)

MASAKO: I know, Mama. We can take the Victrola! We can play records for Mrs. Oka. Then nobody has to talk.

(MURATA laughs.)

Scene 2

That evening. The exterior wall of the Okas' weathered house. There is a workable screen door and a large screened window. Outside there is a wide wooden bench that can accommodate three or four people. There is one separate chair, and a lantern stands against the house.

The last rays of the sun light the area in a soft golden glow. This light grows gray as the scene progresses, and it is quite dark by the end of the scene.

Through the screened window, EMIKO can be seen walking erratically back and forth. She wears drab cotton but her grace and femininity come through. Her hair is bunned back in the style of the Issei women of the era.

OKA sits cross-legged on the bench. He wears a Japanese summer robe (yukata) and fans himself with a round Japanese fan.

The MURATAS enter. MURATA carries towels and a bottle of sake. HANA carries the Victrola, and MASAKO, a package containing their yukata.

OKA: (standing to greet the MURATAS) Oh, you've come. Welcome!

MURATA: *Yah* . . . Good of you to ask us.

HANA: (bowing) Yes, thank you very much. (to MASAKO) Say hello, Masako.

MASAKO: Hello.

HANA: And thank you.

MASAKO: Thank you.

(OKA makes motions of protest. EMIKO stops her pacing and watches from the window.)

HANA: (glancing briefly at the window) And how is Emiko-san this evening?

OKA: (turning to the house) Emi! Emiko!

HANA: That's all right. Don't call her out. She must be busy.

OKA: Emiko!

(EMIKO comes to the door. HANA starts a bow toward the house.)

MURATA: *Konbanwa!?* (Good evening)

HANA: Konbanwa, Emiko-san. I feel so badly about this intrusion. (pause) Your husband has told you our bathhouse was destroyed by fire, and he graciously invited us to come use yours.

(EMIKO shakes her head.)

OKA: I didn't have a chance to . . .

(HANA recovers and nudges MASAKO.)

HANA: Say hello to Mrs. Oka.

MASAKO: Hello, Mrs. Oka.

(HANA lowers the Victrola to the bench.)

OKA: What's this? You brought a phonograph?

MASAKO: It's a Victrola.

HANA: (laughing indulgently) Yes. Masako wanted to bring this over and play some records.

MURATA: (extending the wine) Brought a little sake too.

OKA: (taking the bottle) Ah, now that I like. Emiko, bring out the cups.

(OKA waves at his wife, but she doesn't move. He starts to ask again but decides to get them himself. He enters the house and returns with two cups.)

(EMIKO seats herself on the single chair. The MURATAS unload their paraphernalia; OKA pours the wine, the men drink, HANA chatters and sorts the records. MASAKO stands by helping her.)

HANA: Yes, our Masako loves to play records. I like records too, and Papa, he . . .

MURATA: (watching EMIKO) They take me back home. The only way I can get there. In my mind.

HANA: Do you like music, Emiko-san?

(EMIKO looks vague, but smiles.)

HANA: (continuing) Oka-san, you like them, don't you?

OKA: Yeah. But I don't have a player. No chance to hear them.

MURATA: I had to get this for them. They wouldn't leave me alone until I got it. Well . . . a phonograph . . . what the hell; they got to have *some* fun.

HANA: We don't have to play them, if you'd rather not.

OKA: Play. Play them.

HANA: I thought we could listen to them and relax. (She extends some records to EMIKO.) Would you like to look through these, Emiko-san?

(EMIKO doesn't respond. She pulls out a sack of Bull Durham and begins to roll a cigarette. HANA pushes MASAKO to her.)

HANA: (continuing) Take these to her.

(MASAKO goes to EMIKO with the records. She stands watching her as EMIKO lights a cigarette.)

HANA: (continuing) Some of these are very old. You might know them, Emiko-san. (She sees MASAKO watching EMIKO.) Masako, bring those over here. (She laughs uncomfortably.) You might like this one, Emiko-san. (She starts the player.) Do you know it?

(The record whines out "Kago No Tori." EMIKO listens with her head cocked.)

(She smokes her cigarette. She is wrapped in nostalgia and memories of the past. MASAKO watches her carefully.)

MASAKO: (whispering) Mama, she's crying.

(Startled, HANA and MURATA look toward EMIKO.)

HANA: (pinching MASAKO) Shhh. The smoke is in her eyes.

MURATA: Did you bring the record I like, Mama?

(EMIKO rises abruptly and enters the house.)

MASAKO: They're tears, Mama.

HANA: From yawning, Masako. (regretfully to OKA) I'm afraid we offended her.

OKA: (unaware) Hunh? Aw . . . no . . . pay no attention. No offense.

(MASAKO looks toward the window. EMIKO stands forlornly and slowly drifts into a dance.)

HANA: I'm very sorry. Children, you know . . . they'll say anything. Anything that's on their minds.

(MURATA notices MASAKO looking through the window and tries to divert her attention.)

MURATA: The needles. Masako, where're the needles?

MASAKO: (still watching) I forgot them.

(HANA sees what's going on. OKA is unaware.)

HANA: Masako, go take your bath now. Masako . . .

(MASAKO reluctantly takes her towel and leaves.)

OKA: Yeah, yeah. Take your bath, Masako-chan.

MURATA: (sees EMIKO still dancing) Change the record, Mama.

OKA: (still unaware) That's kind of sad.

MURATA: No use to get sick over a record. We're supposed to enjoy.

(HANA stops the record. EMIKO disappears from the window. HANA selects a lively ondo ["Tokyo Ondo"].)

HANA: We'll find something more fun.

(The three tap to the music.)

HANA: (continuing) Can't you just see the festival? The dancers, the bright kimonos, the paper lanterns bobbing in the wind, the fireflies . . . How nostalgic. Oh, how nostalgic.

(EMIKO appears from the side of the house. Her hair is down; she wears an old straw hat. She dances in front of the MURATAS. They are startled.)

(After the first shock, they watch with frozen smiles. They try to join EMIKO's mood, but something is missing. OKA is grieved. He finally stands as though he's had enough. EMIKO, now close to the door, ducks into the house.)

HANA: That was pretty. Very nice.

(OKA settles down and grunts. MURATA clears his throat, and MASAKO returns from her bath.)

MURATA: You're done already? (He's glad to see her.)

MASAKO: I wasn't very dirty. The water was too hot.

MURATA: Good! Just the way I like it.

HANA: Not dirty?

MURATA: (picking up his towel) Come on, Mama . . . scrub my back.

HANA: (laughing with embarrassment) Oh, oh . . . well . . . (She stops the player.) Masako, now don't forget. Crank the machine and change the needle now and then.

MASAKO: I didn't bring them.

HANA: Oh. Oh . . . all right. I'll be back soon. Don't forget . . . Crank. (She leaves with her husband.)

(OKA and MASAKO are alone. OKA is awkward and falsely hearty.)

OKA: So! So you don't like hot baths, eh?

MASAKO: Not too hot.

OKA: (laughing) I thought you like it real hot. Hot enough to burn the house down.

(MASAKO doesn't laugh.)

OKA: (continuing) That's a little joke.

(MASAKO busies herself to conceal her annoyance.)

OKA: (continuing) I hear you're real good in school. Always top of the class.

MASAKO: It's a small class. Only two of us.

OKA: When Kiyoko comes, you'll help her in school, yeah? You'll take care of her . . . a favor for me, eh?

MASAKO: Okay.

OKA: You'll be her friend, eh?

MASAKO: Okay.

OKA: That's good. That's good. You'll like her. She's a nice girl too.

(OKA stands, yawns, and stretches.)

OKA: (continuing) I'll go for a little walk now. (He touches his crotch to indicate his purpose.)

(MASAKO turns her attention to the records and selects one, "And the Soul Shall Dance," and begins to sway with the music. The song draws EMIKO from the house. She looks out the window, sees MASAKO is alone, and slips into a dance.)

EMIKO: Do you like that song, Masa-chan?

(MASAKO is startled. She remembers her mother's warning. She doesn't know what to do. She nods.)

EMIKO: (continuing) That's one of my favorite songs. I remember in Japan I used to sing it so often. My favorite song. (She sings along with the record.) *Akai kuchibiru / Kappu ni yosete / Aoi sake nomya / Kokoro ga odoru.* Do you know what that means, Masa-chan?

MASAKO: I think so. The soul will dance?

EMIKO: Yes, yes, that's right. The soul shall dance. Red lips against a glass, drink the green . . .

MASAKO: Wine?

EMIKO: (nodding) Drink the green wine . . .

MASAKO: Green? I thought wine was purple.

EMIKO: Wine is purple, but this is a green liqueur.

(EMIKO holds up one of the cups as though it were crystal and looks at the light that would shine through the green liquid.)

EMIKO: (continuing) It's good. It warms your heart.

MASAKO: And the soul dances.

EMIKO: Yes . . .

MASAKO: What does it taste like? The green wine?

EMIKO: Oh, it's like . . . it's like . . .

(The second verse starts: Kurai yoru no yume / Setsu nasa yo / Aoi sake nomya / Yume ga odoru.)

MASAKO: In the dark night . . .

EMIKO: Dreams are unbearable . . .

MASAKO: Drink the . . .

EMIKO: Drink the green wine . . .

MASAKO: And the dreams will dance.

EMIKO: (softly) I'll be going back one day.

MASAKO: Where?

EMIKO: My home. Japan. My real home. I'm going back one day.

MASAKO: By yourself?

EMIKO: Oh, yes. It's a secret. You can keep a secret?

MASAKO: Un-hunh. I have lots of secrets. All my own.

(The music stops. EMIKO sees OKA approaching and disappears into the house. MASAKO attends to the record and does not know EMIKO is gone.)

MASAKO: (continuing) Secrets I never tell anyone . . .

OKA: Secrets? What kind of secrets? What did she say?

MASAKO: (startled) Oh! Nothing.

OKA: What did you talk about?

MASAKO: Nothing. Mrs. Oka was talking about the song. She was telling me what it meant . . . about the soul.

OKA: (scoffing) Heh! What does she know about soul? (calming down) Ehhh . . . Some people don't have them—souls.

MASAKO: (timidly) I thought . . . I thought everyone has a soul. I read in a book . . .

OKA: (laughing) Maybe . . . maybe you're right. I'm not an educated man, you know. I don't know too much about books. When Kiyoko comes you can talk to her about it. Kiyoko is very . . .

(From inside the house, we hear EMIKO begin to sing loudly at the name KIYOKO as though trying to drown it out. OKA stops talking, then resumes.)

OKA: (continuing) Kiyoko is very smart. You'll have a good time with her. She'll learn your language fast. How old did you say you are?

MASAKO: Almost twelve.

(By this time OKA and MASAKO are shouting to be heard above EMIKO's singing.)

OKA: Kiyoko is fifteen. Kiyoko . . .

(OKA is exasperated. He rushes into the house seething. MASAKO hears OKA's muffled rage. "Behave yourself" and "Kitchigai" come through. MASAKO slinks to the window and looks in. OKA slaps EMIKO around. MASAKO reacts to the violence. OKA comes out. MASAKO returns to the bench in time. He pulls his fingers through his hair and sits next to MASAKO. She draws away.)

OKA: Want me to light a lantern?

MASAKO: (shaken) No . . . ye . . . okay.

OKA: We'll get a little light here.

(He lights the lantern as the MURATAS return from their bath. They are in good spirits.)

MURATA: Ahhh . . . Nothing like a good hot bath.

HANA: So refreshing.

MURATA: A bath should be taken hot and slow. Don't know how Masako gets through so fast.

HANA: She probably doesn't get in the tub.

MASAKO: I do.

(Everyone laughs.)

MASAKO: (continuing) Well, I do.

(EMIKO comes out. She has a large purple welt on her face. She sits on the separate chair, hands folded, quietly watching the MURATAS. They look at her with alarm. OKA engages himself with his fan.)

HANA: Oh! Emiko-san . . . what . . . a . . . a . . . whaa . . . (She draws a deep breath.) What a nice bath we had. Such a lovely bath. We do appreciate your hos . . . pitality. Thank you so much.

EMIKO: Lovely evening, isn't it?

HANA: Very lovely. Very. Ah, a little warm, but nice. Did you get a chance to hear the records? (turning to MASAKO) Did you play the records for Mrs. Oka?

MASAKO: Ye . . . no. The needle was . . .

EMIKO: Yes, she did. We played the records together.

MURATA: Oh, you played the songs together?

EMIKO: Yes . . . yes.

MURATA: That's nice. Masako can understand pretty good, eh?

EMIKO: She understands everything. Everything I say.

MURATA: (withdrawing) Oh, yeah? Eh, Mama, we ought to be going. (He closes the player.) Hate to bathe and run but . . .

HANA: Yes, yes. Tomorrow is a busy day. Come, Masako.

EMIKO: Please . . . stay a little longer.

MURATA: Eh, well, we got to be going.

HANA: Why, thank you, but . . .

EMIKO: It's still quite early.

OKA: (ready to say good-bye) Enjoyed the music. And the sake.

EMIKO: The records are very nice. Makes me remember Japan. I sang those songs . . . those very songs . . . Did you know I used to sing?

HANA: (politely) Why, no. No. I didn't know that. You must have a very lovely voice.

EMIKO: Yes.

HANA: No, I didn't know that. That's very nice.

EMIKO: Yes, I sang. My parents were very strict. They didn't like it. They said it was frivolous. Imagine?

HANA: Yes, I can imagine. Things were like that . . . in those days singing was not considered proper for nice . . . I mean, only for women in the profess . . .

MURATA: We better get home, Mama.

HANA: Yes, yes. What a shame you couldn't continue with it.

EMIKO: In the city I did do some classics: the dance, and the koto, and the flower, and of course, the tea. (She makes the gestures for the disciplines.) All those. Even some singing. Classics, of course.

HANA: (politely) Of course.

EMIKO: All of it is so disciplined . . . so disciplined. I was almost a *natori*.

HANA: How nice!

EMIKO: But everything changed.

HANA: Oh!

EMIKO: I was sent here to America. (She glares at OKA.)

HANA: Oh, too bad. I mean, too bad about your *natori*.

MURATA: (loudly to OKA) So did you see Nagata-san today?

OKA: Oh, yeah, yeah.

MURATA: What did he say? Is he interested?

OKA: Yeah. Yeah. He's interested.

MURATA: He likes the horse, eh?

OKA: Ah . . . yeah.

MURATA: I knew he'd like him. I'd buy him myself if I had the money.

OKA: Well, I have to take him over tomorrow. He'll decide then.

MURATA: He'll buy. He'll buy. You'd better go straight over to the ticket agent and get that ticket. Before you (ha-ha) spend the money.

OKA: (ha-ha) Yeah.

HANA: It'll be so nice when Kiyoko-san comes to join you. I know you're looking forward to it.

EMIKO: (confused) Oh . . . oh . . .

HANA: Masako is so happy. It'll be good for her too.

EMIKO: I had more freedom in the city. I lived with an aunt and she let me . . . she wasn't so strict.

(MURATA and MASAKO have their gear together and are ready to leave.)

MURATA: Good luck on the horse tomorrow.

OKA: Yeah.

HANA: (bowing) Many, many thanks.

OKA: Thanks for the sake.

HANA: (bowing again) Good night, Emiko-san. We'll see you again soon. We'll bring the records too.

EMIKO: (softly) Those songs. Those very songs.

MURATA: Let's go, Mama.

(The MURATAS pull away. Light follows them and grows dark on the OKAS. The MURATAS begin walking home.)

HANA: That was uncomfortable.

MASAKO: What's the matter with . . .

HANA: Shhh!

MURATA: I guess Oka has his problems.

MASAKO: Is she really *kitchigai*?

HANA: Of course not. She's not crazy. Don't say that word.

MASAKO: I heard Mr. Oka call her that.

HANA: He called her that?

MASAKO: I . . . I think so.

HANA: You heard wrong, Masako. Emiko-san isn't crazy. She just likes her drinks. She had too much to drink tonight.

MASAKO: Oh.

HANA: She can't adjust to this life. She can't get over the good times she had in Japan. Well, it's not easy. But one has to know when to bend . . . like the bamboo. When the winds blow, bamboo bends. You bend or crack. Remember that, Masako.

MURATA: (wryly) Bend, eh? Remember that, Mama.

HANA: (softly) You don't know. It isn't ever easy.

MASAKO: Do you want to go back to Japan, Mama?

HANA: Everyone does.

MASAKO: Do you, Papa?

MURATA: I'll have to make some money first.

MASAKO: I don't. Not me. Not Kiyoko.

HANA: After Kiyoko-san comes, Emiko will have company and things will straighten out. She has nothing to live on but memories. She doesn't have any friends. At least I have my friends at church. At least I have that. She must get awful lonely. . . .

MASAKO: I know that. She tried to make friends with me.

HANA: She did? What did she say?

MASAKO: Well, sort of . . .

HANA: What did she say?

MASAKO: She didn't say anything. I just felt it. Maybe you should be her friend, Mama.

MURATA: Poor woman. We could have stayed longer.

HANA: But you wanted to leave. I tried to be friendly. You saw that. It's not easy to talk to Emiko. She either closes up, you can't pry a word from her, or else she goes on and on. All that . . . that . . . about the koto and tea and the flower . . . I mean, what am I supposed to say? She's so unpredictable. And the drinking . . .

MURATA: All right, all right, Mama.

MASAKO: Did you see her black eye?

HANA: (calming down) She probably hurt herself. She wasn't very steady.

MASAKO: Oh, no. Mr. Oka hit her.

HANA: I don't think so.

MASAKO: He hit her. I saw him.

HANA: You saw? Papa, do you hear that? She saw them. That does it. We're not going there again.

MURATA: Aw . . . Oka wouldn't do that. Not in front of a kid.

MASAKO: Well, they didn't do it in front of me. They were in the house.

MURATA: You see?

HANA: That's all right. You just have to fix the bathhouse. Either that or we're going to

bathe at home . . . in a bucket, if we have to. We're not going . . . we'll bathe at home.

(MURATA mutters to himself.)

HANA: What?

MURATA: I said all right, it's the bucket then. I'll get to it when I can.

(HANA passes MURATA and walks ahead.)

Scene 3

The same evening. The exterior of the Oka house. The MURATAS have just left. EMIKO sits on the bench, her back to OKA. OKA, still standing, looks at her contemptuously as she pours herself a drink.

OKA: Nothing more disgusting than a drunk woman.

(EMIKO ignores him.)

OKA: (continuing) You made a fool of yourself. You made a fool of *me!*

EMIKO: One can only make a fool of one's self.

OKA: You learn that in the fancy schools, eh?

(EMIKO examines the pattern of her cup.)

OKA: (continuing) Eh? Ehhh? (pause) Answer me!

(EMIKO ignores him.)

OKA: (continuing) I'm talking to you. Answer me! (threatening) You don't get away with that. You think you're so fine. . . .

(EMIKO looks off at the horizon. OKA roughly turns her around.)

OKA: (continuing) When I talk, you listen!

(EMIKO turns away again. OKA pulls the cup from her hand.)

OKA: (continuing) Goddammit! What'd you think my friends think of you? What kind of ass they think I am?

(He grabs her shoulders.)

EMIKO: Don't touch me. Don't touch (me) . . .

OKA: Who the hell you think you are? "Don't touch me, don't touch me." Who the hell! High and mighty, eh? Too good for me, eh? Don't put on the act for me. I know who you are.

EMIKO: Tell me who I am, Mister Smart Peasant.

OKA: Shut your fool mouth, goddammit! Sure. I'll tell you. I know all about you. Shizue told me. The whole village knows.

EMIKO: Shizue!

OKA: Yeah, Shizue. Embarrassed the hell out of her, your own sister.

EMIKO: Embarrassed? I have nothing to be ashamed of. I don't know what you're talking about.

OKA: (derisively) You don't know what I'm talking about. I know. The whole village knows. They're all laughing at you. At me! Stupid Oka got stuck with a secondhand woman. I didn't say anything because . . .

EMIKO: I'm not secondhand!

OKA: Who you trying to fool? I know. Knew long time ago. Shizue wrote me all about your . . . your affairs in Tokyo. The men you were mess(ing) . . .

EMIKO: Affairs? Men?

OKA: That man you were messing with. I knew all along. I didn't say anything because you . . . I . . .

EMIKO: I'm not ashamed of it.

OKA: You're not ashamed! What the hell! Your father thought he was pulling a fast one on me . . . thought I didn't know nothing . . . thought I was some kind of dumb ass . . . I didn't say nothing because Shizue's dead. Shizue's dead. I was willing to give you a chance.

EMIKO: (laughing) A chance? Give me a chance?

OKA: Yeah. A chance! Laugh! Give a *joro* another chance. Sure, I'm stupid . . . dumb.

EMIKO: I'm not a whore. I'm true. He knows I'm true.

OKA: True! (Hah!)

EMIKO: You think I'm untrue just because I let . . . let you . . . There's only one man for me.

OKA: Let me (obscene gesture)? I can do what I want with you. Your father palmed you off on me—like a dog or cat—animal. Couldn't do nothing with you. Even the rich dumb Yamato wouldn't have you. Your

father—greedy father—so proud . . . making big plans for you . . . for himself. (Humh!) the whole village laughing at him.

(EMIKO hangs her head.)

OKA: (continuing) Shizue told me. And she was working like a dog . . . trying to keep your goddam father happy . . . doing my work and yours.

EMIKO: My work?

OKA: Yeah, your work too! She killed herself working. She killed herself. (He has tender memories of his uncomplaining wife.) Up in the morning getting the fires started, working the bellows, cleaning the furnace, cooking, and late at night working with the sewing . . . tending the baby. (He mutters.) The goddam family killed her. And you . . . you out there in Tokyo with the fancy clothes, doing the (sneering) dance, the tea, the flower, the (obscene gesture) . . .

EMIKO: (hurting) Ahhhhh . . .

OKA: Did you have fun? Did you have fun on your sister's blood?

(EMIKO doesn't answer.)

OKA: (continuing) Did you? He must have been a son-of-a-bitch. What would make that goddam greedy old man send his prize mare to a plow horse like me? What kind of bum was he that your father would . . .

EMIKO: He's not a bum. He's not a bum.

OKA: Was he Korean? Was he *Etta?* That's the only thing I could figure.

EMIKO: I'm true to him. Only him.

OKA: True? You think he's true to you? You think he waits for you? Remembers you? *Aho!* Think he cares?

EMIKO: He does.

OKA: And waits ten years? *Baka!* Go back to Japan and see. You'll find out. Go back to Japan. *Kaire!*

EMIKO: In time.

OKA: In time. How about now?

EMIKO: I can't now.

OKA: (Hah!) Now! Go now! Who needs you? Who needs you? You think a man waits ten years for a woman? You think you're some kind of . . . of diamond . . . treasure . . . he's going to wait his life for you? Go to him. He's probably married with ten kids. Go to him. Get out! Goddam *joro*. Go! Go!

(OKA sweeps EMIKO off the bench.)

EMIKO: Ahhh! I . . . I don't have the money. Give me money to . . .

OKA: If I had money I would give it to you ten years ago. You think I been eating this *kuso* for ten years because I like it?

EMIKO: You're selling the horse. Give me the (money) . . .

OKA: (scoffing) That's for Kiyoko. I owe you nothing.

EMIKO: Ten years, you owe me.

OKA: Ten years of what? Misery? You gave me nothing. I give you nothing. You want to go, pack your bag and start walking. Try cross the desert. When you get dry and hungry, think about me.

EMIKO: I'd die out there.

OKA: Die? You think I didn't die here?

EMIKO: I didn't do anything to you.

OKA: No, no, you didn't. All I wanted was a little comfort and you . . . no, you didn't. No. So you die. We all die. Shizue died. If she was here, she wouldn't treat me like this. Ah, I should have brought her with me. She'd be alive now. We'd be poor but happy like . . . like Murata and his wife . . . and the kid.

EMIKO: I wish she were alive too. I'm not to blame for her dying. I didn't know. I was away. I loved her. I didn't want her to die. I . . . .

OKA: (softening) I know that. I'm not blaming you for that. And it's not my fault what happened to you either.

(OKA is encouraged by EMIKO's silence which he mistakes for a change of attitude.)

OKA: (continuing) You understand that, eh? I didn't ask for you. It's not my fault you're here in this desert with . . . with me.

(EMIKO weeps. OKA reaches out.)

OKA: (continuing) I know I'm too old for you. It's hard for me too. But this is the way it is. I just ask you be kinder . . . understand it wasn't my fault. Try make it easier for me. For yourself too.

(OKA touches her and she shrinks from his hand.)

EMIKO: Ach!

OKA: (humiliated again) Goddam it! I didn't ask for you! *Aho!* If you was smart, you'da done as your father said . . . cut out that *saru shibai* with the *Etta* . . . married the rich Yamato. Then you'd still be in Japan. Not here to make my life so miserable.

(EMIKO is silent.)

OKA: (continuing) And you can have your *Etta* . . . or anyone else you want. Take them all on.

(OKA is worn out. It's hopeless.)

OKA: (continuing) God, why do we do this all the time? Fighting all the time. There must be a better way to live. There must be another way.

(OKA waits for a response, gives up, and enters the house. EMIKO watches him leave and pours another drink. The storm has passed, the alcohol takes over.)

EMIKO: I must keep the dream alive. The dream is all I live for. I am only in exile now. If I give in, all I've lived before will mean nothing . . . will be for nothing. Nothing. If I let you make me believe this is all there is to my life, the dream would die. I would die.

(She pours another drink and feels warm and good.)

ACT TWO

Scene 1

Mid-September afternoon. Muratas' kitchen. The calendar reads September. MASAKO is at the kitchen table with several books. She thumbs through a Japanese magazine. HANA is with her sewing.

231

MASAKO: Do they always wear kimonos in Japan, Mama?

HANA: Most of the time.

MASAKO: I wonder if Kiyoko will be wearing a kimono like this.

HANA: (looking at the magazine) They don't dress like that. Not for every day.

MASAKO: I wonder what she's like.

HANA: Probably a lot like you. What do you think she's like?

MASAKO: She's probably taller.

HANA: Mr. Oka isn't tall.

MASAKO: And pretty.

HANA: (laughing) Mr. Oka . . . Well, I don't suppose she'll look like her father.

MASAKO: Mrs. Oka is pretty.

HANA: She isn't Kiyoko-san's real mother, remember?

MASAKO: Oh, that's right.

HANA: But they are related. Well, we'll soon see.

MASAKO: I thought she was coming in September. It's already September.

HANA: Papa said Oka-san went to San Pedro a few days ago. He should be back soon with Kiyoko-san.

MASAKO: Didn't Mrs. Oka go too?

HANA: (glancing toward the Oka house) I don't think so. I see lights in their house at night.

MASAKO: Will they bring Kiyoko over to see us?

HANA: Of course. First thing, probably. You'll be very nice to her, won't you?

(MASAKO finds another book.)

MASAKO: Sure. I'm glad I'm going to have a friend. I hope she likes me.

HANA: She'll like you. Japanese girls are very polite, you know.

MASAKO: We have to be or our mamas get mad at us.

HANA: Then I should be getting mad at you more often.

MASAKO: It's often enough already, Mama. (She opens the book.) Look at this, Mama. I'm going to show her this book.

HANA: She won't be able to read at first.

MASAKO: I love this story. Mama, this is about people like us—settlers—it's about the prairie. We live in a prairie, don't we?

HANA: Prairie? Does that mean desert?

MASAKO: I think so.

HANA: (looking at the bleak landscape) We live in a prairie.

MASAKO: It's about the hardships and the floods and droughts and how they have nothing but each other.

HANA: We have nothing but each other. But these people . . . they're white people.

MASAKO: Sure, Mama. They come from the east. Just like you and Papa came from Japan.

HANA: We come from the far far east. That's different. White people are different from us.

MASAKO: I know that.

HANA: White people among white people . . . that's different from Japanese among white people. You know what I'm saying?

MASAKO: I know that. How come they don't write books about us . . . about Japanese people?

HANA: Because we're nobodies here.

MASAKO: If I didn't read these, there'd be nothing for me.

HANA: Some of the things you read, you're never going to know.

MASAKO: I can dream though.

HANA: (sighing) Sometimes the dreaming makes the living harder. Better to keep your head out of the clouds.

MASAKO: That's not much fun.

HANA: You'll have fun when Kiyoko-san comes. You can study together, you can sew, and sometime you can try some of those fancy American recipes.

MASAKO: Oh, Mama. You have to have chocolate and cream and things like that.

HANA: We'll get them.

(We hear the sound of Oka's old car. MASAKO and HANA pause and listen. MASAKO runs to the window.)

MASAKO: I think it's them!

HANA: Oka-san?

MASAKO: It's them! It's them!

(HANA stands and looks out. She removes her apron and puts away her sewing.)

HANA: Two of them. Emiko-san isn't with them. (pause) Let's go outside.

(OKA and KIYOKO enter. OKA is wearing his going-out clothes: a sweater, white shirt, dark pants, but no tie. KIYOKO walks behind him.)

(KIYOKO is short, broad-chested, and very self-conscious. Her hair is straight and banded into two shucks. She wears a conservative cotton dress, white socks, and two-inch heels.)

(OKA is proud. He struts in, his chest puffed out.)

OKA: Hello, hello! We're here. We made it! (He pushes KIYOKO forward.) This my daughter, Kiyoko. (to KIYOKO) Murata-san. Remember, I was talking about? My friends . . .

KIYOKO: (bowing deeply) *Hajime mashite yoroshiku onegai shimasu.*

HANA: (also bowing deeply) I hope your journey was pleasant.

OKA: (pushing KIYOKO to MASAKO while she still bows) This is Masako-chan; I told you about her.

(MASAKO is shocked at KIYOKO's appearance. The girl she expected is already a woman. She stands with her mouth agape and withdraws noticeably. HANA rushes in to fill the awkwardness.)

HANA: Say hello, Masako. My goodness, where are your manners? (She laughs apologetically.) In this country they don't make much to-do about manners. (She stands back to

examine KIYOKO.) My, my, I didn't picture you so grown up. My, my . . . Tell me, how was your trip?

OKA: (proudly) We just drove in from Los Angeles this morning. We spent the night in San Pedro, and the next two days we spent in Los Angeles . . . you know, Japanese town.

HANA: How nice!

OKA: Kiyoko was so excited. Twisting her head this way and that—couldn't see enough with her big eyes. (He imitates her fondly.) She's from the country, you know . . . just a big country girl. Got all excited about the Chinese dinner—we had a Chinese dinner. She never ate it before.

(KIYOKO covers her mouth and giggles.)

HANA: Chinese dinner!

OKA: Oh, yeah. Duck, *pakkai,* chow mein, seaweed soup . . . the works!

HANA: A feast!

OKA: Oh, yeah. Like a holiday. Two holidays. Two holidays in one.

(HANA pushes MASAKO forward.)

HANA: Two holidays in one! Kiyoko-san, our Masako has been looking forward to meeting you.

KIYOKO: (bowing again) *Hajime mashite . . .*

HANA: She's been planning all sorts of things she'll do with you: sewing, cooking . . .

MASAKO: Oh, Mama . . .

(KIYOKO covers her mouth and giggles.)

HANA: It's true, Kiyoko-san. She's been looking forward to having a best friend.

(KIYOKO giggles and MASAKO pulls away.)

OKA: Kiyoko, you shouldn't be so shy. The Muratas are my good friends, and you should feel free with them. Ask anything, say anything. Right?

HANA: Of course, of course. (She is annoyed with MASAKO.) Masako, go in and start the tea.

(MASAKO enters the house.)

HANA: (continuing) I'll call Papa. He's in the yard. Papa! Oka-san is here! (to KIYOKO) Now tell me, how was your trip? Did you get seasick?

KIYOKO: (bowing and nodding) Eh (affirmative). A little.

OKA: Tell her. Tell her how sick you got.

(KIYOKO covers her mouth and giggles.)

HANA: Oh, I know, I know. I was too. That was a long time ago. I'm sure things are improved now. Tell me about Japan. What is it like now? They say it's so changed . . . modern.

OKA: Kiyoko comes from the country . . . backwoods. Nothing changes much there from century to century.

HANA: Ah! That's true. That's why I love Japan. And you wanted to leave. It's unbelievable. To come here!

OKA: She always dreamed about it.

HANA: Well, it's not really that bad.

OKA: No, it's not that bad. Depends on what you make of it.

HANA: That's right. What you make of it. I was just telling Masako today . . .

(MURATA enters. He rubs his hands to remove the soil and comes in grinning. He shakes OKA's hand.)

MURATA: *Oi, oi . . .*

OKA: *Yah* . . . I'm back. This is my daughter.

MURATA: No! She's beautiful!

OKA: Finally made it. Finally got her here.

MURATA: (to KIYOKO) Your father hasn't stopped talking about you all summer.

HANA: And Masako too.

KIYOKO: (bowing) *Hajime mashite . . .*

MURATA: (with a short bow) *Yah.* How'd you like the trip?

OKA: I was just telling your wife . . . had a good time in Los Angeles. Had a couple of great dinners, took in the cinema—Japanese pictures, bought her some American clothes . . .

HANA: Oh, you bought that in Los Angeles.

MURATA: Got a good price for your horse, eh? Lots of money, eh?

OKA: Nagata-kun's a shrewd bargainer. Heh. It don't take much money to make her happy. She's a country girl.

MURATA: That's all right. Country's all right. Country girl's the best.

OKA: Had trouble on the way back.

MURATA: Yeah?

OKA: Fan belt broke.

MURATA: That'll happen with these old cars.

OKA: Lucky I was near a gasoline station. We were in the mountains. Waited in a restaurant while it was getting fixed.

HANA: Oh, that was good.

OKA: Guess they don't see Japanese much. Stare? Terrible! Took them a long time to wait on us. Dumb waitress practically threw the food at us. Kiyoko felt bad.

HANA: Ah! That's too bad . . . too bad. That's why I always pack a lunch when we take trips.

MURATA: They'll spoil the day for you . . . those barbarians!

OKA: Terrible food too. Kiyoko couldn't swallow the dry bread and bologna.

HANA: That's the food they eat!

MURATA: Let's go in . . . have a little wine. Mama, we got wine? This is a celebration.

HANA: I think so. A little.

(They enter the house talking. MASAKO has made tea and HANA serves the wine.)

HANA: (continuing) How is your mother? Was she happy to see you?

KIYOKO: Oh, she . . . yes.

HANA: I just know she was surprised to see you so grown up. Of course, you remember her from Japan, don't you?

KIYOKO: (nodding) *Eh* (affirmative). I can barely remember. I was very young.

HANA: Of course. But you do, don't you?

KIYOKO: She was gone most of the time . . . at school in Tokyo. She was very pretty, I remember that.

HANA: She's still very pretty.

KIYOKO: Yes. She was always laughing. She was much younger then.

HANA: Oh, now, it hasn't been that long ago.

(MASAKO goes outside. The following dialogue continues muted as the light goes dim in the house and focuses on MASAKO. EMIKO enters, is drawn to the Murata window, and listens.)

OKA: We stayed at an inn on East First Street. *Shizuokaya.* Whole inn filled with Shizuoka people . . . talking the old dialect. Thought I was in Japan again.

MURATA: That right?

OKA: Felt good. Like I was in Japan again.

HANA: (to KIYOKO) Did you enjoy Los Angeles?

KIYOKO: Yes.

OKA: That's as close as I'll get to Japan.

MURATA: *Mattakuna!* That's for sure. Not in this life.

(Outside MASAKO is aware of EMIKO.)

MASAKO: Why don't you go in?

EMIKO: Oh. Oh. Why don't you?

MASAKO: They're all grown-ups in there. I'm not grown up.

EMIKO: (softly) All grown-ups. Maybe I'm not either. (Her mood changes.) Masa-chan, do you have a boyfriend?

MASAKO: I don't like boys. They don't like me.

EMIKO: Oh, that will change. You will change. I was like that too.

MASAKO: Besides, there's none around here . . . Japanese boys. There are some at school, but they don't like girls.

HANA: (calling from the kitchen) Masako . . .

(MASAKO doesn't answer.)

EMIKO: Your mother is calling you.

MASAKO: (to her mother) *Nani?* (What?)

HANA: (from the kitchen) Come inside now.

EMIKO: You'll have a boyfriend one day.

MASAKO: Not me.

EMIKO: You'll fall in love one day. Someone will make the inside of you light up, and you'll know you're in love. Your life will change . . . grow beautiful. It's good, Masa-chan. And this feeling you'll remember the rest of your life . . . will come back to you . . . haunt you . . . keep you alive . . . five, ten years . . . no matter what happens. Keep you alive.

HANA: (from the house) Masako . . . Come inside now.

(MASAKO turns aside to answer and EMIKO slips away.)

MASAKO: What, Mama?

(HANA comes out.)

HANA: Come inside. Don't be so unsociable. Kiyoko wants to talk to you.

MASAKO: (watching EMIKO leave) She doesn't want to talk to me. You're only saying that.

HANA: What's the matter with you? Don't you want to make friends with her?

MASAKO: She's not my friend. She's your friend.

HANA: Don't be silly. She's only fourteen.

MASAKO: Fifteen. They said fifteen. She's your friend. She's an old lady.

HANA: Don't say that.

MASAKO: I don't like her.

HANA: Shhh! Don't say that.

MASAKO: She doesn't like me either.

HANA: Ma-chan. Remember your promise to Mr. Oka? You're going to take her to school, teach her the language, teach her the ways of Americans.

MASAKO: She can do it herself. You did.

HANA: That's not nice, Ma-chan.

MASAKO: I don't like the way she laughs. (She imitates KIYOKO holding her hand to her mouth and giggling and bowing.)

HANA: Oh, how awful! Stop that. That's the way the girls do in Japan. Maybe she doesn't like your ways either. That's only a difference in manners. What you're doing now is considered very bad manners. (She changes her tone.) Ma-chan, just wait: when she learns to read and speak, you'll have so much to say to each other. Come on, be a good girl and come inside.

MASAKO: It's just old people in there, Mama. I don't want to go in.

(HANA calls to KIYOKO inside.)

HANA: Kiyoko-san, please come here a minute. Maybe it's better for you to talk to Masako alone.

(KIYOKO dutifully goes outside.)

HANA: (continuing) Masako has a lot of things to tell you . . . about what to expect in school and . . . things.

MURATA: (calling from the table) Mama, put out something . . . chiles—for Oka-san.

(HANA enters the house. KIYOKO and MASAKO stand awkwardly facing each other, KIYOKO glancing shyly at MASAKO.)

MASAKO: Do you like it here?

KIYOKO: (nodding) *Eh* (affirmative).

(There is an uncomfortable pause.)

MASAKO: School will be starting next week.

KIYOKO: (nodding) *Eh.*

MASAKO: Do you want to walk to school with me?

KIYOKO: (nodding) *Hai.*

(MASAKO rolls her eyes and tries again.)

MASAKO: I leave at 7:30.

KIYOKO: *Eh.*

(There's a long pause. MASAKO gives up and moves offstage.)

MASAKO: I have to do something.

(KIYOKO watches her leave and uncertainly moves back to the house. HANA looks up at KIYOKO coming in alone, sighs, and quietly pulls out a chair for her.)

Scene 2

November night. Interior of the Murata home. Lamps are lit. The family is at the kitchen table.

HANA sews, MASAKO does her homework, MURATA reads the paper. They're dressed in warm robes and are having tea.

Outside, thunder rolls in the distance and lightning flashes.

HANA: It'll be *ohigan* (autumn festival) soon.

MURATA: Something to look forward to.

HANA: We'll need sweet rice for *omochi* (rice cakes).

MURATA: I'll order it next time I go to town.

HANA: (to MASAKO) How is school? Getting a little harder?

MASAKO: Not that much. Sometimes the arithmetic is hard.

HANA: How is Kiyoko-san doing? Is she getting along all right?

MASAKO: She's good in arithmetic. She skipped a grade already.

HANA: Already? That's good news. Only November and she skipped a grade! At this rate she'll be through before you.

MASAKO: Well, she's older.

MURATA: Sure, she's older, Mama.

HANA: Has she made any friends?

MASAKO: No. She follows me around all day. She understands okay, but she doesn't talk. She talks like, you know . . . she says "ranchi" for lunch and "ranchi" for ranch too, and like that. Kids laugh and copy behind her back. It's hard to understand her.

HANA: You understand her, don't you?

MASAKO: I'm used to it.

HANA: You should tell the kids not to laugh. After all, she's trying. Maybe you should help her practice those words . . . show her what she's doing wrong.

MASAKO: I already do. Our teacher told me to do that.

MURATA: (looking up from his paper) You ought to help her all you can.

HANA: And remember, when you started school, you couldn't speak English either.

MASAKO: I help her.

(MURATA goes to the window. The night is cold. Lightning flashes and the wind whistles.)

MURATA: Looks like a storm coming up. Hope we don't have a freeze.

HANA: If it freezes, we'll have another bad year. Maybe we ought to start the smudge pots.

MURATA: (listening) It's starting to rain. Nothing to do now but pray.

HANA: If praying is the answer, we'd be in Japan now. Rich.

MURATA: (wryly) We're not dead yet. We still have a chance.

(HANA glares at the small joke.)

MURATA: (continuing) Guess I'll turn in.

HANA: Go to bed, go to bed. I'll sit up and worry.

MURATA: If worrying was the answer, we'd be around the world twice and in Japan. Come on, Mama. Let's go to bed. It's too cold tonight to be mad.

(There's an urgent knock on the door. The MURATAS react.)

MURATA: (continuing) *Dareh da!* (Who is it?)

(MURATA goes to the door and hesitates.)

MURATA: (continuing) Who is it!

KIYOKO: (weakly) It's me . . . help me . . .

(MURATA opens the door and KIYOKO stumbles in. She wears a kimono with a shawl thrown over. Her legs are bare except for a pair of straw zori. Her hair is wet and stringy, and she trembles uncontrollably.)

MURATA: My God! Kiyoko-san! What's the matter?

HANA: (overlapping) Kiyoko-san! What is it?

MURATA: What happened?

KIYOKO: They're fighting, they're fighting!

MURATA: Oh, don't worry. Those things happen. No cause to worry. Mama, make tea for her. Sit down and catch your breath. Don't worry. I'll take you home when you're ready.

HANA: Papa, I'll take care of it.

MURATA: Let me know when you're ready to go home.

HANA: It must be freezing out there. Try to get warm. Try to calm yourself.

MURATA: Kiyoko-san, don't worry. (He puts his robe around her.)

(HANA waves MASAKO and MURATA off. MURATA leaves. MASAKO goes to her bed in the kitchen.)

HANA: Papa, I'll take care of it.

KIYOKO: (looking at MURATA'S retreating form) But I came to ask your help. . . .

HANA: You ran down here without a lantern? You could have fallen and hurt yourself.

KIYOKO: I don't care . . . I don't care . . .

HANA: You don't know, Kiyoko-san. It's treacherous out there—snakes, spiders . . .

KIYOKO: I must go back! I . . . I . . . you . . . please come with me. . . .

HANA: First, first we must get you warm. Drink your tea.

KIYOKO: But they'll kill each other. They're fighting like animals. Help me stop them!

(HANA warms a pot of soup.)

HANA: (calmly) I cannot interfere in a family quarrel.

KIYOKO: It's not a quarrel. It's a . . . a . . .

HANA: That's all it is. A family squabble. You'll see. Tomorrow . . .

(KIYOKO pulls at HANA's arm.)

KIYOKO: Not just a squabble! Please . . . please . . .

(KIYOKO starts toward the door, but HANA stops her.)

HANA: Now listen. Listen to me, Kiyoko-san. I've known your father and mother a little while now. I suspect it's been like this for years. Every family has some kind of trouble.

KIYOKO: Not like this, not like this.

HANA: Some have it better, some worse. When you get married, you'll understand. Don't worry. Nothing will happen. (She takes a towel and dries KIYOKO's hair.) You're chilled to the bone. You'll catch your death.

KIYOKO: I don't care. . . . I want to die.

HANA: Don't be silly. It's not that bad.

KIYOKO: It is! They started drinking early in the afternoon. They make some kind of brew and hide it somewhere in the desert.

HANA: It's illegal to make it. That's why they hide it. That home brew is poison to the body. The mind too.

KIYOKO: It makes them crazy. They drink it all the time and quarrel constantly. I was in the other room studying. I try so hard to keep up with school.

HANA: We were talking about you just this evening. Masako says you're doing so well. You skipped a grade?

KIYOKO: It's hard . . . hard. I'm too old for the class and the children . . .

(She remembers all her problems and starts crying again.)

HANA: It's always hard in a new country.

KIYOKO: They were bickering and quarreling all afternoon. Then something happened. All of a sudden they were on the floor . . . hitting and . . . and . . . He was hitting her in the stomach, the face . . . I tried to stop them, but they were so . . . drunk.

HANA: There, there. It's probably all over now.

KIYOKO: Why does it happen like this? Nothing is right. Everywhere I go. Masa-chan is so lucky. I wish my life was like hers. I can hardly remember my real mother.

HANA: Emiko-san is almost a real mother to you. She's blood kin.

KIYOKO: She hates me. She never speaks to me. She's so cold. I want to love her, but she won't let me. She hates me.

HANA: I don't think so, Kiyoko-san.

KIYOKO: She does! She hates me.

HANA: No. I don't think you have anything to do with it. It's this place. She hates it. This place is so lonely and alien.

KIYOKO: Then why didn't she go back? Why did they stay here?

HANA: You don't know. It's not so simple. Sometimes I think . . .

KIYOKO: Then why don't they make the best of it here? Like you?

HANA: That isn't easy either. Believe me. (She leaves KIYOKO to stir the soup.) Sometimes . . . sometimes the longing for home . . . the longing fills me with despair. Will I never return again? Will I never see my mother, my father, my sisters again? But what can one do? There are responsibilities here . . . children . . . (pause) And another day passes . . . another month . . . another year. (She takes the soup to KIYOKO.) Did you have supper tonight?

KIYOKO: (bowing) Ah. When my . . . my aunt gets like this, she doesn't cook. No one eats. I don't get hungry anymore.

HANA: Cook for yourself. It's important to keep your health.

KIYOKO: I left Japan for a better life.

HANA: It isn't easy for you, is it? But you must remember your filial duty.

KIYOKO: It's so hard.

HANA: But you can make the best of it here, Kiyoko-san. And take care of yourself. You owe that to yourself. Eat. Keep well. It'll be better, you'll see. And sometimes it'll seem worse. But you'll survive. We do, you know.

HANA: (continuing) It's getting late.

KIYOKO: (apprehensively) I don't want to go back.

HANA: You can sleep with Masako tonight. Tomorrow you'll go back. And you'll remember what I told you. (She puts her arm around KIYOKO.) Life is never easy, Kiyoko-san. Endure. Endure. Soon you'll be marrying and going away. Things will not always be this way. And you'll look back on this . . . this night and you'll . . .

(There is a rap on the door. HANA exchanges glances with KIYOKO and opens the door a crack.)

(OKA has come looking for KIYOKO. He wears an overcoat and holds a wet newspaper over his head.)

OKA: Ah! I'm sorry to bother you so late at night—the fact is . . .

HANA: Oka-san.

OKA: (jovially) Good evening, good evening. (He sees KIYOKO.) Oh, there you are. Did you have a nice visit?

HANA: (irritated) Yes, she's here.

OKA: (still cheerful) Thought she might be. Ready to come home now?

HANA: She came in the rain.

OKA: (ignoring HANA's tone) That's foolish of you, Kiyoko. You might catch cold.

HANA: She was frightened by your quarreling. She came for help.

OKA: (laughing with embarrassment) Oh! Kiyoko, that's nothing to worry about. It's just we had some disagreement.

HANA: That's what I told her, but she was frightened just the same.

OKA: Children are . . .

HANA: Not children, Oka-san. Kiyoko. Kiyoko was terrified. I think that was a terrible thing to do to her.

OKA: (rubbing his head) Oh, I . . . I . . .

HANA: If you had seen her a few minutes ago . . . hysterical . . . shaking . . . crying . . . wet and cold to the bone . . . out of her mind with worry.

OKA: (rubbing his head) Oh, I don't know what she was so worried about.

HANA: You. You and Emiko fighting like you were going to kill each other.

OKA: (lowering his head in penitence) Aaaaaaahhhhhhhh . . .

HANA: I know I shouldn't tell you this, but there's one or two things I have to say: You sent for Kiyoko-san, and now she's here. You said yourself she had a bad time in Japan, and now she's having a worse time. It's not easy for her in a strange country; the least you can do is try to keep from worrying her . . . especially about yourselves. I think it's terrible what you're doing to her . . . terrible!

OKA: (bowing in deep humility) I am ashamed.

HANA: I think she deserves better. I think you should think about that.

OKA: (still bowing) I thank you for this reminder. It will never happen again. I promise.

HANA: I don't need that promise. Make it to Kiyoko-san.

OKA: Come with Papa now. He did a bad thing. He'll be a good Papa from now. He won't worry his little girl again. All right?

(They move toward the door. KIYOKO tries to return Murata's robe.)

KIYOKO: Thank you so much.

OKA: Thank you again.

HANA: (to KIYOKO) That's all right. You can bring it back tomorrow. Remember . . . remember what we talked about. (loudly) Good night, Oka-san.

(They leave. HANA goes to MASAKO, who pretends to sleep. She covers her. MURATA appears from the bedroom. He's heard it all. He and HANA exchange a quick glance and together they retire to their room.)

Scene 3

The next morning. The Murata house and yard. HANA and MURATA have already left the house to examine the rain damage in the fields.

MASAKO prepares to go to school. She puts on a coat and gets her books and lunch bag. Meanwhile, KIYOKO slips quietly into the yard. She wears a coat and carries Murata's robe and sets it on the outside bench.

MASAKO walks out and is surprised to see KIYOKO.

MASAKO: Hi. I thought you'd be . . . sick today.

KIYOKO: Oh. I woke up late.

MASAKO: (scrutinizing KIYOKO's face) Your eyes are red.

KIYOKO: (averting her face) Oh. I . . . got . . . sand in it. Yes.

MASAKO: Do you want eye drops? We have eye drops in the house.

KIYOKO: Oh, no. That's all right.

MASAKO: That's what's called bloodshot.

KIYOKO: Oh.

MASAKO: My father gets it a lot. When he drinks too much.

KIYOKO: Oh.

(MASAKO notices KIYOKO doesn't carry a lunch.)

MASAKO: Where's your lunch bag?

KIYOKO: I . . . forgot it.

MASAKO: Did you make your lunch today?

KIYOKO: Yes. Yes, I did. But I forgot it.

MASAKO: Do you want to go back and get it?

KIYOKO: No. (pause) We will be late.

MASAKO: Do you want to practice your words?

KIYOKO: (thoughtfully) Oh . . .

MASAKO: Say, "My."

KIYOKO: My?

MASAKO: Eyes . . .

KIYOKO: Eyes.

MASAKO: Are . . .

KIYOKO: Are.

MASAKO: Red.

KIYOKO: Red.

MASAKO: Your eyes are red.

(KIYOKO will not repeat it.)

MASAKO: (continuing) I . . .

(KIYOKO doesn't cooperate.)

MASAKO: (continuing) Say, "I."

KIYOKO: I.

MASAKO: Got . . .

KIYOKO: Got.

MASAKO: Sand . . .

(KIYOKO balks.)

MASAKO: (continuing) Say, "I."

KIYOKO: (sighing) I.

MASAKO: Reft . . .

KIYOKO: Reft.

MASAKO: My . . .

KIYOKO: My.

MASAKO: Runch.

KIYOKO: Run . . . Lunch. (pause) Masako-san, you are mean. You are hurting me.

MASAKO: It's a joke! I was just trying to make you laugh!

KIYOKO: I cannot laugh today.

MASAKO: Sure you can. You can laugh. Laugh! Like this! (She makes a hearty laugh.)

KIYOKO: I cannot laugh when you make fun of me.

MASAKO: Okay, I'm sorry. We'll practice some other words then, okay?

(KIYOKO doesn't answer.)

MASAKO: (continuing) Say, "Okay."

KIYOKO: (reluctantly) Okay.

MASAKO: Okay, then . . . um . . . um . . . Say . . . um . . . (rapidly) "She sells seashells by the seashore."

(KIYOKO turns away indignantly.)

MASAKO: (continuing) Aw, come on, Kiyoko! It's just a joke. Laugh!

KIYOKO: (sarcastically) Ha-ha-ha. Now you say, "Kono kyaku wa yoku kaki ku kyaku da!"

MASAKO: Sure I can say it. Kono kyaku waki ku kyoku kaku . . .

KIYOKO: That's not right.

MASAKO: Koki kuki kya . . .

KIYOKO: No. No-no-no.

MASAKO: Okay, then. You say, "Sea sells she shells . . . shu . . . sh."

(They both laugh, KIYOKO with her hands over her mouth. MASAKO takes KIYOKO's hands away.)

MASAKO: Not like that. Like this! (She makes a big laugh.)

KIYOKO: Like this? (She imitates MASAKO.)

MASAKO: Yeah, that's right! (pause) You're not mad anymore?

KIYOKO: I'm not mad anymore.

MASAKO: Okay. You can share my lunch because we're . . .

KIYOKO: "Flends?"

(MASAKO looks at KIYOKO. They giggle and move on.)

(HANA and MURATA come in from assessing the storm's damage. They are dressed warmly. HANA is depressed. MURATA tries to be cheerful.)

MURATA: It's not so bad, Mama.

HANA: Half the ranch is flooded. At least half.

MURATA: No-no. Quarter, maybe. It's sunny today. It'll dry.

HANA: The seedlings will rot.

MURATA: No-no. It'll dry. It's all right. Better than I expected.

HANA: If we have another bad year, no one will lend us money for the next crop.

MURATA: Don't worry. If it doesn't drain by tomorrow, I'll replant the worst places. We still have some seed left. Yeah, I'll replant.

HANA: More work.

MURATA: Don't worry, Mama. It'll be all right.

HANA: (quietly) Papa, where will it end? Will we always be like this—always at the mercy of the weather . . . prices . . . always at the mercy of the Gods?

MURATA: (patting HANA's back) Things will change. Wait and see. We'll be back in Japan by . . . in two years. Guarantee. Maybe sooner.

HANA: (dubiously) Two years . . .

MURATA: (finding the robe on the bench) Ah, look, Mama. Kiyoko-san brought back my robe.

HANA: (sighing) Kiyoko-san . . . poor Kiyoko-san. And Emiko-san . . .

MURATA: Ah, Mama. We're lucky. We're lucky, Mama.

Scene 4

The following spring afternoon. Exterior of the Oka house. OKA is dressed to go out. He wears a sweater, long-sleeved white shirt, dark pants, no tie. He puts his foot to the bench to wipe off his shoe with the palm of his hand. He straightens his sleeve, removes a bit of lint, and runs his fingers through his hair. He hums softly.

KIYOKO comes from the house. Her hair is frizzled in a permanent wave, she wears a gaudy new dress and a pair of new shoes. She carries a movie magazine.

OKA: (appreciatively) Pretty. Pretty.

KIYOKO: (turning for him) It's not too *hadeh?* I feel strange in colors.

OKA: Oh, no. Young girls should wear bright colors. Time enough to wear gray when you get old. Old-lady colors.

(KIYOKO giggles.)

OKA: (continuing) Sure you want to go to the picture show? It's such a nice day . . . shame to waste in a dark hall.

KIYOKO: Where else can we go?

OKA: We can go to Murata-san's.

KIYOKO: All dressed up?

OKA: Or Nagata-san's. I'll show him what I got for my horse.

KIYOKO: I love the pictures.

OKA: We don't have many nice spring days like this. Here the season is short. Summer comes in like a dragon . . . right behind . . . breathing fire . . . like a dragon. You don't know the summers here. They'll scare you.

(He tousles KIYOKO's hair and pulls a lock of it. It springs back. He shakes his head in wonder.)

OKA: (continuing) Goddam. Curly hair. Never thought curly hair could make you so happy.

KIYOKO: (giggling) All the American girls have curly hair.

OKA: Your friend Masako like it?

KIYOKO: (nodding) She says her mother will never let her get a permanent wave.

OKA: She said that, eh? Bet she's wanting one.

KIYOKO: I don't know about that.

OKA: Bet she's wanting some of your pretty dresses too.

KIYOKO: Her mother makes all her clothes.

OKA: Buying is just as good. Buying is better. No trouble that way.

KIYOKO: Masako's not interested in clothes. She loves the pictures, but her mother won't let her go. Someday, can we take Masako with us?

OKA: If her mother lets her come. Her mother's got a mind of her own. Stiff back.

KIYOKO: But she's nice.

OKA: (dubiously) Oh, yeah. Can't be perfect, I guess. Kiyoko, after the harvest I'll have money, and I'll buy you the prettiest dress in town. I'm going to be lucky this year. I feel it.

KIYOKO: You're already too good to me . . . dresses, shoes, permanent wave . . . movies . . .

OKA: That's nothing. After the harvest, just wait . . .

KIYOKO: . . . magazines. You do enough. I'm happy already.

OKA: You make me happy too, Kiyoko. You make me feel good . . . like a man again. (That bothers him.) One day you're going to make a young man happy.

(KIYOKO giggles.)

OKA: (continuing) Someday we going to move from here.

KIYOKO: But we have good friends here, Papa.

OKA: Next year our lease will be up and we got to move.

KIYOKO: The ranch is not ours?

OKA: No. In America Japanese cannot own land. We lease and move every two to three years. Next year we going go someplace where there's young fellows. There's none good enough for you here. Yeah. You going to make a good wife. Already a good cook. I like your cooking.

KIYOKO: (a little embarrassed) Shall we go now?

OKA: Yeah. Put the magazine away.

KIYOKO: I want to take it with me.

OKA: Take it with you?

KIYOKO: Last time, after we came back, I found all my magazines torn in half. Even the new ones.

OKA: (looking toward the house) Torn?

KIYOKO: This is the only one I have left.

OKA: All right, all right.

(The two prepare to leave when EMIKO lurches through the door. Her hair is unkempt—she looks wild. She holds an empty can in one hand, the lid in the other.)

EMIKO: Where is it?

(OKA tries to make a hasty departure.)

KIYOKO: Where is what?

(OKA pushes KIYOKO ahead of him, still trying to make a getaway.)

EMIKO: Where is it? Where is it? What did you do with it?

(EMIKO moves toward OKA.)

OKA: (with false unconcern to KIYOKO) Why don't you walk on ahead to Murata-san's.

KIYOKO: We're not going to the pictures?

OKA: We'll go. First you walk to Murata-san's. Show them your new dress. I'll meet you there.

(KIYOKO enters the house, pushing past EMIKO, emerges with a small package, and exits, looking worriedly back at OKA and EMIKO. OKA sighs and shakes his head.)

EMIKO: (shaking the can) Where is it? What did you do with it?

OKA: (feigning surprise) With what?

EMIKO: You know what. You stole it. You stole my money.

OKA: *Your* money?

EMIKO: I've been saving that money.

OKA: Yeah? Well, where'd you get it? Where'd you get it, eh? You stole it from me! Dollar by dollar! You stole it from me! Out of my pocket!

EMIKO: I saved it!

OKA: From *my* pocket!

EMIKO: It's mine! I saved for a long time. Some of it I brought from Japan.

OKA: *Bakayuna!* What'd you bring from Japan? Nothing but some useless kimonos.

(OKA tries to leave, but EMIKO hangs on to him.)

EMIKO: Give back my money! Thief!

(OKA swings around and balls his fists but doesn't strike.)

OKA: Goddam! Get off me!

EMIKO: (now pleading) Please give it back . . . please . . . please . . .

(EMIKO strokes his legs, but OKA pulls her hands away and pushes her from him.)

EMIKO: (continuing) *Oni!*

OKA: (seething) *Oni?* What does that make you? *Oni-baba?* Yeah, that's what you are . . . a devil!

EMIKO: It's mine! Give it back!

OKA: The hell! You think you can live off me and steal my money too? How stupid you think I am?

EMIKO: (tearfully) But I've paid. I've paid . . .

OKA: With what?

EMIKO: You know I've paid.

OKA: (scoffing) You call that paying?

EMIKO: What did you do with it?

OKA: I don't have it.

EMIKO: It's gone? It's gone?

OKA: Yeah! It's gone. I spent it. The hell! Every last cent.

EMIKO: The new clothes . . . the curls . . . restaurants . . . pictures . . . shoes . . . My money. My going-home money.

OKA: You through?

EMIKO: What will I do? What (will) . . .

OKA: I don't care what you do. Walk. Use your feet. Swim to Japan. I don't care. I give you no more than you gave me. Now I don't want anything. I don't care what you do. (He walks away.)

(EMIKO still holds the empty can. Offstage we hear OKA's car start off. Accustomed to crying alone, she doesn't utter a sound. Her shoulders shake, her dry soundless sobs turn to a silent laugh. She wipes the dust gently from the can as though comforting a friend. Her movements grow sensuous, her hands move to her own body, around her throat, over her breasts, to her hips, caressing, soothing, reminding her of her lover's hands.)

Scene 5

Same day, late afternoon. Exterior of the Murata house. The light is soft. HANA sweeps the yard; MASAKO hangs a glass wind chime on the wall.

HANA: (directing MASAKO) There. There. That's a good place.

MASAKO: Here?

HANA: (nodding) It must catch the slightest breeze. (sighing and listening) It brings back so much. That's the reason I never hung one before. I guess it doesn't matter much anymore.

MASAKO: I thought you liked to think about Japan.

HANA: (laughing softly) I didn't want to hear that sound too often . . . get too used to it. Sometimes you hear something too often, after a while you don't hear it anymore. I didn't want that to happen. The same thing happens to feelings too, I guess. After a while, you don't feel anymore. You're too young to understand that yet.

MASAKO: I understand, Mama.

HANA: Wasn't it nice of Kiyoko-san to give you the *furin?*

MASAKO: I love it. I don't know anything about Japan, but it makes me feel something too.

HANA: Maybe someday when you're grown up, gone away, you'll hear it and remember yourself as this little girl . . . remember this old house, the ranch, and . . . your old mama.

MASAKO: That's kind of scary.

(EMIKO enters unsteadily. She carries a bundle wrapped in a colorful scarf (furoshiki). In the package are two beautiful kimonos.)

HANA: Emiko-san! What a pleasant surprise! Please sit down. We were just hanging the wind chime. It was so sweet of Kiyoko-san to give it to Masako. She loves it.

(EMIKO looks mildly interested. She acts as normal as she can throughout the scene, but at times drops the facade, revealing her desperation.)

EMIKO: Thank you. (She sets the bundle on the bench but keeps her hand on it.)

HANA: Your family was here earlier.

(EMIKO smiles vaguely.)

HANA: (continuing) On their way to the pictures, I think. Make tea for us, Ma-chan.

EMIKO: Please don't.

HANA: Kiyoko-san was looking so nice . . . her hair all curly. Of course, in our day, straight black hair was desirable. Of course, times change.

EMIKO: Yes . . .

HANA: But she did look fine. My, my, a colorful new dress, new shoes, a permanent wave—looked like a regular American girl. Did you choose her dress?

EMIKO: No . . . I didn't go.

HANA: You know, I didn't think so. Very pretty though. I liked it very much. Of course, I sew all Masako's clothes. It saves money. It'll be nice for you to make things for Kiyoko-san too. She'd be so pleased. I know she'd be pleased.

(While HANA talks, EMIKO plucks nervously at the package. She waits for HANA to stop.)

HANA: (continuing) Emiko-san, is everything all right?

EMIKO: (smiling nervously) Yes.

HANA: Masako, please go make tea for us. See if there aren't any more of those crackers left. Or did you finish them? (to EMIKO) We can't keep anything in this house. She eats everything as soon as Papa brings it home. You'd never know it, she's so skinny. We never have anything left for company.

MASAKO: We hardly ever have company anyway.

(HANA gives MASAKO a strong look before MASAKO leaves. EMIKO is lost in her own thoughts.)

HANA: Is there something you . . . I can help you with? (very gently) Emiko-san?

EMIKO: (suddenly frightened) Oh, no. I was thinking . . . Now that . . . now that . . . Masa-chan is growing up . . . older . . .

HANA: Oh, yes.

EMIKO: I was thinking . . .

(She stops, puts the package on her lap, and is lost again.)

HANA: Yes, she is growing. Time goes so fast. I think she'll be taller than me soon. (She laughs weakly but looks puzzled.)

EMIKO: Yes . . .

(EMIKO's depression pervades the atmosphere. HANA is affected by it. The two women sit in silence. A small breeze moves the wind chimes. At the moment, light grows dim on the two lonely figures.)

(MASAKO brings the tray of tea. The light returns to normal.)

HANA: (gently) You're a good girl.

(MASAKO looks first to EMIKO, then to her mother. She sets the tray on the bench and stands near EMIKO. EMIKO seems to notice her for the first time.)

EMIKO: How are you?

(HANA pours the tea.)

HANA: Emiko-san, is there something I can do for you?

EMIKO: There's . . . I was . . . I . . . Masa-chan will be a young lady soon. . . .

HANA: Well, I don't know about "lady."

EMIKO: Maybe she would like a nice . . . nice . . . (She unwraps the package.) I have kimonos I wore in Japan for dancing. Maybe she can . . . if you like, I mean. They'll be nice on her. She's so slim.

(EMIKO shakes out a robe. HANA and MASAKO are impressed.)

HANA: Ohhh! Beautiful!

MASAKO: Oh, Mama! Pretty!

(They touch the material.)

MASAKO: (continuing) Gold threads, Mama.

HANA: Brocade!

EMIKO: Maybe Masa-chan would like them. I mean for her school programs . . . Japanese school.

HANA: Oh, no! Too good for country. People will be envious of us . . . wonder where we got them.

EMIKO: I mean for festivals. *Obon, Hana Matsuri* . . .

HANA: Oh, but you have Kiyoko-san now. You should give them to her. Has she seen them?

EMIKO: Oh. No.

HANA: She'll love them. You should give them to her—not our Masako.

EMIKO: I thought . . . I mean, I was thinking of . . . if you could give me a little . . . if you could pay . . . manage to give me something for . . .

HANA: But these gowns, Emiko-san—they're worth hundreds.

EMIKO: I know, but I'm not asking for that. Whatever you can give. Only as much as you can give.

MASAKO: Mama?

HANA: Masako, Papa doesn't have that kind of money.

EMIKO: Anything you can give. Anything . . .

MASAKO: Ask Papa.

HANA: There's no use asking. I *know* he can't afford it.

EMIKO: (looking at MASAKO) A little at a time . . .

MASAKO: Mama?

HANA: (firmly) No, Masako. This is a luxury.

(HANA folds the gowns and puts them away. EMIKO is decimated. HANA sees this and tries to find a way to help.)

HANA: (continuing) Emiko-san, I hope you understand.

(EMIKO is silent, trying to gather her resources.)

HANA: (continuing) I know you can sell them and get the full price somewhere. Let's see . . . a family with lots of growing daughters . . . someone who did well last year. Nagata-san has no girls. Umeda-san has girls but no money. Well, let's see . . . Maybe not here in this country town. Ah . . . you can take them to the city—Los Angeles—and sell them to a store. Or Terminal Island. Lots of wealthy fishermen there. Yes, that would be the place. Why, it's no problem, Emiko-san. Have your husband take them there. I know you'll get your money. He'll find a buyer. I know he will.

EMIKO: Yes . . . (She ties the bundle and sits quietly.)

HANA: Please have your tea. I'm sorry. I really would like to take them for Masako, but it just isn't possible. You understand, don't you?

(EMIKO nods.)

HANA: (continuing) Please don't feel so . . . so bad. It's not really a matter of life or death, is it? Emiko-san?

(EMIKO nods again. HANA sips her tea.)

MASAKO: Mama? If you could ask Papa . . .

HANA: Oh, the tea is cold. Masako, could you heat the kettle?

EMIKO: No more. I must be going. (She picks up her package and rises slowly.)

HANA: (helplessly) So soon? Emiko-san, please stay.

(EMIKO starts to go.)

HANA: (continuing) Masako will walk with you. (She pushes MASAKO forward.)

EMIKO: It's not far.

HANA: Emiko-san? You'll be all right?

EMIKO: Yes . . . yes . . . yes . . .

HANA: (calling after EMIKO) I'm sorry, Emiko-san.

EMIKO: Yes.

(MASAKO and HANA watch as EMIKO leaves. The light grows dim as though a cloud passed over. HANA strokes MASAKO's hair.)

HANA: Your hair is so black and straight . . . nice.

(They stand close. The wind chimes tinkle; light grows dim. Light returns to normal.)

(MURATA enters. He sees the tableau of mother and child and is puzzled.)

MURATA: What's going on here?

(The women part.)

HANA: Oh . . . nothing. Nothing.

MASAKO: Mrs. Oka was here. She had two kimo(nos) . . .

HANA: (putting her hand on MASAKO's shoulder) It was nothing.

MURATA: Eh? What'd she want?

HANA: Later, Papa. Right now, I'd better fix supper.

MURATA: (looking at the sky) Strange how that sun comes and goes. Maybe I didn't need to irrigate . . . looks like rain. (He remembers.) Ach! I forgot to shut the water!

MASAKO: I'll do it, Papa.

HANA: Masako, that gate's too heavy for you.

MURATA: She can handle it. Take out the pin and let the gate fall all the way down. All the way. And put the pin back. Don't forget to put the pin back.

HANA: And be careful. Don't fall in the canal.

(MASAKO leaves.)

MURATA: What's the matter with that girl?

HANA: Nothing. Why?

MURATA: Usually have to *beg* her to (do) . . .

HANA: She's growing up.

MURATA: Must be that time of the month.

HANA: Oh, Papa, she's too young for that yet.

MURATA: (genially as they enter the house) Got to start sometime. Looks like I'll be outnumbered soon. I'm outnumbered already.

(HANA glances at him and quietly begins preparations for supper. MURATA removes his shirt and picks up a paper. Light fades slowly.)

Scene 6

Same evening. Exterior, desert. There is at least one shrub, a tumbleweed maybe. MASAKO walks slowly. From a distance we hear EMIKO singing the song, "And the Soul Shall Dance." MASAKO looks around, sees the shrub, and crouches by it. EMIKO appears. She wears her beautiful kimono tied loosely at her waist. She carries a branch of sage. Her hair is loose.

EMIKO: *Akai kuchibiru / Kappu ni yosete / Aoi sake nomya / Kokoro ga odoru / Kurai yoru no yume / Setsu nasa yo. . . .*

(EMIKO breaks into a dance, laughs mysteriously, turns round and round acting out a fantasy. MASAKO stirs uncomfortably. EMIKO senses a presence. She stops, drops her branch, empties out her sleeve of imaginary flowers at MASAKO, and exits singing.)

EMIKO: (continuing) *Aoi sake nomya / Yume ga odoru. . . .*

(MASAKO watches as EMIKO leaves. She rises slowly and picks up the branch EMIKO has left. She moves forward a step and looks off to the point where EMIKO disappeared.)

Light slowly fades on MASAKO, and the image of her forlorn form remains etched on the retina.

Producing *And the Soul Shall Dance*

Introduction to East West Players

The Oregon Shakespeare Festival, discussed in Chapter 3, is firmly rooted in the English (European) theatre tradition. The next producing company we discuss, East West Players, represents another tradition and community altogether. The primary focus of East West Players is presenting the voices of Asian/Pacific Americans as writers, actors, and producers. The repertoire of East West Players emphasizes American plays that reflect the experiences of Asian/Pacific Americans.

The theatre's early productions most frequently featured plays by Americans of Japanese, Chinese, and Korean heritage; more recently, performances have expanded to include the work of Southeast Asians and Pacific Islanders. Although there is an international influence, that influence is first Asian and then European. And when European plays are performed, they are acted by Asian American or multiracial casts. A production by East West Players of Ibsen's *Hedda Gabler*, for example, was set in Japan rather than Norway, and the roles were played by Asian American actors. The name East West Players reflects this theatre's goal of serving as a cultural bridge between the East and the West.

History of East West Players

In 1965 a group of Japanese American, Chinese American, and Korean American actors came together in Los Angeles to form East West Players, the first Asian American theatre company in the United States. Tired of the demeaning and frequently ridiculous, stereotypical roles they were playing in films and theatre, such as subservient "houseboys," exotic and treacherous women, or sinister villains, these actors were determined to create a theatre in their own image, where they could choose how they were represented on the stage.

As with so many other struggling young theatre groups, the first performances of East West Players took place in a church basement. In 1968, however, they made the triumphant move to their own space. At first the Asian American casts performed plays written by Europeans and non-Asian Americans; actors at long last had the opportunity to play major, complex roles rather than one-dimensional characters.

The group also supported the development of new plays by Asian American playwrights. These plays recorded the experiences of Asian immigrants to the United States and their Asian American children, histories that had not been recorded elsewhere. They were stories of farming California's agricultural valleys in the 1930s, of struggling for survival in the internment camps in the 1940s, of creating new families when American soldiers returned from World War II with Japanese "war brides." They were about dislocation, the clash of cultures, and the struggle for identity. These stories were dramatized for audiences made up largely of Asian Americans who recognized themselves and the stories of their own lives in the plays.

Location and Physical Space

And the Soul Shall Dance was produced by East West Players for the second time in 1996, when they still performed in their long-standing home, a renovated garment factory in a run-down section of Santa Monica Boulevard in Los Angeles. With only ninety-nine seats, East West Players was at that time an Equity waiver theatre—a professional theatre that because of its limited seating was exempt from certain regulations of the Actors Equity union.

To get to the theatre, audiences had to drive past factories and industrial yards cluttered with trucks, pipes, and metal fittings. There were few shops or restaurants within walking distance of

In the late 1990s, East West Players moved from the renovated garment factory to a larger and more graceful theatre space housed in the centrally located Union Center for the arts, which is also home to Visual Communication and L.A. Art Core, two other arts organizations. The David Henry Hwang Theatre provides expanded seating, including a balcony and sophisticated technical support for lights, sound, and scenery. Tim Dang is the current producing artistic director of East West Players.

the theatre. The external ambience of East West Players was light-years away from the slow pace and charm of Ashland, Oregon, with its quiet streets, cafés, and parks.

Since the production of *And the Soul Shall Dance* in 1996, East West Players, having more than outgrown its space on Santa Monica Boulevard, moved to the Union Center for the Arts in the Little Tokyo area of downtown Los Angeles. The company now has a 236-seat theatre, expanded rehearsal and classroom spaces, sophisticated technology, and comfortable parking for the staff and audiences. But the creativity that was generated in the cramped old space, the careers that were launched, and the barriers that were broken all reflected a wealth of talent and commitment not dependent on an impressive physical plant. In fact, for many theatre practitioners, the satisfaction is greater in a theatre of limited resources, where gold seems to be spun out of straw.

For our production analysis, we return to the experience of the performance at the garment factory where East West Players spent its first thirty years. Inside the theatre, the audience steps away from the grubby Los Angeles street into a tiny but lively and congenial lobby crowded with photographs and posters from previous productions. The audience is drawn largely from the Asian American community, and for this play,

And the Soul Shall Dance, most noticeably from the Japanese American community. Many audience members know each other and exchange friendly greetings over coffee and cookies. Older members of the audience recall the original production of the play, staged eighteen years ago. Younger members of the audience seeing the play for the first time are prepared to be introduced to one of the classics of the Asian American theatre.

Staging the Play

The Director's Prologue

The small stage (measuring twenty by thirty feet) of East West Players is completely empty except for a muslin scrim (curtain) that hangs around the upstage perimeter of the playing

The set design for *And the Soul Shall Dance*, by Yuki Nakamura, featured two small rolling house units that were unfolded ingeniously in view of the audience. The walls were either cut down or covered with transparent material to allow the audience a full view of the interiors.

space. A small elevated platform juts out over the audience at one side. On the platform are Japanese wind and percussion instruments, including shakuhachi (bamboo) flutes of various lengths, taiko drums of different sizes, Tibetan cymbals, and Japanese wind chimes. While the house lights are still up, a light comes up on the platform, where a musician (either George Abe or Masakazu Yoshizawa) in a Japanese *yukata* (a loose tunic) and *hakama* (wide-cut pants) appears. He begins to beat the large taiko drum, sending sharp reverberations through the small theatre, announcing the beginning of the play. At the end of the short drum overture, the lights go down on both the audience and the stage space.

The sound of the wind comes over the theatre's speakers, and the musician begins to play long, mournful notes on the largest shakuhachi flute. A dim light illuminates a single shape on the stage. The shape is a piece of tumbleweed. A **kuroko**—a hooded actor dressed completely in black—who seems to blend in with the darkness of the stage, rolls and lifts the tumbleweed through the air as if it is being blown by the wind.

With these simple elements—the sounds of the wind, the haunting notes of the flute, and

the single piece of blowing, rolling tumbleweed—the production creates the sense of a vast, open, lonely space. Suddenly a sharp clicking sound is heard, and two more hooded figures dressed in black rush silently onto the stage and sweep aside half of the curtain hanging at the back. Using highly stylized, choreographed movement, the three kurokos roll forward and unfold what will become the walls of the Muratas' house. As the simple frame of the house takes shape, one of the kurokos whirls in first with a table and then with chairs. All of the movement suggests that it is the wind that is blowing the small dwelling and its simple furnishings onto the stage. The walls of the house are suggestive rather than complete. They are cut low to allow the audience to see all the action inside. A table and chairs, a bed, a stove, a sink, and dishes give the sense of a functional but spartan household.

The drumming that has accompanied the scene shift gives way to the sound of fire. The actors playing the Murata family enter, dismayed over the loss of the bathhouse, and the play as it is written in the script begins: the realistic story of a child who has been careless; an anxious, scolding mother; and a weary father. But in the few minutes that precede their entrance, a vivid atmosphere has been created for their story. With a few strokes of sound and stage imagery, like the brushstrokes of Japanese calligraphy, the characters have been placed spatially and emotionally in the emptiness and desolation of the Imperial Valley.

The Influence of Asian Theatre

The presence of the kurokos, in combination with the sounds of the musical instruments, also introduces the cultural background of the characters. They are clearly tied to Asia. The director of the production, Jim Ishida, says, "No matter how long the Issei, first-generation, are here, there is still that connection to their cultural heritage."[6] Through the references to Asian theatre, the director, in collaboration with the scene designer Yuki Nakamura, who has also designed the sound, establishes the production's theatrical style. Realism is combined with a simple, concentrated, poetic expression to take us into the daily lives of the characters and beyond, into their "souls."

> **JIM ISHIDA:** I wanted to incorporate as much of Eastern theatre technique as I possibly could. So therefore we thought of kabuki and the use of kurokos and the cycs (**cyclorama**—cloth that forms the background for the action) rising and everything coming out in a big flurry. I like actors to be very physical. I like the actors to be part of the wind, bringing the tumbleweed in, creating the nothing space into something.
>
> The kurokos are based on figures from the traditional kabuki theatre of Japan. In kabuki the kuroko changes the scenery, helps actors make onstage costume changes, and brings in props. The role of the kuroko has its own history in Japanese theatre tradition. Just as acting certain parts was handed down from father to son, so the position of kuroko was passed down through certain families.

In the production of *And the Soul Shall Dance*, the kurokos serve a double purpose. They serve first to change the scenery and the props. But the movement of the kurokos is also meaningful choreographically. As they whirl about the stage, they suggest the feeling of the wind; and the audience accepts the notion that the kurokos are invisible. The kurokos allow for a certain kind of theatrical magic that does not depend on highly complex or expensive technical equipment. The actors playing the kurokos have prepared for their roles by studying dance and the stylized movement of the Japanese theatre. In contrast, the actors playing Yamauchi's characters must create a physically and psychologically believable rendering of Japanese American life in the 1930s.

Through the stylized movement of the kurokos and the realistic acting of the characters, the production blends the poetic and concrete elements of the play. Another example of blending is the mixture of expressive musical accompaniment with realistic sound effects. The production is a fusion of lyricism and realism.

Staging a Period Play: The Work of the Director and the Actors

In rehearsing the actions of the characters, in constructing the realistic life of poor families struggling with hardship, Jim Ishida finds the starting point in "Japanese behavior." The characters' manners, their posture and gestures, and their speech rhythms must echo the conduct of Japanese immigrants to the United States in the early part of the twentieth century.

> **JIM ISHIDA:** That was the hardest work, the physical work, the dance and the behavior. To eliminate the actors' Western colloquialisms, their Western behavior. They've lived their lives as Westerners. In a short period of time they've had to find Japanese behavior. The way they bow, the way farmers hold their hands, the way they drink.

Acquiring such specialized mannerisms is a highly complex task. The actors, third- and fourth-generation descendents of immigrant families, must learn from the outside what was a way of life for their grandparents and great-grandparents.

> **DENISE IKETANI (EMIKO):** We are so American. The culture has changed. I'm fourth-generation. In terms of how we talk to our parents and how our parents talked to their parents and how their parents talked to their parents, each generation is completely different.

Period Style   In the American theatre, specialists typically coach actors in what is called **period style,** the deportment, manners, attitudes, and gestures of times past. Frequently, actors take classes in various aspects of period behavior, particularly combat and dance, which are excellent sources of posture and gesture in addition to being useful for their own sake when a fight must be staged or movement sequences choreographed. Dance styles and the martial arts codify physical attitudes in forms that can be passed down through generations. Paintings and, more recently, photographs and films offer additional sources for details of period behavior.

Another essential source for understanding the movement and posture of other eras is period clothing. If a character must wear a garment that binds the body in various ways—a military uniform or a kimono, for example—the garment structure determines to a large degree how the character will stand and walk. Although the period of *And the Soul Shall Dance*, the 1930s, does not seem very long ago, in fact the cultural circumstances of that time pose a geographic and temporal distance that cannot be bridged without assistance.

Movement and Gesture   Ishida and the actors turn to a variety of sources for the period information they need. Ishida draws on his memory of the actions and attitudes of his grandparents, as well as observations made during recent travels to Japan. The actors watch Japanese films and observe the interactions of senior members of the community. In this production Ishida takes responsibility for coaching the men, and Mary Tamaki is invited to join the production staff to coach the women's movement and to choreograph Emiko's dance sequences. Mary Tamaki has spent years studying the classical dance of Japan and is designated *natori*, the level of achievement that the character Emiko had aspired to.

For this production, the director has another special consultant—the playwright, Wakako Yamauchi. Playwrights are frequently unavailable for consultation after the original production of a play, and theatre companies feel honored if the playwrights come to see their particular productions. But in this case, Wakako Yamauchi attends rehearsals and makes suggestions to Ishida. The play, of course, represents her own experience, the times that she lived through as a child.

During the early rehearsals, Jim Ishida and Mary Tamaki coach the actors on the basics of movement and social interaction—how to walk and stand, how to bow, how to greet each other. Although ultimately Ishida will give the actors much freedom to experiment and make choices, this beginning work is all done through imitation and drill, with endless precise corrections.

For example, the male characters—Murata and Oka— meet twice in the two opening scenes and drink sake. The greeting between them is far from a contemporary American handshake or slap on the back. They make repeated shallow, sharp bows to each other and greet each other heartily, with a guttural, barking kind of laughter. In the first scene they sit together to drink—as if it is understood that the privilege of the sake and the table is theirs—while Hana as dutiful wife waits on them. They drink their sake quickly, with short bursts of energy. When the chiles are called for, Hana serves them, head down, using chopsticks to take them out of the jar. The men punctuate their speech with Japanese rather than American exclamations. After eating the chiles, both men cover their mouths and pick their teeth while continuing their conversation.

The movement work for the women is very difficult. American women have a freedom of movement and a lift in their walk that is incompatible with the style necessary to give authenticity to the production.

MARY TAMAKI: The women must learn to walk with the center of gravity lower, which is the more traditional Japanese style, shuffling the feet. Japanese women do not pick up their feet. They shuffle, wearing the zoris (Japanese sandals). They must be demure. There's no loud laughing, and they must cover their mouths when they want to smile.

Mary Tamaki brings kimonos to rehearsals to facilitate the learning of the necessary body positions and walking style, even though the actors will not wear kimonos in the production.

MARY TAMAKI: These are not natural movements . . . to walk with your knees slightly bent, to shuffle along taking tiny steps. It is a style that you learn. It is not part of our Western nature to be so humble. When you're in kimonos the movements become so much more natural. You are slightly bound in them, so your movements of course are restricted. The way you walk is definitely restricted by the kimono.

DENISE IKETANI (EMIKO): Having to wear the kimono completely changes the way you move. When you put on a kimono it's very tight. It's even hard to breathe sometimes. That just affects what you can and cannot do.

ANNA QUIRINO (MASAKO): When you wear the kimono, it can't flap open at the bottom. Once you see the flap you know you're walking wrong. It has to be like a cylinder walking, so the steps are very small and pigeon-toed.

In rehearsal under Mary Tamaki's guidance, the women practice entering a room, bowing, and greeting each other. They learn the correct way to pour tea and to sit down.

MARY TAMAKI: I walked for them. Then I would remind them to bend their knees more. Don't bounce. Shuffle along. Keep your hands to your side.

Dance   Mary Tamaki also works separately with Denise Iketani on the dances that come from Emiko's past. Tamaki choreographs a dance of two minutes that is based on five basic movements from the classical Japanese dance. One minute of this dance will be used when Emiko dances inside her house and first captivates Masako. Denise Iketani will use the full two-minute piece as the basis for the improvised movements she does outside at other points in the play. Mary Tamaki and Denise Iketani rehearse the two-minute dance sequence for ten hours during different rehearsals. Tamaki feels the pressure of the time limit. In her own dance studies, a ten-minute dance would be rehearsed for over a year. However, in the theatre, time is always measured. In a concentrated period of time, choreography that serves the needs of the production must be created and learned.

The period movement that Jim Ishida, Mary Tamaki, and the actors have worked hard to achieve gives the play a certain authenticity, a texture of the times. It establishes the cultural background that makes clear the standards of propriety, what is expected of or acceptable for men and for women.

MARY TAMAKI: As far as the women's role at that time, the women were second to the men. They had no large gestures. They were not usually able to express themselves in public in front of the men. The wife was able to express herself inside the home but not outside of the home.

But most important, the period movement provides the starting point for the development of character. In Jim Ishida's words, "emotionality must come out of the Japanese behavior." What begin as general standards of deportment and social interaction evolve into highly individuated characters.

Speech Rhythms   Another element Yamauchi uses to create a realistic atmosphere for her play is the suggestion that the adult characters are all speaking Japanese. She includes a number of Japanese words in the text, but it is the rhythm of the speeches that is most important and that also poses another significant task for the actors. They must learn their lines in English, of course, but with Japanese inflection and intonation. In addition to the physical work they must do to

Oka (Benjamin Lum) and Murata (Nelson Mashita) share painful memories as Hana (Sharon Omi) and Masako (Anna Quirino) look on.

develop the characters' behavior, they must study and acquire Japanese speech rhythms. Speech and dialect coaching plays a regular part in the American theatre, preparing actors to speak with foreign or regional accents.

Only the actor playing Masako speaks an Americanized English. The Americanization of Masako's speech rhythms and the freedom of her movement obviously set her apart from the other characters. She is of a new generation, without her parents' ties to Japan. Whereas her parents maintain their identities through observing Japanese traditions and long to return to Japan, Masako looks to the future. She seeks a wider view of the world and her place in it.

Building Character Relationships

To further examine the way realism and lyricism are combined to shape character and to establish crucial character relationships, we consider now the staging of act 1, scene 2 of *And the Soul Shall Dance* at East West Players. Following scene 1, the kurokos roll away the Murata house, and the other half of the curtain is pulled back to allow the unfolding of a second small house on the right side of the stage. The shakuhachi flute is heard again as the Oka house appears.

The sweeping aside of the curtains to reveal each little house is an actual and figurative expression of the opening of memory. What the audience sees is what Masako remembers. When the curtain is brushed aside and the Murata house appears in scene 1, we go back with Masako to the day she burned down the bathhouse. The significance of the burning of the bathhouse becomes clear as the curtain draws back on scene 2, the memory of the Oka house. It is through this small catastrophe that Masako encounters the elusive, withdrawn Emiko.

As act 1, scene 2 begins, Oka, Murata, and Hana sit amicably together on a bench by the

Denise Iketani (Emiko) and Anna Quirino (Masako) rehearse a sequence that uses choreography developed by Mary Tamaki. Quirino uses a kimono for rehearsal although she will not wear one in the play.

door to the Oka house while Masako kneels in front of them with the Victrola. At Oka's insistence, Emiko finally, but reluctantly, comes outside and moves to the other side of the door, where she sits in a chair with her face turned partly away. As the script is written, Emiko does not speak until she is alone with Masako. This means that in the first part of the scene, everything that Emiko communicates must be expressed physically.

As the other characters uneasily make cheerful but forced small talk about the records and the Victrola, Emiko begins to roll herself a cigarette. The rolling of the cigarette is clearly called for in the stage directions: "She pulls out a sack of Bull Durham and begins to roll a cigarette." The playwright has chosen this detail very carefully. Emiko does not speak. She does not greet her guests or offer to serve them tea. But she does roll herself a cigarette. This single action speaks volumes about Emiko's attitude. She is rebellious and defiant; she does not care to be seen as a proper, traditional Japanese woman.

Hana attempts to break the tension of this moment by sending Masako to Emiko with a stack of records. As Masako timidly approaches Emiko with her arms folded around the record albums, Emiko finishes rolling her cigarette. Then, holding the cigarette in one hand and the pouch of tobacco in the other, Emiko inclines her head and pulls the string to close the bag of tobacco sharply with her teeth. This tough, masculine gesture secures Masako's attention.

Emiko then turns her head to look at Masako for the first time. She has the cigarette in her mouth and a defiant look on her face, an attitude that makes a large impression on an eleven-year-old girl raised by a very proper mother.

ANNA QUIRINO (MASAKO): When she pulls out the cigarette . . . that's the big thing for me. Wow! Who is this woman? Because my mother is so traditional. She wants me to be polite. Hana would never do this. She's very strong, especially against my father. She can speak up. But here is Emiko who is very quiet in her corner. But what she's doing! My character is so fascinated by her, scared too in the beginning. At first I just don't want to be there. But the taking out of the cigarette. I've never seen a woman do that before.

The second sequence of actions that draws Masako to Emiko begins when Emiko reenters the house after they begin to play the Japanese

The attitude of Masako (Emily Keiko Pruiksma) contrasts with that of her parents, Murata and Hana (Ken Chin and Kathy Hsieh) in the production of *And the Soul Shall Dance* at Northwest Asian American Theatre in Seattle, directed by Judi Nihei.

records on the Victrola. Emiko dances by herself inside the house, and the audience can see her because the walls are partially cut away or constructed in places with transparent mesh. The adult characters outside are unaware of the dancing, but Masako, on her way to the bath, stops at the window and stares in at Emiko dancing. She is now captivated by the strangeness and wonder of a Japanese woman who drinks and smokes and is also trained in classical movement.

Masako's relationship to Emiko continues to grow when the other adults exit and Masako is left alone on the stage. She puts "And the Soul Shall Dance" on the Victrola and becomes lost in the music. When Emiko returns and sees Masako with a distant expression on her face, she recognizes some kinship between them.

DENISE IKETANI (EMIKO): The song, of course. "And the Soul Shall Dance" *Kokoro ga odoru.* The fact that Masako plays this song that was Emiko's favorite song and that she understands—that's the instant connection. The whole world that she lives in right now is just so horrible. This one little thing that Masako does—it amazes her that Masako does understand. She knows that she's found some sort of bonding, a kinship, with this person even though she is a child. She sees this child who understands what it is about your soul dancing.

Emiko begins to sing with the voice on the record, and after a moment Masako sings too. With warmth growing between them, Emiko crosses to Masako, and the two seem bound in the same spell. They kneel together by the Victrola, and Emiko speaks for the first time: "Do you like that song, Masa-chan?" Their intimacy deepens, and Emiko rises to dance again, now easily and fluidly. The woman and the child speak the words of the song together while Emiko dances. She seems to be dancing out the feeling of the green wine as Masako watches, enchanted.

EMIKO: Drink the green wine . . .

MASAKO: Green? I thought wine was purple.

EMIKO: Wine is purple, but this is a green liqueur. It's good. It warms your heart.

MASAKO: And the soul dances.

EMIKO: Yes . . .

MASAKO: What does it taste like? The green wine?

EMIKO: Oh, it's like . . . it's like . . .

MASAKO: In the dark night . . .

EMIKO: Dreams are unbearable . . .

MASAKO: Drink the . . .

EMIKO: Drink the green wine . . .

MASAKO: And the dreams will dance. (act 1, scene 2)

The two actors speak the words as if together they understand a special language that lifts them out of the present. The song provides a vocabulary,

In the Northwest Asian American Theatre production, Emiko (Sherryl Ray) attracts Masako's attention with her cigarette and her mysterious attitude.

a rhythm, a melody, and an atmosphere that allow for a shift in consciousness. Emiko's soul emerges through the grace of the dance, and Masako's spirit seems to join in the dance of the soul with her. It is a transcendent moment.

All too quickly the moment is interrupted by Oka's return. In this scene Masako is exposed to abuse, the battery of Emiko by her husband, and she sees a drunk Japanese woman smoking a cigarette. But she also experiences Emiko's passion for music and dance. She catches a glimpse of a way of life not limited by the unending cycle of protecting seedlings from freezes, irrigating fragile crops, and paying bills.

ANNA QUIRINO (MASAKO): Masako has dreams that go way beyond the ranch. That's why her books are so important to her. And Masako has a rebellious streak. Watching

Emiko being able to break away from tradition. She's almost a hero. She sees in Emiko this whole other world.

Contrasting Productions: East West Players and Northwest Asian American Theatre

To deepen our understanding of *And the Soul Shall Dance*, we examine now three points of contrast between the production by East West Players in 1996 and a production by Northwest Asian American Theatre in Seattle in 1994. Different productions of the same play may offer strikingly different interpretations of the playwright's material, or through more subtle distinctions they may turn the audience's attention to one idea instead of another.

Scene Design and the Physical Space

A tangible difference that is relatively easy to assess is the arrangement of the physical space. Northwest Asian American Theatre was located in the basement space under the Wing Luke Asian Museum in the International District of Seattle. Like East West Players when they were located in the renovated factory, Northwest Asian American Theatre had a small stage space and little technical support for elaborate scenic effects. But given similar stage limitations, the two productions take entirely different approaches to staging.

In the play the two small houses are isolated and set apart in the desert landscape. The script simply calls for an alternation between the Murata kitchen and yard and the Oka yard. At East West Players, a design was created by Yuki Nakamura to keep the space as open and empty as possible through the use of the rolling and unfolding house units. Only one house appears on the stage at a time, suggesting that each exists in a completely separate space.

In the design of the Seattle production by Jan Tominaga, both houses are permanent structures on the stage, placed immediately next to each other. To suggest the distance between the two locations, the actors move through the aisles of the audience area. This approach to staging highlights certain meanings in the play. The proximity of the houses reinforces the contrast between the responses of the two families to the hostile environment in which they find themselves. The Muratas create a home that will sustain them and nurture Masako's aspirations. The Okas engage in a mutually destructive relationship fed by alcohol and despair. One house is a home that may be entered; the other features only a window that reveals fragments of the misery inside. The physical presentation of the houses symbolizes the life of those within.

There are two key differences in the visual images presented by these companies. First, in contrast to the Seattle production, the Los Angeles production emphasizes the sense of isolation, of two tiny houses in the vast, dusty Imperial Valley, widely separated from neighbors and community. The physical isolation speaks eloquently of the spiritual isolation. The windblown effect of the scene shifts heightens the idea of lives at the mercy of the elements. Second, in contrast to the Los Angeles production, the Seattle production features dissimilar house exteriors to comment on the health or dysfunction of the families. In the Los Angeles production, each family has essentially the same physical environment; the difference is the response to that environment.

Interpreting Family Relationships

In addition to the differences in scene design, the two productions approach relationship issues differently. For example, after Emiko exits with her kimonos, the play describes a moment of closeness between Hana and Masako.

Masako and Hana watch as Emiko leaves. The light grows dim as though a cloud passed over. Hana strokes Masako's hair.

HANA: Your hair is so black and straight . . . nice.

They stand close. The wind chimes tinkle; light grows dim. Light returns to normal. Murata enters. He sees the tableau of mother and child and is puzzled. (act 2, scene 5)

Hana's line is an understated way of expressing her love for her daughter. At this painful moment when she recognizes Emiko's desperation and Masako's longing, Hana pulls Masako to her with this gentle remark about straight hair, which so obviously contrasts with the loss of identity represented by Kiyoko's curly permanent. Hana underlines the health of their relationship and her determination to protect her daughter's childhood and her heritage. The stage directions imply that the father, Murata, is outside this intimacy between mother and daughter and that he is "puzzled" by it, although he recognizes the growing bond between them.

The production at Northwest Asian American Theatre accentuates the father's distance at this particular moment. However, the East West Players' production opens up this moment to reinforce the family bond. The stage directions indicate that "the wind chimes tinkle." At East West Players, it is Murata who sounds the chimes. As he enters, the actor playing Murata responds with delight to the newly hung *furin* (wind chimes) and brushes his hand across them, sharing his obvious pleasure at their sound with Masako. The smile that the father and daughter share creates a sense of family that builds on the moment shared by Hana and Masako. The director, Jim Ishida, said he saw the foundation for his interpretation of the play in the short story: "the beautiful little thing . . . the Murata family . . . this combination of people makes life bearable." The emphasis at the end of the play is on the shared responsibility of the parents and the strength that both share with their daughter.

The production at Northwest Asian American Theatre focuses instead on the inner lives of Emiko and Hana and on their isolation. The director, Judi Nihei, looks for moments where that isolation might be broken. For example, Nihei sees in Hana and Masako a reinvention of the mother–daughter relationship that responds to their unique environment and the difficulties and opportunities that it presents.

> **JUDI NIHEI:** Masako gets away with murder. If I had spoken to my mother the way Masako speaks to her mother, I wouldn't be sitting here today. I always take the writer at their word. So if this is who Wakako Yamauchi was writing about, then there is obviously something more going on here than what we might assume to be a typical mother–daughter relationship. So that says something to me about Hana and how she sees her daughter in her life.

The director and the actor playing Hana, Kathy Hsieh, together develop an approach to this character that depends not on the certainty of an experienced mother who is confident of what is best for her child but on a continuous process of discovery. Kathy Hsieh is actually younger than her character; her youth immediately reminds the audience of the enormous difficulty of facing life in a hostile country without the benefit of family and social structure. She has no mother or sisters to turn to for advice. Her only support comes from the women she knows at church.

Hsieh's age and performance choices clarify the struggle of the character to invent solutions to the challenges of dislocation and racism. There is no ready-made wisdom that can be transferred easily from her Japanese background to the circumstances of raising a Japanese American daughter caught between cultures. Each challenge from her daughter leads to introspection and experimentation. We see her puzzling out each decision. The answers come not from the past but from an attempt to imagine the future. Although there is a very special bond between mother and daughter, the very spirit of openness and shared discovery that distinguishes the relationship will eventually lead to separation.

In the Northwest Asian American Theatre production of *And the Soul Shall Dance,* Hana holds the kimonos that she knows she cannot accept for her daughter. She recognizes Emiko's desperation and Masako's longing. The kimonos also bring back her own memories of life in Japan.

KATHY HSIEH (HANA): She wants her daughter to have those dreams, but she doesn't want her to be disappointed at things that don't come true. She wants her daughter to study and learn, but the things that she is learning and the language that she is studying are all about American people, white people, and English, not Japanese. There are more and more things that her daughter is learning about that Hana will never be able to understand, because she doesn't read English. She knows Masako is learning a whole different world than the world Hana knows. And she realizes that that is creating distance between her and her daughter.

Nihei and Hsieh also look for connections between Hana and Emiko that may be discovered in the subtext rather than in their guarded conversations.

JUDI NIHEI: I really wanted to make more of a relationship between Emiko and Hana even though they don't really have one scene seriously together. To have Hana not be judgmental of Emiko but have much more sympathy for her, just not have a venue in which to express it. And that's a cultural conflict and a cultural imposition on a woman that even if you'd want to align yourself with your sex in support, you may not have that opportunity.

Sexuality and Gender

An aspect of Emiko's character that receives considerable attention in the Seattle production is her sexuality. More powerful than her memory of dancing and singing in her kimonos is her immersion in her memory of desire. When Emiko is alone, the actress playing the role touches herself as her lover may have touched her. She expresses herself as a sensual woman who defines herself at least in part through her own sexual response. What she seeks is control of her own body. All her acts of defiance are related to this claiming of herself.

By contrast, in the Los Angeles production, Emiko's character is built through withdrawal, defiance, and escape into a dreamworld of dance and music. But her state of mind does not lead to overt expression of sexual desire. In fact, her life with Oka seems to have robbed her of connections to the world around her and even to herself. The dancing of Denise Iketani (East West Players) is ethereal and leads the character away from earthly or bodily concerns. For Sherryl Ray (Northwest Asian American Theatre), her own body and the comfort of sexual response are a primary focus of the characterization.

In Japan, Emiko's point of contention with her parents was her sexuality and ownership of her body. They saw her as a commodity to be traded to the "rich Yamato." Yamato is the name of the older, wealthy merchant to whom Emiko's parents had expected to marry her, but it is also a name that refers to all of Japan. Thus, it contains a suggestion of the position of women in the social hierarchy of Japan. In the eyes of Emiko's father, when she had engaged in a sexual relationship of her own choosing, she had become damaged goods, no longer of value in the marriage market. For this reason, Emiko was married by proxy to Oka against her wishes and sent to the United States.

Oka has been dispossessed by both the Japanese and the American economic and social structures. In Japan he gave up his name and self-respect as an apprentice to his father-in-law. In the United States he is an alien ineligible for citizenship, unable to purchase land and make a home for his family. But he is still in a position to regard Emiko as his property.

The confrontation between Emiko and Oka in act 1, scene 3 results largely from her challenge to his authority. He sees her drunkenness as a personal affront to him: "You made a fool of *me!*" Infuriated that she will not speak to him, he attacks her physically. When Emiko asserts her autonomy—"Don't touch me. Don't touch me"—he is outraged: "Who the hell you think you are? . . . Too good for me?" And when Emiko answers his accusations of promiscuity by assuming ownership of her body—"Just because I let . . . let you . . ."—he responds, "Let me (obscene gesture)? I can do what I want with you. Your father palmed you off on me—like a dog or cat— animal." While Oka struggles to maintain the patriarchal view of a woman as property, Emiko, for all of her self-destructive actions, is set on self-determination. Emiko's rebellion against the traditional social structures is all the more striking when possession of her own sexuality is joined with her sense of herself as an artist.

Theatre production is an interpretive art. The three points of contrast identified here—the design of the houses and the arrangement of the physical space, the handling of the wind chimes scene, and the treatment of Emiko's sexuality— underscore the kinds of choices that may be made in different productions of the same play. The directors, actors, and designers all add layers of meaning to the words written by the playwright.

Summary

In *And the Soul Shall Dance*, the playwright presents the harsh lives of immigrant farmers eking out a living in the Imperial Valley in the 1930s. The past, the characters' Japanese background, is an important factor in shaping the present, as is the hostile attitude of Americans toward Asian immigrants. The playwright tells her story through small domestic incidents such as the bathhouse burning down. Although the details seem to come from ordinary circumstances, they are selected to express the characters' spirits. Emiko's longing to return to Japan is bound up in her kimonos. Masako's search for inspiration draws her to Emiko's music and dance.

In the East West Players' performance of *And the Soul Shall Dance*, realistic style was mixed with the more abstract style of the kabuki theatre. Scenes were performed with attention to period authenticity in speech, in characters' attitudes and manners, and in dress. But the scenery was made up of unfolding houses that were whirled around by dancing figures dressed in black, and Japanese percussion and wind instruments were used to create a musical background for the characters' lives. Realism is frequently modified by more abstract elements.

Another production of *And the Soul Shall Dance* at Northwest Asian American Theatre in Seattle demonstrates how two productions of the same play may differ. The scene design in Seattle focused on the contrast between the homes of the Okas and the Muratas, whereas the scene design of the Los Angeles production emphasized the isolation of all the characters. The Seattle production explored gender conflict, whereas the Los Angeles production was concerned with family connections that are sustaining.

Topics for Discussion and Writing

1. Early in *And the Soul Shall Dance*, the neighbor Oka is finally able to bring his daughter Kiyoko from Japan. What are the different aspects of Oka's history that contribute to his determination to make Kiyoko feel successful in the United States?

2. The director Judi Nihei of Northwest Asian American Theatre observes that "Masako gets away with murder" in her behavior toward her mother. What is the nature of their relationship? How does Masako challenge her mother, and in what ways does Hana allow her extra freedom? What does the mother want for her daughter?

3. Is Emiko's memory of her former life in Japan real or imagined?

● For suggested readings and other resources related to this chapter, please visit **www.mhhe.com/creativespirit6e**

CHAPTER 9

Understanding Style: Theatricalism

The two plays we have examined in depth—*Joe Turner's Come and Gone* and *And the Soul Shall Dance*—are largely realistic, both in their dramatic construction and in their staging. Although realism has had a prominent position in theatre and film since the early twentieth century, another style of theatre, nonrealistic theatre, has provided a different way of expressing many of the tensions and uncertainties of modern life. Nonrealistic theatre takes a variety of startling forms that continue to be invented. Audacity and challenge are fundamental to the highly theatrical expression of

nonrealism, which theatre practitioners and audiences alike find energizing and compelling, as well as sometimes puzzling and disturbing.

As we discussed in Chapter 7, the period of realism in the theatre began with the work of European playwrights and theatre practitioners in the second half of the nineteenth century. Realism continues to be a popular style today, particularly in Western theatre and film and also in many non-Western nations. Realists have sought to focus on the social problems engulfing ordinary people by examining psychologically coherent characters placed in detailed environments.

Shortly after the advent of realism, however, some theatre practitioners rejected the idea that constructing an illusion of reality was the most revealing way to examine the human condition. Other styles arose in the arts and in the theatre that were inspired both by the limitations of the realistic theatre and by the tremendous changes in social organization and in scientific and philosophical thought. The Industrial Revolution, for example, drastically changed the nature of human labor and threatened individual identity. The increasingly destructive weaponry of World War I and World War II brought the human community closer to annihilation. Religious skepticism increased in the face of the meaningless slaughter of millions. Changing views of the nature of the universe, such as that provided by Einstein's general theory of relativity, contributed to growing uncertainty about the existence of absolute truths. All these developments prompted the emergence of new styles in the theatre.

These new theatre styles have been referred to collectively as "nonrealistic theatre" or "antirealism" because of their specific reaction against realism. However, they have more in common than just their opposition to realism. If the realistic theatre depends on carefully chosen surface details, then the nonrealistic theatre seeks ways of going beneath the surface to identify something essential about human existence and then to express that essence through theatrical imagery. The theatrical image is an abstraction of or a poetic metaphor for some aspect of life. In the next play we read, *Angels in America* (Chapter 10), an angel appears on the stage. The angel is presented not as part of an actual event in the lives of the characters but as a fantastic creature in both appearance and behavior who symbolizes the characters' struggle to change. The angel is an imagistic way of expressing a complex structure of ideas about religion, psychology, and politics. Although the styles that make up the nonrealistic theatre take many forms, most of these forms rely on bold **theatricalism** that interprets the human condition in concentrated images. Theatricalism expands the concept of nonrealism by indicating a theatre composed of images. *Eurydice* by Sarah Ruhl is such a play, in which the complexity of human relationships is expressed through a highly symbolic journey. For our purposes, we use the terms *nonrealism* and *theatricalism* interchangeably.

Plays that use the style of theatricalism are often concerned with expressing the interior journeys of their characters. Frequently the point of view is expressed subjectively; that is, we see the world as the character sees it. Distortion, grotesque images, and nightmare visions are projected onto the stage from the character's mind, such as Eurydice's encounters in the underworld. In contrast to the realistic concrete world of work, home, and everyday activities in which the characters are viewed objectively by the playwright, the subjective landscape is often bizarre and highly personal. In *Angels in America*, one of the characters is seen largely through her hallucinations; she places herself in a frozen landscape of ice to avoid confronting fears that threaten to destroy her.

Theatricalism also often involves poetic or extravagant language, which frequently blends with the visual imagery to heighten the play's expressiveness. Many twentieth-century nonrealistic plays that focus on the failure of human beings to communicate with each other use fragmented or even nonsensical speech to explore the absence of meaning in human interactions.

The production of *Apollo* that has been discussed in two previous chapters is another example of theatricalism. The story that is told about the efforts to put a man on the moon is presented as a collage pieced together with fragments of history, fantasy, and parody. Images composed of movement, language, music, props, light, and projections are layered to build themes rather than a tightly knit plot. Large questions about American principles and ideals tie together the wide-ranging episodes. The visionary quest for the moon is expressed through many differing views of rockets, which are sometimes seen as playthings, sometimes as powerful missiles. The rocket images are crafted through props, costumes, and projections as well as through movement sequences like the astronauts floating in space (see page 128 and the online slide show). The loss of life associated with the Nazi rockets is expressed through metaphoric objects: the appearance of a pair of small white shoes; a bundle of ashes untied and poured from hand to hand. When the performance shifts to consider the quest for civil rights, the small white shoes and ashes reappear. Like a musical composition, motifs recur and transform. The dramaturg Tom Bryant observes that the director Nancy Keystone is working with certain instances of history but not relying on "realism" as the means of presenting the past. "She's translating these historical transactions or these historical events in theatricalized ways."

Exposing the Mechanics of the Theatre

In addition to concentrated imagery, the subjective point of view, and exaggerated speech, theatricalism changes the actor–audience relationship that is the goal of realism. Although we as audience members always know at the deepest level that we are in the theatre, the realistic theatre tries to make us forget where we are, whereas the nonrealistic theatre tends to remind us that what we are watching is a theatrical creation. In the realistic theatre, the tricks of the theatre are hidden. We do not watch the set changes or the costume changes. Certainly, the East West Players' production added nonrealistic elements of kabuki theatre to the scene changes of an otherwise realistic production of *And the Soul Shall Dance.* But in the Oregon Shakespeare Festival's production of *Joe Turner's Come and Gone,* the backstage areas were blocked off or masked so the audience would not be distracted by what was going on in the wings. The audience's awareness of such activity would have broken the illusion that was being carefully constructed onstage.

Additionally, in realistic staging the actors consciously remain in character the entire time they are onstage. Sometimes offstage sound effects are used in realistic theatre to suggest that the characters' fictional lives continue even when they have exited the stage. We can then imagine them in conversations or actions that continue their stage life when they are no longer in view. The intrusion of the mechanics of the theatre into the realistic illusion onstage would be like watching a film in which a microphone hanging above the actors is accidentally shown on camera. We are instantly taken out of the fictional world of the film and reminded of the devices used to construct the illusion.

In the nonrealistic theatre, the mechanics of the theatre are frequently exposed or the stage effects are so obviously executed that they call attention to themselves as theatrical gestures rather than as subtle elements of a realistic whole. The descent of the raining elevator in *Eurydice* is such a gesture as is the metamorphosis of the Lord of the Underworld from a bizarre stranger to a child to an enormous figure of the devil. In the nonrealistic theatre we may see the ropes that support the scenery or the movements of the stagehands. In *Angels in America,* the actors themselves change the scenery in view

of the audience. A scenic effect such as moonlight, which might be handled in the realistic theatre by a soft light coming through a window, might be presented in the nonrealistic theatre as a cardboard cutout of a moon attached to a stick.

The words *representational* and *presentational* are used to identify the distinction between realistic and nonrealistic theatre. **Representational staging** refers to the creation of a completely realistic illusion, and **presentational staging** refers to staging that recognizes the audience's awareness of theatrical manipulation. Presentational staging demands more of the audience's imagination than does representational staging, in which all of the details have already been filled in. The presentational, nonrealistic theatre frequently uses bold images, and abstract ideas or concepts are given symbolic expression through character, character action, and design as well as through language.

Expressionism

In the early part of the twentieth century, a loosely knit group of theatre artists and visual artists experimented with a form that would become known as **German expressionism.** Although the movement of German expressionism itself lasted from 1905 to 1922, the influences of the German expressionists extend until the present. For example, a contemporary experimental Japanese form, *butoh,* was inspired by the work of the German expressionists.

The word **expressionism** is also frequently used in a more general way to indicate the various developments in Western painting, sculpture, architecture, dance, film, and theatre that were concerned with the abstraction of form. The painters Pablo Picasso and Marc Chagall, the composer Igor Stravinsky, and the choreographer Martha Graham are all included in a long list of expressionist artists. The playwright August Strindberg, whose work is discussed in Chapter 7, turned to a more subjective, abstracted form of theatre in his plays *The Ghost Sonata* and *The Dream Play,* which broke ground for the later expressionists. Early in his career,

The film *Metropolis* (1927), by Fritz Lang, drew on many of the techniques developed in the German expressionist theatre to create the bitter mechanical world inhabited by oppressed workers. The style and scale of the images have been influential ever since the film was made.

Bertolt Brecht was part of the German expressionist movement. The innovations and concerns of the expressionists can still be seen in a play such as *Angels in America*.

German Expressionism

German expressionist theatre was infused with a sense of anguish. It has even been called the theatre of the shriek or the cry; its aim was to put into theatrical terms the feeling that was expressed in Edvard Munch's then highly influential painting *The Scream*. The German expressionists were horrified by the arms buildup in Germany and the militarization of their country. Their theatre performances were a cry for humanitarianism to replace the brutality they saw around them. The expressionists, of course, proved to be prophetic. Many of them fled Germany during Hitler's rise in the 1930s, but those who didn't died in the concentration camps.

The silent film *Metropolis*, by the great German filmmaker Fritz Lang, uses many of the techniques developed in the German expressionist theatre. At this point we briefly examine the techniques used in *Metropolis* because this classic film is readily accessible on video and provides an excellent opportunity to experience the fundamental principles and themes of the German expressionist movement.

The plot of *Metropolis* focuses on the attempt of an industrialist's son to stop the manufacture of poison gas in his father's chemical plant. The film is dominated by striking visual images of the gleaming modern city above ground, inhabited by the unthinking rich; and the brutal factory below, where the workers live out their hopeless days. The workers have become dehumanized cogs in the operation of the vast factory. Almost lifeless, dressed in identical clothes like prisoners, they go through choreographed sequences that integrate their stylized, repetitive, robotlike movements with the workings of the wheels and pulleys of the machinery and the giant hands of a huge, regulatory clock. The enormous scenic images of the factory below and the skyscrapers above dwarf the tiny human characters, who have become insignificant in the world of relentless machines.

The scenes are presented as a sequence of episodes enacted by characters without names who are meant to be types rather than individuals and who speak (in subtitles) in abbreviated bursts of dialogue. The actors' stylized movements and the visual images are as important as the spoken language—or even more important. Although some of the acting is humorous by today's standards because of the exaggerated facial expressions and body language, the power of the workers' segments is undiminished by time.

American Expressionism: Eugene O'Neill

Early in the twentieth century, a number of American playwrights were drawn to expressionism as a style suited to exploring the contradictions and anxieties of American life. Elmer Rice wrote about the dehumanization of the machine world in *The Adding Machine*; Sophie Treadwell explored gender conflicts in *Machinal* (1927); and Eugene O'Neill used expressionistic elements in a number of his plays. Of these playwrights O'Neill has had the most lasting influence.

Eugene O'Neill (1888–1953) grew up in an Irish American family dominated by his father, James O'Neill, a well-known actor. James O'Neill played the lead in *The Count of Monte Cristo* for years, unable to give up the role for fear of financial failure. Thus Eugene O'Neill's youth was steeped in nineteenth-century melodrama. O'Neill remains a seminal figure in the American theatre because of his attempt to lift the level of the medium above nineteenth-century melodrama and spectacle and find an authentic American voice in playwriting that would approach the eloquence of the Europeans Ibsen and Strindberg.

No established form of serious American drama existed when O'Neill began writing one-act plays for the Provincetown Players in 1915. O'Neill's career as a playwright was marked by his experimentation with form, as he searched for the language and dramatic structures that would express his understanding of the American experience. He was concerned with the way human beings deceive themselves with illusions of success or love and then become paralyzed when those illusions are shattered.

Early in his career, in his plays *The Emperor Jones* (1920) and *The Hairy Ape* (1922), O'Neill used expressionism to present the distorted, nightmarish worlds of his characters. Borrowing a convention of the ancient Greek theatre, O'Neill used masks in *The Great God Brown* (1925). And in *Strange Interlude* (1928), which took many hours to perform, he had the characters speak their **inner monologues** and **subtext** aloud. He turned in yet another direction when he wrote *Mourning Becomes Electra* (1931), a trilogy modeled on Greek tragedy. Set during and after the Civil War, the three plays explore the destructive passions of the Mannon family.

O'Neill finally came to a bitter kind of realism in his last and most successful plays, *The Iceman Cometh* (produced posthumously in 1956), *Hughie* (produced posthumously in 1958), *A Moon for the Misbegotten* (1947), and *Long Day's Journey into Night* (produced posthumously in 1957).

Willem Dafoe and Kate Valk appeared in a new production (1997) of Eugene O'Neill's *The Hairy Ape,* produced by the Wooster Group and directed by Elizabeth LeCompte.

The Irish American personages of his youth figure prominently in O'Neill's work, and in the last two plays, he turns to the searing history of his own family, destroyed by alcoholism and drug addiction. These four late plays continue to draw the participation of America's finest actors on Broadway and in regional theatre.

Epic Theatre: Bertolt Brecht

Bertolt Brecht (1898–1956) was a prolific playwright and director who began his work in the theatre as part of the German expressionist movement. Brecht envisioned a new theatre experience to replace what he perceived as the failings

of the realistic theatre. Brecht's **epic theatre** has achieved an influence on the development of the modern theatre equal to the influence of Stanislavsky's system on the development of contemporary psychological acting. Following World War II, Brecht moved to East Berlin. There he founded the famous Berliner Ensemble theatre, where he directed highly regarded performances of his plays. We investigate Brecht's theories of theatre here at some length because of their continuing importance to the modern theatre and because of their influence on the major playwright we study in Chapter 10, Tony Kushner.

Brecht believed that there was a danger in the audience becoming too deeply engrossed or

Bertolt Brecht, who began his theatre work in Germany, became an exile in the United States during World War II. The repressive political climate in the United States following the war encouraged Brecht to return to East Germany, where he founded the Berliner Ensemble, which became one of the most distinguished theatres of the century.

lost in the story of a play. For Brecht, the goal of realism—to make the audience members forget that they were in the theatre—made the theatre into a kind of anesthetic. He wanted to find ways to make the audience step back from the drama in order to encourage analysis rather than empathy or identification. He wanted to provoke questioning so that audiences would maintain an active, internal dialogue with the performance. From Brecht comes the idea, then, of interruption, of breaking the narrative to snap the audience out of what Brecht saw as a hypnotic state.

Brecht also did not want the experience of the play to be completed within the time and space of the performance. Rather, he saw theatre as a call to action. He hoped the performance would be a beginning point or part of a process in which audience members and actors would become engaged in social action. Therefore, Brecht did not look to provide the audience with the kind of experience that involves empathy and then the emotional release often referred to as **catharsis.** Brecht wrote:

> The spectator was no longer in any way allowed to submit to an experience uncritically (and without practical consequences) by means of simple empathy with the characters in a play. . . .
>
> The dramatic [realist] theatre's spectator says: Yes, I have felt like that too—Just like me—It's only natural—It'll never change—The sufferings of this man appall me, because they are inescapable—That's great art; it all seems the most obvious thing in the world—I weep when they weep, I laugh when they laugh.
>
> The epic theatre's spectator says: I'd never have thought it—That's not the way—That's extraordinary, hardly believable—It's got to stop—The sufferings of this man appall me, because they are unnecessary—That's great art: nothing obvious in it—I laugh when they weep, I weep when they laugh.[1]

Brecht's Concept of Alienation

To bring the audience to this receptive or alert mental state, Brecht employed techniques to achieve an **alienation effect,** or, in German, the *Verfremdungseffekt (V-effekt)*. In Brecht's vocabulary, *alienation* did not mean "withdrawal"; rather, it meant "to make strange." He saw this strangeness as a way of interrupting the audience's involvement in the fiction created onstage.

As a director and a playwright, Brecht used a number of theatrical devices to create the alienation effect. The mechanics of the theatre were exposed to destroy any sense of magic or illusion.

In this 2007 production of Brecht's *Mother Courage* at the Berkeley Repertory Theatre, the action of the play is broken with cabaret-style singing. Here Yvette, played by Katie Barrett, sings one of the songs composed by Gina Leishman, with Mark Danisovszky at the piano, in the production directed by Lisa Peterson.

do in British and American musicals, songs in Brecht's plays change the mood and demand the audience's attention. Brecht's goal was to separate the music from the other elements of the drama, whereas in musical or lyrical theatre the goal is to integrate the music into the drama. According to Tony Kushner, the music in Brecht's plays provokes thought rather than provides a mental break:

> When it's good, [Brecht's music is] harder to listen to than the dialogue. It's more upsetting and more difficult. Which sort of reverses the traditional notion of musical theatre, at least American musical theatre, where the music is sort of your rest from thinking. And I think that really great composers for Brecht respond to the lyrics by writing something ugly and hard and difficult.[2]

Set pieces and props were simple and suggestive. Titles posted at the beginning of each new scene told the audience in advance what would happen to interrupt the development of suspense. Slide projections and films were introduced to provide information that clarified or contradicted the situations of the characters. In Brecht's conception, epic theatre encourages spectators to question why the characters make the choices that they do.

Brecht also used music to interrupt the action and to comment on the situation. Rather than heighten the emotional mood of scenes as songs

Brecht's Approach to Acting

Brecht's approach to acting was one of his most intriguing and challenging ideas about changing the nature of the theatre. Brecht was opposed to Stanislavsky's idea of complete identification with the character. Brecht suggested a new approach to performance in which the actor would comment on the character, that is, stand both inside and outside the character—as if the actor were describing his or her conduct and in some way engaging in a dialogue with the

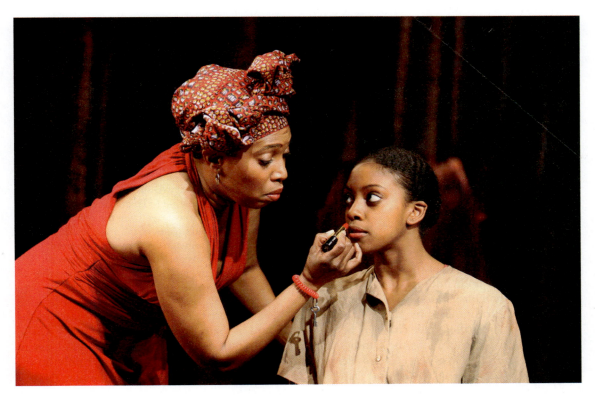

Lynn Nottage has written a new play, inspired in part by *Mother Courage,* entitled *Ruined,* which won the Pulitzer Prize for drama in 2009. Nottage moves the location of the play to the Congo, where an ongoing war currently brutalizes that country. In fact, the playwright interviewed Congolese women in preparing to write the play. In Brecht's version of the play, the character Mother Courage is a peddler who sells food and other goods to the warring armies. Lynn Nottage sets the action in a brothel, where Mama, the Mother Courage figure, played here by Saidah Arrika Ekulona, prepares Sophie, Condola Rashad, to sing for their customers. The play's premiere shown here is a co-production by the Goodman Theatre of Chicago and the Manhattan Theater Club, directed by Kate Whoriskey in 2009.

audience about the character. This technique is sometimes referred to as **acting in quotes.** In Brecht's words:

> The actor does not allow himself to become completely transformed on the stage into the character he is portraying. He is not Lear, Harpagon, Schweik; he shows them.[3]

Brecht is very clear in his writings that he did not mean that the actor should not be emotionally invested in the characterization or that the emotions of the audience should remain disengaged.

Instead, he wanted both the actor and the audience to bring a critical attitude to their participation in the theatre event so that they could consider what was possible under the circumstances:

> Human behavior is shown as alterable; man himself as dependent on certain political and economic factors and at the same time as capable of altering them. . . . The idea is that the spectator should be put in a position where he can make comparisons about everything that influences the way in which human beings behave.[4]

Brecht focused his plays on characters forced to make difficult choices. The plays are written in long sequences of short scenes that reveal the various forces affecting the characters' decision-making process. Brecht also presented a comprehensive history of the situation rather than entering the story line at a late point, as did Ibsen, whose plays begin just before the characters' major crises. For example, *Mother Courage*, which Brecht wrote in collaboration with Margarete Steffin, takes place during the Thirty Years' War of the seventeenth century. Concerned with the devastation of war, Brecht and Steffin created some historical distance so that the audience could consider the effect of all wars. The central character is a peddler who crosses back and forth over the battlefields, selling her wares to both sides in the conflict. She is a pragmatist who is committed to her own survival. But during the many years of the war, she ends up losing her own children because of decisions she makes about the family's economic welfare. Brecht's play *Galileo* demonstrates the influences on the central character Galileo as he first proposes his notion that the earth revolves around the sun and then recants his position after being threatened by the Catholic Church.

Theatre of the Absurd

In the 1950s another dramatic style evolved in response to the devastation of modern warfare, this time World War II. Based more on philosophical or metaphysical explorations than was the overtly political German expressionist theatre, the **theatre of the absurd** was created by a group of international playwrights who all lived and wrote in Paris: the Irish Samuel Beckett; the Romanian Eugène Ionesco; the Russian Arthur Adamov; and the French Jean Genet, who began writing in a prison cell.

In the face of the horrendous slaughter of World War II and the complicity of various segments of European society in the extermination of huge groups of innocent people, the playwrights of the absurd found traditional value systems bankrupt. They wrote about the meaninglessness of human existence and the inability of language to communicate in an effective way. The ultimate isolation of human beings shaped the images of futility that emerged from the absurdist movement. In his definitional study on absurdism, Martin Esslin writes:

> The Theatre of the Absurd . . . tends toward a radical devaluation of language, toward a poetry that is to emerge from the concrete and objectified images of the stage itself. The element of language still plays an important part in this conception, but what happens on the stage transcends and often contradicts the words spoken by the characters.[5]

The most famous play of the theatre of the absurd is Samuel Beckett's *Waiting for Godot*. Two tramps wait by the side of the road, essentially a physical "void" interrupted only by the presence of a shriveled tree. In the play the two characters wait for another character, named Godot, who never comes. While they wait, they struggle to fill the empty time with patter and activity reminiscent of clowning routines from vaudeville. But each attempt at interaction is more futile than the last. Long silences surround and break their speeches. The tree is the only visual detail that breaks the bleakness of the physical space, just as their meaningless chatter may be seen as only a brief interruption of the vast silence of the universe.

Although the two characters speak of parting from each other, they don't. They speak of leaving, yet they are unable to exit from the stage. They simply go on waiting. The nature of Godot is never defined; he is a puzzle that has led to intense speculation about what he may represent. Interpreted simply, Godot represents a reason for the characters to go on waiting, and that must suffice. In his play, Beckett constructs a powerful and disturbing image of life itself: Life is reduced to the act

Endgame is another major play by Samuel Beckett that, like *Waiting for Godot,* explores the futility of human existence and the trivial activities which people concoct to pass the time. And like *Godot,* the vivid language of the characters presents the bleakness of their situation at the same time that it offers biting humor and opportunities for theatrical brilliance. Here Alvin Epstein plays Nag and Elaine Stritch plays Nell, two characters confined to garbage cans for the entire play, in a 2008 production directed by Andrei Belgrader at the Brooklyn Academy of Music.

of waiting for something that never comes. Beckett's plays are extremely dark in spite of their humor.

Eugène Ionesco also wrote about the uselessness of human activity, but sometimes in a more playful way than Beckett. Ionesco delighted in creating situations in plays, such as *The Bald Soprano*, in which characters speak to each other at length in various forms of nonsense. Ionesco was particularly concerned with the failure of language to provide us with a means of reaching one another, as is Tony Kushner, whose *Angels in America* includes a scene in which an assembly of angels blather empty phrases simultaneously.

A Revolution in Movement: Martha Graham

The expressionists and the absurdists made major changes in the use of language, in plot structure, in characterization, and in the nature of stage action. It would require an artist of a different sensibility to contribute a way of approaching stage movement to match the other innovations of expressionism and absurdism. Martha Graham (1893–1991) stands out as one of the most innovative and influential artists of the twentieth century, comparable to Picasso in visual art and James Joyce in literature. Her work has changed the way we understand the expressive possibilities of the human figure in space and the interactions of the figure with objects and costumes. Although Graham's contributions are most evident in modern dance and theatre, her influence, like that of other seminal artists and thinkers, spreads across many disciplines.

Martha Graham was a dancer, choreographer, actress, and playwright. Dance was her language, but her compositions took the form of drama. Graham was an actor who communicated through her body her own versions of Greek and American myths. She began her independent work as a choreographer in the early 1930s and continued to compose dramatic dance works until her death in 1991. The enormous output of this visionary artist spanned the twentieth century.

A New Dance Vocabulary

All the innovators of modern theatre in the West, from the realists to the expressionists to Brecht to the absurdists, sought new styles of acting that would fully engage the body of the actor as well as the voice, to make performance more

Early in her career, Martha Graham choreographed and performed *Lamentation,* a dance of grief that recalls images of the German expressionists.

than posed figures declaiming speeches. Many of these theatre practitioners were inspired by the brilliance of the moving actor in the Asian theatre but frustrated by the lack of a comparable movement tradition in the West. Graham revolutionized what was possible in movement on the stage. Strongly influenced by Asian forms, Graham developed a movement system that contributed to both the technique and the climate that would enable Western experimentation with Eastern forms.

Until the early part of the twentieth century, the available dance vocabulary came from the ballet. In Graham's work, the bare, flexed foot replaced the pointed foot in ballet toe shoes. Angular, asymmetrical movement contrasted sharply with the symmetrical elegance of ballet. The pelvis and abdomen became a primary center for movement so the body could contract and then release rather than always maintain a vertical line. And fundamental to the movement of both women and men was the expression of the body's weight. The floor became a partner in this exploration of the substance of the human body rather than a springboard. The fall, the pull of gravity, was central to Graham's movement system; dancers pressed up from the floor, using their visible power to oppose gravity. Graham herself was a virtuoso performer with an astounding technique and a riveting dramatic presence. She opened the way for much of what would follow in the twentieth-century experimental theatre.

Costume and Set as Partners in Dance

Graham also approached scenic and costume elements as partners to the dancers rather than as decorations or representations of period, although they also served both of these functions. Sewing her own costumes and working with designers such as Isamu Noguchi, who created sculptures for her settings, Graham used design elements to give further definition to the dancing figure and to provide for the development of character through movement. In an early piece entitled *Lamentation*, the dancer is cloaked and hooded by a piece of draped fabric. In this dance of grief, the dancer pushes with angular, stretching gestures against the fabric that surrounds her. The tension of the dance and its emotional content are generated by the way the fabric resists the efforts of the dancer to displace or break through its binding force.

An example of a sculptural set piece by Noguchi is a free-form metal frame bed that he created for a dance about Jocasta, the mother and wife of Oedipus, in Graham's work *Night Journey*. The bed has a strong symbolic presence. It serves first as the place where Jocasta gave birth to Oedipus, second as the site of their incestuous relationship, and third as the funeral bier that carries Jocasta's body to her grave. The bed has physical importance as well. It is central to the movement of Jocasta and Oedipus as they dance out their relationship on its slanted surface. The hard metal frame supports the dancers' bodies and sets in relief the strength and the vulnerability of their characters: Oedipus, who will lose his eyes; and Jocasta, who will lose her life.

Total Theatre: Robert Wilson

Another American theatre artist, Robert Wilson (1941–   ), has become one of the dominant figures shaping today's theatre of images. Wilson's theatrical style is connected to a movement called **total theatre,** a form that stretches back to the mid-nineteenth century and the operas of Richard Wagner. Since Wagner's time, many theatre artists have been drawn to a vision of theatre that fuses music, dance, language, scenic image, and light; this is exactly what Wilson aims at. He creates works on a very large scale in terms of (1) the numbers of performers and collaborators involved, sometimes more than 150; (2) the duration of the performances, which can last up to twelve hours; and (3) the size and complexity of the images he constructs. Wilson begins his theatre pieces with scenic images and with music and dance. Language is frequently used, but text is neither the starting point nor the foundation of what is communicated.

Wilson's expectation of the audience experience is very different from that of most of the other theatre artists we have discussed so far. Wilson is not attempting to build a visible and coherent structure of ideas or to interpret character psychology; nor is he offering a social critique. He seeks to trigger associations in the minds of audience members. Rather than consciously constructing work that interprets themes, Wilson and his collaborators present loosely related images that the audience members must then organize and interpret according to their individual responses. Wilson creates stage images that seem to come from the world of dreams and hallucinations.

Wilson's Experience

Robert Wilson brings to his work a unique combination of training and personal experience. A brief consideration of his background is helpful in understanding his point of view and his approaches to his theatre pieces. Wilson studied painting in Paris before he returned to the United States to earn an undergraduate degree in architecture. He experimented with various visual art forms, including large outdoor installations. His first involvement in the New York theatre was as a scene designer. Wilson is a visual thinker; he develops scenes through long sequences of drawings rather than dialogue.

Another profound influence on Wilson's life is dance. As a child Wilson had a pronounced stutter, which inhibited his ability to communicate verbally. At seventeen he began to study dance with a remarkable seventy-year-old teacher, Bird Hoffman. Through controlled movement and relaxation, Wilson was able to overcome his stutter. His studies with Hoffman inspired Wilson's work with children and adults with disabilities, in

which he encouraged creative responses, in part through the use of slow, controlled repetitions of patterned movement. Eventually he incorporated this approach to movement into his theatre performances. He also invited the participation of some of the children he worked with, and he used their contributions onstage. Wilson frequently communicates nonverbally with the performers in his pieces as he works with them on stylized gestures and abstract movements. There is none of the discussion of character or motivation that is so important to the realistic theatre.

The Interior Landscape

Wilson's work includes *The Life and Times of Joseph Stalin*, *A Letter to Queen Victoria*, *Einstein on the Beach*, and *The Life and Times of Sigmund Freud*. As the titles suggest, Wilson uses large subjects that can be interpreted in many ways. He frequently focuses on a major historical figure whose influence has been felt across generations and continents; he builds collages of images in response to the impact of the central figure. The images relate to each other thematically, often in a very loose sense. The critic John Rockwell summarizes Wilson's approach to these subjects:

> What Wilson really is concerned with is deeper questions of authority, terror, fear and hope and the smaller (deeper?) human quirks of such seemingly overpowering figures.[6]

In Wilson's work one image slowly dissolves to the next: immense architectural backgrounds; enormous figures; characters in elaborate costumes from different periods; dancers; animals such as bears, elephants, and fish; suspended objects and people; burning houses. Various pieces of text are read or spoken, sometimes in several different languages. Exploratory work that was done for a production of *King Lear* involved a complete reordering of Shakespeare's text, spoken sometimes in English and sometimes in German, with an early Russian film version of *King Lear* playing in the background. Music also

Time Rocker, designed and directed by Robert Wilson with music by Lou Reed and based on H. G. Wells's *Time Machine,* is the last piece of a trilogy of rock operas. Wilson produces his work more frequently in Europe than in the United States, and *Time Rocker* was created in Hamburg, Germany, before being produced at the Théâtre de L'Odeon in Paris.

takes a prominent role in Wilson's work. Some of his work has featured the compositions of the **avant-garde** musicians Philip Glass and Laurie Anderson and the voice of the opera singer Jessye Norman. Through the intersection of abstract scenic imagery, hauntingly strange music, hypnotic dance, and pedestrian and poetic fragments of text, Wilson pushes back the boundaries of theatrical expression to reveal, in Martha Graham's words, "the interior landscape."

A New Meeting of East and West: Shen Wei

Both Martha Graham and Bertolt Brecht were deeply influenced by Asian performance styles. Graham's movement vocabulary and Brecht's approach to playwriting and acting reflect their contact with dancers and actors from India, Japan, and China. As Western theatre practitioners adopted ideas from Asian sources, Western performance traditions also have had a major impact on Asian culture. The Japanese perform Shakespeare in the kabuki style, and the Chinese have been exploring realistic spoken drama through performance of plays, like Arthur Miller's *Death of a Salesman,* translated into Chinese or new plays written by Chinese playwrights that use Western-style spoken dialogue instead of dialogue sung in the style of Chinese opera. Most recently, the fusion of Eastern and Western traditions has achieved a striking new direction in the work of Shen Wei.

From Opera to Modern Dance

Shen Wei (1968–) is a Chinese-born dance theatre artist now working in the United States. His father, an actor and a director, and his mother, a producer, both worked in the Chinese opera company in Xianying and were displaced by the Cultural Revolution. Some of Shen's early childhood was spent in harsh circumstances while his parents were forced to do agricultural work in the countryside. He says, "After the Cultural Revolution, the government tried to get back all that had been lost" and some of the Chinese opera schools and companies were reopened.[7] At the age of nine, Shen Wei left his family to study at the Hunan Arts School and prepare for his own career as an opera performer. Classes began at 5:30 in the morning and continued until 8:00 at night. They included movement, acrobatics, martial arts, acting, speech, singing, and learning the roles of different characters. "It was difficult as a young child to get up at 5:30 in the

Shen Wei created *Folding* on a visit to China in 2000 and then re-created it for his company Shen Wei Dance Arts in the United States. Taking his inspiration from the action of folding paper or fabric or any other item, he choreographed a work in which the dancers engage in slow folding and unfolding of their bodies. Dressed in long, draped costumes of red and black and wearing shaped headdresses to extend their height, the dancers have a sculptural quality as they move across a white floor and in front of a huge painting of fish swimming through a mysterious sea. Shen Wei is responsible for the choreography and the set, costume, and makeup design. The lighting is by David Ferri.

morning, to do your own laundry by hand with no hot water. I saw my parents twice a year. You had to be independent very early. It was really, really hard."

In 1984, at the age of sixteen, Shen started his professional career in the theatre. For the next five years he performed with the Hunan State Opera Company, where he specialized in the roles of the acrobatic warrior hero. By this time, not only was Shen an accomplished actor and singer, he was also skilled in music, calligraphy, poetry, and painting. He explains that he was raised in a tradition where an educated person was expected to develop multiple artistic abilities

in order "to achieve spiritual development." And in addition to his mastery of traditional Chinese art forms, he began to teach himself to paint in the Western style that was becoming visible as Chinese society became more open. Just when his interest in painting had become the focus of his creative energies, on a trip to Beijing in 1987, Shen was exposed to yet another art form, Western modern dance. The restless young artist had found the basis of his future work.

The first Chinese modern dance company, Guangdong Modern Dance Company, was established in 1989. Shen Wei was the only member of the new company who did not have

In contrast to the slow meditative movement of *Folding*, *Rite of Spring* demands the dancers to move with lightning speed while they execute complicated sequences of turns and falls. Choreographed to music by Stravinsky, the movement draws on vocabulary from both the Chinese opera and contemporary dance. The costumes and set including the floor are realized in colors of black, white, and gray as the dancers perform abstract sequences of movement connected to Stravinsky's phrases and rhythms.

a firm background in ballet or classical Chinese dance forms. "I was the only one from Chinese opera. But the director saw my paintings and recognized that I had an open mind, so even though I lacked classical dance training, I was accepted." Studying with visiting teachers from the Martha Graham, José Limón, and Paul Taylor companies, Shen quickly became as interested in choreography as he was in dancing.

The evolution of Shen Wei's artistic journey reflects the rapidity of change in China in the last twenty-five years and the way that change is transforming its culture. However, in 1995 Shen Wei decided to leave China for the United States in search of more opportunities and greater artistic freedom. Drawing on his training in both modern dance and Chinese opera; his skills as a painter; and his knowledge of music, makeup, and costuming, Shen formed his own company in 2000 and began to create new theatre works that merge East and West, performing arts and visual arts.

Choreographer and Designer

In creating his theatre works, Shen is like Martha Graham in the way he choreographs and dances in the pieces and then also designs the makeup and costumes, which are very important to shaping the movement. And like Robert Wilson, he designs his own sets. However, as a choreographer, Shen Wei is unique in an important way. Rather than defining himself through a signature movement style that forms an identifiable foundation for his pieces as a group, he attempts to develop a new dance vocabulary for each new work he undertakes. So the rehearsal process always begins with training the dancers in the new movement he has invented or is exploring. He is known for some works that use very slow, repetitive, meditative movement passages in which stillness is an essential part of the composition. In these works, the dancers seem to inhabit a dreamlike world in which their bodies change shape and have the ability to move in entirely new ways. In other pieces, the movement is lightning-fast and percussive, with the dancers leaping or rolling on the floor with breathtaking speed. Uniting the different pieces is a sense that the dancers' bodies and movement patterns are clearly connected to the world of painting and sculpture. In *Connect Transfer*, a canvas covers the entire stage floor and the dancers have paint on their bodies, with which they color the floor in the patterns of their movements. In *Folding* and *Deep Resonance*, the dancers' bodies themselves seem to be the evolving sculptural forms. A more recent work, *Second Visit to the Empress* (2005), offers a restaging of a prominent opera from the Chinese repertoire in which Shen Wei returns to his roots. But now the traditionally costumed singing characters share the stage with contemporary dancers, an interplay between forms of East and West and the past and the present. In 2008 Shen Wei brought his talents and international perspective to the world stage as the principal choreographer for the spectacular opening ceremonies of the Beijing Olympics.

Handspring Puppet Company

To be surprised by a performance is one of the greatest gifts the theatre can give us. The play *War Horse* works this particular magic when we see horses on stage that are clearly puppets, but at the same time seem completely real. *War Horse* tells a story of the part played by horses in the battles of World War I with the focus on one heroic horse, Joey, and the boy who loves him. Stories of animal and human interactions are frequent subjects of film and television, from highly realistic adventures filmed in nature to absurdly rendered creatures dreamed up through animation. But the horses of *War Horse* are neither live animals nor cartoon figures. They exist in another dimension entirely, the world of the puppet. And the puppet brings with it a unique theatricality different from any of the heightened forms we have considered thus far.

War Horse was developed in a collaborative production by the National Theatre of Britain and the Handspring Puppet Company of South Africa. *War Horse* was first presented in England in 2007 and then across the United States and around the world. As the production enters its seventh year of continuous performance, it has proven to be a remarkably popular theatre event for adults and children and a vivid demonstration of the ingenuity of the Handspring Puppet Company in crafting new approaches to an ancient form.

A total of nine horses make up the puppet cast of *War Horse* with one of them, Joey, a stiff-legged colt who flies apart in pieces when he is transformed into a galloping adult. The horses are scaled to appear full-size in comparison to the numerous human characters, first English villagers and then soldiers, who share the stage with the horses. In addition to the actors playing characters, there are three puppeteers onstage for each horse. The puppeteers do not double as actors playing other roles in the play. They have a dedicated responsibility. Each horse has two puppeteers manipulating it from the inside and one puppeteer on the outside adding further refinements to the horse's movements. The puppeteers also vocalize all of the horses' sound effects from neighs and whinnies to snorts and other sounds of breath. All three puppeteers are

In this photo, the puppet horse, Joey, is startled by a tank on the battlefield, while another horse lies dead on the stage. The future of warfare is clear. The old strategies of soldiers on foot and on horseback will be replaced by more terrible and destructive weapons of war. The open cane work of the horse construction is repeated in the tank. The 2007 production of *War Horse* was directed by Tom Morris and Marianne Elliott. The set design was by Rae Smith. The play was adapted by Nick Stafford from a novel by Michael Morpurgo.

always visible. No effort is made to hide them. The horses and puppeteers move freely around the entire space. They are never presented behind some kind of limiting puppet stage. They can gallop, rear up, carry soldiers into battle on their backs, pull wagons loaded with weapons, and die from injury, starvation, and exhaustion in the midst of all of the human characters.

The puppeteers are dressed in keeping with the environment in which the horses are placed. When the horses are on a rural farm in England, the puppeteers are dressed as stable hands. When the horses are on the battlefield, the puppeteers are costumed as soldiers. The horses are fabricated from molded cane and nylon mesh, which depending on the lighting can be opaque or transparent. The articulation of their leg joints, the movement potential of their ears and tails, and the sense of their breathing created through the rising and falling of necks and backs, give the horses a compelling sense of life. When the puppeteers are on the stage, they look only at the horse they are animating. They never look at another actor or at the audience. This specific style of

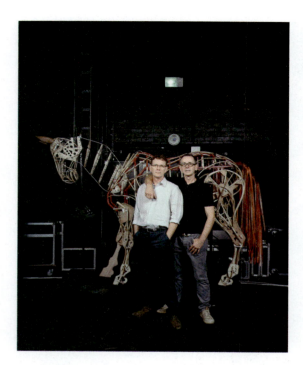

Adrian Kohler and Basil Jones stand in front of the prototype of the horse puppet designed by Kohler for *War Horse*. The brilliant horse puppets were the culmination of thirty years of experience and experimentation with puppet design and manipulation. Kohler and Jones have not only co-directed the Handspring Puppet Company since its founding, they have been two of the principle puppeteers in many of the productions.

puppet performance has been evolving since Adrian Kohler and Basil Jones, together with Jill Joubert and Jon Weinberg, founded the Handspring Puppet Company in Cape Town in 1981.

We first considered the work of the Handspring Puppet Company in Chapter 2 when we discussed theatre and social change in South Africa. The same company that is currently dazzling the world with a heartwarming, universal story about horses and war also produced one of the most compelling pieces of theatre about apartheid, *Ubu and the Truth Commission* (see page 41). Over its thirty-year history, Handspring has

explored the way puppets, often in combination with live actors, can express complex ideas about the human condition in theatre pieces that are created for an adult audience.

The work of the Handspring Puppet Company has been distinguished by a number of factors. Key participants have been leading visual artists as well as theatre practitioners. Adrian Kohler, the company's artistic director and principle puppet designer and sculptor, and Basil Jones, the executive producer, both trained as visual artists before committing their careers to "the artistry of the performing object."[8] In addition to experimenting continuously with new expressive possibilities, Kohler and Jones have also turned to the rich heritage of mask and puppet traditions in Africa through collaborations with the Sogolon Puppet Troupe from Mali and Koffi Koho from Benin. And they have invited leading South African avant-garde theatre directors such as Malcolm Purkey and William Kentridge to join in their process of developing new work that would do justice to the conflicts in their society. Like other South African theatre practitioners working during apartheid, they were determined to create pieces that addressed the precarious nature of life in their country. The vexing problems of identity in South Africa compounded by the views and restrictions of apartheid offered rich material for a theatre using both puppets and humans as actors.

One area of prolonged exploration involved the development of a new style of puppets to be used in combination with animation. William Kentridge, who had trained in theatre as well as in visual art, worked with Adrian Kohler and Basil Jones on four groundbreaking productions: *Ubu and the Truth Commission*, *Woyzeck on the Highveld*, *Faustus in Africa*, and *Il Ritorno d'Ulisse*, an opera. Kentridge is known for his hand-drawn charcoal animations that are now shown in museums around the world that he calls "drawings for projections."[9] Some of the early investigations that he did into this form of animation were undertaken to provide visual imagery for the plays he was producing with Handspring. The creative

The crocodile puppet appears with Ma Ubu, Busi Zokufa, in *Ubu and the Truth Commission* performed at the Market Theatre, Johannesburg, in 1997. The crocodile's head was carved from wood. His body was made from an old briefcase, appropriate to his consumption of vast quantities of documents. Busi Zokufa, who was both a puppeteer and an actor in this production, is a central member of the Handspring Puppet Company. The director and animation designer was William Kentridge.

partners found that the animations "could assist the audience in reaching into the thoughts of the puppets."[10] Kohler began designing wooden puppets in human form that expressed concentrated emotions augmented by the animations and strange versions of animals that presented human qualities through association: a crocodile, a hyena, a rhinoceros. The rough and provocative Kentridge animations intersected with the carving aesthetic used by Adrian Kohler on the wooden puppets in these pieces, which clearly showed the marks of his chisel, and the junk-like found objects that were used as props or even became part of the puppets.

Each of the four plays that Kentridge worked on with Handspring examined the struggles in South Africa from a different perspective, perspectives that were specific to South Africa but universal at the same time. These plays also connect directly to theatre movements discussed earlier in this chapter. *Ubu and the Truth Commission*, arranged by Jane Taylor, uses characters and text from *Ubu Roi* by Alfred Jarry, a play that is often considered as the beginning of the absurdist movement. The grotesque characters from *Ubu Roi* are used in the South African version to parody corrupt leaders such as the character Pa Ubu, played by a human actor, who is

In *Woyzeck on the Highveld,* performed at the Market Theatre, Johannesburg, 2008, Woyzeck reaches for his baby while his lover Maria stands in the background. The puppeteers are Louis Seboko and Adrian Kohler. The animation of the night sky on the projection screen reflects Woyzeck's anguish as he considers Maria's infidelity. The animation was by William Kentridge, who was also the director.

accompanied by a puppet of a three-headed dog. Another *Ubu* character is a crocodile whose body is a briefcase. The crocodile serves as a kind of paper shredder, voraciously eating incriminating documents. *Ubu and the Truth Commission* also draws on a number of Brechtian devices to set off the testimonies of witnesses at the hearings of the Truth and Reconciliation Commission. *Woyzeck on the Highveld* is an adaptation of a German play by Georg Buchner that is a foundational text in the development of expressionism. The Buchner play examines the mental disintegration of a poor soldier who eventually kills his lover with whom he has a child. *Woyzeck* is one of the most frequently produced plays in the international repertory. The oppressive conditions for workers of color in South Africa provide a poignant environment for the desperation of Buchner's central character.

By using puppets to reinterpret these well-known plays, Handspring opens up a wider conversation by challenging how we understand the nature of the actor in the theatre. The puppet characters/actors of the Handspring plays provoke a different kind of relationship with the audience than we have seen in other styles of performance.

First of all, puppet performance depends on audience members projecting deep feelings onto inanimate objects. And then the essential starting point for character creation is neither the playwright nor the actor, but the hand and the imagination of the puppet sculptor. The sculptor determines how the puppet will look, the materials to be used, the style of carving or fabrication, and the kinds of movements that are built into the puppet's basic construction. The details selected for the puppet's appearance and the style and capacity of the puppet's body for articulate movement is a form of script writing. Basil Jones points out that the work of the puppet sculptor is a kind of "authorship."[11] The story of the character is embedded in the puppet's figure. That scripted figure is then given life by the puppeteer, the energy of the entrances and exits, the quality of the gestures large and small, the rhythm and timing, and a sense that the puppet has its own breath. These inanimate objects which we endow with life in a magical transformation can then conjure new worlds that are both human and beyond human.

WORKING IN THE THEATRE

Festivals—Grahamstown

Many of the productions from South Africa discussed in this book, including the plays of the Handspring Puppet Company, have something in common besides their national home. Their premiere performances were presented at the National Arts Festival of Grahamstown in the Eastern Cape in the southern part of the country. Grahamstown is a university town that sponsors an annual arts festival which draws together experienced and emerging theatre practitioners, musicians, dancers, and visual artists to share their work with each other and audiences from around Africa and the world. Thousands of performances fill every possible presentation space in the small community, which explodes each July with artistic energy. For decades the Grahamstown festival has served as a crossroads for artistic exchange where artists could receive support and encouragement. During apartheid and afterward, the festival provided an arena for the presentation of new ideas that challenged the status quo aesthetically and politically.

Arts festivals take place in a variety of locations around the world and take numerous forms. The best-known and largest festival takes place at the end of each summer in Edinburgh, Scotland. In fact, the Grahamstown festival is second in size only to Edinburgh. Other major festival sites include Avignon in France and the Spoleto Festival in Charleston, South Carolina. Arts festivals provide the opportunity for new artists to be seen and for major new works to be developed.

*To learn more about the National Arts Festival in Grahamstown and its significance for young artists, see the film on our Web site.

Summary

In response to what many saw as realism's failure to completely reveal the human condition, new theatre styles arose in the early twentieth century. These theatrical forms communicated through overtly theatrical images, through stylized movement and poetic language, through the abstract rather than the concrete, through a concentration of expression rather than through the accumulation of detail. Although these theatre styles are often grouped under the category of nonrealism, or theatricalism, no single term adequately defines the many forms of theatre that seek to express the inner life of human beings.

Since the beginning of the twentieth century, many playwrights, choreographers, and directors have taken various approaches to theatrical expression. In the theatre of the German expressionists, plays often took the form of protest against war, industrialization, and inhumanity. Characters and language were reduced to their essence and supported by stylized movement and distorted scenic images to produce an effect of anguish. The American playwright Eugene O'Neill used expressionism in much of his early work. Bertolt Brecht sought an alienation effect to interrupt the audience's emotional involvement in the drama in order to encourage analysis of the dramatic event. Absurdist playwrights such as Samuel Beckett and Eugène Ionesco used theatrical imagery to explore philosophical rather than social issues.

Other theatre artists have created unique styles through the use of movement, music, and scenic image rather than language. Martha Graham invented a movement vocabulary to explore the passions of archetypal characters engaged in mythic dramas. Robert Wilson creates a dreamlike total theatre in which enormous scenic images, evocative music, and dancing figures suggest mysterious relationships. Shen Wei draws together theatre, dance, and visual art traditions of China and the West. The Handspring Puppet Company explores the potential of puppets in combination with actors and animation to challenge perceptions about human identity and create deeply felt, concentrated expressions of human experiences.

Topics for Discussion and Writing

1. Research the works of such artists as Edvard Munch, Pablo Picasso, Salvador Dalí, and Käthe Kollwitz that distort and fracture the represented figures, landscapes, or environments. What kinds of commentary about the human condition do these paintings make? How do they diverge from more realistic image making?

2. What changes in the nature of the actor–audience relationship were proposed by Bertolt Brecht? How do Brecht's ideas about acting contrast with those of Stanislavsky outlined in Chapter 7? We frequently see evidence of Stanislavsky's approach to acting in theatre and film today. Cite some examples of Brecht's approach to acting, in which actors call attention to themselves as actors.

3. Compare the plot of *Waiting for Godot* with that of *Joe Turner's Come and Gone* or *And the Soul Shall Dance*. What is the difference in the kinds of actions performed by the characters, and what is the significance of those actions? What is the difference in the endings and what we imagine will happen to the characters after the plays have ended?

● For suggested readings and video resources related to this chapter, please visit **www.mhhe.com/creativespirit6e**

CHAPTER 10

Expressing a Worldview through Theatricalism

Looking at *Angels in America: Millennium Approaches*
by Tony Kushner

Tony Kushner was born in New York in 1956 but grew up in Lake Charles, Louisiana. Both of his parents were professional musicians, and Kushner was raised in an artistic world rich with music and theatre. Although he was raised in a close-knit and supportive Jewish family, life was a struggle

for a politically concerned teenager coming to terms with his identity as a gay man. Kushner chose to attend Columbia University in the hope that New York City would provide a more hospitable social and political environment than he had found in Louisiana. At Columbia, Kushner discovered that his interests in political activism and theatre complemented each other. Through his studies of Bertolt Brecht, Kushner began to envision an idea of theatre that would address the social inequities that he saw damaging the fabric of American life. Kushner pursued his theatre studies further at New York University, where he received a master of fine arts in directing, before turning his energies to playwriting.

Kushner had completed only one major play, *A Bright Room Called Day,* before he began work on *Angels in America,* which would become one of the most celebrated plays of the 1990s and, for some, one of the most important American plays of the twentieth century. Since writing *Angels in America,* Kushner has written *Slavs!*—a play set against the experience of Soviet repression—as well as adaptations of major works from different historical periods, including *Stella,* by the German romantic playwright Johann Wolfgang von Goethe; *The Illusion,* by the seventeenth-century playwright Pierre Corneille; *The Good Woman of Sezuan,* by Bertolt Brecht; and *The Dybbuk,* a play from the Yiddish theatre early in the twentieth century by Solomon Ansky. Recent work includes two plays: *Homebody/Kabul* (2001), about the political turmoil in Afghanistan; and *Caroline, or Change* (2003), an autobiographical musical with a score by Jeanine Tesori. Kushner also wrote the screenplays for the films *Munich* (2005) and *Lincoln* (2012).

In May 2009, Kushner's play entitled *The Intelligent Homosexual's Guide to Capitalism and Socialism with a Key to the Scriptures* premiered at the Guthrie Theatre in Minneapolis as part of a festival dedicated to Kushner's works. This new work has a more realistic structure than *Angels in America* but continues to focus on themes of identity, politics, and the nature of philosophical conflicts in contemporary America.

Angels in America is a brilliant example of the kind of experimentation with form that is characteristic of the nonrealistic theatre. In constructing his play, Tony Kushner draws on elements of expressionism, absurdism, and epic theatre, as well as realism. *Angels in America*, in fact, is not one play but two: *Millennium Approaches* and *Perestroika*. Each play lasts about three and a half hours; the two plays are sometimes presented on alternate days or in marathon sessions beginning in the afternoon, breaking for dinner, and then going on until late into the night. The

Louis (Michael Ornstein, left) and Joe (Michael Scott Ryan) begin their friendship in *Angels in America: Millennium Approaches,* produced at the Eureka Theatre under the direction of David Esbjornson in 1991.

presentation of *Angels in America* was considered a major theatrical event because of the scale of the undertaking, the sheer theatricality of the work, and the themes and issues that the two plays address.

Our study focuses on the first play, *Millennium Approaches*, with a more limited discussion of *Perestroika*. In the production analysis following the playscript, we examine the development of the play itself in relation to its production at the Eureka Theatre, a small theatre in San Francisco; and at the Mark Taper Forum in Los Angeles. In both the introduction to the play and the production analysis, we consider how Kushner juxtaposes realistic and theatricalized elements to create his vision of life in the United States in the late twentieth century.

Exploring the Text of *Angels in America: Millennium Approaches*

Angels in America comprises a complicated mix of characters, plot incidents, and ideas. The playwright, Tony Kushner, tells a broad sweep of a story that involves love and betrayal, politics and religion. Subtitled "A Gay Fantasia on National Themes," *Angels in America* examines American life in the 1980s from a gay male point of view that is heavily influenced by the AIDS epidemic.

Plot and Characters: a World in Spiritual Collapse

The plot of *Angels in America: Millennium Approaches* focuses on two troubled couples living in New York City. Louis and Prior are gay lovers who have been together for four years when Prior is diagnosed with AIDS. Unable to cope with the grim realities of the disease and the ever-present threat of death, Louis abandons

THE AUTHOR SPEAKS

Tony Kushner

I believe that the playwright should be a kind of public intellectual, even if only a crackpot public intellectual: someone who asks her or his thoughts to get up before crowds, on platforms, and entertain, challenge, instruct, annoy, provoke, appall. I'm amused and horrified when I realize that, on occasion, I'm being taken seriously. But of course being taken seriously is my ambition, semisecretly-and-very-ambivalently held. I enjoy the tension between responsibility and frivolity; it's where my best work comes from.[1]

This photo of Tony Kushner was taken at the 12th annual BAFTA/LA Tea Party in 2006 in Century City, California.

Prior. Harper and Joe Pitt are a young, married Mormon couple who have moved from Utah so that Joe, an ambitious lawyer, can take a job clerking for a federal judge. Joe is struggling with his own closeted homosexuality or bisexuality and eventually abandons Harper, having been absent emotionally for some time already. Harper is a frightened young woman, addicted to Valium, who hallucinates about a man attacking her with knives and despairs about the depletion of the earth's ozone layer. Louis, a passionately liberal Jew; and Joe, a conservative Republican, become lovers in spite of the apparent conflicts in their political and religious backgrounds.

This personal drama of abandonment and self-gratification is intricately connected to Kushner's larger social and political concerns. The play takes place in the 1980s during Ronald Reagan's presidency. Both Louis and Joe work for the federal government, and their personal behavior clearly mirrors Kushner's interpretation of the Reagan administration's attitude toward those in need. Louis and Joe both have strong political and religious affiliations, yet neither traditional politics nor religion provides a moral or spiritual guide for the times in which they find themselves. They have become, as Louis says, "Reagan's children. Selfish and greedy and loveless and blind."[2]

The two characters whom Louis and Joe abandon each embody the cancers of the body and soul spreading through the country. Prior struggles with the ravages brought on by HIV infection. Harper is obsessed with the damage to the earth's atmosphere. The health crisis of the gay community links to the environmental crisis of the planet.

The Role of Roy Cohn

Kushner introduces one more major character who also serves to expand the play's frame of reference beyond the domestic drama of the two couples. This character, the lawyer Roy Cohn, is an extreme representative of the moral decay of the country. The character of Cohn is based on a real person who, in fact, moved in the upper echelons of Republican power and died of AIDS in 1986, never having publicly acknowledged his homosexuality.

In the play, Joe Pitt, the ambitious young lawyer, turns to Roy Cohn as a kind of mentor, and Cohn eagerly looks to exploit the younger man in his own illegal schemes and power struggles. With the obscene and self-serving character of Cohn serving as background to the rest of the action, Kushner presents us with a nation in physical, moral, and spiritual collapse. Under such circumstances, Kushner asks, how do we restore compassion to our lives? Faced with such enormous obstacles, where do we find the will to change?

The Shifting Point of View

Like August Wilson and Wakako Yamauchi, Kushner is concerned with the impact of historical and sociological issues on his characters' lives. For Wilson and Yamauchi, social and economic injustices—racism, prejudice, slavery, anti-immigration policies—are a basic part of the environment, the fabric against which we see the characters' lives take shape. Kushner also addresses social and economic issues—the deeply ingrained homophobia of American society and the greed and lack of compassion that he perceives were represented by national policies in the 1980s.

But Kushner's approach to his material is different in essential ways from that of Wilson and Yamauchi. Wilson and Yamauchi focus on the interior movement of the characters' psyches, a progression of struggle, recognition, and awareness. As members of the audience, we are aware of the social background, but our principal concern is the story of the characters. Kushner changes this focus; he asks the audience for analysis as much as for empathy.

Wilson and Yamauchi draw us deeper and deeper into a created world that remains constant. We see their characters from a consistent point of view. Kushner, however, keeps shifting the perspective, alternating between domestic intimacy and spectacle, between a realistic representation of relationships and a surrealistic presentation of dreams and hallucinations. The nature of the created world changes abruptly, going through wild swings of imagery and point of view. Sometimes we see the characters objectively from the outside; sometimes we see them subjectively from the inside. We move inside the characters' minds and see distorted views of experience that have been brought on by illness or addiction. Sometimes the characters enter each other's dreams, and the view of reality seems to be objective and subjective at the same time. And sometimes the play becomes fantasy, with the entrance of historical characters into the present or the appearance of supernatural characters.

Influences on Kushner as Playwright: Bertolt Brecht and Caryl Churchill

As we discussed in Chapter 9, the work of Bertolt Brecht has had a significant influence on Tony Kushner. Epic theatre, whose ideas come largely from Brecht's plays and productions as they evolved from the 1930s to the 1950s, has also shaped the playwriting of another source of inspiration for Kushner: the British playwright Caryl Churchill (1938–   ). Churchill has refined the Brechtian approach to respond to such contemporary concerns as race, gender, class, and economics. She has developed her own vocabulary of alienation devices. For example, in her play *Cloud 9*, Churchill uses **cross-gender casting** and **nontraditional casting;** that is, some of the female roles are played by men, some of the male roles are played by women, and a white actor plays the role of a black character. The purpose of such casting is to raise questions about how attitudes toward gender and race have originated. This casting calls attention to the idea that much human behavior is a result of social conditioning—that the way we perceive other people is the result of social expectations. These theatrical strategies challenge stereotypical thinking and ask us to question the social values regarding race and gender that limit human potential. In *Angels in America*, Tony Kushner employs this particular strategy of Churchill's by specifying in the script that some of the male roles be played by women actors.

Churchill develops her Brechtian approach further by creating a panorama that juxtaposes contemporary characters with historical figures who comment on the situations of the contemporary characters. She essentially widens the

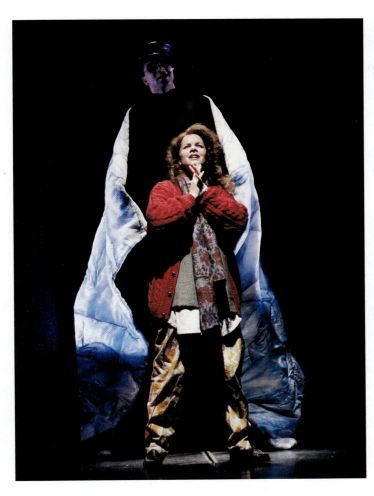

Mr. Lies emerges from Harper's hallucinations to help her escape when the reality of living with Joe Pitt becomes overwhelming, as seen in the New York production of *Angels in America* directed by George C. Wolfe in 1993. Jeffrey Wright plays Mr. Lies; Marsha Gay Harden plays Harper.

respective times. Much of the political theatre that exploded in the United States in the 1960s and afterward was heavily influenced by Brecht. And Caryl Churchill has had a similar impact on American theatrical expression since the 1980s. Although Tony Kushner is generally associated with the Brechtian tradition, his dramatic structure is very specifically shaped by Churchill's influence. She has provided him with a method of bringing together the private and public aspects of his vision and then of placing the contemporary situation in a historical framework.

The Historical Framework of *Angels in America*

frame surrounding her characters to expose more than their daily lives and their physical and psychological environments. In the frame she places historical figures whose presence connects the characters' situations to larger economic and political concerns. In her play *Top Girls*, the difficult lives of ordinary, contemporary Englishwomen and their children are placed against a background of remarkable women from different periods in history. Dialogues occur between characters from different centuries and between historical and fictional characters.

Brecht and Churchill are among the most influential theatre practitioners of their

An obvious example of a historical framework in *Millennium Approaches* is the appearance of two ghostlike characters, both named Prior Walter, in act 3, scene 1. Prior Walter is also the name of the central character of *Angels in America*, who becomes a representative of the gay community and the larger American community through his suffering with AIDS and then his transcendence of both illness and despair. Prior 1 and Prior 2 are the English ancestors of the twentieth-century Prior: Prior 1 from the thirteenth century and Prior 2 from the seventeenth century. Prior 1 and Prior 2 visit the contemporary

Caryl Churchill's *Top Girls* begins with a scene in which a contemporary business executive, Marlene (Deborah Kassner), meets extraordinary women from earlier centuries. This scene from a production at Lewis and Clark College, directed by Stephanie Arnold, shows Lady Nijo (Sakiko Taoka), a thirteenth-century Buddhist nun; Dull Gret (Christine Calfas), a figure from a Breughel painting; and Pope Joan (Heidi Van Schoonhoven), a pope from the eighth century who was discovered to be a woman when she gave birth to a child.

Prior while he is in bed one night to warn him of the coming of the Angel (a character who makes a spectacular appearance at the end of *Millennium Approaches*), much like the ghosts who appear to Scrooge in Dickens's *Christmas Carol*. Prior 1 and Prior 2 were both victims of the plague, the thirteenth century's "spotty monster" and the seventeenth century's "Black Jack." The presence of these plague victims puts the AIDS epidemic in historical perspective; the Prior ancestors place the twentieth-century Prior in a long line of descendents that can be seen as the human family. We see outbreaks of plague as illnesses that affected entire societies, not as historically unique events or as punishments visited on any one group of people for their sins.

The Character Roy Cohn as a Historical Figure

Kushner's most complex and original development of Churchill's historical framework comes in the character Roy Cohn. Cohn is central to Kushner's dramatic vision and his commentary on history and politics.

Roy Cohn (John Bellucci, center) seeks to persuade Joe Pitt (Michael Scott Ryan) to become a "Royboy" in the premiere production of *Angels in America* at the Eureka Theatre. The part of Martin Heller (*left*) is played by a woman, Anne Darragh.

Born in 1927, Roy Cohn first achieved national prominence during the cold war of the late 1940s and 1950s. He served as an assistant to the prosecutor in the trial of Julius and Ethel Rosenberg, who in 1951 were found guilty of selling atomic secrets to the Soviet Union and in 1953 were executed in the electric chair. Cohn claimed that he personally influenced the judge to sentence the Rosenbergs to death. Cohn then became counsel and sidekick to Senator Joseph McCarthy, who launched the anticommunist "witch hunts" of the early 1950s that destroyed the lives and careers of many American writers, artists, and intellectuals. McCarthy died in 1957, discredited and censured, but Cohn lived on,

finding new allies in right-wing politics and new opportunities as a lawyer to the wealthy. He died of AIDS in 1986.

Because of Roy Cohn's position in U.S. history, the character Roy Cohn brings onstage with him a long trail of historical baggage. His appearance evokes the excesses of the cold war and especially the execution of the Rosenbergs. But he is also a contemporary reference, with his connections to the Reagan administration and his death from AIDS.

A study in contradictions, Cohn is a homophobic homosexual; a Jew whose harshest judgments were made against other Jews; a lawyer who twisted the law for his own

IN CONTEXT

The Life and Times of Roy Cohn

Date	Event
1927	Birth of Roy Cohn.
1938	Formation of the House Committee on Un-American Activities (HUAC). The committee focuses on subversive, communist activity, contributing to the climate of suspicion that would prepare the way for the unfounded accusations of Joe McCarthy and Roy Cohn.
1946	Joseph McCarthy is elected to the U.S. Senate as a Republican from Wisconsin.
1947	Bertolt Brecht is called to testify before the HUAC. Scrutiny of artists and intellectuals expands.
1951	Espionage trial of Julius and Ethel Rosenberg begins. Roy Cohn is appointed assistant to the prosecutor, Irving Saypol. The Rosenbergs are convicted of stealing atomic secrets for the Soviet Union, although the case against Ethel Rosenberg indicates minimal involvement. Judge Irving Kaufman sentences both Rosenbergs to die in the electric chair against even the recommendation of the FBI. Roy Cohn claims that he personally influenced the judge on the sentencing.
1952	Joseph McCarthy is reelected to the U.S. Senate in a campaign that focuses on the communist menace. He accuses the Democratic administrations of Franklin Roosevelt and Harry Truman of "twenty years of treason." McCarthy receives the chairmanship of the Senate's Government Operations Committee, which gives him a platform for attacking individuals in the Eisenhower administration, in public life, and in the Senate. Eisenhower tolerates such attacks no matter how outrageous and damaging to individuals and to the atmosphere in the nation as long as they seem to benefit the Republican Party.
1953	Following Roy Cohn's successful participation in the Rosenberg trial, McCarthy appoints him as the chief counsel for his Senate committee.
1953	Execution of Julius and Ethel Rosenberg.
1954	Army-McCarthy hearings, in which the tactics and "above the law" attitude of McCarthy and Cohn are exposed on television.
1954	Cohn resigns as McCarthy's chief counsel. McCarthy is "condemned" by the Senate. Cohn begins his career as lawyer to the wealthy. He cultivates connections and trades favors with the powerful in business and government.
1956	Arthur Miller is called to testify before the HUAC.
1957	McCarthy dies, apparently of acute alcoholism.
1986	Roy Cohn dies of AIDS. He never publicly acknowledges his homosexuality.

enrichment, self-gratification, and aggrandizement. Condensed in the character of Cohn is a large share of the contradictions in American life that are the subjects of Kushner's play. Cohn, real and fictionalized, historical and contemporary, is placed in the center of Kushner's plot structure as a background to the rest of the action.

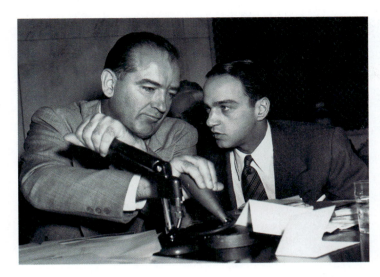

Roy Cohn is shown here (right) as assistant to Joseph McCarthy during the Army-McCarthy hearings in 1954.

Belize. Of course, these tangled interactions at crucial points are calculated. There is no pretense here that all of these characters' paths would intersect in such convenient ways in the natural course of events, as there would be in a realistic play. Kushner wants us to see these lives in contrast with each other; he cleverly and boldly arranges the circumstances to enable such encounters.

Roy Cohn and the Plot of *Angels in America*

Kushner brings Cohn into the construction of *Angels in America: Millennium Approaches* through two subplots. In the first subplot, Cohn faces disbarment proceedings because of his shady dealings as a lawyer. He is therefore searching for an attractive, loyal, young Republican man to place in the Justice Department in a desperate attempt to outmaneuver the disbarment. The young lawyer on whom Cohn fixes his attention and hopes for salvation is Joe Pitt, the Mormon husband at a crossroads in his own life.

The second subplot develops when Cohn's health deteriorates and he becomes part of the AIDS community inhabited by Prior and Prior's close friend and nurse,

Roy Cohn and Ethel Rosenberg

Toward the end of *Millennium Approaches*, Kushner expands the focus on Cohn as a historical figure by providing him with a disturbing companion. He creates a fictional version of Ethel Rosenberg as she might have appeared had she lived to be an older woman. The association of

Prior (Stephen Spinella) is comforted by Belize (Harry Waters, Jr.) in the Eureka Theatre production of *Angels in America* in 1991.

Julius and Ethel Rosenberg were convicted of stealing atomic secrets for the Soviet Union in 1951 and executed for treason in 1953.

Cohn with the execution of Ethel Rosenberg (1953) is the most heinous of the various crimes against humanity that Kushner draws on in his construction of the Cohn character.

Although few historians continue to argue that Julius Rosenberg was framed by the government, the degree of Ethel Rosenberg's involvement as a spy is uncertain. Some conclude that she provided her husband a minimal amount of support; others maintain that her only crime was knowledge of Julius Rosenberg's treason. Government documents released in 1980 make clear that the execution of this young mother of two children was a ploy to gain information from her husband. It was also part of the government's anticommunist propaganda campaign. Above all, the execution of Ethel Rosenberg was far in excess of any reasonable sentence for her limited participation in espionage. For people who

lived through the repressive climate of the 1950s in the United States, the appearance of Ethel Rosenberg on the stage in *Angels in America* is shocking.

The character that Kushner creates for Ethel Rosenberg bears little resemblance to the historical woman, at least as she has been interpreted by historians. A young woman when she died, she now appears as a comfortable Jewish grandmother with a toughness beneath the recognizable stereotypical role. In keeping with Kushner's outrageous approach to his material, Cohn and Rosenberg banter and bicker as if they are old friends rather than mortal enemies.

Like the figure of Cohn, the character of Ethel Rosenberg is loaded with complex significance. She seems to represent the angel of death, coming for Cohn at the end of his

Ethel Rosenberg (Kathleen Chalfant) approaches the bedside of the dying Roy Cohn (Ron Liebman) in *Angels in America: Perestroika*, produced at the Mark Taper Forum under the direction of Oskar Eustis and Tony Taccone in 1992.

life. She is an accusation and a reminder. But perhaps most startling, there is also forgiveness in this character, a character who would have less reason than anyone in the United States to forgive Roy Cohn and his colleagues for their transgressions.

Angels in America: Millennium Approaches

TONY KUSHNER

CHARACTERS

Roy M. Cohn, a successful New York lawyer and unofficial power broker.

Joseph Porter Pitt, chief clerk for Justice Theodore Wilson of the Federal Court of Appeals, Second Circuit.

Harper Amaty Pitt, Joe's wife, an agoraphobic with a mild Valium addiction.

Louis Ironson, a word processor working for the Second Circuit Court of Appeals.

Prior Walter, Louis's boyfriend. Occasionally works as a club designer or caterer, otherwise lives very modestly but with great style off a small trust fund.

Hannah Porter Pitt, Joe's mother, currently residing in Salt Lake City, living off her deceased husband's army pension.

Belize, a former drag queen and former lover of Prior's. A registered nurse. Belize's name was originally Norman Arriaga; Belize is a drag name that stuck.

The Angel, four divine emanations, Fluor, Phosphor, Lumen, and Candle; manifest in One: the Continental Principality of America. She has magnificent steel-gray wings.

Other Characters in Part One

Rabbi Isidor Chemelwitz, an orthodox Jewish rabbi, played by the actor playing Hannah.

Mr. Lies, Harper's imaginary friend, a travel agent, who in style of dress and speech suggests a jazz musician; he always wears a large lapel badge emblazoned "IOTA" (The International Order of Travel Agents). He is played by the actor playing Belize.

The Man In The Park, played by the actor playing Prior.

The Voice, the voice of The Angel.

Henry, Roy's doctor, played by the actor playing Hannah.

Emily, a nurse, played by the actor playing The Angel.

Martin Heller, a Reagan Administration Justice Department flackman, played by the actor playing Harper.

Sister Ella Chapter, a Salt Lake City real-estate saleswoman, played by the actor playing The Angel.

Prior 1, the ghost of a dead Prior Walter from the 13th century, played by the actor playing Joe. He is a blunt, gloomy medieval farmer with a guttural Yorkshire accent.

Prior 2, the ghost of a dead Prior Walter from the 17th century, played by the actor playing Roy. He is a Londoner, sophisticated, with a High British accent.

The Eskimo, played by the actor playing Joe.

The Woman In The South Bronx, played by the actor playing The Angel.

Ethel Rosenberg, played by the actor playing Hannah.

PLAYWRIGHT'S NOTES

A Disclaimer

Roy M. Cohn, the character, is based on the late Roy M. Cohn (1927–1986), who was all too real;

for the most part the acts attributed to the character Roy, such as his illegal conferences with Judge Kaufmann during the trial of Ethel Rosenberg, are to be found in the historical record. But this Roy is a work of dramatic fiction; his words are my invention, and liberties have been taken.

A Note about the Staging

The play benefits from a pared-down style of presentation, with minimal scenery and scene shifts done rapidly (no blackouts!), employing the cast as well as stagehands—which makes for an actor-driven event, as this must be. The moments of magic—the appearance and disappearance of Mr. Lies and the ghosts, the Book hallucination, and the ending—are to be fully realized, as bits of wonderful *theatrical* illusion—which means it's OK if the wires show, and maybe it's good that they do, but the magic should at the same time be thoroughly amazing.

> In a murderous time
> the heart breaks and breaks
> and lives by breaking.
> —Stanley Kunitz
> "The Testing-Tree"

ACT ONE

Bad News
October–November 1985

Scene 1

The last days of October. Rabbi Isidor Chemelwitz alone onstage with a small coffin. It is a rough pine box with two wooden pegs, one at the foot and one at the head, holding the lid in place. A prayer shawl embroidered with a Star of David is draped over the lid, and by the head a yarzheit candle is burning.

RABBI ISIDOR CHEMELWITZ (He speaks sonorously, with a heavy Eastern European accent, unapologetically consulting a sheet of notes for the family names): Hello and good morning. I am Rabbi Isidor Chemelwitz of the Bronx Home for Aged Hebrews. We are here this morning to pay respects at the passing of Sarah Ironson, devoted wife of Benjamin Ironson, also deceased, loving and caring mother of her sons Morris, Abraham, and Samuel, and her daughters Esther and Rachel; beloved grandmother of Max, Mark, Louis, Lisa, Maria . . . uh . . . Lesley, Angela, Doris, Luke and Eric. (Looks more closely at paper) Eric? This is a Jewish name? (Shrugs) Eric. A large and loving family. We assemble that we may mourn collectively this good and righteous woman.

(He looks at the coffin)

This woman. I did not know this woman. I cannot accurately describe her attributes, nor do justice to her dimensions. She was. . . . Well, in the Bronx Home of Aged Hebrews are many like this, the old, and to many I speak but not to be frank with this one. She preferred silence. So I do not know her and yet I know her. She was . . .

(He touches the coffin)

. . . not a person but a whole kind of person, the ones who crossed the ocean, who brought with us to America the villages of Russia and Lithuania—and how we struggled, and how we fought, for the family, for the Jewish home, so that you would not grow up *here,* in this strange place, in the melting pot where nothing melted. Descendants of this immigrant woman, you do not grow up in America, you and your children and their children with the goyische names. You do not live in America. No such place exists. Your clay is the clay of some Litvak shtetl, your air the air of the steppes—because she carried the old world on her back across the ocean, in a boat, and she put it down on Grand Concourse Avenue, or in Flatbush, and she worked that earth into your bones, and you pass it to your children, this ancient, ancient culture and home.

(Little pause)

You can never make that crossing that she made, for such Great Voyages in this world do not any more exist. But every day of your lives the miles that voyage between that place and this one you cross. Every day. You understand me? In you that journey is.

So . . .

She was the last of the Mohicans, this one was. Pretty soon . . . all the old will be dead.

Scene 2

Same day. Roy and Joe in Roy's office. Roy at an impressive desk, bare except for a very elaborate phone system, rows and rows of flashing buttons which bleep and beep and whistle incessantly, making chaotic music underneath Roy's conversations. Joe is sitting, waiting. Roy conducts business with great energy, impatience and sensual abandon: gesticulating, shouting, cajoling, crooning, playing the phone, receiver and hold button with virtuosity and love.

ROY (Hitting a button): Hold. (To Joe) I wish I was an octopus, a fucking octopus. Eight loving arms and all those suckers. Know what I mean?

JOE: No, I . . .

ROY (Gesturing to a deli platter of little sandwiches on his desk): You want lunch?

JOE: No, that's OK really I just . . .

ROY (Hitting a button): Ailene? Roy Cohn. Now what kind of a greeting is. . . . I thought we were friends, Ai. . . . Look Mrs. Soffer you don't have to get. . . . You're upset. You're yelling. You'll aggravate your condition, you shouldn't yell, you'll pop little blood vessels in your face if you yell. . . . No that was a joke, Mrs. Soffer, I was joking. . . . I already apologized sixteen times for that, Mrs. Soffer, you . . . (While she's fulminating, Roy covers the mouthpiece with his hand and talks to Joe) This'll take a minute, eat already, what is this tasty sandwich here it's—(He takes a bite of a sandwich) Mmmmm, liver or some. . . . Here.

(He pitches the sandwich to Joe, who catches it and returns it to the platter.)

ROY (Back to Mrs. Soffer): Uh huh, uh, huh. . . . No, I already told you, it wasn't a vacation, it was business, Mrs. Soffer, I have clients in Haiti, Mrs. Soffer, I. . . . Listen, Ailene, YOU THINK I'M THE ONLY GODDAM LAWYER IN HISTORY EVER MISSED A COURT DATE? Don't make such a big fucking. . . . Hold. (He hits the hold button) You HAG!

JOE: If this is a bad time . . .

ROY: *Bad* time? This is a *good* time! (Button) Baby doll, get me. . . . Oh fuck, wait . . . (Button, button) Hello? Yah. Sorry to keep you holding, Judge Hollins, I. . . . Oh Mrs. Hollins, sorry dear deep voice you got. Enjoying your visit? (Hand over mouthpiece again, to Joe) She sounds like a truckdriver and he sounds like Kate Smith, very confusing. Nixon appointed him, all the geeks are Nixon appointees . . . (To Mrs. Hollins) Yeah yeah right good so how many tickets dear? Seven. For what, *Cats, 42nd Street,* what? No you wouldn't like *La Cage,* trust me, I know. Oh for godsake. . . . Hold. (Button, button) Baby doll, seven for *Cats* or something, anything hard to get, I don't give a fuck what and neither will they. (Button; to Joe) You see *La Cage?*

JOE: No, I . . .

ROY: Fabulous. Best thing on Broadway. Maybe ever. (Button) Who? Aw, Jesus H. Christ, Harry, *no,* Harry, Judge John Francis Grimes, Manhattan Family Court. Do I have to do every goddam thing myself? *Touch* the bastard, Harry, and don't call me on this line again, I told you not to . . .

JOE (Starting to get up): Roy, uh, should I wait outside or . . .

ROY (To Joe): Oh sit. (To Harry) You hold. I pay you to hold fuck you Harry you jerk. (Button) Half-wit dick-brain. (Instantly philosophical) I see the universe, Joe, as a kind of sandstorm in outer space with winds of mega-hurricane velocity, but instead of grains of sand it's shards and splinters of glass. You ever feel that way? Ever have one of those days?

JOE: I'm not sure I . . .

ROY: So how's life in Appeals? How's the Judge?

JOE: He sends his best.

ROY: He's a good man. Loyal. Not the brightest man on the bench, but he has manners. And a nice head of silver hair.

JOE: He gives me a lot of responsibility.

ROY: Yeah, like writing his decisions and signing his name.

JOE: Well . . .

ROY: He's a nice guy. And you cover admirably.

JOE: Well, thanks, Roy, I . . .

ROY (Button): Yah? Who is *this?* Well who the fuck are you? Hold—(Button) Harry? Eighty-seven grand, something like that. Fuck him. Eat me. New Jersey, chain of porno film stores in, uh, Weehawken. That's—Harry, that's the beauty of the law. (Button) So, baby doll, what? *Cats?* Bleah. (Button) *Cats!* It's about cats. Singing cats, you'll love it. Eight o'clock, the theatre's always at eight. (Button) Fucking tourists. (Button, then to Joe) Oh live a little, Joe, *eat* something for Christ sake—

JOE: Um, Roy, could you . . .

ROY: What? (To Harry) Hold a minute. (Button) Mrs. Soffer? Mrs. . . . (Button) God-fucking-dammit to hell, where is . . .

JOE (Overlapping): Roy, I'd really appreciate it if . . .

ROY (Overlapping): Well she was here a minute ago, baby doll, see if . . .

(The phone starts making three different beeping sounds, all at once.)

ROY (Smashing buttons): Jesus fuck this goddam thing . . .

JOE (Overlapping): I really wish you wouldn't . . .

ROY (Overlapping): Baby doll? Ring the *Post* get me Suzy see if . . .

(The phone starts whistling loudly.)

ROY: CHRIST!

JOE: *Roy.*

ROY (Into receiver): Hold. (Button; to Joe) What?

JOE: Could you please not take the Lord's name in vain?

(Pause)

I'm sorry. But please. At least while I'm . . .

ROY (Laughs, then): Right. Sorry. Fuck. Only in America. (Punches a button) Baby doll, tell 'em all to fuck off. Tell 'em I died. You handle Mrs. Soffer. Tell her it's on the way. Tell her I'm schtupping the judge. I'll call her back. I *will* call her. I *know* how much I borrowed. She's got four hundred times that stuffed up her. . . . Yeah, tell her I said that. (Button. The phone is silent)

So, Joe.

JOE: I'm sorry Roy, I just . . .

ROY: No no no no, principles count, I respect principles, I'm not religious but I like God and God likes me. Baptist, Catholic?

JOE: Mormon.

ROY: Mormon. Delectable. Absolutely. Only in America. So, Joe. Whattya think?

JOE: It's . . . well . . .

ROY: Crazy life.

JOE: Chaotic.

ROY: Well but God bless chaos. Right?

JOE: Ummm . . .

ROY: Huh. Mormons. I knew Mormons, in, um, Nevada.

JOE: Utah, mostly.

ROY: No, these Mormons were in Vegas. So. So, how'd you like to go to Washington and work for the Justice Department?

JOE: Sorry?

ROY: How'd you like to go to Washington and work for the Justice Department? All I gotta do is pick up the phone, talk to Ed, and you're in.

JOE: In . . . what, exactly?

ROY: Associate Assistant Something Big. Internal Affairs, heart of the woods, something nice with clout.

JOE: Ed . . .?

ROY: Meese. The Attorney General.

JOE: Oh.

ROY: I just have to pick up the phone . . .

JOE: I have to think.

ROY: Of course.

(Pause)

It's a great time to be in Washington, Joe.

JOE: Roy, it's incredibly exciting . . .

ROY: And it would mean something to me. You understand?

(Little pause.)

JOE: I . . . can't say how much I appreciate this Roy, I'm sort of . . . well, stunned, I mean. . . . Thanks, Roy. But I have to give it some thought. I have to ask my wife.

ROY: Your wife. Of course.

JOE: But I really appreciate . . .

ROY: Of course. Talk to your wife.

Scene 3

Later that day. Harper at home, alone. She is listening to the radio and talking to herself, as she often does. She speaks to the audience.

HARPER: People who are lonely, people left alone, sit talking nonsense to the air, imagining . . . beautiful systems dying, old fixed orders spiraling apart . . .

When you look at the ozone layer, from outside, from a spaceship, it looks like a pale blue halo, a gentle, shimmering aureole encircling the atmosphere encircling the earth. Thirty miles above our heads, a thin layer of three-atom oxygen molecules, product of photosynthesis, which explains the fussy vegetable preference for visible light, its rejection of darker rays and emanations. Danger from without. It's a kind of gift, from God, the crowning touch to the creation of the world: guardian angels, hands linked, make a spherical net, a blue-green nesting orb, a shell of safety for life itself. But everywhere, things are collapsing, lies surfacing, systems of defense giving way. . . . This is why, Joe, this is why I shouldn't be left alone.

(Little pause)

I'd like to go traveling. Leave you behind to worry. I'll send postcards with strange stamps and tantalizing messages on the back. "Later maybe." "Nevermore . . ."

(Mr. Lies, a travel agent, appears.)

HARPER: Oh! You startled me!

MR. LIES: Cash, check or credit card?

HARPER: I remember you. You're from Salt Lake. You sold us the plane tickets when we flew here. What are you doing in Brooklyn?

MR. LIES: You said you wanted to travel . . .

HARPER: And here you are. How thoughtful.

MR. LIES: Mr. Lies. Of the International Order of Travel Agents. We mobilize the globe, we set people adrift, we stir the populace and send nomads eddying across the planet. We are adepts of motion, acolytes of the flux. Cash, check or credit card. Name your destination.

HARPER: Antarctica, maybe. I want to see the hole in the ozone. I heard on the radio . . .

MR. LIES (He has a computer terminal in his briefcase): I can arrange a guided tour. Now?

HARPER: Soon. Maybe soon. I'm not safe here you see. Things aren't right with me. Weird stuff happens . . .

MR. LIES: Like?

HARPER: Well, like you, for instance. Just appearing. Or last week . . . well never mind.

People are like planets, you need a thick skin. Things get to me, Joe stays away and now. . . . Well look. My dreams are talking back to me.

MR. LIES: It's the price of rootlessness. Motion sickness. The only cure: to keep moving.

HARPER: I'm undecided. I feel . . . that something's going to give. It's 1985. Fifteen years till the third millennium. Maybe Christ will come again. Maybe seeds will be planted, maybe there'll be harvests then, maybe early figs to eat, maybe new life, maybe fresh blood, maybe companionship and love and protection, safety from what's outside, maybe the door will hold, or maybe . . .

maybe the troubles will come, and the end will come, and the sky will collapse and there will be terrible rains and showers of poison light, or maybe my life is really fine, maybe Joe loves me and I'm only crazy thinking otherwise, or maybe not, maybe it's even worse than I know, maybe . . . I want to know, maybe I don't. The suspense, Mr. Lies, it's killing me.

MR. LIES: I suggest a vacation.

HARPER (Hearing something): That was the elevator. Oh God, I should fix myself up, I. . . . You have to go, you shouldn't be here . . . you aren't even real.

MR. LIES: Call me when you decide . . .

HARPER: Go!

(The Travel Agent vanishes as Joe enters.)

JOE: Buddy?

Buddy? Sorry I'm late. I was just . . . out. Walking. Are you mad?

HARPER: I got a little anxious.

JOE: Buddy kiss.

(They kiss.)

JOE: Nothing to get anxious about.

So. So how'd you like to move to Washington?

Scene 4

Same day. Louis and Prior outside the funeral home, sitting on a bench, both dressed in funeral finery, talking. The funeral service for Sarah Ironson has just concluded and Louis is about to leave for the cemetery.

LOUIS: My grandmother actually saw Emma Goldman speak. In Yiddish. But all Grandma could remember was that she spoke well and wore a hat.

What a weird service. That rabbi . . .

PRIOR: A definite find. Get his number when you go to the graveyard. I want him to bury me.

LOUIS: Better head out there. Everyone gets to put dirt on the coffin once it's lowered in.

PRIOR: Oooh. Cemetery fun. Don't want to miss that.

LOUIS: It's an old Jewish custom to express love. Here, Grandma, have a shovelful. Latecomers run the risk of finding the grave completely filled.

She was pretty crazy. She was up there in that home for ten years, talking to herself. I never visited. She looked too much like my mother.

PRIOR (Hugs him): Poor Louis. I'm sorry your grandma is dead.

LOUIS: Tiny little coffin, huh?

Sorry I didn't introduce you to. . . . I always get so closety at these family things.

PRIOR: Butch. You get butch. (Imitating) "Hi Cousin Doris, you don't remember me I'm Lou, Rachel's boy." Lou not Louis, because if you say Louis they'll hear the sibilant S.

LOUIS: I don't have a . . .

PRIOR: I don't blame you, hiding. Bloodlines. Jewish curses are the worst. I personally would dissolve if anyone ever looked me in the eye and said "Feh." Fortunately WASPs don't say "Feh." Oh and by the way, darling, cousin Doris is a dyke.

LOUIS: No.

Really?

PRIOR: You don't notice anything. If I hadn't spent the last four years fellating you I'd swear you were straight.

LOUIS: You're in a pissy mood. Cat still missing?

(Little pause.)

PRIOR: Not a furball in sight. It's your fault.

LOUIS: It is?

PRIOR: I warned you, Louis. Names are important. Call an animal "Little Sheba" and you can't expect it to stick around. Besides, it's a dog's name.

LOUIS: I wanted a dog in the first place, not a cat. He sprayed my books.

PRIOR: He was a female cat.

LOUIS: Cats are stupid, high-strung predators. Babylonians sealed them up in bricks. Dogs have brains.

PRIOR: Cats have intuition.

LOUIS: A sharp dog is as smart as a really dull two-year-old child.

PRIOR: Cats know when something's wrong.

LOUIS: Only if you stop feeding them.

PRIOR: They know. That's why Sheba left, because she knew.

LOUIS: Knew what?

(Pause.)

PRIOR: I did my best Shirley Booth this morning, floppy slippers, housecoat, curlers, can of Little Friskies; "Come back, Little Sheba, come back. . . . " To no avail. Le chat, elle ne reviendra jamais, jamais . . .

(He removes his jacket, rolls up his sleeve, shows Louis a dark-purple spot on the underside of his arm near the shoulder)

See.

LOUIS: That's just a burst blood vessel.

PRIOR: Not according to the best medical authorities.

LOUIS: What?

(Pause.)

Tell me.

PRIOR: K.S., baby. Lesion number one. Lookit. The wine-dark kiss of the angel of death.

LOUIS (Very softly, holding Prior's arm): Oh please . . .

PRIOR: I'm a lesionnaire. The Foreign Lesion. The American Lesion. Lesionnaire's disease.

LOUIS: Stop.

PRIOR: My troubles are lesion.

LOUIS: Will you *stop.*

PRIOR: Don't you think I'm handling this well? I'm going to die.

LOUIS: Bullshit.

PRIOR: Let go of my arm.

LOUIS: No.

PRIOR: Let go.

LOUIS (Grabbing Prior, embracing him ferociously): No.

PRIOR: I can't find a way to spare you baby. No wall like the wall of hard scientific fact. K.S. Wham. Bang your head on that.

LOUIS: Fuck you. (Letting go) Fuck you fuck you fuck you.

PRIOR: Now that's what I like to hear. A mature reaction.

Let's go see if the cat's come home.

Louis?

LOUIS: When did you find this?

PRIOR: I couldn't tell you.

LOUIS: Why?

PRIOR: I was scared, Lou.

LOUIS: Of what?

PRIOR: That you'll leave me.

LOUIS: Oh.

(Little pause.)

PRIOR: Bad timing, funeral and all, but I figured as long as we're on the subject of death . . .

LOUIS: I have to go bury my grandma.

PRIOR: Lou?

(Pause)

Then you'll come home?

LOUIS: Then I'll come home.

Scene 5

Same day, later on. Split scene: Joe and Harper at home; Louis at the cemetery with Rabbi Isidor Chemelwitz and the little coffin.

HARPER: Washington?

JOE: It's an incredible honor, buddy, and . . .

HARPER: I have to think.

JOE: Of course.

HARPER: Say no.

JOE: You said you were going to think about it.

HARPER: I don't want to move to Washington.

JOE: Well I do.

HARPER: It's a giant cemetery, huge white graves and mausoleums everywhere.

JOE: We could live in Maryland. Or Georgetown.

HARPER: We're happy here.

JOE: That's not really true, buddy, we . . .

HARPER: Well happy enough! Pretend-happy. That's better than nothing.

JOE: It's time to make some changes, Harper.

HARPER: No changes. Why?

JOE: I've been chief clerk for four years. I make twenty-nine thousand dollars a year. That's ridiculous. I graduated fourth in my class and I make less than anyone I know. And I'm . . . I'm tired of being a clerk, I want to go where something good is happening.

HARPER: Nothing good happens in Washington. We'll forget church teachings and buy furniture at . . . at *Conran's* and become yuppies. I have too much to do here.

JOE: Like what?

HARPER: I *do* have things . . .

JOE: What things?

HARPER: I have to finish painting the bedroom.

JOE: You've been painting in there for over a year.

HARPER: I know, I. . . . It just isn't done because I never get time to finish it.

JOE: Oh that's . . . that doesn't make sense. You have all the time in the world. You could finish it when I'm at work.

HARPER: I'm afraid to go in there alone.

JOE: Afraid of what?

HARPER: I heard someone in there. Metal scraping on the wall. A man with a knife, maybe.

JOE: There's no one in the bedroom, Harper.

HARPER: Not now.

JOE: Not this morning either.

HARPER: How do you know? You were at work this morning. There's something creepy about this place. Remember *Rosemary's Baby?*

JOE: *Rosemary's Baby?*

HARPER: Our apartment looks like that one. Wasn't that apartment in Brooklyn?

JOE: No, it was . . .

HARPER: Well, it looked like this. It did.

JOE: Then let's move.

HARPER: Georgetown's worse. The *Exorcist* was in Georgetown.

JOE: The devil, everywhere you turn, huh, buddy.

HARPER: Yeah. Everywhere.

JOE: How many pills today, buddy?

HARPER: None. One. Three. Only three.

LOUIS (Pointing at the coffin): Why are there just two little wooden pegs holding the lid down?

RABBI ISIDOR CHEMELWITZ: So she can get out easier if she wants to.

LOUIS: I hope she stays put.

I pretended for years that she was already dead. When they called to say she had died it was a surprise. I abandoned her.

RABBI ISIDOR CHEMELWITZ: "Sharfer vi di tson fun a shlang iz an umdankbar kind!"

LOUIS: I don't speak Yiddish.

RABBI ISIDOR CHEMELWITZ: Sharper than the serpent's tooth is the ingratitude of children. Shakespeare. *Kenig Lear.*

LOUIS: Rabbi, what does the Holy Writ say about someone who abandons someone he loves at a time of great need?

RABBI ISIDOR CHEMELWITZ: Why would a person do such a thing?

LOUIS: Because he has to.

Maybe because this person's sense of the world, that it will change for the better with struggle, maybe a person who has this neo-Hegelian positivist sense of constant historical progress towards happiness or perfection or something, who feels very powerful because he feels connected to these forces, moving uphill all the time . . . maybe that person can't, um, incorporate sickness into his sense of how things are supposed to go. Maybe vomit . . . and sores and disease . . . really frighten him, maybe . . . he isn't so good with death.

RABBI ISIDOR CHEMELWITZ: The Holy Scriptures have nothing to say about such a person.

LOUIS: Rabbi, I'm afraid of the crimes I may commit.

RABBI ISIDOR CHEMELWITZ: Please, mister. I'm a sick old rabbi facing a long drive home to the Bronx. You want to confess, better you should find a priest.

LOUIS: But I'm not a Catholic, I'm a Jew.

RABBI ISIDOR CHEMELWITZ: Worse luck for you, bubbulah. Catholics believe in forgiveness. Jews believe in Guilt. (He pats the coffin tenderly)

LOUIS: You just make sure those pegs are in good and tight.

RABBI ISIDOR CHEMELWITZ: Don't worry, mister. The life she had, she'll stay put. She's better off.

JOE: Look, I know this is scary for you. But try to understand what it means to me. Will you try?

HARPER: Yes.

JOE: Good. Really try.

I think things are starting to change in the world.

HARPER: But I don't want . . .

JOE: Wait. For the good. Change for the good. America has rediscovered itself. Its sacred position among nations. And people aren't ashamed of that like they used to be. This is a great thing. The truth restored. Law restored. That's what President Reagan's done, Harper. He says "Truth exists and can be spoken proudly." And the country responds to him. We become better. More good. I need to be a part of that, I need something big to lift me up. I mean, six years ago the world seemed in decline, horrible, hopeless, full of unsolvable problems and crime and confusion and hunger and . . .

HARPER: But it still seems that way. More now than before. They say the ozone layer is . . .

JOE: Harper . . .

HARPER: And today out the window on Atlantic Avenue there was a schizophrenic traffic cop who was making these . . .

JOE: Stop it! I'm trying to make a point.

HARPER: So am I.

JOE: You aren't even making sense, you . . .

HARPER: My point is the world seems just as . . .

JOE: It only seems that way to you because you never go out in the world, Harper, and you have emotional problems.

HARPER: I do so get out in the world.

JOE: You don't. You stay in all day, fretting about imaginary . . .

HARPER: I get out. I do. You don't know what I do.

JOE: You don't stay in all day.

HARPER: No.

JOE: Well. . . . Yes you do.

HARPER: That's what you think.

JOE: Where do you go?

HARPER: Where do you go? When you walk. (Pause, then angrily) And I DO NOT have emotional problems.

JOE: I'm sorry.

HARPER: And if I do have emotional problems it's from living with you. Or . . .

JOE: I'm sorry buddy, I didn't mean to . . .

HARPER: Or if you do think I do then you should never have married me. You have all these secrets and lies.

JOE: I want to be married to you, Harper.

HARPER: You shouldn't. You never should.

(Pause)

Hey buddy. Hey buddy.

JOE: Buddy kiss . . .

(They kiss.)

HARPER: I heard on the radio how to give a blowjob.

JOE: What?

HARPER: You want to try?

JOE: You really shouldn't listen to stuff like that.

HARPER: Mormons can give blowjobs.

JOE: Harper.

HARPER (Imitating his tone): Joe.

It was a little Jewish lady with a German accent.

This is a good time. For me to make a baby.

(Little pause. Joe turns away.)

HARPER: Then they went on to a program about holes in the ozone layer. Over Antarctica. Skin burns, birds go blind, icebergs melt. The world's coming to an end.

Scene 6

First week of November. In the men's room of the offices of the Brooklyn Federal Court of Appeals; Louis is crying over the sink; Joe enters.

JOE: Oh, um. . . . Morning.

LOUIS: Good morning, counselor.

JOE (He watches Louis cry): Sorry, I . . . I don't know your name.

LOUIS: Don't bother. Word processor. The lowest of the low.

JOE (Holding out hand): Joe Pitt. I'm with Justice Wilson . . .

LOUIS: Oh, I know that. Counselor Pitt. Chief Clerk.

JOE: Were you . . . are you OK?

LOUIS: Oh, yeah. Thanks. What a nice man.

JOE: Not so nice.

LOUIS: What?

JOE: Not so nice. Nothing. You sure you're . . .

LOUIS: Life sucks shit. Life . . . just sucks shit.

JOE: What's wrong?

LOUIS: Run in my nylons.

JOE: Sorry . . .?

LOUIS: Forget it. Look, thanks for asking.

JOE: Well . . .

LOUIS: I mean it really is nice of you.

(He starts crying again)

Sorry, sorry, sick friend . . .

JOE: Oh, I'm sorry.

LOUIS: Yeah, yeah, well, that's sweet.

Three of your colleagues have preceded you to this baleful sight and you're the first one to ask. The others just opened the door, saw me, and fled. I hope they had to pee real bad.

JOE (Handing him a wad of toilet paper): They just didn't want to intrude.

LOUIS: Hah. Reaganite heartless macho asshole lawyers.

JOE: Oh, that's unfair.

LOUIS: What is? Heartless? Macho? Reaganite? Lawyer?

JOE: I voted for Reagan.

LOUIS: You did?

JOE: Twice.

LOUIS: Twice? Well, oh boy. A Gay Republican.

JOE: Excuse me?

LOUIS: Nothing.

JOE: I'm not . . .

Forget it.

LOUIS: Republican? Not Republican? Or . . .

JOE: What?

LOUIS: What?

JOE: Not gay. I'm not gay.

LOUIS: Oh. Sorry.

(Blows his nose loudly) It's just . . .

JOE: Yes?

LOUIS: Well, sometimes you can tell from the way a person sounds that . . . I mean you *sound* like a . . .

JOE: No I don't. Like what?

LOUIS: Like a Republican.

(Little pause. Joe knows he's being teased; Louis knows he knows. Joe decides to be a little brave.)

JOE (Making sure no one else is around): Do I? Sound like a . . .?

LOUIS: What? Like a . . .? Republican, or . . .? Do *I*?

JOE: Do you what?

LOUIS: Sound like a . . .?

JOE Like a . . .?

I'm . . . confused.

LOUIS: Yes.

My name is Louis. But all my friends call me Louise. I work in Word Processing. Thanks for the toilet paper.

(Louis offers Joe his hand, Joe reaches, Louis feints and pecks Joe on the cheek, then exits.)

Scene 7

A week later. Mutual dream scene. Prior is at a fantastic makeup table, having a dream, applying the face. Harper is having a pill-induced hallucination. She has these from time to time. For some reason, Prior has appeared in this one. Or Harper has appeared in Prior's dream. It is bewildering.

PRIOR (Alone, putting on makeup, then examining the results in the mirror; to the audience): "I'm ready for my closeup, Mr. DeMille."

One wants to move through life with elegance and grace, blossoming infrequently but with exquisite taste, and perfect timing, like a rare bloom, a zebra orchid. . . . One wants. . . . But one so seldom gets what one wants, does one? No. One does not. One gets fucked. Over. One . . . dies at thirty, robbed of . . . decades of majesty.

Fuck this shit. Fuck this shit.

(He almost crumbles; he pulls himself together; he studies his handiwork in the mirror)

I look like a corpse. A corpsette. Oh my queen; you know you've hit rock-bottom when even drag is a drag.

(Harper appears.)

HARPER: Are you. . . . Who are you?

PRIOR: Who are you?

HARPER: What are you doing in my hallucination?

PRIOR: I'm not in your hallucination. You're in my dream.

HARPER: You're wearing makeup.

PRIOR: So are you.

HARPER: But you're a man.

PRIOR (Feigning dismay, shock, he mimes slashing his throat with his lipstick and dies, fabulously tragic. Then): The hands and feet give it away.

HARPER: There must be some mistake here. I don't recognize you. You're not. . . . Are you my . . . some sort of imaginary friend?

PRIOR: No. Aren't you too old to have imaginary friends?

HARPER: I have emotional problems. I took too many pills. Why are you wearing makeup?

PRIOR: I was in the process of applying the face, trying to make myself feel better—I swiped the new fall colors at the Clinique counter at Macy's. (Showing her)

HARPER: You stole these?

PRIOR: I was out of cash; it was an emotional emergency!

HARPER: Joe will be so angry. I promised him. No more pills.

PRIOR: These pills you keep alluding to?

HARPER: Valium. I take Valium. Lots of Valium.

PRIOR: And you're dancing as fast as you can.

HARPER: I'm not *addicted.* I don't believe in addiction, and I never . . . well, I *never* drink. And I *never* take drugs.

PRIOR: Well, smell *you,* Nancy Drew.

HARPER: Except Valium.

PRIOR: Except Valium; in wee fistfuls.

HARPER: It's terrible. Mormons are not supposed to be addicted to anything. I'm a Mormon.

PRIOR: I'm a homosexual.

HARPER: Oh! In my church we don't believe in homosexuals.

PRIOR: In my church we don't believe in Mormons.

HARPER: What church do . . . oh! (She laughs) I get it.

I don't understand this. If I didn't ever see you before and I don't think I did then I don't think you should be here, in this hallucination, because in my experience the mind, which is where hallucinations come from, shouldn't be able to make up anything that wasn't there to start with, that didn't enter it from experience, from the real world. Imagination can't create anything new, can it? It only recycles bits and pieces from the world and reassembles them into visions. . . . Am I making sense right now?

PRIOR: Given the circumstances, yes.

HARPER: So when we think we've escaped the unbearable ordinariness and, well, untruthfulness of our lives, it's really only the same old ordinariness and falseness rearranged into the appearance of novelty and truth. Nothing unknown is knowable. Don't you think it's depressing?

PRIOR: The limitations of the imagination?

HARPER: Yes.

PRIOR: It's something you learn after your second theme party: It's All Been Done Before.

HARPER: The world. Finite. Terribly, terribly. . . . Well . . .

This is the most depressing hallucination I've ever had.

PRIOR: Apologies. I do try to be amusing.

HARPER: Oh, well, don't apologize, you. . . . I can't expect someone who's really sick to entertain me.

PRIOR: How on earth did you know . . .

HARPER: Oh that happens. This is the very threshhold of revelation sometimes. You can see things . . . how sick you are. Do you see anything about me?

PRIOR: Yes.

HARPER: What?

PRIOR: You are amazingly unhappy.

HARPER: Oh big deal. You meet a Valium addict and you figure out she's unhappy. That doesn't count. Of course I. . . . Something else. Something surprising.

PRIOR: Something surprising.

HARPER: Yes.

PRIOR: Your husband's a homo.

(Pause.)

HARPER: Oh, ridiculous.

(Pause, then very quietly)

Really?

PRIOR (Shrugs): Threshhold of revelation.

HARPER: Well I don't like your revelations. I don't think you intuit well at all. Joe's a very normal man, he . . .

Oh God. Oh God. He. . . . Do homos take, like, lots of long walks?

PRIOR: Yes. We do. In stretch pants with lavender coifs. I just looked at you, and there was . . .

HARPER: A sort of blue streak of recognition.

PRIOR: Yes.

HARPER: Like you knew me incredibly well.

PRIOR: Yes.

HARPER: Yes.

I have to go now, get back, something just . . . fell apart.

Oh God, I feel so sad . . .

PRIOR: I . . . I'm sorry. I usually say, "Fuck the truth," but mostly, the truth fucks you.

HARPER: I see something else about you . . .

PRIOR: Oh?

HARPER: Deep inside you, there's a part of you, the most inner part, entirely free of disease. I can see that.

PRIOR: Is that. . . . That isn't true.

HARPER: Threshhold of revelation.

Home . . .

(She vanishes.)

PRIOR: People come and go so quickly here . . .

(To himself in the mirror) I don't think there's any uninfected part of me. My heart is pumping polluted blood. I feel dirty.

(He begins to wipe makeup off with his hands, smearing it around. A large gray feather falls from up above. Prior stops smearing the

307

makeup and looks at the feather. He goes to it and picks it up.)

A VOICE (It is an incredibly beautiful voice): Look up!

PRIOR (Looking up, not seeing anyone): Hello?

A VOICE: Look up!

PRIOR: Who is that?

A VOICE: Prepare the way!

PRIOR: I don't see any . . .

(There is a dramatic change in lighting, from above.)

A VOICE:

> Look up, look up,
> prepare the way
> the infinite descent
> A breath in air
> floating down
> Glory to . . .

(Silence.)

PRIOR: Hello? Is that it? Helloooo!

What the fuck . . .? (He holds himself)

Poor me. Poor poor me. Why me? Why poor poor me? Oh I don't feel good right now. I really don't.

Scene 8

That night. Split scene: Harper and Joe at home; Prior and Louis in bed.

HARPER: Where were you?

JOE: Out.

HARPER: Where?

JOE: Just out. Thinking.

HARPER: It's late.

JOE: I had a lot to think about.

HARPER: I burned dinner.

JOE: Sorry.

HARPER: Not my dinner. My dinner was fine. Your dinner. I put it back in the oven and turned everything up as high as it could go and I watched till it burned black. It's still hot. Very hot. Want it?

JOE: You didn't have to do that.

HARPER: I know. It just seemed like the kind of thing a mentally deranged sex-starved pill-popping housewife would do.

JOE: Uh huh.

HARPER: So I did it. Who knows anymore what I have to do?

JOE: How many pills?

HARPER: A bunch. Don't change the subject.

JOE: I won't talk to you when you . . .

HARPER: No. No. Don't do that! I'm . . . I'm fine, pills are not the problem, not our problem, I WANT TO KNOW WHERE YOU'VE BEEN! I WANT TO KNOW WHAT'S GOING ON!

JOE: Going on with what? The job?

HARPER: Not the job.

JOE: I said I need more time.

HARPER: Not the job!

JOE: Mr. Cohn, I talked to him on the phone, he said I had to hurry . . .

HARPER: Not the . . .

JOE: But I can't get you to talk sensibly about anything so . . .

HARPER: SHUT UP!

JOE: Then what?

HARPER: Stick to the subject.

JOE: I don't know what that is. You have something you want to ask me? Ask me. Go.

HARPER: I . . . can't. I'm scared of you.

JOE: I'm tired, I'm going to bed.

HARPER: Tell me without making me ask. Please.

JOE: This is crazy, I'm not . . .

HARPER: When you come through the door at night your face is never exactly the way I remembered it. I get surprised by something . . . mean and hard about the way you look. Even the weight of you in the bed at night, the way you breathe in your sleep seems unfamiliar.

You terrify me.

JOE (Cold): I know who you are.

HARPER: Yes. I'm the enemy. That's easy. That doesn't change.

You think you're the only one who hates sex; I do; I hate it with you; I do. I dream that you batter away at me till all my joints come apart, like wax, and I fall into pieces. It's like a punishment. It was wrong of me to marry you. I knew you . . . (She stops herself) It's a sin, and it's killing us both.

JOE: I can always tell when you've taken pills because it makes you red-faced and sweaty and frankly that's very often why I don't want to . . .

HARPER: Because . . .

JOE: Well, you aren't pretty. Not like this.

HARPER: I have something to ask you.

JOE: Then ASK! ASK! What in hell are you . . .

HARPER: Are you a homo?

(Pause)

Are you? If you try to walk out right now I'll put your dinner back in the oven and turn it up so high the whole building will fill with smoke and everyone in it will asphyxiate. So help me God I will.

Now answer the question.

JOE: What if I . . .

(Small pause.)

HARPER: Then tell me, please. And we'll see.

JOE: No. I'm not.

I don't see what difference it makes.

LOUIS: Jews don't have any clear textual guide to the afterlife; even that it exists. I don't think much about it. I see it as a perpetual rainy Thursday afternoon in March. Dead leaves.

PRIOR: Eeeugh. Very Greco-Roman.

LOUIS: Well for us it's not the verdict that counts, it's the act of judgment. That's why I could never be a lawyer. In court all that matters is the verdict.

PRIOR: You could never be a lawyer because you are oversexed. You're too distracted.

LOUIS: Not distracted; abstracted. I'm trying to make a point:

PRIOR: Namely:

LOUIS: It's the judge in his or her chambers, weighing, books open, pondering the evidence, ranging freely over categories: good, evil, innocent, guilty; the judge in the chamber of circumspection, not the judge on the bench with the gavel. The shaping of the law, not its execution.

PRIOR: The point, dear, the point . . .

LOUIS: That it should be the questions and shape of a life, its total complexity gathered, arranged and considered, which matters in the end, not some stamp of salvation or damnation which disperses all the complexity in some unsatisfying little decision—the balancing of the scales . . .

PRIOR: I like this; very zen; it's . . . reassuringly incomprehensible and useless. We who are about to die thank you.

LOUIS: You are not about to die.

PRIOR: It's not going well, really . . . two new lesions. My leg hurts. There's protein in my urine, the doctor says, but who knows what the fuck that portends. Anyway it shouldn't be there, the protein. My butt is chapped from diarrhea and yesterday I shat blood.

LOUIS: I really hate this. You don't tell me . . .

PRIOR: You get too upset, I wind up comforting you. It's easier . . .

LOUIS: Oh thanks.

PRIOR: If it's bad I'll tell you.

LOUIS: Shitting blood sounds bad to me.

PRIOR: And I'm telling you.

LOUIS: And I'm handling it.

PRIOR: Tell me some more about justice.

LOUIS: I am handling it.

PRIOR: Well Louis you win Trooper of the Month.

(Louis starts to cry.)

PRIOR: I take it back. You aren't Trooper of the Month.

This isn't working . . .
Tell me some more about justice.

LOUIS: You are not about to die.

PRIOR: Justice . . .

LOUIS: . . . is an immensity, a confusing vastness. Justice is God.
Prior?

PRIOR: Hmmm?

LOUIS: You love me.

PRIOR: Yes.

LOUIS: What if I walked out on this?
Would you hate me forever?

(Prior kisses Louis on the forehead.)

PRIOR: Yes.

JOE: I think we ought to pray. Ask God for help. Ask him together . . .

HARPER: God won't talk to me. I have to make up people to talk to me.

JOE: You have to keep asking.

HARPER: I forgot the question.
Oh yeah. God, is my husband a . . .

JOE (Scary): Stop it. Stop it. I'm warning you. Does it make any difference? That I might be one thing deep within, no matter how wrong or ugly that thing is, so long as I have fought, with everything I have, to kill it. What do you want from me? What do you want from me, Harper? More than that? For God's sake, there's nothing left, I'm a shell. There's nothing left to kill.

As long as my behavior is what I know it has to be. Decent. Correct. That alone in the eyes of God.

HARPER: No, no, not that, that's Utah talk, Mormon talk, I hate it, Joe, tell me, say it . . .

JOE: All I will say is that I am a very good man who has worked very hard to become good and you want to destroy that. You want to destroy me, but I am not going to let you do that.

(Pause.)

HARPER: I'm going to have a baby.

JOE: Liar.

HARPER: You liar.

A baby born addicted to pills. A baby who does not dream but who hallucinates, who stares up at us with big mirror eyes and who does not know who we are.

(Pause.)

JOE: Are you really . . .

HARPER: No. Yes. No. Yes. Get away from me. Now we both have a secret.

PRIOR: One of my ancestors was a ship's captain who made money bringing whale oil to Europe and returning with immigrants—Irish mostly, packed in tight, so many dollars per head. The last ship he captained foundered off the coast of Nova Scotia in a winter tempest and sank to the bottom. He went down with the ship—la Grande Geste—but his crew took seventy women and kids in the ship's only longboat, this big, open rowboat, and when the weather got too rough, and they thought the boat was overcrowded, the crew started lifting people up and hurling them into the sea. Until they got the ballast right. They walked up and down the longboat, eyes to the waterline, and when the boat rode low in the water they'd grab the nearest passenger and throw them into the sea. The boat was leaky, see; seventy people; they arrived in Halifax with nine people on board.

LOUIS: Jesus.

PRIOR: I think about that story a lot now. People in a boat, waiting, terrified, while implacable, unsmiling men, irresistibly strong, seize . . . maybe the person next to you, maybe you, and with no warning at all, with time only for a quick intake of air you are pitched into freezing, turbulent water and salt and darkness to drown.

I like your cosmology, baby. While time is running out I find myself drawn to anything that's suspended, that lacks an ending—but it seems to me that it lets you off scot-free.

LOUIS: What do you mean?

PRIOR: No judgment, no guilt or responsibility.

LOUIS: For me.

PRIOR: For anyone. It was an editorial "you."

LOUIS: Please get better. Please.
Please don't get any sicker.

Scene 9

Third week in November. Roy and Henry, his doctor, in Henry's office.

HENRY: Nobody knows what causes it. And nobody knows how to cure it. The best theory is that we blame a retrovirus, the Human Immunodeficiency Virus. Its presence is made known to us by the useless antibodies which appear in reaction to its entrance into the bloodstream through a cut, or an orifice. The antibodies are powerless to protect the body against it. Why, we don't know. The body's immune system ceases to function. Sometimes the body even attacks itself. At any rate it's left open to a whole horror house of infections from microbes which it usually defends against.

Like Kaposi's sarcomas. These lesions. Or your throat problem. Or the glands.

We think it may also be able to slip past the blood-brain barrier into the brain. Which is of course very bad news.

And it's fatal in we don't know what percent of people with suppressed immune responses.

(Pause.)

ROY: This is very interesting, Mr. Wizard, but why the fuck are you telling me this?

(Pause.)

HENRY: Well, I have just removed one of three lesions which biopsy results will probably tell us is a Kaposi's sarcoma lesion. And you have a pronounced swelling of glands in your neck, groin, and armpits—lymphadenopathy is another sign. And you have oral candidiasis and maybe a little more fungus under the fingernails of two digits on your right hand. So that's why . . .

ROY: This disease . . .

HENRY: Syndrome.

ROY: Whatever. It afflicts mostly homosexuals and drug addicts.

HENRY: Mostly. Hemophiliacs are also at risk.

ROY: Homosexuals and drug addicts. So why are you implying that I . . .

(Pause)

What are you implying, Henry?

HENRY: I don't . . .

ROY: I'm not a drug addict.

HENRY: Oh come on Roy.

ROY: What, what, come on Roy what? Do you think I'm a junkie, Henry, do you see tracks?

HENRY: This is absurd.

ROY: Say it.

HENRY: Say what?

ROY: Say, "Roy Cohn, you are a . . ."

HENRY: Roy.

ROY: "You are a. . . . " Go on. Not "Roy Cohn you are a drug fiend." "Roy Marcus Cohn, you are a . . ."
Go on, Henry, it starts with an "H."

HENRY: Oh I'm not going to . . .

ROY: *With an "H,"* Henry, and it isn't "Hemophiliac." Come on . . .

HENRY: What are you doing, Roy?

ROY: No, say it. I mean it. Say: "Roy Cohn, you are a homosexual."

(Pause)

And I will proceed, systematically, to destroy your reputation and your practice and your career in New York State, Henry. Which you know I can do.

(Pause.)

HENRY: Roy, you have been seeing me since 1958. Apart from the facelifts I have treated you for everything from syphilis . . .

ROY: From a whore in Dallas.

HENRY: From syphilis to venereal warts. In your rectum. Which you may have gotten from a whore in Dallas, but it wasn't a female whore.

311

(Pause.)

ROY: So say it.

HENRY: Roy Cohn, you are . . .

You have had sex with men, many many times, Roy, and one of them, or any number of them, has made you very sick. You have AIDS.

ROY: AIDS.

Your problem, Henry, is that you are hung up on words, on labels, that you believe they mean what they seem to mean. AIDS. Homosexual. Gay. Lesbian. You think these are names that tell you who someone sleeps with, but they don't tell you that.

HENRY: No?

ROY: No. Like all labels they tell you one thing and one thing only: where does an individual so identified fit in the food chain, in the pecking order? Not ideology, or sexual taste, but something much simpler: clout. Not who I fuck or who fucks me, but who will pick up the phone when I call, who owes me favors. This is what a label refers to. Now to someone who does not understand this, homosexual is what I am because I have sex with men. But really this is wrong. Homosexuals are not men who sleep with other men. Homosexuals are men who in fifteen years of trying cannot get a pissant antidiscrimination bill through City Council. Homosexuals are men who know nobody and who nobody knows. Who have zero clout. Does this sound like me, Henry?

HENRY: No.

ROY: No. I have clout. A lot. I can pick up this phone, punch fifteen numbers, and you know who will be on the other end in under five minutes, Henry?

HENRY: The President.

ROY: Even better, Henry. His wife.

HENRY: I'm impressed.

ROY: I don't want you to be impressed. I want you to understand. This is not sophistry. And this is not hypocrisy. This is reality. I have sex with men. But unlike nearly every other man of whom this is true, I bring the guy I'm screwing to the White House and President Reagan smiles at us and shakes his hand. Because *what* I am is defined entirely by *who* I am. Roy Cohn is not a homosexual. Roy Cohn is a heterosexual man, Henry, who fucks around with guys.

HENRY: OK, Roy.

ROY: And what is my diagnosis, Henry?

HENRY: You have AIDS, Roy.

ROY: No, Henry, no. AIDS is what homosexuals have. I have liver cancer.

(Pause.)

HENRY: Well, whatever the fuck you have, Roy, it's very serious, and I haven't got a damn thing for you. The NIH in Bethesda has a new drug called AZT with a two-year waiting list that not even I can get you onto. So get on the phone, Roy, and dial the fifteen numbers, and tell the First Lady you need in on an experimental treatment for liver cancer, because you can call it any damn thing you want, Roy, but what it boils down to is very bad news.

ACT TWO

In Vitro
December 1985–January 1986

Scene 1

Night, the third week in December. Prior alone on the floor of his bedroom; he is much worse.

PRIOR: Louis, Louis, please wake up, oh God.

(Louis runs in.)

PRIOR: I think something horrible is wrong with me I can't breathe . . .

LOUIS (Starting to exit): I'm calling the ambulance.

PRIOR: No, wait, I . . .

LOUIS: *Wait?* Are you fucking crazy? Oh God you're on fire, your head is on fire.

PRIOR: It hurts, it hurts . . .

LOUIS: I'm calling the ambulance.

PRIOR: I don't want to go to the hospital, I don't want to go to the hospital please let me lie here, just . . .

LOUIS: No, no, God, Prior, stand up . . .

PRIOR: DON'T TOUCH MY LEG!

LOUIS: We have to . . . oh God this is so crazy.

PRIOR: I'll be OK if I just lie here Lou, really, if I can only sleep a little . . .

(Louis exits.)

PRIOR: Louis?

NO! NO! Don't call, you'll send me there and I won't come back, please, please Louis I'm begging, baby, please . . .
(Screams) LOUIS!!

LOUIS (From off; hysterical): WILL YOU SHUT THE FUCK UP!

PRIOR (Trying to stand): Aaaah. I have . . . to go to the bathroom. Wait. Wait, just . . . oh. Oh God. (He shits himself)

LOUIS (Entering): Prior? They'll be here in . . . Oh my God.

PRIOR: I'm sorry, I'm sorry.

LOUIS: What did . . .? What?

PRIOR: I had an accident.

(Louis goes to him.)

LOUIS: This is blood.

PRIOR: Maybe you shouldn't touch it . . . me. . . . I . . . (He faints)

LOUIS (Quietly): Oh help. Oh help. Oh God oh God oh God help me I can't I can't I can't.

Scene 2

Same night. Harper is sitting at home, all alone, with no lights on. We can barely see her. Joe enters, but he doesn't turn on the lights.

JOE: Why are you sitting in the dark? Turn on the light.

HARPER: No. I heard the sounds in the bedroom again. I know someone was in there.

JOE: No one was.

HARPER: Maybe actually in the bed, under the covers with a knife.

Oh, boy. Joe. I, um, I'm thinking of going away. By which I mean: I think I'm going off again. You . . . you know what I mean?

JOE: Please don't. Stay. We can fix it. I pray for that. This is my fault, but I can correct it. You have to try too . . .

(He turns on the light. She turns it off again.)

HARPER: When you pray, what do you pray for?

JOE: I pray for God to crush me, break me up into little pieces and start all over again.

HARPER: Oh. Please. Don't pray for that.

JOE: I had a book of Bible stories when I was a kid. There was a picture I'd look at twenty times every day: Jacob wrestles with the angel. I don't really remember the story, or why the wrestling—just the picture. Jacob is young and very strong. The angel is . . . a beautiful man, with golden hair and wings, of course. I still dream about it. Many nights. I'm. . . . It's me. In that struggle. Fierce, and unfair. The angel is not human, and it holds nothing back, so how could anyone human win, what kind of a fight is that? It's not just. Losing means your soul thrown down in the dust, your heart torn out from God's. But you can't not lose.

HARPER: In the whole entire world, you are the only person, the only person I love or have ever loved. And I love you terribly. Terribly. That's what's so awfully, irreducibly real. I can make up anything but I can't dream that away.

JOE: Are you . . . are you really going to have a baby?

HARPER: It's my time, and there's no blood. I don't really know. I suppose it wouldn't be a great thing. Maybe I'm just not bleeding because I take too many pills. Maybe I'll give birth to a pill. That would give a new meaning to pill-popping, huh?

I think you should go to Washington. Alone. Change, like you said.

JOE: I'm not going to leave you, Harper.

HARPER: Well maybe not. But I'm going to leave you.

Scene 3

One A.M., the next morning. Louis and a nurse, Emily, are sitting in Prior's room in the hospital.

EMILY: He'll be all right now.

LOUIS: No he won't.

EMILY: No. I guess not. I gave him something that makes him sleep.

LOUIS: Deep asleep?

EMILY: Orbiting the moons of Jupiter.

LOUIS: A good place to be.

EMILY: Anyplace better than here. You his . . . uh?

LOUIS: Yes. I'm his uh.

EMILY: This must be hell for you.

LOUIS: It is. Hell. The After Life. Which is not at all like a rainy afternoon in March, by the way, Prior. A lot more vivid than I'd expected. Dead leaves, but the crunchy kind. Sharp, dry air. The kind of long, luxurious dying feeling that breaks your heart.

EMILY: Yeah, well we all get to break our hearts on this one.

He seems like a nice guy. Cute.

LOUIS: Not like this.

Yes, he is. Was. Whatever.

EMILY: Weird name. Prior Walter. Like, "The Walter before this one."

LOUIS: Lots of Walters before this one. Prior is an old old family name in an old old family. The Walters go back to the Mayflower and beyond. Back to the Norman Conquest. He says there's a Prior Walter stitched into the Bayeux tapestry.

EMILY: Is that impressive?

LOUIS: Well, it's old. Very old. Which in some circles equals impressive.

EMILY: Not in my circle. What's the name of the tapestry?

LOUIS: The Bayeux tapestry. Embroidered by La Reine Mathilde.

EMILY: I'll tell my mother. She embroiders. Drives me nuts.

LOUIS: Manual therapy for anxious hands.

EMILY: Maybe you should try it.

LOUIS: Mathilde stitched while William the Conqueror was off to war. She was capable of . . . more than loyalty. Devotion.

She waited for him, she stitched for years. And if he had come back broken and defeated from war, she would have loved him even more. And if he had returned mutilated, ugly, full of infection and horror, she would still have loved him; fed by pity, by a sharing of pain, she would love him even more, and even more, and she would never, never have prayed to God, please let him die if he can't return to me whole and healthy and able to live a normal life. . . . If he had died, she would have buried her heart with him.

So what the fuck is the matter with me?

(Little pause)

Will he sleep through the night?

EMILY: At least.

LOUIS: I'm going.

EMILY: It's one A.M. Where do you have to go at . . .

LOUIS: I know what time it is. A walk. Night air, good for the. . . . The park.

EMILY: Be careful.

LOUIS: Yeah. Danger.

Tell him, if he wakes up and you're still on, tell him goodbye, tell him I had to go.

Scene 4

An hour later. Split scene: Joe and Roy in a fancy (straight) bar; Louis and a Man in the Rambles in Central Park. Joe and Roy are sitting at the bar; the place is brightly lit. Joe has a plate of food in front of him but he isn't eating. Roy occasionally reaches over the table and forks small bites off Joe's plate. Roy is drinking heavily, Joe not at all. Louis and the Man are eyeing each other, each alternating interest and indifference.

JOE: The pills were something she started when she miscarried or . . . no, she took some before that. She had a really bad time at home, when she was a kid, her home was really bad. I think a lot of drinking and physical stuff. She doesn't talk about that, instead she talks about . . . the sky falling down, people with knives hiding under sofas. Monsters. Mormons. Everyone thinks Mormons don't come from homes like that, we aren't supposed to behave that way, but we do. It's not lying, or being two-faced. Everyone tries very hard to live up to God's strictures, which are very . . . um . . .

ROY: Strict.

JOE: I shouldn't be bothering you with this.

ROY: No, please. Heart to heart. Want another. . . . What is that, seltzer?

JOE: The failure to measure up hits people very hard. From such a strong desire to be good they feel very far from goodness when they fail.

What scares me is that maybe what I really love in her is the part of her that's farthest from the light, from God's love; maybe I was drawn to that in the first place. And I'm keeping it alive because I need it.

ROY: Why would you need it?

JOE: There are things. . . . I don't know how well we know ourselves. I mean, what if? I know I married her because she . . . because I loved it that she was always wrong, always doing something wrong, like one step out of step. In Salt Lake City that stands out. I never stood out, on the outside, but inside, it was hard for me. To pass.

ROY: Pass?

JOE: Yeah.

ROY: Pass as what?

JOE: Oh. Well. . . . As someone cheerful and strong. Those who love God with an open heart unclouded by secrets and struggles are cheerful; God's easy simple love for them shows in how strong and happy they are. The saints.

ROY: But you had secrets? Secret struggles . . .

JOE: I wanted to be one of the elect, one of the Blessed. You feel you ought to be, that the blemishes are yours by choice, which of course they aren't. Harper's sorrow, that really deep sorrow, she didn't choose that. But it's there.

ROY: You didn't put it there.

JOE: No.

ROY: You sound like you think you did.

JOE: I am responsible for her.

ROY: Because she's your wife.

JOE: That. And I do love her.

ROY: Whatever. She's your wife. And so there are obligations. To her. But also to yourself.

JOE: She'd fall apart in Washington.

ROY: Then let her stay here.

JOE: She'll fall apart if I leave her.

ROY: Then bring her to Washington.

JOE: I just can't, Roy. She needs me.

ROY: Listen, Joe. I'm the best divorce lawyer in the business.

(Little pause.)

JOE: Can't Washington wait?

ROY: You do what you need to do, Joe. What *you* need. *You.* Let her life go where it wants to go. You'll both be better for that. *Somebody* should get what they want.

MAN: What do you want?

LOUIS: I want you to fuck me, hurt me, make me bleed.

MAN: I want to.

LOUIS: Yeah?

MAN: I want to hurt you.

LOUIS: Fuck me.

MAN: Yeah?

LOUIS: Hard.

MAN: Yeah? You been a bad boy?

(Pause. Louis laughs, softly.)

LOUIS: Very bad. Very bad.

MAN: You need to be punished, boy?

LOUIS: Yes. I do.

MAN: Yes what?

(Little pause.)

LOUIS: Um, I . . .

MAN: Yes *what,* boy?

LOUIS: Oh. Yes sir.

MAN: I want you to take me to your place, boy.

LOUIS: No, I can't do that.

MAN: No *what?*

LOUIS: No sir, I can't, I . . .
I don't live alone, sir.

MAN: Your lover know you're out with a man tonight, boy?

LOUIS: No sir, he . . .
My lover doesn't know.

MAN: Your lover know you . . .

LOUIS: Let's change the subject, OK? Can we go to your place?

MAN: I live with my parents.

LOUIS: Oh.

ROY: Everyone who makes it in this world makes it because somebody older and more powerful takes an interest. The most precious asset in life, I think, is the ability to be a good son. You have that, Joe. Somebody who can be a good son to a father who pushes them farther than they would otherwise go. I've had many fathers, I owe my life to them, powerful, powerful men. Walter Winchell, Edgar Hoover. Joe McCarthy most of all. He valued me because I am a good lawyer, but he loved me because I was and am a good son. He was a very difficult man, very guarded and cagey; I brought out something tender in him. He would have died for me. And me for him. Does this embarrass you?

JOE: I had a hard time with my father.

ROY: Well sometimes that's the way. Then you have to find other fathers, substitutes, I don't know. The father-son relationship is central to life. Women are for birth, beginning, but the father is continuance. The son offers the father his life as a vessel for carrying forth his father's dream. Your father's living?

JOE: Um, dead.

ROY: He was . . . what? A difficult man?

JOE: He was in the military. He could be very unfair. And cold.

ROY: But he loved you.

JOE: I don't know.

ROY: No, no, Joe, he did, I know this. Sometimes a father's love has to be very, very hard, unfair even, cold to make his son grow strong in a world like this. This isn't a good world.

MAN: Here, then.

LOUIS: I. . . . Do you have a rubber?

MAN: I don't use rubbers.

LOUIS: You should. (He takes one from his coat pocket) Here.

MAN: I don't use them.

LOUIS: Forget it, then. (He starts to leave)

MAN: No, wait.
Put it on me. Boy.

LOUIS: Forget it, I have to get back. Home. I must be going crazy.

MAN: Oh come on please he won't find out.

LOUIS: It's cold. Too cold.

MAN: It's never too cold, let me warm you up. Please?

(They begin to fuck.)

MAN: Relax.

LOUIS (A small laugh): Not a chance.

MAN: It . . .

LOUIS: What?

MAN: I think it broke. The rubber. You want me to keep going? (Little pause) Pull out? Should I . . .

LOUIS: Keep going.

Infect me.

I don't care. I don't care.

(Pause. The Man pulls out.)

MAN: I . . . um, look, I'm sorry, but I think I want to go.

LOUIS: Yeah.

Give my best to mom and dad.

(The Man slaps him.)

LOUIS: Ow!

(They stare at each other.)

LOUIS: It was a joke.

(The Man leaves.)

ROY: How long have we known each other?

JOE: Since 1980.

ROY: Right. A long time. I feel close to you, Joe. Do I advise you well?

JOE: You've been an incredible friend, Roy, I . . .

ROY: I want to be family. Familia, as my Italian friends call it. La Familia. A lovely word. It's important for me to help you, like I was helped.

JOE: I owe practically everything to you, Roy.

ROY: I'm dying, Joe. Cancer.

JOE: Oh my God.

ROY: Please. Let me finish.

Few people know this and I'm telling you this only because. . . . I'm not afraid of death. What can death bring that I haven't faced? I've lived; life is the worst. (Gently mocking himself) Listen to me, I'm a philosopher.

Joe. You must do this. You must must must. Love; that's a trap. Responsibility; that's a trap too. Like a father to a son I tell you this: Life is full of horror; nobody escapes, nobody; save yourself. Whatever pulls on you, whatever needs from you, threatens you. Don't be afraid; people are so afraid; don't be afraid to live in the raw wind, naked, alone. . . . Learn at least this: What you are capable of. Let nothing stand in your way.

Scene 5

Three days later. Prior and Belize in Prior's hospital room. Prior is very sick but improving. Belize has just arrived.

PRIOR: Miss Thing.

BELIZE: Ma cherie bichette.

PRIOR: Stella.

BELIZE: Stella for star. Let me see. (Scrutinizing Prior) You look like shit, why yes indeed you do, comme la merde!

PRIOR: Merci.

BELIZE (Taking little plastic bottles from his bag, handing them to Prior): Not to despair, Belle Reeve. Lookie! Magic goop!

PRIOR (Opening a bottle, sniffing): Pooh! What kinda crap is that?

BELIZE: Beats me. Let's rub it on your poor blistered body and see what it does.

PRIOR: This is not Western medicine, these bottles . . .

BELIZE: Voodoo cream. From the botanica 'round the block.

PRIOR: And you a registered nurse.

BELIZE (Sniffing it): Beeswax and cheap perfume. Cut with Jergen's Lotion. Full of good vibes and love from some little black Cubana witch in Miami.

PRIOR: Get that trash away from me, I am immune-suppressed.

BELIZE: I *am* a health professional. I *know* what I'm doing.

PRIOR: It stinks. Any word from Louis?

(Pause. Belize starts giving Prior a gentle massage.)

PRIOR: Gone.

BELIZE: He'll be back. I know the type. Likes to keep a girl on edge.

PRIOR: It's been . . .

(Pause.)

BELIZE (Trying to jog his memory): How long?

PRIOR: I don't remember.

BELIZE: How long have you been here?

PRIOR (Getting suddenly upset): I don't remember, I don't give a fuck. I want Louis. I want my fucking boyfriend, where the fuck is he? I'm dying, I'm dying, where's Louis?

BELIZE: Shhhh, shhh . . .

PRIOR: This is a very strange drug, this drug. Emotional lability, for starters.

BELIZE: Save a tab or two for me.

PRIOR: Oh no, not this drug, ce n'est pas pour la joyeux noël et la bonne année, this drug she is serious poisonous chemistry, ma pauvre bichette.

And not just disorienting. I hear things. Voices.

BELIZE: Voices.

PRIOR: A voice.

BELIZE: Saying what?

(Pause.)

PRIOR: I'm not supposed to tell.

BELIZE: You better tell the doctor. Or I will.

PRIOR: No no don't. Please. I want the voice; it's wonderful. It's all that's keeping me alive. I don't want to talk to some intern about it.

You know what happens? When I hear it, I get hard.

BELIZE: Oh my.

PRIOR: Comme ça. (He uses his arm to demonstrate) And you know I am slow to rise.

BELIZE: My jaw aches at the memory.

PRIOR: And would you deny me this little solace—betray my concupiscence to Florence Nightingale's storm troopers?

BELIZE: Perish the thought, ma bébé.

PRIOR: They'd change the drug just to spoil the fun.

BELIZE: You and your boner can depend on me.

PRIOR: Je t'adore, ma belle nègre.

BELIZE: All this girl-talk shit is politically incorrect, you know. We should have dropped it back when we gave up drag.

PRIOR: I'm sick, I get to be politically incorrect if it makes me feel better. You sound like Lou.

(Little pause)

Well, at least I have the satisfaction of knowing he's in anguish somewhere. I loved his anguish. Watching him stick his head up his asshole and eat his guts out over some relatively minor moral conundrum—it was the best show in town. But Mother warned me: if they get overwhelmed by the little things . . .

BELIZE: They'll be belly-up bustville when something big comes along.

PRIOR: Mother warned me.

BELIZE: And they do come along.

PRIOR: But I didn't listen.

BELIZE: No. (Doing Hepburn) Men are beasts.

PRIOR (Also Hepburn): The absolute lowest.

BELIZE: I have to go. If I want to spend my whole lonely life looking after white people I can get underpaid to do it.

PRIOR: You're just a Christian martyr.

BELIZE: Whatever happens, baby, I will be here for you.

PRIOR: Je t'aime.

BELIZE: Je t'aime. Don't go crazy on me, girlfriend, I already got enough crazy queens for one lifetime. For two. I can't be bothering with dementia.

PRIOR: I promise.

BELIZE (Touching him; softly): Ouch.

PRIOR: Ouch. Indeed.

BELIZE: Why'd they have to pick on you?

And eat more, girlfriend, you really do look like shit.

(Belize leaves.)

PRIOR (After waiting a beat): He's gone.

Are you still . . .

VOICE: I can't stay. I will return.

PRIOR: Are you one of those "Follow me to the other side" voices?

VOICE: No. I am no nightbird. I am a messenger . . .

PRIOR: You have a beautiful voice, it sounds . . . like a viola, like a perfectly tuned, tight string, balanced, the truth. . . . Stay with me.

VOICE: Not now. Soon I will return, I will reveal myself to you; I am glorious, glorious; my heart, my countenance and my message. You must prepare.

PRIOR: For what? I don't want to . . .

VOICE: No death, no:

A marvelous work and a wonder we undertake, an edifice awry we sink plumb and straighten, a great Lie we abolish, a great error correct, with the rule, sword and broom of Truth!

PRIOR: What are you talking about, I . . .

VOICE:

I am on my way; when I am manifest, our Work begins:
Prepare for the parting of the air,
The breath, the ascent,
Glory to . . .

Scene 6

The second week of January. Martin, Roy and Joe in a fancy Manhattan restaurant.

MARTIN: It's a revolution in Washington, Joe. We have a new agenda and finally a real leader. They got back the Senate but we have the courts. By the nineties the Supreme Court will be block-solid Republican appointees, and the Federal bench-Republican judges like land mines, everywhere, everywhere they turn. Affirmative action? Take it to court. Boom! Land mine. And we'll get our way on just about everything: abortion, defense, Central America, family values, a live investment climate. We have the White House locked till the year 2000. And beyond. A permanent fix on the Oval Office? It's possible. By '92 we'll get the Senate back, and in ten years the South is going to give us the House. It's really the end of Liberalism. The end of New Deal Socialism. The end of ipso facto

secular humanism. The dawning of a genuinely American political personality. Modeled on Ronald Wilson Reagan.

JOE: It sounds great, Mr. Heller.

MARTIN: Martin. And Justice is the hub. Especially since Ed Meese took over. He doesn't specialize in Fine Points of the Law. He's a flatfoot, a cop. He reminds me of Teddy Roosevelt.

JOE: I can't wait to meet him.

MARTIN: Too bad, Joe, he's been dead for sixty years!

(There is a little awkwardness. Joe doesn't respond.)

MARTIN: Teddy Roosevelt. You said you wanted to. . . . Little joke. It reminds me of the story about the . . .

ROY (Smiling, but nasty): Aw shut the fuck up Martin.

(To Joe) You see that? Mr. Heller here is one of the mighty, Joseph, in D.C. he sitteth on the right hand of the man who sitteth on the right hand of The Man. And yet I can say "shut the fuck up" and he will take no offense. Loyalty. He . . .

Martin?

MARTIN: Yes, Roy?

ROY: Rub my back.

MARTIN: Roy . . .

ROY: No no really, a sore spot, I get them all the time now, these. . . . Rub it for me darling, would you do that for me?

(Martin rubs Roy's back. They both look at Joe.)

ROY (To Joe): How do you think a handful of Bolsheviks turned St. Petersburg into Leningrad in one afternoon? Comrades. Who do for each other. Marx and Engels. Lenin and Trotsky. Josef Stalin and Franklin Delano Roosevelt.

(Martin laughs.)

ROY: *Comrades,* right Martin?

MARTIN: This man, Joe, is a Saint of the Right.

JOE: I know, Mr. Heller, I . . .

ROY: And you see what I mean, Martin? He's special, right?

MARTIN: Don't embarrass him, Roy.

ROY: Gravity, decency, smarts! His strength is as the strength of ten because his heart is pure! And he's a Royboy, one hundred percent.

MARTIN: We're on the move, Joe. On the move.

ROY: Mr. Heller, I . . .

MARTIN (Ending backrub): We can't wait any longer for an answer.

(Little pause.)

JOE: Oh. Um, I . . .

ROY: Joe's a married man, Martin.

MARTIN: Aha.

ROY: With a wife. She doesn't care to go to D.C., and so Joe cannot go. And keeps us dangling. We've seen that kind of thing before, haven't we? These men and their wives.

MARTIN: Oh yes. Beware.

JOE: I really can't discuss this under . . .

MARTIN: Then *don't* discuss. Say yes, Joe.

ROY: Now.

MARTIN: Say yes I will.

ROY: Now.

Now. I'll hold my breath till you do, I'm turning blue waiting. . . . *Now,* goddammit!

MARTIN: Roy, calm down, it's not . . .

ROY: Aw, fuck it. (He takes a letter from his jacket pocket, hands it to Joe)

Read. Came today.

(Joe reads the first paragraph, then looks up.)

JOE: Roy. This is . . . Roy, this is terrible.

ROY: You're telling me.

A letter from the New York State Bar Association, Martin.

They're gonna try and disbar me.

MARTIN: Oh my.

JOE: Why?

ROY: Why, Martin?

MARTIN: Revenge.

ROY: The whole Establishment. Their little rules. Because I know no rules. Because I don't see the Law as a dead and arbitrary collection of antiquated dictums, thou shall, thou shalt not, because, because I know the Law's a pliable, breathing, sweating . . . *organ,* because, because . . .

MARTIN: Because he borrowed half a million from one of his clients.

ROY: Yeah, well, there's that.

MARTIN: *And* he forgot to *return* it.

JOE: Roy, that's. . . . You borrowed money from a client?

ROY: I'm deeply ashamed.

(Little pause.)

JOE (Very sympathetic): Roy, you know how much I admire you. Well I mean I know you have unorthodox ways, but I'm sure you only did what you thought at the time you needed to do. And I have faith that . . .

ROY: Not so damp, please. I'll deny it was a loan. She's got no paperwork. Can't prove a fucking thing.

(Little pause. Martin studies the menu.)

JOE (Handing back the letter, more official in tone): Roy I really appreciate your telling me this, and I'll do whatever I can to help.

ROY (Holding up a hand, then, carefully): I'll tell you what you can do.

I'm about to be tried, Joe, by a jury that is not a jury of my peers. The disbarment committee: genteel gentleman Brahmin lawyers, country-club men. I offend them, to these men . . . I'm what, Martin, some sort of filthy little Jewish troll?

MARTIN: Oh well, I wouldn't go so far as . . .

ROY: Oh well I would.

Very fancy lawyers, these disbarment committee lawyers, fancy lawyers with fancy corporate clients and complicated cases. Antitrust suits. Deregulation. Environmental control. Complex cases like these need Justice

Department cooperation like flowers need the sun. Wouldn't you say that's an accurate assessment, Martin?

MARTIN: I'm not here, Roy. I'm not hearing any of this.

ROY: No. Of course not.

Without the light of the sun, Joe, these cases, and the fancy lawyers who represent them, will wither and die.

A well-placed friend, someone in the Justice Department, say, can turn off the sun. Cast a deep shadow on my behalf. Make them shiver in the cold. If they overstep. They would fear that.

(Pause.)

JOE: Roy. I don't understand.

ROY: You do.

(Pause.)

JOE: You're not asking me to . . .

ROY: Sssshhhh. Careful.

JOE (A beat, then): Even if I said yes to the job, it would be illegal to interfere. With the hearings. It's unethical. No. I can't.

ROY: Un-ethical.

Would you excuse us, Martin?

MARTIN: Excuse you?

ROY: Take a walk, Martin. For real.

(Martin leaves.)

ROY: Un-ethical. Are you trying to embarrass me in front of my friend?

JOE: Well it is unethical, I can't . . .

ROY: Boy, you are really something. What the fuck do you think this is, Sunday School?

JOE: No, but Roy this is . . .

ROY: This is . . . this is gastric juices churning, this is enzymes and acids, this is intestinal is what this is, bowel movement and blood-red meat—this stinks, this is *politics*, Joe, the game of being alive. And you think you're. . . . What? Above that? Above alive is what? Dead! In the clouds! You're on earth, goddammit! Plant a foot, stay a while.

I'm sick. They smell I'm weak. They want blood this time. I must have eyes in Justice. In Justice you will protect me.

JOE: Why can't Mr. Heller . . .

ROY: Grow up, Joe. The administration can't get involved.

JOE: But I'd be part of the administration. The same as him.

ROY: Not the same. Martin's Ed's man. And Ed's Reagan's man. So Martin's Reagan's man.

And you're mine.

(Little pause. He holds up the letter)

This will never be. Understand me?

(He tears the letter up)

I'm gonna be a lawyer, Joe, I'm gonna be a lawyer, Joe, I'm gonna be a goddam mother-fucking legally licensed member of the bar lawyer, just like my daddy was, till my last bitter day on earth, Joseph, until the day I die. (Martin returns.)

ROY: Ah, Martin's back.

MARTIN: So are we agreed?

ROY: Joe?

(Little pause.)

JOE: I will think about it.

(To Roy) I will.

ROY: Huh.

MARTIN: It's the fear of what comes after the doing that makes the doing hard to do.

ROY: Amen.

MARTIN: But you can almost always live with the consequences.

Scene 7

That afternoon. On the granite steps outside the Hall of Justice, Brooklyn. It is cold and sunny. A Sabrett wagon is selling hot dogs. Louis, in a shabby overcoat, is sitting on the steps contemplatively eating one. Joe enters with three hot dogs and a can of Coke.

JOE: Can I . . .?

LOUIS: Oh sure. Sure. Crazy cold sun.

JOE (Sitting): Have to make the best of it. How's your friend?

LOUIS: My . . .? Oh. He's worse. My friend is worse.

JOE: I'm sorry.

LOUIS: Yeah, well. Thanks for asking. It's nice. You're nice. I can't believe you voted for Reagan.

JOE: I hope he gets better.

LOUIS: Reagan?

JOE: Your friend.

LOUIS: He won't. Neither will Reagan.

JOE: Let's not talk politics, OK?

LOUIS (Pointing to Joe's lunch): You're eating *three* of those?

JOE: Well . . . I'm . . . hungry.

LOUIS: They're really terrible for you. Full of rat-poo and beetle legs and wood shavings 'n' shit.

JOE: Huh.

LOUIS: And . . . um . . . irridium, I think. Something toxic.

JOE: You're eating one.

LOUIS: Yeah, well, the shape, I can't help myself, plus I'm *trying* to commit suicide, what's your excuse?

JOE: I don't have an excuse. I just have Pepto-Bismol.

(Joe takes a bottle of Pepto-Bismol and chugs it. Louis shudders audibly.)

JOE: Yeah I know but then I wash it down with Coke.

(He does this. Louis mimes barfing in Joe's lap. Joe pushes Louis's head away.)

JOE: Are you *always* like this?

LOUIS: I've been worrying a lot about his kids.

JOE: Whose?

LOUIS: Reagan's. Maureen and Mike and little orphan Patti and Miss Ron Reagan Jr., the you-should-pardon-the-expression heterosexual.

JOE: Ron Reagan Jr. is *not*. . . . You shouldn't just make these assumptions about people. How do you know? About him? What he is? You don't know.

LOUIS (Doing Tallulah): Well darling he never sucked *my* cock but . . .

JOE: Look, if you're going to get vulgar . . .

LOUIS: No no really I mean. . . . What's it like to be the child of the Zeitgeist? To have the American Animus as your dad? It's not really a *family,* the Reagans, I read *People,* there aren't any connections there, no love, they don't ever even speak to each other except through their agents. So what's it like to be Reagan's kid? Enquiring minds want to know.

JOE: You can't believe everything you . . .

LOUIS (Looking away): But . . . I think we all know what that's like. Nowadays. No connections. No responsibilities. All of us . . . falling through the cracks that separate what we owe to our selves and . . . and what we owe to love.

JOE: You just. . . . Whatever you feel like saying or doing, you don't care, you just . . . do it.

LOUIS: Do what?

JOE: It. Whatever. Whatever it is you want to do.

LOUIS: Are you trying to tell me something?

(Little pause, sexual. They stare at each other. Joe looks away.)

JOE: No, I'm just observing that you . . .

LOUIS: Impulsive.

JOE: Yes, I mean it must be scary, you . . .

LOUIS (Shrugs): Land of the free. Home of the brave. Call me irresponsible.

JOE: It's kind of terrifying.

LOUIS: Yeah, well, freedom is. Heartless, too.

JOE: Oh you're not heartless.

LOUIS: You don't know.

Finish your weenie.

(He pats Joe on the knee, starts to leave.)

JOE: Um . . .

(Louis turns, looks at him. Joe searches for something to say.)

JOE: Yesterday was Sunday but I've been a little unfocused recently and I thought it was Monday. So I came here like I was going to work. And the whole place was empty. And at first I couldn't figure out why, and I had this moment of incredible . . . fear and also. . . . It just flashed through my mind: The whole Hall of Justice, it's empty, it's deserted, it's gone out of business. Forever. The people that make it run have up and abandoned it.

LOUIS (Looking at the building): Creepy.

JOE: Well yes but. I felt that I was going to scream. Not because it was creepy, but because the emptiness felt so *fast*.

And . . . well, good. A . . . happy scream.

I just wondered what a thing it would be . . . if overnight everything you owe anything to, justice, or love, had really gone away. Free.

It would be . . . heartless terror. Yes. Terrible, and . . .

Very great. To shed your skin, every old skin, one by one and then walk away, unencumbered, into the morning.

(Little pause. He looks at the building)

I can't go in there today.

LOUIS: Then don't.

JOE (Not really hearing Louis): I can't go in, I need . . .

(He looks for what he needs. He takes a swig of Pepto-Bismol)

I can't be this anymore. I need . . . a change, I should just . . .

LOUIS (Not a come-on, necessarily; he doesn't want to be alone): Want some company? For whatever?

(Pause. Joe looks at Louis and looks away, afraid. Louis shrugs.)

LOUIS: Sometimes, even if it scares you to death, you have to be willing to break the law. Know what I mean?

(Another little pause.)

JOE: Yes.

(Another little pause.)

LOUIS: I moved out. I moved out on my . . . I haven't been sleeping well.

JOE: Me neither.

(Louis goes up to Joe, licks his napkin and dabs at Joe's mouth.)

LOUIS: Antacid moustache.

(Points to the building) Maybe the court won't convene. Ever again. Maybe we are free. To do whatever.

Children of the new morning, criminal minds. Selfish and greedy and loveless and blind. Reagan's children.

You're scared. So am I. Everybody is in the land of the free. God help us all.

Scene 8

Late that night. Joe at a payphone phoning Hannah at home in Salt Lake City.

JOE: Mom?

HANNAH: Joe?

JOE: Hi.

HANNAH: You're calling from the street. It's . . . it must be four in the morning. What's happened?

JOE: Nothing, nothing, I . . .

HANNAH: It's Harper. Is Harper. . . . Joe? Joe?

JOE: Yeah, hi. No, Harper's fine. Well, no, she's . . . not fine. How are you, Mom?

HANNAH: What's happened?

JOE: I just wanted to talk to you. I, uh, wanted to try something out on you.

HANNAH: Joe, you haven't . . . have you been drinking, Joe?

JOE: Yes ma'am. I'm drunk.

HANNAH: That isn't like you.

JOE: No. I mean, who's to say?

HANNAH: Why are you out on the street at four A.M.? In that crazy city. It's dangerous.

JOE: Actually, Mom, I'm not on the street. I'm near the boathouse in the park.

HANNAH: What park?

JOE: Central Park.

HANNAH: CENTRAL PARK! Oh my Lord. What on earth are you doing in Central Park at this time of night? Are you . . .

Joe, I think you ought to go home right now. Call me from home.
(Little pause)
Joe?

JOE: I come here to watch, Mom. Sometimes. Just to watch.

HANNAH: Watch what? What's there to watch at four in the . . .

JOE: Mom, did Dad love me?

HANNAH: What?

JOE: Did he?

HANNAH: You ought to go home and call from there.

JOE: Answer.

HANNAH: Oh now really. This is maudlin. I don't like this conversation.

JOE: Yeah, well, it gets worse from here on.

(Pause.)

HANNAH: Joe?

JOE: Mom. Momma. I'm a homosexual, Momma.

Boy, did that come out awkward.

(Pause)
Hello? Hello?
I'm a homosexual.

(Pause)
Please, Momma. Say something.

HANNAH: You're old enough to understand that your father didn't love you without being ridiculous about it.

JOE: What?

HANNAH: You're ridiculous. You're being ridiculous.

JOE: I'm . . .
What?

HANNAH: You really ought to go home now to your wife. I need to go to bed. This phone call. . . . We will just forget this phone call.

JOE: Mom.

HANNAH: No more talk. Tonight. This . . .
(Suddenly very angry) Drinking is a sin! A sin! I raised you better than that. (She hangs up)

Scene 9

The following morning, early. Split scene: Harper and Joe at home; Louis and Prior in Prior's hospital room. Joe and Louis have just entered. This should be fast and obviously furious; overlapping is fine; the proceedings may be a little confusing but not the final results.

HARPER: Oh God. Home. The moment of truth has arrived.

JOE: Harper.

LOUIS: I'm going to move out.

PRIOR: The fuck you are.

JOE: Harper. Please listen. I still love you very much. You're still my best buddy; I'm not going to leave you.

HARPER: No, I don't like the sound of this. I'm leaving.

LOUIS: I'm leaving.
I already have.

JOE: Please listen. Stay. This is really hard. We have to talk.

HARPER: We are talking. Aren't we? Now please shut up. OK?

PRIOR: Bastard. Sneaking off while I'm flat out here, that's low. If I could get up now I'd beat the holy shit out of you.

JOE: Did you take pills? How many?

HARPER: No pills. Bad for the . . . (Pats stomach)

JOE: You aren't pregnant. I called your gynecologist.

HARPER: I'm seeing a new gynecologist.

PRIOR: You have no right to do this.

LOUIS: Oh, that's ridiculous.

PRIOR: No right. It's criminal.

JOE: Forget about that. Just listen. You want the truth. This is the truth.

I knew this when I married you. I've known this I guess for as long as I've known anything, but . . . I don't know, I thought maybe that with enough effort and will I could change myself . . . but I can't . . .

PRIOR: Criminal.

LOUIS: There oughta be a law.

PRIOR: There is a law. You'll see.

JOE: I'm losing ground here, I go walking, you want to know where I walk, I . . . go to the park, or up and down 53rd Street, or places where. . . . And I keep swearing I won't go walking again, but I just can't.

LOUIS: I need some privacy.

PRIOR: That's new.

LOUIS: Everything's new, Prior.

JOE: I try to tighten my heart into a knot, a snarl, I try to learn to live dead, just numb, but then I see someone I want, and it's like a nail, like a hot spike right through my chest, and I know I'm losing.

PRIOR: Apartment too small for three? Louis and Prior comfy but not Louis and Prior and Prior's disease?

LOUIS: Something like that.

I won't be judged by you. This isn't a crime, just—the inevitable consequence of people who run out of—whose limitations . . .

PRIOR: Bang bang bang. The court will come to order.

LOUIS: I mean let's talk practicalities, schedules; I'll come over if you want, spend nights with you when I can, I can . . .

PRIOR: Has the jury reached a verdict?

LOUIS: I'm doing the best I can.

PRIOR: Pathetic. Who cares?

JOE: My whole life has conspired to bring me to this place, and I can't despise my whole life. I think I believed when I met you I could save you, you at least if not myself, but . . .

I don't have any sexual feelings for you, Harper. And I don't think I ever did.

(Little pause.)

HARPER: I think you should go.

JOE: Where?

HARPER: Washington. Doesn't matter.

JOE: What are you talking about?

HARPER: Without me.

Without me, Joe. Isn't that what you want to hear?

(Little pause.)

JOE: Yes.

LOUIS: You can love someone and fail them. You can love someone and not be able to . . .

PRIOR: You *can*, theoretically, yes. A person can, maybe an editorial "you" can love, Louis, but not *you*, specifically you, I don't know, I think you are excluded from that general category.

HARPER: You were going to save me, but the whole time you were spinning a lie. I just don't understand that.

PRIOR: A person could theoretically love and maybe many do but we both know now you can't.

LOUIS: I do.

PRIOR: You can't even say it.

LOUIS: I love you, Prior.

PRIOR: I repeat. Who cares?

HARPER: This is so scary, I want this to stop, to go back . . .

PRIOR: We have reached a verdict, your honor. This man's heart is deficient. He loves, but his love is worth nothing.

JOE: Harper . . .

HARPER: Mr. Lies, I want to get away from here. Far away. Right now. Before he starts talking again. Please, please . . .

JOE: As long as I've known you Harper you've been afraid of . . . of men hiding under the bed, men hiding under the sofa, men with knives.

PRIOR (Shattered; almost pleading; trying to reach him): I'm dying! You stupid fuck! Do you know what that is! Love! Do you know what love means? We lived together four-and-a-half years, you animal, you idiot.

LOUIS: I have to find some way to save myself.

JOE: Who are these men? I never understood it. Now I know.

HARPER: What?

JOE: It's me.

HARPER: It is?

PRIOR: GET OUT OF MY ROOM!

JOE: I'm the man with the knives.

HARPER: You are?

PRIOR: If I could get up now I'd kill you. I would. Go away. Go away or I'll scream.

HARPER: Oh God . . .

JOE: I'm sorry . . .

HARPER: It is you.

LOUIS: Please don't scream.

PRIOR: Go.

HARPER: I recognize you now.

LOUIS: Please . . .

JOE: Oh. Wait, I. . . . Oh!
(He covers his mouth with his hand, gags, and removes his hand, red with blood)

  I'm bleeding.
(Prior screams.)

HARPER: Mr. Lies.

MR. LIES (Appearing, dressed in antarctic explorer's apparel): Right here.

HARPER: I want to go away. I can't see him anymore.

MR. LIES: Where?

HARPER: Anywhere. Far away.

MR. LIES: Absolutamento.

(Harper and Mr. Lies vanish. Joe looks up, sees that she's gone.)

PRIOR (Closing his eyes): When I open my eyes you'll be gone.

(Louis leaves.)

JOE: Harper?

PRIOR (Opening his eyes): Huh. It worked.

JOE (Calling): Harper?

PRIOR: I hurt all over. I wish I was dead.

Scene 10

The same day, sunset. Hannah and Sister Ella Chapter, a real-estate saleswoman, Hannah Pitt's closest friend, in front of Hannah's house in Salt Lake City.

SISTER ELLA CHAPTER: Look at that view! A view of heaven. Like the living city of heaven, isn't it, it just fairly glimmers in the sun.

HANNAH: Glimmers.

SISTER ELLA CHAPTER: Even the stone and brick it just glimmers and glitters like heaven in the sunshine. Such a nice view you get, perched up on a canyon rim. Some kind of beautiful place.

HANNAH: It's just Salt Lake, and you're selling the house *for* me, not *to* me.

SISTER ELLA CHAPTER: I like to work up an enthusiasm for my properties.

HANNAH: Just get me a good price.

SISTER ELLA CHAPTER: Well, the market's off.

HANNAH: At least fifty.

SISTER ELLA CHAPTER: Forty'd be more like it.

HANNAH: Fifty.

SISTER ELLA CHAPTER: Wish you'd wait a bit.

HANNAH: Well I can't.

SISTER ELLA CHAPTER: Wish you would. You're about the only friend I got.

HANNAH: Oh well now.

SISTER ELLA CHAPTER: Know why I decided to like you? I decided to like you 'cause you're the only unfriendly Mormon I ever met.

HANNAH: Your wig is crooked.

SISTER ELLA CHAPTER: Fix it.

(Hannah straightens Sister Ella's wig.)

SISTER ELLA CHAPTER: New York City. All they got there is tiny rooms.

I always thought: People ought to stay put. That's why I got my license to sell real estate. It's a way of saying: Have a house! Stay put! It's a way of saying traveling's no good. Plus I needed the cash. (She takes a pack of cigarettes out of her purse, lights one, offers pack to Hannah)

HANNAH: Not out here, anyone could come by.

There's been days I've stood at this ledge and thought about stepping over.

It's a hard place, Salt Lake: baked dry. Abundant energy; not much intelligence. That's a combination that can wear a body out. No harm looking someplace else. I don't need much room.

My sister-in-law Libby thinks there's radon gas in the basement.

SISTER ELLA CHAPTER: Is there gas in the . . .

HANNAH: Of course not. Libby's a fool.

SISTER ELLA CHAPTER: 'Cause I'd have to include that in the description.

HANNAH: There's no gas, Ella. (Little pause) Give a puff. (She takes a furtive drag of Ella's cigarette) Put it away now.

SISTER ELLA CHAPTER: So I guess it's good-bye.

HANNAH: You'll be all right, Ella, I wasn't ever much of a friend.

SISTER ELLA CHAPTER: I'll say something but don't laugh, OK?

This is the home of saints, the godliest place on earth, they say, and I think they're right. That mean there's no evil here? No. Evil's everywhere. Sin's everywhere. But this . . . is the spring of sweet water in the desert, the desert flower. Every step a Believer takes away from here is a step fraught with peril. I fear for you, Hannah Pitt, because you are my friend. Stay put. This is the right home of saints.

HANNAH: Latter-day saints.

SISTER ELLA CHAPTER: Only kind left.

HANNAH: But still. Late in the day . . . for saints and everyone. That's all. That's all.

Fifty thousand dollars for the house, Sister Ella Chapter; don't undersell. It's an impressive view.

ACT THREE

Not-Yet-Conscious, Forward Dawning

January 1986

Scene 1

Late night, three days after the end of Act Two. The stage is completely dark. Prior is in bed in his apartment, having a nightmare. He wakes up, sits up and switches on a nightlight. He looks at his clock. Seated by the table near the bed is a man dressed in the clothing of a 13th-century British squire.

PRIOR (Terrified): Who are you?

PRIOR 1: My name is Prior Walter.

(Pause.)

PRIOR: My name is Prior Walter.

PRIOR 1: I know that.

PRIOR: Explain.

PRIOR 1: You're alive. I'm not. We have the same name. What do you want me to explain?

PRIOR: A ghost?

PRIOR 1: An ancestor.

PRIOR: Not *the* Prior Walter? The Bayeux tapestry Prior Walter?

PRIOR 1: His great-great grandson. The fifth of the name.

PRIOR: I'm the thirty-fourth, I think.

PRIOR 1: Actually the thirty-second.

PRIOR: Not according to Mother.

PRIOR 1: She's including the two bastards, then; I say leave them out. I say no room for bastards. The little things you swallow . . .

PRIOR: Pills.

PRIOR 1: Pills. For the pestilence. I too . . .

PRIOR: Pestilence. . . . You too what?

PRIOR 1: The pestilence in my time was much worse than now. Whole villages of empty houses. You could look outdoors and see Death walking in the morning, dew dampening the ragged hem of his black robe. Plain as I see you now.

PRIOR: You died of the plague.

PRIOR 1: The spotty monster. Like you, alone.

PRIOR: I'm not alone.

PRIOR 1: You have no wife, no children.

PRIOR: I'm gay.

PRIOR 1: So? Be gay, dance in your altogether for all I care, what's that to do with not having children?

PRIOR: Gay homosexual, not bonny, blithe and . . . never mind.

PRIOR 1: I had twelve. When I died.

(The second ghost appears, this one dressed in the clothing of an elegant 17th-century Londoner.)

PRIOR 1 (Pointing to Prior 2): And I was three years younger than him.

(Prior sees the new ghost, screams.)

PRIOR: Oh God another one.

PRIOR 2: Prior Walter. Prior to you by some seven-teen others.

PRIOR 1: He's counting the bastards.

PRIOR: Are we having a convention?

PRIOR 2: We've been sent to declare her fabulous incipience. They love a well-paved entrance with lots of heralds, and . . .

PRIOR 1: The messenger come. Prepare the way. The infinite descent, a breath in air . . .

PRIOR 2: They chose us, I suspect, because of the mortal affinities. In a family as long-descended as the Walters there are bound to be a few carried off by plague.

PRIOR 1: The spotty monster.

PRIOR 2: Black Jack. Came from a water pump, half the city of London, can you imagine? His came from fleas. Yours, I understand, is the lamentable consequence of venery . . .

PRIOR 1: Fleas on rats, but who knew that?

PRIOR: Am I going to die?

PRIOR 2: We aren't allowed to discuss . . .

PRIOR 1: When you do, you don't get ancestors to help you through it. You may be surrounded by children but you die alone.

PRIOR: I'm afraid.

PRIOR 1: You should be. There aren't even torches, and the path's rocky, dark and steep.

PRIOR 2: Don't alarm him. There's good news before there's bad.

We two come to strew rose petal and palm leaf before the triumphal procession. Prophet. Seer. Revelator. It's a great honor for the family.

PRIOR 1: He hasn't got a family.

PRIOR 2: I meant for the Walters, for the family in the larger sense.

PRIOR (Singing):

All I want is a room somewhere,
Far away from the cold night air . . .

PRIOR 2 (Putting a hand on Prior's forehead): Calm, calm, this is no brain fever . . .

(Prior calms down, but keeps his eyes closed. The lights begin to change. Distant Glorious Music.)

PRIOR 1 (Low chant):

Adonai, Adonai,
Olam ha-yichud,
Zefirot, Zazahot,
Ha-adam, ha-gadol
Daughter of Light,
Daughter of Splendors,
Fluor! Phosphor!
Lumen! Candle!

PRIOR 2 (Simultaneously):

Even now,
From the mirror-bright halls of heaven,
Across the cold and lifeless infinity of space,
The Messenger comes
Trailing orbs of light,
Fabulous, incipient,
Oh Prophet,
To you . . .

PRIOR 1 and PRIOR 2:

Prepare, prepare,
The Infinite Descent,
A breath, a feather,
Glory to . . .
(They vanish.)

Scene 2

The next day. Split scene: Louis and Belize in a coffee shop. Prior is at the outpatient clinic at the hospital with Emily, the nurse; she has him on a pentamidine IV drip.

LOUIS: Why has democracy succeeded in America? Of course by succeeded I mean comparatively, not literally, not in the present, but what makes for the prospect of some sort of radical democracy spreading outward and growing up? Why does the power that was once so carefully preserved at the top of the pyramid by the original framers of the Constitution seem drawn inexorably downward and outward in spite of the best effort of the Right to stop this? I mean it's the really hard thing about being Left in this country, the American Left can't help but trip over all these petrified little fetishes: freedom, that's the worst; you know, *Jeane Kirkpatrick* for God's sake will go on and on about freedom and so what does that mean, the word freedom, when she talks about it, or human rights; you have Bush talking about human rights, and so what are these people talking about, they might as well be talking about the mating habits of Venusians, these people don't begin to know what, ontologically, freedom is or human rights, like they see these bourgeois property-based Rights-of-Man-type rights but that's not enfranchisement, not democracy, not what's implicit, what's potential within the idea, not the idea with blood in it. That's just liberalism, the worst kind of liberalism, really, bourgeois tolerance, and what I think is that what AIDS shows us is the limits of tolerance, that it's not enough to be tolerated, because when the shit hits the fan you find out how much tolerance is worth. Nothing. And underneath all the tolerance is intense, passionate hatred.

BELIZE: Uh huh.

LOUIS: Well don't you think that's true?

BELIZE: Uh huh. It is.

LOUIS: *Power* is the object, not being tolerated. Fuck assimilation. But I mean in spite of all this the thing about America, I think, is that ultimately we're different from every other nation on earth, in that, with people here of every race, we can't. . . . Ultimately what defines us isn't race, but politics. Not like any European country where there's an insurmountable fact of a kind of racial, or ethnic, monopoly, or monolith, like all Dutchmen, I mean Dutch people, are well, Dutch, and the Jews of Europe were never Europeans, just a small problem. Facing the monolith. But here there are so many small problems, it's really just a collection of small problems, the monolith is missing. Oh, I mean, of course I suppose there's the monolith of White America. White Straight Male America.

BELIZE: Which is not unimpressive, even among monoliths.

LOUIS: Well, no, but when the race thing gets taken care of, and I don't mean to minimalize how major it is, I mean I know it is, this is a really, really incredibly racist country but it's like, well, the British. I mean, all these blue-eyed pink people. And it's just weird, you know, I mean I'm not all that Jewish-looking, or . . . well, maybe I am but, you know, in New York, everyone is . . . well, not everyone, but so many are but so but in England, in London I walk into bars and I feel like Sid the Yid, you know I mean like Woody Allen in *Annie Hall,* with the payess and the gabardine coat, like never, never anywhere so much—I mean, not actively despised, not like they're Germans, who I think are still terribly anti-Semitic, and racist too, I mean black-racist, they pretend otherwise but, anyway, in London, there's just . . . and at one point I met this black gay guy from Jamaica who talked with a lilt but he said his family'd been living in London since before the Civil War—the American one—and how the English never let him forget for a minute that he wasn't blue-eyed and pink and I said yeah, me too, these people are anti-Semites and he said yeah but the British

Jews have the clothing business all sewed up and blacks there can't get a foothold. And it was an incredibly awkward moment of just. . . . I mean here we were, in this bar that was *pub,* you know, the beams and the plaster and those horrible little, like, two-day-old fish and egg sandwiches—and just so British, so *old,* and I felt, well, there's no way out of this because both of us are, right now, too much immersed in this history, hope is dissolved in the sheer age of this place, where race is what counts and there's no real hope of change—it's the racial destiny of the Brits that matters to them, not their political destiny, whereas in America . . .

BELIZE: Here in America race doesn't count.

LOUIS: No, no, that's not. . . . I mean you *can't* be hearing that . . .

BELIZE: I . . .

LOUIS: It's—look, race, yes, but ultimately race here is a political question, right? Racists just try to use race here as a tool in a political struggle. It's not really about race. Like the spiritualists try to use that stuff, are you enlightened, are you centered, channeled, whatever, this reaching out for a spiritual past in a country where no indigenous spirits exist—only the Indians, I mean Native American spirits and we killed them off so now, there are no gods here, no ghosts and spirits in America, there are no angels in America, no spiritual past, no racial past, there's only the political, and the decoys and the ploys to maneuver around the inescapable battle of politics, the shifting downwards and outwards of political power to the people . . .

BELIZE: POWER to the People! AMEN! (Looking at his watch) *OH MY GOODNESS!* Will you look at the time, I gotta . . .

LOUIS: Do you. . . . You think this is, what, racist or naive or something?

BELIZE: Well it's certainly *something.* Look, I just remembered I have an appointment . . .

LOUIS: What? I mean I really don't want to, like, speak from some position of privilege and . . .

BELIZE: I'm sitting here, thinking, eventually he's got to run out of steam, so I let you rattle on and on saying about maybe seven or eight things I find really offensive.

LOUIS: What?

BELIZE: But I know you, Louis, and I know the guilt fueling this peculiar tirade is obviously already swollen bigger than your hemorrhoids.

LOUIS: I don't have hemorrhoids.

BELIZE: I hear different. May I finish?

LOUIS: Yes, but I don't have hemorrhoids.

BELIZE: So finally, when I . . .

LOUIS: Prior told you, he's an asshole, he shouldn't have . . .

BELIZE: You promised, Louis. Prior is not a subject.

LOUIS: You brought him up.

BELIZE: I brought up hemorrhoids.

LOUIS: So it's indirect. Passive-aggressive.

BELIZE: Unlike, I suppose, banging me over the head with your theory that America doesn't have a race problem.

LOUIS: Oh be fair I never said that.

BELIZE: Not exactly, but . . .

LOUIS: I said . . .

BELIZE: . . . but it was close enough, because if it'd been that blunt I'd've just walked out and . . .

LOUIS: You deliberately misinterpreted! I . . .

BELIZE: Stop interrupting! I haven't been able to . . .

LOUIS: Just let me . . .

BELIZE: NO! What, *talk?* You've been running your mouth nonstop since I got here, yaddadda yaddadda blah blah blah, up the hill, down the hill, playing with your MONOLITH . . .

LOUIS (Overlapping): Well, you could have joined in at any time instead of . . .

BELIZE (Continuing over Louis): . . . and girlfriend it is truly an *awesome* spectacle but I got better things to do with my time than sit here listening to this racist bullshit just because I feel sorry for you that . . .

LOUIS: I am not a racist!

BELIZE: Oh come on . . .

LOUIS: So maybe I am a racist but . . .

BELIZE: Oh I really hate that! It's no fun picking on you Louis; you're so guilty, it's like throwing darts at a glob of jello, there's no satisfying hits, just quivering, the darts just blop in and vanish.

LOUIS: I just think when you are discussing lines of oppression it gets very complicated and . . .

BELIZE: Oh is that a fact? You know, we black drag queens have a rather intimate knowledge of the complexity of the lines of . . .

LOUIS: *Ex*-black drag queen.

BELIZE: Actually ex-ex.

LOUIS: You're doing drag again?

BELIZE: I don't. . . . Maybe. I don't have to tell you. Maybe.

LOUIS: I think it's sexist.

BELIZE: I didn't ask you.

LOUIS: Well it is. The gay community, I think, has to adopt the same attitude towards drag as black women have to take towards black women blues singers.

BELIZE: Oh my we *are* walking dangerous tonight.

LOUIS: Well, it's all internalized oppression, right, I mean the masochism, the stereotypes, the . . .

BELIZE: Louis, are you deliberately trying to make me hate you?

LOUIS: No, I . . .

BELIZE: I mean, are you deliberately transforming yourself into an arrogant, sexual-political Stalinist-slash-racist flag-waving thug for my benefit?

(Pause.)

LOUIS: You know what I think?

BELIZE: What?

LOUIS: You hate me because I'm a Jew.

BELIZE: I'm leaving.

LOUIS: It's true.

BELIZE: You have no basis except your . . .

Louis, it's good to know you haven't changed; you are still an honorary citizen of the Twilight Zone, and after your pale, pale white polemics on behalf of racial insensitivity you have a flaming *fuck* of a lot of nerve calling me an anti-Semite. Now I really gotta go.

LOUIS: You called me Lou the Jew.

BELIZE: That was a joke.

LOUIS: I didn't think it was funny. It was hostile.

BELIZE: It was three years ago.

LOUIS: So?

BELIZE: You just called yourself Sid the Yid.

LOUIS: That's not the same thing.

BELIZE: Sid the Yid is different from Lou the Jew.

LOUIS: Yes.

BELIZE: Someday you'll have to explain that to me, but right now . . .

You hate me because you hate black people.

LOUIS: I do not. But I do think most black people are anti-Semitic.

BELIZE: "Most black people." *That's* racist, Louis, and *I* think most Jews . . .

LOUIS: Louis Farrakhan.

BELIZE: Ed Koch.

LOUIS: Jesse Jackson.

BELIZE: Jackson. Oh really, Louis, this is . . .

LOUIS: Hymietown! Hymietown!

BELIZE: Louis, you voted for Jesse Jackson. You send checks to the Rainbow Coalition.

LOUIS: I'm ambivalent. The checks bounced.

BELIZE: All your checks bounce, Louis; you're ambivalent about everything.

LOUIS: What's that supposed to mean?

BELIZE: You may be dumber than shit but I refuse to believe you can't figure it out. Try.

LOUIS: I was never ambivalent about Prior. I love him. I do. I really do.

BELIZE: Nobody said different.

LOUIS: Love and ambivalence are. . . . Real love isn't ambivalent.

BELIZE: "Real love isn't ambivalent." I'd swear that's a line from my favorite bestselling paperback novel, *In Love with the Night Mysterious,* except I don't think you ever read it.

(Pause.)

LOUIS: I never read it, no.

BELIZE: You ought to. Instead of spending the rest of your life trying to get through *Democracy in America.* It's about this white woman whose Daddy owns a plantation in the Deep South in the years before the Civil War—the American one—and her name is Margaret, and she's in love with her Daddy's number-one slave, and his name is Thaddeus, and she's married but her white slave-owner husband has AIDS: Antebellum Insufficiently Developed Sexorgans. And there's a lot of hot stuff going down when Margaret and Thaddeus can catch a spare torrid ten under the cotton-picking moon, and then of course the Yankees come, and they set the slaves free, and the slaves string up old Daddy, and so on. Historical fiction. Somewhere in there I recall Margaret and Thaddeus find the time to discuss the nature of love; her face is reflecting the flames of the burning plantation—you know, the way white people do—and his black face is dark in the night and she says to him, "Thaddeus, real love isn't ever ambivalent."

(Little pause. Emily enters and turns off IV drip.)

BELIZE: Thaddeus looks at her; he's contemplating her thesis; and he isn't sure he agrees.

EMILY (Removing IV drip from Prior's arm): Treatment number . . . (Consulting chart) four.

PRIOR: Pharmaceutical miracle. Lazarus breathes again.

LOUIS: Is he. . . . How bad is he?

BELIZE: You want the laundry list?

EMILY: Shirt off, let's check the . . .

(Prior takes his shirt off. She examines his lesions.)

BELIZE: There's the weight problem and the shit problem and the morale problem.

EMILY: Only six. That's good. Pants.

(He drops his pants. He's naked. She examines.)

BELIZE: And. He thinks he's going crazy.

EMILY: Looking good. What else?

PRIOR: Ankles sore and swollen, but the leg's better. The nausea's mostly gone with the little orange pills. BM's pure liquid but not bloody anymore, for now, my eye doctor says everything's OK, for now, my dentist says "Yuck!" when he sees my fuzzy tongue, and now he wears little condoms on his thumb and forefinger. And a mask. So what? My dermatologist is in Hawaii and my mother . . . well leave my mother out of it. Which is usually where my mother is, out of it. My glands are like walnuts, my weight's holding steady for week two, and a friend died two days ago of bird tuberculosis; bird tuberculosis; that scared me and I didn't go to the funeral today because he was an Irish Catholic and it's probably open casket and I'm afraid of . . . something, the bird TB or seeing him or. . . . So I guess I'm doing OK. Except for of course I'm going nuts.

EMILY: We ran the toxoplasmosis series and there's no indication . . .

PRIOR: I know, I know, but I feel like something terrifying is on its way, you know, like a missile from outer space, and it's plummeting down towards the earth, and I'm ground zero, and . . . I am generally known where I am known as one cool, collected queen. And I am ruffled.

EMILY: There's really nothing to worry about. I think that shochen bamromim hamtzeh menucho nechono al kanfey haschino.

PRIOR: What?

EMILY: Everything's fine. Bemaalos k'doshim ut'horim kezohar horokeea mazhirim . . .

PRIOR: Oh I don't understand what you're . . .

EMILY: Es nishmas Prior sheholoch leolomoh, baavur shenodvoo z'dokoh b'ad hazkoras nishmosoh.

PRIOR: Why are you doing that? Stop it! Stop it!

EMILY: Stop what?

PRIOR: You were just . . . weren't you just speaking in Hebrew or something.

EMILY: *Hebrew?* (Laughs) I'm basically Italian-American. No. I didn't speak in Hebrew.

PRIOR: Oh no, oh God please I really think I . . .

EMILY: Look, I'm sorry, I have a waiting room full of. . . . I think you're one of the lucky ones, you'll live for years, probably—you're pretty healthy for someone with no immune system. Are you seeing someone? Loneliness is a danger. A therapist?

PRIOR: No, I don't need to see anyone, I just . . .

EMILY: Well think about it. You aren't going crazy. You're just under a lot of stress. No wonder . . . (She starts to write in his chart)

(Suddenly there is an astonishing blaze of light, a huge chord sounded by a gigantic choir, and a great book with steel pages mounted atop a molten-red pillar pops up from the stage floor. The book opens; there is a large Aleph inscribed on its pages, which bursts into flames. Immediately the book slams shut and disappears instantly under the floor as the lights become normal again. Emily notices none of this, writing. Prior is agog.)

EMILY (Laughing, exiting): Hebrew . . .

(Prior flees.)

LOUIS: Help me.

BELIZE: I beg your pardon?

LOUIS: You're a nurse, give me something, I . . . don't know what to do anymore, I. . . . Last week at work I screwed up the Xerox machine like permanently and so I . . . then I tripped on the subway steps and my glasses broke and I cut my forehead, here, see, and now I can't see much and my forehead . . . it's like the Mark of Cain, stupid, right, but it won't heal and every morning I see it and I think, Biblical things, Mark of Cain, Judas Iscariot and his silver and his noose, people who . . . in betraying what they love betray what's truest in themselves, I feel . . . nothing but cold for myself, just cold, and every night I miss him, I miss him so much but then . . . those sores, and the smell and . . . where I thought it was going. . . . I could be . . . I could be sick too, maybe I'm sick too. I don't know.

Belize. Tell him I love him. Can you do that?

BELIZE: I've thought about it for a very long time, and I still don't understand what love is. Justice is simple. Democracy is simple. Those things are unambivalent. But love is very hard. And it goes bad for you if you violate the hard law of love.

LOUIS: I'm dying.

BELIZE: He's dying. You just wish you were.

Oh cheer up, Louis. Look at that heavy sky out there.

LOUIS: Purple.

BELIZE: *Purple?* Boy, what kind of a homosexual are you, anyway? That's not purple, Mary, that color up there is (Very grand) *mauve.*

All day today it's felt like Thanksgiving. Soon, this . . . ruination will be blanketed white. You can smell it—can you smell it?

LOUIS: Smell what?

BELIZE: Softness, compliance, forgiveness, grace.

LOUIS: No . . .

BELIZE: I can't help you learn that. I can't help you, Louis. You're not my business. (He exits)

(Louis puts his head in his hands, inadvertently touching his cut forehead.)

LOUIS: Ow FUCK! (He stands slowly, looks towards where Belize exited) Smell what?

(He looks both ways to be sure no one is watching, then inhales deeply, and is surprised) Huh. Snow.

Scene 3

Same day. Harper in a very white, cold place, with a brilliant blue sky above; a delicate snow-fall. She is dressed in a beautiful snowsuit. The sound of the sea, faint.

HARPER: Snow! Ice! Mountains of ice! Where am I? I . . .

I feel better, I do, I . . . feel better. There are ice crystals in my lungs, wonderful and sharp. And the snow smells like cold, crushed peaches. And there's something . . . some current of blood in the wind, how strange, it has that iron taste.

MR. LIES: Ozone.

HARPER: Ozone! Wow! Where am I?

MR. LIES: The Kingdom of Ice, the bottommost part of the world.

HARPER (Looking around, then realizing): Antarctica. This is Antarctica!

MR. LIES: Cold shelter for the shattered. No sorrow here, tears freeze.

HARPER: Antarctica, Antarctica, oh boy oh boy, LOOK at this, I. . . . Wow, I must've really snapped the tether, huh?

MR. LIES: Apparently . . .

HARPER: That's great. I want to stay here forever. Set up camp. Build things. Build a city, an enormous city made up of frontier forts, dark wood and green roofs and high gates made of pointed logs and bonfires burning on every street corner. I should build by a river. Where are the forests?

MR. LIES: No timber here. Too cold. Ice, no trees.

HARPER: Oh details! I'm sick of details! I'll plant them and grow them. I'll live off caribou fat, I'll melt it over the bonfires and drink it from long, curved goat-horn cups. It'll be great. I want to make a new world here. So that I never have to go home again.

MR. LIES: As long as it lasts. Ice has a way of melting . . .

HARPER: No. Forever. I can have anything I want here—maybe even companionship, someone who has . . . desire for me. You, maybe.

MR. LIES: It's against the by-laws of the International Order of Travel Agents to get involved with clients. Rules are rules. Anyway, I'm not the one you really want.

HARPER: There isn't anyone . . . maybe an Eskimo. Who could ice-fish for food. And help me build a nest for when the baby comes.

MR. LIES: There are no Eskimo in Antarctica. And you're not really pregnant. You made that up.

HARPER: Well all of this is made up. So if the snow feels cold I'm pregnant. Right? Here, I can be pregnant. And I can have any kind of a baby I want.

MR. LIES: This is a retreat, a vacuum, its virtue is that it lacks everything; deep-freeze for feelings. You can be numb and safe here, that's what you came for. Respect the delicate ecology of your delusions.

HARPER: You mean like no Eskimo in Antarctica.

MR. LIES: Correcto. Ice and snow, no Eskimo. Even hallucinations have laws.

HARPER: Well then who's that?

(The Eskimo appears.)

MR. LIES: An Eskimo.

HARPER: An antarctic Eskimo. A fisher of the polar deep.

MR. LIES: There's something wrong with this picture.

(The Eskimo beckons.)

HARPER: I'm going to like this place. It's my own National Geographic Special! Oh! Oh! (She holds her stomach) I think . . . I think I felt her kicking. Maybe I'll give birth to a baby covered with thick white fur, and that way she won't be cold. My breasts will be full of hot cocoa so she doesn't get chilly. And if it gets really cold, she'll have a pouch I can crawl into. Like a marsupial. We'll mend together. That's what we'll do; we'll mend.

Scene 4

Same day. An abandoned lot in the South Bronx. A homeless Woman is standing near an oil drum in which a fire is burning. Snowfall.

Trash around. Hannah enters dragging two heavy suitcases.

HANNAH: Excuse me? I said excuse me? Can you tell me where I am? Is this Brooklyn? Do you know a Pineapple Street? Is there some sort of bus or train or . . .?

I'm lost, I just arrived from Salt Lake. City. Utah? I took the bus that I was told to take and I got off—well it was the very last stop, so I had to get off, and I *asked* the driver was this Brooklyn, and he nodded yes but he was from one of those foreign countries where they think it's good manners to nod at everything even if you have no idea what it is you're nodding at, and in truth I think he spoke no English at all, which I think would make him ineligible for employment on public transportation. The public being English-speaking, mostly. Do you speak English?

(The Woman nods.)

HANNAH: I was supposed to be met at the airport by my son. He didn't show and I don't wait more than three and three-quarters hours for *anyone.* I should have been patient, I guess, I. . . . Is this . . .

WOMAN: Bronx.

HANNAH: Is that. . . . The *Bronx?* Well how in the name of Heaven did I get to the Bronx when the bus driver said . . .

WOMAN (Talking to herself): Slurp slurp slurp will you STOP that disgusting slurping! YOU DISGUSTING SLURPING FEEDING ANIMAL! Feeding yourself, just feeding yourself, what would it matter, to you or to ANYONE, if you just stopped. Feeding. And DIED?

(Pause.)

HANNAH: Can you just tell me where I . . .

WOMAN: Why was the Kosciusko Bridge named after a Polack?

HANNAH: I don't know what you're . . .

WOMAN: That was a joke.

HANNAH: Well what's the punchline?

WOMAN: I don't know.

HANNAH (Looking around desperately): Oh for pete's sake, is there anyone else who . . .

WOMAN (Again, to herself): Stand further off you fat loathsome whore, you can't have any more of this soup, slurp slurp slurp you animal, and the—I know you'll just go pee it all away and where will you do that? Behind what bush? It's FUCKING COLD out here and I . . .

Oh that's right, because it was supposed to have been a tunnel!

That's not very funny.

Have you read the prophecies of Nostradamus?

HANNAH: Who?

WOMAN: Some guy I went out with once somewhere, Nostradamus. Prophet, outcast, eyes like. . . . Scary shit, he . . .

HANNAH: Shut up. Please. Now I want you to stop jabbering for a minute and pull your wits together and tell me how to get to Brooklyn. Because you know! And you are going to tell me! Because there is no one else around to tell me and I am wet and cold and I am very angry! So I am sorry you're psychotic but just make the effort—take a deep breath—DO IT!

(Hannah and the Woman breathe together.)

HANNAH: That's good. Now exhale.

(They do.)

HANNAH: Good. Now how do I get to Brooklyn?

WOMAN: Don't know. Never been. Sorry. Want some soup?

HANNAH: Manhattan? Maybe you know . . . I don't suppose you know the location of the Mormon Visitor's . . .

WOMAN: 65th and Broadway.

HANNAH: How do you . . .

WOMAN: Go there all the time. Free movies. Boring, but you can stay all day.

HANNAH: Well. . . . So how do I . . .

WOMAN: Take the D Train. Next block make a right.

HANNAH: Thank you.

WOMAN: Oh yeah. In the new century I think we will all be insane.

Scene 5

Same day. Joe and Roy in the study of Roy's brownstone. Roy is wearing an elegant bathrobe. He has made a considerable effort to look well. He isn't well, and he hasn't succeeded much in looking it.

JOE: I can't. The answer's no. I'm sorry.

ROY: Oh, well, apologies . . .

   I can't see that there's anyone asking for apologies.

(Pause.)

JOE: I'm sorry, Roy.

ROY: Oh, well, apologies.

JOE: My wife is missing, Roy. My mother's coming from Salt Lake to . . . to help look, I guess. I'm supposed to be at the airport now, picking her up but. . . . I just spent two days in a hospital, Roy, with a bleeding ulcer, I was spitting up blood.

ROY: Blood, huh? Look, I'm very busy here and . . .

JOE: It's just a job.

ROY: A job? A *job? Washington!* Dumb Utah Mormon hick shit!

JOE: Roy . . .

ROY: *WASHINGTON!* When Washington called me I was younger than you, you think I said "Aw fuck no I can't go I got two fingers up my asshole and a little moral nosebleed to boot!" When Washington calls you my pretty young punk friend you go or you can go fuck yourself sideways 'cause the train has pulled out of the station, and you are *out,* nowhere, out in the cold. Fuck you, Mary Jane, get outta here.

JOE: Just let me . . .

ROY: Explain? Ephemera. You broke my heart. Explain that. Explain that.

JOE: I love you. Roy.

There's so much that I want, to be . . . what you see in me, I want to be a participant in the world, in your world, Roy, I want to be capable of that, I've tried, really I have but . . . I can't do this. Not because I don't believe in you, but because I believe in you so much, in what you stand for, at heart, the order, the decency. I would give anything to protect you, but. . . . There are laws I can't break. It's too ingrained. It's not me. There's enough damage I've already done. Maybe you were right, maybe I'm dead.

ROY: You're not dead, boy, you're a sissy.

   You love me; that's moving, I'm moved. It's nice to be loved. I warned you about her, didn't I, Joe? But you don't listen to me, why, because you say Roy is smart and Roy's a friend but Roy . . . well, he isn't nice, and you wanna be nice. Right? A nice, nice man!

(Little pause)

   You know what my greatest accomplishment was, Joe, in my life, what I am able to look back on and be proudest of? And I have helped make Presidents and unmake them and mayors and more goddam judges than anyone in NYC ever—AND several million dollars, tax-free—and what do you think means the most to me?

   You ever hear of Ethel Rosenberg? Huh, Joe, huh?

JOE: Well, yeah, I guess I. . . . Yes.

ROY: Yes. Yes. You have heard of Ethel Rosenberg. Yes. Maybe you even read about her in the history books.

   If it wasn't for me, Joe, Ethel Rosenberg would be alive today, writing some personal-advice column for *Ms.* magazine. She isn't. Because during the trial, Joe, I was on the phone every day, talking with the judge . . .

JOE: Roy . . .

ROY: Every day, doing what I do best, talking on the telephone, making sure that timid Yid nebbish on the bench did his duty to America, to history. That sweet unprepossessing woman, two kids, boo-hoo-hoo, reminded us all of our little Jewish mamas— she came this close to getting life; I pleaded till I wept to put her in the chair. Me. I did that. I would have fucking pulled the switch if they'd have let me. Why? Because I fucking hate traitors. Because I fucking hate communists. Was it legal? Fuck legal. Am I a nice man? Fuck nice. They say terrible things about me in the *Nation*. Fuck the *Nation*. You want to be Nice, or you want to be Effective? Make the law, or subject to it. Choose. Your wife chose. A week from today, she'll be back. SHE knows how to get what SHE wants. Maybe I ought to send *her* to Washington.

JOE: I don't believe you.

ROY: Gospel.

JOE: You can't possibly mean what you're saying.

Roy, you were the Assistant United States Attorney on the Rosenberg case, ex-parte communication with the judge during the trial would be . . . censurable, at least, probably conspiracy and . . . in a case that resulted in execution, it's . . .

ROY: What? Murder?

JOE: You're not well is all.

ROY: What do you mean, not well? Who's not well?

(Pause.)

JOE: You said . . .

ROY: No I didn't. I said what?

JOE: Roy, you have cancer.

ROY: No I don't.

(Pause.)

JOE: You told me you were dying.

ROY: What the fuck are you talking about, Joe? I never said that. I'm in perfect health. There's not a goddam thing wrong with me.
(He smiles)

Shake?

(Joe hesitates. He holds out his hand to Roy. Roy pulls Joe into a close, strong clinch.)

ROY (More to himself than to Joe): It's OK that you hurt me because I love you, baby Joe. That's why I'm so rough on you.

(Roy releases Joe. Joe backs away a step or two.)

ROY: Prodigal son. The world will wipe its dirty hands all over you.

JOE: It already has, Roy.

ROY: Now go.

(Roy shoves Joe, hard. Joe turns to leave. Roy stops him, turns him around.)

ROY (Smoothing Joe's lapels, tenderly): I'll always be here, waiting for you . . .
(Then again, with sudden violence, he pulls Joe close, violently)

What did you want from me, what was all this, what do you want, treacherous ungrateful little . . .

(Joe, very close to belting Roy, grabs him by the front of his robe, and propels him across the length of the room. He holds Roy at arm's length, the other arm ready to hit.)

ROY (Laughing softly, almost pleading to be hit): Transgress a little, Joseph.

(Joe releases Roy.)

ROY: There are so many laws; find one you can break.

(Joe hesitates, then leaves, backing out. When Joe has gone, Roy doubles over in great pain, which he's been hiding throughout the scene with Joe.)

ROY: Ah, Christ . . .

Andy! Andy! Get in here! Andy!
(The door opens, but it isn't Andy. A small Jewish Woman dressed modestly in a fifties hat and coat stands in the doorway. The room darkens.)

ROY: Who the fuck are you? The new nurse?

(The figure in the doorway says nothing. She stares at Roy. A pause. Roy looks at her carefully, gets up, crosses to her. He crosses back to the chair, sits heavily.)

ROY: Aw, fuck. Ethel.

ETHEL ROSENBERG (Her manner is friendly, her voice is ice-cold): You don't look good, Roy.

ROY: Well, Ethel. I don't feel good.

ETHEL ROSENBERG: But you lost a lot of weight. That suits you. You were heavy back then. Zaftig, mit hips.

ROY: I haven't been that heavy since 1960. We were all heavier back then, before the body thing started. Now I look like a skeleton. They stare.

ETHEL ROSENBERG: The shit's really hit the fan, huh, Roy?

(Little pause. Roy nods.)

ETHEL ROSENBERG: Well the fun's just started.

ROY: What is this, Ethel, Halloween? You trying to scare me?

(Ethel says nothing.)

ROY: Well you're wasting your time! I'm scarier than you any day of the week! So beat it, Ethel! BOOO! BETTER DEAD THAN RED! Somebody trying to shake me up? HAH HAH! From the throne of God in heaven to the belly of hell, you can all fuck yourselves and then go jump in the lake because I'M NOT AFRAID OF YOU OR DEATH OR HELL OR ANYTHING!

ETHEL ROSENBERG: Be seeing you soon, Roy. Julius sends his regards.

ROY: Yeah, well send this to Julius!

(He flips the bird in her direction, stands and moves towards her. Halfway across the room he slumps to the floor, breathing laboriously, in pain.)

ETHEL ROSENBERG: You're a very sick man, Roy.

ROY: Oh God . . . ANDY!

ETHEL ROSENBERG: Hmmm. He doesn't hear you, I guess. We should call the ambulance.

(She goes to the phone)

Hah! Buttons! Such things they got now. What do I dial, Roy?

(Pause. Roy looks at her, then:)

ROY: 911.

ETHEL ROSENBERG (Dials the phone): It sings! (Imitating dial tones) La la la . . .

Huh.

Yes, you should please send an ambulance to the home of Mister Roy Cohn, the famous lawyer.

What's the address, Roy?

ROY (A beat, then): 244 East 87th.

ETHEL ROSENBERG: 244 East 87th Street. No apartment number, he's got the whole building.

My name? (A beat) Ethel Greenglass Rosenberg.

(Small smile) Me? No I'm not related to Mr. Cohn. An old friend.

(She hangs up)

They said a minute.

ROY: I have all the time in the world.

ETHEL ROSENBERG: You're immortal.

ROY: I'm immortal. Ethel. (He forces himself to stand)

I have *forced* my way into history. I ain't never gonna die.

ETHEL ROSENBERG (A little laugh, then): History is about to crack wide open. Millennium approaches.

Scene 6

Late that night. Prior's bedroom. Prior 1 watching Prior in bed, who is staring back at him, terrified. Tonight Prior 1 is dressed in weird alchemical robes and hat over his historical clothing and he carries a long palm-leaf bundle.

PRIOR 1: Tonight's the night! Aren't you excited? Tonight she arrives! Right through the roof! Ha-adam, Ha-gadol . . .

PRIOR 2 (Appearing, similarly attired): Lumen! Phosphor! Fluor! Candle! An unending billowing of scarlet and . . .

PRIOR: Look. Garlic. A mirror. Holy water. A crucifix. FUCK OFF! Get the fuck out of my room! GO!

PRIOR 1 (To Prior 2): Hard as a hickory knob, I'll bet.

PRIOR 2: We all tumesce when they approach. We wax full, like moons.

PRIOR 1: Dance.

PRIOR: Dance?

PRIOR 1: Stand up, dammit, give us your hands, dance!

PRIOR 2: Listen . . .

(A lone oboe begins to play a little dance tune.)

PRIOR 2: Delightful sound. Care to dance?

PRIOR: Please leave me alone, please just let me sleep . . .

PRIOR 2: Ah, he wants someone familiar. A partner who knows his steps. (To Prior) Close your eyes. Imagine . . .

PRIOR: I don't . . .

PRIOR 2: Hush. Close your eyes.

(Prior does.)

PRIOR 2: Now open them.

(Prior does. Louis appears. He looks gorgeous. The music builds gradually into a full-blooded, romantic dance tune.)

PRIOR: Lou.

LOUIS: Dance with me.

PRIOR: I can't, my leg, it hurts at night . . .
Are you a ghost, Lou?

LOUIS: No. Just spectral. Lost to myself. Sitting all day on cold park benches. Wishing I could be with you. Dance with me, babe . . .

(Prior stands up. The leg stops hurting. They begin to dance. The music is beautiful.)

PRIOR 1 (To Prior 2): Hah. Now I see why he's got no children. He's a sodomite.

PRIOR 2: Oh be quiet, you medieval gnome, and let them dance.

PRIOR 1: I'm not interfering, I've done my bit. Hooray, hooray, the messenger's come, now I'm blowing off. I don't like it here.

(Prior 1 vanishes.)

PRIOR 2: The twentieth century. Oh dear, the world has gotten so terribly, terribly old.
(Prior 2 vanishes. Louis and Prior waltz happily. Lights fade back to normal. Louis vanishes. Prior dances alone.
Then suddenly, the sound of wings fills the room.)

Scene 7

Split scene: Prior alone in his apartment; Louis alone in the park.

Again, a sound of beating wings.

PRIOR: Oh don't come in here don't come in . . .
LOUIS!!

No. My name is Prior Walter, I am . . . the scion of an ancient line, I am . . . abandoned I . . . no, my name is . . . is . . . Prior and I live . . . *here and now*, and . . . in the dark, in the dark, the Recording Angel opens its hundred eyes and snaps the spine of the Book of Life and . . . hush! Hush!

I'm talking nonsense, I . . .

No more mad scene, hush, hush . . .

(Louis in the park on a bench. Joe approaches, stands at a distance. They stare at each other, then Louis turns away.)

LOUIS: Do you know the story of Lazarus?

JOE: Lazarus?

LOUIS: Lazarus. I can't remember what happens, exactly.

JOE: I don't. . . . Well, he was dead, Lazarus, and Jesus breathed life into him. He brought him back from death.

LOUIS: Come here often?

JOE: No. Yes. Yes.

LOUIS: Back from the dead. You believe that really happened?

JOE: I don't know anymore what I believe.

LOUIS: This is quite a coincidence. Us meeting.

JOE: I followed you.

From work. I . . . followed you here.
(Pause.)

LOUIS: You followed me.

You probably saw me that day in the washroom and thought: there's a sweet guy, sensitive, cries for friends in trouble.

JOE: Yes.

LOUIS: You thought maybe I'll cry for you.

JOE: Yes.

LOUIS: Well I fooled you. Crocodile tears. Nothing . . . (He touches his heart, shrugs)

(Joe reaches tentatively to touch Louis's face.)

LOUIS (Pulling back): What are you doing? Don't do that.

JOE (Withdrawing his hand): Sorry. I'm sorry.

LOUIS: I'm . . . just not . . . I think, if you touch me, your hand might fall off or something. Worse things have happened to people who have touched me.

JOE: Please.

Oh, boy . . .

Can I . . .

I . . . want . . . to touch you. Can I please just touch you . . . um, here?

(He puts his hand on one side of Louis's face. He holds it there)

I'm going to hell for doing this.

LOUIS: Big deal. You think it could be any worse than New York City?

(He puts his hand on Joe's hand. He takes Joe's hand away from his face, holds it for a moment, then) Come on.

JOE: Where?

LOUIS: Home. With me.

JOE: This makes no sense. I mean I don't know you.

LOUIS: Likewise.

JOE: And what you do know about me you don't like.

LOUIS: The Republican stuff.

JOE: Yeah, well for starters.

LOUIS: I don't not like that. I hate that.

JOE: So why on earth should we . . .

(Louis goes to Joe and kisses him.)

LOUIS: Strange bedfellows. I don't know. I never made it with one of the damned before.

I would really rather not have to spend tonight alone.

JOE: I'm a pretty terrible person, Louis.

LOUIS: Lou.

JOE: No, I really really am. I don't think I deserve being loved.

LOUIS: There? See? We already have a lot in common.

(Louis stands, begins to walk away. He turns, looks back at Joe. Joe follows. They exit.)

(Prior listens. At first no sound, then once again, the sound of beating wings, frighteningly near.)

PRIOR: That sound, that sound, it. . . . What is that, like birds or something, like a really big

bird, I'm frightened, I . . . no, no fear, find the anger, find the . . . anger, my blood is clean, my brain is fine, I can handle pressure, I am a gay man and I am used to pressure, to trouble, I am tough and strong and. . . . Oh. Oh my goodness. I . . . (He is washed over by an intense sexual feeling) Ooohhhh. . . . I'm hot, I'm . . . so . . . aw Jeez what is going on here I . . . must have a fever I . . .

(The bedside lamp flickers wildly as the bed begins to roll forward and back. There is a deep bass creaking and groaning from the bedroom ceiling, like the timbers of a ship under immense stress, and from above a fine rain of plaster dust.)

PRIOR: OH!

PLEASE, OH PLEASE! Something's coming in here, I'm scared, I don't like this at all, something's approaching and I. . . . OH!

(There is a great blaze of triumphal music, heralding. The light turns an extraordinary harsh, cold, pale blue, then a rich, brilliant warm golden color, then a hot, bilious green, and then finally a spectacular royal purple. Then silence.)

PRIOR (An awestruck whisper): God almighty . . .

Very Steven Spielberg.

(A sound, like a plummeting meteor, tears down from very, very far above the earth, hurtling at an incredible velocity towards the bedroom; the light seems to be sucked out of the room as the projectile approaches; as the room reaches darkness, we hear a terrifying CRASH as something immense strikes earth; the whole building shudders and a part of the bedroom ceiling, lots of plaster and lathe and wiring, crashes to the floor. And then in a shower of unearthly white light, spreading great opalescent gray-silver wings, the Angel descends into the room and floats above the bed.)

ANGEL:

Greetings, Prophet;
The Great Work begins:
The Messenger has arrived.
(Blackout.)

Producing *Angels in America*

The productions we have studied so far—*And the Soul Shall Dance* at East West Players and at Northwest Asian American Theatre and *Joe Turner's Come and Gone* at the Oregon Shakespeare Festival—began with completed scripts. Each play had already had a number of successful productions and had achieved national recognition. For *Angels in America* we begin at a much earlier time in the life of the play. We examine the development of the play itself and the relationship between a new play and the performance process.

The Eureka Theatre and the Playwright

More and more, American theatre companies are directly involved in the development of new plays. Sometimes playwrights work on their own and submit a new play to a theatre only after it has been completed. But there are also playwrights who are members of theatre companies or are invited or commissioned to write a play for a particular company. A commission involves payment that supports the actual writing of the play. In 1987, a small theatre company in San Francisco, the Eureka Theatre, used a grant from the National Endowment for the Arts to commission Tony Kushner to write a play. That play would become *Angels in America*.

The production history of *Angels in America* begins with Oskar Eustis, the Eureka's artistic director and **dramaturg;** and Tony Taccone, the theatre's producing director at that time. In this case, the development of the play itself was highly dependent on the production process. In the late 1980s, the Eureka Theatre was a small but active theatre committed to a "politically progressive aesthetic" and the production of plays that would be responsive to social issues.[3]

Together, the artistic leaders of the theatre—Taccone and Eustis—sought out new plays or commissioned new work to create a vital and forward-looking repertoire for their theatre and the politically conscious San Francisco audience that it attracted.

Oskar Eustis had just directed Kushner's first play, *A Bright Room Called Day*, and was inspired by the originality of Kushner's presentation of political ideas. In the capacity of dramaturg, Eustis began a dialogue with Kushner about what kind of play he might write for the Eureka Theatre. Kushner says of the origins of the new work, "I began *Angels* as a conversation, real and imaginary, between Oskar and myself."[4]

The Role of the Dramaturg

For years, European theatres have employed dramaturgs, whose role is to work with the playwrights in the shaping of their plays and to advise directors on questions of history, analysis, and interpretation. The position of dramaturg is a fairly recent addition to the production staffs of American theatres. The critic and producer Martin Esslin sees the role of the dramaturg as crucial to expanding the intellectual and cultural foundation of the American theatre: "The American dramaturg not only has to do the basic job of finding and nurturing scripts, but has also to work hard on helping to create that basic cultural atmosphere in which a healthy theatre can operate."[5] Robert Brustein, the founding director of the Yale Repertory Theatre and American Repertory Theatre, calls the dramaturg "the conscience of the theatre."[6] In this sense the dramaturg is concerned with developing a repertoire of plays that will challenge the audience as well as working with playwrights and directors to make sure that ideas are substantial and clearly articulated.

Oskar Eustis had been working in Germany and Switzerland as a director and dramaturg before he returned to the United States and joined the staff of the Eureka Theatre. He explains his original goals in assuming the role of dramaturg at the Eureka Theatre:

> **OSKAR EUSTIS:** Being a dramaturg is an art form, not a science. What I felt needed to be done was to help work with playwrights to create a theatre that was more accessible, more political, more audience-friendly, and therefore more narratively based than the theatre I had done before.[7]

Eustis describes the starting point in the development of two plays he commissioned for the Eureka that eventually went on to larger theatres, including some on Broadway—*Execution of Justice* by Emily Mann and *Angels in America* by Tony Kushner.

> **OSKAR EUSTIS:** In both instances, I took a playwright who the Eureka had already produced and that we had had an exciting relationship with. With Emily Mann we had produced her play *Still Life* and had an amazing experience with it. Emily had loved the production. With Tony I had produced the professional premiere of *A Bright Room Called Day.* They were writers with whom I felt deep affinities, aesthetically, theatrically, and politically.

Eustis wanted to merge the interests of the Eureka Theatre with the concerns of the playwrights. He asked each playwright, "What play does it make sense for you to write for the Eureka Theatre?"

> **OSKAR EUSTIS:** And both of them, for different reasons, ended up focusing on things that had to do with the gay community in San Francisco, with subjects that seemed to speak very directly to the audience that was there for us in San Francisco.

Emily Mann turned to a true story about San Francisco itself. She wrote a courtroom drama based on the trial of Dan White, the city supervisor who shot and killed two city officials: another

---

IN CONTEXT

Production History of *Angels in America*

Date	Event
1987	Oskar Eustis commissions Tony Kushner to write a play for the Eureka Theatre.
1990	*Millennium Approaches* is staged in a workshop production at the Mark Taper Forum in Los Angeles, directed by Oskar Eustis.
1991	*Millennium Approaches* premieres at the Eureka Theatre in San Francisco, directed by David Esbjornson. *Perestroika* is given a staged reading but remains unfinished.
1992	*Millennium Approaches* opens at the Royal National Theatre's small black-box theatre, the Cottesloe, in London, directed by Declan Donnellan. *Perestroika* would be added to the production in 1993.
1992	*Millennium Approaches* and *Perestroika* are produced together for the first time at the Mark Taper Forum in Los Angeles, codirected by Oskar Eustis and Tony Taccone.
1993	*Millennium Approaches* and *Perestroika* are produced together at the Walter Kerr Theatre on Broadway, directed by George C. Wolfe.

---

city supervisor, Harvey Milk, the first openly gay elected official in America; and George Moscone, the mayor of San Francisco. When Tony Kushner was invited to work with the Eureka Theatre, he knew that somehow he wanted to write a play that concerned Roy Cohn, AIDS in the gay community, and Mormons. How those subjects were to be connected, what form the play was to take, was still in the future.

One of the remarkable anecdotes about the evolution of *Angels in America* has to do with the company of the Eureka Theatre. The material that Kushner wanted to pursue had to do with gay men, but the core acting company of the Eureka Theatre was made up of three women and one man. The three women would need parts in whatever Kushner wrote.

> **OSKAR EUSTIS:** The play was modeled after the company members of the Eureka. The reason those parts exist in *Angels* is because that was the company of the Eureka Theatre. We spent a number of sleepless nights while Tony tried to figure out how to put three straight women into a show that is about the experience of gay men. But part of the reason why the show is so great is that Tony had to continually expand the range of the subject matter in order to get those actresses into the play. The play ended up taking on a scope that none of us suspected it was going to when we started.

The Developmental Process

Angels in America went through a long and difficult developmental process that lasted six years until both plays were actually completed. Before the official premiere of *Millennium Approaches* at the Eureka Theatre in 1991, there were six workshop productions in San Francisco, in Los Angeles, and at the Sundance Institute; about a dozen readings; endless informal discussions; and many revised drafts of the play. *Perestroika* was given an abbreviated staged reading when *Millennium Approaches* was being performed at the Eureka Theatre. Kushner did not finish the second play until just before its premiere in Los Angeles. *Perestroika* would be rewritten yet one more time before the entire piece opened on Broadway.

The developmental process was affected both by changes in personnel and by financial complications. After beginning the work on *Angels in America* at the Eureka Theatre, Tony Taccone became the associate artistic director of the Berkeley Repertory Theatre and Oskar Eustis became associate artistic director of the Mark Taper Forum in Los Angeles. David Esbjornson then became the director of the play at the Eureka Theatre. Following the production at the Mark Taper Forum, Eustis and Taccone concluded their formal relationship with the play, and

George C. Wolfe, director of the Public Theater in New York, guided the play on the final part of its journey. Until the play opened at the Mark Taper Forum in Los Angeles, the developmental process was guided by Oskar Eustis.

> **OSKAR EUSTIS:** Many, many different formats were used, and I think all of them were certainly necessary to get us there. There were times when we were focusing on the arc of the characters. At other times we were focusing on the internal shape of the different scenes of different acts. There were times when we were trying to finish the story. And at times we were very much trying to figure out how to produce the thing as a whole, what our production method might be.

Tony Kushner readily acknowledges the help of a variety of dramaturgs, theatre practitioners, and colleagues in the evolution of *Angels in America*. Some people were involved in the development of characters, scenes, and language; others gave crucial advice on cutting the script; and some were engaged with Kushner in dialogues and arguments about the ideas expressed by the play. Each reading or production made a major contribution to the writing process.

> **TONY KUSHNER:** It's deeply suspect that writers—especially male writers—feel that they have to produce everything completely on their own and that the act of writing becomes in part an act of denying that one is in any way reliant on other people. I've thought that maybe other writers simply don't need other people's help as much as I do, or maybe I'm just a bad writer. I suspect that some people are more solitary and really dredge it all out of their own souls. But even there, there may be ways in which people are feeding them about which they're not aware. . . . I haven't been diminished by admitting that other people have participated.[8]

Although Kushner received input from many sources during the six-year gestation of *Angels in America*, the writing and rewriting were his work. Kushner is a playwright who makes continuous adjustments in his material, and *Angels* involved a legendary number of rewrites. Some of the actors who began the production in San Francisco were also part of the cast in Los Angeles and eventually went on to New York, a rather unusual casting history. Ellen McLaughlin, who played the Angel, memorized as many as twenty versions of a crucial scene in *Perestroika* before Kushner was satisfied. The rewrites continued on *Perestroika* throughout most of the rehearsal period in Los Angeles. The directors and actors who were staging two full plays that would run a total of seven hours had only ten weeks to do their preparatory work and had to contend with changes in the script up until days before the production opened.

> **TONY TACCONE:** There were lots of rewrites, and that was both thrilling and scary—thrilling because the writing was fantastic and scary because you have to constantly assess how many changes you can try to incorporate without driving everybody completely insane.

Impact of the Theatre Space
Just as the writing of the play went through many stages, so the production of the play changed from theatre to theatre, and these changes had an enormous impact on the final shape of the play. The home of the Eureka Theatre was a converted warehouse off Market Street in San Francisco. With a stage that measured twenty-five feet by twenty-five feet and an audience space of 200 seats, the theatre was only a little larger than East West Players or Northwest Asian American Theatre. Old wooden bleachers were used to form ten rows of seating accommodating twenty people per row. The existing pipes were exposed across the ceiling, lowering the height of the performance space and increasing the "rough" atmosphere of the interior of the building. The Brechtian idea of exposing the mechanics of the theatre meshed conveniently with the theatre space.

> **TONY TACCONE:** It had a kind of raw but exciting feel. It was always a little too hot or too cold, but it had a lot of energy. Everything was exposed at the Eureka. You could never hide anything.

The limitations of the stage space and the financial resources of the Eureka Theatre encouraged the development of a play that focused on the resources of the actors. For example, in writing the play for the Eureka Theatre, Kushner ended up creating a play with twenty-one characters for a total of eight actors—five men and three women. The range of characters grew out of the needs of the original Eureka company with the addition of four men who were invited to join the group.

And yet as Kushner expanded the scope of the play in response to the company, he found he needed many more characters than there were actors. Kushner's intention was for the actors to play more than one part. The actors then had the responsibility of shifting between characters who existed in the present and characters who came out of the past or between realistic characters and fantasy characters.

Kathleen Chalfant, who played Hannah Pitt, Joe's Mormon mother from Salt Lake City, also played three other roles in *Millennium Approaches*—Ethel Rosenberg; the rabbi who conducts the funeral service for Louis's grandmother at the beginning of the play; and the doctor, Henry, who tells Roy Cohn that he has AIDS. The development of each character was helped by costume changes, varying hairstyles, and, for the rabbi, a long beard. But the emphasis was on Chalfant's creativity in drawing distinct characters and on her skill in quickly moving from character to character in performance. The double casting had stylistic and philosophical implications. Chalfant observed, "Not only did Tony want women to play men, but he wanted women to play male authority figures, which is rare."[9]

The double casting at the Eureka challenged the ingenuity of the actors and kept the audience from identifying each actor with only one role. The audience became more conscious of the actors as actors rather than only as certain characters. There was an awareness of an ensemble of actors working closely together to tell Kushner's complicated story. The actors also did most of the scene changes, reinforcing the audience's perception of the actors as arrangers of the event as well as inhabitants of the play. The necessities of the Eureka Theatre production—the double casting and having the actors change the sets—were subsequently written into the script to be used even at larger theatres with more substantial resources.

Refining the Balance Between Intimacy and Spectacle

The Eureka production emphasized the intimate nature of the character relationships. Most of the scenes in *Angels in America* are between two characters and focus on personal details. In performance at the Eureka, the energy of the work went into the intensity and immediacy of the characters' needs and revelations.

> **TONY TACCONE:** The simplicity of the show when it was done at the Eureka was brilliant. It was really straightforward and wonderfully clear. The play was in the lap of the audience, and that created an intimacy and urgency that made for a fantastic theatre experience.

When the play moved to larger theatres, the spectacle became increasingly important, enlarging the background against which individual lives were seen.

Refining the balance between intimacy and spectacle—expanding Kushner's idea of a "fantasia"—became of primary importance in productions subsequent to the performances at the Eureka. For example, the presence of the Angel took on much larger dimensions at the Mark Taper Forum and then at the Walter Kerr Theatre in New York. The Angel's entrance from eighteen inches at the Eureka Theatre became an entrance from thirty feet above the stage at the Mark Taper Forum.

> **TONY TACCONE:** The Angel was flown in from high above with a halogen light behind her bright enough to light up the city of New York. There was a terrific amount of smoke and a very full sound track. It was spectacular.

The much greater stage height at the Mark Taper and the more sophisticated flying

Ellen McLaughlin appears in her first incarnation as the Angel in the original production of *Angels in America* at the Eureka Theatre.

apparatus allowed the producers to build the image of the Angel as a force of majestic power. This possibility contributed to Kushner's development of the emerging relationship between Prior and the Angel in *Perestroika*.

Act 2, scene 2 of *Perestroika*, a ferocious confrontation between Prior and the Angel, is at the heart of Kushner's vision for the play. This is the scene that Ellen McLaughlin memorized in twenty different versions. It becomes a heroic and symbolic or allegorical battle for Prior's soul. The Angel turns out to be a conservative force who demands that human beings stop moving, that they stop trying to change.

ANGEL: Forsake the Open Road:
Neither Mix nor Intermarry: Let Deep Roots
    Grow:
If you do not Mingle you will Cease to Progress:
Seek Not to Fathom the World and its Delicate
    Particle Logic:
You cannot Understand, You can only
    Destroy, . . .
Turn back. Undo.[10]

By the time *Angels in America* was staged in New York, the Angel, still played by Ellen McLaughlin, had become a stupendous creation that symbolized the entire work. Here, the Angel overwhelms Prior in the second play, *Perestroika*. Prior and the Angel battle for his soul.

Prior comes to understand that if he accepts the Angel's message of "stasis," it becomes his death sentence. He rejects the Angel's vision because he realizes that change is the only course of human action that can lead to "more life."

Taccone describes the scene as a "wild landscape of evocative images that are all designed to create this huge conflict between a dying gay man, struggling to save his life, and an Angel who is not the miracle he is seeking."

In staging this confrontation in Los Angeles, the directors used the technology of the flying apparatus to create what Taccone calls a "fantastic, surreal wrestling match with an angel flying and leaping around the room and an actor who was both stunned and terrified." The scene became a theatricalized encounter between larger-than-life characters playing out a spiritual crisis. The choreographed battle—part dance, part high-wire gymnastics—merged with Kushner's poetic, dreamlike language to create a defining image for the play.

Expanding Opportunities for the Development of New Plays

Many of the most interesting plays come out of small theatres that do not have a commercial focus. Some of these plays may go on to larger regional theatres and to New York. The hallmark of a successful American play used to be its success on Broadway, but Broadway is no longer the final judge of a play's merit. At one time most major American plays originated in New York and then toured the country or moved on to regional theatres. Clearly, the course of many successful plays is now reversed. Like *Angels in America*, a play may originate in a regional theatre and work its way to Broadway. New York still has a remarkable concentration of talent and venues that can generate cutting-edge work and support long-running productions. But exciting theatre can emerge from any part of the country where theatres and audiences meet to consider questions about human existence from a new perspective.

In over twenty years of producing plays, the Eureka Theatre supported the development of more than sixty new plays. Many other theatres also attempt to establish opportunities for new playwrights. In developing new work, theatres understand that they may provide only the starting point for new plays that will become part of the larger American theatre.

Angels in America outgrew the boundaries of the Eureka Theatre. It became an event that took on a life of its own.

TONY TACCONE: It felt like an avalanche. It started out as a snowball and ended up coursing down the mountainside at a speed that none of us could possibly keep up with or predict.

The original producers could have tried to contain the play, to keep it within the limits of the Eureka's production capabilities. No one had bargained for a six-year effort that would lead to a marathon extravaganza. But a good part of the energy that comes out of theatre work has to do with the unpredictable nature of whatever may evolve.

OSKAR EUSTIS: We came to a crisis point where we said, the Eureka cannot produce this play; it's not manageable. The play had taken on a scope that none of us had suspected when we started. It became apparent that it was going to be two evenings long, and that was catastrophic for my poor little theatre company, which had no way of believing that it could work or afford to pay for it.

The work was telling us it had to be this thing that was larger than we could afford, and I really had two choices: to try to cut the ambition and scope of the piece to fit the Eureka or to say, let's go on this ride and see what happens. My decision was obvious. We went on the ride, and it led to extraordinary results. I think it's a perfect little model for what you have to do in this kind of process.

No previous paradigm is sufficient for creating important new work, because the whole point of it, the whole thing that makes it an art form, is that it is being invented and new. Otherwise, what you're doing is trying to fit new wine into old bottles. You might come up with something that sort of works. But you'll never come up with something that has the kind of galvanic effect that *Angels* has, an artwork that is so uniquely, precisely itself. To produce *Angels in America* took years and years. You just have to be willing to get in the trenches and work for as long as it takes. I can't think of anything else that would be more worth doing with your time.

Summary

A play such as *Angels in America* that draws on many sources of theatrical expression reminds us to be wary of trying to define plays according to rigid categories. *Angels in America* tells a sweeping story of American life that functions on political and personal levels at the same time. Among the styles used by the playwright Tony Kushner are realism, epic theatre, expressionism, and absurdism. The rapid shifts between kinds of characters and styles of language are in part influenced by the theatre of Bertolt Brecht. Kushner is also influenced by the plays of Caryl Churchill, who brings together characters from the past and characters from the present to create a historical perspective for contemporary issues. This device is seen in *Angels in America* in the character Ethel Rosenberg, the ancestor Priors, and most of all the character Roy Cohn. The flamboyant presentation of the Angel demonstrates how a theatrical image can be central to a play's expression.

The dramaturg is a relatively new position in the American theatre. In developing *Angels in America* at the Eureka Theatre, the playwright was assisted by Oskar Eustis, who originally commissioned the play and then worked closely on its development. The responsibilities of the dramaturg include new play development as well as research and analysis to help other theatre practitioners in the production of challenging plays.

Topics for Discussion and Writing

If possible, read aloud in class the scenes from *Angels in America* that relate to the following questions:

1. **Act 1, scene 9**
   In Roy Cohn's confrontation with his doctor, what are the points he uses to construct his identity? What does his argument with his doctor convey about how he sees his place in the world? What does he need to defend against? Does his position express self-awareness?

2. **Act 2, scene 9**
   Study the shifts back and forth between the two pairs of characters in the scene. From the audience's viewpoint, how do the lines from one pair of characters comment on or contribute to the meaning of the lines from the other pair of characters? What is the cumulative effect of the split scene?

3. **Act 3, scene 1**
   How do you imagine the staging of the scene with the three Priors? What ideas are suggested by the discussion of the plagues of different centuries? Why would the two ancestor Priors be the ones to announce the coming of the Angel?

● For an interview with Oskar Eustis and other resources related to this chapter, please visit
www.mhhe.com/creativespirit6e

CHAPTER 11

The Musical Theatre

Music and dance are forms of human expression that respond to some of life's most intensely felt moments, when it is neither enough to speak nor to remain silent. Through rhythmic movement or by lifting our voices in song, we express joy or heartache. The blues, Celtic ballads, country music, work songs, rap, and reggae are all connected to essential life experiences.

Music and dance mark our observations of life's defining occasions. At weddings we celebrate through music. Music and dance accompany courtship, from the prom to the nightclub, from rock and roll concerts to moonlight serenades. Fight songs inspire battles and sporting events. The Maori of New Zealand still dance the ferocious *haka* that once motivated their warriors. Most religious worship includes musical expression, from the solemnity of a restrained hymn to the exuberance of gospel. Ecstatic dancing that liberates the spirit is also associated with religious observation throughout the world. We mourn the dead through music as well, in the form of a solemn requiem or the livelier music of a wake or the spontaneous keening and wailing of individual mourners.

Much of our musical expression is formalized in its association with particular events, from worship services to sporting events. We also organize musical participation through orchestras, bands, and choirs. However, spontaneous musical expression is one of life's great pleasures, whether it is the hip-hop danced on street corners or the singing of a lullaby to a child. If music and dance were eliminated from our lives, we would find human existence greatly diminished.

Music and dance have been fundamental to many of the world's great theatre traditions: the Greek choruses danced and sang; bands played before and during the medieval mystery cycles; and Elizabethan theatres had a special place built for musicians. Most forms of Asian theatre involve onstage musicians who play throughout the performances, and many of the actors' lines are sung. The theatre has always recognized the emotional and dramatic expressiveness of music.

Song and dance together give the actor two of the most powerful means of communicating a heightened sense of human experience. The emotional possibilities of the singing voice fusing words with melody and the visual language of the body propelled through space provide a lyrical way of enacting a story that carries the audience beyond everyday reality. Rhythmic structures build the drama and drive the action forward, pulling the audience into their energy and their pulse. The musical is another major example of theatricalism and has its own unique history in the United States.

Origins of Musical Theatre in America

The immigrant groups that made up the U.S. population of the nineteenth century and early twentieth century brought many music and dance traditions with them. Musical entertainment of all kinds grew out of the free-swirling mixture of cultures. For example, tap dancing developed in part because of the incorporation of Irish clog dancing into the developing black tradition of dance.[1] The young nation enjoyed entertainments in which song and dance routines were laced with comedy, and novelty acts brought together the latest in musical styles and dance steps. Minstrel shows and then musical revues and vaudeville eventually led to the development of a **musical theatre** form that presented the popular dancing and singing in a dramatic plot with characters who played out a complete story. A collection of loosely connected routines or variety acts gave way to an integration of spoken text, singing, and dance that developed a dramatic idea. The evolving musical theatre drew on diverse talents and diverse backgrounds. Entertainers from the world of jazz and vaudeville eventually intersected with ballet choreographers and classically trained composers and musicians to create the American musical theatre.

The term *musical comedy* was used for years to describe this theatre form because most of the early works followed the pattern of a troubled love relationship that was accompanied by comic variations and that ended with reconciliation and celebration. In fact, musical comedy in this version fits nicely into the definition of comedy discussed in Chapter 14. However, the musical theatre form has grown and expanded beyond the formulaic romance to include a variety of subjects and situations that do not always lead to reconciliation. We use the term *musical theatre* to include the most open definition of this form.

The Broadway Theatre

Our discussion of musical theatre focuses on Broadway, which continues to be the heart of musical theatre production. For much of the twentieth century, most musicals originated on Broadway. Over time, however, the musical theatre too has been affected by the decentralization of the American theatre. New musicals today are often developed in regional theatres and then move to Broadway, or they may develop in not-for-profit theatres or workshops before achieving a Broadway production. Nonetheless, the goal in most musical theatre is still a Broadway engagement.

Broadway consists of a group of large, elegant theatres located on or close to Broadway and Times Square in New York City. Most of the theatres are found between 41st Street and 50th Street. Broadway theatres usually seat more than 1,000 audience members in an orchestra and two balconies and are equipped with state-of-the-art technology. The price of a ticket for a Broadway musical at $75 and higher makes attendance at this "popular" form of theatre a very expensive proposition. Half-price tickets can be purchased on the day of performance at the TKTS booth in Times Square, and some musicals reserve a number of lower-priced seats for students.

As we examine some of the most celebrated musicals of the American theatre, we focus primarily on the original productions. There we can see the work of the composer, lyricist, and librettist joined to the work of the director and choreographer. In contemporary American theatre, the choreographer has become a major theatre practitioner, contributing significant new ideas to the staging of the drama.

Oklahoma!

Opening on Broadway in 1943, *Oklahoma!* was a musical about farmers and cowboys that reinforced traditional American values at a time when the nation was in the middle of its participation

The dream ballet from *Oklahoma!* features the "Post Card Girls," who suggest another side of life on the American frontier in the choreography by Agnes de Mille.

in World War II. The musical tells a simple love story set against the progression of Oklahoma toward statehood. *Oklahoma!* represented nostalgia for the past at a time when war made for an anxious and uncertain present. Songs such as "Oh What a Beautiful Morning," "The Surrey with the Fringe on Top," and the title song "Oklahoma!" created an onstage sense of optimism and faith in rural American life. *Oklahoma!* was a retreat from the sophisticated subject matter of earlier musical theatre but an advance in the integration of theatrical materials. Each song in *Oklahoma!* contributed to the development of the plot or the emotional state of a character.

Known for its enduring musical score, *Oklahoma!* also established new possibilities for the use of dance in the musical theatre form. Instead of serving as a break in the action to provide variety and show off the skills of talented performers,

dance was used to develop character and express ideas nonverbally. Cowboy posture and movement that derived from actions such as horseback riding and roping were combined with square dancing to give the choreography and the play a distinctive flavor. Significantly, the dance went beyond filling the stage with charming western idioms to accompany the songs. In the most innovative use of dance, a prolonged choreographic sequence was used for psychological development. The central character, Laurey, has foolishly encouraged the attention of Jud Fry, to provoke the hero, Curly. Jud is a hostile, threatening figure, and Laurey's fear of him is played out in an elaborate dream ballet. Curly and Jud fight, and Curly is killed. Laurey is carried off by Jud to live in his sleazy world of violence and used-up dance-hall girls.

Oklahoma! was the first creation of the partnership of Richard Rodgers, who composed the music; and Oscar Hammerstein II, who wrote the **book** (script) and lyrics. Together, Rodgers and Hammerstein later created such popular musicals as *Carousel*, *South Pacific*, *The King and I*, and *The Sound of Music*. All of the Rodgers and Hammerstein collaborations are known for their use of music to define character and to contribute to the structure of the plot. Each of their musicals tells the story of characters, usually in love, who overcome conflicts and obstacles to reach a triumphant ending. Sentimental but inspired melodies and good-humored characters carry the Rodgers and Hammerstein musicals.

For *Oklahoma!* Agnes de Mille joined the Rodgers and Hammerstein team as choreographer. She brought her considerable ballet background into the musical theatre but also drew on tap and folk dance forms. De Mille continued to choreograph Rodgers and Hammerstein productions and became one of the first choreographer-directors. Her approach to the integration of choreography into the musical opened the way for the brilliant innovations in the musical theatre to come. It is interesting to note that the choreographer Susan Stroman, whose work is discussed later in the chapter, restaged Agnes de Mille's original dances for *Oklahoma!* in a new Broadway production that opened in 2001.

West Side Story

Oklahoma! reflected the sensibility of a nation engaged in war abroad that looked to the stage for a comforting, rural view of the home front. In

Jerome Robbins's explosive choreography distinguished *West Side Story* and brought the musical theatre to a new level in the integration of drama and movement. For the Broadway revival of *West Side Story* in 2009, Joey McKneeley reproduced the original Robbins choreography. Here Anita, Karen Olivo, and Bernardo, George Akram, perform in the "Dance at the Gym" during which the Jets and the Sharks continue their rivalry on the dance floor.

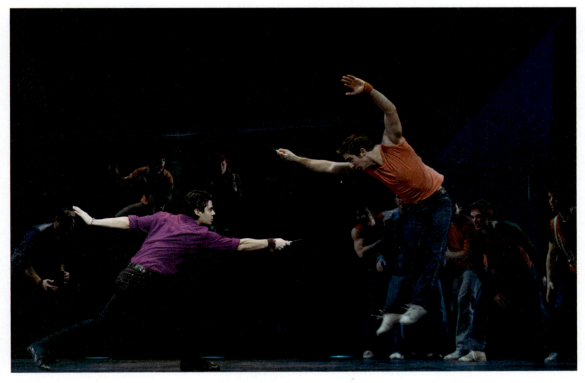

The gang tension in *West Side Story* erupts in a deadly knife fight between Bernardo, George Akram, and Riff, Cody Green, in this recreation of Jerome Robbins's choreography by Joey McKneeley.

1957 a new musical, *West Side Story*, would take on our own urban warfare. Based on the feuding families that doomed the love of Romeo and Juliet, *West Side Story* dramatizes the gang conflict between Puerto Rican and Anglo youths in an impoverished New York City neighborhood. The choreographer-director Jerome Robbins originated the idea for the production and invited the collaboration of the composer and conductor Leonard Bernstein. Robbins and Bernstein had already worked together successfully on a ballet, "Fancy Free," that became a Broadway musical and then a film, *On the Town*. Each had extensive experience in the musical theatre in addition to Robbins's work in the ballet and Bernstein's contributions to the world of classical music. They were both at the top of their professions and were able to merge their formidable talents to create one of the great American works of the modern theatre. The playwright Arthur Laurents adapted Shakespeare's *Romeo and Juliet*; and a young songwriter, Stephen Sondheim, wrote the lyrics. Sondheim would go on to become one of the foremost composers and lyricists of the musical theatre, creating such works as *Company*, *Sweeney Todd*, and *Sunday in the Park with George*.

The young lovers in the 1950s version of Shakespeare's play are Maria and Tony, on opposite sides of the gang conflict. Tony is a former member of the Jets, the gang made up of the sons of European immigrants; Maria is the sister of Bernardo, leader of the Sharks, the Puerto Rican gang. As in its Shakespearean source, hostilities and misunderstandings lead to the deaths of several young men. Yet in the musical version Maria lives. As with much contemporary gang violence, the woman is left to face the consequences of the fighting alone. The entire play focuses on the young people involved: the limitations of their circumstances, their reliance on one another, their alienation from the larger society, their aspirations, and their love.

West Side Story has very little dialogue. Almost the entire story is told through songs and dances, with dance playing a much more important part than it had previously in the American musical theatre. The Bernstein score has an edgy, urban dissonance influenced by jazz and Latin rhythms. Some of the most memorable love songs of the musical theatre come from *West Side Story*, such as "Maria," "Tonight," and "Somewhere." The score is also notable for its use of counterpoint. For example, a love theme is introduced and then returns to be played against the theme of the impending gang fight. The score is percussive, with a drive and urgency that would be adopted by many later musicals.

Matching the intensity of the music, the choreography had the actors flying across the stage and at each other for much of the production. The characters were in constant motion, cruising the streets, looking for fights, dancing at the gym. Intricately choreographed sequences defined character and dramatized the action of the play. Robbins combined a ballet base with a heavy use of jazz and gymnastics to create a tough, jagged street-smart choreography for the gang sequences and a sexy, competitive choreography for the men and women. Latin dance styles were integrated into the movement of the Puerto Rican characters in the "Dance at the Gym" and "America" to physicalize the difference between the backgrounds of the two groups of characters. The raw dancing of the gang members and their girlfriends formed a contrasting background for the softer, lyrical duets of Tony and Maria. Robbins's position as director and choreographer ensured the complete integration of all the staging elements, with dance becoming the central force around which the rest of the production was built.

My Fair Lady

In the mid-1950s, two musicals based on classics of drama from different eras—*Romeo and Juliet*, by Shakespeare; and *Pygmalion* (1912), by George Bernard Shaw (1856–1950)—brought the musical theatre to a new level of artistry. *West Side Story* fulfilled the dance possibilities suggested by *Oklahoma!* and *My Fair Lady* introduced brilliant language to the musical stage. Both used the unique advantages of the musical theatre to create dramas of substance and style.

My Fair Lady (1956) represents the collaborative efforts of another well-known Broadway team, Alan Lerner and Frederick Loewe. Their third collaborator, the English playwright George Bernard Shaw, is sometimes overlooked as one of the creators of this most witty of all Broadway musicals. In *West Side Story*, although the situation resembles *Romeo and Juliet* and some of the plot incidents coincide, the language and terms of expression are entirely reworked. In contrast, much of the strength of *My Fair Lady* derives from the characters and the language written by Shaw.

My Fair Lady tells the story of the transformation of Eliza Doolittle, who sells flowers in Covent Garden, from a "guttersnipe" and "a squashed cabbage leaf" into a young woman of such distinction that she can be passed off as a princess at a royal ball. Her two mentors in this unlikely venture are both noted linguists: the abrasive Professor Henry Higgins and the milder Colonel Pickering. Their project to reinvent Eliza grows out of a bet over how much work it will take to eliminate Eliza's cockney speech patterns and instill in her instead the speech of a lady.

As the lessons proceed, Eliza and Henry engage in a battle of wills and wits that creates one of the more original female–male relationships in the musical theatre. Their verbal sparring is expanded to include the contributions of Eliza's father, the opportunistic Alfred Doolittle, a dustman; and Henry's eminently sensible mother, Mrs. Higgins. The score, which includes the popular

Henry Higgins (Rex Harrison), Eliza Doolittle (Julie Andrews), and Colonel Pickering (Robert Coote) celebrate Eliza's newly achieved mastery of proper pronunciation in "The Rain in Spain" from *My Fair Lady,* with choreography by Hanya Holm and stage direction by Moss Hart.

favorites "I Could Have Danced All Night" and "The Street Where You Live," also has a series of brilliant character songs that are as engaging musically as they are dramatically. Higgins and Eliza carry their skirmishes into musical attacks that are filled with humor and bite.

The casting of Rex Harrison and Julie Andrews in the lead roles became one of the celebrated partnerships of the musical theatre. The director, Moss Hart, who was an exceptional comic playwright himself, staged the play with a sophistication that matched the brilliance of the material. Another major dance figure of the mid-twentieth century, Hanya Holm, did the choreography. The choreography complemented the clever staging by Moss Hart. But it was the music and language that carried *My Fair Lady* to the heights of the musical form.

Cabaret

The 1960s saw major changes in the U.S. political scene and in the theatre. The divisiveness of the Vietnam War and student protests marked the decade, as did new theatre companies concerned with both political issues and new forms of expression. *Cabaret*, a musical first produced in 1966, expressed some of the anxieties of the times and the upheaval in traditional forms while turning back to an earlier era for its subject.

Cabaret draws on *The Berlin Stories* (1945) of Christopher Isherwood and the play *I Am a*

Alan Cumming, as the Master of Ceremonies, is surrounded by the jaded dance girls of the Kit Kat Club in the 1998 revival of *Cabaret* directed by Sam Mendes at the Henry Miller Theatre in New York City, which was turned into a nightclub for the production.

Camera (1951), by John Van Druten, based on the Isherwood material. *Cabaret* presents a sleazy picture of Berlin in the late 1920s, just preceding the Nazis' and Hitler's rise to power in Germany. The musical is set in a trashy nightclub, the Kit Kat Club, inhabited by tacky dance girls dressed in skimpy torn stockings and underwear. These women go through the motions of nightclub routines under the control of the bizarre Master of Ceremonies, a bitterly flamboyant character who directs the false gaiety of all the proceedings. At the Kit Kat Club we come to meet a young American writer, Clifford Bradshaw, who is at first attracted to the decadence that pervades Berlin, symbolized by the Kit Kat Club, and then repelled by it as he realizes that the Nazis are gathering power while careless people indulge their jaded appetites. The world of the musical is seen through Bradshaw's eyes as he becomes involved with a young English expatriate, Sally Bowles, a singer at the Kit Kat Club. When Bowles becomes pregnant, Bradshaw offers to marry her and move with her to the United States, but Bowles chooses an abortion and the chance to go on being part of the Kit Kat Club. The fate of the Jews is particularly focused in the subplot of a Jewish grocer who insists, in the face of increasingly violent anti-Semitism, that normality will return to Germany.

The book for *Cabaret* was written by Joe Masterhoff, the music by John Kander, and the lyrics by Fred Ebb. But rather than telling a straightforward story in the style of *Oklahoma!*

or *My Fair Lady*—which are designated as **book musicals** because of their reliance on traditional dramatic plotting—*Cabaret* created a new style for expressing its content. In collaboration with the director, Harold Prince, the writers created what is called a **concept musical**—a musical that emphasizes a theme in which scenic and performance elements are of greater significance than the plot. This innovation is not unlike the emphasis on imagery in German expressionism and the theatre of the absurd discussed in Chapter 9. In the case of this play, the idea of the world defined as a cabaret shaped the basic concept. And the jangling cabaret music, recalling the jarring music composed by Kurt Weill for Brecht's early plays, became the framing structure for the drama itself rather than a device to complement or fill out the play's dialogue. In his review of the original production for *The New York Times*, Walter Kerr wrote:

> Instead of telling a little story about the decadence of Berlin just before Hitler came to power into which casual musical numbers can be sandwiched whenever politeness permits, *Cabaret* lunges forward to insist on music as mediator between audience and characters, as lord and master of the revels, as mocking conferencier without whose ministrations we should have no show at all. We are inside the music looking out, tapping our feet to establish a cocky rhythm and a satanically grinning style to which the transient people of the narrative must accommodate themselves, through which—in irony and after the fact—they can be known.[2]

The play's tone established by the music was continued in Ronald Field's choreographed sequences set in the Kit Kat Club, which were vulgar and suggestive and backed by a large mirror in which audience members could watch themselves watching the show. Under Harold Prince's direction, the staging shifted the audience's sense of being detached from the action to becoming part of the audience in the Kit Kat Club itself. In the Broadway revival of *Cabaret* in

1998, the audience involvement was heightened by turning the entire seating area of the audience into an extension of the nightclub with tables and chairs, red lamps on the tables, and food and drink served and consumed by audience members during the performance. The atmosphere in that revival emphasized the cheap, harsh sexual exchange that underscores all the action and the bleak, abusive world of the Kit Kat Club. With *Cabaret*, the musical left the romance of the form far behind.

Among the actors in the original production, Joel Grey created a sensation as the Master of Ceremonies and went on to re-create the role in the highly regarded film, which starred Grey and Liza Minelli. Lotte Lenya, who began her career acting with Bertolt Brecht, played the role of Fräulein Schneider, who runs the boardinghouse in which Bowles and Bradshaw live and who ultimately rejects her Jewish suitor when the Nazi presence becomes too ominous. In the revival of 1998, Alan Cumming was scintillating as the Master of Ceremonies, with a more vicious quality yet than that of Joel Grey, a reflection perhaps of our own times. And Natasha Richardson gave the most complete interpretation of Sally Bowles since the musical was first produced. This revival was directed by Sam Mendes, following a production of the same play, which he directed in London in 1993.

Stephen Sondheim

The contributions of Stephen Sondheim to the musical theatre cannot be represented by a single defining work. From his earliest effort as a composer of both music and lyrics in *A Funny Thing Happened on the Way to the Forum*, the works of Stephen Sondheim have followed no formula or pattern. Rather, he is known for his experimentation with subject and form, for being adventurous in a field that has tended to favor predictability. During his time as theatre critic for *The New York Times*, Frank Rich observed that Sondheim was "persistent" in trying "to transform the Broadway musical" and considered him "as adventurous and as accomplished an author, playwrights included, as Broadway has produced over the last two decades."[3] Sondheim has spent his career in the musical theatre, from 1957 to the present, exploring new ways of creating musical dramas.

Stephen Sondheim was a committed student of music composition at Williams College, which he followed with three years of study with the avant-garde composer Milton Babbitt. He wrote his first musicals in high school and was always focused on the goal of composing for the musical stage. As a family friend of Oscar Hammerstein II, he had the unique opportunity of being mentored by the author of some of the most compelling and successful song lyrics in the musical theatre. Sondheim learned much from Hammerstein, but Hammerstein wrote optimistic lyrics about overcoming adversity, the "golden sky and the sweet silver song of a lark" that followed the storm (*Carousel*), and the sustaining power of love, "younger than springtime am I with you" (*South Pacific*). Sondheim would move in a very different direction.

Steeped in musical theatre tradition, Stephen Sondheim began his professional career as lyricist first for *West Side Story* and then for *Gypsy*, collaborating with other major figures in the musical theatre such as Jerome Robbins, Jule Styne, and Harold Prince. When he began to write his own complete scores as well as the lyrics, Sondheim placed increasing responsibility on the music and lyrics as the driving force in the creation of the drama. The book that in earlier musicals told a story through dialogue augmented by songs was replaced by the score itself. Building his works around a theme or an idea rather than a highly structured plot, Sondheim was a major influence in the development of the concept musical.

The subjects of the Sondheim musicals are challenging for audiences: examining the stresses and disappointments of urban life, the difficulties in building satisfactory relationships, the painful and sometimes bitter path to maturity, and the contradictory nature of American values. Whereas many musicals are written and produced to provide audiences with a form of escape from their concerns, Sondheim musicals ask audiences to participate in a thoughtful process. For example, *Pacific Overtures* explores the forced opening of Japan in the nineteenth century to Western commerce and the consequences for Japanese society as it underwent enormous social change. *Sunday in the Park with George* considers the nature of artistic creation, and *Assassins* takes on the disturbing subject of violence in American public life. Music and lyrics in combination are used as social commentary, as narrative, and as reflection or debate as well as the expression of a character's state of mind. In *Pacific Overtures* traditional Japanese instruments create a texture of life in sound whose rhythms are interrupted and distorted by the demands of outside forces. In *Assassins* the style of folk ballads usually associated with a positive sense of American character is used as a point of departure for the confusion expressed by those trying to rewrite U.S. history through murder.

The work of Stephen Sondheim demonstrates particularly the way song lyrics can be seen as poetry set to music. The lyrics are a condensed and eloquent expression of a significant moment in a character's life. The lyrics contain the particularity of the character's voice as well as an intricate verbalization of the changing or developing circumstances of the drama. The sung lyrics must be listened to as carefully as or more carefully than any of the spoken dialogue, and the audience members cannot simply lose themselves in the melody or the staging of a song.

> You try to make the language dance, not only to your own tune, which is a metaphor, but to the actual tune that's there. You try to make the words sit on music, to rhyme them, to make jokes land, to use literary techniques. It's technical, like poetry or any creative art is technical. But, because lyric writing makes you deal with so few words and the language is not so elastic when sung . . . it becomes very crossword puzzle-like.[4]

In 2005 *Sweeney Todd* by Stephen Sondheim was produced on Broadway under the direction of John Doyle, with Michael Cerveris and Patti Lupone playing the central characters. Doyle employed a unique approach to staging a musical by having the actors double as the musicians who accompany each other's singing. Doyle developed this concept of the actor-musician in England before re-staging his interpretation of *Sweeney Todd* in the United States.

Here is the final section of the song "Four Black Dragons" from the musical *Pacific Overtures* (1976) in which the local people and the narrator, the Reciter, sing of their terror at the arrival of U.S. warships off the coast of Japan.

> (Townspeople)
> Four black dragons
> Spitting fire!
> (Reciter)
> Then the hooves clattered
> And the warriors were there,
> Diving quickly through the panic
> Like the gulls.
> Hai! Hai!
> And the swords were things of beauty
> As they glided through the air—
> Hai!
> Like the gulls.

> Hai!
> (Townspeople)
> Hai! Hai!
> Four black dragons,
> Spitting fire!
> (Thief and Company)
> And the sun darkened
> And the sea bubbled,
> And the earth trembled,
> And the sky cracked,
> And I thought it was the end
> Of the world!
> (Reciter)
> And it was.[5]

Through the lyrics Sondheim furthers the drama in a number of ways. He creates the action of the arrival of the ships, the "four black dragons." He captures the fear of the community as the people record this invasion of their private world. He creates explosive visual imagery of the upheaval that it represents, and he foreshadows the transformation to come.

Sondheim's songs have not had nearly the success of the work of other composers as popular songs performed outside their plays, because of the deep connection of the words to the ongoing drama. And Sondheim's works can be hard to appreciate without their proper instrumentation because of the close integration between the lyrics and the score. In spite of the fact that the music and lyrics dominate Sondheim musicals, Sondheim has chosen not to write the spoken dialogue of his plays, relying instead on a series of collaborators. Some of his work has suffered as a result of dramatic construction that lacks the sophistication and skill of the score.

But there is no doubt that Sondheim has created a body of work that is a major force in shaping the musical theatre at the beginning of the twenty-first century. Recent productions of Sondheim musical theatre pieces reflect his continuing importance for the American theatre. In 2002 Sondheim was represented on Broadway by a well-received revival of *Into the Woods*, and *Pacific Overtures* was presented at the Lincoln Center summer festival in a new production by the New National Theatre of Tokyo. At the same time, a major retrospective of six Sondheim musicals was produced at the Kennedy Center in Washington, DC. In June 2003, the Goodman Theatre in Chicago premiered Sondheim's newest work, *Gold*, which returns to U.S. history to look at the lives of the Mizner brothers, trying to grasp the opportunities available to the adventurous as they travel from Alaska to Florida at the beginning of the twentieth century. And a highly regarded production of *Sweeney Todd: The Demon Barber of Fleet Street* began a successful Broadway run in 2005.

A Chorus Line

Before *West Side Story*, musicals relied on a chorus of singers and dancers to dress the stage and carry the choreographic responsibility of the big production numbers. There was a clear delineation between principals and chorus members, and the groups even rehearsed separately. In *West Side Story*, Jerome Robbins essentially eliminated the chorus by making all the roles singing and dancing characters, thereby assigning importance to all the performers. For the first time, the musical cast became an ensemble.

In his musical *A Chorus Line* (1975), with music by Marvin Hamlisch and lyrics by Edward Kleban, Michael Bennett made the chorus the subject of the play. The premise of this musical is based on the endless auditioning required of performers seeking employment as chorus members. Bennett created a musical that told the stories of young singers and dancers desperately hoping for their big break. In a time-honored tradition, the theatrical performance was about the theatre.

Bennett began dancing as a child and served his apprenticeship dancing in the choruses of musicals before becoming a choreographer. Always focused on a theatrical career, he dropped out of high school to become one of the Jets in the international touring company of *West Side Story* and to learn from the master, Jerome Robbins. Bennett's theatre education and training took place in the musical theatre. In 1970, he joined Stephen Sondheim and Harold Prince as the choreographer of *Company* and then became the choreographer and codirector of *Follies*. When he turned to the lives of dancers as the subject for a new musical, he was able to draw on his own experiences from many productions as well as those of a group of dancers he invited to brainstorm with him in a workshop at the Public Theater, then under the direction of Joseph Papp.

In creating *A Chorus Line*, Bennett reduced the musical form to its essence, in the words of one of its famous songs, "the music and the mirror, and the chance to dance." Gone were the sets that had become increasingly lavish for musical theatre production; gone were the

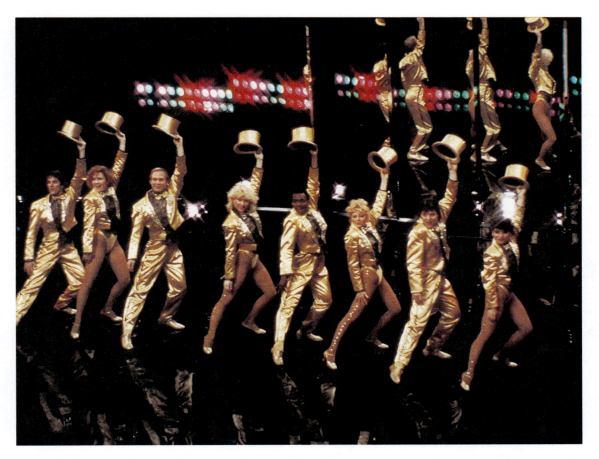

At the end of *A Chorus Line,* the vulnerability and anxiety of the individual actors hoping to be cast is replaced by the confidence and unity of the chorus line. In the musical's finale, the actors have the chance to pull out all the stops as they sing and dance their triumph, wearing the production's signature gold tuxedoes and top hats. *A Chorus Line* is a tribute to the musical form itself.

elaborate costumes and the cast of "thousands." A group of young characters stood in a line at the front of the stage wearing a combination of leotards, tights, jeans, and T-shirts. One at a time, they told the stories that had brought them into the theatre, beginning with spoken words that segued into song and then into dance. Because the play took the form of a fictional audition, the stories were addressed to the character of the director, who was placed at the back of the auditorium behind the audience seats, allowing the actors to speak out directly to the audience.

A Chorus Line has a very thin plot, involving a relationship between the dancer, Cassie, and the director, Zach. Like *Cabaret,* *A Chorus Line* is a concept musical. But the heart of the piece is in the characters' stories and their quest for approval and for a chance to show their worth and to follow their dreams. *A Chorus Line* became a metaphor for a new era of life in the United States.

New Directions for the Musical Theatre

Four musicals have once again turned the musical theatre in new directions at a time when some critics were suggesting that the form had exhausted its possibilities. *Bring in da Noise, Bring in da Funk* (1995) explores historical and contemporary perspectives in black American life through tap dancing. *Rent* (1995) chronicles the lives of artists and their impoverished friends living in the East Village in New York City. *The Lion King* (1997) introduces a style of integrating puppets and moving sculpture into a musical production that makes the director-designer the principal author of the story told onstage. And *Contact* (1999) features the work of the director-choreographer who composes the entire piece through dance and music with spoken dialogue but without songs. Both *Bring in da Noise, Bring in da Funk* and *Rent* deal with serious, sensitive, and controversial issues: oppression and self-determination in *Bring in da Noise, Bring in da Funk* and drug addiction and AIDS in *Rent*. *The Lion King* and *Contact* are recognized more for innovations in style than subject matter. But all four musicals are noted for their high spirits and originality. They were created by young authors and feature very young cast members, some without traditional theatre backgrounds. Although the sound and style of these productions are completely contemporary, these new musicals are tied to musical theatre traditions that are clearly still evolving.

Savion Glover and *Bring in da Noise, Bring in da Funk*

Savion Glover grew up in Newark, New Jersey, but in the shadow of Broadway. By the time he was twelve years old, he was already recognized as a dance prodigy. He tap-danced his way through *The Tap Dance Kid*, *Black and Blue*, and *Jelly's Last Jam* before he was eighteen years old. Dancing with Gregory Hines, Honi Cole, and Jimmy Slyde provided Glover with an education in American tap styles that he merged with his own

sense of rap and reggae to create a new approach, called "the beat."

Savion Glover performs with a style of dance distinctly different from the light and graceful approach frequently associated with African American tap dancers. Glover's dancing is forceful and appears self-involved. He drives his feet into the floor and uses the whole foot in new ways. He dances on his toes and on the sides of his feet. The focus of the dance is in his legs and feet; his head is often down, and he doesn't use his torso or his arms to extend the range of movement. The dancing is very athletic and includes gymnastic and break-dancing elements. This is dance that can express anger and sorrow as well as joy and freedom. Savion Glover represents the tap dancing of a new generation.

George C. Wolfe, the former director of the Public Theater, was the creator and director of *Jelly's Last Jam*, whose premiere production featured Glover as the young Jelly. After this production Wolfe began to consider the significance of African American tap dance as a folk form and its possibilities for expressing the African American experience. He proposed a collaboration with Glover in the development of a performance without a script. Glover brought to the developmental process at the Public Theater four young men with whom he had danced (the oldest among them was twenty-six) and two drummers. They were joined by Ann Duquesnay, an actor and singer who would collaborate on and eventually perform the songs for the show; and Reg Gaines, a poet who was working on the text. Together they evolved a series of scenes, focused in dance, that each addressed a different aspect of black life in the United States.

In *Bring in da Noise, Bring in da Funk*, tap dance is used to depict a lynching, the post-slavery migration to the North, and even the attempts of black men to flag a cab in New York City. *Bring in da Noise, Bring in da Funk* has an episodic organization of scenes related to a theme rather than a traditional plot made up of connected incidents. Like *A Chorus Line*, the show is about the dancers themselves. But in

Savion Glover and his fellow dancers bring the choreography of *Bring in da Noise, Bring in da Funk* into the present. The dancers and drummers celebrate one of the musical's fundamental themes, "In the beginning there was . . . da beat!"

A Chorus Line the dancers are always in character, even though much of the content of their characters' lives may be close to their own. In *Bring in da Noise, Bring in da Funk* the dancers speak for themselves. Their taped voices describing the place of dance in their lives accompany one sequence of their dancing. The actual lives of the actor-dancers are seen as the final movement of history that the play presents.

The black musical was a significant part of the early history of musical theatre in the United States. Musicals such as *Ain't Misbehavin'* and *Jelly's Last Jam* have reinterpreted a tradition that has deep roots in the American theatre. *Bring in da Noise, Bring in da Funk* makes a place for young dancers in the musical

theatre and brings an entirely new sensibility to a choreographed, dramatic form. At age twenty-three, Savion Glover joined Jerome Robbins and Michael Bennett as creators of modern, choreographically created musical theatre pieces at the same time that he reached back to the traditions of African American dance and musical theatre.

Jonathan Larson and *Rent*

Like *Bring in da Noise, Bring in da Funk*, *Rent* grew out of a workshop production, in this case at New York Theatre Workshop; it then moved to the Nederlander Theatre on what is considered the outer perimeter of Broadway. *Bring in da Noise, Bring in da Funk* was the work of young creators

The cast of *Rent* sings and dances "La Vie Bohème" on the tables of the Life Café with choreography by Marlies Yearby. In "La Vie Bohème" the characters sing of their social rebellion. Unlike the more structured choreography of *West Side Story* and *A Chorus Line,* the dancing in *Rent* has an informal, improvisational quality.

and performers but had the very experienced and well-connected hand of George C. Wolfe guiding the process. *Rent* was sustained by the energy and commitment of its creator, Jonathan Larson.

Larson studied acting and musical composition in college; and with encouragement from Stephen Sondheim, he committed himself to a career of writing for the musical theatre. It took fifteen years of living the life represented by the characters in *Rent* to bring his vision of a new musical to the stage. Larson sought to merge the tradition of the musical theatre with music of the 1990s and the sensibility of young people raised

with MTV, film technology, and rapidly changing social values. He wanted to place the heart of rock-and-roll culture on the musical stage in order to tell the story of young people struggling to make sense of life in the midst of poverty and the AIDS epidemic.

Larson found the starting point for what would become *Rent* in a nineteenth-century opera, *La Bohème* (1895), by Puccini; and in the novel *Scenes de la Vie Bohème,* by Henri Murger, on which *La Bohème* was based. From *La Bohème* he took the situation of a group of artists struggling with poverty and illness but sustaining themselves through their friendships and their faith in life. Many of the plot incidents and the characters are suggested by the opera; an example is Mimi, who in the opera dies of tuberculosis and in *Rent* is dying of drug addiction and AIDS.

But *Rent* is definitely a late-twentieth-century creation: a rock band is placed on the stage; the characters all wear head mikes; one of the characters records everything on a video camera; and drug addiction underscores the troubled lives of the characters. The music reflects the mix of pop music culture, all with a rock-and-roll beat. Instead of the slickness and polished finish of most musical theatre productions, Larson sought a roughness and rawness in the performance, in terms of both the singing and the visual presentation. The set appears to be made from found pieces of junk; the costumes are a grungy compilation of worn and frayed cast-off garments or the cheapest of the new. The staging has an improvisational feel. Where there is choreography, there is a sense of looseness and invention in the moment rather than the highly crafted dance structures of Jerome Robbins, Michael Bennett, or Savion Glover.

The story behind the creation of *Rent* is as dramatic as what occurs on the stage. The night before the production's final dress rehearsal, thirty-five-year-old Jonathan Larson died suddenly of an aortic aneurysm. The grief-stricken cast "went on with the show," which met with great success. But the success was mixed with sadness for the young playwright and composer who didn't live to see his music and lyrics lighting up Broadway.

Julie Taymor and *The Lion King*

In 1997 a new musical opened on Broadway that once again took the form in a major new direction. *The Lion King* was adapted from the extraordinarily popular Walt Disney film of the same name and followed the Disney recreation of *Beauty and the Beast* as a stage musical. The stage version of *Beauty and the Beast* was guided by the cartoon imagery of the film, but the stage production of *The Lion King* broke new ground in the musical theatre. The avant-garde director and designer Julie Taymor was invited by Walt Disney Theatrical Productions to interpret the story of *The Lion King* in her own way. Impressed by Taymor's previous intercultural work using astounding sculpted puppets and cinematic design effects, the Disney organization provided the opportunity for highly imaginative exploration in a commercial context. *The Lion King* continues the tradition of Broadway musicals that rely on lavish sets and costumes but integrates these elements into the telling of a story in a significantly new way. The designer-director becomes the driving force behind the expressive elements of the production.

Taymor became a serious student of theatre as a child and expanded her awareness of non-Western theatre traditions when she traveled to India and Sri Lanka during high school. During college she was part of the same experimental theatre company as Bill Irwin at Oberlin College. She also studied mime in Paris, improvisational acting in New York, and puppetry with the Bread and Puppet Theatre. Taymor was always concerned with the anthropological origins of theatre and with mythical subjects. She also showed talent early on as a painter and sculptor as well as a performer, talents that she continued to nurture as she apprenticed with different theatre companies and traditions.

After graduating from college, Taymor spent four years in Indonesia studying its brilliant movement theatre and observing the cultural conditions out of which it emerged. In Indonesia she became part of the Bengkel Theatre, which encouraged her to create a production with the company actors. Her first major work, *Way of Snow*, began her lifelong experimentation with theatre expressed through masks, puppets, live actors, and startling visual effects drawing on myth and ritual to probe the human condition. And she continued to build her design and construction skills in the areas of scene, costume, and puppet design at the same time that she refined her vision as a director. Taymor worked for twenty

Tsidii Le Loka is seen here as the shaman Rafiki in *The Lion King*. Her costume and makeup were designed to suggest the physical characteristics of a baboon.

years directing and designing original works, Shakespeare, and opera before being invited to bring her imaginative approach to *The Lion King*.

Taymor first worked with the original screenwriters of the film to expand and strengthen the narrative of the young lion, Simba, who must undertake a complicated journey to earn his place as king. She became a collaborator on the script itself at the same time that she began to envision the form that the characters should be given and a staging concept that would allow for the extremely adventurous nature of the action. The music from the film also required considerable augmentation, with particular attention paid to its African sources. Elton John and Tim Rice, the original composers who had worked with the South African performer Lebo M, wrote two additional pop-style character songs; Lebo M, Hans Zimmer, and Mark Mancina filled out the score, drawing on Zulu chanting and African rhythms and musical instruments. Just as Taymor's production style would draw on international sources and performance traditions, so the score would be an eclectic blend of American, European, and African styles. But as important as the music and the script were to the production, the greatest excitement would come from the visual presentation.

Taymor determined that various forms of puppets inhabited by actors would bring the animal characters to life and give her the flexibility to create magical action sequences, such as stampeding wildebeests or characters who could fly. The actors were not to be hidden by the puppet forms but rather to exist in puppet form and human form at the same time. The faces of the actors would always be seen. The actors playing lions would wear large masks placed above their own faces and be dressed in gowns of African-inspired fabrics rather than animal bodies. The hippopotamus was designed in full animal form for two actors whose bodies would be inside the large animal but whose heads would appear above the huge puppet. The character of Zazu, the comic bird, was designed as a fully realized rod puppet to be worn on the head of the actor who would sing and dance the role but who would be dressed in a suit that suggested the attitude of the bird character rather than in any kind of costume representing a bird. Human figures were designed into costumes representing plants, vines, and grass. Contraptions were invented such as the Gazelle Wheel, which would allow an actor to push across stage a wheeled vehicle that provided the momentum for the seven leaping figures of gazelle that were attached to it. Other "corporate" puppet forms were designed to enable one actor to present other groups of animals such as a flock of birds. Some of the puppets in *The Lion King* recall the inventions of the Handspring Puppet Company discussed in Chapter 9. Taymor explains her reasons for keeping the actor-puppeteers visible:

> When we see a person actually manipulating an inanimate object like a puppet and making it come alive, the duality moves us. Hidden special effects lack humanity, but when the human spirit visibly animates an object, we experience a special, almost life giving connection. We become engaged by both the method of story telling as well as by the story itself.[6]

Taymor also conceptualized a method of changing scale that would help develop the sense of movement across vast spaces. Characters would be represented by small puppets when they were meant to be seen at a distance, what she calls a "long shot," and then would be played by human actors when they had traveled far enough to be seen in a "close-up." For the wildebeest stampede, the first image seen by the audience is created by painted figures on cloth being turned on rollers at the back of the stage. As the stampede approaches the audience, larger and larger masks are used to create the sense that the animals are coming closer and closer.

Developing this visually stupendous musical involved the creative collaboration of many theatre artists. Michael Curry codesigned the puppets and was responsible for engineering and constructing them; and Taymor was responsible for sculpture and aesthetics. Richard Hudson created the actual scene design after Taymor developed the basic staging concept. Seven of the actors who ultimately appeared in the production were involved in experimentation with puppets and masks throughout the development process to see what would work and what would communicate effectively. In fact, Taymor incorporated puppets in the audition process:

> I also brought puppets to auditions to see how performers would look in relation to specific puppets and how they would respond when asked to animate an inanimate object. And though performers would not be totally immersed within the puppets nor hidden behind the masks, they would have to be willing to accept that the audience is not going to be looking at them alone. Attitude is a very important part of my casting decision. I want an actor who is going to enjoy the challenge and not view it as a burden. Rather than expressly hiring puppeteers, I look for inventive actors who move well. A strong actor gives an idiosyncratic performance, because he infuses the puppet characters with his own personality instead of relying on generic puppetry technique. The thrill of working with a good actor who is new to this medium, is that he will take the form further than I ever imagined.[7]

Designers have frequently created spectacular environments for musicals in the past with astonishing special effects. However, in *The Lion King*, Julie Taymor has investigated ways in which the work of the actor may be extended through her puppet and mask creations. She has returned to ancient theatre traditions and brought them into contemporary performance to challenge the imaginations of both actors and audiences.

Susan Stroman and *Contact*

Susan Stroman called her theatre piece *Contact* (1999) a "dance play" because the essential medium for storytelling in this work was choreographic. Despite the facts that there was no actual singing in *Contact* and that the music for the dancing was recorded rather than played live, the Broadway community chose to extend the term *musical* to include this performance of three loosely related stories, each in its own way based on the central human need for emotional and physical connection to other people. In *Contact* the work of the choreographer, which had become a major force in earlier American musicals such as *West Side Story*, *A Chorus Line*, and *Bring in da Noise, Bring in da Funk*, replaced the work of both the playwright-librettist and the lyricist. Although John Weidman collaborated with Stroman to provide the actor-dancers with small segments of spoken dialogue, it was dance that shaped the characters, the characters' relationships, and the actions of their stories.

In 1997 Andre Bishop, who was the artistic director of Lincoln Center Theater, invited Susan Stroman to create an original piece for his theatre because he admired the excitement and energy her choreography had brought to more traditional musicals such as *Crazy for You* (1992) and the revival of *Show Boat* (1994). Bishop provided rehearsal space and resources to enable Stroman to develop material of her own choosing. *Contact* was inspired by Stroman's own experience in a late-night swing club in which she

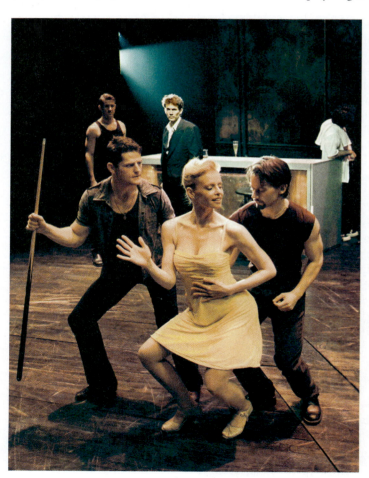

Deborah Yates, the girl in the yellow dress, confident and flirtatious, dances with two of her many admirers while Boyd Gaines looks on from the background, unable to join the dance. *Contact* was choreographed and directed by Susan Stroman with costume design by William Ivey Long.

observed the magnetism of a stunning dancer in a yellow dress. From this seductive image evolved a story of a man who has lost the will to live until he dances with the woman in the yellow dress. The writer John Weidman explains that dance became salvation for a man betrayed by the failure of words: "The character came from a world that was all about language and language was something that failed him. He was going to have to escape from language to get saved."[8]

The story is danced out in the man's lonely apartment, which, in a dreamlike way, keeps changing into the swing club where he first watches from a distance and then finally, overcoming his inhibitions, dances with the woman in the yellow dress. Much of the piece consists of high-voltage swing dancing by characters who have discovered a world of dance that the alienated man is unable to enter. Because the story is set in a dance club, Stroman chose to use recorded jazz and swing music to reinforce the atmosphere of being in a club. When the work was expanded to include two additional stories, Stroman decided to use recorded music for all three vignettes.

The choreography of Susan Stroman is distinguished by invention and by the way dance movement creates character. For example, the first vignette of *Contact*, entitled "Swinging," consists of a playful and exuberant romantic encounter between lovers on a swing. The young man first pushes the woman on the swing and then joins her, sometimes sharing the seat and sometimes doing gymnastics on the ropes holding the swing. As the swing sails back and forth suspended high above the stage, the lovers find numerous ways of using the swing as part of their romance.

Stroman's ability to develop character through dance is exemplified by the second of the three *Contact* pieces, "Did You Move?" The essence of composing dance drama depends on conceptualizing the needs of the characters and the conflicts between them as physical problems. In this piece the central conflict is between a man trying to control his wife by imprisoning her in stillness while she tries to take back her freedom through movement. The woman begins the short story seated opposite her surly, gangsterlike husband in an Italian restaurant. Hunched over his food, he discourages her attempts at conversation, and when he leaves the table to get more food from the buffet, he barks at her, "don't move." The woman overcomes the paralyzing effect of his threats, and during each of her husband's absences she dances out her fantasies with increasing abandon. Gradually she engages all the other people in the restaurant, diners and waiters, in a wild celebration of human connection. Full of humor, the dance evolves into a broad conspiracy involving actor-dancers and food and serving trays to confuse and outwit the joyless, thuggish husband.

Since the success of *Contact*, Susan Stroman has gone on to work as the director-choreographer first of a revival of *The Music Man* and then most notably of *The Producers* (2001). Starring Nathan Lane and Matthew Broderick, *The Producers* was adapted by the comedian Mel Brooks from his film of the same name and is a comedy about the theatre itself. *The Producers* tells a simple story of a down-on-his-luck theatre producer who hits on an outrageous scheme to make money. He persuades a large number of older women, foolishly susceptible to his charms, to invest in his next show, selling each of them a half interest or more, percentages that are clearly too large to be paid back. Then he guarantees that the show will be a catastrophic failure by choosing the most offensive and tasteless material possible, a cheerful musical about Nazi Germany. He is certain the show will close after one night, and he will be able to keep his elderly investors' money. However, audiences believe the show must be a satire and find it so amusing that it becomes a huge success. This success, of course, means that the producer, Max Bialystock, is exposed as a fraud, dashing his fortunes but not his survival instincts. *The Producers* enjoyed a notable success in the months after September 11, 2001, providing audiences with the much needed release of laughter during disturbing times.

The Musical Theatre Today

Large-scale musical productions continue to be mainstays of Broadway and national tours. In addition, regional theatres and smaller New York theatres have become increasingly interested in developing both traditional and new approaches to theatre works that use sung music as a foundational element. Popular music forms from rock and roll to hip hop to reggae to folk music to jazz invigorate the older styles of musical theatre composition. Many musicians who have established careers with bands or as recording artists are finding the musical theatre provides opportunities to add a dimension of storytelling or narrative performance to their music. The pop composer and singer Duncan Sheik wrote a score for an updated version of a German expressionist play, *Spring Awakening* (see page 380). The soul guitarist and singer Stew developed an autobiographical musical performance piece, *Passing Strange* (see page 466). Lin-Manuel Miranda, a rapper and lyricist who wrote *In the Heights* (see page 389), is currently working on developing his song cycle, concept album, *The Hamilton Mixtape*, into a musical biography of Alexander Hamilton. The renowned jazz trumpeter Wynton Marsalis is embarking on a collaboration

The musical *Once* (2012) is based on the 2006 independent film about the love affair of two young folk-rock musicians. The actors in the film, Glen Hansard and Marketa Irglova, are in fact the composers of the music and the love story is their story. Adapted for the stage through a series of workshops at New York Theatre Workshop, *Once* now stars Steve Kazee and Cristin Milioti, with a book written by the playwright Enda Walsh.

The two principal actors in *Once* are musicians as are the members of the ensemble. All of the music is played on the stage with violins, accordion, mandolin, guitars, cello, and piano. The set is a pub designed by Bob Crowley. The director is John Tiffany and the movement is devised by Steven Hogget, whose unique approach to stylized, choreographed movement was discussed in Chapter 5.

with Stephen Sondheim. Bands are developing musical theatre pieces from within their own groups such as Lisps' *Futurity*.

Theatre companies interested in presenting new work regularly invite musicians into developmental processes following the models exemplified by the Public Theater, the New York Theatre Workshop, and Lincoln Center Theater. Theatre practitioners and musicians realize that there is unexplored potential within the musical theatre form to incorporate new uses of music and new subjects. Through voices raised in song, the collected energy and range of musical instruments, the pulse and rhythm of dance, and the heightened use of text, the musical theatre form offers unique storytelling possibilities that can respond to the significant changes in contemporary culture.

 # Summary

Works of musical theatre integrate singing, spoken text, and dance to communicate the drama. The musical theatre is a unique development of the American theatre that has had widespread influence throughout the world. The musical theatre grew out of the minstrel shows, revues, and vaudeville of the nineteenth century, which drew heavily on the various immigrant groups that made up the U.S. population.

Oklahoma! made major advances in drawing together the expressive elements of musical theatre. All the songs in *Oklahoma!* were necessary to the development of plot or character, and dance was also used in a new way to further the ideas of the work. In *West Side Story*, based on William Shakespeare's *Romeo and Juliet*, Jerome Robbins made the choreography equal in importance to the singing. *My Fair Lady* drew on its source, *Pygmalion*, by George Bernard Shaw, to bring brilliant language to the musical stage. *Cabaret* turned the musical theatre away from the carefully plotted book musicals represented by *Oklahoma!*, *West Side Story*, and *My Fair Lady* to a new form, the concept musical, in which theme expressed through scenic and performance elements is of greater importance than the plot. Stephen Sondheim contributed major innovations in subject matter and

dramatic construction and set new standards for the writing of lyrics. *A Chorus Line* continued the evolution of the concept musical with its prominent use of dance to tell the stories of actors auditioning for a musical. New directions in theme and style have been provided by recent musicals such as *Bring in da Noise, Bring in da Funk*; *Rent*; *The Lion King*; and *Contact*.

The use of popular music to convey dramatic ideas and to build character and the centrality of dance in telling a story distinguish the musical theatre form. The popular music of each era has been embraced by the musical theatre, including, most recently, hip-hop and rock and roll. The choreographer-director has emerged as a new theatre creator, as exemplified by Jerome Robbins, Michael Bennett, and Susan Stroman. In *The Lion King*, it was the designer-director, Julie Taymor, who contributed a startling new vision for musical theatre by extending the actors' expressive possibilities through puppets and masks.

Topics for Discussion and Writing

1. Discuss the ways that music is an integral part of student life today. What kinds of music do you listen to or participate in creating? In addition to concerts, where music is the focus of the event, what events that are significant to you have some kind of musical association? What experiences in your life involve some kind of musical expression?

2. How does experiencing musical theatre differ from experiencing the spoken text of

a nonmusical play? Draw on the musicals seen by members of the class, whether on the stage or on film, to discuss the way music changes the nature of theatrical expression and the audience's response. What kinds of material is music especially suited to?

3. What subject material and style of music in a musical production would appeal to an audience of your peers?

● For suggested readings and other resources related to this chapter, please visit **www.mhhe.com/creativespirit6e**

The Nature of Drama
Structure and Genre

Drama is a unique art form with its own particular structural characteristics. We have distinguished theatre from film because theatre is performed live in front of an audience. We may also distinguish drama from other forms of written storytelling because of the way drama is built through character action and dialogue. A novelist writes descriptively, filling in details of the environment, the atmosphere, and the character history and psychology necessary to the reader's understanding of the work. The playwright works in a different medium, one in which the essence of the work is expressed through the nature of the characters and what they do and say.

The last section of the book presents two approaches to assessing dramatic form. Chapter 12 takes up the study of dramatic structure, the parts or elements of the drama and the relationship between those parts. Using the plays that we have read, the chapter looks at the building of the drama through character, plot, language, music, and spectacle. In Chapter 13 we expand our discussion of dramatic structure through the examination of another play and its production, *Water by the Spoonful* by Quiara Alegría Hudes. The innovative structure of *Water by the Spoonful* is composed through scenes that take place alternately between real time and space and the Internet. This play is also part of a trilogy, three plays that look at the lives of these characters as they evolve through different challenges and experiences.

Chapter 14 then introduces another way of identifying dramatic characteristics through the study of genre. Genre divides the drama into categories—tragedy, comedy, melodrama, tragicomedy, and farce—and indicates the area of human experience addressed by the playwright. For example, tragedy confronts the significance of human mortality whereas comedy celebrates our ability to endure. Each genre considers human existence from a different perspective. The study of structure and genre leads to consideration of the dramaturg and the critic, two writers who must analyze the drama to communicate effectively with audiences and theatre practitioners. Chapter 15 concludes Part Four by offering students an opportunity to engage in the creative process and imagine their own production of a play.

CHAPTER 12

The Elements of Drama and Dramatic Structure

We have now studied three plays in some detail and surveyed a number of dramatic traditions. We therefore have the resources to make some observations about the structure of plays. A discussion of dramatic structure provides us with a way of summarizing the work of the playwright.

Fundamental Elements of Structure

At the center of the drama are its characters and the stories they tell through their actions. Character action may show events or human conflict or a movement of the human spirit. Drama is distinguished from fiction because its fundamental expression comes through character action. When the curtain goes up or the stage lights come on, one or more actors must enter the stage, impersonating characters who are involved in some kind of action. To this impersonation of characters all kinds of elaborations are added through plot, language, music, and spectacle.

This list of elements is similar to the one originally proposed by the Greek philosopher Aristotle. Writing in the fourth century B.C.E., Aristotle began a dialogue about the nature of the drama, particularly tragedy, that has continued through the ages to our own time. Aristotle's analysis, consisting of a series of lectures, is known as *The Poetics*. It should be noted, though, that in Aristotle's sequence of dramatic elements, plot comes before **character.**

Many drama teachers and critics have found Aristotle's list of structural elements to be a useful starting point in understanding the unique nature of the drama. To the five elements of the drama already mentioned, Aristotle added theme (or ideas), which he identified as "thought."

All of the first five elements (character, plot, language, music, and spectacle) are completely interrelated. We separate them in the following discussion only for the purpose of analysis rather than to suggest that character and plot or character and language exist independently of each other. Each element defines or shapes the others. We know who characters are by what they say or the actions they perform. But of all six structural elements, the ideas or thoughts in a play are the most difficult to separate from the other elements of dramatic expression. Form—that is, the arrangement of character, plot, language, music, and spectacle—is what creates meaning. As we consider the structural components of the three plays we have read, we will see the emergence of further layers of "thought" created by the playwrights.

Character

The theatre celebrates what is extraordinary about life. The essential agents of the extraordinary in the drama are the characters. The characters who appear on the stage have remarkable qualities that may draw us to them, as we are drawn to Seth and Bertha in *Joe Turner's Come and Gone;* or that may repel us, as we are repelled by Roy Cohn in *Angels in America.* They may be ordinary characters, such as Hana in *And the Soul Shall Dance* or Prior in *Angels in America*, who behave in exceptional ways under difficult conditions. Or, like Emiko in *And the Soul Shall Dance*, they may be characters who are too large for the circumstances in which they are placed. The characters are our point of entry into the world of the play. They must take us with them. The characters must capture our attention and our imagination.

Part of what makes characters compelling is their will, their determination. Whatever the object of that determination, characters have overwhelming desires that propel them to action. Actors frequently begin their preparation for a role by seeking out the characters' motivations, that is, the characters' objectives or intentions. All characters who successfully hold the stage have some urgent goal that they strive to accomplish or some formidable obstacle to overcome. Herald Loomis is driven to find his wife. Seth is determined to make a decent life for himself and his wife, Bertha. Emiko is compelled to maintain her illusion that she will return to her old life in Japan. Roy Cohn is desperate to prevent his disbarment. Even in a play such as *Waiting for Godot*, in which the whole action is based on what could be a passive condition, waiting, the two main characters are driven to fill their time, compelled to converse, obsessed with puzzling out their situation.

Othello and Desdemona, played here by John Douglas Thompson and Juliet Rylance, are characters caught in a catastrophe of jealousy spiraling out of control. Their passionate love for each other is poisoned by the ruinous actions of Iago, who poses as Othello's friend and counselor. Iago is a character formed by maliciousness and spite, whose satisfaction lies in the wanton destruction of others. These three characters are among Shakespeare's most vivid creations. Arin Arbus directed this 2009 production of *Othello* for the Theatre for a New Audience.

Characters are defined by their actions, their motives, their histories, the selection of words that make up their vocabularies, and their reactions and responses to other characters. We learn more about them through what they say about themselves, what others say about them, and the physical descriptions provided by the playwright. For example, in *Angels in America*, the character of Roy Cohn is first defined through his relationship to the telephone. The playwright's description for act 1, scene 2 of the play, in which the character of Roy Cohn first appears, is as follows:

Roy and Joe in Roy's office. Roy at an impressive desk, bare except for a very elaborate phone system, rows and rows of flashing buttons which bleep and beep and whistle incessantly, making chaotic music underneath Roy's conversations. Joe is sitting, waiting. Roy conducts business with great energy, impatience and sensual abandon: gesticulating, shouting, cajoling, crooning, playing the phone, receiver and hold button with virtuosity and love. (*Angels in America: Millennium Approaches*, act 1, scene 2)

The intensity and sensuality of the interaction with the telephone provide a vivid physicalization of the character's nature. Here is one of the great manipulators in American history, the power player par excellence, lovingly plying the tool of his trade. The telephone is his link to the other power players, and the joy of modern technology allows Cohn to expand his influence according to the number of lines he can control. Cohn's opening line is vulgarly exuberant: "I wish I was an octopus, a fucking octopus. Eight loving arms and all those suckers. Know what I mean?" And while he plays the telephone as he would a musical instrument or a lover, he is acutely aware of being watched. Cohn is always "on." He is always dramatizing himself for effect.

Plot

Character action and plot are closely intertwined. The plot is the spine of the play and is made up of all the essential actions or incidents. The significant events, the sequence and pace of character entrances, the confrontations between characters, the changes in the situation, and the outcome of the various actions contribute to the development of the plot. In *Joe Turner's Come and Gone*, the plot revolves around the arrivals of the different characters at the boardinghouse and the interactions between them. Although the actions of all of the characters are important, the most important plot incidents have to do with the arrival of Herald Loomis, his search for his wife, his conflict with Seth, and his exchanges with Bynum.

A plot structure can be very simple, as is the plot of *And the Soul Shall Dance;* or it can be tremendously complicated, as is the plot of *Angels in America: Millennium Approaches,* with its thirty-five scenes. It is through what happens in the drama that playwrights shape their ideas and their worldviews. To illustrate, let's compare the two plays by Yamauchi and Kushner.

In a realistic play, such as *And the Soul Shall Dance,* causality is extremely important to plot structure. The incidents are all closely linked in terms of both time and logic. One action leads directly to another: The characters are brought together because the bathhouse has burned down; because Oka has stolen Emiko's money, Emiko is driven to sell her kimonos. In contrast, the plot structure of *Angels in America* is more arbitrary;

Kushner organizes a sequence of events that lack the organic connections of a realistic drama. His jump-cut style juxtaposes snippets of different stories. It is only once the various plot threads begin to intertwine that we see an external logic at work.

A further example of causality in *And the Soul Shall Dance* is the inclusion of two contradictory characters, Emiko and Oka, who are married by proxy and come to live in hostile and isolated circumstances. Disaster thus becomes inevitable. The characters are set on a collision course from the outset. In contrast, there is no causal logic for the appearance of Prior 1 and Prior 2 in *Angels in America;* nor is there anything inevitable about the arrival of the Angel.

In her play, Yamauchi presents the closely interwoven details of a small domestic drama as a way of illuminating what turns out to be a moment of great significance for all the characters, and particularly for the child, Masako. In contrast, Kushner presents a cosmic drama to comment on the relationship between individual conduct and national priorities.

Language

Although language is not present in all forms of drama and although many modern theatre practitioners have modified the centrality of words in the theatre, language is one of the great sources of vitality in the theatre. Language defines the characters and gives them authenticity and credibility. The speech rhythms and vocabulary of the characters in *And the Soul Shall Dance* and *Joe Turner's Come and Gone* are critical to the audience's perception of time, place, and character history. In *Angels in America,* Tony Kushner has a number of political arguments to make. What gives the play vitality is the gutsy language of the individual characters that makes them resonate as human beings, not as puppets of the playwright delivering prepared speeches. Dramatic language must somehow appeal to the audience's imagination and contribute to the sensory appeal of the play.

The vitality of Tony Kushner's language comes from the wit and biting sarcasm of his

Another issue that affects the language of many plays is translation. Since we regularly perform plays that were written in a language other than English, the sensibility of the translator makes a huge difference in the text that the actors will speak and the audience will hear. There is a growing recognition that an individual's knowledge of languages is not always sufficient to produce an eloquent translation that does justice to the playwright's original text. Playwrights have become active participants in the process of translation. For example, for the 2011 Berkeley Repertory Theatre production of *The Three Sisters* by the Russian playwright Anton Chekhov, a literal translation was prepared by Elise Thoron. The script was then written by Sarah Ruhl. Sarah Ruhl is the prominent American playwright who wrote *Eurydice*. The production was directed by Les Waters. The actors are Natalia Payne, Heather Wood, and Wendy Rich Stetson.

characters. The play is energized by its brashness and its humor. *Angels in America* uses a range of verbal approaches to match the odd and explosive mix of plot devices and characters. Much of the language is the intimate, domestic language of characters who share their lives, and this intimate language is at the heart of the play, the language with which the characters reveal themselves to each other. Frequently this language is sexually charged in an earthy and graphic way. At other times the language incorporates a sexual vocabulary that is hostile and manipulative; in Roy Cohn's mouth, language becomes abuse. Some of the characters also use a kind of **camp** that is associated with the gay community—lines quoted from *The Wizard of Oz*, *A Streetcar Named Desire*, and *Come Back, Little Sheba*. The Angel speaks in heightened, mystic poetry; Hebrew words and phrases are used to imply the Angel's ancient biblical origins. Yiddish brings a sense of Jewish tradition and history to Ethel Rosenberg and Louis. And of great importance

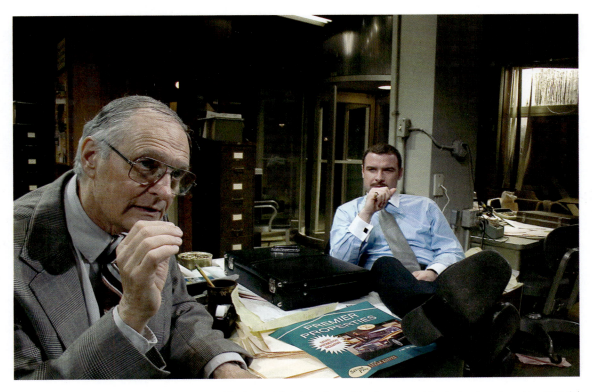

Playwright David Mamet interprets American life through harsh and repetitive language. Vocabulary is reduced to essential phrases to give a concentrated sense of character and situation. In *Glengarry Glen Ross,* cutthroat real estate salesmen viciously compete for sales opportunities. Alan Alda and Liev Schreiber appear here in a 2005 revival of Mamet's play at the Royale Theatre in New York City directed by Joe Mantello.

is the intellectual quality of the language as the characters struggle with ideas and arguments:

VOICE: I can't stay. I will return.

PRIOR: Are you one of those "Follow me to the other side" voices?

VOICE: No. I am no nightbird. I am a messenger . . .

PRIOR: You have a beautiful voice, it sounds . . . like a viola, like a perfectly tuned, tight string, balanced, the truth. . . . Stay with me.

VOICE: Not now. Soon I will return, I will reveal myself to you; I am glorious, glorious; my heart, my countenance and my message. You must prepare.

PRIOR: For what? I don't want to . . .

VOICE: No death, no:
A marvelous work and a wonder we undertake, an edifice awry we sink plumb and straighten, a great Lie we abolish, a great error correct, with the rule, sword and broom of Truth!

PRIOR: What are you talking about, I . . .

VOICE: I am on my way; when I am manifest, our Work begins:
Prepare for the parting of the air,
The breath, the ascent, Glory to . . .
(act 2, scene 5)

Spring Awakening is a play about teenagers struggling with issues of identity, particularly related to sexuality, and was written by Frank Wedekind in 1891. A recent production by the Atlantic Theatre of New York City in 2006 updated the play with a rock music score to create a rhythmic expression of the characters' tensions and frustrations. The music is by Duncan Sheik and the book and lyrics by Steven Sater with direction by Michael Mayer.

The language of Wakako Yamauchi's play is marked by poetic concentration and restraint. Within the framework of Japanese speech rhythms, the characters speak with economy and understatement. The language has none of the over-the-top verbal fireworks of *Angels in America*. It operates as if within a different musical scale. Because the characters function in a culture of public reserve, nuance and subtext become very important:

KIYOKO: She does! She hates me.

HANA: No. I don't think you have anything to do with it. It's this place. She hates it. This place is so lonely and alien.

KIYOKO: Then why didn't she go back? Why did they stay here?

HANA: You don't know. It's not so simple. Sometimes I think . . .

KIYOKO: Then why don't they make the best of it here? Like you?

HANA: That isn't easy either. Believe me. Sometimes . . . sometimes the longing for home . . . the longing fills me with despair. Will I never return again? Will I never see my mother, my father, my sisters again? But what can one do? There are responsibilities here . . . children . . . (pause) And another day passes . . . another month . . . another year. (act 2, scene 2)

August Wilson also brings to the theatre unique dialogue that reflects his many years of writing poetry before becoming a playwright.

Individual characters are defined by their own speech patterns, and yet a strong contrapuntal structure that blends the many rhythms and patterns connects all the speeches to make an almost musical whole. Repetition is one of the devices that Wilson uses in creating these poetic rhythms. A character may repeat himself, or a phrase may be passed from character to character:

BYNUM: You a farming man, Herald Loomis? You look like you done some farming.

LOOMIS: Same as everybody. I done farmed some, yeah.

BYNUM: I used to work at farming . . . picking cotton. I reckon everybody done picked some cotton.

SETH: I ain't! I ain't never picked no cotton. I was born up here in the North. My daddy was a freedman. I ain't never even seen no cotton!

BYNUM: Mr. Loomis done picked some cotton. Ain't you, Herald Loomis? You done picked a bunch of cotton.

LOOMIS: How you know so much about me? How you know what I done? How much cotton I picked? (act 2, scene 2)

The short, probing exchanges that drive the play forward pause sometimes and open out into the storytelling of first one character and then another. As in a jazz solo improvisation, the storyteller lingers over his subject before the momentum of the play resumes.

Music

When Aristotle included music as one of the basic elements of the drama, he was referring to the musical accompaniment for the choruses and to the chorus members themselves, who chanted parts of their text in the Greek tragedies. Almost all forms of theatre use music in one way or another. In opera all of the text is sung, as it is in most forms of Asian theatre. The modern musical alternates between spoken and sung text. In the Asian theatre, musicians almost always appear onstage and are visible throughout the entire performance. Inspired by the Chinese theatre, Bertolt Brecht saw songs as a fundamental way of commenting on the characters' situations and choices. For Robert Wilson music is essential to his strange and elusive images (see Chapter 9). Even plays that don't incorporate music in the dramatic structure use music at various points throughout the production—before the play begins, between scenes, and often during the scenes as a kind of atmospheric background or underscoring of the action. This use of music as underscoring has an enormously important function in film.

For both Wakako Yamauchi and August Wilson, music makes a significant contribution to the rhythms of their plays and the feelings that the characters try to express. Yamauchi uses Japanese folk songs to highlight the texture of the characters' lives. The songs provide a certain nostalgia and connection to a distant homeland; but—more important—they provide the characters with a kind of special text that goes beyond the accepted language of polite social interaction. So the song "And the Soul Shall Dance" provides Emiko and Masako with a basis for communicating their mutual understanding of the life of the spirit. In *Joe Turner's Come and Gone*, folk songs and blues songs are interwoven into the text. Finding one's song is a major metaphor throughout the play. The Juba is a song and dance that all the characters share. The "Joe Turner Blues" has major thematic significance and is also sung by Bynum as a way of approaching Herald Loomis. And the child, Zonia, sings a children's song about tomorrow that develops her relationship to her father's journey.

Spectacle

Spectacle comes at the end of Aristotle's discussion of dramatic structure, and he all but dismisses it as the least important and least artistic element of the drama. Needless to say, there are many who would disagree. **Spectacle** encompasses everything from acting style and the blocking or movement of the actors to the

Moliere's seventeenth-century play *The Miser* is a comedy about the central character Harpagon's grotesque obsession with money. In this 2004 production, Stephen Epp, playing Harpagon, is seen at the center of the stage, driving away both his family and his servants with his rages and demands. Riccardo Hernandez has designed the set of an enormous but almost barren room, emptied out of furniture and comfort. What appears to have been a grand home is now drafty and crumbling with holes in the walls, windows without glass, a leaking roof, and broken flooring. The set directly reflects the grasping stinginess of Harpagon, who forces all the other characters to join him in his impoverished existence in spite of the fortune he keeps hidden away. Theatre de la Jeune Lune collaborated on the production of *The Miser* with the American Repertory Theater and Actors Theatre of Louisville.

most breathtaking scenic and special effects. As we have already observed, the playwright may include descriptions of the proposed spectacle, but the interpretation of a play through spectacle is in the hands of the director, the actors, the designers, and the technicians.

The playwright Henrik Ibsen (see Chapter 7) took great care in detailing the scenic elements of his plays. Particularly because individualized, realistic settings were not the norm at the time he wrote his plays, Ibsen's descriptions of the settings contributed greatly to the developing style

of realism as well as made clear the metaphoric significance of each play's environment. Following is his opening description of the scene for *A Doll's House*, in which the environment is very inviting but ultimately stifling:

> A comfortable room, tastefully, but not expensively furnished. A door to the right in the back wall leads to the entryway; another to the left leads to Helmer's study. Between these doors, a piano. Midway in the left-hand wall a door, and further back a window. Near the window a round table with an armchair and

a small sofa. In the right-hand wall, toward the rear, a door, and nearer the foreground a porcelain stove with two armchairs and a rocking chair beside it. Between the stove and the side door, a small table. Engravings on the walls. An etagère with china figures and other small art objects; a small bookcase with richly bound books; the floor carpeted; a fire burning in the stove. It is a winter day.[1]

In *And the Soul Shall Dance*, the playwright suggests simple settings in keeping with a realistic presentation of the material. The East West Players' production of the play with the kabuki-inspired unfolding houses and the rolling tumbleweed added a layer to the cultural context of the play by placing the Japanese theatre as a backdrop to the Japanese American experience.

For a theatre artist such as Robert Wilson, spectacle is the soul of the drama. Wilson conceptualizes with images rather than with words. His initial plan for a theatre piece consists of sequences of sketches that outline a progression of evolving images. Verbal text plays a part in his dramas, but it is a subsidiary part rather than the foundation.

The twentieth-century theatre philosopher Antonin Artaud wrote in his visionary book *The Theatre and Its Double* that the theatre is a three-dimensional space, which must be filled with a concrete poetry of its own.

> I say that the stage is a concrete physical place which asks to be filled, and to be given its own concrete language to speak.
>
> I say that this concrete language, intended for the senses and independent of speech, has first to satisfy the senses, that there is a poetry of the senses as there is a poetry of language, and that this concrete physical language to which I refer is truly theatrical only to the degree that the thoughts it expresses are beyond the reach of the spoken language.[2]
>
> The problem is to make space speak, to feed and furnish it; like mines laid in a wall of rock which all of a sudden turns into geysers and bouquets of stone.[3]

When Aristotle suggested a diminished place for spectacle in the drama, he may have been deferring to his teacher, the philosopher Plato, who would have eliminated the theatre altogether because of its illusionary nature. But whatever the reason for Aristotle's dismissal of spectacle, the Greek theatre set on a hillside overlooking the sea, with its masked choruses dancing and gods descending from above, had much more in common with the primacy of spatial poetry of which Artaud writes than Aristotle's evaluation admits.

The Organization of the Drama in Space and Time

Some playwrights believe that a credible theatre event depends on not stretching events across too much time or too much space. In certain historical periods of the drama, place was restricted to a single setting and time to a single day. Nevertheless, most playwrights have great faith in the ability of the audience's imagination to keep up with their leaps through the calendar and around the globe. For these dramatists, space and time are organized according to the needs of their material. The plays of Shakespeare are prime examples, with their scenes that shift quickly between castle and battleground or even from nation to nation and with their events that chronicle a span of months or even years.

In *Joe Turner's Come and Gone*, August Wilson creates an action that takes place in Seth and Bertha's boardinghouse over a period of two weeks. The action of *And the Soul Shall Dance* shifts back and forth between two small houses in the Imperial Valley during a time span of about nine months. The time covered by the action of *Angels in America: Millennium Approaches* extends from October 1985 to January 1986 (although *Perestroika* takes the play all the way to 1990). And the thirty-five scenes of the play move between a multiplicity of locations within New York and even to Salt Lake City, as well as into the nightmares and hallucinations of the characters. The time is the late twentieth century, but characters emerge from the past to create a distorted sense of time just as we move in and out of realistic and expressionistic spaces. And although there seems to be a much more concentrated and realistic approach to time in *And the Soul Shall Dance* and *Joe Turner's Come and Gone* than in *Angels in America*, both of these largely realistic plays offer variations on the sequential progression of time. Because *And the Soul Shall Dance* represents Masako's memory, the play may be said to move backward in time as well as forward. And in *Joe Turner's Come and Gone*, the telling of stories interrupts a sequential, realistic sense of time and opens out moments of consciousness into an almost mythical time frame in which large, symbolic actions and legendary figures replace the everyday goings-on of the boardinghouse kitchen.

The Duration of the Performance

In addition to the fictional time created by the stage action, another factor of great importance to the shaping of the drama is the actual time or duration of the theatre event. In Western society, going to the theatre is usually considered an afternoon or evening event. We think of the theatre as providing a concentrated experience that will last from two to three hours; *And the Soul Shall Dance* and *Joe Turner's Come and Gone* fulfill this expectation. But there are also many one-act plays that may range in time from a few minutes to one hour. One-acts are frequently grouped together to form one program or one evening of theatre. Festivals of one-act plays by different playwrights have been popularized by such theatres as Actors Theatre of Louisville, which sponsors the annual Humana Festival. And in recent years various theatres have experimented with very long performances such as the combined parts of *Angels in America*, which lasts about seven hours. Other marathon presentations have featured the work of Robert Wilson and dramatizations of novels such as *Nicholas Nickleby*, by Charles Dickens. Long

productions allow the audience to experience a shift in consciousness. Time seems to become suspended as the audience members become immersed in the world of the performance. In the words of Robert Wilson:

> Most theatre deals with speeded-up time, but I use the kind of natural time in which it takes the sun to set, a cloud to change, a day to dawn. I give you time to reflect, to meditate about other things than those happening on stage. I give time and space in which to think.[4]

It is not uncommon in Asia for the audience to spend all day or all night at the theatre, or even several days at a time. For such productions, unwavering concentration is not expected of the audience. In addition to watching the performance, theatregoers socialize, eat, drink, and even nap during the course of the event.

Building the Drama: The Internal Rhythm

Within the plot structures of all dramas, no matter what form they may take, there is an internal rhythm, a relationship between the parts that involves the audience progressively in the theatre experience. As the play or performance changes and develops, the audience's understanding of and commitment to the theatre work increases. Usually this internal rhythm has to do with conflict and rising tension or suspense. What is at stake becomes increasingly important and at the same time more difficult to obtain. Expectations on the verge of fulfillment collapse, and characters must begin again with greater obstacles or change course altogether. Mistaken assumptions lead to disastrous choices that cannot be reversed or that require a more heroic effort yet. Characters' needs are set against each other in such a way that a physical or psychological battle is inevitable. Sometimes the internal rhythm of the drama has to do with the building or layering of image upon image or the accumulation of sensory experiences. The interplay between the areas of information or the incidents in the presentation of an epic story create a tension of its own. In this last section of the chapter we examine the more traditional conflict structure that is responsible for building the drama in most of the plays we have studied thus far.

Conflict, Rising Tension, and Resolution

Conflict can occur between individual characters, between groups of characters, or between characters and institutions such as governments or religion. Conflict may be internal—that is, within an individual character. Most plays have at least several layers of conflicts, and they have some form of rising tension—a series of escalating confrontations that heighten the conflict and raise the stakes. Frequently, through these confrontations, characters discover new information that changes or reverses their expectations and therefore also intensifies the urgency of their needs or motivations.

In *And the Soul Shall Dance*, the conflict between the Okas generates rising tension that draws in all the other characters. Some of the

hostility we witness directly in their two violent scenes; some we learn of through Kiyoko's distraught response when she escapes in the middle of the night to seek the Muratas' assistance. In the final confrontation between Oka and Emiko, Oka reveals that he has spent Emiko's savings on Kiyoko. With this terrible reversal of her situation, the urgency of Emiko's motivation increases dramatically. She must now part with her only real treasures if she is to retain any

In *Topdog/Underdog* by Suzan-Lori Parks, the Pulitzer Prize–winning play for 2002, two brothers search for their place in America and in their own family. Challenging each other through the street con game three-card monte, the brothers engage in a deadly battle of rising tensions. Here Mos Def and Jeffrey Wright appear in the production at the Public Theater directed by George C. Wolfe in 2002.

In this scene from *And the Soul Shall Dance*, Emiko finally must face the reality of her situation when she realizes that she will not be able to sell her kimonos. Hana, Masako, and Emiko all experience this devastating moment of recognition in the production at East West Players.

hope of returning to Japan. Thus we have the climactic scene in which Emiko tries to sell her kimonos to Hana and Masako.

Frequently, final climactic scenes are explosive, as in *Joe Turner's Come and Gone* when Loomis pulls out his knife; such scenes may build to almost unbearable suspense that catches audiences with its intensity and then allows them to collect themselves in the final moment of resolution that follows. In *And the Soul Shall Dance*, however, the climactic scene, the kimono scene, has a certain stillness. Despite her desperation, Emiko gathers herself and ventures out beyond her own house for the first time in the play to make one last attempt to function in the real world. She is motivated by financial need and the illusion of financial possibilities. We do not know whether Emiko has anything to return to in Japan or whether she has any inner resources left to make a new life for herself. She appears to sustain herself with illusions. Her motive grows more complex as her options shrink. As much as she is concerned about the money for herself, it is Masako to whom she wants the kimonos to

go. She wants to pass something of what she has known to someone for whom it will make a difference.

Yamauchi takes her time with the resolution and ending of her play. The resolution has three parts. First is the defeat or loss for Emiko, her recognition that there is no way out of her situation. Second is the drawing together of the Murata family in response to the disturbance and suffering that they have witnessed in their neighbors' unhappy lives. The play could have conceivably ended with either of these moments, but the playwright chose to finish with the brief scene on the desert between Emiko and Masako. Emiko, dressed in one of her beautiful kimonos, with her hair down, dances and sings. She has now withdrawn completely into her own world. Masako watches her, hidden behind a shrub. When Emiko senses her presence, she makes one further gesture before she exits. She "empties out her sleeve of imaginary flowers at Masako."

This seems to be the passing of her spirit that Emiko could not achieve through the sale of her kimonos. The domestic drama concludes with the previous scene of the kimonos and the wind chimes. The spiritual drama finishes with this silent little epilogue. We do not know if this scene is real or a function of Masako's memory or imagination. What is important is that Masako has received a gift from Emiko that her own mother could not give her. As Masako picks up the branch that Emiko has dropped, we know that her life is forever changed.

Summary

The playwright constructs a drama through character, plot, language, ideas, music, and spectacle. Different playwrights shape the elements according to the needs of the ideas they wish to express. The placement of the play in one or more locations and the movement of the play through time are also important factors in the construction of the drama. Many plays have an internal rhythm that evolves out of conflict.

Rising tension that results in some kind of climactic action is frequently the basis of dramatic plotting. However, a number of dramas move away from this model. The climax may be diffused or the pattern of the characters' interaction or the plot incidents may not move in a linear progression of increasing tension but may use repetition or a layering of images to create a cumulative awareness of the dramatic situation.

Topics for Discussion and Writing

1. How many levels of conflict are part of the structure of *Joe Turner's Come and Gone?* Cite examples of internal conflict, conflict between characters, and conflict between groups of characters or between characters and institutions.

2. Create an idea for a brief two- or three-character play. Make a cast list in which you briefly describe each character. Create a plot outline in which you list the major events of the play. Focus on the characters' important actions and the conflicts between the characters.

3. Choose one of the three plays that we have read thus far. How does the language of the play affect your responses to the material? Does the language provoke images or associations in your own mind? Does the language prompt emotional or physical responses? What mood or feeling does the language create? How would you describe the playwright's use of language to someone who has not read the play?

 For suggested readings and other resources related to this chapter, please visit **www.mhhe.com/creativespirit6e**

CHAPTER 13

Innovations in Dramatic Structure

Looking at *Water by the Spoonful*
by Quiara Alegría Hudes

Quiara Alegría Hudes is a young American playwright who began writing plays at an early age but focused her formal studies in music. She became an accomplished pianist and as an undergraduate at Yale University turned her attention to composition. She composed for a number of different

types of performance including musical theatre, dance, and small and large instrumental groups, and she also played with a band. Her musical interests were broad, ranging from classical European music to American jazz to the traditional music of her family's heritage in Puerto Rico. An early mentor was her aunt Linda Hudes who composed regularly for the Big Apple Circus, and so popular circus music was also part of the extensive world of music in which she grew up.

Following her college graduation, Hudes decided that as much as she loved music, storytelling through characters on the stage was the form of expression that made the best use of her talents and brought her the most satisfaction. Then as she embarked on her playwriting career, first as a graduate student in playwriting at Brown University, and later through the development of her craft as a professional playwright, she found that her study of musical forms and traditions and her experience as a composer exploring musical structures strongly influenced the way she approached dramatic structure.

In one of her first major successes as a playwright, Hudes collaborated with Lin-Manuel Miranda on the book for the musical *In the Heights,* drawing on her abilities to bring language and music together in dramatic form. *In the Heights* won the Tony in 2008 for the best Broadway musical. Working on *In the Heights* provided Hudes further impetus to continue exploring new territory in developing theatre pieces that would reflect her own personal history integrated with a range of musical traditions.

In the Heights tells a story about the Washington Heights neighborhood of New York City and the Latino families living there whose heritage includes Dominican and Puerto Rican roots. This musical was originally developed by Lin-Manuel Miranda when he was a college student. Later, Miranda invited Quiara Alegría Hudes to rewrite the book for *In the Heights* before its Off-Broadway (2007) and then Broadway (2008) runs. As a musical, the play is distinguished by its Latin and hip hop styles.

Elliot, A Soldier's Fugue: A Quartet for Actors

Before writing *In The Heights*, Hudes had completed an adventurous play inspired by the transformation of her cousin Elliot Ruiz during his tour of duty as a marine fighting in Iraq. She renamed her cousin Elliot *Ortiz* when she created him as a character in a play about what it means for a generation of young American men to go to war. Hudes was inspired to write the play when she met Elliot for the first time after his return from Iraq.

> **QUIARA HUDES:** I just remember the instant I saw him, there was just something changed in his eye. You know, he was still absolutely the same young clown of a cousin I had always known and had grown up with, loving, but there was something different. And I felt that I might never understand it. And that's the simple spark that it came from.[1]

THE AUTHOR SPEAKS ·

Quiara Alegría Hudes

One of the best classes I ever took in my education was orchestration. As a pianist, I learned how all the woodwinds sound, how all the strings sound, how the percussion sounds, in all of their registers. High register flute sounds extremely different than low register flute. High register clarinet sounds wildly different than low register clarinet. You learn the rules of how high and low they can go, what key signatures are trickier and more natural among them and then to experiment with various combinations. What's a piece for four violins versus what's a piece for violin, clarinet, tuba, and percussion? You're going to get two very different results. So I really hear the voices in the play, the characters in the play, like it's orchestration. Each one is its own instrument with its own sound and range and limitation.[2]

The cast of *Elliot, A Soldier's Fugue* appears together in the 2006 premiere production directed by Davis McCallum for Page 73 Productions. From left to right the cast is Elliott, Armando Riesco; Pop, Triney Sandoval; Ginny, Zabryna Guevara; Grandpop, Mateo Gomez. Page 73 Productions focuses on the development and production of new work by "early-career" playwrights.

This play, *Elliot, a Soldier's Fugue* (2006), presents the unfolding consciousness of an eighteen-year-old marine as he is confronted by the realities of war. At first the play focuses on his deployment, and through his dialogue and the narration of two other characters only his experience is presented. He appears to be alone, with the play's action shifting between actuality and his recurring nightmares. But soon Elliot is joined, onstage, by two other soldiers from two different wars: his father, Pop, in Vietnam, and his grandfather, Grandpop, in Korea. The meaning of the word "fugue" from the play's title quickly becomes clear. As a musical term, **fugue** indicates a piece of music in which a theme is introduced and then repeated with some variation by three or four other voices. There is a sense that these instrumental or sung "voices" are answering each other. In the play, the stories of the three

IN CONTEXT

American Military Engagement and *Elliot, A Soldier's Fugue*

Korean War

*Dates of American Involvement: 1950–1953

Warring Nations: American led United Nations Forces versus North Korea and China

**Casualties: U.S. Troops Killed: 54,229
U.S. Troops Missing in Action: 8,142

Character from Play: **Grandpop,** Elliot's Grandfather (65th Infantry Regiment of Puerto Rico)

Vietnam War

*Dates of American Involvement: 1960–1973

Warring Nations: United States and South Vietnam versus North Vietnam

**Casualties: U.S. Troops Killed: 58,220

Characters from Play: **Pop,** Elliot's Father (3rd Cavalry Division)
Ginny, Elliot's Mother (Army Nurse Corps)

Iraq War

*Dates of American Involvement: 2003–2011

Warring Nations: United States and Coalition Forces versus Iraq

**Casualties: American Troops Killed in Iraq: 4,488
American Troops Killed in Afghanistan: 2,061
American Troops Wounded: 50,569
Suicides Amongst Returned Veterans in 2012: 349

Character from Play: **Elliot** (1st Marine Division)

*These dates are open to interpretation. Some analysts would expand the time periods depending on the arrival date and departure date of all American forces.

**The casualty figures are for U.S. troops only. In each conflict many thousands of additional troops, both allies and enemies, were also killed. These figures also do not reflect the enormous loss of civilian life. In Iraq, for example, estimates vary from 600,000 to 1,500,000 civilian lives lost.

soldiers are woven together, each echoing the other: the loneliness and fear of young men far from home, the damage done to bodies by the weapons of war, the damage done to minds by the taking of lives. These are personal stories, not political statements: three generations of men from one Puerto Rican family, repeating variations of the same stories of war. The three men are joined by a fourth character, Ginny, an army nurse who will tend to the wounds of her future husband, and later tend the wounds of her son, Elliot.

Time and space in this play are entirely fluid. The play can be happening in all three war zones at the same time or shift back and forth between them. Sometimes the characters speak for themselves, sometimes they narrate each other's actions. The play is constructed like a piece of music with themes that echo and repeat, voices that are presented in counterpoint. Music is also built into the characters' actions. The grandfather has taken his flute to Korea and plays the music of Bach in a major key when one of his comrades receives a letter from home and in

Elliot relives the moment when he fired at a man he believed to be an armed Iraqi. The staging is suggestive. The actor, Armando Riesco, leans across a bench as if he is handling a rifle.

a minor key when a soldier is lost. The father calls out his own versions of military cadences while Elliot sings along to the rap music on his Walkman. The play can be seen in part as an innovative and poetic continuation of the expressionist movement discussed in Chapter 9.

In the following scene, Elliot is on patrol in Iraq talking casually with his partner when he sees "some hostiles." A similar situation is occurring at the same time with his father in Vietnam. In this scene, Elliot and his father, Pop, are the main characters performing the action of the play. Ginny (Elliot's mother) provides narration for Elliot; Grandpop provides narration for Pop. At the end of the scene, both Elliot and Pop will be faced with removing the identification from the bodies of the men they have killed.

Elliot, A Soldier's Fugue

QUIARA ALEGRÍA HUDES

6. FUGUE

The empty space. Two wallets are on the ground.

GINNY: In my dreams, he said.

> Everything is in green.
>
> Green from the night-vision goggles.
>
> Green Iraq.
>
> Verdant Falluja.
>
> Emerald Tikrit.

(Elliot enters. He puts on night-vision goggles.)

ELLIOT *(To unseen night patrol partner)*: Waikiki man, whatchu gonna eat first thing when you get home? I don't know. Probably start me off with some French toast from Denny's. Don't even get me near the cereal aisle. I'll go crazy. I yearn for some cereal. If you had to choose between Cocoa Puffs and Count Chocula, what would you choose? Wheaties or Life? Fruity Pebbles or Crunch Berry? You know my mom don't even buy Cap'n Crunch. She buys King Vitaman. Cereal so cheap, it don't even come in a box. It comes in a bag like them cheap Jewish noodles.

GINNY: Nightmares every night, he said.

> A dream about the first guy he actually saw that he killed.
>
> A dream that doesn't let you forget a face.

ELLIOT: The ultimate Denny's challenge. Would you go for the Grand Slam or the French Toast Combo? Wait. Or Western Eggs with Hash Browns? Yo, hash browns with ketchup. Condiments. Mustard, tartar sauce. I need me some condiments.

GINNY: Green moon.

> Green star.
>
> Green blink of the eye.

Green teeth.

> The same thing plays over and over.

(Elliot's attention is suddenly distracted.)

ELLIOT: Yo, you see that?

GINNY: The green profile of a machine gun in the distance.

ELLIOT: Waikiki, look straight ahead. Straight, straight at that busted wall. Shit. You see that guy? What's in his hand? He's got an AK. What do you mean, "I don't know." Do you see him?

(Elliot looks out.)

We got some hostiles. Permission to shoot.

(Pause.)

Permission to open fire.

(Pause.)

Is this your first? Shit, this is my first, too. All right. You ready?

GINNY: In the dream, aiming in.

> In the dream, knowing his aim is exact.
>
> In the dream, closing his eyes.

(Elliot closes his eyes.)

ELLIOT: Bang.

(Elliot opens his eyes.)

GINNY: Opening his eyes.

> The man is on the ground.

ELLIOTT: Hostile down. Uh, target down.

(Elliot gets up, disoriented from adrenaline.)

GINNY: In the dream, a sudden movement.

ELLIOT: Bang bang. Oh shit. That fucker moved. Did you see that? He moved, right? Mother f. Target down. Yes, I'm sure. Target down.

GINNY: Nightmares every night, he said.
> A dream about the first guy he actually saw that he killed.

(Pop enters, sits on the ground. He's trying to stay awake. He looks through binoculars.)

GRANDPOP: In my dreams, he said.

GINNY: Walking toward the guy.

> *(Elliot walks to the wallet.)*

GRANDPOP: Everything is a whisper.

GINNY: Standing over the guy.

(Elliot looks down at the wallet.)

GRANDPOP: Breathing is delicate.

GINNY: A green face.

GRANDPOP: Whisper of water in the river.

GINNY: A green forehead.

GRANDPOP: Buzz of mosquito.

GINNY: A green upper lip.

GRANDPOP: Quiet Dong Ha.

GINNY: A green river of blood.

(Elliot kneels down, reaches for the wallet on the ground. He puts his hand on the wallet and remains in that position, frozen.)

GRANDPOP: Echo Vietnam.

POP: Joe Bobb. Wake up, man. Tell me about your gang from Kentucky. What, back in the Bronx? Yeah, we got ourselves a gang, but not a bad one. We help people on our street. Like some kids flipped over an ice-cream stand. It was just a nice old guy, the kids flipped it, knocked the old guy flat. We chased after them. Dragged one. Punched him till he said sorry. We called ourselves the Social Sevens. After the Magnificent Sevens.

GRANDPOP: Nightmares every night, he said.

A dream that doesn't let you forget a voice.

The same sounds echoing back and forth.

POP: Guns? Naw, we weren't into none of that. We threw a lot of rocks and bottles. And handballs. Bronx Handball Champs, 1964. Doubles and singles. Hm? What's a handball?

GRANDPOP: The snap of a branch.

POP: Shh.

GRANDPOP: Footsteps in the mud.

POP: You hear something?

GRANDPOP: Three drops of water.

A little splash.

(Pop grabs his binoculars and looks out.)

POP: VC on us. Ten o'clock. Kneeling in front of the river, alone. He's drinking. Fuck, he's thirsty. Joe Bobb, man, this is my first time. Oh shit. Shit. Bang. (Pause.) Bang.

GRANDPOP: Whisper of two bullets in the air.

Echo of his gun.

A torso falling in the mud.

POP: Got him. I got him, Joe Bobb. Man down. VC down.

(Pop rises, looks out.)

GRANDPOP: Hearing everything.

Walking to the guy.

Boots squishing in the mud.

(Pop walks to the second wallet.)

Standing over the guy.

The guy says the Vietnamese word for "mother."

He has a soft voice.

He swallows air.

A brief convulsion.

Gasp.

Silence.

Water whispers in the river.

POP AND ELLIOTT: Military code.

Remove ID and intel from dead hostiles.

(Pop kneels in front of the dead man's wallet. He reaches out his hand and touches the wallet. Elliot and Pop are in the same position, each of them touching a wallet. They move in unison.)

POP: The wallet.

The body.

The face.

The eyes.

(Elliot and Pop open the wallets.)

ELLIOT: The photo.

The pictures.

Bullet.

(Elliot and Pop each pull a little photo out of the wallets.)

POP: Dog tags.

    The wife.

ELLIOTT: The children.

(They turn over the photo and look at the back of it.)

    Black ink.

POP: A date.

POP AND ELLIOT: Handwriting.

    A family portrait.

(They each drop their photo. They each find a second photo. Lights fade.)[3]

A New Trilogy

Although Hudes received considerable acclaim for her work on *In the Heights*, a successful Broadway musical, it was the world of Elliot Ortiz that called to her. She believed there was more to Elliot's story that should be told and she was eager to experiment further with the integration of musical structures into her playwriting.

> QUIARA HUDES: I wanted to live in that writing world a little more. What I found out was that I couldn't go back, couldn't retrace my footsteps. I wanted to do something new. So I thought about working with music in the same way but using a different type of music so that I would be experiencing the same type of process writing-wise but would be moving forward with a new play. And so I thought about jazz. At the same time my cousin Elliot had some pretty incredible stuff happening in his life. I wanted to continue with this story and use jazz as a musical background.[4]

Hudes determined to write two more plays about her cousin Elliot's return from Iraq and use a different musical foundation for each. And the scope of the work would be expanded with new characters, some based on her family, and some characters of her invention, who shared the experiences that would be central to each play. Including *Elliot, A Soldier's Fugue*, the three interconnected plays would make a new trilogy for the American theatre, that we will call the Elliot trilogy.

> QUIARA HUDES: I love long form. I'm one of those rare audience members who wants things to be longer as opposed to shorter. A trilogy affords a long form without making someone sit through six hours of theatre straight. I think that it's the same attraction to serialized drama over cable. There will be a story arc that will last an entire season or that mini series model where you can really stretch a story for a longer amount of time. And then with the separation of the three different pieces within that long form, there's more room to play. Because each piece is its own event too, I can play with different ideas in each one. Each play has a different style and a different structure, a very different tone; so it doesn't feel too repetitive.

The History of the Trilogy

The **trilogy** is one of the earliest forms in the history of Western drama. At the time of the Greek theatre in the fifth century B.C.E., which we studied in Chapter 1, the Athenian playwrights frequently composed plays in the trilogy form using the three-play structure to develop complex themes. Separately, the individual Greek plays often used remarkable economy in the plot (a single unified action), the setting (one place), and the time frame (twenty-four hours), but the trilogy allowed playwrights to show the evolution of an idea across a broader range of characters and situations. In spite of evidence that many trilogies were written at this time, *The Oresteia* by Aeschylus is the only surviving trilogy from the classical Greek theatre.

The Oresteia tells the story of the return of a general, Agamemnon, from the Trojan War, his subsequent murder by his wife Clytaemnestra, and then the revenge killing of Clytaemnestra by the son of Agamemnon and Clytaemnestra, Orestes. Orestes is pursued by the Furies for his crime until he is brought to a trial by jury. The overarching theme of *The Oresteia* is the search for a system of justice that will stop the cycle of vengeance begun when Agamemnon sacrificed his daughter, Iphigenia, in order to secure favorable winds that would allow the Greek fleet of ships to set sail for Troy to begin the Trojan War. *The Oresteia* has received a number of recent productions around the world because of the way it addresses the cycles of revenge and brutality that we continue to witness in many geographic regions, including our own participation in military conflicts in the Middle East. It is one of the oldest plays and yet it has proven to speak forcefully to our contemporary circumstances. The best-known American trilogy is Eugene O'Neill's *Mourning Becomes Electra*, written in 1931. In fact O'Neill's work is an adaptation of *The Oresteia* that he placed in the American Civil War. Both the Greek and American versions of *The Oresteia* were written to be performed in one continuous presentation.

The trilogy is not a form of dramatic structure that is frequently employed. However, we have seen two major recent experiments in the American theatre with plays that are structurally connected: the two plays that make up *Angels in America* and the ten plays that together create August Wilson's cycle for the twentieth century. Certainly we see a number of experiments with connected episodes in contemporary television and Internet drama.

The Elliot Trilogy

The three plays in the Elliot trilogy are *Elliot, a Soldier's Fugue; Water by the Spoonful;* and *The Happiest Song Plays Last.* Together they trace the story of Elliot's participation in the war and his injury in Iraq and the stages he goes through as a returned veteran who is traumatized and unsure how to find his way forward. Each play looks at a particular time in Elliot's life and then expands and deepens the meaning of his experience by placing it in the context of his relationship to other members of his family. The form of each play is shaped by the significance of these family connections and a form of musical composition that is both a metaphor for the experience

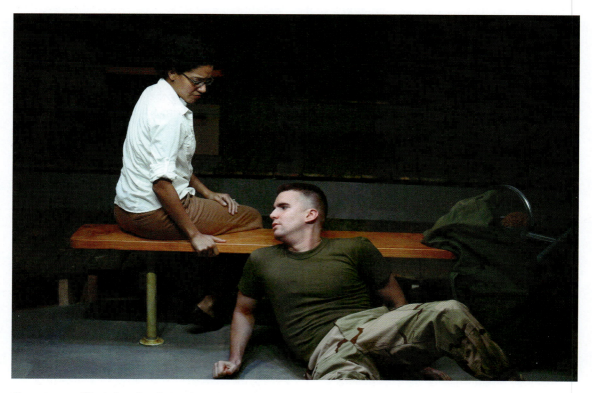

Ginny narrates Elliot's thoughts during the scene in which he is injured outside Tikrit.

represented and a structural component that expresses the nature of the characters' interactions and the human condition being explored.

Elliot, A Soldier's Fugue demonstrates the repetition of young soldiers at war from generation to generation, and the form is shaped as a fugue. *Water by the Spoonful* examines an issue affecting both Elliot and a larger group of other characters, all in recovery from substance abuse. This play is written as three duets for characters discovering ways to support each other. Where the first play in the trilogy is very carefully and economically constructed, *Water by the Spoonful* is a more expansive development of a theme through variation and longer, individual stories. The structures of jazz composition, particularly the music of John Coltrane, are used to reinforce the turmoil experienced by individual characters and the dissonance and conflict within the character relationships.

John Coltrane is recognized as one of the leading jazz musicians of the twentieth century. He rose to prominence during the 1960s and was known as a brilliant performer on both the alto and tenor saxophones. He experimented with the production of sound on his instruments, with extended improvisation, and with both melodic and dissonant compositions. Although he was born in North Carolina, Philadelphia became his musical home. Coltrane died at the age of forty in 1967. His reputation continued to grow following his death and his legacy was an inspiration to Quiara Hudes when she was a young music student in Philadelphia during the 1980s and 1990s. Two of Coltrane's most influential works, *A Love Supreme* and *Ascension*, became touchstones for Hudes when she was writing *Water by the Spoonful*.

QUIARA HUDES: With jazz and Coltrane, one of the things I was interested in was improvisation. He's exploring something about abandon. Just letting oneself go. And I wanted to give myself freedom to make big, bold statements at the risk of being messy. I listened to *Love Supreme* by Coltrane over and over again and I started thinking about what the play was going to sound like, the rush of energy, the movements.

In the last play, *The Happiest Song Plays Last*, Elliot moves toward a form of personal forgiveness. He performs an act of atonement for the taking of human life. He buries the passport that he took in the scene included above from *Elliot, A Soldier's Fugue* and that haunts him throughout *Water by the Spoonful*. He has tried to bury the passport in Jordan and then tried to return it to the widow of the man he killed. Finally, with the help of his cousin Yazmin and his new wife, Shar, who is of Arab heritage, he is able to bury the passport in his mother's garden.

The geographical setting of the third play shifts between Jordan, where Elliot is making a movie about the Iraq War, and Philadelphia, the home of Elliot's family. The play is written to be accompanied by two or three live musicians and includes a number of lively, traditional Puerto Rican songs. The Spanish-language lyrics of these songs augment and punctuate the content of the characters' dialogue and actions. The instruments called for are the guitar and the *cuatro*, central to Puerto Rican music. The playwright also recommends using an *oud*, an instrument from Iraq, which would further underscore the theme of mutual understanding that builds through the play.

Together the parts of the trilogy move from crisis to recovery to agency and reconciliation. Davis McCallum has directed the premieres of both *Elliot, a Soldier's Fugue* and *Water by the Spoonful*. He sees the character of Elliot taking on a larger significance than an isolated individual.

DAVIS McCALLUM: He's just a guy who grew up in the barrio and went to Iraq, like a lot of other people, and came home, like a lot of other people. What's so inspiring about what Quiara has done is to see a cousin, whom she loves, as a kind of everyman. It becomes more than just one guy's story. The trilogy becomes the quintessential American coming-of-age story. Over three plays, we see this guy struggling with what it means to be a man, and to be an American man.

As McCallum points out, Elliot is an ordinary young man caught in circumstances not of his making. He is elevated by his journey of suffering and introspection. And in his struggle to become whole by taking responsibility for his actions, he becomes a representative for the nation.

The Playwright's Sources: Family

Particularly for the Elliot trilogy, Hudes has found the sources for her characters, their stories, and their cultural context in her own family.

> **QUIARA HUDES:** I have to feel that personal connection, at least thus far. It has to come from somewhere in me. When I was at Brown, I took a course with Holly Hughes who is a performance artist. She gave us ten minutes to write a list of our identities. At the end of ten minutes, I had thirty things written on my paper, and as I shared it, I realized only about the first three or four were really *my* identities. The rest were identities of people I was really close with and especially family members. I think I've always taken on the identities of those around me too. So I feel like when I write about family, in some ways it's as personal as autobiography.

In one sense the three plays are something of a family history.

Hudes is inspired by the struggles, the strength, and the wisdom of the people that she has known best and draws on their experiences as the foundation for these plays. In addition to Elliot, another cousin inspired the character of Odessa in *Water by the Spoonful*. Odessa is a recovering addict whose struggles with addiction had "serious repercussions" for other family members. Some characters can be identified specifically; some are composites of two different family members. In the second two plays, some characters are pure inventions. A central character for the entire trilogy is Ginny, who appears only in *Elliot, A Soldier's Fugue*. She is the figure of healing in that play and her presence guides the development of the other two plays even though it is her death at the beginning of *Water by the Spoonful* that precipitates much of the action. Quiara Hudes, in fact, has an Aunt Ginny for whom this character is named. But the character's spirituality also reflects Hudes' mother and her connections to Taíno and Afro-Caribbean rituals as well as her community activism.

In *Elliott, A Soldier's Fugue*, Ginny has a long monologue about the garden she created in her hometown of Philadelphia, in an abandoned lot filled with junk and garbage. The reclaimed garden, which she filled with tropical plants from her native Puerto Rico, serves as a metaphor throughout the trilogy for the reclamation of lives from poverty, addiction, and despair.

> **GINNY:** When Elliot left for Iraq, I went crazy with planting. Begonias, ferns, trees. A seed is a contract with the future. It's saying I know something better will happen tomorrow . . . You have to plant wild. When your son goes to war, you plant every goddamn seed you can find. It doesn't matter what the seed is. So long as it grows. I plant what I like and to hell with the consequences.[5]

Although Ginny dies at the beginning of *Water by the Spoonful*, another character drawn from Hudes' family, Yazmin, gradually grows into the role of family protector during the second two plays.

In developing her characters, Hudes goes beyond writing from memory or observation. She interviews the family members she wants to write about and also discusses with them how she will use the material and takes into account their feelings about having their private lives revealed publicly. She has found "they really do want to talk about their experience and their point of view and tell me their stories." The next step in her process is to undertake research to expand her understanding of the circumstances she wants to work with. Hudes reads widely and interviews additional sources. For *Water by the Spoonful*, that meant extensive research

Ginny describes the tropical garden she created in an abandoned lot in Philadelphia. In *Water by the Spoonful,* the actor Zabryna Guevara, who plays Ginny here, plays the role of Ginny's niece Yazmin, who ends up inheriting her aunt's garden.

about addiction and recovery. She spoke with counselors at the Institute for Living, a recovery institute in Hartford, Connecticut, as well as with Alan Leshner, President of the National Institute for Drug Abuse. Ultimately she spends months or years sifting and processing the material she has gathered.

> Over that long period of time, it is a very slow stream of conscious process. I do a lot of walking and thinking. I think my process is about 70% walking without writing or reading anything.

When Hudes does sit down to write her plays, she enters a new phase of the work, which involves creating a fiction of the life stories and research materials she has absorbed.

The Dual Worlds of *Water by the Spoonful*

In *Water by the Spoonful,* the story of Elliot's reentry into American society connects to his relationship with his birth mother, Odessa. We learn that Ginny from *Elliot, A Soldier's Fugue* is his aunt, who adopted him when Odessa spiraled down into drug use. Another structural component is introduced as a foundation for this character, still locked in a battle with addiction. The play presents Odessa through her online conversations with other recovering substance abusers. The construction of the play alternates between scenes that take place in actual time and space and scenes that take place online, in virtual space.

Whether they appear in the real world or online, all of the characters are hiding truths about themselves. They have retreated in differing degrees from full participation in life. Through the course of this second play of the trilogy, they all seek to repair the damage to their own lives or the damage they have inflicted on others.

QUIARA HUDES: With the real versus the online, the first act basically alternates between the two worlds. Then they come together at the end of act I. The structure breaks down and the worlds start to bleed into each other. I feel very connected to that structure living in 2013 because we live in multiple worlds now all at the same time. Swiftly shifting from world to world on the stage just feels like the way time works and the way that one's traffic moves through the day right now.

Water by the Spoonful

QUIARA ALEGRÍA HUDES
Second Stage production draft

DEDICATION

For Ray Beauchamp.

ACKNOWLEDGEMENTS

This play, its story, and its characters are works of fiction. However, I owe a debt of gratitude to Othet Sauris and Elliot Ruiz, whom I interviewed before writing. Without their generosity of story and spirit, my imagination would not have landed at this play.

More seeds of inspiration came from interviews with Jeremy Cohen, Sandy Moehle, Rik Albani and Alan Leshner. Roger Zepernick, my dear friend, contributed to Scene Ten by sending me a transcript of a speech he gave in Philadelphia along with his permission to adapt it.

Gratitude to all my family, with a special beam of light shining on my mother, Virginia Sanchez. Linda Hudes, Eugenia Burgos and Liz Morales provide ongoing support and inspiration. My siblings keep me young at heart: Gabriela Sanchez, Ariel Hudes and Forrest Hudes. My stepfather, Mercedes Sanchez, told me a tale of his first cold drink. My father, Henry Hudes, sanded the curly maple of my writing desk.

Gratitude to my collaborators. John Buzzetti, your joy is infectious. Michael Wilson, what a champion you are. Davis McCallum, Armando Riesco and Zabryna Guevara—what shall we call our theater company? Hana Sharif and Darko Tresnjak, for steel-beam support at Hartford Stage. Catherine Rush, for drawing the starting line; and Kent Gash, for grabbing the baton along the way. New Dramatists, for seven lovely years.

Gratitude, ongoing, to Paula Vogel.
Gratitude, endless, to Ray.

CHARACTERS

ODESSA ORTIZ, 39, aka Haikumom, founder of www.recovertogether.com, works odd janitorial jobs, lives one notch above squalor.

ELLIOT ORTIZ, 24, an Iraq vet with a slight limp, works at Subway Hoagies, scores an occasional job as a model or actor, Yazmin's cousin, Odessa's birth son.

YAZMIN ORTIZ, 31, adjunct professor of music, Odessa's niece and Elliot's cousin.

FOUNTAINHEAD, 38, aka John, a computer programmer and entrepreneur, lives on Philadelphia's Main Line, white.

CHUTES&LADDERS, 56, lives in San Diego, has worked a low-level job at the IRS since the Reagan years, African-American, his real name is Clayton "Buddy" Wilkie.

ORANGUTAN, 26, a recent community college graduate, Japanese by birth, her real name is Madeleine Mays and before that Yoshiko Sakai.

A GHOST, also plays Professor Aman, an Arabic professor at Swarthmore; also plays a Policeman in Japan.

SETTING

2009. Six years after Elliot left for Iraq. Philadelphia, San Diego, Japan, and Puerto Rico.

The stage has two worlds. The "real world" is populated with chairs. The chairs are from many locations—living rooms, an office, a seminar room, a church, a diner, internet cafes. They all have the worn-in feel of life. A duct-taped La-Z-Boy. Salvaged trash chairs. A busted up metal folding chair from a rec center. An Aero chair. An Eames chair. A chair/desk from a college classroom. Diner chairs. A chair from an internet café in Japan. Living room chairs. Library chairs. A church pew. Facing in all different directions.

The "online world" is an empty space. A space that connects the chairs.

MUSIC

Jazz: John Coltrane. The sublime stuff (*A Love Supreme*). And the noise (*Ascension*).

NOTE

Unless specifically noted, when characters are online, don't have actors typing on a keyboard. Treat it like regular conversation rather than the act of writing or typing. They can be doing things people do in the comfort of their home like eating potato chips, walking around in jammies, cooking, doing dishes, clipping nails, etc.

Scene 1

(Swarthmore College. Elliot and Yaz eat breakfast. Elliot wears a Subway Hoagies polo shirt.)

ELLIOT: This guy ain't coming. How do you know him?

YAZ: We're on a committee together.

ELLIOT: My shift starts in fifteen.

YAZ: Alright, we'll go.

ELLIOT: Five more minutes. Tonight on the way home, we gotta stop by Whole Foods.

YAZ: Sure, I need toothpaste.

ELLIOT: Yaz, you gotta help me with my mom.

YAZ: You said she had a good morning.

ELLIOT: She cooked breakfast.

YAZ: Progress.

ELLIOT: No. The docs said she can't be eating all that junk, it'll mess with her chemo, so she crawls out of bed for the first time in days and cooks eggs for breakfast. In two inches of pork chop fat. I'm like, mom, recycle glass and plastic, not grease. She thinks putting the egg on top of a paper towel after you cook it makes it healthy. I told her, mom you gotta cook egg whites. In Pam spray. But it has to be her way. Like, "That's how we ate them in Puerto Rico and we turned out fine." You gotta talk to her. I'm trying to teach her about quinoa. Broccoli rabe. Healthy shit. So I get home the other day, she had made quinoa with bacon. She was like, "It's healthy!"

YAZ: That's Ginny. The more stubborn she's being, the better she's feeling.

ELLIOT: I gave those eggs to the dogs when she went to the bathroom.

(She pulls some papers from her purse.)

YAZ: You wanna be my witness?

ELLIOT: To what?

(Yaz signs the papers.)

YAZ: My now-legal failure. I'm divorced.

ELLIOT: Yaz. I don't want to hear that.

YAZ: You've been saying that for months and I've been keeping my mouth closed. I just need a John Hancock.

ELLIOT: What happened to "trial separation"?

YAZ: There was a verdict. William fell out of love with me.

ELLIOT: I've never seen you two argue.

YAZ: We did, we just had smiles on our faces.

ELLIOT: That's bullshit. You don't divorce someone before you even have a fight with them. I'm calling him.

YAZ: Go ahead.

ELLIOT: He was just texting me about going to the Phillies game on Sunday.

YAZ: So, go. He didn't fall out of love with the family, just me.

ELLIOT: I'm going to ask him who he's been screwing behind your back.

YAZ: No one, Elliot.

ELLIOT: You were tappin' some extra on the side?

YAZ: He woke up one day and I was the same as any other person passing by on the street, and life is short, and you can only live in mediocrity so long.

ELLIOT: You two are the dog and the owner that look like each other. Y'all are the *Cosby Show*. Conundrum, Yaz and William make a funny, end of episode. You show all us cousins, maybe we can't ever do it ourselves, but it *is* possible.

YAZ: Did I ever say, "It's possible"?

ELLIOT: By example.

YAZ: Did I ever say those words?

(Professor Aman enters.)

AMAN: Yazmin, forgive me. You must be . . .

ELLIOT: Elliot Ortiz. Nice to meet you, I appreciate it.

AMAN: Professor Aman.

(They shake.)

We'll have to make this short and sweet, my lecture begins . . . began . . . well, talk fast.

ELLIOT: Yaz, give us a second?

YAZ: I'll be in the car. (Exits.)

ELLIOT: I'm late, too, so . . .

AMAN: You need something translated.

ELLIOT: Just a phrase. Thanks, man.

AMAN: Eh, your sister's cute.

ELLIOT: Cousin. I wrote it phonetically. You grow up speaking Arabic?

AMAN: English. What's your native tongue?

ELLIOT: Spanglish. (Hands Aman a piece of paper.)

AMAN: Mom-ken men fad-luck ted-dini ga-waz saf-far-i. Momken men-fadluck ted-dini gawaz saffari. Am I saying that right?

ELLIOT: (Spooked.) Spot on.

AMAN: You must have some familiarity with Arabic to remember it so clearly.

ELLIOT: Maybe I heard it on TV or something.

AMAN: An odd phrase.

ELLIOT: It's like a song I can't get out of my head.

AMAN: Yazmin didn't tell me what this is for.

ELLIOT: It's not for anything.

AMAN: Do you mind me asking, what's around your neck?

ELLIOT: Something my girl gave me.

AMAN: Can I see?

(Elliot pulls dog tags from under his shirt.) Romantic gift. You were in the army.

ELLIOT: Marines.

AMAN: Iraq?

ELLIOT: For a minute.

AMAN: Were you reluctant to tell me that?

ELLIOT: No.

AMAN: Still in the service?

ELLIOT: Honorable discharge. Leg injury.

AMAN: When?

ELLIOT: A few years ago.

AMAN: This is a long time to have a phrase stuck in your head.

ELLIOT: What is this, man?

AMAN: You tell me.

ELLIOT: It's just a phrase. If you don't want to translate, just say so.

AMAN: A college buddy is making a film about Marines in Iraq. Gritty, documentary-style.

He's looking for some veterans to interview. Get an authentic point of view. Maybe I could pass your number onto him.

ELLIOT: Nope. No interviews for this guy.

AMAN: You're asking me for a favor. (Pause.) Yazmin told me you're an actor. Every actor needs a break, right?

ELLIOT: I did enough Q&As about the service. People manipulate you with the questions.

AMAN: It's not just to interview. He needs a right-hand man, an expert to help him. How do Marines hold a gun? How do they kick in civilian doors, this sort of thing. How do they say "Ooh rah" in a patriotic manner?

ELLIOT: Are you his headhunter or something?

AMAN: I'm helping with the translations, I have a small stake and I want the movie to be accurate. And you seem not unintelligent. For a maker of sandwiches. (Hands him a business card.) He's in L.A. In case you want a career change. I give you a cup of sugar, you give me a cup of sugar.

ELLIOT: If I have a minute, I'll dial the digits. (Takes the business card.) So what's it mean?

AMAN: Momken men-fadluck ted-dini gawaz saffari. Rough translation, "Can I please have my passport back?"

Scene 2

(Odessa's living room and kitchen. She makes coffee. She goes over to her computer, clicks a button. On a screen we see:)

HAIKUMOM, SITEADMIN
STATUS: ONLINE

HAIKUMOM: Rise and shine, kiddos, the rooster's a-crowin', it's a beautiful day to be sober. (No response.) Your Thursday morning haiku:

if you get restless

buy a hydrangea or rose

water it, wait, bloom

(Odessa continues making coffee. A computer dings and on another screen we see:)

ORANGUTAN
STATUS: ONLINE

ORANGUTAN: Ninety one days. Smiley face.

HAIKUMOM: (Relieved.) Orangutan! Jesus, I thought my primate friend had disappeared back to the jungle.

ORANGUTAN: Disappeared? Yes. Jungle? Happily, no.

HAIKUMOM: I'm trying to put a high-five emoticon but my computer is being a capital B. So, high-five!

(They high-five in the air. Another computer screen lights up:)

CHUTES&LADDERS
STATUS: ONLINE

CHUTES&LADDERS: Orangutan? I was about to send a search party after your rear end. Kid, *log on.* No news is bad news.

ORANGUTAN: Chutes&Ladders, giving me a hard time as usual. I'd expect nothing less.

CHUTES&LADDERS: Your last post says, "Day One. Packing bags, gotta run," and then you don't log on for three months?

ORANGUTAN: I was going to Japan, I had to figure out what shoes to bring.

HAIKUMOM: The country?

CHUTES&LADDERS: What happened to Maine?

ORANGUTAN: And I quote, "Get a hobby, find a new job, an exciting city, go teach English in a foreign country." Did you guys think I wouldn't take your seasoned advice? I was batting 0 for ten, and for the first time, guys, I feel fucking free.

HAIKUMOM: (Nonjudgmental.) Censored.

ORANGUTAN: I wake up and I think, "What's the world got up its sleeve today?" and I look forward to the answer. So, thank you.

CHUTES&LADDERS: We told you so.

ORANGUTAN: (Playful.) Shut up.

HAIKUMOM: You're welcome.

ORANGUTAN: I gave my parents the URL. My user-name, my password. They logged on and read every post I've ever put on here and for once they said they understood. They had completely cut me off but after reading this site they bought me the plane ticket. One way. I teach English in the mornings. I have a class of children, a class of teens, and a class of adults, most of whom are older than me. I am free in the afternoons. I have a paycheck which I use for legal things like ice cream, noodles, and socks. I walk around feeling like maybe I *am* normal. Maybe, just possibly, I'm not that different. Or maybe it's just home-land delusions.

CHUTES&LADDERS AND HAIKUMOM: Homeland?

HAIKUMOM: You're Japanese?

ORANGUTAN: I *was,* for the first eight days of my life. Yoshiko Sakai. Then on day nine I was adopted and moved to Cape Lewiston, Maine, where I became Ma— M.M., and where in all my days I have witnessed *one* other Asian. In the Superfresh. Deli counter.

CHUTES&LADDERS: Japan . . . Wow, that little white rock sure doesn't discriminate.

HAIKUMOM: Amen.

ORANGUTAN: Mango Internet Café. I'm sitting in an orange plastic chair, a little view of the Hokkaido waterfront.

HAIKUMOM: Japan has a waterfront?

CHUTES&LADDERS: It's an island.

HAIKUMOM: Really? Are there beaches? Can you go swimming?

ORANGUTAN: The ocean reminds me of Maine. Cold water, very quiet, fisherman, boats, the breeze. I wouldn't try swimming. I'm just a looker. I was never one to actually have an experience.

CHUTES&LADDERS: Ah, the ocean . . . There's only one thing on this planet I'm more scared of than that big blue lady.

HAIKUMOM: Let me guess: landing on a sliding board square?

CHUTES&LADDERS: Lol, truer words have never been spoken. You know I was born just a few miles from the Pacific. In the fresh salt air. Back in "those days" I'm at Coronado Beach with a few "friends" doing my "thing" and I get sucked up under this wave. I gasp, I breathe in and my lungs fill with water. I'm like, this is it, I'm going to meet my maker. I had never felt so heavy, not even during my two OD's. I was sinking to the bottom and my head hit the sand like a lead ball. My body just felt like an anvil. The next thing I know there's fingers digging in my ankles. This lifeguard pulls me out, I'm throwing up salt water. I say to him, "Hey blondie, you don't know me from Adam but you are my witness: today's the day I start to *live.*" And this lifeguard, I mean he was young with these muscles, this kid looks at me like, "Who is this big black dude who can't even doggy paddle?" When I stand up and brush the sand off me, people *applaud.* An old lady touches my cheek and says, "I thought you were done for." I get back to San Diego that night, make one phone call, the next day I'm in my first meeting, sitting in a folding chair, saying the serenity prayer.

ORANGUTAN: I hate to inflate your already swollen ego, but that was a lucid, touching story. By the way, did you get the lifeguard's name? He sounds hot.

HAIKUMOM: Hey Chutes&Ladders, it's never too late to learn. Most YMCAs offer adult swimming classes.

CHUTES&LADDERS: I'll do the world a favor and stay out of a speedo.

ORANGUTAN: Sober air toast. To lifeguards.

CHUTES&LADDERS/HAIKUMOM: To lifeguards.

ORANGUTAN/CHUTES&LADDERS/HAIKUMOM: Clink.

HAIKUMOM: Chutes&Ladders, I'm buying you a pair of water wings.

Scene 3

(John Coltrane's *A Love Supreme* plays. A Subway Hoagie shop on Philadelphia's Main Line. Elliot sits behind the counter. The phone rings. He gets up, hobbles to it—he walks with a limp.)

ELLIOT: Subway Main Line. Lar! Laaar, what's it doing for you today? Staying in the shade? I got you, how many you need? Listen, the delivery guy's out and my little sports injury is giving me hell so can you pick up? Cool, sorry for the inconvenience. Let me grab a pen. A'ight, pick a hoagie, any hoagie!

(Elliot begins writing the order.

Lights rise to a seminar room at Swarthmore College. We find Yaz mid-class. She hits a button on a stereo and the Coltrane stops playing.)

YAZ: Coltrane's *A Love Supreme*, 1964. Dissonance is still a gateway to resolution. A B-diminished chord is still resolving to? C-major. A tritone is still resolving up to? The major sixth. Diminished chords, tritones, still didn't have the right to be their own independent thought. In 1965 something changed. The ugliness bore no promise of a happy ending. The ugliness became an end in itself. Coltrane democratized the notes. He said, they're all equal. Freedom. It was called Free Jazz but freedom is a hard thing to express musically without spinning into noise. This is from *Ascension*, 1965.

(She plays *Ascension*. It sounds uglier than the first sample.

In the Subway shop, a figure comes into view. It is The Ghost.)

GHOST: Momken men-fadluck ted-dini gawaz saffari?

(Elliot tries to ignore the Ghost, reading off the order.)

ELLIOT: That's three teriyaki onion with chicken. First with hots and onions. Second with everything. Third with extra bacon. Two spicy Italian with American cheese on whole grain. One BMT on flatbread. Good so far?

GHOST: Momken men-fadluck ted-dini gawaz saffari?

ELLIOT: Five chocolate chip cookies, one oat-meal raisin. Three Baked Lays, three Doritos. Two Sprite Zeros, one Barq's, one Coke, two orange sodas. How'd I do?

GHOST: Momken men-fadluck ted-dini gawaz saffari?

ELLIOT: Alright, that'll be ready in fifteen min-utes. One sec for your total.

(Elliot gets a text message. He reads it, his entire demeanor shifts.)

Lar, I just got a text. There's a family emer-gency, I can't do this order right now.

(Elliot hangs up. He exits, limping away.)

YAZ: Oh come on, don't make that face. I know it feels academic. You're going to leave here and become R&B hit makers and Sondheim clones and never think about this noise again. But this is Coltrane, people, this is not Schoenberg! This is jazz, stuff people listen to *voluntarily.* Shopping period is still on, go sit in one session of "Germans and Noise" down the hall and you'll come running back beg-ging for this muzak.

(Yaz turns off the music.)

In fact, change the syllabus. No listening report next week. Instead, I want you to pinpoint the first time you really noticed dissonance. The composer, the piece, the measures. Two pages analyzing the notes and two pages describing the experience person-ally. This is your creation myth. Before you leave this school you better figure out that story and cling to it for dear life or you'll be a stockbroker within a year.

I was thirteen, I worked in a corrugated box factory all summer, I saved up enough to find my first music teacher—up to that point I was self-taught, playing to the radio. I walked into Don Rappaport's room at Settlement Music School. He was old, he had jowls, he was sitting at the piano and he said, "What do you do?" I said, "I'm a composer, sir." Presumptuous, right? I sat down and played Mr. Rappaport a Yazmin original. He said, "It's pretty, everything goes together. It's like an outfit where your socks are blue and your pants, shirt, hat are all blue." Then he said, "Play an F-sharp major in your left hand." Then he said, "Play a C-major in your right hand." "Now play them together." He asked me, "Does it go together?" I told him, "No sir." He said, "Now go home and write." My first music lesson was seven minutes long. I had never really heard dissonance before.

(Yaz's phone vibrates. She sees the caller with concern.)

Let's take five.

(As students file out, Yaz makes a phone call. Lights up on Elliot outside the Subway Hoagie shop.)

YAZ: ("What's the bad news?") You called three times.

ELLIOT: She's still alive.

YAZ: Okay.

ELLIOT: Jefferson Hospital. They admitted her three hours ago, Pop had the courtesy to text me.

YAZ: Are you still at work?

ELLIOT: Just smashed the bathroom mirror all over the floor. Boss sent me out to the parking lot.

YAZ: Wait there. I'm on my way.

ELLIOT: "Your mom is on breathing machine." Who texts that? Who texts that and then doesn't pick up the phone?

YAZ: I'll be there within twenty.

ELLIOT: Why did I come to work today?

YAZ: She had a good morning. You wanted your thing translated.

ELLIOT: She cooked and I wouldn't eat a bite off the fork. There's a Subway hoagies around the corner and I had to work half an hour away.

YAZ: You didn't want your buddies to see you working a normal job.

ELLIOT: Not normal job. Shit job. I'm a butler. A porter of sandwiches.

YAZ: Ginny's been to Hades and back, stronger each time.

ELLIOT: What is Hades?

YAZ: In Greek mythology, the river through the underworld—

ELLIOT: My mom's on a machine and you're dropping vocab words?!

(A ding.)

YAZ: Text message, don't hang up. (She looks at her phone. A moment, then.) You still there?

ELLIOT: It was my dad wasn't it? Yaz, spit it out.

YAZ: It was your dad.

ELLIOT: And? Yaz, I'm about to start walking down Lancaster Avenue for thirty miles til I get back to Philly and I don't care if I snap every wire out my leg and back—I need to get out of here. I need to see mom, I need to talk to her!

YAZ: He said, "Waiting for Elliot til we turn off the machine."

Scene 4

(The chat room. A screen lights up:)
No Image

FOUNTAINHEAD
STATUS: ONLINE

FOUNTAINHEAD: I've uh, wow, hello there everyone. Delete, delete.

Good afternoon. Evening. Delete.

(Deep breath.)

Things I am taking:

-My life into my own hands.

-My gorgeous, deserving wife out for our seventh anniversary.

Me: Mildly athletic, but work twice as hard. Won state for javelin two years straight. Ran a half-marathon last fall. Animated arguer. Two medals for undergrad debate. MBA from Wharton. Beautiful wife, two sons. Built a programming company from the ground up, featured in the New York Times Circuits section, sold it at its peak, bought a yellow Porsche, got a day job to keep myself honest. Salary was 300 K, company was run by morons, got laid off, handsome severance, which left me swimming in cash and free time.

Me & crack: long story short, I was at a conference with our CFO and two programmers and a not-unattractive lady in HR. They snorted, invited me to join. A few weeks later that little rock waltzed right into my hand. I've been using off-and-on since. One eight ball every Saturday, strict rations, portion control. Though the last three or four weeks, it's less like getting high and more like trying to build a time machine. Anything to get back the romance of that virgin smoke.

Last weekend I let myself buy more than my predetermined allotment—I buy in small quantity, because as with my food, I eat what's on my plate. Anyway, I ran over a curb, damaged the underside of my Porsche. Now it's in the shop and I'm driving a rental Mustang. So, not rock bottom but a rental Ford is as close to rock bottom as I'd like to get. Fast forward to tonight. I'm watching my wife's eyelids fall and telling myself, "You are on punishment, poppa. Daddy's on time out. Do not get out of bed, do not tiptoe down those stairs, do not go down to that basement, do not sit beside that foosball table, do not smoke, and please do not crawl on the carpet looking for one last hit in the fibers."

(Pause.)

In kindergarten my son tested into G&T. Gifted and talented. You meet with the school, they tailor the program to the kid. Math, reading, art, whatever the parent chooses. I said, "Teach my son how to learn." How to use a library. How to find original source material, read a map, track down the experts so he becomes the expert. Which gets me to—

You: the experts. It's the first day of school and I'm knocking at your classroom door. I got my number two pencils, I'll sit in the front row, pay attention, and do my homework. No lesson is too basic. Teach me every technique. Any tip so that Saturday doesn't become every day. Any actions that keep you in the driver seat. Healthy habits and rational thoughts to blot out that voice in the back of my head.

Today, I quit. My wife cannot know, she'd get suspicious if I were at meetings all the time. There can be no medical records, so therapy is out. At least it's not heroin, I'm not facing a physical war. It's a psychological battle and I'm armed with two weapons: willpower and the experts.

I'm taking my wife out tomorrow for our seventh anniversary and little does she know that when we clink glasses, I'll be toasting to Day One.

(Odessa is emotional. Chutes&Ladders and Orangutan seem awestruck.)

ORANGUTAN: (Clapping.) That was brave.

CHUTES&LADDERS: What. The.

HAIKUMOM: Careful.

CHUTES&LADDERS: Fuck.

HAIKUMOM: Censored.

ORANGUTAN: I'm making popcorn. Oh, this is gonna be fun!

CHUTES&LADDERS: Fountainhead, speaking of experts, I've been meaning to become an asshole. Can you teach me how?

HAIKUMOM: Censored!

ORANGUTAN: "Tips?" This isn't a cooking website. And what is a half-marathon?

CHUTES&LADDERS: Maybe it's something like a half crack addict. Or a half husband.

ORANGUTAN: Was that an addiction coming out or an online dating profile? "Married Male Dope Fiend. Smokin' hot."

CHUTES&LADDERS: Fountainhead, you sound like the kind of guy who's read *The Seven Habits of Highly Effective People* cover to cover. Was one of those habits crack? Give the essays a rest and type three words. "I'm. A. Crackhead."

ORANGUTAN: You know, adderall is like totes cool. Us crackheads, we're like yucky and stuff. We're like so 90s. Go try the adderall edge!

HAIKUMOM: Hey.

ORANGUTAN: The guy's a hoax. Twenty bucks says he's pranking. Let's start a new thread.

HAIKUMOM: Hi, Fountainhead, welcome. As the site administrator, I want to honestly congratulate you for accomplishing what so many addicts only hope for: one clean day. Any time you feel like using, log on here instead. It's worked for me. When it comes to junkies, I dug lower than the dungeon. Once upon a time I had a beautiful family, too. Now all I have is six years clean. Don't lose what I lost, what Chutes&Ladders lost.

CHUTES&LADDERS: Excuse me.

HAIKUMOM: Orangutan, I just checked and Fountainhead has no aliases and has never logged onto this site before under a different pseudonym, which are the usual markers of a scam.

ORANGUTAN: I'm just saying. Who toasts to their first day of sobriety?

CHUTES&LADDERS: I hope it's seltzer in that there champagne glass.

ORANGUTAN: Ginger ale, shirley temple.

CHUTES&LADDERS: "A toast, honey. I had that seven year itch so I became a crackhead."

CHUTES&LADDER/ORANGUTAN: Clink.

HAIKUMOM: Hey, kiddos. Your smiley administrator doesn't want to start purging messages. For rules of the forums click on this link. No personal attacks.

ORANGUTAN: We don't come to this site for a pat on the back.

HAIKUMOM: I'm just saying. R-e-s-p-e-c-t.

CHUTES&LADDERS: I will always give *crack* the respect it deserves. Some purebred poodle comes pissing on my tree trunk? Damn straight I'll chase his ass out my forest.

HAIKUMOM: This here is my forest. You two think you were all humble pie when you started out? Check your original posts.

ORANGUTAN: Oh, I know mine. "I-am-scared-I-will-kill-myself-talk-me-off-the-ledge."

HAIKUMOM: So unless someone gets that desperate they don't deserve our noble company? "Suffer like me, or you ain't legit?"

ORANGUTAN: Haikumom's growing claws.

HAIKUMOM: Just don't act entitled because you got so low. (To Fountainhead.) Sorry. Fountainhead, forgive us. We get very passionate because—

CHUTES&LADDERS: Fountainhead, your Porsche has a massive engine. You got bulging marathon muscles. I'm sure your penis is as big as that javelin you used to throw.

HAIKUMOM: Censored.

CHUTES&LADDERS: But none of those things come close to the size of your ego. If you can put that aside, you may, *may* stand a chance. Otherwise, you're fucked, my friend.

HAIKUMOM: Message purged.

ORANGUTAN: OH MY GOD, WE'RE DYING HERE, DO WE HAVE TO BE SO POLITE ABOUT IT?

HAIKUMOM: Censored.

ORANGUTAN: Oh my G-zero-D. Democracy or dictatorship?

CHUTES&LADDERS: Hey Fountainhead, why the silence?

(Fountainhead logs off.)

HAIKUMOM: Nice work, guys. Congratulations.

CHUTES&LADDERS: You don't suppose he's . . . crawling on the carpet looking for one last rock??

ORANGUTAN: Lordy lord lord, I'm about to go over his house and start looking for one myself!

HAIKUMOM: That's why you're in Japan, little monkey. For now, I'm closing this thread. Fountainhead, if you want to reopen it, email me directly.

Scene 5

(A flower shop in center city Philadelphia. Yaz looks over some brochures. Elliot enters, his limp looking worse.)

YAZ: I was starting to get worried. How you holding?

ELLIOT: Joe's Gym, perfect remedy.

YAZ: You went boxing? Really?

ELLIOT: I had to blow off steam. Women don't get it.

YAZ: Don't be a pig. You've had four leg surgeries, no more boxing.

ELLIOT: Did Odessa call?

YAZ: You know how she is. Shutting herself out from the world.

ELLIOT: We need help this week.

YAZ: And I got your back.

ELLIOT: I'm just saying, pick up the phone and ask, "Do you need anything, Elliot?"

YAZ: I did speak to your dad. Everyone's gathering at the house. People start arriving from PR in a few hours. The next door neighbor brought over two trays of pigs feet.

ELLIOT: I just threw up in my mouth.

YAZ: Apparently a fight broke out over who gets your mom's pocketbooks.

ELLIOT: Those pleather things from the ten-dollar store?

YAZ: Thank you, it's not like she had Gucci purses!

ELLIOT: People just need to manufacture drama.

YAZ: He said they were tearing through Ginny's closets like it was a shopping spree. "I want this necklace!" "I want the photo album!" "Yo, those chancletas are mine!" I'm like, damn, let Ginny be buried first.

ELLIOT: Yo, let's spend the day here.

YAZ: (Handing him some papers.) Brochures. I was being indecisive so the florist went to work on a wedding bouquet. I ruled out seven, you make the final call. Celebration of Life, Blooming Garden, Eternity Wreath.

ELLIOT: All of those have carnations. I don't want a carnation within a block of the church.

YAZ: You told me to eliminate seven. I eliminated seven. Close your eyes and point.

ELLIOT: Am I a particularly demanding person?

YAZ: Yes. What's so wrong with a carnation?

ELLIOT: You know what a carnation says to the world? That they were out of roses at the 7-Eleven. It should look something like Mom's garden.

YAZ: (In agreement.) Graveside Remembrances? That looks something like it . . . I'm re-nominating Graveside Remembrances. Putting it back on the table.

ELLIOT: You couldn't find anything tropical? Yaz, you could find a needle in a damn haystack and you couldn't find a bird of paradise or something?

YAZ: He just shoved some brochures in my hand.

ELLIOT: (Stares her down.) You have an awful poker face.

YAZ: Now, look here.

ELLIOT: You did find something.

YAZ: No. Not exactly.

ELLIOT: How much does it cost? Yaz, this is my mom we're talking about.

YAZ: Five hundred more. Just for the casket piece.

ELLIOT: You can't lie for shit, you never could.

YAZ: Orchid Paradise.

(Yaz hands him another brochure. They look at it together.)

ELLIOT: Aw damn. Damn. That looks like Mom's garden.

YAZ: Spitting image.

ELLIOT: (Pointing.) I think she grew those.

YAZ: Right next to the tomatoes.

ELLIOT: But hers were yellow. Fuck.

YAZ: It's very odd to order flowers when someone dies. Because the flowers are just gonna die, too. "Would you like some death with your death?"

ELLIOT: (A confession.) I didn't water them.

YAZ: (Getting it.) What, are you supposed to be a gardener all of a sudden?

ELLIOT: It doesn't rain for a month and do I grab the hose and water Mom's garden one time?

YAZ: You were feeding her. Giving her meds. Bathing her. I could've come over and watered a leaf. A single petal.

ELLIOT: The last four days, she'd wake me up in the middle of the night. "Did you water the flowers?" "Yeah, Mom, just like you told me to yesterday." "Carry me out back, I want to see." "Mom, you're too heavy, I can't carry you down those steps one more time today."

YAZ: Little white lies.

ELLIOT: Can you do the sermon?

YAZ: This is becoming a second career.

ELLIOT: Because you're the only one who doesn't cry.

YAZ: Unlike Julia.

ELLIOT: (Imitating.); "¡Ay dios mio! ¡Ay! ¡Ay!"

YAZ: I hate public speaking.

ELLIOT: You're a teacher.

YAZ: It's different when it's ideas. Talking about ideas isn't saying something, it's making syllables with your mouth.

ELLIOT: You love ideas. All you ever wanted to do was have ideas.

YAZ: It was an elaborate bait and switch. The ideas don't fill the void, they just help you articulate it.

ELLIOT: You've spoken at City Hall. On the radio.

YAZ: You're the face of Main Line Chevrolet. (Pause.) Can I do it in English?

ELLIOT: You could do it in Russian for all I care. I'll just be in the front row acting like my cheek is itchy so no one sees me crying.

YAZ: The elders want a good Spanish sermon.

ELLIOT: Mami Ginny was it. You're the elder now.

YAZ: I'm thirty-one.

ELLIOT: But you don't look a day over fifty.

YAZ: You gotta do me a favor in return. I know this is your tragedy but . . . Call William. Ask him not to come to the funeral.

ELLIOT: Oh shit.

YAZ: He saw the obit in the *Daily News*.

ELLIOT: They were close. Mami Ginny loved that blonde hair. She was the madrina of your wedding.

YAZ: William relinquished mourning privileges. You fall out of love with me, you lose certain rights. He calls talking about, "I want the condo." That I decorated, that I painted. "Oh, and where's the funeral, by the way?" You know, he's been to four funerals in the Ortiz clan and I could feel it, there was a part of him, under it all, that was disgusted. The open casket. The prayers.

ELLIOT: It is disgusting.

YAZ: Sitting in the pew knowing what freaks we are.

ELLIOT: He's good people.

YAZ: Truth is I was at his side doing the same thing, acting like I'm removed, that I'm somehow different.

ELLIOT: Hey, hey, done.

YAZ: One more condition. I go to Puerto Rico with you. We scatter her ashes together.

ELLIOT: Mami Ginny couldn't be buried in Philly. She had to have her ashes thrown at a waterfall in El Yunque, just to be the most Puerto Rican motherfucker around.

YAZ: I saw your Colgate ad.

ELLIOT: Dang, cousin Yaz watches Spanish TV?

YAZ: Shut up.

ELLIOT: I walked into the casting office, flashed my pearly whites, showed them my military ID and I charmed them.

YAZ: Do it.

ELLIOT: Give me a dollar.

YAZ: For that big cheeseburger smile?

(She gives him a dollar.)

ELLIOT: (Smiling.) "Sonrisa, baby!"

(Yaz cracks up laughing, which devolves into tears.)

How we gonna pay for Orchid Paradise?

YAZ: They should have a frequent flower card. They punch a hole. Buy nine funeral bouquets, get the tenth free. We'd be living in a house full of lilies. Look at that guy. Arranging his daisies like little treasures. What do you think it's like to be him? To be normal?

ELLIOT: Normal? A hundred bucks says that dude has a closet full of animal porno at home.

YAZ: I bet in his family funerals are rare occasions. I bet he's never seen a cousin get arrested. Let alone one under the age of eighteen. I bet he never saw his eight-year-old cousin sipping rum through a twisty straw or . . . I just remembered this time cousin Maria was babysitting me . . .

ELLIOT: Fat Maria or buck tooth Maria?

YAZ: Pig. I was dyeing her hair. I had never dyed hair before so I asked her to read me the next step and she handed me the box and said, "You read it." And I said, "My rubber gloves are covered in toxic goop, I can't really hold that right now." And so she held it in front of my eyes and said, "You gonna have to read it because I sure as hell can't."

ELLIOT: I been knowed that.

YAZ: I said, "But you graduated from high school." She said "They just pass you, I just stood in the back." I was in fourth grade. I could read! (Pause.) I have a degree written in Latin that I don't even understand. I paid seventeen thousand dollars for my piano.

ELLIOT: Oh shit.

YAZ: I have a mortgage on my piano. Drive two miles north? William told me every time I went to North Philly, I'd come back different. His family has Quaker Oats for DNA. They play Pictionary on New Years. I'd sit there wishing I could scoop the blood out my veins like you scoop the seeds out a pumpkin and he'd be like, "Whatchu thinking about, honey?" and I'd be like, "Nothing. Let's play some Pictionary."

ELLIOT: Yo, being the scholarship case at an all-white prep school really fucked with your head, didn't it?

YAZ: I should've gone to Edison.

ELLIOT: Public school in el barrio. You wouldn't have survived there for a day.

YAZ: Half our cousins didn't survive there.

ELLIOT: True. But you would've pissed your pants. At least their pants was dry when they went down.

YAZ: I thought abuela dying, that would be the end of us. But Ginny grabbed the torch. Christmas, Easter. Now what? Our family may be fucked-up but we had somewhere to go. A kitchen that connected us. Plastic-covered sofas where we could park our communal asses.

ELLIOT: Pop's selling the house. And the plastic-covered sofas. He's moving back to the Bronx, be with his sisters.

YAZ: You going with him? (Elliot shrugs.) Wow. I mean, once that living room is gone, I may never step foot in North Philly again.

ELLIOT: I could go out to L.A. and be a movie star.

YAZ: You need a manager? Shoot I'm coming witchu. Forget Philly.

ELLIOT: Change of scene, baby. Dream team.

YAZ: Probably we should order some flowers first, though. Don'tcha think?

ELLIOT: Orchid Paradise? (Yaz hands him the brochure. To the florist:) Sir?

Scene 6

(The chat room. Orangutan is online, seems upset.)

ORANGUTAN: 2:38 A.M. Tuesday. The witching hour.

(Chutes&Ladders logs on.)

CHUTES&LADDERS: 1:38 P.M. Monday. The lunch hour.

ORANGUTAN: I'm in a gay bar slash internet café in the city of Sapporo. Deafening dance music.

CHUTES&LADDERS: Sure you should be in a bar, little monkey?

ORANGUTAN: (Disappointed.) I flew halfway around the world and guess what? It was still me who got off the plane. (Taking comfort.) Sapporo is always open. The world turns upside down at night.

CHUTES&LADDERS: You're in a city named after a beer sitting in a bar. Go home.

ORANGUTAN: Everything in this country makes sense but me. The noodles in soup make sense. The woodpecker outside my window every evening? Completely logical. The girls getting out of school in their miniskirts and shy smiles? Perfectly natural. I'm floating. I'm a cloud. My existence is one sustained out-of-body experience. It doesn't matter if I change my shoes, there's not a pair I've ever been able to fill. I'm a baby in a basket on an endless river. Wherever I go I don't make sense there.

CHUTES&LADDERS: Hey little monkey. How many days you got?

ORANGUTAN: I think day ninety-six is when the demons really come out to play.

CHUTES&LADDERS: Ninety-six? Girl, hang your hat on that.

ORANGUTAN: I really really really want to smoke crack.

CHUTES&LADDERS: Yeah, well *don't*.

ORANGUTAN: Distract me from myself. What do you really really really want, Chutes&Ladders?

CHUTES&LADDERS: I wouldn't say no to a new car— my Tercel is one sorry sight.

ORANGUTAN: What else?

CHUTES&LADDERS: Tuesday's crossword. On Monday I'm done by the time I sit at my desk. I wish every day could be a Tuesday.

ORANGUTAN: What about your son? Don't you really really really want to call him?

CHUTES&LADDERS: By all accounts, having me be a stranger these ten years has given him the best decade of his life.

ORANGUTAN: I've known you for how long?

CHUTES&LADDERS: Three Christmas Eves. When you logged on you were a stone-cold user. We sang Christmas carols online all night. Now you've got ninety days.

ORANGUTAN: Can I ask you a personal question? What's your day job?

CHUTES&LADDERS: IRS. GS4 paper pusher.

ORANGUTAN: Got any vacation days?

CHUTES&LADDERS: A solid collection. I haven't taken a vacation in ten years.

ORANGUTAN: Do you have money?

CHUTES&LADDERS: Enough to eat steak on Friday nights. Enough to buy pay-per-view boxing.

ORANGUTAN: Yeah, I bet that's all the pay-per-view you buy. (Pause.) Enough money to fly to Japan?

(Pause.)

CHUTES&LADDERS: You should know I'm fifty years old on a good day, I eat three and a half donuts for breakfast and save the remaining half for brunch, I have small hands, six toes on my left foot, and my face resembles a corgi.

ORANGUTAN: If I was looking for a hot screw I wouldn't be logging onto this site.

CHUTES&LADDERS: Damn, was it something I said?

ORANGUTAN: (With honest admiration.) I've been on this planet for twenty six years and you're the only person I've ever met who's more sarcastic than I am yet still believes in god.

CHUTES&LADDERS: (Taking the compliment.) Says the agnostic.

ORANGUTAN: The atheist. Who is very envious of believers. My brain is my biggest enemy— always arguing my soul into a corner. (Pause.) I like you. Come to Japan. We can go get an ice cream. I can show you the countryside.

CHUTES&LADDERS: I don't have a passport. If my Tercel can't drive there, I generally don't go.

ORANGUTAN: Come save me in Japan. Be my knight in shining armor.

CHUTES&LADDERS: I'll admit, I'm a dashing concept. If you saw my flesh and blood, you'd be disappointed.

ORANGUTAN: I see my flesh and blood every day and I've learned to live with the disappointment.

CHUTES&LADDERS: I'm the squarest of the square. I live in a square house on a square block watching a square box eating square-cut fries.

ORANGUTAN: I get it. You were the kid who colored inside the lines.

CHUTES&LADDERS: No, I was the kid who ate the crayons. Was. I went clean and all personality left my life. Flew right out the window. I had to take life on life's terms. Messy, disappointing, bad shit happens to good people, coffee stains on my necktie, boring life.

ORANGUTAN: Maybe we could hang out and have a relationship that has very little to do with crack or addiction or history. We could watch DVDs and microwave popcorn and take walks on the waterfront while we gossip about celebrities. It could be the land of the living.

CHUTES&LADDERS: Stay in the box. Keep things in their place. It's a simple, effective recipe for ten clean years.

ORANGUTAN: Forget simple. I want a goddamn challenge.

CHUTES&LADDERS: You're in recovery and work in a foreign country. That's a challenge.

ORANGUTAN: No. No it's fucking not. Not if I just stay anonymous and alone. Like every day of my shit life so far. A friend, the kind that is nice to you and you are nice to in return. *That* would push the comfort zone. The invitation is open. Come tear my shyness open.

CHUTES&LADDERS: Alright, now you're being weird. Can we change the subject?

(Haikumom appears. She's reading the newspaper.)

HAIKUMOM: Orangutan, cover your ears.

ORANGUTAN: Big Brother, always watching.

HAIKUMOM: Cover your ears, kiddo.

ORANGUTAN: That doesn't really work online.

HAIKUMOM: Okay, Chutes&Ladders, can we g-chat? One on one?

ORANGUTAN: Come on! No talking behind backs.

HAIKUMOM: Fine. Chutes&Ladders, you listening?

CHUTES&LADDERS: Lord have mercy spit it out.

HAIKUMOM: Orangutan may be immature . . .

ORANGUTAN: Hey.

HAIKUMOM: She may be annoying at times . . .

ORANGUTAN: What the f?

HAIKUMOM: She may be overbearing and self-obsessed and a little bit of a concern troll and she can type faster than she can think which often leads to diarrhea of the keyboard—

CHUTES&LADDERS: Your point?

HAIKUMOM: But she's telling you, "Be my friend." When's the last time someone opened your closet door, saw all them skeletons, and said, "Wassup?! Can I join the party?"

CHUTES&LADDERS: Alright, my wrist is officially slapped. Thank you, oh nagging wives.

HAIKUMOM: Internal Revenue Service, 300 North Los Angeles Street 90012? Is that you?

CHUTES&LADDERS: Need my name, too? It's Wilkie. I'll leave it at that.

HAIKUMOM: I'm sending you a care package. Orangutan, you can uncover your ears now. I love you.

ORANGUTAN: Middle finger.

(Fountainhead's logon appears.)

FOUNTAINHEAD: Hey all, thanks for the warm two by four to my head.

HAIKUMOM: Alright, look who's back.

FOUNTAINHEAD: Knives sharpened? Last night we ran out of butter while my wife was cooking and she sent me to the store and it took every bit of strength I could summon not to make a "wrong turn" to that parking lot I know so well. I got the butter and on the car ride home, I couldn't help it, I drove by the lot, and there was my dealer in the shadows. My brain went on attack. "Use one more time just to prove you won't need another hit tomorrow." I managed to keep on driving and bring the butter home. Major victory. And my wife pulls it out of the plastic bag and says, "This is unsalted. I said salted." Then she feels guilty so she says never mind, never mind, she'll just add a little extra salt to the pie crust but I insist. "No, no, no, my wife deserves the right kind of butter and she's gonna get it!" I mean, I bark it, I'm already halfway out the door, my heart was racing all the way to the parking lot and raced even harder when I sat in the car and smoked. So, Michael Jordan is benched with a broken foot. But he'll come back in the finals.

HAIKUMOM: Thanks for the update, Fountainhead. You may not believe this, but we were missing you and worried about you. Don't beat yourself up about the slip. You had three days clean. This time you'll make it to day four.

FOUNTAINHEAD: Be ambitious. Why not reach for a whopping five?

ORANGUTAN: Maybe you'll make it to day thirty if you tell your wife.

FOUNTAINHEAD: I told you, I have my reasons, I cannot do that. My wife has some emotional issues.

ORANGUTAN: (Sarcastic.) No!

FOUNTAINHEAD: Listen? Please? Are you capable of that? She's in therapy twice a week. Depression, manic. I don't want to be the reason she goes down a tailspin. I actually have her best interest in mind.

CHUTES&LADDERS: Yawn.

FOUNTAINHEAD: Ah, Chutes&Ladders. I could feel you circling like a vulture. Weigh in, by all means.

CHUTES&LADDERS: And I repeat. Yawn.

FOUNTAINHEAD: Chutes&Ladders, why do I get the feeling you'd be the first in line for tickets to watch me smoke again? That you'd be in the bleachers cheering if I relapse?

CHUTES&LADDERS: How can you relapse when you don't even think you're addicted?

FOUNTAINHEAD: If you read my original post clearly, I wrote that it's a psychological addiction, not like heroin.

CHUTES&LADDERS: Well see then, you're not a junkie after all.

FOUNTAINHEAD: What is this, first grade recess?

CHUTES&LADDERS: No, this is a site for crackheads trying not to be crackheads anymore. If you're not a crackhead, leave, we don't want you, you are irrelevant, get off my lawn, go.

HAIKUMOM: Chutes&Ladders, please.

CHUTES&LADDERS: I got this.

ORANGUTAN: He's still logged on.

CHUTES&LADDERS: Hey Fountainhead, why did you come to this website?

FOUNTAINHEAD: Because I thoroughly enjoy getting shit on.

HAIKUMOM: Censored.

CHUTES&LADDERS: Why do you want to be here?

FOUNTAINHEAD: Want? The two times I've logged on here I've *wanted* to vomit.

CHUTES&LADDERS: Well? Did you receive some sort of invitation? Did one of us ask you here?

FOUNTAINHEAD: Look, I'm the first to say it. I have a problem.

CHUTES&LADDERS: Adam had problems. Eve had problems. Why are *you here?*

FOUNTAINHEAD: To get information.

CHUTES&LADDERS: Go to Wikipedia. Why are you *here?*

FOUNTAINHEAD: Because I smoke crack.

CHUTES&LADDERS: Go to a dealer. Why are you here?

FOUNTAINHEAD: Because I plan to stop smoking crack.

CHUTES&LADDERS: Fine, when your son has a tummy-ache in the middle of the night and walks in on you tweaking and geeking just tell him, "Don't worry, Junior, daddy's sucking on a glass dick—"

HAIKUMOM (overlaps): Hey!

CHUTES&LADDERS: "—but daddy makes 300K and this is all a part of Daddy's Plan!"

FOUNTAINHEAD: I'M A FUCKING CRACKHEAD.

HAIKUMOM: (Apologetic.) Censored.

FOUNTAINHEAD: Fuck you, Chutes&Ladders.

HAIKUMOM: Bleep.

FOUNTAINHEAD: Fuck you . . . Don't talk about my sons. Don't fucking talk about my boys.

HAIKUMOM: Bleep again.

FOUNTAINHEAD: Are you happy, Chutes&Ladders?

CHUTES&LADDERS: Absolutely not, my friend. I'm a crackhead too and I wouldn't wish it on my worst enemy.

FOUNTAINHEAD: And I *made* 300K, I'm currently unemployed. An unemployed crackhead. At least I still have all my teeth. (They laugh.) Better than I can say for my dealer.

CHUTES&LADDERS: (Being a friend.) Ex-dealer, man.

FOUNTAINHEAD: Ex-dealer. Thank you.

HAIKUMOM: Fountainhead, welcome to the dinner party. Granted, it's a party we never wanted to be invited to, but pull up a chair and pass the salt. Some people here may pour it in your wounds. Just like you, we've all crawled on the floor with a flashlight. We've thrown out the brillo and bought some more. But guess what? You had three days. For three days straight, you didn't try to kill yourself on an hourly basis. Please. Talk to your wife about your addiction. You need every supporting resource. You are in for the fight of your life. You mentioned Wharton. I live in Philly. If you're still in the area and you have an emergency or even a craving, email me directly. Any time of night. Don't take it lightly when I say a sober day for you is a sober day for me. I know you can do this but I know you can't do it alone. So stop being a highly functioning isolator and start being a highly dysfunctional *person*. The only way out it is through it.

ORANGUTAN: (Nostalgic.) Slogans . . .

HAIKUMOM: Y'all know I know em all.

CHUTES&LADDERS: They saved my life.

ORANGUTAN: Your personal favorite. Go.

HAIKUMOM: "Nothing changes if nothing changes."

(Elliot appears at the boxing gym, punching a bag. The Ghost watches him.)

GHOST: Momken men-fadluck ted-dini gawaz saffari?

ORANGUTAN: "It came to pass, it didn't come to stay."

FOUNTAINHEAD: "I obsessively pursue feeling good, no matter how bad it makes me feel."

CHUTES&LADDERS: Okay, now!

ORANGUTAN: Nice!

HAIKUMOM: Rookie don't play!

GHOST: Momken men-fadluck ted-dini gawaz saffari?

(Yaz appears with a pen and notepad, writing.)

YAZ: "We are gathered here in remembrance."

ORANGUTAN: "One hit is too many, one thousand never enough."

HAIKUMOM: "Have an at-ti-tude of gra-ti-tude."

CHUTES&LADDERS: "If you are eating a shit sandwich, chances are you ordered it."

ORANGUTAN: Ding ding ding. We have a winner!

HAIKUMOM: Censored. But good one.

YAZ: (Crossing out, scribbling) "Today we send off our beloved, Ginny P. Ortiz."

GHOST: Momken men-fadluck ted-dini gawaz saffari?

HAIKUMOM: (Turning a page in the paper.) Oh shit!

ORANGUTAN: CENSORED!!!!!! YES!!!!!! Whooooooo!

HAIKUMOM: You got me.

ORANGUTAN: (Victorious.) You know how long I've been waiting to do that?!

HAIKUMOM: My sister Ginny's in the *Daily News!* A nice big picture!

GHOST: Momken men-fadluck ted-dini gawaz saffari?

YAZ: (Scribbling, erasing) "Ginny P. Ortiz was known to many as Mami Ginny."

HAIKUMOM: "Ginny P. Ortiz, A Force For Good In Philadelphia!" That's my sister alright! Page 46 . . .

(Haikumom looks for the page. Elliot punches harder. His leg is starting to bother him.)

ELLIOT: Your leg feels great. Your leg feels like a million bucks. No pain. No pain.

HAIKUMOM: (Finding the page) Obituaries? "In lieu of flowers contributions may be made to . . ."

(Haikumom drops the newspaper.
The Ghost blows on Elliot, knocking him to the floor.)

Intermission

Scene 7

(A diner. Odessa and John, aka Fountainhead, sit in a booth.)

ODESSA: To lapsed Catholics. (They clink coffee mugs.) And you thought we had nothing in common.

JOHN: When did you become interested in Buddhism?

ODESSA: My older brother used to terrorize me during mass. He would point to a statue, tell me about the evil spirit hiding behind it. Fangs, claws. I thought Saint Lazarus was gonna come to life and suck my eyes out. Buddhism? Not scary. If there's spirits, they're hiding inside you.

JOHN: Aren't those the scariest kind?

ODESSA: So, how many days do you have? It should be two now.

JOHN: I put my son's picture on my cell phone so if I get the urge, I can just look at him instead.

ODESSA: How many days?

JOHN: (Small talk.) I love Puerto Rico. On my honeymoon we stayed at that hotel in Old San Juan, the old convent. (Odessa shrugs.) And that Spanish fort at the top of the city? El Morro?

ODESSA: I've always been meaning to make it there.

JOHN: There are these keyholes where the cannons used to fit, and the view of the waves through them, you can practically see the Spanish armada approaching.

ODESSA: I mean, one of these days I've gotta make it to PR.

JOHN: Oh. I just figured . . .

ODESSA: The Jersey shore. Atlantic City. The Philadelphia airport. Oh, I've been places.

JOHN: On an actual plane?

ODESSA: I only fly first class, and I'm still saving for that ticket.

(Odessa's cell phone rings.)

JOHN: You're a popular lady.

ODESSA: (Into her phone, her demeanor completely changing.) What? I told you, the diner on Spring Garden and Third. I'm busy, come in an hour. One hour. Now stop calling me and asking fucking directions. (She hangs up.)

JOHN: Says the one who censors.

ODESSA: My sister died.

JOHN: Right. You sure you're okay?

ODESSA: She's dead, ain't nothing left to do. People act like the world is going to fall apart.

JOHN: You write very Zen messages. And yet.

ODESSA: My family knows every button to push.

JOHN: My condolences. (Pause.) You don't strike me as a computer nerd. I used to employ an entire floor of them.

ODESSA: You should've seen me at first, pecking with two fingers. Now I'm like an octopus with ten little tentacles. In my neck of the woods staying clean is like trying to tap dance on a minefield. The website fills the hours. So how are we gonna fill yours, huh? When was the last time you picked up a javelin?

JOHN: Senior year of high school.

ODESSA: (Hands him a sheet of paper.) There's a sober softball league. Fairmount Park, games on Sundays. Sober bowling on Thursdays.

JOHN: I lied in my first post. I've been smoking crack for two years. I've tried quitting hundreds of times. Day two? Please, I'm in the seven hundredth day of hell.

ODESSA: You got it out of your system. Most people lie at one time or another on the site. The good news is, two years in, there's still time. (Hands him another sheet of paper.) Talbot Recovery Center in Atlanta. It's designed for professionals with addictions. Paradise Recovery in Hawaii. They actually check your income before admitting you. Just for the wealthy. This place in Jersey, it's right over the bridge, they have an outpatient program for professionals like you.

JOHN: I'm tenacious. I'm driven. I love my parents.

ODESSA: Pitchforks against tanks.

JOHN: I relish in paying my taxes.

ODESSA: And you could be dead tomorrow. (Pause.) Is your dealer male or female?

JOHN: I had a few. Flushed their numbers down the toilet like you suggested.

ODESSA: Your original connection. The one who got you hooked.

JOHN: Female.

ODESSA: Did you have sex with her?

JOHN: You don't beat around the bush do you?

ODESSA: I'll take that as a yes. (No answer.) Do you prefer sex when you're high to sex when you're sober?

JOHN: I've never really analyzed it.

ODESSA: It can be a dangerous cocktail. Some men get off on smoking and fucking.

JOHN: All men get off on fucking.

ODESSA: Are you scared your wife will find out you're addicted to crack? Or are you scared she'll find out what came of your wedding vows?

JOHN: I should go.

ODESSA: We just ordered.

JOHN: I promised my son. There's a science fair tomorrow. Something about dioramas and crazy glue.

ODESSA: Don't talk about them. Get sober for them.

JOHN: Fuck you.

ODESSA: Leave me three bucks for your coffee.

(He pulls out three dollars. She throws the money back at him.)

You picked up the phone and called me.

JOHN: (He sits down again.) I don't know how to do this. I've never done this before.

ODESSA: I have and it usually doesn't end up so good. One in twenty, maybe, hang around. Most people just don't write one day and then thirty days and then you're wondering . . . And sometimes you get the answer. Cuz their wife looks on their computer and sees the website and logs on and writes, "I found him face down in the snow."

JOHN: How many day ones did you have?

ODESSA: Seven years' worth.

JOHN: Do you still crave?

ODESSA: On the good days, only every hour. Would you rather be honest with your wife, or would you rather end up like me? (Pause.) That wasn't rhetorical.

JOHN: You're not exactly what I wanted to be when I grew up.

ODESSA: Truth. Now we're talking.

(Elliot and Yaz enter.)

YAZ: There she is.

(Elliot and Yaz sit down in the booth.)

ELLIOT: You were supposed to meet us at the flower place.

YAZ: The deposit was due at nine.

ODESSA: My alarm clock didn't go off.

ELLIOT: Were you up on that chat room all night?

ODESSA: (Ignoring him.) Can I get a refill, please?

ELLIOT: Where's the money?

ODESSA: I told you I don't have any money.

ELLIOT: And you think I do? I been paying for Mami Ginny's meds for six months straight—

ODESSA: Well get it from Yaz's mom.

YAZ: My mom put in for the headstone. She got an expensive one.

ODESSA: Headstone? She's getting cremated.

YAZ: She still needs a proper Catholic piece of granite. Right beside abuela, right beside your dad and sister and brother.

ELLIOT: And daughter.

YAZ: Everyone agreed.

ODESSA: No one asked my opinion.

ELLIOT: Everyone who showed up to the family meeting.

ODESSA: I wasn't invited.

YAZ: I texted you twice.

ODESSA: I was out of minutes.

ELLIOT: We just spoke on the phone.

ODESSA: Whatchu want me to do, Elliot, if I say I ain't got no fucking money, I ain't got no money.

JOHN: Hi, I'm John, nice to meet you.

YAZ: Yazmin.

ELLIOT: You one of mom's rehab buddies?

JOHN: We know each other from work.

ELLIOT: You scrub toilets?

ODESSA: (To John.) I'm a practitioner of the custodial arts.

ELLIOT: Is she your sponsor?

JOHN: (To Odessa.) I thought this was going to be a private meeting.

ELLIOT: I'm her son.

JOHN: (To Odessa.) You must have been young.

ELLIOT: But I was raised by my aunt Ginny and that particular aunt just died. (To Odessa.) So now, you got three hours to find some money to pay for one basket of flowers in her funeral.

YAZ: We're all supposed to be helping out.

ODESSA: You both know I run out of minutes all the time. No one could be bothered to drive by and tell me face to face?

ELLIOT: Because you always bothered to drive by and say hello to Mami Ginny when you knew she was sick? Because you bothered to hit me up one time this week and say, "Elliot, I'm sorry your mom died."

ODESSA: You still got one mom alive.

ELLIOT: Really? You want to go there?

YAZ: The flower place needs the money today.

ODESSA: She was my sister and you are my son, too.

YAZ: Guys. Two hundred dollars by end of business day.

ODESSA: That's my rent.

ELLIOT: Then fifty.

ODESSA: I just spent fifty getting my phone back on.

ELLIOT: Ten dollars. For the woman who raised your son! Do we hear ten dollars? Going once!

ODESSA: I spent my last ten at the post office.

ELLIOT: Going twice!

(John goes into his wallet.)

JOHN: Here's fifty.

(They all look at him like he's crazy. He pulls out some more money.)

JOHN: Two hundred?

(Elliot pushes the money back to John with one pointer finger, like the bills might be contaminated.)

ELLIOT: No offense, I don't take money from users.

JOHN: I'm not . . . I think that was my cue.

ODESSA: Sit down. My son was just going.

ELLIOT: Did World's Best Mom here tell you about her daughter?

ODESSA: I'm about to throw this coffee in your fucking face.

YAZ: Come on, Elliot, I'll pay for the flowers.

(Elliot doesn't get up.)

ELLIOT: I looked at that chat room once. The woman I saw there? She's literally not the same person I know. (To John.) Did she tell you how she became such a saint?

JOHN: We all have skeletons.

ELLIOT: Yeah well she's an archaeological dig. Did she tell you about her daughter?

ODESSA: (Suddenly resigned.) Go ahead, I ain't got no secrets.

YAZ: (Getting up.) Excuse me.

ELLIOT: Sit here and listen, Yaz. You were born with a silver spoon and you can't stand how it was for me.

YAZ: I said I'd pay for the goddamn flowers so LET'S GO. NOW!

ELLIOT: My sister and I had the stomach flu, right? For a whole day we couldn't keep nothing down.

ODESSA: Three days . . . You were vomiting three days straight.

ELLIOT: Medicine, juice, anything we ate, it would come right back up. Your co-worker here took us to Children's Hospital.

ODESSA: Jefferson.

ELLIOT: It was wall-to-wall packed. Every kid in Philly had this bug. ERs were turning kids away. They gave us a flier about stomach flu and sent us home. Bright blue paper. Little cartoon diagrams. It said give your kids a spoonful of water every five minutes.

ODESSA: A teaspoon.

ELLIOT: A small enough amount that they can keep it down. Five minutes. Spoon. Five minutes. Spoon. I remember thinking, wow, this is it. Family time. Quality time. Just the three of us. Because it was gentle, the way you said, "Open up." I opened my mouth, you put that little spoon of water into my mouth. That little bit of relief. And then I watched you do the same thing with my little sister. And I remember being like, "Wow, I love you, mom. My moms is alright." Five minutes. Spoon. Five minutes. Spoon. But you couldn't stick to something simple like that. You couldn't sit still like that. You had to have your thing. That's where I stop remembering.

ODESSA: I left.

ELLIOT: A Department of Human Services report. That's my memory. Six hours later a neighbor kicks in the door. Me and my sister are lying in a pile of laundry. My shorts was all messed up. And what I really don't remember is my sister. Quote. "Female infant, approximately two years, pamper and tear ducts dry, likely cause of death, dehydration." Cuz when you dehydrate you can't form a single tear.

JOHN: (To Elliot.) I'm very sorry . . . (He puts some money on the table.) For the coffee. (Exits.)

ELLIOT: That's some friend you got there.

(Pause.)

YAZ: Mary Lou. We never say her name out loud. Mary Lou. Mary Lou. (To Odessa.) One time you came to babysit me, you brought Elliot and Mary Lou—she had just learned to use a straw and she had this soda from 7-Eleven. She didn't want to give me a sip. You yelled at her so bad, you totally cursed her out and I said, "You're not supposed to yell at people like that!" And you said, "No, Yaz, she's gotta learn that y'all are cousins, y'all are flesh and blood, and we share everything. In this family we share everything." You walked out of the room, came back from the kitchen with four straws, sat us down on the floor in a circle, pointed to me and said, "You first." I took a sip. "Elliot's turn." He sipped. "Mary Lou's turn." She sipped. Then you sipped. You made us do like that, taking turns, going around the circle, til that cup was empty.

(Odessa hands Elliot a key.)

ODESSA: The pawn shop closes at five. Go into my house. Take my computer. Pawn it. However much you get, put towards a few flowers, okay?

(Odessa exits.)

Scene 8

(Split scene. Odessa's living room and the chat room. Chutes&Ladders holds a phone.)

ORANGUTAN: Did you hit the call button yet?

CHUTES&LADDERS: I'm working on it.

ORANGUTAN: Where are you? Are you at home?

CHUTES&LADDERS: *Jeopardy!*'s on mute.

ORANGUTAN: Dude, turn off the tube. This is serious. Did you even dial?

CHUTES&LADDERS: Yeah, yeah. (He does.) Alright, it's ringing. What am I going to say?

ORANGUTAN: "Hi, Son, it's Dad."

CHUTES&LADDERS: Wendell. That's his name. (Hangs up.) No answer.

ORANGUTAN: As in, you hung up?

CHUTES&LADDERS: Yes. I hung up.

ORANGUTAN: Dude, way too quick!

CHUTES&LADDERS: What do you have, a stop watch? Do you know the average time before someone answers a telephone?

ORANGUTAN: 3.2 rings.

CHUTES&LADDERS: According to . . .

ORANGUTAN: I don't reveal my sources.

CHUTES&LADDERS: Look, my son's a grown man with a good life.

ORANGUTAN: Quit moping and dial Wendell's number.

CHUTES&LADDERS: This Japan thing is cramping my style. Different networks, different time zones. No concurrent *Jeopardy!* watching.

ORANGUTAN: Deflection: nostalgia.

CHUTES&LADDERS: Humor me.

ORANGUTAN: (Humoring him.) How's my little Trebeky doing?

CHUTES&LADDERS: He's had work done. Man looks younger than he did twenty years ago.

ORANGUTAN: Needle or knife?

CHUTES&LADDERS: Needle. His eyes are still in the right place.

ORANGUTAN: Well, it's working. Meow. Purrrrr. Any good categories?

CHUTES&LADDERS: Before and After.

ORANGUTAN: I love Before and After! But I'll go with . . . Quit Stalling for two hundred. (She hums the *Jeopardy!* theme.)

CHUTES&LADDERS: It's ringing.

ORANGUTAN: My stopwatch is running.

CHUTES&LADDERS: Still ringing.

ORANGUTAN: You're going to be great.

CHUTES&LADDERS: It rang again.

ORANGUTAN: You're a brave soul.

(We hear a man's voice at the other end of the line say, "Hello?" Chutes&Ladders hangs up.)

CHUTES&LADDERS: He must not be around.

ORANGUTAN: Leave a voice mail.

CHUTES&LADDERS: Maybe next time.

(Chutes&Ladders logs off.)

ORANGUTAN: Hey! Don't log off, come on. Chutes&Ladders. Whatever happened to tough love? Log back on, we'll do a crossword. You can't fly before "Final Jeopardy!" Sigh. Anyone else online? Haikumom? I'm still waiting for that daily poem . . . Bueller? Bueller?

(In Odessa's living room, Elliot and Yaz enter.)

YAZ: Wow, look at that computer. Stone age.

ELLIOT: Fred Flinstone shit.

YAZ: Positively Dr. Who.

ELLIOT: Dr. Who?

YAZ: That computer is actually worse than what they give the adjuncts at Swarthmore.

ELLIOT: What does "adjunct" even mean?

YAZ: Exactly. It's the nicest thing she owns.

ELLIOT: Let's not act like this is some heroic sacrifice. Like this makes her the world's martyr.

YAZ: We're not going to get more than fifteen bucks for it.

ELLIOT: Symbols matter, Yaz. This isn't about the money. This is shaking hands. This is tipping your hat. This is holding the door open. This is the bare minimum, the least effort possible to earn the label "person." (Looks at the screen.) What do you think her password is? (Types.) "Odessa." Nope. "Odessaortiz." Nope.

YAZ: It's probably Elliot.

(He types. Haikumom's log-on appears.)

ELLIOT: The irony.

YAZ: I think legally that might be like breaking and entering.

ELLIOT: (Typing.) Hello? Oh shit it posted.

ORANGUTAN: Haikumom! Hit me with those seventeen syllables, baby!

YAZ: Haikumom? What the hell is that?

ELLIOT: Her username. She has the whole world thinking she's some Chinese prophet.

YAZ: Haiku are Japanese.

ELLIOT: "Haiku are Japanese." (Typing.) Hello, Orangutan. How are you?

ORANGUTAN: (Formal.) I am fine. How are you?

ELLIOT: (Typing.) So, I guess you like monkeys, huh?

ORANGUTAN: An orangutan is a primate.

YAZ: Elliot.

ELLIOT: Chill.

ORANGUTAN: And this primate has ninety-eight days. That deserves a poem, don't you think?

ELLIOT: (Typing.) I don't have a poem, but I have a question. What does crack feel like?

ORANGUTAN: What?

YAZ: Elliot, cut it out.

ELLIOT: (Typing.) Sometimes I'm amazed I don't know firsthand.

ORANGUTAN: Who is this?

ELLIOT: (Typing.) How does it make your brain feel?

ORANGUTAN: Like it's flooded with dopamine. Listen, cyberstalker, if you came here for shits and giggles, we are a sadly unfunny bunch.

ELLIOT: (Typing.) Are you just a smoker or do you inject it right into your eyeballs?

ORANGUTAN: Who the fuck is this?

ELLIOT: (Typing.) Haikumom.

ORANGUTAN: Bullshit, you didn't censor me. Quit screwing around, hacker, who are you?

YAZ: You think Ginny would want you acting this way?

ELLIOT: I think Mami Ginny would want Mami Odessa to pay for a single flower on her fucking casket.

YAZ: (Types.) This is not Haikumom. It's her son.

ORANGUTAN: Well, if you're looking for the friends and family thread, you have to go to the home page and create a new logon. This particular forum is for people actually in recovery. Wait, her son the actor? From the Crest ad?

ELLIOT: (Typing.) Colgate.

ORANGUTAN: "Sonrisa baby!" I saw that on YouTube! Your teeth are insanely white. Ever worked in Hollywood?

ELLIOT: (Typing.) Psh. I just had this guy begging me to do a feature film. Gritty, documentary-style, about Marines in Iraq. I just don't want to do anything cheesy.

ORANGUTAN: So you're the war hero . . .

ELLIOT: (Typing.) Haikumom brags.

ORANGUTAN: How's your recovery going? (No answer.) This is the crack forum, but there's a really good pain-meds forum on this site, too. Link here.

YAZ: What is she talking about?

ORANGUTAN: There's a few war vets on that forum, just like you. You'd be in good company.

YAZ: Pain meds? Elliot? (He doesn't respond. Yaz types.) What are you talking about?

ORANGUTAN: Haikumom told us about your history.

YAZ: (Typing.) What history?

ORANGUTAN: Sorry. Maybe she told us in confidence.

ELLIOT: Confidence? They call this shit "world wide" for a reason.

YAZ: (Typing.) I can search all the threads right now.

ORANGUTAN: That you had a bunch of leg surgeries in Iraq. That if a soldier said they hurt, the docs practically threw pills at them. That you OD'd three times and were in the hospital for it. She was real messed up about it. I guess she had hoped the fruit would fall a little farther from the tree.

YAZ: (To Elliot.) Is this true?

ELLIOT: I wasn't a soldier. I was a Marine. Soldiers is the army.

YAZ: Oh my god.

ELLIOT: (Takes the keyboard, types.) What I am: sober. What I am not and never will be: a pathetic junkie like you.

(He unplugs the computer. He throws the keyboard on the ground. He starts unplugging cables violently.)

YAZ: Hold on. Just stop it, Elliot! Stop it!

ELLIOT: The one time I ever reached out to her for anything and she made me a story on a website.

YAZ: Why wouldn't you ask me for help? Why would you deal with that alone?

ELLIOT: The opposite of alone. I seen barracks that looked like dope houses. It was four months in my life, it's over. We've chopped up a lot of shit together, Yaz, but we ain't gonna chop this up. This shit stays in the vault. You got me?

YAZ: No!

ELLIOT: Yaz. (He looks her straight in the eye.) Please. Please.

YAZ: I want to grab the sky and smash it into pieces. Are you clean?

ELLIOT: The only thing I got left from those days is the nightmares. That's when he came, and some days I swear he ain't never gonna leave.

YAZ: Who?

(Elliot tries to walk away from the conversation, but the Ghost is there, blocking his path.)

Who?!

ELLIOT: (Almost like a child.) Please, Yaz. Please end this conversation. Don't make me beg, Yaz.

YAZ: The pawn shop closes in fifteen minutes. I'll get the monitor, you grab the computer.

Scene 9

(Chutes&Ladders is at work, on his desk phone. A bundled pile of mail is on his desk. He takes off the rubber band, browses. Junk, mostly.)

CHUTES&LADDERS: (Into the work phone.) That's right. Three W's. Dot. Not the word, the punctuation mark. I-R-S. Not F like flamingo, S like Sam. Dot. Yup, another one. Gov. Grover orange victor.

(Orangutan appears, online.)

ORANGUTAN: I'm doing it. I'm almost there. *And* I can chat! Japan is so advanced. Internet cafés are like parking meters here.

CHUTES&LADDERS: Where are you and what are you doing?

ORANGUTAN: Sapporo train station. Just did some research. Get this: in the early 80's, they straightened all the rivers in Hokkaido.

CHUTES&LADDERS: Why?

ORANGUTAN: To create jobs the government straightened the rivers! Huge bodies of water, manual laborers, scientists, engineers, bulldozers, and the rivers became straight! How nuts is that?

CHUTES&LADDERS: People can't leave good enough alone. Why are humans so damn restless?

ORANGUTAN: It's not restlessness. It's ego. Massive, bizarre ego.

CHUTES&LADDERS: Can't let a river be a river. (Into the phone.) The forms link is on the left.

ORANGUTAN: Now it's the aughts, people keep being born, jobs still need creating, but there's no curves left to straighten, so, drum roll, the government is beginning a new program to put all the original turns back in the rivers! Ever heard of Kushiro?

CHUTES&LADDERS: Is that your new boyfriend's name?

ORANGUTAN: Ha. Ha ha ha. It's home of the hundred-mile-long Kushiro River, which is the pilot project, the first river they're trying to re-curve.

CHUTES&LADDERS: Kushiro River. Got it. Burned in the brain. One day I'll win a Trivial Pursuits wedge with that. (Into the phone.) You, too, ma'am. (He hangs up.)

ORANGUTAN: My train to Kushiro leaves in twenty minutes. My heart is pounding.

CHUTES&LADDERS: I don't follow.

ORANGUTAN: Kushiro is the town where I was born. I'm going. I'm doing it.

CHUTES&LADDERS: Hold on, now you're throwing curve balls.

ORANGUTAN: In my hand is a sheet of paper. On the paper is the address of the house where my birth parents once lived. I'm going to knock on their door.

(Chutes&Ladder's desk phone rings.)

CHUTES&LADDERS: (Into the phone.) Help desk, please hold. (To Orangutan.) How long have you had that address for?

ORANGUTAN: It's been burning a hole in my pocket for two days. I hounded my mom before I left Maine. She finally wrote down the name of the adoption agency. The first clue, the first evidence of who I was I ever had. I made a vow to myself, if I could stay sober for three months, I would track my parents down. So a few days ago class ended early, I went to the agency, showed my passport, and thirty minutes later I had an address on a piece of paper. Ask me anything about Kushiro. All I've done the last two days is research it. I'm an expert. Population, 190,000. There's a tech school, there's an airport.

CHUTES&LADDERS: Why are you telling me this? To get my blessing?

ORANGUTAN: I tell you about the things I do.

CHUTES&LADDERS: You don't want my opinion, you want my approval.

ORANGUTAN: Hand it over.

CHUTES&LADDERS: No.

ORANGUTAN: Don't get monosyllabic.

CHUTES&LADDERS: Take that piece of paper and use it as kindling for a warm winter fire.

ORANGUTAN: Jeez, what did they slip into your Wheaties this morning?

CHUTES&LADDERS: Do a ritual burning and never look back. You have three months. Do you know the worth in gold of three months? Don't give yourself a reason to go back to the shadows.

ORANGUTAN: I'm in recovery. I have no illusions about catharsis. I realize what will most likely happen is nothing. Maybe something tiny. A microscopic butterfly flapping her microscopic wings.

CHUTES&LADDERS: Live in the past, follow your ass.

ORANGUTAN: Don't you have the slightest ambition?

CHUTES&LADDERS: Yes, and I achieve it every day. Don't use and don't hurt anyone. Two things

I used to do on a daily basis. I don't do them anymore. Done. Dream realized. No more dreaming.

(His phone rings again.)

(Into the phone.) Continue holding, please.

ORANGUTAN: When was the last time you went out on a limb?

CHUTES&LADDERS: Three odd weeks ago.

ORANGUTAN: Did you try Hazelnut instead of French Roast?

CHUTES&LADDERS: There's a new secretary down the hall, she's got a nice smile. I decided to go say hello. We had a little back and forth, I said, let's have lunch, she said maybe but meant no, I turned away, looked down and my tie was floating in my coffee cup.

ORANGUTAN: I waited three months to tell you this, every step of the way, the train ride, what the river looks like. What their front door looks like. (Pause.) I'm quitting this site. I hate this site. I fucking hate this site.

CHUTES&LADDERS: You're already losing it and you haven't even gotten on the train.

ORANGUTAN: Three days ago I suggested you and I meet face to face and you blew a fucking gasket.

CHUTES&LADDERS: That's what this is about?

ORANGUTAN: Don't flatter yourself. This is about me wanting relationships. With humans, not ones and zeroes. So we were once junkies. It's superficial. It's not real friendship.

CHUTES&LADDERS: I beg to differ.

ORANGUTAN: Prove me wrong.

CHUTES&LADDERS: Search down that address and a hundred bucks says your heart comes back a shattered light bulb.

ORANGUTAN: You mean, gasp, I'll actually FEEL something?

CHUTES&LADDERS: What are you going to do if the address is wrong? What if the building's been bulldozed? What if some new tenant lives there? What if the woman who gave you birth then gave you away answers the door?

ORANGUTAN: I DON'T KNOW! A concept you clearly avoid at all costs. Learn how to live, that's all I'm goddamn trying to do!

(His phone rings. He picks up the receiver and hangs it up.)

CHUTES&LADDERS: I have three grandsons. You know how I know that? Because I rang my son's doorbell one day. Step 9, make amends. And his wife answered, and I don't blame her for hating me. But I saw three little boys in that living room and one of those boys said, "Daddy, who's that man at the door?" And my son said to *my grandson*, "I don't know. He must be lost." My son came outside, closed the door behind him, exchanged a few cordial words and then asked me to go.

ORANGUTAN: So I shouldn't even try.

CHUTES&LADDERS: I had five years sober until that day.

ORANGUTAN: You really believe in your heart of hearts I should not even try. (Pause.) Coward.

(His phone rings. He unplugs the phone line.)

CHUTES&LADDERS: You think it's easy being your friend?

ORANGUTAN: Sissy. You walk the goddamn earth scared of your own shadow, getting smaller and smaller, until you disappear.

CHUTES&LADDERS: You tease me. You insult me. It's like breathing to you.

ORANGUTAN: You fucking idiot. Why do little girls tease little boys on the playground at recess? Why the fuck were cooties invented? You fucking imbecile!

CHUTES&LADDERS: You disappeared for three months. I couldn't sleep for three months!

ORANGUTAN: I wanted to impress you. I wanted to log on and show you I could be better. And I was an idiot because you're just looking for cowards like you. I'm logging off. This is it. It's over.

CHUTES&LADDERS: Orangutan.

ORANGUTAN: Into the abyss I climb, looking for a flesh and blood hand to grasp onto.

CHUTES&LADDERS: Little monkey, stop it.

ORANGUTAN: I'm in the station. My train is in five minutes, you gave me all the motivational speech I need, I'm going to the platform, I'm getting on the train, I'm going to see the house where I was born.

(She logs off. Chutes&Ladders grabs his phone and hurls it into his wastebasket. He throws his calculator, his mail pile, his pen cup to the ground. Left on his desk is one padded envelope.)

CHUTES&LADDERS: "To Chutes&Ladders Wilkie." "From Haikumom Ortiz."

(He rips it open, pulls out a deflated orange water wing, puts it over his hand.)

Scene 10

(Split scene. Lights rise on a church. Elliot and Yaz stand at the lectern.)

YAZ: It is time to honor a woman.*

ELLIOT: A woman who built her community with a hammer and nails.

YAZ: A woman who knew her nation's history. Its African roots. European roots. Indigenous roots. A woman who refused to be enslaved but lived to serve.

ELLIOT: A carpenter, a nurse, a comedian, a cook.

YAZ: Eugenia Ortiz.

ELLIOT: Mami Ginny.

(Lights rise on Odessa's house. She sits on her floor. She scoops a spoonful of water from a mug, pours it onto the floor in a slow ribbon.)

YAZ: She grew vegetables in her garden lot and left the gate open so anyone could walk in and pick dinner off the vine.

ELLIOT: She drank beer and told dirty jokes and even the never-crack-a-smile church ladies would be rolling laughing.

YAZ: She told me every time I visited, "Yaz, you're going to Juilliard."

---

*This eulogy is inspired by and owes much debt to Roger Zepernick's eulogy for Eugenia Burgos.

ELLIOT: Every morning when I left for school, "Elliot, nobody can make you invisible but you."

(Lights rise on the Sapporo train station. Orangutan is on the platform. We hear a loudspeaker boarding announcement in Japanese.)

YAZ: Zero.

ELLIOT: Birth children.

YAZ: One.

ELLIOT: Adopted son.

(Odessa pours another spoonful of water on the floor. Again, it creates a slow ribbon.)

YAZ: Three.

ELLIOT: Years in the army nurse corps.

YAZ: Three.

ELLIOT: Arrests for civil disobedience. I was in Iraq and she was demonstrating for peace.

YAZ: Forty seven.

ELLIOT: Wheelchair ramps she installed in homes with disabled children or elderly.

(Odessa pours another spoonful of water to the floor. A small pool is forming.)

YAZ: Twelve.

ELLIOT: Abandoned lots she turned into city-recognized public gardens.

(Another spoonful.)

YAZ: Twenty-two.

ELLIOT: Godchildren recognized by this church.

(Another spoonful.)

YAZ: One hundred and thirty.

ELLIOT: Abandoned homes she refurbished and sold to young families.

(In the Sapporo station we hear a final loud-speaker boarding announcement. Orangutan is still on the platform. She seems frozen, like she cannot move.)

YAZ: All while having a fresh pot of rice and beans on the stove every night. For any hungry stranger. And the pilgrims stopped. And they planted roots, because she was here. We are the living, breathing proof.

427

ELLIOT: I am the standing . . . Excuse me.

(He exits.)

YAZ: Elliot is the standing, walking testimony to a life. She. Was. Here.

(Odessa turns the cup upside down. It is empty.)

Scene 11

(Chutes&Ladders at his desk. In front of him: an inflated orange water wing.)

CHUTES&LADDERS: (On the phone.) Yeah, it's a 1995 Tercel. Midnight blue. It's got a few miles. A hundred and twenty thousand. But like I said, I'll give it to you for three hundred below Kelley Blue Book. Yup, automatic. Just got new brake pads. Cassette deck, mint condition. I'll even throw in a few tapes. Tina Turner and Lionel Richie. Oh, hold on, call waiting.

(He presses mute. Sings to himself.)

A tisket, a tasket.

A green and yellow basket.

I bought a basket for my mommy.

On the way I dropped it.

Was it red? No no no no!
Was it brown? No no no no!

(Back into the phone.) Sorry about that. I got someone else interested. No, it's alright, I have them on hold. You need to see this thing tonight if you're serious. I put this listing up thirty minutes ago, my phone is ringing off the hook. 6:30? Hey I didn't mention. Little lady has racing stripes.

Scene 12

(Split scene. Lights rise in the Sapporo train station, same as before. Orangutan has laid down on the platform and fallen asleep, her backpack like a pillow.

Lights rise on Odessa's house, that night. Her phone rings. We hear loud knocking.)

ELLIOT: (Offstage.) Mami Odessa! Open the door!

(More ringing.)

ELLIOT: (Offstage.) Yo, mom!

YAZ: (Offstage.) She's not there.

ELLIOT: (Offstage.) Can't you hear her phone ringing? Move out the way.

YAZ: (Offstage.) Be careful, your leg!

(A few kicks and the door bursts open. Yaz and Elliot enter, switch on the lights. Odessa is in a heap, motionless, on the floor. Yaz runs and holds Odessa in her arms.)

YAZ: Oh shit. Odessa! Odessa! Wake up.

(She slaps her face a few times.)

YAZ: Her pulse is racing. (Yaz opens her cell phone, dials.)

(Elliot finds a spoon on the floor.)

ELLIOT: Oh no. Oh no you fucking didn't! MOM!!! Get up!

YAZ: (Into the phone.) Hi, I need an ambulance. I have someone unconscious here. I think it's an overdose, crack cocaine. Yes, she has a pulse. 33 Ontario Street. No, no seizures, she's just a lump. Well what should we do while we wait? Okay. Yes. (She hangs up.) They're on their way. Elevate her feet.

ELLIOT: Help me get her to the sofa. One, two, three.

(Elliot lifts her with Yaz's help. They struggle under her weight. In fact they lift the air. Odessa stands up, lucid, and watches the action: Elliot and Yaz struggling under her invisible weight.)

YAZ: Watch her head.

ELLIOT: Aw, fuck, my leg.

YAZ: Careful.

(They set "Odessa" on the sofa, while Odessa watches, unseen, calm.)

ODESSA: I must be in the terminal. Between flights. The layover.

YAZ: Oh god, not two in one day, please.

ELLIOT: She's been through this shit a million times. She's a survivor! WAKE UP! Call your mom. She'll get here before the ambulance.

(Yaz dials.)

ODESSA: I've been to the airport, one time. My dad flew here from Puerto Rico. First time

I was gonna meet him. We stood by the baggage claim, his flight was late, we waited forever. There was one single, lone suitcase, spinning around a carousel.

YAZ: (To Elliot.) Voice mail. (Into the phone.) Mom? Call me back immediately, it's an emergency.

ELLIOT: Give me that. (Grabs the phone.) Titi, Odessa fucking OD'd and she's dying in her living room and I can't take this anymore! COME GET US before I walk off and leave her on the sofa! (He hangs up.)

YAZ: If you need to, go. No guilt. I got this.

ELLIOT: She's my *mom.* Can I be angry? Can you let me be angry?

YAZ: Why is this family plagued? (Elliot gets up.) Where are you going?

ELLIOT: To find something fragile.

(He exits. We hear something shatter.)

ODESSA: Everyone had cleared away from the carousel. Everyone had their bags. But this one was unclaimed. It could still be there for all I know. Spiraling. Spinning. Looking for an owner. Abandoned.

(In the Sapporo station, a policeman enters with a bright, beaming flashlight and points it at Orangutan.

In Odessa's house, a radiant white light suddenly pours in from above. Odessa looks up, is overwhelmed. It is beautiful. Yaz sees it.)

YAZ: Dear god, do you see that?

ELLIOT: (Enters, looks up, not seeing it.) What?

YAZ: (To Odessa.) It's okay Odessa, go, go, we love you, I love you Titi, you are good, you *are* good. Oh my god, she's beautiful.

ELLIOT: What are you talking about?

YAZ: It's okay, it's okay. We love you Odessa.

POLICEMAN: (In Japanese.) Miss, miss, are you okay?

ORANGUTAN: (Waking.) English, please.

POLICEMAN: No sleeping on the floor.

ORANGUTAN: (Getting up slowly.) Sorry.

POLICEMAN: Are you sick?

ORANGUTAN: No.

POLICEMAN: Are you intoxicated?

ORANGUTAN: No. I'm very sorry. I just got tired. I'll go. I'm going.

POLICEMAN: Please, can I give you a hand?

ORANGUTAN: No. I got it.

(Orangutan exits. The policeman turns off his flashlight, exits.

The sound of an ambulance siren and suddenly the white light disappears. Odessa crawls onto the couch and slips into Yaz's arms, where she's been all along.)

YAZ: Holy shit . . .

ELLIOT: What's happening, Yaz? What the fuck was that?

YAZ: You've got to forgive her, Elliot. You have to.

Scene 13

(The chat room.)

CHUTES&LADDERS: Oh nagging wives? Orangutan? Hello? Earth to Orangutan. Come on, three days straight I been worrying about you. I have time-sensitive information. Ground control to major Orangutan.

ORANGUTAN: Ta da.

CHUTES&LADDERS: Where you been?

ORANGUTAN: Here. There. Morrisey and Nine Inch Nails on loop.

CHUTES&LADDERS: Is that what the kids like these days?

ORANGUTAN: (Rolls eyes.) That was me rolling my eyes.

CHUTES&LADDERS: Guess what I did.

ORANGUTAN: (She shrugs.) That was me shrugging.

CHUTES&LADDERS: Guess.

ORANGUTAN: Guess what I didn't do?

CHUTES&LADDERS: Meet your birth parents?

ORANGUTAN: Board the train.

CHUTES&LADDERS: Sorry.

ORANGUTAN: Don't apologize. You had my number.

CHUTES&LADDERS: Guess what I did.

ORANGUTAN: Told me so. Had my shit pegged.

CHUTES&LADDERS: I sold my Tercel. My plane lands in Narita Airport on Wednesday.

ORANGUTAN: What?

CHUTES&LADDERS: American Airlines flight 3312. Arriving 10:01 A.M.

ORANGUTAN: You're a dumb ass. Tokyo? Do you have any idea how far that is from Hokkaido? And how much a ticket on the train costs? Oy, and how the hell am I going to get out of teaching that day? Oh, you doll-face, you duckie!

CHUTES&LADDERS: I'll be wearing a jean jacket and a Padres cap. That's how you'll know me.

ORANGUTAN: Oh Chutes&Ladders. You old bag of bones, you! You old so-and-so, you mensch, you human being! Why the hell didn't you tell me?

CHUTES&LADDERS: I'm just hoping I have the guts to get on the plane.

ORANGUTAN: Of course you're getting on that damn plane! For me you did this?

(Fountainhead logs on.)

FOUNTAINHEAD: Hey everyone. I managed to find one computer here at the hospital that works. Odessa asked me to post a message on her behalf. She landed on "Go." Hit reset on the timer. Back to day one.

ORANGUTAN: Who's Odessa?

FOUNTAINHEAD: Sorry. Haikumom.

ORANGUTAN: What? Do you log on here just to mock us?

CHUTES&LADDERS: Hold on, is she okay?

FOUNTAINHEAD: Cardiac arrest. They said she was one hair from a coma. She hadn't used in six years and her system went nuts.

CHUTES&LADDERS: So she's alive?

FOUNTAINHEAD: And just barely ticking. Tubes in and out of her nose. She's responsive, she mumbled a few words.

ORANGUTAN: You can't be serious.

CHUTES&LADDERS: Why are you there? Were you using with her?

FOUNTAINHEAD: No.

CHUTES&LADDERS: Did you sell her the stuff?

FOUNTAINHEAD: No, Jesus, of course not. She gave them my number, I'm her emergency contact. Why, I have no idea, we're practically strangers. Getting here to the hospital, seeing her like that . . . I don't mean this as an insult, but she looked not human. Bones with skin covering. Mummy-like.

ORANGUTAN: Fuck. You.

FOUNTAINHEAD: I'm being descriptive. I'm being honest. The thought of my boys walking in on me like that. My wife finding me . . .

ORANGUTAN: That woman is the reason I'm. Oh god, you get complacent for one second! One second! You get comfortable for one minute!

CHUTES&LADDERS: Fountainhead, does she have family there? Has anyone come through her room?

FOUNTAINHEAD: Apparently a son and a niece but they had to catch a flight to San Juan.

CHUTES&LADDERS: No parents? No other children? A friend? A neighbor?

FOUNTAINHEAD: None showed up.

CHUTES&LADDERS: Fountainhead. You have a family, I absolutely understand that, and I mean zero disrespect when I say, when I beg of you this: your job on this earth has just changed. It's not to be a husband or a father or a CEO. It's to stay by that woman's side. Make sure she gets home safe. Bathe her. Feed her. Get her checked into a rehab, inpatient. Do not leave her side for a second. Can you do this?

FOUNTAINHEAD: I have one day clean. I'm not meant to be a saint.

CHUTES&LADDERS: Tell me now, swear on your mother's name, otherwise I'm on the first flight to Philadelphia.

FOUNTAINHEAD: I don't know.

CHUTES&LADDERS: Look man, do you believe in God?

FOUNTAINHEAD: Sure, along with unicorns and the boogeyman.

CHUTES&LADDERS: How about miracles?

FOUNTAINHEAD: When the Phils are winning.

CHUTES&LADDERS: How about actions? I bet you believe in those.

FOUNTAINHEAD: Yeah.

CHUTES&LADDERS: Your lifeboat has just arrived. Get on board or get out of the way.

FOUNTAINHEAD: I'll take care of Odessa. You have my word. My solemn word. (Pause.) She did manage to say one thing. Someone has to take over site admin. She doesn't want the chatroom full of curse words.

(Fountainhead's phone rings.)

I gotta go.

CHUTES&LADDERS: You gave us your word. Don't be a stranger.

(He logs off. Into the phone.)

FOUNTAINHEAD: Hi, honey, sorry I haven't called sooner. Listen, I'm not coming home tonight, just order in. I have a friend who got sick, she's having an emergency. No, it's not a romantic friend but she needs my help. Honey? Honey . . .

(The call is over.)

Scene 14

(Puerto Rico. A hotel room. Yaz works on her laptop as a screen lights up:)

FREEDOM&NOISE
STATUS: ONLINE

FREEDOM&NOISE: Hello, I am Freedom&Noise. Current location: Rainforest B&B, Puerto Rico. This is my job app for interim site admin. Experience with chat rooms: zero. Experience with drugs: one doobie in high school. But Fountainhead said it was up to you guys if you would have me so please hear me out. Haikumom is my aunt. For a few years she was my crazy babysitter. The baddest hide-and-seek player north of Girard Avenue. Dress up, booby traps, forts. Until I was eight and, poof, she disappeared. New babysitter, zero explanation. So my first Thanksgiving home from college I walk in and there's Haikumom, stuffing pasteles in the kitchen. Hadn't seen her in ten years. "What up, little niece? Congratulations on college." She planted a big wet one on my cheek and pulled a necklace from her shirt and said, "You know what these gold letters mean? The N is for Narcotics, the A is for Anonymous, and today is my two-year anniversary of being clean." (Pause) I remember sitting next to her at that Thanksgiving table, this question first rooting itself deep in my gut. "What did I do to earn all that I have? Have I done anything difficult in my whole life?" So if you'll have me while Haikumom recovers, I'll be paying a babysitter back for all the times she let me win at Uno. Five-seven-five right? (Counting syllables on her fingers) Box full of ashes . . .

(Elliot enters from the bathroom, freshly showered, pulling on a shirt.)

ELLIOT: Whatchu looking at, Willis?

YAZ: Sh. I'm counting syllables.

(Elliot looks over her shoulders at the computer.)

ELLIOT: Hold up. Don't read that shit, Yaz.

YAZ: You know how Odessa got into haiku in the first place?

ELLIOT: For real, close the computer.

YAZ: I went through this Japanese minimalist phase freshman year. Rock Gardens, Zen Buddhism, the works. I gave her a haiku collection for Christmas.

ELLIOT: Yeah, and you gave me a midget tree that died by New Year's.

YAZ: Bonsai. You didn't water it.

ELLIOT: (Closing her laptop.) For the two days I'm away from Philly, let me be away from Philly?

YAZ: You know where I was gonna be by thirty? Two kids. Equal-housework marriage. Tenure, no question. Waaaay tenured, like by the age of twenty-four. Carnegie Hall debuts Yazmin Ortiz's "Oratorio for Electric Guitar and Children's Choir." I wrote a list on a piece of paper and dug a hole in Fairmount Park and put it in the ground and said, "When I turn thirty, I'll dig it up and cross it all off." And I promise you I'll never have the courage to go to that spot with a shovel and face my list full of crumbs, decoys, and bandaids.

ELLIOT: Married with kids, what an awful goal.

YAZ: Odessa's done things.

ELLIOT: Well, when you throw her a parade, don't expect me to come.

YAZ: You've done things.

ELLIOT: I wouldn't come to my own parade either.

YAZ: Ginny did things. What have I done?

ELLIOT: Second-grade Language Arts. You glued my book report.

YAZ: I couldn't stop your leg from getting chewed up.

ELLIOT: Fairmount little league basketball. You kept score, you brought our equipment.

YAZ: I didn't hold your hand when you were in the desert popping pills trying to make yourself disappear. I didn't keep Odessa away from that needle. I didn't water a single plant in Ginny's garden. We're in PR and I'm gonna dig a new hole and I'm not putting a wish or a list in there, I'm putting a scream in there. And I'm gonna sow it like the ugliest foulest and most necessary seed in the world and it's going to bloom! This time it's going to fucking bloom!

ELLIOT: My eyes just did this weird thing. For a second, it was Mom standing in front of me.

YAZ: Odessa?

ELLIOT: Ginny.

YAZ: Elliot, your birth mother saved your life by giving you away. You think she's the one holding you back? Nobody can make you invisible but you.

(Elliot doesn't respond. Yaz begins gathering her stuff hastily.)

Now we got some ashes to throw. El Yunque closes in an hour and a half.

ELLIOT: Maybe we should do this tomorrow.

YAZ: I gotta make a call. I'll be in the lobby!

(She exits.)

ELLIOT: Yaz?

(The Ghost appears. He's probably been there the whole time.)

Yaz!

GHOST: Momken men-fadluck ted-dini gawaz saffari?

(The Ghost reaches out his hand to touch Elliot.)

Momken men-fadluck ted-dini gawaz saffari?

(The second they make contact, Elliot spins on his heels and grabs the Ghost. The Ghost defends himself, pulling away. They start pushing, grabbing, fighting. The Ghost is looking for something—is it Elliot's wallet?)

Momken men-fadluck ted-dini gawaz saffari?

(The Ghost finds Elliot's wallet and tears through it, hurling its contents onto the floor. Elliot attacks again, but this time the Ghost reaches out his hand and touches Elliot's face. Elliot freezes, unable to move, as the Ghost's hands glide across his features, considering each one with authority, taking inventory.)

Momken men-fadluck ted-dini gawaz saffari?

(The Ghost is gone. Elliot catches his breath, shaken. He reaches into his pocket and pulls out a bottle of pills. He puts one pill in his hand. Then he empties the entire bottle of pills into his hand. He stares at the pills, wanting to throw them away.)

Scene 15

(Split scene. Odessa's bathroom. The bathtub is filled with water. John enters, carrying a very weak Odessa. Odessa is wearing shorts and a bra, a modest outfit for bathing. John lowers her gently into the bathtub.)

JOHN: Does that feel okay?

(Odessa barely nods.)

It's not too hot or cold?

(Odessa shakes her head.)

I don't know how to do this. These are things women do. Take care of sick people. Make the wounds go away.

(He takes a sponge and starts to bathe her.)

Is this okay?

(He lifts her arms and washes her armpits. Embarrassed at first, but quickly gets the swing of it.)

We check you in at 4:30 so we have plenty of time to clean you up and get you in good clothes, okay? You'll go in there looking like a decent woman.

(He stops.)

I spoke to my wife while you were sleeping. I told her to go under my bookmarks, find the website. I gave her my logon, my password. She's probably reading it right now. So, uh, thank you.

(Odessa whispers something inaudible.)

What was that?

(She gestures for him to lean in. She whispers into his ear.)

One more time.

(She whispers a little louder.)

Did someone take swimming lessons?

(She whispers again.)

Did someone put on water wings?

(She nods. He continues to bathe her, gently, in silence as:

Lights rise on Tokyo. Narita Airport. Orangutan sits on the floor by the luggage carousel. At her feet is a sign that says CHUTES&LADDERS. She throws the sign like a Frisbee across the floor and gets up to leave. Chutes&Ladders enters, rolling a suitcase behind him. He waves to Orangutan.)

CHUTES&LADDERS: Orangutan?

ORANGUTAN: What the holy hell?

CHUTES&LADDERS: Sorry. Sorry. I tried calling but my cell doesn't work here. I told you I'm no good at this fancy kind of living.

ORANGUTAN: You were supposed to land yesterday, you were too scared to get on the plane. You rebook, you were supposed to land today, three hours ago. Everyone got their luggage already. The last person pulled the last suitcase from the carousel half an hour ago. I thought, wow, this one sure knows how to play a joke on the ladies. I thought you had left me at the fucking altar.

CHUTES&LADDERS: I got sick on the flight. Totally embarrassing. I had a panic attack as the plane landed and I started tossing into the doggy bag right next to this nice old lady. I've been sitting on the bathroom floor emptying my stomach. Then I had to find a toothbrush and toothpaste and mouthwash because I didn't want to greet you with bad breath and all.

(She looks skeptical. She sniffs his mouth quickly.)

ORANGUTAN: Minty. (Pause.) Oh, you dummy, you big old dummy. Put her here, you San Diego Padre.

(She extends her hand, he takes it. A long handshake. Their first physical contact.)

ORANGUTAN: What's your name?

CHUTES&LADDERS: Clay. Clayton Buddy Wilkie.

ORANGUTAN: I'm Madeleine Mays.

CHUTES&LADDERS: It's weird, huh?

ORANGUTAN: Totally weird. The land of the living.

(They hug. They melt into each other's arms. A hug of basic survival and necessary friendship. Then they exit, rolling his suitcase off as lights rise in:

Puerto Rico. A rock outcropping looking out over a waterfall. Elliot is there, looking down at the water.)

ELLIOT: (Looking down.) Oh shit! Yaz, you gotta see this! Yaz? Fucking Johnny Appleseed of El Yunque.

(Yaz enters holding a soil-covered flower bulb. She compares the root against a field book.)

YAZ: I found my spiral ginger! This is going right next to the aloe by the kitchen door, baby!

ELLIOT: Yo, this science experiment ain't getting past security.

YAZ: Experiment my ass. I'm planting these in Ginny's garden.

ELLIOT: Customs gonna sniff that shit from a mile away.

YAZ: (Putting the bulb in a Ziploc baggie full of dirt and bulbs.) China rose . . . Seagrape . . . Some kind of fern . . .

ELLIOT: When they cuff those wrists, I don't know you.

YAZ: I'll hide them in my tampon box.

ELLIOT: That don't work. My first trip to PR, Mami Ginny smuggled a coquí back with her Kotex and got arrested. Front page of the *Daily News*.

YAZ: Good shit. (A dirty little secret.) You know what grandma did?

ELLIOT: Do I want to?

YAZ: She used to smuggle stuff back, too. She'd tuck it below her boobs. She had storage space under there!

ELLIOT: Yo you think if I jumped off this rock right now and dove into that water, I'd survive?

YAZ: Just watch out for the huge boulders and the footbridge.

ELLIOT: It's tempting. That spray. (His phone beeps.) Reception in the rainforest.

YAZ: Kind of ruins the romance.

ELLIOT: (Reads a text message.) Damn, that was fast.

YAZ: What?

ELLIOT: Pop sold the house. Did he even put out a listing?

YAZ: Not that I know of.

ELLIOT: That's like a VW bus going from zero to sixty in three seconds. Don't make no sense.

YAZ: Must have been an inside job.

ELLIOT: I guess so.

YAZ: A way way inside job . . .

ELLIOT: Yaz . . .

YAZ: (Conspiratorially.) Yeeeees?

ELLIOT: What did you do?

YAZ: (Very conspiratorially.) Nothing . . .

ELLIOT: Holy shit!

YAZ: Put my Steinway on craigslist. Got four responses before you made it down to the lobby. My eighty-eight keys are worth more than Ginny's whole house. Sadly. I'll buy an upright.

ELLIOT: You are one crazy motherfucking adjunct! Yo, I don't know if el barrio is ready for you. I don't know if they can handle you!

YAZ: Oh, they gonna handle me. It'll be the Cousins House. We'll renovate the kitchen. You redo the plumbing, I'll hook up a little tile backsplash.

ELLIOT: I watched Bob Villa with Pop, but I ain't no handyman.

YAZ: Just wait, Mr. Home Depot. You're gonna be like, "Fuacata, fuacata, fuacata" with your power drill and nail gun and vice grips.

ELLIOT: Something like that.

YAZ: Well? Get to it. Toss 'em.

ELLIOT: Me? Why the hell do you think I let you come along?

(He hands Yaz the box.)

YAZ: Well then say something. Pray.

ELLIOT: I'm all out of prayers.

YAZ: Me, too. Make a toast.

ELLIOT: To LAX. I'm not flying back with you.

YAZ: What do you mean?

ELLIOT: I called from the hotel and changed my flight. One way ticket. Watch out, Hollywood. (Pause.) You know how you had to shake me awake last night?

YAZ: (Demeanor shifting.) You were literally sobbing in your sleep.

ELLIOT: This dream was different than usual. I'm fixing a Subway hoagie, I feel eyes on the back of my neck, I turn around and expect to see him, the first guy I shot down in Iraq. But instead it's Mami Ginny. Standing next to the bread oven, smiling. You know how her eyes smile?

YAZ: Best smile in the world.

ELLIOT: Looking at me, her son. Coming to say goodbye.

YAZ: That's beautiful.

ELLIOT: She puts on her glasses to see my face even better. She squints and something changes. The moment I come into focus, she starts trembling. Then she starts to cry. Then she starts to scream loud, like, "Ahhh! Ahhh!" She won't stop looking at me, but she's terrified, horrified by what she sees. And I'm touching my face like, is my lip bleeding, is there a gash on my forehead? Or is she looking through my eyes and seeing straight into my fucking soul?

YAZ: Jesus.

ELLIOT: I wanted Mami Odessa to relapse, Yaz. I wanted her to pick up that needle. I knew precisely what to do, what buttons to push, I engineered that shit, I might as well have pushed the thing into her vein. Because I thought, why would God take the good one? Yo, take the bad mom instead! I was like, why wouldn't you take the bad fucking mom? If I stay in Philly, I'm gonna turn into it. I'm gonna become one of them. I'm already halfway there. You've got armor, you've got ideas, but I don't.

YAZ: Go. Go and don't you ever, ever look back.

(She takes his hand.)

But if you do, there will be a plastic-covered sofa waiting for you.

(Below them, in Philadelphia, John is done bathing Odessa. He lifts her and holds her like an angel above the bathtub. She is dripping wet and seems almost radiant, and yet deeply, deeply sick.)

I'm the elder now. I stay home. I hold down the fort.

ELLIOT: I'm walking.

YAZ: On three?

YAZ/ELLIOT:

One.

Two.

Three.

(They toss the ashes. Blackout.)

Producing *Water by the Spoonful*

Second Stage

Second Stage is an Off-Broadway, New York theatre organization founded in 1979, dedicated to the development and presentation of contemporary plays. Until recently they produced plays by both emerging and established playwrights in two spaces: a 108-seat theatre on the Upper West Side and a 296-seat theatre on West 43rd Street. In 2013 they were in the process of expanding to include a Broadway presence as well by starting to produce plays at the Helen Hayes Theatre. With these three different venues, the Second Stage mission remains the same: to focus on the presentation of new works for the theatre and to provide an opportunity for the growth of young theatre artists. The newly acquired Helen Hayes Theatre will be one of only four not-for-profit theatres on Broadway.

In January 2013, Second Stage produced the New York premiere of *Water by the Spoonful* at its midsize theatre on West 43rd Street. Although this theatre is only a few blocks from Times Square and the elaborate theatres on Broadway, it offers a much simpler, stripped down theatre environment to producers and audiences. This was New York's first opportunity to see the play that had won the Pulitzer Prize for 2012 and had received its world premiere at Hartford Stage, Connecticut, in 2011.

In accordance with its mission, Second Stage provided a "second" opportunity for the artists who had produced *Water by the Spoonful* in Hartford to continue their work on the play. The playwright Quiara Hudes made major revisions to the script based on the earlier production as well as through considering input from the creative staff and some of the actors who had become close collaborators in the process. Those revisions are part of the script of the play presented in this book. The director and designers made adjustments to the staging to bring greater clarity to the complex storytelling and in response to the new theatre space, an end stage instead of the thrust at Hartford Stage (see page 166). And the actors deepened their understanding of the characters.

Dramatic Structure and Spectacle

Design

The structure of *Water by the Spoonful* with its scenes that alternate between the real world and the online world presents particular challenges for the production team. The director and the scene designer must create a spatial arrangement that will clearly and quickly guide the audience between the two kinds of scenes. All of the designers must determine how much visual information is necessary to the telling of this story and the kind of detail that provides the appropriate background to help define the characters' lives. And since the play moves between several actual geographic locations, as well as into virtual space, the creative staff must decide what will bring unity to the many different elements of the play. For the production of *Eurydice* discussed in Chapter 6, we saw an abstract, lyrical approach to solving similar kinds of problems. For *Water by the Spoonful*, an entirely different approach was taken. *Eurydice* is a poetic play that explores relationships through a mythical, even fantastic, form of play making. *Water by the Spoonful* comes from a gritty, urban environment that gives us harshly realistic details of social breakdown.

If we were to list the actual geographic locations in the play we would see Philadelphia, San Diego, Japan, and the El Yunque Rain Forest of Puerto Rico. Within Philadelphia we would need to add the Swarthmore College campus, the Subway shop, Odessa's house, the diner, and the flower shop. And prominently placed would be the chat room with its links to the lives and

In 1999 renowned Dutch architect Rem Koolhass and New York architect Richard Gluckman were commissioned by Second Stage to create a theatre in a historic bank building. This became Second Stage's intermediate size theatre on West 43rd Street. The box office is in what was once the bank's vault; the second floor was converted to an end stage theatre space. Usually theatres are built without windows to create as dark a space as possible. But here the windows remain to allow a view of the city when it is appropriate. As Koolhass observed, "Second Stage Theatre will be the only theatre that can claim Manhattan itself as its décor." This is the theatre space where *Water by the Spoonful* was staged. All of the audience members share the same view of the stage.

locations of the group of characters who connect with each other online. The first challenge for the scene designer Neil Patel is "to keep the play moving and flowing from scene to scene, which is critical." But the spectacle needs to go beyond simply accounting for many different locations. Underlying the jump cuts between scenes and the movement from real space to virtual space

and back is a state of mind. The spectacle needs to support the progression of this particular plot, which involves the characters moving toward each other across physical and mental distances and breaking free of their old limitations and old spaces to enter each others' spaces. There is a psychological environment that the characters share that unifies the action of the play.

Neil Patel tracks the movement of a play by storyboarding the scenes with rough models that he creates scene by scene. He spent three months developing storyboards for *Water by the Spoonful* in collaboration with the director, Davis McCallum, well before the beginning of rehearsals. Each scene is constructed in model form, which is then photographed. Lights and projections are also tested on the models. The models were essential to working out the speed and ease of transitions to allow the play to "flow as seamlessly as possible from scene to scene." In all, he made seventeen scene models for the Second Stage production. This first model shows the stage at the beginning of the play, with the walls closed and the bench set for the opening scene between Elliot and Yazmin on the Swarthmore campus. The white cardboard figure is used to establish scale.

This model shows the walls slid apart with furniture placed to allow Odessa, Orangutan, and Chutes&Ladders to be onstage together in Scene 2, each communicating online from their own private locations. Stage right is Odessa's kitchen, which was given more detail than the spaces of the other online characters. Stage left is the Chutes&Ladders desk from which he doesn't move until the end of the play. In the center is simply a chair for Orangutan, which indicates an Internet cafe in Japan. The gray walls, with greenery growing through the cracks, are used as the background for all of the scenes. The walls can be transformed with lights and can also be transparent.

Neil Patel describes two essential visual components of that psychological environment as an "urban, oppressive look and the hopeful life represented through gardens." Both were to be found in the Philadelphia of Quiara Hudes' childhood now inhabited by her principle trio of characters: Elliot, Odessa, and Yazmin. For Patel the starting point for his work on the play was "pictures of abandoned lots with overgrown plants."

> The images we were looking at were abandoned lots with plants growing through cracked concrete and broken walls, life breaking through as it does. And in the same way the characters in this play do. Through all kinds of hardship and suffering, there's this kind of vibrant and undefeatable life popping through. And because everything is vertical,

This third model shows the scenic arrangement for the end of the play: upstage Elliot and Yazmin prepare to scatter Ginny's ashes at the waterfall in the El Yunque Rain Forest; downstage is the bathtub where Fountainhead will bathe Odessa before she checks into a rehabilitation facility. A functional scaffold is used to make a cliff for Elliot and Yazmin to stand on.

we were also looking at vertical gardens, something you see on buildings now, mostly in Europe. And it was sort of interesting to imagine a garden growing out of the side of a building. So it was really the actual urban lots in Philadelphia and the urban gardens that were our inspiration. And I think you get it, as an audience, that it ties into the tropical scenery at the end. And then we added flowers so it's related to the idea of the flowers and the flower shops, but they aren't tropical flowers. They are flowers that would grow in a back lot in Philadelphia, or an urban vertical garden.

The director, Davis McCallum, saw Ginny's garden, first described in *Elliot, A Soldier's Fugue*, as the "deep metaphor for the play."

Ginny's garden began in an abandoned lot, which she turned into city-recognized public gardens. Flowers and planting seeds, things that come to bloom is one of the big poetic images of the play. And I feel there is a certain amount of isolation—something inhospitable about the world of the play, but it's not that the play is cold or forbidding. Even in difficult circumstances, life is always growing. So that central idea, which was a starting place for the play, came from these pictures of Philadelphia.

It also incidentally came from a children's book that Quiara has written called *El Barrio ABC*, which I read to my children at night. It's one of those alphabet books for kids. And it's all about barrio. It feels a lot like Washington Heights, but it's also based on the neighborhood in North Philadelphia where Elliot grew up. And for "Q"—which is always a hard thing in an alphabet book— Q is for the word *quemar*, which is Spanish for "to burn." In the book, the image shows a row of houses where a house has burned to the ground and it becomes this empty space where a house just was, like a row of teeth, missing one tooth. That triggered the thought, "Oh, between two buildings, there is this no man's land that could be turned into a place of fecundity and life and growth."

Vertical walls looming over small abandoned lots provided a structural framework for the stage and continued the metaphoric ideas in the set. And as a functional device, the walls slid into different configurations, allowing the stage to be transformed quickly from one location to another to indicate the change of scenes. Designed as grids, the walls could look like they were made up of concrete blocks or metallic squares. They could be part of a decaying urban landscape or suggest a representation of separate locations on the Internet.

> **NEIL PATEL:** We wanted to have a complex, abstract environment with gray, industrial materials. We tried to avoid the slick, high tech manifestation of Internet which seemed antithetical to the play. The text did not seem like it belonged on a slick, clean surface.

The grungy, hard-edged appearance of the gridded walls was continued in the selection of the stage furniture. Odessa's house was sparsely furnished with small, rectangular, rundown, thrift store appliances. Chutes&Ladders's IRS office was indicated with a grubby, metal desk. The lighting was done with squares and rectangles on the floor, creating an impression of characters who were separated from each other and isolated in boxes. Even if they were close together on stage, the audience understood the psychic distances that would need to be bridged for the characters to achieve sustaining connections.

Acting

The online sequences and multiple narratives contained in the rapidly shifting scenes also presented technical challenges for the director and the actors. The director was guided by a statement from the playwright in choosing how to stage the Internet conversations. "It's a play about a family, except they're online." He therefore chose to stage these conversations to suggest that there is a domestic intimacy among the online characters. They are regular visitors in one another's lives.

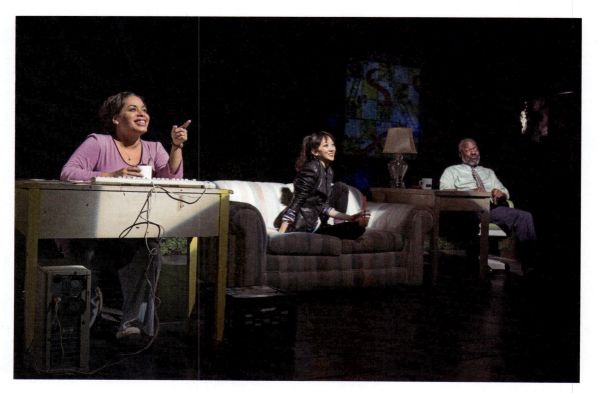

In the chat room scenes all of the actors behave as if they are continuing with their lives in their own private spaces. They do not type their thoughts into their computers but perform mundane tasks of daily life or speak as if they are talking to friends. When these three characters first appear in the chat room it is clear that they have already been communicating with each other for a long period of time. A major convention of the staging is that the characters in the chat room do not look at any of the other actors. They look out into the audience as if they are connecting to the other characters in a separate dimension. From left to right the actors are Liza Colón-Zayas (Odessa), Sue Jean Kim (Orangutan), and Frankie Faison (Chutes&Ladders).

DAVIS MCCALLUM: We see Odessa in her apartment, and she goes over to the kitchen and putters around and then comes to the computer, which is a desk with a keyboard but not a monitor. She punches in the code and we see projections of icons for all the online people. But now, her friends from the chat room come into her apartment and they use her apartment *as if* they are in their own real spaces. So that's a vocabulary that we set up in the first part of the play. Then whoever starts the next chat room scene, we use that as a kind of anchor.

However, in order to maintain the illusion of Internet conversations, in spite of the implied familiarity, the online characters do not look at each other. Instead they deliver their lines looking out into the auditorium. In fact, the director had headshots taken of the actors and placed strategically in the auditorium to guide the actors among focal points. Liza Colón-Zayas, who played Odessa, identifies one of the problems in observing this convention. "I always have to be on guard not to look in the wrong direction. It's hard, facing straight out, with bright lights in my eyes." But beyond the concentration issues is the very important need to build connections and emotional energy between the characters.

In most traditional theatre scene work, the tension in a scene is built through the give and take between actors playing off of each other, making eye contact, responding to all of the shifts in another actor's body language, facial expression, and vocal tone. So the early rehearsals for the online scenes were done with the actors facing each other to develop that crucial rapport before they made the change to the outward focus that would be used in performance.

Furthermore, the actors were directed to be very physical in their individual performances, moving actively through the stage space and sometimes standing or sitting close to the other characters even though they are not looking at each other. Their blocking was determined by character issues. For example, Chutes&Ladders protects himself by staying in one place. Davis McCallum says, "his rootedness offers him a kind of stability, but then it becomes a prison." On the other hand, Orangutan's "hunger" to find herself drives her into continuous, restless motion.

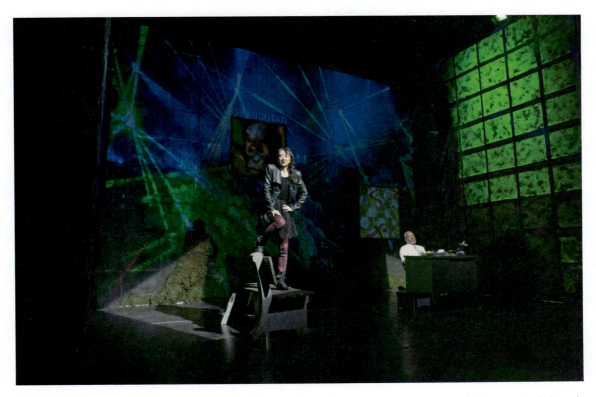

Orangutan and Chutes&Ladders begin the play on different continents, but gradually are able to take the steps to help each other overcome their paralysis and cement a deep friendship. A lighting effect is used to reinforce the distance encompassed by the Internet and the number of other people who may also be online. Lines across the back wall indicate the many connections being made; specific icons represent the characters Orangutan, the monkey, and Chutes&Ladders, the game board. The lighting design is by Russell H. Champa; the projection design is by Aaron Rhyne.

The staging sets up an internal tension shared by the online characters. As long as they communicate via their computers, they can be open, direct, warm or scathingly honest in their responses to each other. But each character uses the Internet to keep from taking the steps that would expose them to greater risks.

LIZA COLÓN-ZAYAS (speaking of her character, Odessa): She maintains sobriety by isolating from her triggers. But she has relied too heavily on the online world because there you can remake yourself and you're not disappointing people. Whereas going to therapy and going to actual meetings with real people, you don't get to hide behind that.

Because a number of storylines are maintained throughout the play, the actors also face the challenge of connecting the pieces of their narratives that are interrupted or not shown onstage. For example, scenes involving Elliot and Yazmin alternate with scenes that take place in the chat room, involving other characters. The actors

The play opens on the downstage bench that indicates the Swarthmore College campus where Elliot is waiting to meet the professor whom he hopes will translate the phrase that haunts him from his tour of duty in Iraq, "please give me back my passport." The vitality of the actors is evident in the warmth and ease of their relationship as cousins. This relationship will become the foundation for a renewal of their family, after the death of their Aunt Ginny. Following this scene, the scenes involving Elliot and Yazmin alternate with scenes for the online characters until Act II. The actors must maintain their throughlines as well as imagine parts of the story that are taking place offstage. Yazmin is played by Zabryna Guevara and Elliot is played by Armando Riesco. Riesco, who originated the role of Elliot in the first play of the trilogy, also played Elliot in the premiere production of the third play, *The Happiest Song Plays Last,* at the Goodman Theatre in Chicago in 2013.

must stay connected to the evolution of their own part of the story and return to the stage for each new scene as if the events being described just happened. Armando Riesco says, "You've got to stay in it between scenes, which is the hardest part of playing this."

> ZABRYNA GUEVARA: It doesn't stop. I'm onstage every other scene. There are no two scenes that happen without us showing up on the other end of it. For instance, Ginny dies in between scenes 3 and 5. All that has to happen offstage. Between my finding out Elliot overdosed while he was in the service and the eulogy, a lot happens. The whole funeral has been prepared. And after the eulogy, there's the tracking of how Odessa's absence has affected us. We come down the stairs from the eulogy, take off mic pacs, put on a coat, get a phone, Elliot takes off his military top half, and all that is happening while we're mentally thinking about the events that have transpired to get us to the door knocking and Elliot's line, "Odessa, open the door, open the door." The play is still happening offstage.

Defining the Characters

By assembling scenes that take place in the real world and online, Quiara Hudes is able to draw together a surprisingly disparate group of characters. Through this gathering of individuals we see that the struggles of her characters take place in multiple American communities, not just one. In *Elliot, A Soldier's Fugue*, the playwright uses a structure of repetition to focus on circumstances that recur from generation to generation within the same family. In *Water by the Spoonful*, she uses a structure that ripples out from the family to connect people across a broader spectrum. The traumatic experiences that lead people into isolation and destructive behavior occur in a variety of social environments. But Hudes' characters are not **types** who simply represent categories of behavior or social background. They have their own highly individual personal histories and obstacles that the actors must fill out to

bring the play fully to life. Davis McCallum says, "You believe the people are real and you feel you could walk up on stage and introduce yourself to them."

Researching the Social Environment

To create authentic characters, the actors did extensive research into the social issues that define the world of the play as well as psychological exploration of their characters' given circumstances and interior journeys. When Armando Riesco prepared to play Elliot in the first play of the trilogy, his research focused on combat, through conversations with marines about their tours of duty and watching documentaries about troops deployed to Afghanistan such as *Restrepo* and *Armadillo*. For *Water by the Spoonful*, he turned to the experiences of young veterans returning from the Iraq War and the way those experiences fall disproportionately on certain communities. He looked at the difficulty vets have finding work and the way that erodes self-esteem.

> ARMANDO RIESCO: Many returning vets are unemployed or underemployed, a much higher rate than the regular civilian population. A great number of them struggle daily with anger issues and such. It's the really mundane stuff they come back to and they can't deal with. It's no coincidence that Elliot is working at Subway when the Ghost first visits him.

He studied the web site of IAVA, Iraq and Afghanistan Veterans of America, and found a documentary of a young man like his character, Elliot, with a similar injury.

> ARMANDO RIESCO: The very first story I found in my research was a 24 year old who did not know what to do with his anger. He regularly drove at 90 miles an hour through his town, got into fights at bars for no reason. He was constantly tempting fate.

He read accounts of veterans who are addicted to pain medications and examined statistics on suicide.

> **ARMANDO RIESCO:** How many veterans are killing themselves? The figures from 2012 detail the numbers: 22 per day. Suicides outnumbered soldier combat deaths in the Iraq conflict.

He found the state of mind of a returning veteran in a short story by Phil Klay entitled "Deployment" to be influential in understanding the disorientation of young men unable to reconcile their lives in Iraq with their lives in the United States.

Liza Colón-Zayas worked in a variety of social service settings while she was building her career as an actor. For this play she drew on what she learned working in support groups with high-risk women and men in lock down facilities and as a teaching artist in homeless shelters and in jails. In addition to her personal experiences, she watched videos and documentaries, confronting the painful realities of behavior related to addiction and overdose. Colón-Zayas explains her understanding of her character, drawing on her analysis of the text and her awareness of circumstances surrounding substance abuse.

> Odessa is a recovering addict. She's had six years clean. She's had over twenty years of struggling with a crack-cocaine addiction. She had an episode which got her locked up which I think was the thing to help her get on the road to recovery. But because of this tragedy in her life, she's been an outcast. So she created an online recovery web site. She's created this community of relationships that are as real to her as family. And they check in regularly on the web site, focusing on retaining their sobriety and sharing their stories, supporting each other. And on this particular day, she get's the rug pulled out. The thing that she's been trying to escape comes back and she ends up back in the life, at least momentarily. I grew up in the South Bronx when it was on fire. So I've seen a lot of this first hand and I've seen people, from one moment to the next,

become Jekyll and Hyde. So, I wanted to be truthful about that, and not judge that, because it's real. You can be sober and still not have worked out your issues. And so, I wanted to show that dichotomy. I wanted to show the extreme mood changes that can take place and still give her heart, and empathy, and humanity and focus on how fragile sobriety is. Because I can easily play someone who is rough around the edges, but I was resisting that in this play because I didn't want people to judge her unfairly. I didn't want her to just be a stereotype.

The Interior Journey

Like the process described by Liza Colón-Zayas, each of the actors was faced with imaginatively constructing his or her character's autobiography and then building a progression of attempts to take control of situations made increasingly difficult by new reversals or setbacks. Much of the rehearsal process involved lengthy conversations with the director, the playwright Quiara Hudes (who was frequently in rehearsals), and the other actors about key points in each character's development. Given the painful nature of these characters' lives, this is a process that requires a deep emotional investment on the part of the actors in order to be genuinely open to the truth of the characters' circumstances. As Armando Riesco says, "I think when you don't open yourself 110% you are doing a disservice to the play. Your job is to try every single time to open yourself completely and to be in the moment and to feel all these terrible things." However, he also makes clear that the focus of each actor's work cannot be on the enormity of the character's hardships but rather on what the character is doing to overcome those obstacles.

> The baggage is evident. You read the play and the given circumstances are there. The trick to making this play fly is that you have to have those given circumstances deeply weighing you down. But then your action is not to show how you're weighted down. It's the

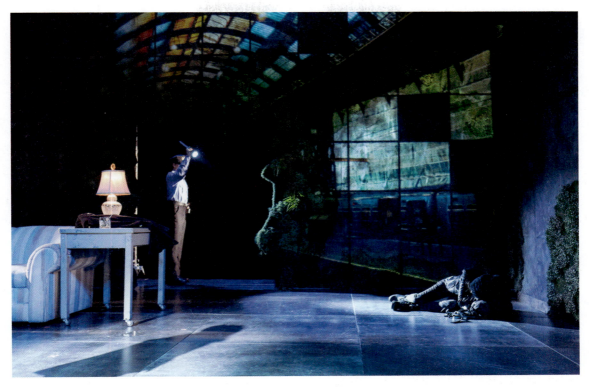

The Sapporo train station is created through lights and projections at the same time that Odessa's house exists on another part of the stage. Orangutan has fallen into a confused sleep in the train station at the same time that Odessa has overdosed. The lines from the two different scenes overlap and each connects to the meaning in the other scene. The lowest points in the progressions of Odessa's and Orangutan's characters coincide in this scene.

opposite of that. And in between that weight that's pulling you down and you trying to stay above water, now we have a play.

The Language of Resilience

One of the coping mechanisms written into the play is the characters' earthy language that is laced with humor. Sarcasm and jokes, some self-deprecating, some aimed at other characters, are a way of negotiating painful subjects without giving in to self-pity. The characters use humor as a form of self-protection, a kind of armor to defend against showing their true feelings. It is one of the ways to try to prove that they are not "weighted down,"

that they are surviving. Although the humor is noteworthy in four of the characters' language: Yazmin, Elliot, Madeleine Mays (Orangutan), and Clayton Wilkie (Chutes&Ladders), it is not generic, but comes out of each character's particular circumstances, some of which are cultural. In performance, the effective use of humor by the actors makes an important contribution to building the energy of the production.

ZABRYNA GUEVARA (speaking from the viewpoint of her character, Yazmin): I think that the sarcasm you see comes from a real sense of heartbreak and a need for love, a *real* need to be understood and for me to love *me*. Elliot and I love each other unconditionally.

But up until now, I have love from my family in the form of admiration for my achievements. I went to school. I play music. I'm a composer. Nobody knows me. I don't know them. There's a mutual disconnect. And then my husband divorces me and I don't even have that. He fell *out* of love with me. Maybe he loved me at some point, but it was probably admiration. I didn't even have what I thought I had. But we're not self-indulgent sentimental people, so there's bite behind it, because otherwise you'll just lay down and cry. So if you're not going to let that overtake you, then there's bite behind the comment to lay a spine in the pain. It doesn't just double you over and kill you. There's got to be strength in it. I have anger through the pain and it keeps you up, it keeps you going, it gets you to the eulogy, it gets you past the eulogy, it gets you past the OD. It's a coping mechanism. I think it is in the language and it's definitely cultural. Just to get through really hard times, in my family, you make light, you make jokes, throw this anger, just to make you feel better.

The Musical Environment

We began our discussion of Quiara Hudes' work as a playwright by considering the importance of music in the structure of her plays, particularly for the Elliot trilogy. The musical idea behind *Water by the Spoonful* is first introduced into the play in Yazmin's speech when she is giving a lecture to her students about the music of the great jazz composer John Coltrane. She challenges them to think about dissonance in their lives and introduces them to the idea of "free jazz." In free jazz, the compositional structure lacks the harmony and resolution of other musical forms, but instead offers continuing sequences of notes that clash, producing a discordant sound. Improvisation is an essential component of free jazz and the form depends on the improvisational contributions of all the performing participants rather than a single composer.

The jazz of John Coltrane and the concept of free jazz had implications for the production in a number of ways. Davis McCallum believes that

the entire text of the play is like a jazz score, but also that instrumental music is "invited" into the text in important places. It became clear to him that John Coltrane should be considered the play's "composer," and he asked Josh Schmidt to be the production's sound designer because of his expertise in jazz and composition as well as sound design. Together they listened to many hours of Coltrane pieces and then carefully chose selections from *Ascension*, *Love Supreme*, and other works that emphasized drum rhythms rather than saxophone. During the first act there was some reggaeton to suggest the barrio, Puerto Rican music for the scene in the flower shop, and club music for the scene in the Japanese nightclub. But there was no jazz other than Coltrane, and Coltrane was played increasingly in act 2 as the play moved to conclusion. For example, loops from *Ascension*, which is the dissonant piece that Yazmin's character says spins toward "noise," was heard each time the Ghost appeared. And in fact, the first entrance of the Ghost occurs immediately after the "dissonance" speech. *Love Supreme*, with its more focused, pure, haunting notes, was heard at the beginning of act 2.

McCallum also encouraged the actors to find "the jazz in the language."

The language was coming out clearly and honestly, but rather straight, almost square. I wanted them to feel the freedom, to rediscover some of their own idiosyncrasies; their individuality in the way they approached the language; to linger on one word, to vary their speed, tempo, rhythm, and pitch, so we could regain a more varied color.

In terms of a musical analogy, McCallum sees the jazz inspiration for *Water by the Spoonful* leading to a "wilder" form of staging than the tightly choreographed staging of *Elliot, A Soldier's Fugue*. The "collision" between the needs of the different characters and the turmoil of their emotional lives brings an undercurrent of chaos to the intersecting narrative strands.

DAVIS MCCALLUM: People are fighting for their lives, not just in the chat room, in the

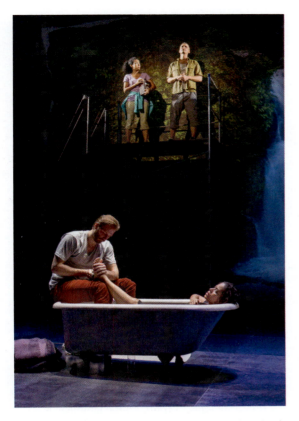

All four characters in this scene participate in healing rituals that are part of their path of recovery. Fountainhead is played by Bill Heck.

real world. They're battling with addiction; they're battling with each other; they're battling with themselves. That fight needs to be a brawl. There's blood on the floor.

These battles uncover enough vulnerability to allow the characters to approach connections with each other that will make recovery possible. Through these connections, they gain the courage to face the most painful knowledge about themselves. Liza Colón-Zayas says the play is "not just about recovery. It's about redemption. It's about forgiveness. People of all colors, from all stations of life. Every single person on that stage needs some sort of forgiveness."

Because of these mutually supportive relationships, all of the characters are able to change the directions of their lives. The chat room characters move beyond their online dialogues to accept each other in real space. They give up their identities as Internet icons with symbolic names. The actors stop facing out and turn to each other in intimate ways. John gently bathes Odessa, a form of touch that allows them both a moment of peace. Clayton Wilkie and Madeleine Mays embrace joyfully in the Tokyo airport. And as Elliot and Yazmin scatter Ginny's ashes, they are able to let go of parts of the past that have kept them from beginning a new journey into the future.

Summary

Quiara Alegría Hudes has written a new American trilogy consisting of three plays: *Elliot, A Soldier's Fugue, Water by the Spoonful,* and *The Happiest Song Plays Last.* Together the three plays examine the experiences of a young marine who is injured during combat in the Iraq War and his struggles to find a place for himself when he returns to the United States. The first play also includes the experiences of Elliot's father and grandfather who served in two previous wars in Vietnam and Korea. The second play introduces additional characters from Elliot's family, his mother Odessa and his cousin Yazmin, but also expands the frame of reference to present characters who enter the lives of this family via the Internet. In writing her plays, Hudes draws on the stories of actual members of her own family, which she uses as the foundation for some of the characters. Many of the characters in *Water by the Spoonful* are struggling with substance abuse and the play focuses on the interactions among the characters that lead them toward recovery.

Hudes is an accomplished musician and musical structures were an important factor in writing these plays. In *Elliot, A Soldier's Fugue*, the repeating war experiences of the three generations are expressed through language and action that are tightly woven together in a pattern of themes that echo each other. *Water by the Spoonful* is influenced by the jazz compositions of John Coltrane. The structure of this play is expansive with a number of different character narratives and speeches that suggest jazz improvisation. The structure of *Water by the Spoonful* is also distinguished by scenes that alternate between characters who meet face-to-face and characters who interact online. The play is written as duets for three sets of characters, who come from very different walks of life.

The last play, *The Happiest Song Plays Last*, opens up the frame of reference further yet to include international characters. The musical background is provided through Puerto Rican traditional songs. Other notable trilogies in dramatic history include *The Oresteia* by the Greek playwright Aeschylus and *Mourning Becomes Electra* by the American playwright Eugene O'Neill.

Topics for Discussion and Writing

1. Read the scene from *Elliot, A Soldier's Fugue*, beginning on page 394, aloud. How do you think the scene should be staged to bring out the differences between the active characters, Elliot and Pop, and the characters who serve as narrators in this scene, Ginny and Grandpop? How would you describe the different kinds of language spoken by the characters in the scene, and what is the effect of the differing styles?

2. The line spoken by the Ghost of a dead Iraqi in *Water by the Spoonful* repeats a number of times, first in Arabic and then in English: "Please, give me back my passport." How do you interpret the meaning of this line for the character of the Ghost? What is the significance of the passport and the appearances of the Ghost for Elliot? How does this line apply to the other characters?

3. The playwright Quiara Alegría Hudes sees online language being distinct from the language that we use in face-to-face conversations. She says, "I think online language is more formal than conversational language, which is more casual and fumbling. You get language that is being used in a more thoughtful way. It is heightened and uninhibited." Do you agree with her statement? What do you think distinguishes the way people communicate online? How would you stage the scenes that take place in the chat room?

● For suggested readings and interviews with the playwright, director, scenic designer, and actors, please visit **www.mhhe.com/creativespirit6e**

CHAPTER 14

Genre

In the preceding chapters we looked at the playwright's artistic vision and the development of that vision through style and dramatic construction. In this chapter we consider another dimension of playwriting: the way the drama views human existence or divides human experience. In simple terms, we divide drama into the serious and the comic, into tragedy and comedy. To these divisions we can add tragicomedy, a form of drama that moves between serious and comic views. The term **genre** refers to a specific division, or classification, of drama. The most frequently used classifications, or genres, of drama are tragedy, comedy, melodrama, tragicomedy, and farce. Following our consideration of genre, we turn our attention to writers whose work involves analyzing plays and performances. These writers, the dramaturg and the critic, must understand the nature of theatrical communication on the stage and the elements of dramatic construction and classification, which are the subjects of Chapters 12, 13, and 14.

Introduction to Genre

In thinking about genres, we must remember that categorization is a tool for exploration, not an end itself. Furthermore, genres frequently merge or overlap rather than stay within neat and tidy boundaries. The organization of the drama into genres offers a way to examine the shifting viewpoint on human experience and a comparable shift in the audience's response to the drama.

What makes the study of genre worthwhile is the insight that each particular form of drama contributes to our understanding of the relationship between human beings and the world or the universe. Studying genre leads us to consider some of the most troublesome questions about human existence. How much control do we have over our own lives? Are human beings responsible for their own actions? Are we merely victims of circumstance? Are human beings capable of heroic action, or do we often blunder at the critical moment or fail to recognize the significant issues? How high or low is our aim? Are we free, or is there an external force, either divine or random, that ultimately controls, contradicts, or renders meaningless all of our actions?

ARTISTIC FOUNDATIONS

Characteristics of Comedy

- Comedy celebrates the continuation of life, the success of generations through love and rebirth.

- The plot of comedy usually involves an outrageous idea or fantastic scheme that disrupts the normal workings of the community and leads to chaos.

- Comedy usually looks at characters as part of a social group.

- Comic characters tend to reflect human weakness.

- Comedy often takes place in the realm of the ludicrous.

- The world of comedy is a protected world where there is no pain.

- Comedy ends with a reconciliation or happy resolution, frequently including an engagement or marriage.

- Comedy exists to make us laugh, but its underlying subject matter is often serious and involves some kind of social critique.

- The performance of comedy depends on broad physicality, timing, and rapport between actor and audience.

Tragedy and Comedy

Genre begins with tragedy and comedy, the most basic—though not necessarily opposite—parts of the dramatic experience. Tragedy and comedy are two different ways of understanding the fundamental rhythms of the human life cycle. Tragedy frequently ends in disaster. Although violence and death are central to most tragedies, it is the awareness of our mortality that seems most relevant to the tragic understanding of life. Tragedy explores the notion that no matter how great our human achievement, life is finite. We cannot overcome our mortality, nor can we overcome the hostilities or inconsistencies in the universe. The limitations of human mortality are addressed in the following passage from the Greek poet Pindar:

> One is the race of gods and of men; from one mother we both draw our breath. Yet are our powers poles apart; for we are nothing, but for them the brazen Heaven endures forever, their secure abode.[1]

Pindar suggests that human beings are godlike in their aspirations. But the gods, however we interpret them or whatever forces they represent, are constant. They do not die. Human beings, for all their intelligence, courage, and will, can never achieve the immortality of the gods or the constant forces of the universe.

Molière (1622–1673) is a beloved playwright of comedies whose works are widely produced and translated into many languages. In *A Doctor In Spite of Himself* a woodcutter masquerades as a doctor in a satire of pretense and hypocrisy. One of Molière's broader escapades, this piece invites theatrical invention such as the puppets, silent film costumes, rap music and opera, slapstick and sight gags featured in the 2012 production at Berkeley Repertory Theatre, directed by Christopher Bayes. The actors are Liam Craig, Renata Friedman, Steven Epp, and Julie Briskman.

In contrast to tragedy, comedy looks to the continuation of life rather than to its finality. In spite of all the pitfalls and the setbacks, in spite of the pettiness of human behavior and our foolish self-importance, life goes on. Comedy focuses on the success of generations rather than on the mortality of the individual. Through love and rebirth, there is continuance.

The plot of comedy usually begins with an outrageous idea or a fantastic scheme that disrupts the normal workings of the community. Incongruous events are frequently complicated by mistaken identity and misunderstandings. Gullibility, greed, egotism, and hypocrisy appear to rule the day. Lovers are separated, fortunes are lost, and chaos seems to reign supreme. But common sense prevails, the misunderstandings are resolved, and the reconciliation of all the separated factions leads to the affirmation of true love. Comedies frequently end in marriage or engagements.

Comedy exists to make us laugh. But the brilliance of comedy lies in its ability to take on the most serious subjects while evoking the deepest laughter. Perhaps we laugh hardest at the exposure of things that concern us the most or, as Bill Irwin has observed, that frighten us the most. War, religion, politics, generational conflict, and sexual relationships are common subjects of comedy.

Origins in Greek Drama

The original designations of tragedy and comedy in the theatre were arrived at simply. In the early Greek theatre, all plays that dealt with lofty and serious subjects were called tragedies. The word *tragedy* is derived from the Greek word that means "goat song"—a song that was sung in honor of Dionysus. Plays that dealt with human weakness and folly were called comedies.

The Greeks were certainly aware of the proximity of tragedy and comedy in describing human experience. Originally, comedies were performed as companion pieces to tragedies to complete the picture of human endeavor. The tragic side looked to the human actor engaged in noble causes. The comic side revealed that underneath the heroic guise, humans are terrified and capable of the most ridiculous posturing and mistakes. In the Greek theatre the genres were maintained as separate but complementary entities. In contrast, contemporary playwrights frequently mix comic and tragic elements in the same play because that approach seems to most effectively reflect their understanding of life's rhythms in today's world.

Aristotle on Tragedy and Comedy

In his series of lectures that were collected under the title *The Poetics* (see Chapter 12), Aristotle described the nature of tragedy. In defining tragedy, he included a few asides on the nature of comedy. Aristotle summarized the distinction between tragedy and comedy in two statements. In the first he wrote:

> Comedy aims at representing men as worse,
> Tragedy as better than in actual life.[2]

We may interpret "better than in actual life" to mean that the characters in tragedy come from noble houses. And Aristotle in fact writes later in *The Poetics* that a tragic character must be "highly renowned and prosperous."[3] Tragic characters, by their royal birth, are distinguished from ordinary citizens. But Aristotle's "better" refers more significantly to character, behavior, and choices. In tragic characters, nobility of conduct corresponds to nobility of position.

In his second statement on comedy Aristotle wrote:

> Comedy is, as we have said, an imitation of characters of a lower type—not, however, in the full sense of the word bad, the Ludicrous being merely a subdivision of the ugly. It consists in some defect or ugliness which is not painful or destructive. To take an obvious example, the comic mask is ugly and distorted, but does not imply pain.[4]

Comedy's "imitation of characters of a lower type" suggests conduct that may make audience members feel superior—or that may make them recognize themselves at their worst. Aristotle uses the word *ludicrous* to further delineate the particular area of behavior comedy addresses. *Ludicrous* implies the contradictions in life that make our efforts ridiculous. When Harpo Marx uses huge scissors to cut off pieces of a formal dinner jacket worn by a pompous diplomat while he is conducting serious business, we are in the realm of the ludicrous. Ludicrous has to do with the loss of control, with the incongruous, with the undermining of whatever we take too seriously.

Comedy: A World Without Pain
In his second statement, Aristotle made another simple observation about comedy that has far greater significance than the words communicate at first reading: "It consists in some defect or ugliness which is not painful or destructive. To take an obvious example, the comic mask is ugly and distorted, but does not imply pain." The implication here is that comic characters may do all kinds of ridiculous things and may suffer temporary losses, but they are not in pain. And most particularly,

the audience does not respond to them as if they were suffering. When we laugh in the theatre, we laugh at the incongruous, we laugh at the foolish, we laugh at ourselves, but we do not laugh if we believe that people are genuinely in pain.

Tragedy: Catharsis and Awareness

The audience's experience in tragedy is quite different from that in comedy. In tragedy we feel

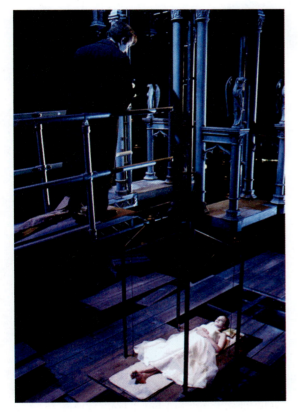

Romeo and Juliet by William Shakespeare is a tragedy of young lovers separated by their feuding families. While trying to escape together, misunderstandings bring about both of their deaths. Here a family member, Paris, played by Lee Mark Nelson, comes upon the apparently dead body of Juliet, played by Christine Marie Brown, in a 2004 production at the Guthrie Theater in Minneapolis directed by Ethan McSweeney.

the pain and suffering of the characters intensely. The audience empathizes with the tragic characters and shares in their inner journeys. The identification with the suffering in tragedy brings about an emotional release or cleansing of the spirit that is referred to as catharsis. Catharsis is one of the most discussed and debated concepts in the study of drama. To understand catharsis, imagine that you have witnessed an ordeal and have been caught up in the terrible tensions of the situation. When those conflicts and tensions are finally resolved, you feel both relief and heightened awareness. The same emotional experience occurs in tragedy: the tragic character comes to a new understanding or a greater wisdom through his or her suffering, and we in the audience come to a new awareness of life's meaning. This experience that combines emotional sensitivity with insight into life's most difficult questions brings us a degree of exhilaration at the same time that we are deeply moved by the struggle we have witnessed.

Plot Summaries of Selected Tragedies

Today we are surrounded by comedies—on the stage, on television, and in the movies. We have abundant material to draw on in our attempt to identify the distinguishing qualities of comedy. But we have only a generalized sense of the "tragic," which we tend to think of in terms of painful incidents that end in loss, disaster, or death. We do not have a large, well-known body of contemporary theatre works to create a frame of reference for identifying that part of human experience explored by tragedy.

To provide a partial foundation for our discussion of tragedy, we include here brief plot summaries of the plays most frequently cited in discussions of tragedy. To the tragedies listed, written in either the fifth century B.C.E. or Elizabethan England, could be added more plays from either of these periods as well as the tragedies of Racine, written in seventeenth-century

Another famous tragic drama of generational conflict is Sophocles' *Electra,* which tells the story of Electra's determination to revenge herself on her mother, Clytaemnestra, for the death of her father, Agamemnon. The plot of Electra is drawn from the same material as the plot of *The Oresteia* described in this chapter. The contemporary playwright Luis Alfaro has adapted *Electra* in a new version he has titled *Electricidad* and set in the middle of gang warfare in Southern California. In this photograph, the brother of Electricidad, Orestes, played by Maximino Arciniega Jr., considers the murder that his sister is asking him to commit in a 2006 production at the Goodman Theatre in Chicago. Nino is played by Edward Torres.

France. But even with these additions, we quickly see that a huge area of literary and dramatic study is based on a very small sample of plays.

Oedipus Rex (Sophocles)

When Oedipus is a young man, he is told by an oracle that he is fated to kill his father and marry his mother and have children with her. Horrified at such a future, he leaves the home and kingdom of his parents, not knowing that he is, in fact, an adopted child. Unwittingly, he travels to the city of his actual parents, where the prophecy comes true. Oedipus murders his father King Laius and marries his mother Queen Jocasta. Because Laius is dead, the people of Thebes choose Oedipus to be their new king. The play focuses on the day, many years after Oedipus's arrival in Thebes, the true city of his birth, that Oedipus comes to know who he really is.

Antigone (Sophocles)

The sons of Oedipus, Eteocles and Polyneices, have both been killed battling each other for the throne. Their uncle, Creon, declares that one is a hero and will be buried appropriately and that the other is a traitor and will be left unburied with his remains to be destroyed by the elements. Creon, who has become the king on the death of Oedipus's sons,

further decrees that anyone attempting to bury the abandoned body will be stoned to death. The young men's sister, Antigone, refuses to obey her uncle's decree and performs burial rites for her brother. Creon has Antigone imprisoned in a cave, where she commits suicide.

The Oresteia (Aeschylus)

Agamemnon, the Greek king and general who leads the Greek army against Troy in the ten-year Trojan war, is killed by his wife, Clytaemnestra, on his return from the war. Clytaemnestra is then killed by her son, Orestes, as revenge for his father's death. Orestes is tried for murder in a trial by jury and acquitted.

Hamlet (Shakespeare)

Hamlet's father, King Hamlet, is murdered by his uncle Claudius, who is the dead king's brother. Claudius then marries Hamlet's mother, Gertrude, and takes the throne of Denmark. Young Prince Hamlet fears that his uncle has murdered his father but lacks conclusive proof. In the course of Hamlet's attempt to prove his uncle a murderer and avenge his father's death, violence claims eight lives, including those of Hamlet, Claudius, and Gertrude.

Macbeth (Shakespeare)   Macbeth is presented with visions of future power by three witches whom he meets on the heath. The witches' mysterious prophecies fire his own ambitions. He and his wife Lady Macbeth embark on a course of murder, beginning with the reigning king, that ultimately leads to their downfall.

King Lear (Shakespeare)   Seeking to bind his three daughters more closely to him, King Lear divides up his kingdom and bestows what would be his children's inheritance in advance of his death. He announces the division of his kingdom in a public ceremony, in which he expects his daughters to declare their love for him above all else. His treacherous older daughters easily proclaim the adulation they know he awaits. However, Cordelia, his youngest daughter (for whom the ceremony is probably staged), refuses to compromise herself with false flattery to surpass her sisters. Lear banishes Cordelia, opening the way for a vicious power struggle that results in the deaths of both Lear and Cordelia.

Common Themes of Tragedy

A Struggle Over Succession
As these six plot summaries show, the major tragedies all deal with power struggles over succession. Oedipus unknowingly kills the legitimate king, his father, and then taints his own children and heirs through incest. Creon imprisons his rebellious niece, Antigone, to consolidate his own power as king following the deaths of the two legitimate heirs to the throne. Clytaemnestra kills her husband to avenge the death of their daughter and then assumes the leadership of the state; Orestes, Clytaemnestra's son, kills his mother to reclaim the throne he believes by right should be his. Claudius and Macbeth both scheme for power and murder the legitimate king. By giving up his power prematurely, King Lear unleashes a bloody struggle for control of the kingdom. And in *Medea*, Jason leaves his wife to form a new

marital alliance that will make him successor to the throne of the aging king of Corinth.

Although succession is not necessarily the primary focus of tragedy, it is integral to many of the works of the past that we categorize as tragedy. A crisis over succession exposes a society at its most vulnerable. Tragedy explores a breakdown or challenge to a society's system of values. And it is during these times of vulnerability that the moral choices of the characters are the most difficult and significant.

A Rupturing of Family and Societal Bonds
Classical tragedies test the moral foundations of human civilization. Tragedies take place when the bonds that tie human society together are ruptured. The family is almost always at the center of tragedy, and it is a royal family that represents both the larger society and the essential relationships between family members. Tragic characters become engaged in

---

ARTISTIC FOUNDATIONS

Characteristics of Tragedy

- Tragedy deals with serious subjects and characters who are confronted with their own mortality.
- Many tragic plots revolve around a crisis over succession to a throne, representing a rupture in the bonds that tie families and society together.
- Murder and death occur frequently in tragedy and usually as a result of the transgression of sacred principles.
- Tragic characters come from aristocratic or royal families and usually exhibit admirable behavior.
- Tragic characters act alone and take responsibility for their choices and actions.
- The audience empathizes with tragic characters, identifies with their suffering, and often experiences catharsis.

conflict leading to or in response to the transgression of principles deemed sacred by the community. All the major tragedies involve royal or artistocratic characters who kill members of their own families. The health or disruption in the royal family is intricately tied to the social and political health of the community.

The relationship of the tragic characters to this wrenching of fundamental values changes from play to play and playwright to playwright. Some characters—such as Oedipus, unknowingly; and King Lear, knowingly—initiate all the events that lead to catastrophe. Others, such as Hamlet and Antigone, must respond to situations initiated by others. What the characters share is an unwillingness to let other characters or circumstances shape their individual destinies. They are determined, even at the cost of their own lives and sometimes the lives of others, to find a course of action that is true to their own natures and true to a value system as they understand it. Some of them, such as King Lear, Creon, and Macbeth, make enormous errors of judgment or miscalculations. Some, such as Oedipus, are caught in such a tangled web that extrication is impossible. Some, such as Hamlet and Antigone, give their lives to restore justice. For all these tragic characters, great suffering results from the actions they choose, and through that suffering comes not only wisdom but also self-determination. They have defined themselves.

Isolation of the Tragic Character

Whereas comedies look at characters as part of a social unit, tragedies examine characters who stand alone. Hamlet was part of the court of Denmark before the play opens; he had family, friends, a woman who loved him, and the highest regard of the people of Denmark. Part of his tragedy is that he becomes increasingly isolated as he pursues his course of action. His father is dead. He is betrayed by his friends Rosencrantz and Guildenstern, attacked by his uncle Claudius, rejected by Ophelia, and abandoned by his mother. In *Medea* the central character is viewed as an outsider who should be banished.

Isolated, the tragic hero or character struggles with a hideous situation: Hamlet's father has been murdered, and the apparent murderer now wears the crown and has married Hamlet's mother; the body of Antigone's brother lies unburied, to be torn apart by wild dogs and vultures, and the king has decreed that anyone burying the body will be stoned to death; Oedipus's people are dying of plague because an old murder goes unpunished; Medea's husband has left her for another woman and she has become a social outcast. The tragic character determines to follow his or her own conscience in addressing these situations rather than accept the solutions of others or the supposed decrees of fate.

The Acceptance of Responsibility

Although the circumstances with which they are presented are not always of their own making, tragic characters take full responsibility for their actions. Tragedy is about human potential and our ability to choose for ourselves and take responsibility for the consequences of those choices. It is no coincidence that the great tragedies were written in periods of optimism about the ability of human beings to control their own destinies. The fifth century B.C.E. saw the rise of both Athenian democracy and the Athenian empire. In Shakespeare's time, the English navy defeated the Spanish armada and then pursued Queen Elizabeth's goals of building an empire.

Can Tragedy Exist Today?

Because the drama has changed and our philosophical perspective has changed, we might question whether tragedy can exist today. Certainly, the tragedies that we use as our reference points were written during times when dramatists saw royal characters rather than common characters as the best personages to convey their meaning. These characters were seen as larger than life as they undertook epic struggles with the universe.

Medea is so obsessed with revenging herself on Jason for his lack of fidelity that she kills their children. At the end of the play, Medea (Fiona Shaw) cradles the body of one of her dead sons while Jason (Jonathan Cake) denounces her actions. But he is too late to stop the course of events that his duplicity set in motion. The tragedy, *Medea,* was produced by the Abbey Theatre in 2002 and directed by Deborah Warner.

They spoke a poetic, highly charged language that also lifted them out of the realm of ordinary existence. And they were further enlarged by their relationship to myths or legends. They were characters ready to fight the gods or fate.

Today, much of our drama frames human action in realistic terms and examines the struggles of average people to overcome economic and social problems. Our sense of the universe and our place in it has changed. The vastness of the universe defies comprehension; human beings have become no more than flecks barely registering on the surface of endless space and time. Because so much of our lives seems out of our control, much of today's nonrealistic drama

has focused on the absurd, on our inability to give meaning to our brief passage on the planet. The idea of taking responsibility for our actions, which is at the heart of tragedy, may seem impossible or irrelevant.

If indeed tragedy is possible today, it cannot be produced from the models of Greek or Elizabethan tragedy. It will have to take a different course. The very nature of democracy, for example, precludes a tragedy of the aristocracy. In the mid-twentieth century several playwrights, including Arthur Miller and Eugene O'Neill, contributed to an American idea of tragedy. And, as part of his epic cycle on America, the playwright August Wilson provides tantalizing

Early film made the most of melodramatic plots in which young women were threatened by villains. The scene depicted here comes from a film of 1919: *Chelsea 7750*. Although such damsel-in-distress scenes are the most vivid representations of melodramatic form, melodrama encompasses a range of plots in which good and evil are clearly opposed.

possibilities of a tragic view in *Joe Turner's Come and Gone*. The central figure, Herald Loomis, has a larger-than-life quality that comes from both the intensity of his feelings and the symbolic nature of his character. And he speaks a language that is poetic and charged. His name, Herald Loomis, suggests that he brings redemption; he is the "herald" of the light. He emerges from a background of slavery and the chain gang, a background comparable to the harrowing circumstances of classical tragedy.

Just as the tragic figures of ancient Greece or Elizabethan England represented their communities, so Herald Loomis represents his community—all of the enslaved. He endures terrible suffering, and through that suffering he comes to wisdom. Like Oedipus, he is searching for himself, and he reviews his past and those closest to him as he comes to recognize and take his place in the world. Although, like Hamlet, much of his suffering is not of his own making, the play focuses on his spiritual crisis, for which he *is* responsible. And ultimately he chooses the path of self-determination, acting symbolically when he cuts himself. Freedom is central to classical tragedy, and it is central to Herald Loomis. He is not waiting for someone else to bleed or suffer for him. He will suffer for himself. And in that moment of accepting himself, he discharges the spectral chains of Joe Turner.

In its own way, *Joe Turner's Come and Gone* may also deal with the struggle over succession. Herald Loomis may not be a king, but he is a representative of a people enslaved by another people. By throwing off the oppressor and reclaiming himself, Herald Loomis asserts the rights of black people to participate fully in society. His actions help bring change in succession to the rights of the nation. August Wilson places his characters in a world that has meaning and a moral framework.

Melodrama

We may see very little tragedy in the theatre and films of today, yet we do see a great deal of another genre, **melodrama.** Melodrama has its origins in very simple conflicts of good and evil. Melodrama externalizes the cause of our problems; there is little internal conflict or probing of moral issues. The nature of good and evil is clear at the outset. The hero or heroine may have terrifying obstacles to overcome. But the heroic figures are not their own primary obstacles nor do they set in motion the forces that threaten them.

In traditional melodrama, a helpless young woman would be held hostage in some gruesome way by an obvious villain—only to be rescued at the last possible moment by a courageous and virtuous young man. This was a celebrated formula on the early American stage that has transitioned into many Hollywood movies. For example, a version of the young woman in distress takes place in the third film of George

Kneehigh is a theatre company from Cornwall, England, that is known for its adventurous approaches to theatrical storytelling. *The Wild Bride* is based on a Grimm's fairy tale entitled, "The Handless Maiden." The heroine, played here by Audrey Brisson, is plunged into a nightmare journey when her father makes a careless bargain with the devil. In the photograph the character's hands have been cut off to satisfy the devil's escalating frustration as he finds he is unable to possess the innocent and virtuous young bride. In the spirit of early melodrama, the play relies on music to shape its changing moods, in this case lively bluegrass with dance that also lighten the darker plot episodes. The production was adapted and directed by Emma Rice, the co-artistic director of Kneehigh, and is shown in performance at Berkeley Repertory Theatre in 2013.

Lucas's *Star Wars* trilogy, *Return of the Jedi*. Princess Leia and Han Solo have been taken captive by the evil and disgusting Jabba the Hutt. Solo,

weak and blinded from having been imprisoned in ice, is temporarily unable to defend Leia from the vile Jabba, "the slimy piece of worm-ridden filth." Leia, for all her modern courage and independence, is dressed seductively in a bikini with a metal collar and chain about her neck. Jabba holds the chain and uses it to pull Leia closer to his voluminous flesh. It is a particularly gross version of the villain taking advantage of the heroine, a new way of tying her to the railroad tracks. At this point Luke Skywalker, now a Jedi knight, arrives. But he must face more evil before he can win the release of his friends. First he must outwit the horrible Rancor, and then they must all take on the dreaded Sarlac, the vast, pulsing mouth on the desert floor, filled with hundreds of tusk-like teeth. As the battle builds, the well-known *Star Wars* theme music supports the action. Like the early stage melodramas from which the name of this genre is taken, music is an extraordinarily important part of the action film experience, building a sense of fear or triumph as needed.

Different versions of melodramatic stories involving the good guy who takes on the many incarnations of the forces of evil, all with state-of-the-art special effects, are at the heart of a long list of Hollywood movies, from *Star Wars* to *Indiana Jones* and James Bond to *Spiderman* and *Mission Impossible*. Sometimes there are whole cities of innocent people to be rescued instead of an individual woman, but the basic premise is the same. However, we do see a shift in gender roles as more women characters participate actively in the battle for salvation, such as in *The Hunger Games*.

The popularity of such movies is due to more than simply the rush of the special effects. The world is a difficult place. Contemporary life is stressful. We worry about everything from financial difficulties to crime to international tensions to climate change and its effect on the environment. There is great and simple satisfaction in being clear on the distinction between good and evil and in seeing the triumph of the good and the crushing of the bad. Although we may celebrate such triumph at the moment, we know that life is much more complicated than in the movies and that celluloid villains and heroes are as thin as the film on which their exploits are recorded.

Pure melodrama is most easily identified in action movies and popular drama from the nineteenth century. More serious drama that clearly opposes the forces of good and evil can also be described in part by the term *melodrama*. With Roy Cohn as the obvious villain, *Angels in America* can be seen to have some melodramatic tendencies. And the work of the playwright Lillian Hellman (discussed in Chapter 7) is also sometimes categorized as melodrama because it examines the way evil spreads when good people do not fight it.

Tragicomedy

Tragicomedy is a form of drama that has particular resonance today. The plays that fall into this classification are not merely plays that combine serious and comic elements. *Hamlet*, for example, has a generous amount of comedy and humor, yet we are clear that it is a tragedy. Similarly, there are some tragicomic—as well as melodramatic—tendencies in *Angels in America*; yet because the play focuses on the possibility of social and personal change, it does not fall under the category of tragicomedy.

Tragicomic plays are concerned with human awareness rather than a program of social change. In particular, they tend to explore an existential philosophical position. In simple terms, existentialism has to do with relativity—a belief that no fixed meaning underlies human existence and that the best we can do is to invent a framework for meaning that will be highly personal and individual and will inevitably have to change. What distinguishes tragicomedy is the way one perspective undercuts or changes the other. There is an interplay between the serious and comic sides of a situation that results in an unstable landscape, a kind of shifting terrain where the footing is hard to secure. The truth of the situation becomes elusive or impossible to ascertain, as is the case in Luigi Pirandello's 1922 play, *Six Characters in Search of an Author*.

Six Characters in Search of an Author presents a bizarre situation in which a group of characters arrive at a theatre where actors are rehearsing a play. The characters request and then insist that the actors put on the story of the characters' lives instead of the play that they are rehearsing. The characters claim that their playwright abandoned them partway through the process of making them into a play, and now they are desperate to have the opportunity to play out their drama. The six characters want to perform their play for the actors and then have the actors restage that play with the characters as the audience. Built into this confusing structure of real actors playing stage actors who are then impersonating characters who are actually present are all kinds of questions about the nature of reality. The Father, who is one of the six characters, expresses his fear that human beings cannot understand each other:

We all have a world of things inside ourselves and each one of us has his own private world. How can we understand each other if the words I use have the sense and the value that I expect them to have, but whoever is listening to me inevitably thinks that those same words have a different sense and value, because of the private world he has inside himself too? We think that we understand each other, but we never do.[5]

Later he comments to the director on the slippery, changing nature of reality:

I'm only asking to try to find out if you really see yourself now in the same way that you saw yourself, for instance, once upon a time in the past, with all the illusions you had then, with everything inside and outside yourself as it seemed then—and not only seemed, but really

The tormented family of "characters" reappears mysteriously at the end of *Six Characters in Search of an Author* at the Oregon Shakespeare Festival's second company in Portland, Oregon (now Portland Center Stage). Because each of the characters tells a different version of their tormented family history, it is impossible for either the actors whose rehearsal they interrupt or the actual audience members to determine what is the truth of the characters' situation. Pirandello leaves us with an unsolvable puzzle.

was! Well then, look back on those illusions, those ideas that you don't have anymore, on all those things that no longer seem the same to you. Don't you feel that not only this stage is falling away from your feet but so is the earth itself, and that all these realities of today are going to seem tomorrow as if they had been an illusion?[6]

Pirandello's play challenges the audience members not to be relentless in pursuing the truth about one another, because the truth is impossible to ascertain. In the difficult areas of human relationships, Pirandello suggests that compassion may be the best we can offer.

Plays that communicate the existential, tragicomic perspective embodied by *Six Characters* range from the realistic plays of Anton Chekhov to the absurd plays of Samuel Beckett. Tragicomedy probably offers the least affirmation of any of the theatrical genres. These plays are usually disturbing and present more questions than answers. The mixture of forms as well as the frequently provoking stage images are deliberate challenges to complacency or certainty. Tragicomedy offers neither the catharsis of tragedy, nor the moral satisfaction of melodrama, nor the emotional release through laughter of comedy or farce. The laughter of tragicomedy is laughter that is interrupted when we are reminded once again of how genuinely painful the situation actually is.

In tragicomedy, the characters are cut off from a fixed value system and at the same time are cut off from one another. The condition of loneliness or alienation is at the heart of tragicomedy. We have observed that tragic characters are also alone, but their isolation heightens the grandeur and courage of their actions. The scale of the characters in tragicomedy is greatly reduced. These are small characters beset by anxiety, failure, and emptiness.

American playwrights who write tragicomedy include both Edward Albee and Sam Shepard. Both Albee and Shepard focus on breakdowns in the American family—breakdowns that result from the spiritual isolation of the characters. In *Buried Child* and *True West*, Shepard's distinctly American characters are rough around the edges, restless, and in search of something that can be called home. Humor in Shepard's plays is interrupted by the very real threat of violence that always simmers underneath the surface. By contrast, Albee's characters, in such plays as *Who's Afraid of Virginia Woolf?* and *A Delicate Balance*, are more educated and upper-class than Shepard's, but their education becomes part of the source of their spiritual crisis.

Like the American tragicomic playwrights, the Russian playwright Anton Chekhov focuses on a realistic social group of family, friends, and associates. Of all the tragicomic playwrights, Chekhov seems to be the most gentle with his characters and yet the most unforgiving. As a group, his plays present situations in which the gulf between people cannot be bridged. The isolation and self-focus are complete. For example, in the poignant final moments of his play *The Cherry Orchard*, the characters are making plans to depart. But they are so absorbed with their personal needs that they fail to provide for the care of their aged servant, Firs. Each exits thinking someone else has arranged to take Firs to a nursing home. As they go off, calling out their good-byes, with the house bolted from the outside, it becomes apparent to the audience that Firs has been forgotten. The last image of the play is of Firs, locked alone in the house to die, with the sound first of a breaking string and then of an ax chopping down the cherry trees.

The ending of Beckett's *Waiting for Godot* is widely considered a definitional moment in tragicomedy, when the two tramps repeat for the last time, "Let's go." But once again, they cannot leave the stage and remain sitting, waiting into eternity as the light fades. What sustains these two characters in the end is their companionship, however difficult and contentious. There is genuine affection between the two characters, and they choose to stay together rather than part.

Tragicomic plays involve human desperation, yet they are some of the most eloquent theatrical works of our times. In their arresting and imaginative creation lies the challenge of the playwright to confront our own illusions—about ourselves and the world we inhabit—without any of the protective devices that we usually employ to hold back the truth.

Farce

Whereas comedy generally takes as its subject some kind of social critique, **farce** is concerned with the humorous possibilities of the moment. Farce attacks pretentiousness of all kinds and uses the social situation as a launching pad for the ridiculous. Farce is about anarchy, about breaking all the rules. Taking on authority is one of the trademarks of farce, and frequently the characters are only one step ahead of the law. In the film *Animal House*, the Deltas, a group of low-life fraternity brothers, scheme to destroy the obnoxious dean and his pal the mayor as well as the rich and condescending members of the student elite. This film is a classic example of a farce involving a rowdy assault on authority. Similarly, in the Marx Brothers' films, Groucho, Harpo, and Chico invade various forms of high society and bring them crashing down.

Troublemaker, or The Freaking Kick-A Adventures of Bradley Boatright offers a title that captures the spirit of rebellion permeating this play by Dan LeFranc. A fantasy adventure that shifts between the home shared by a twelve-year-old boy and his mother and the world of comic book superheroes, this production (2013) is part of the new play development program at Berkeley Repertory Theatre. The actors are Ben Mehl, Chad Goodridge, and Matt Bradley, directed by Lila Neugebauer.

Farce almost always highlights actors rather than playwrights. Performances are memorable not because of the playwright's words but because of the comic genius of the actor. Farce has a brilliant history in the United States if we consider as a whole the work of actors on the stage, in film, and on television. It is not surprising that farce would flourish in a nation whose origins are revolutionary and whose goals are democratic. The actors of farce rebel against notions of aristocracy, against the imposition of high culture, against institutions that have lost touch with the people, against all forms of arbitrary rules and hierarchical power structures.

Jim Carrey is an actor known for creating characters who have a wild, anarchic streak. He performs with a highly energized physical abandon that seems to defy the bodily limitations of most humans. In films such as *The Mask* (1994) and *Liar Liar* (1997) he challenges authority with an attitude of defiance well suited to contemporary farce. His film *The Mask* offers another model of a typical plot in farce. Carrey's character, Stanley Ipkiss, is the little man at the bottom of the ladder at the bank where he works. He is taken advantage of by everyone, abused by his landlady, swindled by his auto mechanics. He wears the ultimate in "geek" ties and pajamas.

The Marx Brothers honed their acting skills in vaudeville before turning their special brand of lunacy into films. Animals were frequently featured as part of their performance onstage and in the movies. The French theatre practitioners Antonin Artaud and Samuel Beckett acknowledged the Marx Brothers' influence on their own work well before the comedy team was taken seriously in the United States. Major films of the Marx Brothers include *Duck Soup* and *A Night at the Opera*.

But by placing a mysterious mask on his face, Carrey breaks through all the social restraint of his "Mr. Nice Guy" role, throws caution to the wind, and becomes the embodiment of physical and spiritual anarchy. With a ludicrous green face and an outrageously suave wardrobe, he robs the bank where he works, defeats the town gangsters, and has the police dancing in the streets while he plays the maracas in his persona as "Cuban Pete." With the broadest possible physical humor, sometimes even rendered through cartoon images, he revenges himself on

everyone who previously pushed him around. Carrey's character says of the power of the mask, "It brings your innermost desires to life." The same could be said of farce.

Writing about the Theatre

The unique structural elements of the drama discussed in Chapter 12 and the views of human existence that shape dramatic genres are foundational for the work of the playwright. The study of structure and genre is also essential to the

Stanley Ipkiss, played by Jim Carrey, re-creates himself as a bizarre, but romantic, hero dancing with Cameron Diaz in *The Mask*. The masked character fulfills the fantasies of the nice guy who always finishes last.

work of two other theatre writers: the dramaturg and the critic. The dramaturg and the critic are particularly concerned with analyzing the work of the playwright in connection with the production of plays. They seek to understand what distinguishes the ideas in the play and what distinguishes the play as a work of art. Frequently dramaturgs and critics have similar backgrounds and interests. They must both be broadly educated in the theatre and be strong and creative writers. In fact, the same individual may work sometimes as a dramaturg and sometimes as a critic. For example, for many years Michael

Feingold served as the chief critic of *The Village Voice* in New York City and currently writes for *TheaterMania*. He is also a highly regarded dramaturg as well as a translator and adaptor. Each of these roles requires a different perspective.

The dramaturg can be seen as a writer and thinker engaged at the beginning of theatre making, whereas the critic participates at the end. The dramaturg is part of the collaborative process of creating the work; the critic assesses the work when it is performed onstage for an audience. The dramaturg is on the inside, the critic on the outside. But the dramaturg must maintain a certain independence if he or she is to serve the production well. And the critic must be an engaged and respectful member of the larger theatre community in order to be effective, while remaining entirely independent of the production process. Michael Feingold could not review a production for which he was dramaturg. We now consider the contributions of these two important theatre writers who serve both theatre practitioners and theatre audiences.

The Dramaturg

More and more frequently, resident theatre companies—organizations producing a season of plays—employ at least one staff member who works as a dramaturg. The dramaturg is an ongoing member of the company and is involved continuously with the selection of plays and research and writing about those plays. Although the dramaturg is a relatively new position in the American theatre, the idea of the dramaturg is much older; it is usually credited to the German critic G. E. Lessing, who wrote in the late eighteenth century. Stephen Weeks, who is both a dramaturg and a teacher of dramaturgy and playwriting, sees the dramaturg as occupying a unique position in a theatre organization:

> Dramaturgy is a fluid enterprise and dramaturgs wear many hats. Whereas we might think of actors or directors as having specific, well-defined responsibilities, the dramaturg is

Passing Strange (2007) is a new musical by the composer and performer Stew, produced at the Public Theater where one of Oskar Eustis's primary goals as artistic director is the development of new work. "On a piece like *Passing Strange* it started with a singer in Joe's Pub to whom we said, 'Have you ever thought of making a theatre piece out of your songs?' and he said, 'I've never been to a piece of theatre.' Now he's opening on Broadway next month. It takes three and a half years to do that. You invest the time and figure out the way for each particular art form."[7]

a theatrical generalist. The dramaturg makes connections, starts conversations, builds bridges.[8]

In Chapter 10, we discussed the work of Oskar Eustis, who served as the dramaturg at the Eureka Theatre in San Francisco and collaborated with the playwright Tony Kushner on the development of *Angels in America*. Eustis is now the artistic director of the Public Theater in New York City. As dramaturg at the Eureka Theatre, he focused on encouraging the development of new plays and bringing those plays into production. Like Eustis, dramaturgs at other theatre companies provide feedback and assistance to playwrights who are creating new work; and, as Stephen Weeks observes, they must demonstrate great sensitivity to the needs of the play and the needs of the playwright:

> The goal is usually to assist the writer to realize his or her vision for the play. This is a complex task, and the dramaturg might need to serve as a guide, a cheerleader, a surrogate audience member, a critic, or all of these things. A good dramaturg will also know when to leave the playwright to his or her own devices and good judgment.

Tom Bryant, dramaturg for *Apollo*, contrasts the perspective of the dramaturg with that of the director, who is also often concerned with new play development.

Directors tend to be very pragmatic. They have to focus on immediate production results. Given production demands, directors tend to ask, "What can I do with this text onstage? What kind of actor choices would I make here? What kind of choices would the designers make?" These are all production-oriented choices. The dramaturg looks at the text, beyond the current production choices, and asks, "Does this work as a scene? Does this work as an act? Is there strong momentum here?" They think beyond the current production to the play's future productions. When directors face literary issues in a script they sometimes tend to compensate for the material by production adjustments. They think, "Oh, this isn't working so well. Maybe what I'll do is create a piece of staging that really makes the rhythm faster here." This may solve the problem in the current production but it doesn't necessarily solve the inherent literary problem in terms of the text of the play. So part of what the specialization in dramaturgy becomes is helping the playwright fix those problems on the page.[9]

The dramaturg also works with the artistic director of the theatre to select a provocative and complementary group of plays for the season and must have a wide knowledge of classical as well as recent plays. Another part of the dramaturg's work is to research background materials related to a particular play—first to provide necessary information to the director and the actors, and then to write introductory material for the audience to be presented in the program or possibly in a lobby display. Research that the dramaturg does for the theatre company may be

WORKING IN THE THEATRE

Summary of the Dramaturg's Responsibilities

- To keep up with developments in the drama.
- To assist playwrights in the development of new plays.
- To advise the artistic director on selecting plays.
- To study the play text.
- To research appropriate historical materials for the director, designers, and actors.
- To research production history.
- To provide assistance with textual analysis and meaning of words.
- To assist with cuts or adaptation of the text if appropriate.
- To attend rehearsals and provide the director with feedback.
- To write program notes.
- To prepare lobby displays.
- To contribute to public relations materials.
- To lead discussions before or after the show.

presented through discussion or informally written notes or summaries. Dramaturgs frequently participate in the table work sessions at the beginning of the rehearsal period to explain the historical and philosophical background of the play and to provide resource materials such as photographs, maps, and biographies. They may also be responsible for locating highly specialized information. For example, Nilo Cruz's Pulitzer Prize–winning play *Anna in the Tropics* takes place in a cigar factory, and the actors must learn how to roll cigars. The dramaturg may arrange for a cigar maker to come to one or more rehearsals to demonstrate these skills. The areas of research the dramaturg may be called upon to pursue are limitless.

Once the rehearsal process is under way, the dramaturg must engage in more formal

ARTISTIC FOUNDATIONS

Necessary Skills and Talents of the Dramaturg

- Love of dramatic literature.
- Fascination with research.
- Wide knowledge of dramatic literature and theatre history.
- Strong analytical skills.
- Strong writing skills.
- Commitment to collaborative work.
- Teaching skills.
- Ability to clearly articulate observations made in rehearsals.

writing for the program and, sometimes, for lobby displays. The lobby display is being used by an increasing number of theatres to expand the amount of contextual information available to audience members. The lobby display also offers the dramaturg an opportunity to use visual materials such as photographs, historical objects, and video clips to support written statements. In the program notes and the lobby display, the dramaturg communicates why the company has chosen to do a particular play and why this play is important for the community that makes up the audience. Background materials are presented to enrich the audience's understanding of the significance of the events in the play. Most of all, the dramaturg shares the excitement that the theatre company feels in undertaking the production, an excitement that should be infectious for the audience.

The Critic

The critic has been in existence almost as long as there has been theatre. Aristotle's writing on

drama, which has been part of our discussion of structure and genre, is considered a work of criticism. In *The Poetics*, Aristotle writes about what makes a successful and admirable play. Over the centuries, critics have followed Aristotle with heated arguments about what makes good theatre or art and what place theatre should have in a particular society. Most critics are passionate about their views and recognize something vital and essential in the theatre, although they have strongly divided opinions about what the essence of good theatre is.

Sometimes a critic's ideas are formulated slowly and represent a cumulative process of evaluation. But often criticism is written quickly, particularly when it takes the form of a review composed immediately following a play's opening to be published in a newspaper or online within a day or two. Some writers and theatre practitioners would separate critics and reviewers into different categories, concluding that the role of the critic is to try to answer larger questions about the significance of a work of theatre than a reviewer can tackle in the sprint to the deadline. But with that reservation in mind, we will examine the role of the contemporary critic in relationship to the theatre.

When the dramaturg writes a program note or prepares a lobby display, it is quite clear who the targeted readers are: the people who have chosen to come to see this particular play. And when the dramaturg provides analysis and research early on in the production process, he or she knows the director and the actors for whom that work is intended and how it is to be used. It is less clear for whom the critic is writing, and so it is profitable to explore who the critic's audience is in order to assess the role the critic plays.

The most immediate source in which a critic may publish an article or review in response to a play is a newspaper, a magazine, or an online site. The readers of this publication may or may not become audience members, and many of them will look to a review to provide guidance about whether a production is worth their time and money. In this regard the review functions as advice for the consumer and there is no doubt that commentary published immediately after a play opens is expected to offer judgment about the production's overall merit. But the critic has a larger obligation to the general reader than merely to indicate thumbs-up or thumbs-down.

Julius Novick, a well-known critic who has spent decades writing about the theatre, sees his responsibility as communicating the experience of the performance as fully as possible to the reader who has not yet seen the play:

> But our obligation and our joy as writers is to convey what we have seen and heard and thought and felt at the theatre, as truthfully and vividly, as gracefully and clearly, and with as deep an understanding as we can, and, if possible, to refract the truth about the show we've just seen through our individual selves to a larger truth about the theatre and a still larger truth about the world.[10]

In Novick's judgment the critic must be open and sensitive to the theatre event and then be ready to put that experience into words in order to distill its meaning. There is also a recognition that describing and interpreting one's own experience of an event is not a simple matter. Writing good criticism is itself an art form, requiring creative choices and drawing the significant parts into a coherent whole.

As a way of organizing one's responses to a performance, Novick proposes that the critic answer four questions.

1. What is the work itself trying to do?
2. How well has it done it?
3. Was it worth doing?
4. Why was it or wasn't it worth doing?

WORKING IN THE THEATRE

Summary of the Critic's Responsibilities

- To do appropriate preparation before the performance such as reading the play and researching background on the play, playwright, or performance style.
- To attend the performance in an alert and receptive state of mind.
- To write a review that focuses on the particular production, not the preferences or cleverness of the reviewer.
- To provide readers with a vivid sense of the audience's experience and the style and ideas of the play and the production.
- To provide theatre practitioners with constructive feedback about their work.
- To engage in a public dialogue about the significance of work being done in the theatre.

And he says of the fourth question, "That's where the bones are buried. That can get us into the relation between the work and the world, the subject to which all the great critics are drawn."[11] In these questions, Novick leads the critic away from judging a theatre work according to personal preference and instead asks the critic to consider the terms of the play itself and the production of that play.

Furthermore, when critics ask Novick's four questions, they are setting up an apparatus to address a second set of readers in addition to potential audience members: the theatre practitioners who have produced the play. A productive review, which serves the theatre profession well, gives the practitioners vital feedback about how successfully they communicated their ideas and how their work was received. Directors, actors, and designers work very hard to craft their storytelling and expressive stage metaphors. A thoughtful response from an insightful critic can be very important to the theatre artists in assessing the impact of their work. The actor Billy Crudup says he hopes that critics will engage in a dialogue with the production by answering important questions for him:

> What was successful? What wasn't successful? Why? Is that interpretation an interesting interpretation?[12]

Of course, all theatre practitioners seek approval of their stage efforts. But the responsible critic contributes far more to the health of the theatre by considering the artistic choices made than by merely announcing which actor was a hit and which one wasn't and whether the scenery and costumes were dazzling.

ARTISTIC FOUNDATIONS

The Necessary Skills and Talents of the Critic

- Enthusiasm for the theatre.
- Belief in the importance of the arts in the life of the community.
- Wide knowledge of dramatic literature and theatre history.
- Understanding of the contributions of playwrights, directors, actors, and designers.
- Strong writing skills.
- Ability to communicate the experience of the theatre performance through lively, accessible language.
- Ability to understand symbolic and metaphorical constructs.
- Ability to interpret the meaning of a play in relation to philosophical, cultural, or political concerns of the community.
- Ability to generate interest and excitement about the theatre for readers.

Although critics are writing most obviously for those who are involved with a production as audience members or producers, they are also participating in a larger conversation about art and culture that extends to many people beyond the immediate radius of a particular production. Criticism is read by those interested in the arts and in the relationship between art and society whether they are other critics, appreciators of art, producers of art, or academics and students of all backgrounds. Frank Rich was for many years the head theatre critic of *The New York Times.* He now writes what may be called cultural criticism that is particularly concerned with the direction of our country and the various forces that affect political decision making. He draws heavily on his involvement with the theatre to explain contemporary actions through comparisons with characters of great playwrights and by considering political performances in light of the way actors construct stage identities.

Through their writing, critics also address readers of the future by creating a record of the impact of the theatre performance. One of the defining factors of theatre production is its nature as a live event. As we observed at the beginning of the book, the theatre actually exists only during the performance itself with an audience present. Films are by their very nature preserved for future generations. A theatre performance can be documented through video or film, but that documentation does not re-create the actual event of the performance. By exploring the visual, aural, kinesthetic, emotional, and intellectual experience of being an audience member at a particular performance, the critic leaves a written impression, however imperfect, of the nuances and excitement communicated by the actors' work. This written record of the most eloquent details of the performance offers students of the art of theatre the chance to understand what was meaningful in a given time and place, years after the actors and designers who made the work no longer hold forth on the stage.

Two Reviews of *Medea*

Following are two reviews of contemporary productions of the Greek tragedy *Medea*. The first review considers the production done by the Classical Theatre of Harlem; the second evaluates the production done by the Abbey Theatre of Ireland. Both reviews were published in *The New York Times* in 2002. The reviews of *Medea* are included here because they allow us to continue our discussion of this play begun in Chapter 2 in the section on ancient Greek theatre and continued in this chapter's examination of genre and tragedy. The reviews also illustrate the manner in which two different critics approach constructing a review. In each case, the critic creates a vivid sense of the performance by describing the work of the actors and the arrangement of the physical space. Both critics also tell us what distinguishes these productions and how the play's conflicts are interpreted for modern audiences. The reviews demonstrate that the critics have studied the play, its history, and other productions in order to be authoritative in assessing the work of the theatre companies involved.

Passions of *Medea*, Brought Up to Date
By D. J. R. Bruckner, *The New York Times*, April 16, 2002

Every performance of "Medea" is an adaptation. Euripides' text is a highly selective commentary on a hugely popular series of legends about this semidivine psychotic, and we can only dimly perceive aspects of what he meant to say about them. We also have far from perfect knowledge of stagecraft in the fifth century B.C. So even those rare performances given in Euripides' own language are adaptations.

That said, the one adapted and directed by Alfred Preisser for the Classical Theatre of Harlem, running until April 28 at the Harlem School of the Arts, is special. Its language is current street talk. Its chorus dances, chants spare lines and occasionally sings to music of striking ingenuity by Kelvyn Fell and David Red Harrington. But this chorus does not carry the burden of the narrative as in Euripides. Here the whole story is told by the three characters: Medea (April Yvette Thompson), Kreon (Arthur French) and Jason (Lawrence Winslow).

This radical personalizing of the lethal conflicts among men and a woman, between different nations, and between mortals and divinities brings out surprising qualities and instabilities in the characters. I suspect that no matter how many versions I see in the future, my perception of them all will be affected by the revelations here.

It is very clear that Kreon, King of Corinth, is not arrogant or unfeeling when he banishes Medea so that Jason will be free to marry the king's daughter; he simply cannot perceive the justice of this barbarian woman's refusal to lose her husband and her sons. And Jason really believes he honors Medea by leaving her and marrying a princess so that Medea's sons will become royal heirs.

As for Medea herself, the transformation is haunting. There is no mistaking her outrage and injury when she spits curses of defiance at both men and reminds them of the murderous betrayals of her own people she committed in the past for Jason's glory. But in this version her tenderness toward her children touches Kreon and Jason at times, and her fury at Jason's betrayal makes her murder of those children appear to be an act of passionate satisfaction.

At 70 minutes, Mr. Preisser's "Medea" is considerably shorter than most, but it sends one away with more to think about than most. It also causes more anxiety and excitement in the audience. Viewers sit on opposite sides of a relatively intimate space, and the rising hostility between Jason and Medea seems to spill out into the audience. That a couple of audience members uttered audible replies to a few of the lines at the performance I saw cannot be a rare occurrence. It is very hard to remain silent.

Inevitably, in a revision so extensive, some things are lost. The gritty idiom removes the aura of mystery surrounding the action in Euripides' play. And there are other disjunctures. But do they add up to too great a price? Probably not, for most.

This ambitious undertaking puts 19 actors onstage. But of course the overall effect depends most on the principal three. Mr. French gives Kreon the appearance of stunned dignity that is absolutely demanded by Mr. Preisser's reading of the story. Mr. Winslow makes Jason so honestly ignorant of how mortal is his betrayal of Medea that he elicits more pity than scorn. And Ms. Thompson's Medea is a real hell cat, a bundle of contradictions that are all the more threatening for seeming so natural in someone who is half human but who has power no human can control or even comprehend.

MEDEA By Euripides; adapted and directed by Alfred Preisser; choreography by Tracy Johnson and Angela Hughes; sets by Anne Lomel; lighting by Christopher McElroen; costumes by Kimberly Glennon; sound by Stefan Jacobs; stage manager, Frantz Cayo; fight direction by T. J. Glenn; original music and songs by Kelvyn Bell and David Red Harrington. Presented by the Classical Theatre of Harlem, Mr. McElroen, co-founder and executive director; Mr. Preisser, co-founder and artistic director. At the Harlem School of the Arts Theatre, 645 St. Nicholas Avenue, near 141st Street, Hamilton Heights.

WITH: Arthur French (Kreon), Joan Green (Nurse), Angela Hughes (Fate), Zainab Jah (Choral Leader/Death), April Yvette Thompson (Medea) and Lawrence Winslow (Jason).

Next Wave Review; A *Medea* Fit for the World of Today
By Ben Brantley, *The New York Times*, October 4, 2002

The word has gone out in Corinth that there's a celebrity in pain in the vicinity. And when the groupies who sniff for blood wounds among the incredibly famous arrive at her house, Medea doesn't disappoint.

There she is, as embodied with a harrowing lack of vanity by the brilliant Fiona Shaw, her recognizable features smudged by unhappiness, her eyes hidden by the formal shield of dark glasses, her mismatched wardrobe a thrown-on hash of running shoes, a cardigan and a little print dress. Why, she might have stepped from those pages of The National Enquirer devoted to stars foolish enough to leave home without makeup. The question is: Will she talk to us? Will she let us in on her truly sensational problems?

You bet she will. How satisfying, after all, can revenge be unless you have an audience to reflect it, to magnify it, to turn it into legend? Without their urging, how will you know who you really are?

In the thrilling Abbey Theatre production of Euripides' "Medea," which runs at the Harvey Theatre of the Brooklyn Academy of Music through Oct. 12, Greek tragedy's most spectacularly vengeful woman has rematerialized in the dawning years of the 21st century. And it is, to tell the truth, a little frightening to see how comfortably this volcanically uncomfortable woman fits into the world of today.

What Ms. Shaw and the director, Deborah Warner,

who collaborated so memorably on their staging of T. S. Eliot's "Waste Land," have achieved here seems so obvious, when you think about it, that you're amazed it hasn't been done before. For this "Medea" homes in on the parallels between the very form of Greek tragedy—with its dialogue between uncommon heroes and heroines and the common folk of the chorus—and an age in which private breakdowns, breakups and humiliations have become public rituals.

Of course if this were the only point of Ms. Warner's "Medea," it wouldn't have turned out to be the most essential ticket of this theatre season. This isn't one of those stagings in which a clever concept reduces characters to glossy illustrations.

The miracle of this "Medea" is how completely it integrates its ideas of a latter-day culture of celebrity into a classic text, freshly translated by Kenneth McLeish and Frederic Raphael, without ever seeming to warp the spirit of the original. The anxious perfume that saturates this production is a compound of the passion, terror and existential ambivalence that have plagued humans for as long as they have been able to think.

Ms. Shaw's Medea has little in common with the usual majestically angry sorceress who is guided by one idée fixe: to avenge herself on her husband, Jason, for whom she betrayed her homeland and who has now left her for the young princess of Corinth. There is scant evidence of the commanding icy intellect so elegantly incarnated by Diana Rigg in Jonathan Kent's production of a proto-feminist "Medea" on Broadway in 1994.

It's not that you doubt the intelligence of Ms. Shaw's Medea. But her lacerating misfortunes have broken the circuits of that intelligence, and her responses are a toxic jumble. She seems to wear her nerves outside her skin. Numbness and excruciating pain, shrill anger and mordant, bizarre humor flit across her raw features in disjunctive parade.

Set in a half-finished courtyard littered with children's toys and cinder blocks (the designer is Tom Pye), suggesting a life interrupted, the entire production seems to occur in that heightened, instinct-addling realm that occurs during times of emergency. The evening begins in a state of breathlessness that never really lets up. And as upsetting as much of it is, the show radiates such high theatrical energy and insight that you can't help grinning through most of it.

The first image is of Medea's Nurse (Siobhan McCarthy), represented here as a student au pair type, rushing onto the stage with a handful of knives. She is also, it turns out, carrying bottles of pills. And she proceeds to hide these commonplace household objects, which in this context have suddenly turned threatening.

This interpolated scene is inspired in its banal immediacy, translating abstract terror into specific and familiar physical terms. You can't help feeling like a visitor who has showed up at just the wrong moment. Of course, you keep staring. And if you don't, there's the chorus of five townswomen who emerge from the audience and swarm onto the stage as if to act as your proxy.

They have the feverish look of fans addicted to real-life soap operas, like the kind of people who rushed to the site of Nicole Simpson's murder and stood in line for the trial of Michael C. Skakel. Their relentless talk to Medea, shaped by a sooty mix of empathy and prurience, seems perfectly natural. So, more surprisingly, does Medea's willingness to respond to them.

Then again, as a notorious exile now spurned by even the husband who brought her here, who else does she have to talk to? Besides, as Jason (Jonathan Cake) later says nastily, he and Medea have become people who would "rather be sung about than sing."

This production acutely accents the talk of reputation and fame and its rewards. And you can see that Jason and, in her more befuddled way, Medea are quite keen to put forth their respective versions of their lives together. Medea knows very well she is playing to a crowd and, by extension, to history. She accepts as her due the applause that the chorus gives after she has successfully pleaded with Kreon (Struan Rodger), the king of Crete, to postpone her exile.

If it sounds as if Ms. Shaw's Medea is a smooth spinmeister, then I'm misrepresenting her. What's so mesmerizing and truly frightening about her performance is how cogently she evokes a mind that is anything but clear. This Medea is an all too sensitive instrument played upon by overwhelming forces that come from both without and within.

Among these is simple brute lust. The superb Mr. Cake's vanity-driven Jason may not be his wife's match in ingenuity. But he knows exactly where to touch Medea to turn her into jelly. Their most rancorous arguments are punctuated by perverse sexual sparks that threaten to subdue Medea into passivity. And then the spell is broken, and she emerges all the more addled and angry.

The play's grotesque climax (mercilessly rendered here), in which Medea murders her two sons, does not seem a foregone conclusion. Ms. Shaw and Ms. Warner have created a Medea who isn't even sure herself how she will act from one moment to the next. There are stretches, as Medea rants about her diabolical plans for vengeance,

when you think, "Oh, she's just playing," or to use the preferred psychobabble, "acting out."

For this Medea has a wide-ranging mind that, even in abject pain, keeps shifting perspectives on her. Suddenly, without warning, she'll do something like pick up a toy gun and simulate murder with a goofy smile. And she's funny when she's deriding her husband and his bride-to-be, finding the idea of them so unspeakable that she's reduced to making "bleah" and "ick" noises. But the noises also suggest an eloquent woman for whom words are no longer adequate.

When, toward the play's end, a messenger (Derek Hutchinson) arrives to describe the excruciating deaths of Kreon and his daughter, Jason's intended, Ms. Shaw's face goes dead white and still, showing flickers of gratification and just as often of incomprehension that her plan has come to fruition.

And therein lies the real genius of Ms. Shaw's portraiture. Real life seldom affords the tidy motives of murder mysteries or the stark psychological blueprints of novels about serial killers. And the recent spate of reality television serials have confirmed that famous people are never just the cleanly drawn cartoons we would like them to be. Witness the on-camera disintegration of Anna Nicole Smith.

Ms. Shaw and Ms. Warner have created one of the most

human Medeas ever, precisely because they have refused to simplify her. Medea's acts may be monstrous, but the woman who performs them is a mass of confused impulses and thwarted drives that elude easy categorization. It is this very blurriness that makes her so vivid, so haunting and so damningly easy to identify with.

MEDEA By Euripides; directed by Deborah Warner; translated by Kenneth McLeish and Frederic Raphael; set by Tom Pye; costumes by Jacqueline Durran; original lighting by Peter Mumford; associate lighting designer, Michael Gunning; soundscape, Mel Mercier; sound by David Meschter. Produced in association with Max Weitzenhoffer, Roger Berlind, Old Vic Productions, Nica Burns for the Really Useful Theaters and Jedediah Wheeler. The Abbey Theatre presented by the Brooklyn Academy of Music, Alan H. Fishman, chairman; William I. Campbell, vice chairman; Karen Brooks Hopkins, president; Joseph V. Melillo, executive producer. At the Brooklyn Academy of Music, Harvey Theatre, 651 Fulton Street, Fort Greene.

WITH: Fiona Shaw (Medea), Siobhan McCarthy (Nurse), Robin Laing (Tutor), Struan Rodger (Kreon), Jonathan Cake (Jason), Joseph Mydell (Aegeus), Dylan Denton (Son) and Derek Hutchinson (Messenger).

Summary

The division of drama into genres is a way of identifying different perspectives on human existence. Tragedy focuses on human mortality and often ends in death or disaster. But tragedy is not a pessimistic form of drama. Tragic characters assume heroic stature as they struggle to control their own destinies and take responsibility for the consequences of their actions. Tragedy flourished as a form of drama in the Greek and Elizabethan theatres, which produced such masterpieces as *Oedipus Rex* and *Hamlet*.

Comedy is concerned with the human ability to endure. Comedy looks at the way human weakness leads to the ridiculous and the ludicrous. But in spite of all their failures, comic characters find a way to go on. Comedy frequently involves a group of characters separated by misunderstanding who are reconciled in the end.

Tragicomedy reflects the anxiety of life. Plays of this genre shift between serious and comic perspectives, and each view undermines the other. In plays such as *Six Characters in Search of an Author* and *Waiting for Godot*, the nature of reality is uncertain, and no fixed meaning underlies the characters' existence. The plays emphasize the characters' frailty and isolation. Tragicomedy also challenges traditional ideas of dramatic structure by questioning the ability of language to communicate or the ability of characters to act in any purposeful way.

Two other genres, melodrama and farce, have become very popular on television and in film as well as in the theatre. Melodrama builds on clear-cut conflicts between good and evil. Farce is a comic form that attacks pretentiousness and all forms of authority.

The dramaturg is an additional member of a theatre company who is responsible for assisting playwrights to develop new work and helping directors and actors interpret plays they are preparing for production. The dramaturg may provide background research as well as dramatic analysis in the service of both the rehearsal process and publications related to a production. The critic evaluates a theatre production when it is performed for an audience. The critic is responsible for analyzing the production for potential audience members and also for providing constructive feedback to the theatre practitioners.

Topics for Discussion and Writing

1. What are the fundamental differences between tragedy and comedy? How can they be considered as complementary genres rather than as opposites?

2. How does comedy offer social criticism? Where do you see social criticism in comedies in the theatre or in films? Because we laugh, do we take social criticism less seriously in comedy than in other genres?

3. What is the philosophical perspective expressed by tragicomedy? What view of life is expressed by the situation of the characters in *Waiting for Godot?*

● For interviews with some of the dramaturgs in this chapter and other resources, please visit
www.mhhe.com/creativespirit6e

CHAPTER 15

The Project

In our study of theatre, we have moved from the most basic element of theatre—the impulse in human nature to perform—to the complex development of that performance impulse in the production of plays. In coming to understand the theatre, we have examined the structure of plays, the work of theatre artists, and the relationship between the expression of ideas in performance and the audience. The purpose of this final chapter is to give you an opportunity to integrate the materials presented in the book by participating in the production process. The goal of this culminating project is for groups of students to collaborate on the hypothetical production of a scene or a play. You will need to study the play to be produced, consider the ideas of the playwright, and contribute to an interpretation of those ideas in a theatre of your choosing for an audience of your peers.

Several approaches to the production project are possible, depending on the size and organization of your class. The project may be collaborative or individual. It may culminate in the presentation of scenes to your class or in the presentation of a production plan, or both. If the project is done individually, your results may be turned in to the instructor rather than presented to the class. The collaborative project is designed for small classes or large classes that also have discussion sections. Large classes without discussion sections will need to modify the collaborative process or use the individual approach.

The project has been structured to allow you to work from a complete play, *Water by the Spoonful,* or from a scene, Scene 6 from *Elliot, A Soldier's Fugue,* both included in Chapter 13. Some staging, scenic, music, and projection ideas have already been introduced for these two plays, but each text is flexible enough to allow a variety of other choices in addition to those we have discussed. The assignments may be adapted to other modern American plays including the other three plays in this book. Additional contemporary plays recommended for the production project are *Dead Man's Cellphone* by Sarah Ruhl, and *Rabbit Hole* by David Lindsay-Abaire. As one further alternative, some classes may wish to explore a play from an earlier period chosen by the instructor.

Preparing a Production

The collaborative project should be done in groups of approximately five to seven. If possible, groups should include students who are interested in design and students who are interested in performance. After the groups have been organized, each group will meet and decide who will take on the different individual responsibilities as they are described in the "Project Assignments" section of this chapter. One person needs to assume the role of the director. Each group does not need to do all of the possible assignments. Students should choose the area which interests them most and with which they are most comfortable.

After reading the play, each group will hold its first meeting to decide on the distribution of responsibilities. Then each student will begin work on his or her particular assignment. The group should meet for the second time when the members have completed enough preliminary thinking to allow the group to brainstorm and make the group decisions listed on page 478.

Group members will present their production plan to the class, showing the poster design, scene design, and costume designs; outlining the stylistic choices they have made; and explaining how those choices interpret the ideas in the play. The production presentation may also include the presentation of a scene from the play. If time restrictions do not allow a class presentation, the director will write an overview of the stylistic choices. As an alternative presentation plan, each group may display the visual materials its members have developed, and the class time may be used for the presentation of scenes.

If the project is to be completed individually, each student should choose one of the assignments and develop his or her project as described in the "Project Assignments" section. Each student will need to make the decisions listed under "Group Decisions" on an individual basis.

Alternative Plays

Dead Man's Cell Phone, by Sarah Ruhl
Dramatic Comedy

> Four women, two men
> Unit set that shifts among multiple locations
> A comic play about what happens if you answer someone else's cell phone and enter that person's life. The central character is unable to resist the persistent ring of an unanswered phone and then through half-truths and inventions, she claims a place in the family of the man who had failed to answer his phone because he was dead. The play is a satire about the place of technology in our lives and about human connections, told through bizarre details and slippery, shifting circumstances. Strong two- and three-person scenes with male-female and female-female casting.

Rabbit Hole, by David Lindsay-Abaire
Drama

> Three women, two men
> Realistic interior of family home
> The play examines the struggles of family members with their own guilt and with each other after the death of a four-year-old child. The grief of the individual characters is shaded with humor that provides an essential coping mechanism for the characters and the audience. Strong two-person scenes with male-female and female-female casting.

Working on the Project

Sequence of Work

1. Select and read the play.
2. *Group Meeting 1.* Begin group discussion topics. Choose individual assignments. Choose a director. Decide *if* you are going to present a scene, and, if so, cast actors.
3. Begin individual research. Begin scene rehearsals.

4. *Group Meeting 2.* Work through group decisions. Establish a calendar for completion of
   the work. Share initial findings.

5. Complete research and continue rehearsals.

6. Complete design for each area, including
   set, costumes, music, poster, program note.

7. *Group Meeting 3.* Present designs to other
   members of the group. Hold a final dress
   rehearsal with everyone present if you are
   presenting a scene.

8. Present project to class.

Topics for Group Discussion (Group Meeting 1)

1. How would you describe the world of the
   play? Where is the play located in space
   and time? What does this world look
   and sound like? What factors govern the
   characters lives?

2. What is most compelling about the characters? What surprises or intrigues you
   about the character relationships? What
   events from the past are most important in
   the characters lives? What burdens do they
   carry with them?

3. What are the major issues framing the
   action of the play? Which background issues
   do you feel you need to have more familiarity with to understand the characters in the
   play? Do you have knowledge of any of the
   specific social issues in the play that you can
   share with other students in the group?

4. What theme or idea in the play seems most
   important in drawing the elements of the
   play together? What do you think the play
   is about?

5. If you are working on *Water by the Spoonful,*
   discuss the significance of the Ghost in the
   play. How many appearances does the Ghost
   make? What does the Ghost reveal about
   Elliot's character? What are possible ways of
   staging the Ghost's appearances?

If you have decided to work on the scene from
Elliot, A Soldier's Fugue, following are the playwright's notes on the Set and Time.

> The set has two playing areas. The "empty
> space" is minimal, it transforms into many
> locations. It is stark, sad. When light enters,
> it is like light through a jailhouse window or
> through the dusty stained glass of a decrepit
> chapel. The "garden space," by contrast, is
> teeming with life. It is a verdant sanctuary,
> green speckled with magenta and gold. Both
> spaces are holy in their own way.
>
> Time within the "Fugue" scenes is fluid
> and overlaps. When Elliot steps into the
> "Fugue" scenes, he's in 2003 Iraq. When
> Pop steps into the "Fugue" scenes, he's in
> late 1960s, Vietnam. When Grandpop steps
> into the "Fugue" scenes, he's in 1950 Korea.
> Often, these disparate time periods occur
> simultaneously.

Group Decisions (Group Meeting 2)

1. What theatre is to be used for your hypothetical production? What would be the
   most appropriate spatial arrangement (proscenium? thrust? arena?) and actor–audience
   relationship? How large should the theatre
   be? How close should the audience be to
   the action? If possible, choose a theatre on
   your campus or in your community that you
   think would be a good space in which to
   produce the play. Find out the dimensions
   of the theatre and the number of seats in the
   auditorium.

2. What style do you think will be appropriate
   for your production? How realistic should
   the sets and costumes be? How much detail
   should they have? Is the setting to be complete with walls and windows, or is the set
   to be suggestive or expressionistic? Does the
   environment give the appearance of reality,
   or is it distorted in some way? Are there
   pieces of furniture or architectural features
   that seem essential? Do the costumes seem

real, or are they exaggerated or simplified? Would projected images help express the content of the play or establish the appropriate environment?

3. What metaphors or images seem helpful in thinking about the play?

4. What colors best communicate the feelings of the play?

5. What style of music is appropriate to the play and how much music should be used? Bring in examples of Bach or John Coltrane as well as other music that you might consider for your production to listen to together and give feedback on to your sound/music designer.

Project Assignments

The Director

The director will lead the discussion on the group topics and questions. The director will develop a written response to questions 8 and 9 in the "Scene Design" section (page 480) and question 6 in the "Costume Design" section (page 481). These issues should be discussed at Group Meeting 2.

The director will write a summary of the ideas for the production based on his or her understanding of the play and the group's responses. If scenes from the same play are to be presented to the class, the directors from the different groups will meet to make sure each group produces a different scene. As part of the director's written project, the director will analyze the content of the scene and its relationship to the play; that is, he or she will identify the important actions or issues in the scene and determine how they contribute to the play's meaning.

Character Analysis

Choose one character. Anyone performing a scene should do the analysis for the character that he or she is playing. If scenes are not to be presented, the character analysis may be done for any character.

1. What does your character say about himself or herself? Make a list quoting all the lines by act and scene.

2. What do the other characters say about your character? Make a list quoting all the lines by act and scene.

3. What are the motives that drive your character? List the things that he or she wants from the other characters in the play. What seems to be the dominant motive for your character?

4. How does your character change during the course of the play? What are the important realizations that your character comes to during the play? What provokes the realizations? Where does the character begin? Where does the character end?

5. What is the history of your character? Put together all the information given by the playwright, your character, and the other characters.

6. What is your character's relationship to other significant characters? How does it change?

7. What does your character look like? Find several pictures that show clothes, physicality, or outlook.

Scene Design

This assignment may be shared by two students.

Assessing The Environment:

1. How does the playwright describe the setting?

2. How do the characters refer to the environment and how do they feel about it? Does the environment offer them protection or is it threatening?

3. How many different locations does the setting need to provide for? What is the relative importance of each location? What solutions will allow the play's action to move easily between the different locations?

4. What are the basic actions of the characters in the play? What are the necessary entrances and exits and the physical actions that the stage space must accommodate and support?

5. How does the socio-economic background of the characters impact any elements of the setting or the environment?

6. What pieces of furniture or kinds of environmental detail such as a fence or a boulder are referred to by the characters or in the stage directions? Make a list of everything that is necessary to the action of the play. What other furniture pieces or environmental details seem useful to the characters' actions or to communicating the circumstances of the characters?

7. What artifacts from the characters' lives might be part of the physical environment? In what ways is the environment personalized? Is one character's point of view more important than another's in determining the details of the physical environment? Does someone seem to own or dominate the space?

8. Does the stage need to be enclosed in some way or shaped by scenery or should the stage be open? Does the stage need to have multiple levels? How could those levels be created? Stairs? Platforms? Benches?

9. Are there projected images that would help define some part of the setting or contribute to the atmosphere of the environment? If projected images would be useful to your concept for the production, how would a projection surface be worked into the set design?

10. Collect pictures that give you ideas about the way any part of the environment might look.

Designing the Set

1. *Ground plan.* In collaboration with the director, work out a ground plan that will allow for the kind of locations and interactions indicated in the script. What are the necessary pieces of furniture? What would be the most effective placement of entrances, doors, walls, pieces of furniture, or other elements that would shape the space? Where would you place levels such as steps or platforms that would change the terrain of the stage floor? If possible, consult with the scene designer in your theatre department or with a scene design student on the development of your ground plan. The ground plan may be drawn very simply on a diagram of the stage that you are using, with geometric shapes indicating levels and furniture drawn to scale. See the ground plan included with the discussion of scene design for *Eurydice* in Chapter 6.

2. *Optional.* Draw or paint a rendering of your set, *or* build a model of the set.

3. If you do not do a rendering or a model of your set, then use pictures from your research to accompany the ground plan to demonstrate the atmosphere of the scenic environment and the style of any architectural elements or furniture.

Costume Design

1. Make a list of all the references in the stage directions to costuming.

2. Make a list of the references in the dialogue to articles of clothing.

3. What symbols are associated with the costumes?

4. What period or periods do the costumes come from?

5. What range of colors seems appropriate to the world of the play? How can contrasting

colors appropriately identify differences between the characters?

6. What qualities of the characters help identify the kind of clothing each character might wear? What clothing pieces seem appropriate, given circumstances such as jobs or activities performed, social status, and the characters' outlook? How do you think the characters feel about what they wear? Do they hide or cover themselves in some way with their clothes? Do any of the characters try to call attention to themselves with their clothing? Are there major costume changes during the play? What do the costume changes signify?

7. Draw or find pictures of costumes that you think would be appropriate for each character. Go to a fabric store and buy small pieces of fabric that you would use to make the costumes for each character. Attach the appropriate fabric swatches to the drawing of each costume.

Sound/Music Design

Decide on the range of music that best supports your group's staging of the play or scene. Decide where you will use the music indicated by the playwright and where you will use other selections. Also, decide if there are sound effects to be used in addition to the music and how those sound effects will be produced. Make a compilation of representative samples of all the music and sound effects. Make a cue sheet that indicates each place in the script that music is to be played and the title of the selection you have chosen or the kind of sound effect to be used. Write a brief paper to accompany your compilation and cue sheet that explains how each selection supports the moment in the play for which it is intended.

Program Note

Write a program note for a production of the play. In writing the program note, decide what kind of information would be most helpful and also most interesting to an audience of your peers. The program note may include biographical material on the playwright, historical background on issues in the play, thematic exploration of the play itself (which could also include references to other plays of the playwright), and previous noteworthy productions of the same play.

Poster

Design a poster to advertise your group's production. Look at posters from the theatre department of your college or university or from another theatre in your community to determine the kind of information that should go on the poster. Decide on fictional dates and times for your production for the purposes of your poster. Consult with the director and the costume and set designers for possible images and colors for the poster.

In designing the poster you should focus on clarity. The lettering of the play's title and the playwright's name is very important in communicating effectively to potential ticket buyers; the lettering needs to be strong and clear. Further, any image you decide to use must be compelling and give some sense of the mood of the production. Poster imagery must be fairly simple, given the limited amount of space available and the need to attract the viewers' attention quickly.

Conclusion

You are preparing a hypothetical production. You are working with unfamiliar materials and new approaches and methods. You may come up with ideas that might not work in an actual production, although you might just as likely arrive at some remarkable ideas. What is important is starting from a point of exploration, asking questions rather than beginning with answers. The production project is meant to allow you to participate in a process of discovery. To do that you must be willing to take risks, to try out possibilities and see where they may lead. If such a process is to be successful, it requires commitment on your part—commitment to be prepared, to be open with the other members of your group, to follow through on your part of the production.

This kind of commitment is the starting point for all theatre practitioners. The theatre continues in every age because of the passionate commitment of theatre artists to work collectively to bring stories, images, and ideas to life on the stage. Every group of theatre artists shares something with the actors, playwrights, directors, and designers who have created the productions in this book and for whom working in the theatre is an affirmation of life itself. The live performance produced by theatre artists in the presence of the audience is a celebration of the human spirit.

Appendix: Guided Writing Assignments

The assignments presented here focus on the analytical and writing skills used by dramaturgs and critics, as discussed in Chapter 14. Three different writing projects ask you to consider the ideas in a play or production while drawing on your own perceptions and creativity. Underlying all three assignments should be a goal articulated by Ben Brantley, the chief theatre critic for *The New York Times:* "to generate excitement about the theatre . . . [and] open a window for people to look in."

Assignment 1: Write a Review

Write a four-page review of a campus, community, or professional theatre production. Imagine that you will publish the review in your school newspaper, to be read by your college community, students, and faculty. Your readers will also include the participants in the production. The review should explore the content of the play and the stylistic choices made by the director, actors, and designers.

Purpose

The basic goals of writing a review are to come to a greater understanding of the production and to communicate to your readers the experience of being an audience member. A productive review will provide valuable information for potential audience members as well as useful and respectful feedback to the theatre practitioners involved. In order to determine the focus for your review, keep in mind the four questions posed by Julius Novick, a critic for *The Village Voice*, summarized in Chapter 14:

1. What is the work itself trying to do?
2. How well has it done it?
3. Was it worth doing?
4. Why was it or wasn't it worth doing?

A play that offers a hard look at a controversial problem on your campus may be worth doing. But so is a comedy that really makes us laugh or a musical with great music and characters we love. What is important in writing the review is to take the production on its own terms and think about the success of its various elements in building a convincing whole. The question "Was it worth doing?" covers a broad range of theatre experiences that may balance entertainment and ideas in very different ways.

Preparation

Read the play shortly before attending the performance, if possible. Learn what you can about the playwright and the production history of the play. What other plays has the playwright written? Have they been produced in your community? Does the playwright's biography enhance your understanding of the play? What themes or storytelling devices seem most compelling to you when you read the play?

Watching the Play

An essential part of your work as a reviewer takes place during the performance itself. You need to be fully alert and in a receptive state of mind when you go to the play in order to get the most out of the experience and retain what you have seen. Therefore, you should be well rested when you go to the theatre. Arrive at the theatre early enough to comfortably take your seat and read the program. Be sure to take a small notebook and pen.

Your experience of the play and the many observations you make during the performance about staging, design elements, and characterization will be the basis of your review. It is essential that you take notes immediately after the performance while the details of the production are still fresh in your mind. You may take some notes at intermission. However, it is counterproductive to take notes during the performance itself because writing interrupts your own involvement with the performance and may be distracting to the people sitting around you.

Here are some points to consider as you watch the play. How is the performance created for the audience members? What is the layout of the theatre: proscenium? in the round? three sides? Where does the audience sit in relation to the stage, and how close is the audience to the stage? How large is the audience? What do the sets and costumes look like? Are there special effects? What is the sound design? Is there live music? Is the acting realistic and psychologically shaded, or do the actors play to the audience with broad gestures? What are the production's particular strengths? What surprises you? What is particularly moving or disturbing or funny? What do you find yourself thinking about after the performance? Have your own ideas been challenged or changed in some way by this experience?

As you write rough notes after the performance, try to settle on what you think this production was about. What is the central action that drives the different parts of the performance? Is there a theme that ties all the pieces together? What is the story that has been told, and what incidents form the plot?

Writing the Review

The foundation for your introductory paragraph should be a statement summarizing what you think the performance was about. For example, you could say that a production of *Joe Turner's Come and Gone* was about a man's search to find himself, or about the changes that a group of people are going through together as they move from one situation in life to another. What you establish as central to the production in this introductory paragraph will help you decide how to develop the rest of your review in order to explain the development of this major idea or theme.

Some kind of plot summary is important as the next step, but you should not give an overly detailed description of the plot. "First this happened, then that happened" can take up most of your review without providing appropriate interpretation. The plot summary should be approximately one substantial paragraph unless you must explain one aspect of the plot in more detail. The goal of the review is to get underneath the plot to the inner life of the characters and the ramifications of their situation. What you include about the plot should explain how the action of the play develops or should give a summary of the story. What is it that the main characters are trying to accomplish? What are the obstacles they have to overcome to get what they want?

Following the introductory paragraph and the plot summary, explore the production elements of acting and design. Explain how the story was told through acting, sets, costume, lighting, and sound. Here, specific description becomes extremely important for two reasons: (1) You are trying to communicate the experience of being an audience member as vividly as possible; (2) the only way to distinguish effectively between different kinds of plays and interpretations is to evaluate the details and the way they form a whole. Therefore, in writing your review you need to include a good deal of careful description of what you saw and heard.

Ultimately, your review should address one or more of the following questions. What ideas are essential to the play, and how did the production help to shape those ideas? What original interpretations by the producers and actors cast new light on the material? What qualities of the performance captured your imagination and drew you into the world of the play? What performance elements were emphasized, and what did that emphasis mean for the audience? A musical that has an energetic score and exciting choreography offers a different kind of experience from a sad story of lost love or a wild comedy that parodies contemporary politics. What was it like to be an audience member at this event?

The review should focus more on explaining the experience of being an audience member than on judgments about the work of the actors, director, and designers. A useful question to answer in terms of the degree of success of the performance is whether you would recommend it to others. What are the elements that you think are particularly noteworthy? In what ways could the performance be improved in order to be more appealing or compelling? This takes us back to Julius Novick's second question: How well has the work done what it was trying to do? In the end, did the theatre practitioners believe in what they were doing, and did they make you believe?

Assignment 2: Prepare a Lobby Display

The instructor will assign a play that has research problems suitable for a lobby display and provide a list of possible topics, issues, or questions that would benefit from investigation. After you have read the play, choose a topic of interest to you and research the history of this subject by consulting books, journals, newspapers, Web sites, or photo archives. Write two pages of text supported by two or three strong visual images that help the audience understand the place of your subject in the play. Arrange the written text and the visual images to make an eye-catching panel for a lobby display.

Purpose

The purpose of a lobby display is to offer the audience important background material on the play in an exciting and inviting presentation that combines text and visual materials. The material should be thought-provoking. It should connect the play to historical issues, contemporary issues, or both. In addition to providing information, the lobby display creates another gathering space for audience members and encourages them to leave their seats at intermission but still stay in touch with the play. Moving around the display may also facilitate interactions between audience members as well as enhance their experience before and after the play. In order to prepare an authoritative and compelling presentation, you must develop your own expertise about the play's background.

Sample Background of a Lobby Display: The *Elliot* Trilogy

Chapter 13 focuses on two plays by Quiara Alegría Hudes: *Elliot, A Soldier's Fugue* and *Water by the Spoonful*. These plays are also recommended for a group theatre production project in Chapter 15. A lobby display for either or both of these plays could include an exploration of materials drawn from exploring some of the following questions and issues.

Elliot, A Soldier's Fugue tells the interwoven stories of three American soldiers who fought in different wars. Many Americans today do not know the history of these conflicts. Each of these wars changed America's position in the world as well as having a profound impact on the lives and perceptions of people in the United States and in the other nations involved.

The In Context Box in Chapter 13 provides you with the dates, the nations involved, and some information about casualties for each of these conflicts. In addition, it would be informative for audiences to know the basis for the U.S. decisions to become involved in conflicts so far from American territory. In each case young American soldiers were called on to enter cultures with which they were unfamiliar. An exploration of cultural conditions could examine political systems, religious beliefs, and economic structures. Maps would be useful for demonstrating geographic relationships. The natural resources of the nations involved would also cast light on what larger nations might have at stake in battling over smaller nations. It would also be important to know which Americans undertook the burden of fighting these wars by joining the military. Each conflict had an uneasy resolution, which reflected both the difficulty of achieving military solutions and divisions among Americans about waging these wars. Learning the outcome of each war and the nature of the debates among Americans about what we were fighting for and why would contribute to an understanding of the climate that soldiers entered when they returned home following their tours of duty.

Since a major focus of the trilogy is Elliot's struggle to find himself following his military service, a study of the difficulties of returning veterans would be helpful in explaining the world of the play. Armando Riesco, who has played Elliot in the premiere productions of all three plays, provides suggestions for resources in his comments about preparing to play the role. In their interview comments, both playwright Quiara Alegría Hudes and actor Liza Colón-Zayas identify some of the resources on substance abuse that could be helpful in developing background materials on the current battle going on with drug addiction and recovery in our country.

Assignment 3: Interview a Theatre Practitioner and Present the Interview in Writing or in an Electronic Format

Interview a theatre practitioner who is currently engaged in or has just finished working on the production of a specific play on your campus or in your community. You may choose a professional or a student practitioner. A written version of the interview will be three to four pages. An electronic format will be edited to about ten to fifteen minutes.

Purpose

The purpose of an interview is to allow theatre practitioners to express their own insights about their craft and their ideas about or reactions to the play they are working on. For readers, this form of article increases their contact with the art of making theatre through a personal story. The words of an individual bring a subject to life. Anecdotes, emotional responses, examples of the work involved, obstacles to be overcome, and biographical details together weave a story that should capture the reader's attention and illuminate why people are drawn to the theatre and what sustains their efforts. A good interview allows the reader to share in the passion of actors and playwrights for the work they do.

Preparation

Select someone to interview who in your judgment is doing work that merits your attention or from whom you can learn about important issues. At least a week in advance, contact this person to request an interview and arrange for a specific day and time. Determine an appropriate meeting place, and make sure it is available. Although coffee shops and restaurants are popular places for interviews, the noise level at such places can often interfere with your ability to successfully record the conversation.

An interview must be recorded. Otherwise you cannot have an accurate version of your subject's words. You may make an audio recording, or you may use video. Ultimately, the finished presentation of your interview can be in the form of a written article in which you will transcribe parts of the recorded conversation; or you can present the work electronically on a CD or a DVD. Whatever the final form, part of your preparation will involve securing an appropriate recording device, which could be borrowed from your audiovisual department or connected to your own computer. Choose a possible site for the publication or broadcast presentation of the interview, such as your school newspaper, a television station, or a Web site for your class. This will help you determine the audience for the material and the format, whether the interview actually appears at this site or not.

In preparation for the interview, you should read the play in which your subject is involved and, if possible, attend either a rehearsal or a performance. If biographical information about your interviewee is not available, this could become one of the topics for your interview. Consider what is intriguing to you about both the play currently being performed and the work of the artist. What would you like to know about the challenges of this production and the circumstances of personal history, training, or experience that guide artistic decisions? Develop a written list of questions, which you will refer to when you are conducting the interview.

Conducting the Interview

In conducting an interview, the emphasis must be on the person being interviewed, not the person asking the questions. Your job as an interviewer is to encourage your subject to speak while you remain an alert and engaged listener. It is certainly appropriate to briefly explain your background and point of view when you meet with the subject, and in editing the interview material. Observing a time limit of about thirty to forty minutes is appropriate. Avoid the temptation to speak longer. You need to be respectful of your interviewee's schedule, and you will end up with more material than you can use. The time limit does require you to remain focused on your questions and to gently guide your subject back to the point if the conversation begins to wander. Practicing some of your questions with a roommate or friend is a good strategy to help you be more comfortable when you are actually conducting the interview.

Editing the Interview

Select the comments of your subject that are the most vivid and that offer helpful specific examples and details. Eliminate passages or phrases that are redundant, vague, or tangential to the major points you are trying to develop. For a written version of the interview, you should edit out words that meander, whether they fall within a sentence or between sentences that carry clearly focused ideas. For a video or audio presentation, editing out rambling sections will be more practical than trying to tighten up individual sentences. Write a brief introduction that provides the essential background and focus for the interview. The introduction should make two points: why you did the interview, and what may be of greatest interest to the reader. Group statements that are related or contribute to developing the same idea. Choose those questions of yours that successfully introduce and frame the responses you have selected. For example, an interview could be organized around three major topics such as why your subject chose to go into the theatre, what kind of training he or she had, and what was most interesting or challenging about the work on the play you saw.

Notes

Chapter 1

1. The description of this performance draws on details provided in "Postscript: The Treasures of Siwidi," by Judith Ostrowitz and Aldona Jonaitis in Jonaitis, Aldona, *Chiefly Feasts*, New York: American Museum of Natural History, 1991.

2. Bill Irwin, quoted in Bruce Weber, "Just Clowning Around with Intellect," *New York Times*, March 3, 1993, C1.

3. Olga Sanchez interview with the author, December 2005.

4. Dorothy K. Washburn, *Hopi Kachina: Spirit of Life* (San Francisco: California Academy of Sciences, 1980), 40.

5. Washburn, 41.

6. Euripides, *Medea and Other Plays*, translated and edited by James Morwood (Oxford: Oxford University Press, 1998), 32.

7. Jose Luis Valenzuela interview with the author, December 2008.

Chapter 2

1. *Hamlet*, in *The Complete Plays and Poems of William Shakespeare*, ed. William Allen Neilson and Charles Jarvis Hill (Cambridge: Riverside Press, 1942), 1049. (I, i)

2. *King Lear*, in *The Complete Plays*, ed. Neilson and Hill, 1158. (III, ii)

3. *Henry V*, in *The Complete Plays*, ed. Neilson and Hill, 711. (Prologue)

4. *Hamlet*, 1068. (III, ii)

5. *Hamlet*, 1068. (III, ii)

6. Jane Taylor, Writer's Note for *Ubu and the Truth Commission* (Cape Town: University of Cape Town Press, 2007), ii.

7. Malcolm Purkey and Craig Higginson, interview with the author, July 1, 2010.

Chapter 3

1. August Wilson, preface to *Three Plays* (Pittsburgh: University of Pittsburgh Press, 1991), viii.

2. Richard Bernstein, "August Wilson's Voices from the Past," *New York Times*, March 27, 1988, sec. 2, 1.

3. Wilson, preface to *Three Plays*, viii.

4. Wilson, preface to *Three Plays*, ix.

5. Imamu Amira Baraka [LeRoi Jones], *Blues People* (New York: Morrow, 1963), 61.

6. William Barlow, *Looking Up at Down* (Philadelphia: Temple University Press, 1989), 7–8.

7. August Wilson, foreword to Myron Schwartzman, *Romare Bearden: His Life and Art* (New York: Abrams, 1990), 8.

8. Wilson, foreword to *Romare Bearden*, 9.

9. To hear Bessie Smith's version, listen to Bessie Smith, "Nobody Knows You When You're Down and Out," *The Complete Recordings*, Vol. 4, Columbia, 1993.

10. Bernstein, sec. 2, 1.

11. August Wilson, *Joe Turner's Come and Gone* (New York: New American Library, 1988), 67.

12. W. C. Handy, *The Father of the Blues* (New York: Collier, 1941), 146.

13. All quotations in the production analysis are from the author's interviews.

14. The early death of LeWan Alexander was a loss to the nation's theatre community.

Chapter 4

1. Billy Crudup quoted in Laurie Stuhlbarg, "Brilliant and Brutal Theatre: Interview with Billy Crudup and Michael Stuhlbarg," *Scene 4 Magazine*, January 2006.

2. David Warrilow, quoted in Laurie Lassiter, "David Warrilow: Creating Symbol and Cypher," in

Acting (Re)Considered, ed. Phillip B. Zarrilli (London: Routledge, 1995), 321.

3. BW Gonzalez, interview with the author, July 17, 2002.

4. Stephen Spinella, quoted in Janet Sonenberg, *The Actor Speaks* (New York: Random House, 1996), 252.

5. Gonzalez interview.

6. Sean McNall, interview with the author, November 2007.

7. Spinella, quoted in Sonenberg, 278.

8. Heather Robison, interview with the author, November 2008.

9. James Earl Jones, quoted in Holly Hill, *Actors' Lives: On and off the American Stage, Interviews by Holly Hill* (New York: Theatre Communications Group, 1993), 19.

10. Richard Gallegos, interview with the author, January 2009.

11. McNall interview.

12. Gallegos interview.

13. Gordon Davidson, quoted in Gordon Hunt, *How to Audition* (New York: HarperCollins, 1995), 203.

14. Hunt, 184.

15. Jack Bowdan, quoted in Heltie Lynee Hurtes, *The Back Stage Guide to Casting Directors* (New York: Watson-Guptill, 1998), 15.

16. Stuart Ostrow, quoted in Hunt, 168.

17. Tamu Gray, interview with the author, March 24, 1993.

18. James Earl Jones, quoted in Hill, 9–10.

19. Kathleen Chalfant, quoted in Sonenberg, 102–103.

20. Robison interview.

21. Joe Mantello, quoted in Sonenberg, 141–42.

22. Gonzalez interview.

23. Brandon J. Dirden quoted in Erik Piepenburg, "Speaking August Wilson's Words Can Change You," *New York Times*, December 27, 2012.

24. *King Lear*, in *The Complete Works of Shakespeare*, ed. David Bevington (New York: HarperCollins, 1992), 1173. (I, i)

25. Nancy Keystone, interview with the author, February 2009.

26. Gallegos interview.

27. Valerie Spencer, interview with the author, January 2009.

28. Mary-Louise Parker, quoted in Mervyn Rothstein, "Getting *Proof* to Work is a Delicate Equation," *New York Times*, June 3, 2001, 7.

29. Ray Ford, interview with the author, February 2009.

30. Spencer interview.

31. Cate Blanchett, quoted in Matt Dobkin, "New York Theatre, Hedda Steam," *New York Magazine*, February 27, 2006.

32. Sarah Jessica Parker, quoted in Bruce Weber, "The Starry 'Three Sisters' Cast Reveals a Trend," *New York Times*, February 9, 1997, 31.

33. Spencer interview.

Chapter 5

1. Libby Appel interview with the author, July 17, 2002.

2. Harold Clurman, "In a Different Language," in *Directors on Directing*, ed. Toby Cole and Helen Krich Chinoy (New York: Bobbs-Merrill, 1963), 275.

3. Peter Brook, *There Are No Secrets: Thoughts on Acting and Theatre* (London: Methuen, 1993), 25.

4. Brook, 52–53.

5. Jerzy Grotowski, "Towards a Poor Theatre," in *Towards a Poor Theatre*, ed. Jerzy Grotowski (New York: Simon and Schuster, 1968), 17.

6. Jerzy Grotowski, quoted in Naim Kattan, "Theatre Is an Encounter: An Interview with Jerzy Grotowski," in Grotowski, 58.

7. Ludwik Flaszen, "*Akropolis:* Treatment of the Text," in Grotowski, 62.

8. Grotowski, 164.

9. Russell Vandenbrouke, *Truths the Hand Can Touch: The Theatre of Athol Fugard* (New York: Theatre Communications Group, 1985), 106.

10. Athol Fugard, Introduction to *Statements* (New York: Theatre Communications Group, 1986), vii.

11. Ping Chong interview with the author, October 6, 2005.

12. Elizabeth LeCompte, quoted in David Savran, *The Wooster Group, 1975–1985: Breaking the Rules* (Ann Arbor, MI: Books on Demand, 1986), 115–116.

13. Declan Donnellan, quoted in Maria M. Delgado and Paul Heritage, *In Contact with the Gods? Directors Talk Theatre* (Manchester: Manchester University Press, 1996), 89.

14. Lloyd Richards, quoted in April Austin, "Lloyd Richards and August Wilson: A Winning Partnership Plays On," *Christian Science Monitor*, September 18, 1995, 13.

15. Lloyd Richards, quoted in "Theater-Maker at Yale," *Fairpress* (Norwalk, Conn., June 21, 1990), F3.

16. Richards, quoted in "Theater-Maker at Yale," F3.

17. Appel interview.

18. Tisa Chang interview with the author, June 23, 1995.

19. William Ball, *A Sense of Direction* (New York: Drama Book Publishers, 1984), 36.

20. Keystone interview.

21. William Shakespeare, *Macbeth* (New York: Applause, 1996), 46.

22. Ford interview.

23. Ball, 111.

Chapter 6

1. All of the commentary by the theatre practitioners about the SCR production of *Eurydice* by Sarah Ruhl is derived from the author's interviews in 2012.

2. Angela Wendt, quoted in Evelyn McDonnell and Katherine Silberger, *Rent: Book, Music, and Lyrics by Jonathan Larson* (New York: Morrow, 1997), 153.

3. Joan Arhelger interview with the author, August 5, 2002.

Chapter 7

1. Ruby Cohn, *Currents in Contemporary Drama* (Bloomington: Indiana University Press, 1969), 54–55.

2. Jiao Juyin, quoted in program for *The Teahouse*, ed. Meng Shanshan Yang Jing, trans. Wu Zhuhong (Beijing, China: Beijing People's Art Theatre, 2005).

3. Lin Zhaohua interview with the author, November 6, 2005.

Chapter 8

1. Wakako Yamauchi, "And the Soul Shall Dance," in *Songs My Mother Taught Me: Stories, Plays, and Memoir*, ed. Garrett Hongo (New York: Feminist Press, 1994).

2. Sources are Roger Daniels, *The Politics of Prejudice: The Anti-Japanese Movement in California and the Struggle for Japanese Exclusion* (New York: Atheneum, 1977), 63, 88; Ronald Takaki, *Strangers from a Different Shore: A History of Asian Americans* (Boston: Little, Brown, 1989), 180, 203–209; and the Wing Luke Asian Museum, Seattle.

3. Chiura Obata, quoted in *Chiura Obata's Topaz Moon: Art of the Internment*, ed. Kimi Kodani Hill (Berkeley: Heyday Books, 2000), 105.

4. Wakako Yamauchi, quoted in preface to *Songs My Mother Taught Me*, vii.

5. Wakako Yamauchi, quoted in Stephanie Arnold, "Dissolving the Half Shadows," in *Making a Spectacle*, ed. Lynda Hart (Ann Arbor: University of Michigan Press, 1988), 181–182.

6. All quotations in the production analysis are from the author's interviews.

Chapter 9

1. Bertolt Brecht, *Brecht on Theatre*, ed. and trans. John Willett (New York: Hill and Wang, 1964), 71.

2. Wendy Arons, "Preaching to the Converted: An Interview with Tony Kushner," *Communications from the International Brecht Society*, 23, no. 2 (1994): 59.

3. Brecht, 137–138.

4. Brecht, 86.

5. Martin Esslin, *The Theatre of the Absurd* (London: Penguin, 1988), 26.

6. John Rockwell, *Robert Wilson: The Theatre of Images* (New York: Harper and Row, 1984), 27.

7. Shen Wei interview with the author, October 6, 2005.

8. TED Lecture, Adrian Kohler and Basil Jones, March 2011.

9. Jane Taylor, editor, *Handspring Puppet Company* (Parkwood, South Africa: David Krut Publishing, 2009), 69.

10. *Handspring Puppet Company*, 73.

11. *Handspring Puppet Company*, 253.

Chapter 10

1. Tony Kushner, *Thinking about the Longstanding Problems of Virtue and Happiness* (New York: Theatre Communications Group, 1995), x.

2. Tony Kushner, *Angels in America: Millennium Approaches* (New York: Theatre Communications Group, 1993), 74.

3. Tony Taccone interviews with the author, June 13 and 16, 1996. All of Taccone's comments in this chapter come from these interviews.

4. Tony Kushner, acknowledgments to *Angels in America: Part Two, Perestroika* (New York: Theatre Communications Group, 1994), xi.

5. Martin Esslin, "Towards an American Dramaturg," in *Dramaturgy in American Theatre*, ed. Susan Jonas and Geoffrey S. Proehl (Orlando, FL: Harcourt Brace, 1997), 27.

6. Robert Brustein, "From 'The Future of an Un-American Activity'," in *Dramaturgy in American Theatre*, ed. Jonas and Proehl, 36.

7. Oskar Eustis interview with the author, June 2, 1996. All of Eustis's remarks in this chapter come from this interview.

8. Susan Jonas, "Tony Kushner's Angels," in *Dramaturgy in American Theatre*, ed. Jonas and Proehl, 473.

9. Kathleen Chalfant, quoted in Eric Grode, "Two Men and a Mormon (and Ethel Rosenberg)," *TheaterWeek*, September 20–26, 1993, 15.

10. Kushner, *Angels: Perestroika*, 52–53.

Chapter 11

1. Richard A. Long, *The Black Tradition in Dance* (New York: Rizzoli, 1990), 11.

2. Walter Kerr, *New York Times*, December 4, 1966, 5.

3. Frank Rich, "A Musical Theatre Breakthrough," *New York Times*, October 21, 1984, sec. 6, 53.

4. Stephen Sondheim quoted in Linda Winer, "Sondheim in His Own Words," *American Theatre*, II, no. 2 (May 1985): 12.

5. Stephen Sondheim and John Weidman, *Pacific Overtures* (New York: Theatre Communications Group, 1991), 20–21.

6. Julie Taymor, *The Lion King: Pride Rock on Broadway* (New York: Hyperion, 1999), 28.

7. Taymor, 136.

8. John Weidman, quoted in Robin Pogrebin, "Making 'Contact' without Conflict," *New York Times*, October 18, 1999, E3.

Chapter 12

1. Henrik Ibsen, *A Doll House*, in *Henrik Ibsen: The Complete Major Prose Plays*, trans. Rolfe Fjelde (New York: New American Library, 1978), 125. Fjelde translates the title as *A Doll House*, though most American productions use the title *A Doll's House*.

2. Antonin Artaud, *The Theatre and Its Double* (New York: Grove, 1958), 37.

3. Artaud, 98.

4. Robert Wilson, quoted in a brochure from UCLA Extension, "Robert Wilson: Artist in Residence," May 1985.

Chapter 13

1. All of the quotes in Chapter 13 are from the author's interviews unless otherwise noted.

2. Jeff Lunden, Morning Edition, NPR, January 8, 2013.

3. From *Elliot, A Soldier's Fugue* by Quiara Alegría Hudes, used by arrangement with Theatre Communications Group, Inc.

4. Marcus Gardley, "Music is her Muse: Quiara Alegría Hudes and her Path to the Pulitzer," The Brooklyn Rail, August 2012.

5. From *Elliot, A Soldier's Fugue* by Quiara Alegría Hudes, Theatre Communications Group, Inc, 2012, 22.

Chapter 14

1. Pindar, quoted in H. D. F. Kitto, *The Greeks* (Baltimore, MD: Penguin, 1962), 10.

2. Aristotle, *The Poetics*, trans. S. H. Butcher (New York: Hill and Wang, 1968), 52.

3. Aristotle, 76.

4. Aristotle, 59.

5. Luigi Pirandello, *Six Characters in Search of an Author*, trans. John Linstrum (London: Methuen, 1986), act 1.

6. Pirandello, act 3.

7. Oskar Eustis interview with the author, November 2007.

8. Stephen Weeks, correspondence with the author, May 10, 2006.

9. Tom Bryant interview with the author, February 2009.

10. Julius Novick, "Perspectives in Criticism: The Critic as Writer," talk presented at the Friars Club, February 4, 2005.

11. Novick, "Perspectives in Criticism."

12. Billy Crudup, quoted in "The Actor and the Critic," *American Theatre*, May–June 2006, 66.

Glossary

A

act 1. To play a role on the stage in front of an audience. 2. The basic division of a play. *Joe Turner's Come and Gone* is divided into two acts.

acting in quotes The Brechtian concept of acting in which actors comment on the actions of the characters they are playing rather than maintain continuous identification with the character.

action The movement of the actors and the unfolding of a play's events. Action may be physical or psychological.

actor The central artist of the theatre who creates a dramatic story on the stage through words and gestures. Frequently the actor expresses the language of a playwright; theatre, however, can exist without playwrights, but it cannot exist without actors.

alienation effect The Brechtian idea of distancing the audience from a performance through breaks in the narrative and the suspense to promote critical awareness.

amplification The augmentation of sound through electronic means.

apartheid Former government policy of South Africa enforcing disenfranchisement and repression of citizens based on race.

arena stage A round or square stage completely surrounded by the audience.

audition The process through which actors seeking roles in a play or positions with a theatre company present monologues or scene readings for a director.

aural Of or relating to the ear or to the sense of hearing.

avant-garde New ideas of drama and performance that push back boundaries and challenge the assumptions of accepted theatre traditions.

B

beat The basic units of an actor's role defined by changes in character motivation.

Beijing Opera A form of Chinese theatre first introduced in 1790 that relies on music, singing, and acrobatics to express dramas based on the traditional Chinese way of life. Domestic relationships and military conquests are frequently the subjects of Beijing Opera, which also uses mythical subjects to reinforce accepted values.

black box A flexible theatre space in which the stage space and the configuration of the audience space can be changed from production to production.

blocking All of the movement of the actors on the stage during a play.

blues Songs that are part of the African American oral tradition. Descended from slave songs, the blues became a major outlet for community concerns and stories.

book The scripted action and dialogue of a musical—as distinguished from the music and lyrics of the songs.

book musical A musical with an integrated plot such as *Oklahoma!* and *My Fair Lady*.

Broadway The long street that runs through the heart of Manhattan, home to the largest concentration of professional theatres in New York City.

C

camp A linguistic form of parody.

catharsis The release of emotion experienced by audience members watching a play. Aristotle understood this emotional release to be one of the essential elements of the experience of watching a tragedy.

character The people in a play. The theatre is distinguished from other forms of storytelling because of the presence of characters onstage who are engaged in action.

chorus In classical Greek theatre, a group of fifteen or more actors who chanted their lines in unison and sometimes functioned as a character in the play and sometimes provided commentary on

493

the dramatic situation. The chorus added to the rhythmic structure of the performances through singing and dancing.

City Dionysia A festival in ancient Athens that became a major event for the presentation of drama. The festival was held in honor of the god Dionysus, who is closely associated with the Greek theatre.

collaborative art The group effort required to produce theatre, as opposed to the separate work of individuals.

comedy The dramatic genre that focuses on human weakness through humor. Comedy celebrates the regeneration of life through love and reconciliation.

community aesthetics The artistic expression formulated over many years that has precise meaning for a particular community; includes accepted traditions and conventions.

concept musical A musical organized around a theme, with the songs or musical numbers functioning as connected episodes; examples include *A Chorus Line* and *Bring in da Noise, Bring in da Funk.*

costume designer The theatre artist responsible for interpreting plays through the costumes created for the actors.

cross-gender casting The casting of actors of the opposite sex in roles written for either men or women. In many early theatres, men played the roles of women characters. In recent productions, cross-gender casting has been used as a strategy to explore issues of gender identity.

cue The line of dialogue, musical moment, or piece of stage action that is the signal for a character entrance or any change in lights or scenery. For a play to run smoothly, every participant must pay scrupulous attention to the cues.

Cultural Revolution The cultural upheaval initiated by Mao Zedong and his wife Jiang Qing in 1966 with the goal of reforming Chinese society. During the Cultural Revolution, traditional forms of theatre were repressed and replaced with model performances that presented an obvious political point of view.

cyclorama A very large piece of light-colored fabric stretched across the back of the stage that serves to create expansive lighting effects and to silhouette actors.

D

dialogue The language spoken by two or more characters in a play.

Dionysus The Greek god of fertility in whose honor plays were performed in ancient Greece.

director The theatre practitioner who has primary responsibility for the interpretation of a play. The director creates the stage action and unifies all the elements of the production.

dissonance Musical term referring to chords that clash in such a way as to produce tension in the listener. May also refer to inner conflicts in individual human or collective community behavior.

downstage The front of the stage or area of the stage closest to the audience.

drama The written text of a play as it is constructed by the playwright.

dramatic ritual A ceremony, frequently religious, that expresses community values or beliefs through performance. Participants enact community stories that have been passed down through generations. Dramatic rituals are performed for the welfare of the community and usually involve repetition of the drama in a set form.

dramaturg A theatre practitioner concerned with selecting plays for a theatre company, working with playwrights on the development of new scripts, and working with directors on research issues.

E

ekkyklema The wheeling cart on which the bodies of dead characters were displayed in Greek tragedy. The ekkyklema showed the results of violence that had taken place offstage.

end stage A theatre, usually square or rectangular, with the audience on one side only. The stage may or may not be framed with a proscenium arch.

ensemble A group of actors who work closely together and share the responsibility for the performance of a play.

environmental sound Sound effects that may be live or recorded that contribute to the interpretation of the play or are an expressive part of the performance.

epic theatre A theatrical style that emphasizes a historical approach to the subject and uses an episodic structure. Epic theatre also uses devices such as songs and signs to interrupt the action of the play so that emotional distance is created.

episodic art Visual art and theatre that tell a story through a sequence of connected images or episodes. The church-related art of the Middle Ages was particularly known for employing an episodic form.

equity theatre A theatre company or producing organization that performs in a theatre space that seats an audience of one hundred or more patrons and that pays its actors according to a union contract.

equity waiver theatre A professional theatre with ninety-nine or fewer seats that is thereby exempt from certain regulations of the Actors Equity union.

expressionism A theatrical style that uses exaggeration and distortion in both design and acting to reflect the interior world of the characters.

external acting approach An acting approach that begins with text and movement rather than the psychological analysis of character.

F

farce An extreme form of comedy involving challenges to authority that frequently result in anarchy.

found space Found space refers to a venue used for a theatre performance that was not constructed to be a theatre. A found space can be inside or outside and is a space that offers unusual or surprising opportunities for theatre production. A found space can be a space that is regularly used for daily activity other than theatre such as a house or it can be a space that is currently abandoned.

fugue Repetition and variation of a theme by multiple voices in musical or literary composition.

G

genre The division of dramas into categories such as tragedy and comedy as they represent different kinds of human experience.

German expressionism An artistic movement in the visual and performing arts that prevailed in Germany from 1905 to 1922; it merged aesthetic and political views.

gestural acting An approach to acting influenced by Bertolt Brecht and Asian performance techniques that relies on distilling the essence of character through concentrated physical gestures.

glory A scenic device used in the Italian court theatre to fly large groups of characters such as angels.

gobo A stencil placed inside a lighting instrument to create a pattern of reflected light on the floor or on a cyclorama or scenic unit.

ground plan The basic diagram for the placement of furniture, walls, doors, and levels such as stairs; evolves through collaboration by the scene designer and the director.

H

HUAC The Congressional committee organized to monitor "un-American activities." From the late 1930s to the 1950s the committee functioned to censor the content of American theatre and film.

I

improvisation The spontaneous invention of actors used to explore text, character, or situation; a tool used by actors to freely create actions and language. Improvisation can be used in either rehearsal or performance.

inner monologue The unspoken thoughts that accompany an actor's lines in method acting. The actor responds to the character's situation with a stream of spontaneous thoughts as if the actor were in the character's place.

internal acting approach An acting approach that is based on a psychological investigation of character and actor identification with character; involves imagining character history and placing oneself in the character's position.

interpretive art Theatre performance that evolves out of the interpretation of the playwright's script. Directors, actors, and designers are interpretive artists.

K

kabuki A popular Japanese theatre form that began in the sixteenth century; highly stylized with elaborate action, exaggerated gestures and speech patterns, and magnificent costumes, makeup, and wigs.

kachina cycle A sequence of ritual ceremonies performed by the Hopi people of the American Southwest that promotes the welfare of their community. The kachinas are the guardian spirits of the Hopi, who believe that the kachinas participate with them in dramatic ceremonies performed to ensure the success of the harvest and to preserve the Hopi way of life.

kathakali A form of dance drama from southern India in which the actors express a story through movement and complex hand gestures accompanied by musicians and singers who communicate the text. The actors play character types as in the Beijing Opera and spend years in intense training to perfect the strenuous and complicated movement skills. The dramas themselves are based on the *Ramayana* and the *Mahabharata*, two epic Sanskrit poems.

kuroko A performer dressed in black (with a hood) in the tradition of the kabuki theatre; changes scenery and props and helps actors with onstage costume changes.

L

language The dialogue of a play written from the multiple points of view of the characters. Dramatic language may be realistic or poetic.

light plot A diagram that shows the position and type of each lighting instrument to be used for a given production. This diagram is used as a tool in discussion between the lighting designer and the director and is also used by the technicians who hang the lights in the theatre.

lighting designer The theatre artist responsible for interpreting plays through the use of light to create atmosphere and imagery and to make the action visible.

M

mask A fundamental device for establishing character that covers the human face and has been used in dramatic presentations throughout the world since the beginning of theatre.

melodrama A dramatic genre that presents the conflict between good and evil.

method acting An internal approach to acting used in the United States that was influenced by the work of Constantin Stanislavsky. Method acting uses a close study of character psychology to determine the character's sequence of intentions or objectives. Method acting also relies on the actor's own life experiences as a major source of material for character creation.

musical theatre A form of theatre in which dialogue, singing, and dance are integrated to communicate character and plot.

mystery cycle A medieval theatre form based on biblical teachings. Episodic in structure, the mystery cycles were composed of many individual playlets.

N

nonrealism A theatrical style that offers a way of interpreting human experience different from the illusion of daily life created by realism. Some nonrealistic theatrical styles are expressionism, symbolism, and surrealism. Nonrealistic styles emphasize bold theatrical imagery and gestural acting.

nontraditional casting The casting of actors of different racial backgrounds in plays that were written for a nonpluralistic society, such as the plays of Shakespeare.

P

pageant wagons Traveling stages drawn by horses or people on which the playlets of the medieval mystery cycles were performed in England.

parody The imitation of a style of writing (for example, songs or plays) for comic effect or ridicule.

perform To engage in the presentation of theatre, dance, or music. In the theatre, performance involves the manipulation of the persona presented by the actor.

performance The live presentation of a play.

period style Presentational elements such as character movement and dress that are determined by the theatrical and social conventions of a particular era.

perspective The painting technique used to create a sense of depth in painted scenery on the stage.

playwright The theatre artist who authors the playscripts that are frequently the starting point for theatrical creation. The playwright uses language to express dramatic action.

plot The sequence of actions that determines what happens in a play; the events that make up the play's story.

poetic realism Realism that is heightened through symbols, the selection of details, and eloquent language.

poor theatre A term introduced by Polish director Jerzy Grotowski to identify theatre that uses only those materials necessary to extend the expression of the actor. At the Polish Laboratory Theatre, scenery and costumes were made of the simplest, least costly materials, and no scenic elements were used merely to provide background or ornamentation.

potlatch A ceremonial festival observed by Native people of the Northwest coast of the United States and the Southwest coast of Canada. The potlatch includes feasts and elaborate dramatizations, which present community history and important rites of passage. The wealth and status of the host is confirmed through the presentation of valuable gifts to guests.

presentational staging Staging that makes obvious use of the theatre's resources.

preview A performance that is presented to an invited audience or at a reduced ticket price to allow actors to work in front of an audience before the official opening of a play.

progression The sequence of changes that defines character development.

proscenium arch The frame, like a picture frame, defining the opening of a proscenium stage. The proscenium arch creates the sense that the audience is looking into a contained space from which one wall has been removed.

proscenium stage A rectangular theatre with the stage at one end of the rectangle.

R

realism A theatrical style that creates an illusion of daily life through the presentation of a detailed environment, natural actions, and language that sounds as if it were overheard in ordinary circumstances.

rehearsal The process of exploration and repetition used to prepare a play for public presentation.

rehearsal costume A temporary costume worn during rehearsal to give the actor the opportunity to construct character in response to physical costume restrictions and the psychological dimensions of the costume.

rendering A sketch or painting of scenery or costumes that is used as a visual aid by the director, the other designers, and the actors in the development of a production.

repertory The alternating presentation of more than one play at a time practiced by a theatre company such as the Oregon Shakespeare Festival.

representational staging The creation of a complete, realistic illusion on the stage that makes audience members forget that they are in the theatre.

S

scene 1. The smaller units that make up the acts in a play. 2. A particular moment in the performance of a play. 3. The arrangement of the scene design elements.

scene designer The theatre artist responsible for interpreting plays through shaping and defining the stage space.

scenography The work of the scene designer or combined work of the scene designer, costume designer, lighting designer, and sound designer; also known as stage design.

script The dialogue, stage directions, and character descriptions that together constitute the printed text of a play.

sound reinforcement The use of microphones and amplifiers to augment the sound of actors' voices, particularly in the musical theatre.

spectacle The visual elements of a performance, including scenery, lights, costumes, and the movement of actors.

spine According to Constantin Stanislavsky, the through line of a role or the entire play that the director and actors must identify in their preparation for performance.

stage left Stage left indicates the side of the stage to the left of an actor standing at the center of the stage facing the audience in an end stage theatre arrangement. The identification of the stage directions is based on the actor's perspective, not the perspective of the audience.

stage picture The arrangement of actors on the stage to communicate character relationships.

stage right Stage right indicates the side of the stage to the right of an actor standing at the center of the stage facing the audience in an end stage theatre arrangement. The identification of the stage directions is based on the actor's perspective, not the perspective of the audience.

style The combination of expressive choices made by the playwright and the director, designers, and actors that construct the world of the play.

subtext The thoughts and feelings of the character that are unspoken but expressed through gesture, facial expression, and phrasing.

superobjective A term used in method acting to identify the central motivation for a character in a play that brings together in a coherent way all of the character's smaller desires and intentions during the course of the play.

T

table work The reading and discussion of a play done by the cast and the director at the beginning of the rehearsal process.

technical rehearsal A rehearsal dedicated to the integration of scenery, costumes, and lighting cues into the production.

terrain The use of steps, ramps, and levels to reshape the stage floor.

theatre in the round A theatre in which the audience surrounds the stage on all sides.

theatre of the absurd Plays that focus on the lack of meaning in human existence, such as those written by Samuel Beckett, Eugène Ionesco, and Jean Genet.

theatrical conventions Elements of dramatic construction and performance accepted by theatre practitioners and audience members in a given community that facilitate the presentation of plays. Conventions of the Greek theatre include masked actors and offstage violence.

theatricalism A style of playwriting or theatrical production that makes bold use of the resources of the theatre. Theatricalism is nonrealistic and employs vivid imagery and heightened language to express the playwright's meaning. Plays produced in a theatricalist style frequently call attention to the mechanics of the theatre itself.

thespian A term used for "actor" taken from the name of Thespis, the first recognized Greek actor.

through line The arc or progression of an actor's role that ties together all of the character's words and actions.

thrust stage A theatre space in which the audience is placed on three sides of the stage.

total theatre A theatrical style that integrates sound, words, movement, light, music, and color to create a performance that emphasizes gesture and imagery as much as or more than language.

tragedy The dramatic genre initiated by ancient Greek playwrights such as Aeschylus, Sophocles, and Euripides. Tragedy focuses on suffering and loss but celebrates the will of the individual to choose his or her own course of action.

tragicomedy A dramatic genre in which the perspective shifts between serious and comic perspectives.

trilogy Tragedies in ancient Greece were originally written as three interrelated plays called a trilogy.

typecasting A method of choosing actors for roles in a play that relies on generalizations or stereotypical notions of what characters should look like.

types Character types represent a generalized interpretation of human behavior. A character type demonstrates a category of social background or position in contrast to a fully developed, realistic character with varied and specific qualities.

U

upstage The area of the stage farthest away from the audience.

Credits

p. 41, Librado Romero/*The New York Times*; p. 42, Courtesy The Market Theatre

Part II p. 45, © Berkeley Repertory Theatre, Courtesy kevinberne.com

Chapter 3 p. 46, Joan Marcus; p. 47, ASP Images/Ted S. Warren; p. 48, Joan Marcus; p. 50, © Berkeley Repertory Theatre, Courtesy of kevinberne.com; p. 52, © 2009 The Jacob and Gwendolyn Lawrence Foundation, Seattle/Artists Rights Society (ARS), New York; p. 54, © Bettmann/CORBIS; p. 56, Art © Romare Bearden Foundation/Licensed by VAGA, New York, NY; p. 57, © Bettmann/CORBIS; p. 58, Christopher Briscoe, Courtesy Oregon Shakespeare Festival; p. 97, Christopher Briscoe, Courtesy Oregon Shakespeare Festival; p. 99, Christopher Briscoe, Courtesy Oregon Shakespeare Festival; p. 101, Christopher Briscoe, Courtesy Oregon Shakespeare Festival; p. 102, Christopher Briscoe, Courtesy Oregon Shakespeare Festival; p. 103, Scene design courtesy Mike Fish; p. 103, Christopher Briscoe, Courtesy Oregon Shakespeare Festival; p. 105, Costume design courtesy Candice Cain; p. 106, Costume design courtesy Candice Cain; p. 107, Christopher Briscoe, Courtesy Oregon Shakespeare Festival

Chapter 4 p. 110, Photo by Jenny Graham; p. 111, Joan Marcus; p. 112, Irene Young; p. 114, Courtesy Stephanie Arnold; p. 115, Joan Marcus; p. 116, Photo by Carol Rosegg, 2007, Courtesy Pearl Theatre; p. 117, Courtesy Mark Prieto; p. 118, Courtesy Arena Stage; p. 120, Photo by Carol Rosegg, 2007, Courtesy Pearl Theatre; p. 121, Joan Marcus; p. 123, Photo by David Cooper; p. 123, Photo by Jenny Graham; p. 124, T. Charles Erickson; p. 126, Mike Paul/ACT ONE; p. 128, Photo by Nancy Keystone; p. 130, Photo by Nancy Keystone; p. 131, Joan Marcus

Chapter 5 p. 134, Richard Termine; p. 135, ©Sovfoto; p. 136, ©Sovfoto; p. 138, Richard Termine; p. 139, PaulCooperPhotography; p. 140, Photo of the Laboratory Theatre, The Grotowski Institute; p. 140, Photo of the Laboratory Theatre, The Grotowski Institute; p. 142, T. Charles Erickson; p. 143, Courtesy Ping Chong & Company; p. 144, Courtesy Ping Chong & Company; p. 145, Photo: © Paula Court; p. 148, Photo by Nancy Keystone; p. 150, Courtesy Erik Hansen-Hansen; p. 151, Photo by David Cooper; p. 153, Photo by Nancy Keystone; p. 155, Photo by Michael Palma; p. 156, Manuel Harlan; p. 157, Courtesy American Repertory Theater

Chapter 6 p. 162, Henry DiRocco, Courtesy South Coast Repertory; p. 163, Henry DiRocco, Courtesy South Coast Repertory; p. 165, Henry DiRocco, Courtesy South Coast Repertory; p. 166, T. Charles Erickson; p. 167, Photo by David Cooper; p. 168, Lee Celano; p. 173, Courtesy Gerard Howland; p. 174, Courtesy Gerard Howland; p. 176, Henry DiRocco, Courtesy South Coast Repertory; p. 176, Henry DiRocco, Courtesy South Coast Repertory; p. 177, Henry DiRocco, Courtesy South Coast Repertory; p. 178, Henry DiRocco, Courtesy South Coast Repertory; p. 181, Henry DiRocco, Courtesy South Coast Repertory; p. 182, Henry DiRocco, Courtesy South Coast Repertory; p. 183, Henry DiRocco, Courtesy South Coast Repertory; p. 184, Henry DiRocco, Courtesy South Coast Repertory; p. 185, Henry DiRocco, Courtesy South Coast Repertory

Part III p. 193, © Simon Annand

Chapter 7 p. 194, Photo by ©Paul Kolnik; p. 197, Steven Siewert/Fairfax Photos; p. 198, © Bettman/CORBIS; p. 199, Gautier Deblonde, Courtesy Ahmanson Theatre; p. 200, Pavel Antonov; p. 201, © Bettman/CORBIS; p. 202, Photo courtesy of mellopix.com, ©Berkeley Repertory Theatre; p. 203, Photo by ©Paul Kolnik; p. 203, AP Images; p. 204, © Bettmann/CORBIS; p. 205, Courtesy American Repertory Theater; p. 206, Michael Brosilow

Chapter 8 p. 209, Courtesy Stephanie Arnold; p. 210, Courtesy Gary M. Kuwahara; p. 211, Corky Lee, Courtesy Pan Asian Repertory Company; p. 213, Chiura Obata, Courtesy Kimi Kodani Hill; p. 214, Courtesy Gary M. Kuwahara; p. 215, Courtesy Stephanie Arnold; p. 216, Chiura Obata, Courtesy Kimi Kodani Hill; p. 218, Courtesy Gary M. Kuwahara; p. 248, Jay Africa, Courtesy East-West Players; p. 249, James Ishida, Courtesy East-West Players; p. 253, Courtesy Gary M. Kuwahara; p. 254, Courtesy Gary M. Kuwahara; p. 255, Rick Wong, Courtesy NWAAT;

p. 256, Rick Wong, Courtesy NWAAT; p. 258, Rick Wong, Courtesy NWAAT

Chapter 9 p. 261, Bruce R. Feeley, Courtesy Shen Wei Dance Arts; p. 264, mptvimages.com; p. 266, Mary Gearhart/The Wooster Group; p. 267, © Bettmann/CORBIS; p. 268, Manuel Rotenberg, ©Berkeley Reptertory Theatre; p. 269, Joan Marcus; p. 271, Richard Termine; p. 272, Time Life Pictures/Getty Images; p. 275, © Stephanie Berger; p. 276, Bruce R. Feeley, Courtesy Shen Wei Dance Arts; p. 277, Zen Qian, Courtesy Shen Wei Dance Arts; p. 279, ©Simon Annand; p. 280, Courtesy Handspring Puppet Theatre; p. 281, ©Ruphin Coudyzer FPPSA-www.ruphin.com; p. 282, ©Ruphin Coudyzer FPPSA-www.ruphin.com

Chapter 10 p. 285, Joan Marcus; p. 286, Katy Raddatz; p. 287, Giulio Marrocchi/Sipa Press; p. 289, Joan Marcus; p. 290, Owen Carey; p. 291, Katy Raddatz; p. 293, © Bettmann/CORBIS; p. 293, Katy Raddatz; p. 294, © Bettmann/CORBIS; p. 295, Jay Thompson, Courtesy Mark Taper Forum; p. 296, Katy Raddatz; p. 345, Katy Raddatz; p. 346, Joan Marcus

Chapter 11 p. 349, Joan Marcus; p. 351, Photofest; p. 352, Joan Marcus; p. 353, Joan Marcus; p. 355, Photofest; p. 356, Joan Marcus; p. 359, Photo by © Paul Kolnik; p. 361, Photofest; p. 363, Photo by Michal Daniel; p. 364, Joan Marcus; p. 366, Joan Marcus; p. 368, Photo by © Paul Kolnik; p. 370, Joan Marcus; p. 371, Joan Marcus

Part IV p. 373, Monica Carboni

Chapter 12 p. 374, Photo courtesy of mellopix.com, © Berkeley Repertory Theatre; p. 376, © 2009 Gerry Goodstein; p. 378, Photo courtesy of mellopix. com, © Berkeley Repertory Theatre; p. 379, Scott Landis; p. 380, Sarah Krulwich/*The New York Times*; p. 382, Photo by Michal Daniel; p. 385, Photo by Michal Daniel; p. 386, Courtesy Gary M. Kuwahara

Chapter 13 p. 388, Richard Termine; p. 389, Joan Marcus; p. 390, Courtesy Quiara Alegría Hudes; p. 390, Monica Carboni; p. 392, Monica Carboni; p. 398, Monica Carboni; p. 401, Monica Carboni; p. 437, Courtesy Second Stage; p. 438, Courtesy Neil Patel; p. 438, Courtesy Neil Patel; p. 438, Courtesy Neil Patel; p. 440, Photo by Richard Termine; p. 441, Photo by Richard Termine; p. 442, Photo by Richard Termine; p. 445, Photo by Richard Termine; p. 447, Photo by Richard Termine

Chapter 14 p. 449, Photo courtesy Steve Tanner, © Berkeley Repertory Theatre; p. 451, Photo courtesy kevinberne.com, ©Berkeley Repertory Theatre; p. 453, Photo by Michal Daniel; p. 454, Michael Brosilow; p. 457, © Stephanie Berger; p. 458, mptvimages.com; p. 459, Photo courtesy Steve Tanner, © Berkeley Repertory Theatre; p. 461, Rick Adams Photography; p. 463, Photo courtesy of kevinberne.com, ©Berkeley Repertory Theatre; p. 464, mptvimages.com/Ted Allan; p. 465, mptvimages.com/Rico Torres; p. 466, Photo courtesy of kevinberne.com, © Berkeley Repertory Theatre

Chapter 15 p. 476, Photo by Richard Termine

Index

Page numbers in **bold** represent definitions; those in *italics* represent pictures.